CCNA

Guide to Cisco Networking

Third Edition

Kelly Cannon, Kelly Caudle

THOMSON

COURSE TECHNOLOGY

Australia • Canada • Mexico • Singapore • Spain • United Kingdom • United States

CCNA Guide to Cisco Networking, Third Edition

is published by Course Technology

Managing Editor
William Pitkin III

Product Manager
Amy M. Lyon

Developmental Editor
Dan Seiter

Production Editor
Philippa Lehar

Technical Editor
Chris Ward

Quality Assurance Testing
Marianne Snow, Chris Scriver

Product Marketing Manager
Jason Sakos

Senior Manufacturing Coordinator
Trevor Kallop

Associate Product Managers
David Rivera, Mirella Misiaszek

Editorial Assistant
Amanda Piantedosi

Cover Design
Nancy Goulet

Text Design
GEX Publishing Services

Compositor
GEX Publishing Services

BRIEF
Contents

TABLE OF

Contents

Preface

The proliferation of networks in the workplace and the popularity of the Internet have contributed to an increasing need for networking professionals with both LAN and WAN configuration skills. Employers are looking for qualified people to fill the demand for these networking jobs, and certification is a great way to prove you have what it takes. The primary objective of this book is to help you prepare for and pass the Cisco Certified Network Associate Exam (CCNA), the foundation certification upon which other Cisco certifications are built. The undisputed worldwide leader in networking equipment, Cisco manufactures routers, switches, access servers, and network management software designed to interconnect LANs and WANs around the globe.

Hands-on learning is the best way to master the networking skills necessary for both the CCNA exam and a career in wide-area networking. This book contains more than 50 hands-on exercises that apply networking concepts, such as IP addressing, routing, and switching, as they would be applied on Cisco equipment in the real world and on CCNA Exam #640-801. In addition, each chapter offers multiple review questions to reinforce mastery of the CCNA topics.

The inclusion of the lab manual at the end of this text provides a substantial and effective learning experience. In addition, the appendices provide crucial test-taking information such as a list of essential commands, as well as troubleshooting techniques and references.

This book is suitable for use in any Cisco CCNA course. As a prerequisite, students should have basic networking knowledge, such as the skills learned in an introductory networking course.

Intended Audience

CCNA Guide to Cisco Networking, Third Edition serves as a comprehensive guide for anyone who wants to obtain a solid background in basic Cisco networking concepts, and is an ideal tool to use to prepare for CCNA certification. This book guides you through the basics of networking, configuration, and troubleshooting of Cisco routers and switches. To best understand the material in this book, you should have a background in basic computer concepts and have worked with PC hardware. This book is intended for use in a classroom or an instructor-led training environment with access to Cisco routers and switches. When you finish the book, you should understand and be able to perform all objectives covered in CCNA Exam #640-801.

Chapter Descriptions

Here is a summary of the topics covered in each chapter of this book:

Chapter 1, "Introducing Networks," introduces the OSI reference model and identifies why the industry uses this layered approach to networking. It also explores the five steps of data encapsulation, the function of a MAC address, and the difference between connection-oriented and connectionless network service.

In **Chapter 2**, "Network Devices," you learn all about the different devices used on a network and the advantages and disadvantages of using particular devices. The devices include hubs and repeaters, bridges and switches, brouters and routers, and gateways. Devices are discussed in the context of network segmentation, because it is important to understand which devices segment the network and which do not.

In **Chapter 3**, "TCP/IP and IP Addressing," you learn about TCP/IP—the language of the Internet. TCP/IP is a suite of many protocols, including ICMP, UDP, TCP, ARP, and RARP. IP addressing and subnetting are also covered in this chapter. Finally, you learn about benefits of using ping and trace to troubleshoot IP.

In **Chapter 4**, "Network Topology and Design," you review physical and logical LAN topologies as well as cabling standards. Items such as media and network architecture are presented. The chapter also offers a review of various network management tools.

In **Chapter 5**, "WAN Concepts," you are introduced to the various WAN physical standards and data link protocols operating on WAN links today. The chapter includes an introduction to various WAN technologies and protocols, including ATM, T1, ISDN, X.25, Frame Relay, PPP, HDLC, and SDLC.

In **Chapter 6**, "Router and IOS Basics," you learn about the components of the router and the basic configuration commands. This includes various configuration modes and prompts, passwords, context-sensitive help, and enhanced editing features. It also includes instructions on how to configure the HyperTerminal program in Windows to access the router, and how to configure the router using the system configuration dialog. You additionally receive an introduction to the Cisco 1900 series switch user interface.

Chapter 7, "Router Startup and Configuration," explains the boot process in a Cisco router and how to manipulate the process. You are introduced to CDP, a proprietary protocol of Cisco, which is enabled by default on all Cisco routers and switches. In addition, configuration of IP on the router and the 1900 series switch are discussed. Finally, this chapter details troubleshooting connection problems using show commands, ping, trace, and telnet.

In **Chapter 8**, "Routing Protocols and Network Address Translation," you learn to differentiate among routable, nonroutable, and routing protocols. Routing protocols are categorized as either Exterior Gateway Protocols or Interior Gateway Protocols. The focus of this chapter is Interior Gateway Protocols and the two categories therein, which include distance-vector and link-state. You learn about the count-to-infinity problem with distance-vector routing protocols, along with different ways to combat this problem. Finally, you learn how to configure the two most popular distance-vector routing protocols, RIP and Cisco's proprietary IGRP.

Chapter 9, "Advanced Routing Protocols," introduces several new concepts on the 640-801 exam. Classful and classless routing are described in detail. The chapter introduces RIPv2, Enhanced Interior Gateway Routing Protocol (EIGRP), and Open Shortest Path First (OSPF). Static and default routes are also covered.

Chapter 10, "Access Lists," covers the dual purpose of access lists, which are flow control and security. You learn the syntax of the two types of lists found on the CCNA exam. These include standard IP and extended IP lists. You learn the usage and rules of access lists and how to configure and apply them. You also learn how to control access to the VTY line with access lists. Finally, you learn how to monitor your lists on the router.

In **Chapter 11**, "PPP and ISDN," you learn about PPP encapsulation and how to configure PPP and its options on a Cisco router. You also learn about PPP multilink and how to enable it. This chapter teaches you how to implement ISDN BRI and dial-on-demand routing on Cisco routers, and how to configure an ISDN BRI connection.

In **Chapter 12**, "Frame Relay," you learn about Frame Relay standards and equipment, and about the role of virtual circuits and performance parameters in Frame Relay. This chapter covers the various Frame Relay topologies and how to configure and monitor Frame Relay on Cisco routers.

In **Chapter 13**, "Switching and VLANs," features and benefits of Fast Ethernet are taught, as well as its guidelines and distance limitations. In addition, you learn about defining full- and half-duplex Ethernet operation. This chapter shows you how to distinguish between cut-through and store-and-forward LAN switching, and how to define the operation of the Spanning Tree Protocol and its benefits. You also learn about the benefits of virtual LANs and how to route between VLANs. Finally, you discover the configuration basics for the Cisco 1900 series switch and the Cisco 2950 series switch.

Appendix A, "CCNA Certification Objectives," lists each CCNA certification objective and the chapter in which it is covered.

Appendix B, "Additional Resources," provides additional sources of information on subjects covered in this course.

Appendix C, "A Networking Professional's Toolkit," provides pictures of networking tools, along with their proper names and uses.

Appendix D, "Command Summary," provides a list of the commands presented in this course. You should review these commands before you attempt the CCNA certification examination.

Appendix E, "Troubleshooting Summary," provides a list of commonly used troubleshooting commands and a description of their output. You should review these commands before you attempt the CCNA certification examination.

The Lab Manual chapters map to the main text chapters and provide necessary hands-on skills for working with networking equipment in general, and for configuring Cisco routers and switches. The Cisco CCNA certification Exam #640-801 includes simulation questions that mirror actual router and switch configuration. Configuration of the routers and switches in the lab is essential to performing successfully on the CCNA exam. Even students who are not interested in passing the CCNA exam still need to master the equipment if they will configure it on the job. In addition, working with the networking equipment enhances students' understanding of the material presented in their lectures. Finally, students work on the labs in teams. They help each other and learn from each other's successes and mistakes.

Book Features

To aid you in fully understanding Cisco networking concepts, this book includes many features designed to enhance your learning experience:

- **Chapter Objectives**—Each chapter begins with a detailed list of the concepts to be mastered. This list gives you a quick reference to the chapter's contents, and is a useful study aid.

- **Chapter Summary**—Each chapter's text is followed by a bulleted summary of the concepts introduced in that chapter. These summaries provide a helpful way to recap and revisit the major ideas covered in each chapter.

- **Key Terms**—All the terms within the chapter that were introduced with boldfaced text are collected in the Key Terms list at the end of the chapter. This list helps you check your understanding of all the terms introduced.

- **Review Questions**—The end-of-chapter assessment begins with a set of review questions that reinforce the ideas introduced in each chapter. Answering these questions ensures that you have mastered the important concepts. The review questions can also be used to help prepare for the CCNA exam.

- **Case Projects**—At the end of each chapter, there are several case projects. In these extensive case examples, you implement the skills and knowledge gained in the chapter through real design and implementation scenarios.

Lab Manual Features

To ensure a successful experience for instructors and students alike, this book includes the following sections for each lab:

- **Lab Objectives**: Every lab has a brief description and list of learning objectives.

- **Materials Required**: Every lab includes information on hardware, software, and other materials you need to complete the lab.

- **Estimated Completion Time**: Every lab has an estimated completion time, so that you can plan your activities accurately.

- **Activity**: The actual lab activity is presented in this section. Logical and precise step-by-step instructions guide you through the lab.

- **Certification Objectives**: Each chapter lists the relevant objectives from Cisco's CCNA Exam #640-801.

- **Review Questions**: Every lab provides follow-up questions to help reinforce concepts presented in the lab.

Text and Graphic Conventions

Additional information and exercises have been added to this book to help you better understand what is being discussed. Icons throughout the text alert you to these additional materials. The icons used in this book are described below.

Notes present additional helpful material related to the subject being discussed.

Tips offer extra information on resources, how to attack problems, and time-saving shortcuts.

The Caution icon identifies important information about potential mistakes or hazards.

Case projects are more involved, scenario-based assignments. In these extensive case project examples, you are asked to independently apply what you have learned in the chapter.

Each hands-on activity in the Lab Manual is accompanied by the Activity icon.

Instructor's Materials

The following supplemental materials are available when this book is used in a classroom setting. All of the supplements available with this book are provided to the instructor on a single CD-ROM.

Electronic Instructor's Manual. The Instructor's Manual that accompanies this textbook includes additional instructional material to assist in class preparation, including suggestions for classroom activities, discussion topics, and additional projects.

Solutions. This supplement provides answers to all end-of-chapter materials, including Review Questions, Case Projects, and the Activity projects in the Lab Manual.

ExamView®. This textbook is accompanied by ExamView, a powerful testing software package that allows instructors to create and administer printed, computer (LAN-based), and Internet exams. ExamView includes hundreds of questions that correspond to the topics covered in this text, enabling students to generate detailed study guides that include page references for further review. The computer-based and Internet testing components allow students to take exams at their computers, and they save the instructor time by grading each exam automatically.

PowerPoint Presentations. This book comes with Microsoft PowerPoint slides for each chapter. They can be used as a teaching aid for classroom presentation, can be made available to students on the network for chapter review, or can be printed for classroom distribution. Instructors, please feel at liberty to add your own slides for additional topics that you introduce to the class.

Figure Files. All of the figures in the book are reproduced on the Instructor Resources CD, in bitmap format. Similar to the PowerPoint presentations, these can be used as a teaching aid for classroom presentation, can be made available to students for review, or can be printed for classroom distribution.

Test Prep Software

Two kinds of exam preparation software are included on the CD-ROM at the back of this book:

CoursePrep software from MeasureUp provides hundreds of sample exam questions that mirror the look and feel of the CCNA 640-801 exam. For more information about MeasureUp test prep products, or to order the complete version of this software, visit their Web site at *www.measureup.com*.

CertBlaster software from DataTrain, Inc. also offers hundreds of sample exam questions in a variety of testing modes: Study, Certification, Assessment, Flash Drill, and Adaptive. For more information about CertBlaster and other DataTrain products, visit their Web site at *www.certblaster.com*.

ACKNOWLEDGMENTS

Many talented people participated in the creation of this book. The Development team thanks the Production Editor, Philippa Lehar, for her creativity and flexibility, and the

Technical Editor, Chris Ward, for his diligent work. Our thanks also go to Chris Scriver for the quality assurance testing on the Lab Manual chapters, and to the reviewers, Brian Goodman and John Sanns, for their dedication to the project, and for their very helpful feedback.

Kelly Caudle

First, as I try to do with each project, I want to thank the Lord for blessing me each and every day. I must also thank Amy Lyon at Course Technology and Dan Seiter for their patience when I was late (which was often) and for their hard work. Furthermore, I want to thank Kelly Cannon for all her hard work during this project; without Cannonball, the book would not be nearly as error-free as it is. A special thanks also goes to my colleagues at Stanly Community College, who put up with me during my "book" sessions. I want to especially thank Mike Hogan for helping me out of jams more than once. Last, I thank my wonderful wife Susan for her love, support, and encouragement.

Kelly Cannon

I thank Course Technology for the opportunity to be involved in the world of academic publishing. I also thank my writing partner Kelly Caudle for working with me on this project. Although we were always miles apart, whenever we communicated, we were in agreement. In addition, I am grateful to Dan Seiter and Amy Lyon for all of their hard work. They are both great at what they do, and I hope to work with them again in the near future. Of course, I want to thank my wonderful family, Jim, Veronica, and Adrienne, and my parents, who had the foresight to bring me to the greatest country in the world, where I continue to be blessed with opportunities.

HARDWARE REQUIREMENTS

The following is a list of hardware required to complete all the labs in the book. Many of the individual labs do not have all of these requirements. In terms of routers and switches, if you have a Cisco Academy CCNA lab setup, you have the necessary equipment for the labs in Chapter 6 through the end of the book. The hardware required for Chapters 1 through 5 is minimal. The routing and switching lab setup, in addition to any other hardware required, is as follows:

- Four 2501 series routers with power cables (could substitute a different series but must have two serial interfaces and one Ethernet interface)

- One 2514 series router with power cable (could substitute a different series but must have two serial interfaces and two Ethernet interfaces)

- One or two Cisco series 1900 switches (or other appropriate series switch) with power cord

- Five hubs with power cables (can substitute switches)
- Three V.35 DTE cables (male) with serial end to match serial interface on routers
- Three V.35 DCE cables (female) with serial end to match serial interface on routers
- Six Ethernet 10BaseT UTP-to-AUI transceivers (do not need these if the Ethernet interfaces on the routers are RJ-45 transceivers)
- Five RJ-45 to DB-25 or DB-9 connectors
- Five RJ-45 to RJ-45 rollover cables for the routers
- A rollover cable for the switch
- Six computers running any Microsoft Windows platform, with NICs installed
- HyperTerminal installed on all Windows computers
- One Windows Internet computer with a NIC configured and the TCP/IP protocol configured
- Transceivers for the router Ethernet ports, if these ports use an AUI connection instead of RJ-45
- TFTP server software on a diskette (preferably Cisco's, which is TFTPSERV.EXE)
- Power strips
- Nineteen UTP patch cables
- One CSU/DSU (you can substitute a router if necessary, and it doesn't have to work; it is for simulation purposes only, and is only used in Lab 2.1)
- One bridge (doesn't have to work; it is for simulation purposes only, and is only used in Lab 2.1)
- Transceivers for the bridge connections if the bridge uses AUI connections instead of RJ-45 (only used in Lab 2.1)
- Three hubs (don't have to work; they are for simulation purposes only, and are only used in Lab 2.1)
- Nine NICs with RJ-45 transceivers to simulate nine host computers (don't have to work; they are for simulation purposes only, and are only used in Lab 2.1)
- One serial cable with a compatible connector for a serial interface on a router on one end and a V.35 connector on the other end to attach to the CSU/DSU. If another router will be used instead of the CSU/DSU, the cable connector should match the serial interface on the additional router (doesn't have to work; it is for simulation purposes only, and is only used in Lab 2.1)

- One UTP cable crimper and one pair of wire cutters for every four students (Labs 4.1, 4.2, and 4.4 only)
- A box or spool of CAT 5 UTP cable (Labs 4.1, 4.2, and 4.4 only)
- Box of RJ-45 connectors (Labs 4.1, 4.2, and 4.4 only)
- One UTP continuity tester (or other cable tester) for every four students (Labs 4.1, 4.2, and 4.4 only)
- Thinnet sample (Lab 4.3 only)
- Thicknet sample (Lab 4.3 only)
- Category 5 UTP sample (Lab 4.3 only)
- Category 3 UTP sample (Lab 4.3 only)
- Multimode fiber sample (Lab 4.3 only)
- Single-mode fiber sample (Lab 4.3 only)
- STP sample (Lab 4.3 only)
- T-connector (Lab 4.3 only)
- RJ-45 connector (Lab 4.3 only)
- RG-58 terminator (Lab 4.3 only)
- Plenum cable sample (Lab 4.3 only)
- One patch panel for every four students, preferably mounted on a rack to hold it steady (used in Lab 4.4 only)
- One Krone tool or other punch-down tool for every four students (used in Lab 4.4 only)
- A folder named SWITCHTEST containing enough files to equal at least 100 MB on the desktops of the lab-b, lab-d, and lab-e computers (Labs 13.3 and 13.4 only)
- A stopwatch (Labs 13.3 and 13.4 only)

1

INTRODUCING NETWORKS

> **After reading this chapter and completing the exercises, you will be able to:**
>
> ◆ Identify and describe the functions of each of the seven layers of the OSI reference model
>
> ◆ Identify the reasons why the networking industry uses a layered model
>
> ◆ Define and explain the conversion steps of data encapsulation
>
> ◆ Define and describe the function of a MAC address
>
> ◆ Describe connection-oriented network service and connectionless network service, and identify the key differences between them

This chapter introduces the fundamentals and evolution of computer networking. You will learn about the reasons for networking, some networking terminology, and a bit about the different types of networks. Specifically, you will learn about networking standards and types of networking equipment. As the course progresses, the concepts presented in this chapter will be periodically revisited and expanded upon.

INTRODUCTION TO NETWORKING

A computer network, or simply a **network**, is a term that describes the connection of two or more computers by some type of medium. For example, a computer connected to the Internet over the public telephone system is part of a network. Two computers connected by a wire cable also form a network. In addition to wire cables, you can use **fiber-optic cable**, **infrared**, and radio equipment to create and maintain a connection between two or more systems, thereby forming a network.

Origin of Networking

Industry experts find it difficult to place the actual origin of networking because many devices have been networked throughout history. For example, in the 1930s, electrical engineers used a device called the Network Analyzer for simulating electrical power grids. The earliest mainframe computers also were placed in networks, in that cables connected them in order to share computing power. Today, networks include a wide variety of computers and peripheral components.

Systems that are part of a network do not have to be identical. As a matter of fact, the largest computer network in the world, the Internet, connects a wide variety of computer systems. Mainframes, IBM and IBM-compatible personal computers (PCs), and Macintosh, UNIX, and NetWare systems are all part of the Internet. Televisions, vending machines, and light switches are also part of computer networks today because creative electrical engineers have developed methods to add network interfaces to these devices.

Why Do We Use Networks?

Some people might use the words "efficiency" or "necessity" in answering the preceding question. Realistically, the question could be answered in one word: convenience. As people have grown more dependent on technology, their need for networked devices has increased.

People expect interoperability from electronic devices. For instance, every person who has a videocassette recorder (VCR) expects it to work with the television set. When connected, the two devices are essentially networked to provide the user with the ability to watch television, play movies, and record television programs. Many people integrate their televisions and VCRs with their home stereos to form a larger networked system. In many ways, a computer network is no more complex than a home entertainment system.

Computer networks allow for the transfer of files, data, and even shared applications without copying anything to floppy disk. In addition, networks allow computers to share items such as printers, scanners, fax machines, processors, disk drives, and other resources.

Networked computers can share data and peripherals. Without a network, people have to find other methods for transferring data between computers. These other methods include copying the data to a floppy disk or another type of storage media, and physically moving that data to another system—a method called "sneakernet," because shoes provide the transport medium between computers.

Networking Terminology

New terminology for networking and networking components emerges almost daily. Therefore, the creation of a complete and up-to-date list of networking terminology would be impossible. In this section, you will learn the most widely used networking terminology.

Media

All network connections use **media**. Wire cabling, such as coaxial or the more commonly used twisted-pair, forms the connection in most networks. Some networks employ fiber-optic cable. It is more expensive than wire cabling, but less susceptible to **electromagnetic interference (EMI)**, which is frequently caused by nearby motors or fluorescent lighting. Still other networks use **wireless** transmission media, such as infrared or radio signals. With wireless communication, a connection is made between the devices sending and receiving the signals, with air, rather than cable, used to host the communication.

Client/Server Networks

Client/server networks have computers that are **servers** and computers that act as **clients** to those servers. In a client/server network, the servers host the resources for the clients to use and provide security, while a client is the computer that requests resources from the server. The term client sometimes also refers to a user. For example, a server might have a printer, or resource, attached to it for clients to use. You may see a variety of servers on a network:

- Print server: Hosts the connection to a printer so that clients can send print jobs to the printer
- File server: Maintains storage space for data that is shared with clients
- Database server: Hosts a database that clients can use to read/write and share information in an organized system with other clients
- Remote access server (RAS): Allows clients to dial in, usually over the public telephone system, to establish connections and to access network resources from a remote location
- Web server: Provides content on the Internet for clients to connect to when "browsing" the Internet

Peer-to-Peer

When every computer on a network acts as both a client and a server, the network is a peer-to-peer network. In a **peer-to-peer network**, all computers can share resources, such as files, printers, and applications, with other computers. Peer-to-peer networks are also known as "workgroups" because all computers are on the same level and can share resources with other computers.

LAN, WAN, MAN, SAN

Depending on the size of the network, you can use different terms to describe it. For example, a **local area network (LAN)** is contained within a company or department and located in a single geographic area, usually a building or part of a building. A **wide area network (WAN)** spans multiple geographic areas and is usually connected by common telecommunication carriers. A **metropolitan area network (MAN)** is the intermediate stage between a LAN and a WAN. (The term, which is used infrequently, attempts to describe a network that is within the boundaries of a city, campus, or town, but is also larger than a LAN.) A **storage area network (SAN)** is a relatively new term that describes a series of storage devices, such as tapes, hard drives, and CDs, that are networked together to provide very fast data storage for a network or subnetwork. The devices are physically separate from the servers. This makes the network more scalable and flexible, because any server can exchange data with any storage device and additional storage devices can be added more quickly and simply.

Network Operating System

A **network operating system (NOS)** allows communication, security, and distribution of data, files, and applications over a network. In the early days of PC computing, most PCs could not communicate on a network with other computers. This gave rise to two distinct terms: the stand-alone operating system (OS), which could not communicate on a network, and the networking OS, whose main purpose is network communications.

 Network administrators sometimes call the device or computer at which a user works an **end system**.

NOTE

NIC

A **network interface card (NIC)** is a device that allows a computer or other device to connect to a network through the media. This device is also known as a network adapter, network card, or network interface. The NIC is a physical component that connects to the internal hardware of the computer system. The NIC allows a physical connection to the network media.

Networking Hardware

Networking hardware is a generic term that describes all the physical components of a network, such as the NIC, cable, hub, switch, router, and any related connectors or devices. Any device or physical component that is used to connect computers in a network is considered to be network hardware.

Networking Software

The programs used to run a network are known as networking software. They include the NOS and all client/server networking software programs, such as shared applications like e-mail and database applications.

Virtual Private Networks

A **virtual private network** (**VPN**) is a method of using public communications infrastructure like the Internet to communicate privately between a company LAN and remote employees. These employees work from home or are otherwise not physically sitting at their computer at work. Although there are security issues to address, VPNs provide a relatively inexpensive way to connect remote and mobile users with the company's private network. Very often, businesses want to provide some limited access to their communications infrastructure to non-employees. This may include business partners, suppliers, vendors, and others who deal with the company but are not employees. The part of the company's network that is allowed access by these non-employees is called the **extranet**, which is accessed over or through the Internet. Conversely, the part of the company's network that is allowed access by employees is called the **intranet**, which is completely separate from the Internet. Virtual private networks can be intranet VPNs or extranet VPNs. The alternatives to VPNs include owned or leased lines, which are much more expensive.

UNDERSTANDING THE OSI MODEL

As computer networks became popular in the early 1980s, many different networking implementations were created. In the following years, compatibility and communication problems among these different network implementations became pervasive. The wide variety of hardware and software made communication between heterogeneous systems nearly impossible.

In 1984, the **International Organization for Standardization (ISO)** presented the **Open Systems Interconnection (OSI)** model. In developing the OSI model, ISO examined existing protocols, such as Transmission Control Protocol/Internet Protocol (TCP/IP), Systems Network Architecture (SNA) from IBM, and Digital Equipment Corporation's proprietary networking model (DECNET). Based on their examination of existing protocols, the ISO recommended a seven-layer network model called the OSI model.

Most networking vendors agreed to support the OSI model in one form or another. The model allows vendors to implement networks that permit communication among the wide variety of network implementations. The OSI model is not an absolute standard for computer networks; it is used as a reference model for how networks should be built. Because it is a reference model, it makes an ideal tool for learning how networks function.

Reasons for Layering

As previously mentioned, the OSI model has seven layers. A layered networking model is advantageous because it:

- Simplifies the networking model by dividing it into less complex components, which makes it easier to comprehend and use

- Enables programmers to specialize in a particular level or layer of the networking model

- Provides design modularity, which allows upgrades to a specific layer to remain separate from the other layers

- Encourages interoperability by promoting balance between different networking models

- Allows for standardized interfaces to be produced by networking vendors

Figure 1-1 shows the layers of the OSI model: **Physical layer**, **Data Link layer**, **Network layer**, **Transport layer**, **Session layer**, **Presentation layer**, and **Application layer**. The number beside each layer represents the number associated with that particular layer. For instance, the Network layer is commonly referred to as layer 3.

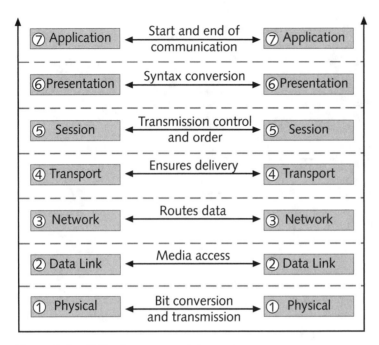

Figure 1-1   OSI reference model

As a group, these layers form the OSI protocol stack. A **protocol** is a defined method for communicating between systems. Computers must use a common protocol to communicate properly. Many different protocols are available for use on networks today; two examples are TCP/IP and IPX/SPX. You can think of a protocol as a common language between two computers. Just as humans must speak a common language to communicate, computers must use a common protocol.

If you need an easy way to remember the seven layers, from layer seven to layer one, use the following saying: All People Seem To Need Data Processing (Application, Presentation, Session, Transport, Network, Data Link, Physical). To remember layer one to layer seven, use Please Do Not Throw Sausage Pizza Away (Physical, Data Link, Network, Transport, Session, Presentation, Application).

Peer OSI Communication

The seven layers of the OSI reference model communicate with one another via **peer communication**. In other words, each layer will only talk to its peer on the opposite side of the communications process. As a result, each layer is unaware of the activities of all other layers of the model. Figure 1-2 shows peer communication, where the layers on the source node only talk with the opposite and equivalent layers on the destination node.

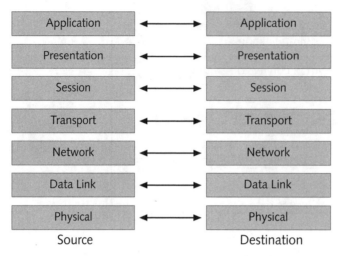

Figure 1-2   Peer communication

Each layer will only communicate with its opposite equivalent. Peer communication allows error checking to occur on two separate layers simultaneously. Even if the Transport layer is already providing reliable transmission of data, the Data Link layer is unaware of what goes on above it and will provide Data Link error control in the form of the **cyclical redundancy check (CRC)**.

Each layer does provide services to the layer above it and receives services from the layer below it, but the layers do not acknowledge these services in any way. Instead, each layer concentrates just on its function in the overall communications process. As a result, each layer of the OSI model takes information from the layer above, encapsulates that information into specific formats, and passes that information to the layer below.

Layer Functions

The OSI model was developed as an industry standard for companies to use when developing network hardware and software to ensure complete compatibility. As previously stated, each layer in the OSI model performs a specific function in the transmission process. Although most modern networks do not implement the OSI model exactly as it is defined, the model remains an excellent reference and learning tool. In light of that, the functions of each layer of the OSI model are defined in the following sections.

NOTE   Although the OSI model specifies seven layers to the communication process, most real-world implementations of protocol stacks do not use seven distinct layers. For example, TCP/IP uses a four-layer approach, while IPX/SPX loosely maps to the OSI model. Still, as mentioned earlier, the model is useful to help conceptualize the network communication process.

Physical (Layer 1)

Layer 1 in the OSI model is the Physical layer. It has the following responsibilities:

- Definition of the physical characteristics of the network hardware, including cable and connectors

- Representation of binary digits as voltages (encoding)

- Transmission of signals on the wire

The Physical layer defines the mechanical, electrical, and procedural events that occur during the physical transmission of electronic signals on the wire. In essence, the Physical layer's job is to transmit the actual signals on the network. This layer defines the physical characteristics of the transmission media (cabling/wire, radio waves, infrared, fiber/glass, etc.), the network card, and other physical items, such as hubs, repeaters, transceivers, connectors, and wall jacks.

As an example of a Physical layer definition, consider the Electronic Industries Association/Telecommunications Industry Association (EIA/TIA) 568B specification. The 568B specification defines a wiring system for data-grade cable, as shown in Figure 1-3.

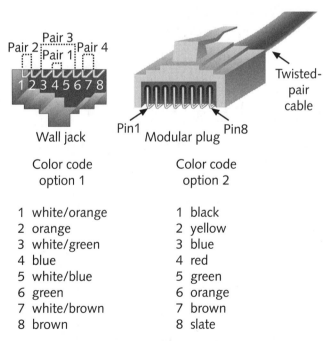

Figure 1-3   568B twisted-pair wiring scheme

Because a computer stores information in binary form (as a one or a zero digit), the Physical layer must convert that information into a signal for physical transmission. The network card at the Physical layer converts the data into electrical, radio, or light signals and transmits the signal on the network media. At a set measurement interval, the receiving NIC detects the presence of a signal as a binary one and its absence as a binary zero. Signals are sent by the source and received by the destination at a common interval so that the code (signal on/signal off) is interpreted correctly at the destination.

Logically, the physical devices must follow some type of standard when encoding and decoding these binary digits into and from electrical signals. The most common standard used in LANs is the Manchester Encoding method. This encoding method defines specific measurement intervals that are to be used when interpreting signals as binary digits.

Connectors, cables, and devices such as **repeaters** and hubs are all items that you can associate with the Physical layer. In the process of choosing cable, network administrators often consider the following criteria:

- Expense
- Physical location
- Distance
- Security requirements
- Transmission speed required

Network devices and networking media will be discussed in greater detail later in this course.

Data Link (Layer 2)

The layer just above the Physical layer on the OSI protocol stack is the Data Link layer. This layer has several responsibilities:

- NIC software functions, including the identification of the source and destination nodes via their physical addresses (Media Access Control addresses)
- Definition of how data is packaged for transport as frames
- Error notification

In the Data Link layer, the information to be transmitted receives its final formatting. The data is prepared for transmission, and a CRC is added. The CRC is information that is used to determine whether data was corrupted during transmission. Once assembled, the data is placed in a frame.

The Data Link layer has two sublayers that further articulate its functions: the **Logical Link Control (LLC) layer** and the **Media Access Control (MAC) layer**. The **Institute of Electrical and Electronics Engineers (IEEE)** created these sublayers to identify and isolate the separate responsibilities required at this level of the protocol stack. The LLC sublayer defines how data is packaged for the network. The LLC function is significant because it allows data frames to be packaged differently for different types of networks. Essentially, the LLC is the portion of the Data Link layer that provides the linking function between the Physical layer and the higher layers. Figure 1-4 shows the OSI layers, including the two sublayers.

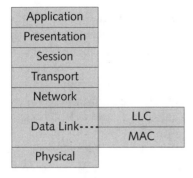

Figure 1-4   Data Link layer subdivision

The MAC sublayer defines the media access method and provides a unique identifier for the network card. The unique identifier, called a MAC address, is a 48-bit address represented as a 12-digit **hexadecimal** number given to each network card during production, as shown in Figure 1-5. Every network interface card on your network must have a unique MAC address. This **physical address** provides a way to distinguish one computer from another on the network.

Figure 1-5   MAC address

When network-card manufacturers produce network cards, they burn the MAC address into the circuitry of the NIC. IEEE assigns the first six hexadecimal digits of a MAC address to NIC manufacturers. Thus each manufacturer has its own six-digit identifier, sometimes called the Organizational Unit Identifier (OUI) or block ID. Large companies such as Cisco and 3Com may have more than one OUI. The last set of six hexadecimal digits is assigned by the vendor itself and is sometimes called the serial number or the device ID. Together, the 12 digits in a MAC address must form a unique number. Note that because the MAC address is added during the manufacturing process, it is a permanent marking. The only way to change your computer's MAC address is to replace the network card.

Because a computer uses a MAC address to identify itself on the network, the MAC address is an integral component when computers open communication pathways to transmit data on the network. On an **Ethernet** or **CSMA/CD** network, when one computer (the source) wants to communicate with another (the destination), the source computer sends the data frame out on the wire. The data frame is then sent to the appropriate portion or segment of the entire network. On that segment, every network interface receives and evaluates the message. When a NIC finds a match between its MAC address and the one listed in the data frame, the frame is copied and passed up the protocol stack. Even when one NIC finds a match, the data frame is still moved along the network until each NIC on the segment has evaluated the frame. When computers send out broadcast messages (messages intended for every machine on a given segment), every computer will accept the frame and pass it up the protocol stack.

Many LANs and WANs contain several segments. Dividing a network into segments enhances performance. If you didn't divide a network, every NIC on that network would take the time to receive and evaluate every message, which is costly. When networks are segmented, regular broadcasts and packets meant for the local segment are not passed to other segments. Because segmentation reduces the amount of packets that each NIC must check and evaluate, it increases network performance.

Network (Layer 3)

Layer 3 in the OSI model is the Network layer. This layer has the following functions:

- Software/logical addressing for data packets, such as IP, IPX, and AppleTalk
- Routes data and provides connectivity
- Best path selection

The Network layer routes data and provides connectivity to remote networks using the best path. The Network layer contains software-addressing information for data packets, which makes network segmentation and routing possible.

The protocols at the Network layer allow computers to route packets to remote networks using a **logical address**. This logical address is used by routers to forward the packet to the correct network. The type of logical address depends on the type of Network layer protocol used. For example, if the network uses the Internet Protocol (IP), an example of a logical address could be the following IP address: 192.168.1.1. Like the MAC address, the logical address must be unique for the computer on the network. Unlike the MAC address, which is permanent, the logical address usually can be assigned and modified by the person in charge of the network.

The Network layer and IP addresses are discussed in greater detail as this course progresses.

Transport (Layer 4)

The Transport layer provides host-to-host data transportation, and is concerned with quality of service and reliability. The responsibilities of the Transport layer include the following:

- End-to-end error-free transmission and delivery
- Flow control
- Data segmentation into maximum transmission unit (MTU) size
- Messaging service for the Session layer

Protocols that reside at the Transport layer can be connection-oriented or connection-less. **Connection-oriented** protocols, such as TCP, require an acknowledgment (ACK) of the receipt of data packets. If an ACK is not returned for a given packet in a given time, the connection-oriented protocol will retransmit the packet. Conversely, **connectionless** protocols, such as UDP, do not require an ACK for received packets.

Connectionless services are often deemed unreliable because they do not ensure that the data was properly received. A packet sent by a connectionless transport is also called a **datagram**. A letter sent through the post office is similar to a datagram. A person who sends regular mail through the post office does not receive an acknowledgment from the post office when the letter is delivered. If the person wants an acknowledgment, he or she has to confirm with the letter recipient. Connection-oriented services are termed reliable because they ensure the receipt of packets. Using the post office analogy again, assume that a letter was sent through the post office with a return receipt requested. This type of delivery could be considered reliable, because the sender receives notification when the letter is successfully delivered. The connection-oriented services of the Transport layer help create a "session" between two computers. Computers that share large amounts of data often establish sessions. This is especially true when computers are linked for application-sharing purposes.

The Transport layer protocols can often be adjusted to alter the packet size for the given network. This type of control allows for optimization of the packet, based on the type of data transfers that are being conducted. Generally, the size of the packet should be correlated to the size of the data transfer. For instance, if a system typically transfers large files over the network, larger packet sizes are used.

Session (Layer 5)

The Session layer enables two applications on the network to have an ongoing conversation or dialog. This is especially useful when applications are shared across the network or when computers are joined for game playing. Examples of Session layer protocols include NetBIOS, **SQL**, **RPC**, and **X-Windows**.

The Session layer provides the following services:

- Control for data exchange (full or half duplex)
- Data synchronization definition
- Failure recovery
- Communication setup and teardown

The Session layer tells the receiving computer where a transmission begins and ends. When a large amount of data must be passed between two computers, the data most likely is broken into several pieces. The Session layer ensures clear identification of the beginning and end of such a data transfer.

The Session layer allows the transfer of a large set of data across the network. For example, if you want to save a file to a network file server, your computer will attempt to open a session with the network server. Once the session is established, your computer will break the data into tiny packets and send the packets across the network until all the packets have been received by the server and written to the file server's disk drive. The Session layer also provides the ability to interrupt and recover the session if there is a need to wait for other data transmissions that are occurring on the local segment. If the line fails momentarily, the Session layer will also attempt to recover the session.

Presentation (Layer 6)

The Presentation layer prepares the data from the Application layer for transmission over the network. It also reformats data received from the lower layers in the protocol stack for the Application layer. Presentation layer components include extensions and coding schemes such as **BMP**, **WAV**, JPEG, MIDI, HTML, **EBCDIC**, and **ASCII**.

The Presentation layer has these responsibilities:

- Data translation
- Data formatting
- Data syntax restructuring
- Data encryption
- Data compression

The Presentation layer receives data from the Application layer. Because the data can come in several different formats, the Presentation layer must translate the data into a format that all computers on the network can interpret. In some cases, the Presentation layer must restructure the data before it can be sent across the network.

This layer also provides encryption services when data encryption is used in network communications. For outbound communications, the Presentation layer will encrypt data prior to transmission. For inbound data, the Presentation layer decrypts the data before passing it up to the Application layer. The Presentation layer may also compress outbound data or decompress inbound data. Data compression reduces the size of the data that is sent across the network and, in many cases, improves network performance.

After the Presentation layer reformats, compresses, and/or encrypts data, no further restructuring of the data takes place. The lower layers add headers and trailers, but they do not reconfigure the data.

Application (Layer 7)

Layer 7 is the Application layer. It has the following responsibilities:

- Initiating the request for network services
- Providing network services to applications such as e-mail and Web browsers

The Application layer is at the very top of the OSI protocol stack. This layer is concerned with user interaction with the computer and the network. In this layer, the user's actions may result in network access and the beginning of communications. The Application layer contains many protocols and utilities, such as telnet, FTP, HTTP, DNS, SMTP, and SNMP, which provide services to network applications. Note that application programs like Microsoft Word, Eudora Mail, and Netscape are not in the Application layer. Application programs, as well as the users of those programs, are outside the model, above the Application layer. For example, a user may use the Outlook e-mail program. That program is not in the Application layer, but the e-mail protocol SMTP (Simple Mail Transfer Protocol) that supports programs such as Outlook is in the layer. Data from the Application layer is passed directly to the Presentation layer.

Data Encapsulation

Data is sent from one computer to another in a data **packet**. The packet contains data from the sending application and more information added by the protocol stack. Prior to transmission across the network, the data is organized into a data **frame** at layer 2.

Each layer in the protocol stack may add a **protocol data unit (PDU)** to the data as it is passed down the layers. A PDU, which is also known as a header or a trailer, is specific information that is sent from one layer on the source computer to the same layer on the destination computer. This type of communication is called peer communication. As the layers pass the data through the stack, the addition of a header and/or trailer is called **encapsulation**. When data is passed down the protocol stack, the header or trailer of the next-lower layer encapsulates it. It is helpful to think of encapsulation as "wrapping."

The data packet is passed over the network from the source computer to the destination computer. It is assembled as it travels down the protocol stack of the source computer and disassembled as it travels up the protocol stack of the destination computer, as shown in Figure 1-6.

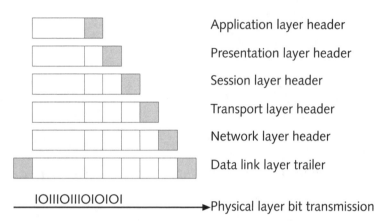

Application layer header

Presentation layer header

Session layer header

Transport layer header

Network layer header

Data link layer trailer

IOIIIOIIIOIOIOI —▶ Physical layer bit transmission

Figure 1-6   Encapsulation

As the destination computer unpacks the data packet, the data is checked. Once the data packet is completely disassembled, the original information that was transmitted is delivered to the receiving application. Table 1-1 lists and describes the five steps of data encapsulation.

Table 1-1   Five steps of data encapsulation

Step Number	Event	Description
1	Data conversion	When the application generates a message to be sent out on the network, the data is converted into a standard data format. This occurs at OSI layers 5, 6, and 7, which are also known as the "upper layers."
2	Segmentation header added	The Transport layer segments the data into maximum transmission units (MTUs) to ensure that hosts on both ends can communicate.
3	Packet creation with network header	Data is placed into a data packet or datagram, and a network header with logical addressing information is added. This occurs at layer 3, the Network layer.
4	Frame header and trailer for network link	The data frame is prepared for the type of network protocol that is in use. A frame header (including the source and destination MAC addresses) and trailer are added at the Data Link layer.
5	Bit transmission	The frame is sent across the wire as bits at the Physical layer; ones and zeros are encoded and transmitted along the physical network as pulses.

CHAPTER SUMMARY

- Two or more computers connected by media form a network. Computers can use a network to share resources such as printers, disk space, and applications.

- Before computers were networked, file transfers were usually conducted by users physically walking copies of data (on floppy disk or other magnetic media) to another computer, a system called "sneakernet."

- The earliest networks had no standardization, so interoperability between the various proprietary network implementations was rare. The ISO developed the OSI model in the mid-1980s to standardize networking models.

- Data transmission can be connection-oriented or connectionless. Connection-oriented transmission requires that packets be acknowledged as received. Connectionless transmission does not require acknowledgments.

- The OSI networking model has seven layers, which simplify the networking model by dividing it into less complex components. This layering allows engineers to specialize in specific layers, and the modularity allows them to upgrade components at one layer without affecting other layers. The layered model also encourages interoperability among the various networking vendors by providing them with a standard architecture.

- The Physical layer, the first and lowest layer of the OSI model, handles the physical transmission of data across the network.

- The Data Link layer, the second layer of the OSI model, interacts with the networking hardware by controlling the link and supporting communications with the network interface; this layer also interacts with the MAC address.

- The Network layer, the third layer of the OSI model, supports logical addressing and routing of data packets.

- The Transport layer, the fourth layer, segments and optimizes data that is to be sent out on the network.

- The Session layer, the fifth layer, establishes and maintains connections between computers during data transfers.

- The Presentation layer, the sixth layer, handles data translation, encryption, and formatting for transmission on the network or for interpretation by the Application layer.

- The Application layer, the seventh and highest layer, handles the interface between the network and the user.

- When the network user sends data to the network, it goes through a five-step data encapsulation process. This process takes place as the data packet travels down the OSI protocol stack.

KEY TERMS

American Standard Code for Information Interchange (ASCII) — A standardized method for formatting binary information and text for communications and printer control. The acronym ASCII is pronounced "ask-ee."

Application layer — The seventh layer of the OSI model, which is responsible for requesting network services and for providing services to applications.

BMP — A Windows Bitmap (BMP) file, a graphical image type used with Microsoft Windows applications.

Carrier Sense Multiple Access with Collision Detection (CSMA/CD) — The network access method used by Ethernet networks.

client — A computer that operates on a network and requests and uses the services of other computers on the network, but does not necessarily provide any services to other computers.

client/server — A type of networking in which a few dedicated computers, called servers, share files, printers, disk drives, and other resources with a group of client computers.

connection-oriented — Network communications that require acknowledgment. On the OSI reference model, the decision to use connection-oriented communications is made at the Transport layer.

connectionless — Network communications that do not require acknowledgment. On the OSI reference model, the decision to use connectionless communications is made at the Transport layer.

cyclical redundancy check (CRC) — The process that ensures that data was not corrupted during transmission. This is accomplished by comparing CRC calculations before and after transmission.

Data Link layer — The second layer of the OSI protocol stack, which defines the rules for sending and receiving information across the network media. It encodes and frames data for transmission and provides error detection and control. This layer has two parts: LLC and MAC.

datagram — A message or packet that is sent across a network and does not require acknowledgment by the destination station.

electromagnetic interference (EMI) — Electronic noise that disrupts signals on cables. This noise is frequently caused by motors and generators, but can also be caused by sunspots and other natural EMI-producing phenomena.

encapsulation — A process that occurs during transmission through the protocol stack, in which data from the higher layers is wrapped in a protocol header and/or trailer.

end system — The location and/or set of controls that the user can manipulate to interact with a computer or a network.

Ethernet — A standard networking architecture that defines the physical layout, lengths, and types of media that can be used. There are many variations of Ethernet but most use the CSMA/CD network access method.

1

Extended Binary Coded Decimal Interchange Code (EBCDIC) — A standardized formatting method for both binary and text files for communications and printer control. IBM developed EBCDIC. The acronym EBCDIC is pronounced "eb-see-dick."

extranet — An area of a company's network allowed access by non-employees such as business partners, vendors, and suppliers.

fiber-optic cable — A type of cable that conducts light signals through glass or plastic to generate network signals. Fiber-optic cable allows for transmission rates of 100 megabits per second or greater. It is impervious to electromagnetic interference because it sends light signals rather than electric signals along the cable.

frame — A segment of data. The words "frame" and "data packet" are often used interchangeably, although technically a frame is found at layer 2 of the OSI model and a packet is found at layer 3.

hexadecimal — A numbering method that relies on a base of 16. Hexadecimal digits can be 0, 1, 2, 3, 4, 5, 6, 7, 8, 9, A, B, C, D, E, or F.

infrared — Invisible light at the upper end of the electromagnetic spectrum. It is used in most hand-held remote control devices for televisions, stereos, and videocassette players. It is also used in some types of computer networking, especially for data transfers between laptop and desktop systems.

Institute of Electrical and Electronics Engineers (IEEE) — A technical professional society that fosters national and international standards. Its Web site is *www.ieee.org.*

International Organization for Standardization (ISO) — A multi-industry association that attempts to standardize and define items that increase communication and compatibility in many different industries.

intranet — The part of a company's network that is restricted to employee use only.

local area network (LAN) — A group of computers and other devices typically connected by a cable. A LAN is normally located in a single geographic region such as a building or floor in a building.

logical address — A network address that can be assigned and modified by the person in charge of the network. This type of address appears at the Network layer of the OSI model.

Logical Link Control (LLC) layer — A sublayer of the Data Link layer that forms the connection between the other software in the protocol stack and the networking hardware (such as the NIC and the cables).

media — The cable, glass, or telephone lines that host the signal from one computer to another on a network.

Media Access Control (MAC) layer — A sublayer of the Data Link layer that defines the hardware address of the physical network interface. In addition, it discards corrupted packets and identifies which packets were directed to the local system.

metropolitan area network (MAN) — An intermediate specification that defines networks confined to a fairly restricted geographic area, such as a campus, town, or city. These private networks span multiple geographically separate locations that are near one another.

network — Two or more computers connected by some type of media.

network interface card (NIC) — A hardware device that transmits and receives electronic signals on a network.

Network layer — The third layer of the OSI conceptual networking model, which allows communications to be routed on a network. It provides a logical address for computers on a network.

network operating system (NOS) — Operating software that has networking components built into its structure.

Open Systems Interconnection (OSI) — A seven-layer reference model created by the International Organization for Standardization (ISO) to define and separate networking hardware and software into distinct layers and functions. This model makes it easy for developers and manufacturers to ensure that their networking implementations are compatible with other implementations in the industry.

packet — A group of data that is transmitted across a network.

peer-to-peer network — A type of network in which the clients can also function as servers.

peer communication — The method of communication among the levels of the OSI model, in which each protocol in the OSI protocol stack encodes its own protocol data unit into the network hierarchy, so that it can communicate with the equivalent layer on the destination computer.

physical address — Also called the MAC address. It is burned into the network interface card (NIC) during the manufacturing process.

Physical layer — The first layer of the OSI conceptual networking model, which defines the physical media and electronic transmission methods used in networking.

Presentation layer — The sixth layer of the OSI network model, responsible for data formatting and encryption.

protocol — A definition of rules for communication between two or more computers. Computers must have a common protocol (or a translator) in order to communicate.

protocol data unit (PDU) — Information added to a data packet by the layers of the protocol stack. It can be header or trailer information that is attached to the data packet prior to transmission.

Remote Procedure Call (RPC) — A method used to establish communications between computer systems at the Session layer.

repeater — A device that repeats or boosts a network signal along network wire. It reduces signal degradation and increases the maximum usable length of network cable.

server — A computer that shares resources with other devices on a network.

Session layer — The fifth layer of the OSI model, which controls the connection between two computers sharing data. It maintains, defines, and recovers connections that are established between two computers.

storage area network (SAN) — A subsystem of networked storage devices that are physically separate from the servers.

Structured Query Language (SQL) — A computer language used to query, manipulate, and communicate with databases.

Transport layer — The fourth layer of the OSI reference model, which segments and reassembles data frames. It also provides for connection-oriented and connectionless communications.

virtual private network (VPN) — A private communications link over public communications infrastructure, such as the Internet.

WAV — A Windows Audio file, an audio file format used with Microsoft Windows applications.

wide area network (WAN) — A network that spans two or more geographically diverse locations and typically uses public telecommunications carriers to connect its individual segments.

wireless — Communications that are not conducted over physical wires or cables. These communications can include infrared, radio, and other types of transmissions that are sent through the air between two or more locations.

X-Windows — A standard graphical user interface (GUI) used on UNIX systems.

REVIEW QUESTIONS

1. Which of the following best describes the Presentation layer?

   a. Establishes, maintains, and manages sessions between applications

   b. Translates, encrypts, or prepares data from the Application layer for network transmission

   c. Handles routing information for data packets

   d. Provides the electrical and mechanical transmission of data

   e. Handles link control and uses the MAC address on the network interface card (NIC)

2. Which of the following best describes the Network layer?

   a. Handles routing information for data packets

   b. Provides the electrical and mechanical transmission of data

   c. Handles link control and uses the MAC address on the NIC

   d. Establishes, maintains, and manages sessions between applications

   e. Translates, encrypts, or prepares data from the Application layer for network transmission

3. Which of the following best describes the Session layer?

   a. Translates, encrypts, or prepares data from the Application layer for network transmission

   b. Handles routing information for data packets

   c. Provides the electrical and mechanical transmission of data

   d. Handles link control and uses the MAC address on the NIC

   e. Establishes, maintains, and manages sessions between applications

4. Which of the following best describes the Transport layer?

   a. Provides the electrical and mechanical transmission of data

   b. Handles link control and uses the MAC address on the NIC

   c. Establishes, maintains, and manages sessions between applications

   d. Segments and reassembles data and provides either connection-oriented or connectionless communications

   e. Translates, encrypts, or prepares data from the Application layer for network transmission

5. Which of the following best describes the Data Link layer?

   a. Provides the electrical and mechanical transmission of data

   b. Handles link control and uses the MAC address on the NIC

   c. Establishes, maintains, and manages sessions between applications

   d. Translates, encrypts, or prepares data from the Application layer for network transmission

   e. Handles routing information for data packets

6. Which of the following best describes the Physical layer?

   a. Establishes, maintains, and manages sessions between applications

   b. Translates, encrypts, or prepares data from the Application layer for network transmission

   c. Provides the electrical and mechanical transmission of data

   d. Handles link control and uses the MAC address on the NIC

   e. Provides network services to the user

7. Which of the following best describes the Application layer?

   a. Establishes, maintains, and manages sessions between applications

   b. Translates, encrypts, or prepares data for network transmission

   c. Provides network services to the user

   d. Handles routing information for data packets

   e. Provides the electrical and mechanical transmission of data

8. Which of the following accurately describe the Media Access Control (MAC) address? (Choose all that apply.)

a. It is a physical number set during the manufacturing process.

b. This address is a layer in a network segment.

c. MAC addresses contain 12 hexadecimal numbers.

d. Computers use this address to uniquely identify themselves on the network.

e. An IP address is one example of this type of address.

9. Which of the following accurately describe the network address? (Choose all that apply.)

a. It is a physical number set during the manufacturing process.

b. This address is used when routing communications between different network segments.

c. The Data Link layer uses this address.

d. This address is set at layer 3 of the OSI model.

e. An example of this type of address is an IP address.

10. Connection-oriented services are also known as _____ services.

a. reliable

b. unreliable

c. datagram

11. Connectionless services are also called _____ services.

a. reliable

b. acknowledgment

c. unreliable

12. Which of the following services receive an acknowledgment from the destination? (Choose all that apply.)

a. Datagram

b. Reliable

c. Connection-oriented

d. Connectionless

e. Unreliable

13. Place the following steps of data encapsulation in their correct descending order:

a. Frame headers and trailers added

b. Segment header added

c. Bit transmission

d. Packet creation and network header

e. Data conversion

14. Which of the following correctly defines a WAN?

    a. A network contained within a single geographic location and usually connected by a privately maintained medium

    b. A network spread over multiple geographic areas and usually connected by publicly and privately maintained media

    c. A network spread over a single metropolitan area

15. Which of the following best describes a LAN?

    a. A network that is contained in a single geographic area such as a building or floor in a building

    b. A countywide network that spans multiple geographic locations

    c. A large network that is connected by both publicly and privately maintained cabling spread over multiple geographic regions

16. Which of the following reasons for providing a layered OSI architecture are correct? (Choose all that apply.)

    a. To provide design modularity, which allows upgrades to a specific layer to remain separate from the other layers

    b. To simplify the networking model by dividing it into 14 layers and 12 sublayers

    c. To discourage interoperability between disparate networking models

    d. To enable programmers to specialize in a particular layer

    e. To allow for standardized interfaces from networking vendors

17. On a network, computers must use a common _____ in order for communication to occur.

    a. protocol

    b. operating system

    c. manufacturer

    d. hardware platform

18. Before networks, what did people use to transfer files?

    a. Sneakernet

    b. Protocols

    c. Interface cards

    d. Ethernet

19. A protocol is to a computer as a(n) _____ is to a person.

    a. identity

    b. personality

    c. language

    d. personal philosophy

1

20. Which of the following are network hardware? (Choose all that apply.)
    a. NIC
    b. NOS
    c. LLC
    d. Network media
    e. Connectors

21. Which of the following are network software? (Choose all that apply.)
    a. Components that map to the Application layer of the OSI model
    b. NIC
    c. NOS
    d. Media connectors

22. All networking vendors follow the OSI model and design seven-layer architectures. True or False?

23. Communications on a network originate at the _____.
    a. destination
    b. breaker
    c. peak
    d. source

24. Transmitted signals are bound for a _____ computer.
    a. destination
    b. breaker
    c. peak
    d. source

25. Information transmitted on a network is called a(n) _____.
    a. package
    b. expresser
    c. data destination
    d. data packet
    e. E-pack

26. Which of the following are layers of the OSI model? (Choose all that apply.)
    a. OSI
    b. Physical
    c. IEEE
    d. Data Link

27. Which layer of the OSI model is responsible for media access and packaging data into frames?

   a. Network layer

   b. Physical layer

   c. Data Link layer

   d. Transport layer

28. At which layer of the OSI model will encryption and compression occur?

   a. Presentation layer

   b. Session layer

   c. Application layer

   d. Network layer

29. Which of the following lists the layers of the OSI model from layer 7 to layer 1?

   a. Application, Session, Transport, Network, Presentation, Data Link, Physical

   b. Physical, Data Link, Network, Transport, Session, Presentation, Application

   c. Application, Presentation, Session, Transport, Network, Data Link, Physical

   d. Presentation, Application, Session, Network, Transport, Data Link, Physical

30. The _____ layer is responsible for finding the best path to route packets within an internetwork.

   a. Transport

   b. Network

   c. Session

   d. Data Link

CASE PROJECTS

CASE PROJECTS

1. Jennifer, Moe, and Lisa recently passed the Network+ certification exam and have been hired to perform network support at your company. Moe has been complaining that memorizing the layers of the OSI model was difficult and a waste of time. He understands why protocol developers need to know about it, but thinks that network administrators and support people only need to know which protocols are operating on the network in question. Explain to Moe the reasons for using the OSI model. How could detailed knowledge of the model be valuable in Moe's network-support position?

2. Lisa overhears your conversation with Moe and asks your opinion about data encapsulation. She is confused about the layers in which encapsulation occurs. Explain the five steps of data encapsulation to her.

1

3. Jennifer is unsure in which layer the MAC addresses function. Because the MAC is on the NIC and is associated with the physical media, she asks why this address is associated with the Data Link layer. Explain to Jennifer the functions of the Data Link layer and the sublayers within this layer. Where exactly does the MAC address fit in?

4. Give Jennifer, Moe, and Lisa a helpful way to remember the layers of the OSI model. Identify three words to associate with each layer.

5. This afternoon, you will be explaining the OSI model to senior management. Design a flow chart showing how the OSI model facilitates the transferring of data from a source to a destination node.

2

NETWORK DEVICES

After reading this chapter and completing the exercises, you will be able to:

♦ Explain the uses, advantages, and disadvantages of repeaters

♦ Explain the uses, advantages, and disadvantages of hubs

♦ Define wireless access points

♦ Define network segmentation

♦ Explain network segmentation using bridges

♦ Explain network segmentation using switches

♦ Explain network segmentation using routers

♦ Explain network segmentation using brouters and gateways

Many devices help control and extend the usable size of a growing net-work. These devices have a wide variety of functions and are added to networks to allow a greater number of computers to exist on the network; to extend the usable distance of the network; to segment, or localize, traffic on the network; to subdivide the network so problems are easier to isolate; and to join existing networks together. In this chapter, you will learn about the different devices that can be used to accomplish the preceding objectives. These devices include repeaters, hubs, bridges, switches, routers, brouters, and gateways.

REPEATERS

The number of **nodes** on a network and the length of cable used influence the quality of communication on the network. As data leaves the source, or transmitting station, the NIC converts the data to electrical impulses if copper wire is used, or to light signals if a fiber-optic cable is used. As the signal travels the length of the cable, the distance that it must traverse weakens it. The nodes that copy and pass the signal on also degrade it. This degradation of signal clarity is called **attenuation**.

Repeaters work against attenuation by repeating signals that they receive on a network, typically cleaning and boosting the digital transmission in the process. For example, a digital signal communicates one of two different states (one or zero) in its communication stream. On a network connected by wire media, the presence of voltage creates a one, and the absence of voltage creates a zero. However, as attenuation occurs, the digital signal may become increasingly difficult to decipher. If left uncorrected, attenuation could make the signal unreadable. A repeater takes the attenuated signal, cleans it up, and then sends the clear and crisp digital stream to the rest of the network, as shown in Figure 2-1.

Figure 2-1   Repeater

Note that on **analog** networks, devices that boost the signal are called **amplifiers**. These devices do not have the same signal regeneration capabilities as repeaters because they must maintain the shape of the received signal. Therefore, noise tends to be amplified with the signal.

Because repeaters work with the actual physical signal, and do not attempt to interpret the data being transmitted, they are Physical layer (layer 1) devices on the OSI model. This means that most repeaters cannot tell the difference between a good signal and a corrupt signal. Thus, they normally repeat everything. On optical networks, signal amplification is handled by **optical repeaters**. Optical repeaters use either a light-emitting diode (LED) or diode laser per optical signal. The type of fiber, multimode or single mode, and distance of the cable run determine the necessary type of optical repeater.

Some repeaters can be used to connect two physically different types of cabling. For example, a repeater might connect a twisted-pair cable to a coaxial cable. However, repeaters cannot reformat, resize, or otherwise manipulate the data packet. In other words, when a network uses different physical media but the same data type and packet structure, a repeater can be used as a connection device. Figure 2-2 shows a repeater on a bus network.

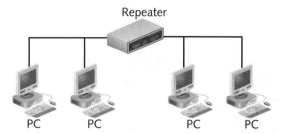

Figure 2-2   Repeater in the network

HUBS

A **hub** is a generic connection device used to tie several networking cables together to create a link between different stations on a network. Hubs that are plugged into electric power are called **active hubs**. They usually amplify or repeat signals that pass through them. Because they have multiple inbound and outbound connections, these hubs are also known as multiport repeaters. A hub that merely connects different cables on a network and provides no signal regeneration is called a **passive hub** and is not a repeater.

NOTE

"Hub" is a generic term applied to many different network-connection devices. A hub can accomplish two different tasks: if it only connects cables together, it is a passive hub; if it actually boosts the network signal, it is an active hub. If a hub in some way **segments** or subdivides the traffic on a network, it is an intelligent, or switching, hub. For the purposes of the CCNA exam, the term hub, by itself, is a device that does not segment the network.

Often, a hub forms a central point on a network where the cables come together. A star topology often has a hub at its center. **Topology** usually refers to the physical layout of network cable and devices. When all stations are connected to a central hub, the topology is known as a star because of its appearance. Figure 2-3 shows a star topology with a hub in the center.

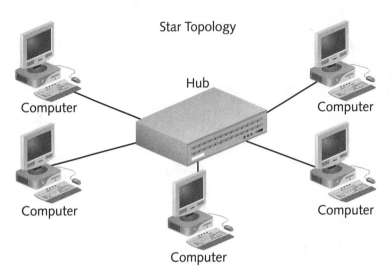

Figure 2-3   Star topology

ADVANTAGES AND DISADVANTAGES OF REPEATERS AND HUBS

Because repeaters simply repeat, amplify, and clean up a signal, network administrators mainly use them to increase the usable distance of a network. Repeaters have little impact on network speed because they do not do any packet processing.

Familiarize yourself with the following advantages of using repeaters on your network:

- Repeaters can extend a network's total distance.
- Repeaters do not seriously affect network performance.
- Certain repeaters can connect networks using different physical media.

Although repeaters provide many advantages, they do have disadvantages. The following list describes the disadvantages of using repeaters on the network:

- Repeaters cannot connect different network architectures, such as **Token Ring** and Ethernet.
- Repeaters do not reduce network traffic.
- Repeaters do not segment the network.

Repeaters do not reformat data packets, so they cannot connect networks that require different types of packet structures. Also, they do not reduce network traffic because they repeat everything they receive. Because they repeat everything without discrimination, the number of repeaters must be limited on your network. Too many repeaters on a network could throw off network communication timings by repeating packets after they normally would have been dropped. Such a circumstance would create noise on the wire and increase the likelihood of packet collisions, which would reduce network performance.

Repeaters also do not segment a network. That is, they do not create logical or physical divisions of the network. On an Ethernet network, packets that are broadcast on a given segment may collide. This happens when two or more stations transmit at the same time. Since repeaters do not segment a network, devices that are separated only by a repeater are susceptible to data packet collision, because they are part of the same **collision domain**.

WIRELESS ACCESS POINTS

The proliferation of wireless technologies and **wireless local area networks (WLANs)** has led to the creation of a new network device known as a wireless access point. **Wireless access points** provide cell-based areas where wireless clients can connect to the network via association. Each access point contains a radio transceiver that matches the wireless technology on the network.

In most respects, a wireless access point functions exactly like a hub. Bandwidth on the access point is shared. Therefore, as more clients are associated with an access point, the available bandwidth decreases. In addition, nearly all wireless access points can also function as wireless repeaters, just as hubs can provide this function. Figure 2-4 shows a wireless access point connected to a repeater.

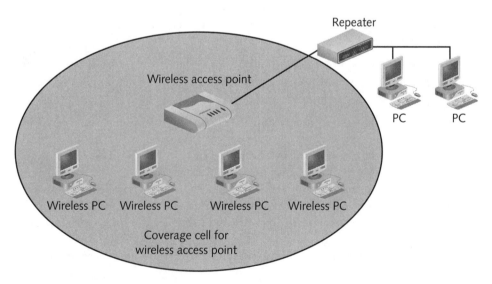

Figure 2-4   Wireless access point in the network

NETWORK SEGMENTATION

Network **segmentation** is an essential concept you must understand to complete the CCNA exam successfully and understand the contents of this book. In particular, you must understand network segmentation using bridges, switches, and routers.

Ethernet networks, which are characterized by the IEEE 802.3 standard, define the use of a **Carrier Sense Multiple Access with Collision Detection (CSMA/CD)** access method. CSMA/CD specifies that each node (before placing packets onto the networking media) must first listen to the network medium to determine if the medium is currently free of packets. If so, the node can place packets on the medium. Obviously, it is possible for two nodes to listen, find a wire empty, and send packets at the same exact time. The result is a collision in which both packets are destroyed. The CSMA/CD access method specifies that nodes involved in a collision on the network perform a **backoff algorithm**, which causes them to wait a random amount of time, called a **backoff period**, before making an attempt to retransmit data. The randomness of the period greatly reduces the likelihood of a second collision.

Problems occur when network administrators place too many nodes on the same network segment. As the number of nodes increases, the amount of traffic on a segment increases, as does the chance that two nodes will transmit data at exactly the same time. This causes the number of collisions to increase. The result is a large amount of network bandwidth being used to retransmit packets that have been destroyed by collisions. Segmentation is the answer to this problem.

Segmentation is the breaking down of a single heavily populated network segment into smaller segments, or collision domains, populated by fewer nodes. Figure 2-5 shows an example of network segmentation.

In Figure 2-5, the upper graphic depicts a network consisting of four nodes sharing a single segment—in other words, a single collision domain. In this unsegmented network, all computers would be affected by the traffic of other nodes. The lower graphic shows a bridge separating the four computers into two collision domains. This segmentation reduces the number of computers that must contend for use of the bandwidth. For example, on a 10-Mbps network, each collision domain shares its own 10 Mbps. In the upper graphic, four computers would share this 10 Mbps. In the lower graphic, only two computers would share the bandwidth. As a result, network collisions and retransmissions are reduced. A bridge is one networking device that can be used to segment networks.

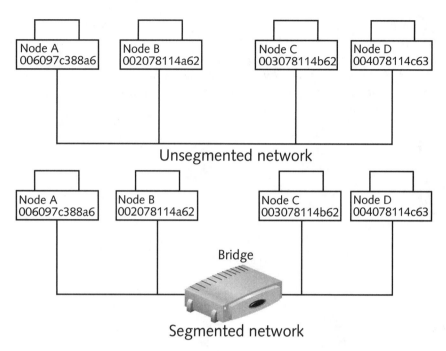

Figure 2-5   Network segmentation

BRIDGES

Bridges operate at the Data Link layer of the OSI model. A bridge filters traffic between network segments by examining the destination MAC address. Based on this destination MAC address, the bridge either forwards or discards the frame. If the destination MAC address is located on a segment other than the originating segment, the bridge forwards it. If the frame was meant for the local segment, the bridge discards the frame. In this way, the bridge reduces network traffic by keeping local traffic on the local segment. However, when a client sends a **broadcast** frame to the entire network, the bridge will always forward the frame. In addition, if a bridge has no destination MAC address in its table, it will send the frame out to all interfaces except the one it came in on.

The bridge functions like a repeater in that it listens to incoming frames and repeats them on other segments. The only real difference is that it actually reads the MAC address and chooses whether to repeat or discard a frame.

Consider the network shown in Figure 2-6. The bridge divides the network into two segments (Segment A and Segment B). Communications between computers on Segment A do not pass through to Segment B, and vice versa. However, communications between computers on Segment A and Segment B will be repeated through the bridge to the other segment. For example, when Computer 1 sends a message to Computer 4, the bridge discards the frame, and only Computers 2, 3, and 4 receive it.

Computer 4 will accept the frame, while Computers 2 and 3 will discard it after determining that it was not destined for their MAC address. However, when Computer 2 sends a frame to Computer 5, all computers on Segment A and Segment B will examine the frame. Only Computer 5 will accept the frame, and the rest will discard it after determining that the MAC address on the frame does not match theirs.

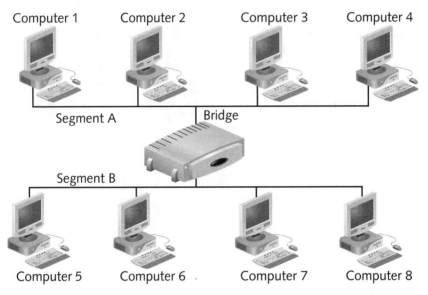

Figure 2-6   Bridge

Bridges can use two different methods to determine which segment includes a specific MAC address. One method is transparent bridging, and the other is source-route bridging.

Transparent Bridges

Transparent bridges are also called learning bridges because they build a table of MAC addresses as they receive frames. This means that they "learn" which addresses are on which segments. When a bridge first receives power, its bridging table is empty. Over time, though, it learns which segments have which MAC addresses as frames are forwarded. The bridge uses the source MAC addresses to determine which addresses are on which segments. By determining a frame's origin, the bridge knows where to send frames in the future. Ethernet networks mainly use transparent bridges. Token Ring networks usually employ source-routing bridges.

Source-Routing Bridges

In Token Ring networks, source-routing bridges rely on the source of the frame transmission to provide the routing information. The source computer determines the best path by sending out explorer frames. When the destination computer receives the explorer frames, it determines the best routes and sends that information back to the source. Then, the source includes the routing information returned by its explorer frames in the frame sent across the network. The bridge uses this information to build its table.

Translation Bridges

Although bridges tend to connect similar networks, translation bridges can connect networks with different architectures, such as Ethernet and Token Ring. These bridges appear as transparent bridges to an Ethernet host and as source-routing bridges to a Token Ring host.

Advantages and Disadvantages of Bridges

Bridges do more than repeaters because they evaluate frames; however, their additional capabilities bring both advantages and disadvantages. The advantages of using a bridge include the following:

- Bridges can extend a network by acting as a repeater.

- Bridges can reduce network traffic on a segment by subdividing network communications.

- Bridges increase the available bandwidth to individual nodes because fewer nodes share a collision domain.

- Bridges reduce the likelihood of network collisions.

- Some bridges connect networks using different media types and architectures.

Because bridges regenerate the network signal when they pass it from segment to segment, they can extend the cable's usable distance. Bridges selectively forward frames, which effectively reduces the number of messages circulating around the network. Because this also reduces the number of frames and broadcasting stations, the likelihood that two stations will broadcast at the same time on the same segment and cause a collision is reduced. Bridges also connect different media types, and some can connect different architectures. Bridges, however, do have some disadvantages:

- Because bridges do more than repeaters by viewing MAC addresses, the extra processing makes them slower than repeaters.

- Bridges forward broadcast frames indiscriminately, so they do not filter broadcast traffic.

- Bridges are more expensive than repeaters.

The fact that bridges forward broadcast traffic can be a major disadvantage on a network during a **broadcast storm**, which happens when two or more stations engage in the transmission of excessive broadcast traffic. For example, Microsoft operating systems use broadcasts to determine which computer will be in charge of creating a browse list (i.e., a map of network resources). In the early Microsoft networks, broadcast storms occurred when two or more machines would not relinquish the browse list responsibility to a higher-ranked machine. Such an error condition can cease network communications altogether. Because bridges simply forward broadcast traffic, they do nothing to reduce the storm.

SWITCHES

Like bridges, switches operate at the Data Link layer of the OSI model. **Switches** increase network performance by reducing the number of packets transmitted to the rest of the network. In an Ethernet network, computers are usually connected directly to a switch. Unlike bridges, a switch opens a **virtual circuit** between the source and the destination. This prevents communications between just two computers from being broadcast to every computer on the network or segment. This is called **microsegmentation** because the segment, or collision domain, is effectively just the sending and receiving nodes.

Sometimes switches are called "switching hubs."

NOTE

When two machines have a virtual circuit, they do not have to share the wire with any other computers. Thus, if the total network transfer capacity is 100 Mbps, the two communicating machines get the full **bandwidth**, which is 100 Mbps in this case. Multiple virtual circuits can be in use at the same time, each with its own 100 Mbps. This is called "switched bandwidth." Conversely, a hub will divide the 100 Mbps among each communicating node connected to its ports. This is called "shared bandwidth." When machines must share a wire and compete for available bandwidth with other machines, they experience **contention**. A switch reduces contention by subdividing a network into virtual circuits. Figure 2-7 shows a star topology that uses a switch.

2

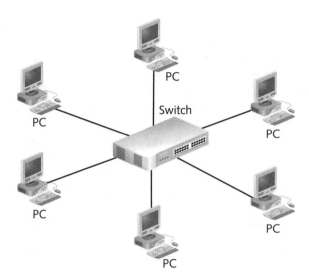

Figure 2-7 Star topology using a switch

Switches filter based on MAC addresses and build tables in memory just like bridges, but the switching table will have a mapping of switch port number to MAC address instead of bridge segment number to MAC address. Switches can have an unlimited number of ports, which can be connected directly to workstations. Usually bridges have fewer than 10 ports, and so those ports are connected to hubs rather than directly to workstations. Bridges are software-based devices while switches are hardware-based.

The advantages of switches include the following:

- Switches increase available network bandwidth.
- With switches, there is reduced workload on individual computers.
- Switches increase network performance.
- There are fewer frame collisions because switches create collision domains for each connection (a process called microsegmentation).
- Switches have an unlimited number of ports and connect directly to workstations.

Even though the benefits of switching are great, switching has its disadvantages. Here are a few to consider:

- Switches are significantly more expensive than bridges.
- Network connectivity problems can be difficult to trace through a switch.
- Broadcast traffic may be troublesome.

Switches usually cost more than bridges, but they do a lot more. Unfortunately, because switches are constantly creating and dropping virtual circuits, network problems may be difficult to trace. Broadcast traffic is also a problem for switches, because the hardware address indicates that all computers should receive a packet. The switch can either block or send these broadcasts. When a switch blocks the broadcasts, network performance improves, but applications that rely on broadcasts to keep track of resources are not able to communicate using broadcasts. However, if the switch sends the broadcasts, they will be transmitted to every machine on the network by the switch. In that case, virtual circuits provide no benefit. Of course, other types of network communications will still benefit from switches' involvement. A switch is the device of choice for improving network performance, and many companies are replacing hubs and bridges with switches.

REFERENCE

Switching, and the Cisco 1900 series switch in particular, are covered in greater detail in Chapter 13.

NOTE

This section discusses Ethernet switches (primarily used in LANs), but several implementations of switching for WAN configurations also exist. Public telecommunications carriers such as AT&T, Sprint, and MCI provide most of these switching services. These services include packet switching, switched-56, AT&T Switched Digital Services, and MCI Communications Virtual Private Data Services.

ROUTERS

As networks grow more complex, network administrators may need to use routers on their networks. **Routers** provide filtering and network traffic control on LANs and WANs. These devices can connect multiple segments and multiple networks. Networks connected by multiple routers are called **internetworks** because they create a larger network of interconnected, smaller networks.

Routers operate at the Network layer of the OSI model. Routers are similar to switches and bridges in that they segment a network and filter traffic. However, instead of filtering traffic based on the physical address of a packet (as do switches and bridges), routers use the logical address. Like bridges and switches, routers use a table to determine how to forward packets.

REFERENCE

You will learn more about routing tables in Chapter 3.

When a router is introduced into a network, it creates more networks. This is because every interface on a router represents a different network. Routers create collision domains and they also create **broadcast domains** because a router will not pass broadcast traffic. A broadcast domain is a group of network devices that will receive LAN broadcast traffic from each other.

Physical vs. Logical Addresses

The NIC manufacturer burns the physical address or MAC address into the network card during the manufacturing process. The MAC address, which is found at the Data Link layer of the OSI model, is used by bridges and switches to make forwarding decisions within a network or **subnetwork**. On the other hand, the type of Network and Transport protocols used by the devices on a network dictate the format of the logical address. For example, the TCP/IP and IPX/SPX protocol suites span the Network layer and Transport layer of the OSI reference model. Both of these protocols are routable, which means that they can be used for communication between networks or subnetworks that are divided by a router or routers.

When TCP/IP is used on an internetwork, the logical address is known as an **IP address**. Routers use the IP address to route packets to the correct network segment. Software, not hardware, implements IP addresses. This means that routers use the logical Network layer software address to route packets to the appropriate network segment. Figure 2-8 illustrates a router connecting four different network segments. Notice that each **port** (connection) on the router has its own unique IP address.

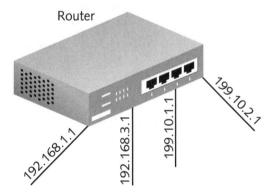

Router

Figure 2-8 Router

Advantages and Disadvantages of Routers

Although routers offer several advantages for the network, they have some inherent disadvantages. First, let us take a look at the advantages:

- Routers can connect different network architectures, such as Ethernet and Token Ring.

- Routers can choose the best path across the network using dynamic routing techniques.

Dynamic routing techniques are described in Chapter 8.

- Routers create collision domains by segmenting the network.
- Routers reduce network traffic because they do not retransmit network broadcast traffic; in other words, they create broadcast domains.

The disadvantages of using routers on the network include the following:

- Routers work only with routable network protocols; not all protocols are routable.
- Routers are more expensive than bridges or repeaters.
- Dynamic router communications (inter-router communication) cause additional network overhead, which results in less bandwidth for user data.
- Routers are slower than bridges or switches because they must analyze a data transmission from the Physical through the Network layer, whereas bridges and switches only read two layers of information: the Physical and Data Link.

Routers are commonly used to connect networks to the Internet. Figure 2-9 displays a network consisting of a switch that uses a physical star topology to connect to the Internet via a router.

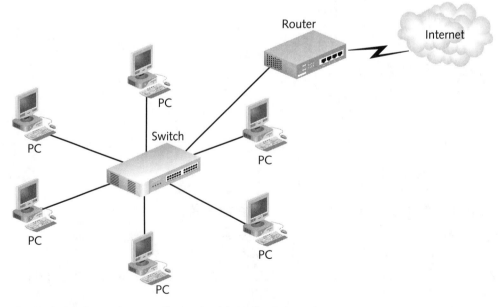

Figure 2-9   Router connecting network to the Internet

BROUTERS

Several types of hybrid devices exist in the networking world. One such device is the **brouter**. A brouter functions as both a bridge for nonroutable protocols and a router for routable protocols.

A brouter provides the best attributes of both a bridge and a router. The brouter acts as a bridge when it receives a packet that contains a nonroutable protocol, such as NetBEUI. To accomplish its bridging task, the brouter uses the MAC address. In contrast, the brouter acts as a router when it receives a packet that contains a routable protocol, such as TCP/IP or IPX/SPX. To accomplish its routing task, the brouter uses network address information. Routers operate at the Network layer of the OSI model; bridges operate at the Data Link layer. Because the brouter performs a dual role, it operates at both the Data Link and Network layers.

GATEWAYS

A **gateway** is usually a combination of hardware and software. Its purpose is to translate between different protocol suites. The packets must be rebuilt not just at the lower levels for conversion between, for example, Ethernet and Token Ring, but at the very upper levels so that the actual data content can be converted into a format the destination can process. Because gateways must rebuild the packets at the upper layers of the OSI model, gateways have the most negative effect on network performance. That is to say, they create the most **latency** of all the devices discussed in this chapter. One example of a common gateway would be Services for Macintosh. This is software installed on a Windows 2000 server so that Macintosh computers, which use the AppleTalk protocol, can communicate with the server, which is most likely using the TCP/IP protocol.

CHAPTER SUMMARY

◻ Network administrators use devices to control and extend the usable size of a network. These devices include repeaters, hubs, bridges, switches, routers, brouters, and gateways.

◻ Repeaters work against attenuation by cleaning and repeating signals that they receive on a network. Repeaters work at the Physical layer of the OSI model. They cannot connect different network architectures. Repeaters do not reduce network traffic or segment the network.

◻ A hub ties several networking cables together to create a link between different stations on a network. An active hub has its own electrical power and acts as a repeater, whereas a passive hub provides no signal regeneration. Hubs operate at the Physical layer of the OSI model and do not segment the network.

◻ Network segmentation is the process of isolating hosts onto smaller segments to reduce the possibility of collisions. Bridges and switches are two devices commonly used to segment networks.

◻ Bridges provide network segmentation by examining the MAC address that is sent in the data frame. Bridges can use transparent bridging or source-route bridging to determine which segment includes a specific physical address. Bridges operate at the Data Link layer of the OSI model.

◻ Switches increase network performance by reducing the number of frames transmitted to the rest of a network. They do this by opening a virtual circuit between the source and the destination. Switches operate at the Data Link layer of the OSI model.

◻ Routers operate at the Network layer of the OSI model and provide filtering and network-traffic control on LANs and WANs. They can connect multiple segments and networks. On a TCP/IP network, routers use IP addresses to route packets to the correct network segment. Routers use information from routing tables to move packets from one network to another.

◻ A brouter is a hybrid device that functions both as a bridge for nonroutable protocols and as a router for routable protocols. Brouters operate at both the Data Link and Network layers.

◻ Gateways are usually a combination of hardware and software and are used to translate between different protocols. They usually operate at layer 4 and above in the OSI model.

KEY TERMS

active hub — A device that connects multiple nodes and/or networks, is connected to external power, and repeats and regenerates signals on a network.

amplifier — A device used to boost analog signals on a broadband network.

analog — A method of signal transmission on broadband networks.

attenuation — The natural degradation of a transmitted signal over distance.

backoff algorithm — A mathematical calculation performed by computers after a collision occurs on a CSMA/CD network, which forces machines to wait a random amount of time before resending the destroyed packet. A backoff algorithm is run by computers to set the length of time for the backoff period.

backoff period — A random time interval used after a collision has been detected on an Ethernet network. Use of a backoff period minimizes the likelihood of another collision.

bandwidth — The available capacity of the network. The greater the network bandwidth, the greater the speed in data transfer.

bridge — A device that operates at the Data Link layer, used to filter traffic between network segments by evaluating the MAC address of packets that are sent to it.

broadcast — A packet meant for the entire network.

broadcast domain — A group of network devices that will receive LAN broadcast traffic from each other.

broadcast storm — Excessive broadcast messages to every host on the network, launched by multiple computers; usually triggered by some error condition on the network.

brouter — A device that functions as a bridge for nonroutable protocols and a router for routable protocols. The brouter operates at both the Data Link and Network layers.

Carrier Sense Multiple Access with Collision Detection (CSMA/CD) — An access method specified by the IEEE Ethernet 802.3 standard. In this method, a node will listen to see if the line is clear and then, if the line is clear, send data. Two nodes may still send at the same time and cause a collision, in which case the two nodes will then perform the backoff algorithm.

collision domain — In Ethernet networking, a single segment on a network. Any station on the same physical segment or separated by a repeater is in the same collision domain. Bridges, routers, and switches (depending on how they are configured) can separate collision domains.

contention — The condition that occurs when computers on a network must share the available capacity of the network wire with other computers.

gateway — A combination of hardware and software that translates between different protocols on a network.

hub — An active or passive device that connects network segments. Passive hubs are connection points; active hubs repeat and regenerate signals.

internetwork — A large network comprised of smaller interconnected networks.

IP address — A 32-bit binary address used on TCP/IP networks; consists of a host portion and a network portion.

latency — A delay on a network caused by a variety of factors, including the addition of devices.

microsegmentation — The type of segmentation that occurs through the use of virtual circuits between switches and nodes. Each connection enjoys the total bandwidth. Bandwidth is not shared as it is through hubs.

node — A connection point or junction on the network. A node can be a terminal or computer connected to the network.

optical repeater — A network device that uses LEDs or diode lasers to amplify optical signals.

passive hub — A device that connects network segments, but does not perform signal regeneration.

port — A connection point, usually for network cable, on a device such as a hub, bridge, switch, or router.

repeater — A device that repeats and cleans signals on the network, and extends the usable distance of the network.

router — A device that connects multiple segments, subdivides a network, filters broadcast traffic, and maintains a routing table. A router uses the logical address to move data packets from point to point.

segment (noun) — A section of a network that has been subdivided by routers, switches, or bridges.

segment (verb) — To subdivide a network with a networking device, such as a bridge, switch, or router.

segmentation — The process of breaking a network into smaller broadcast or collision domains.

subnetwork — A portion of the network created by manipulating a network address and breaking it down into smaller parts.

switch — A device used between nodes on a network or between networks to create virtual circuits between two points. A switch increases bandwidth by isolating traffic between two points.

Token Ring — A networking method developed by IBM that organizes the network into a physical or logical ring. The token is a logical device, and because stations may only broadcast on the network when they have the token, traffic does not collide.

topology — The physical layout of network components. The topology can take the form of a ring, star, or bus.

virtual circuit — A private connection between two points created by a switch that allows the two points to use the entire available bandwidth between them without contention.

wireless access point — A network device that contains a radio transceiver, which allows wireless clients to connect to a WLAN.

wireless local area network (WLAN) — A local area network consisting either entirely of wireless clients or a traditional LAN that contains wireless access points.

REVIEW QUESTIONS

1. Routers operate at which layer of the OSI model?

   a. Data Link

   b. Presentation

   c. Session

   d. Network

2. Bridges operate at which layer of the OSI model?

   a. Network

   b. Data Link

   c. Session

   d. Transport

3. Bridges provide which of the following benefits? (Choose all that apply.)

    a. Reduced network traffic

    b. Reduced broadcast traffic

    c. Minimized collisions

    d. Faster response time than repeaters

4. Which of the following is an appropriate description of a broadcast storm?

    a. Noise on the network

    b. A large amount of traffic that passes directly through routers

    c. An electrical condition caused by the sun

    d. An error condition in which many broadcasts are sent simultaneously across the entire network

5. Which of the following best describes a network segment?

    a. A section of the network that has been separated from other segments by a router, bridge, or switch

    b. A piece of broken twisted-pair cable

    c. A piece of broken coaxial cable

    d. A portion of the network that has been isolated with a repeater

6. A router that has eight ports will require how many IP addresses?

    a. Four

    b. Six

    c. Eight

    d. Nine

    e. Ten

7. If a bridge receives a frame that has a destination MAC address located on the same segment from which it came, what will happen to the frame at the bridge?

    a. It will be forwarded.

    b. It will be dropped.

    c. The source signal will be repeated on all segments.

    d. The destination address will be repeated on all segments.

8. Which of the following is not true about bridges?

    a. Bridges do not forward broadcast traffic.

    b. Bridges segment the network.

    c. Bridges reduce the likelihood of a collision.

    d. Bridges operate at the Data Link layer.

9. Which of the following is not true about routers?

   a. Routers operate at the Network layer.

   b. Routers segment the network.

   c. Routers reduce broadcast traffic.

   d. Routers are faster than repeaters.

10. Which of the following is not true about switches?

    a. Switches operate at the Data Link layer.

    b. Switches create virtual network segments.

    c. Switches do not segment the network.

    d. Switches create private connections between two points.

11. Which type of addresses do routers use?

    a. Logical

    b. Physical

    c. MAC

    d. Data Link

12. A _____ can reduce broadcast traffic.

    a. bridge

    b. router

    c. repeater

    d. connector

13. Which of the following is the correct name for a device that operates at both the Data Link and Network layers of the OSI reference model?

    a. Router

    b. Bridge

    c. Switch

    d. Brouter

    e. Hub

14. When two stations broadcast at the same time on a single segment of an Ethernet network, what happens?

    a. Contention

    b. Crash

    c. Collision

    d. Interruption

2

15. Which type of addresses do bridges use?

    a. Logical

    b. Physical

    c. IP

    d. TCP

16. When must you change the IP address of a given host on a network segmented with routers?

    a. When that computer is moved to a different segment on the network

    b. When the network card is replaced

    c. When the router is replaced

    d. When a bridge is replaced

17. Which of the following OSI layers contains media access control information?

    a. Physical

    b. Data Link

    c. Transport

    d. Presentation

    e. Session

    f. Network

18. A switch divides network communications at which layer of the OSI model?

    a. Presentation

    b. Network

    c. Transport

    d. Data Link

19. Which of the following devices translates between different protocols?

    a. Bridge

    b. Switch

    c. Router

    d. Gateway

20. Rank the following devices from lowest to highest latency.

    a. Hub

    b. Switch

    c. Gateway

    d. Router

21. Typically, which is the best device for increasing performance on your LAN?

    a. Hub

    b. Bridge

    c. Switch

    d. Router

22. What kind of bridges do Ethernet networks use?

    a. Translation

    b. Source-routing

    c. Transparent

    d. Brooklyn

23. What kind of bridges will connect an Ethernet network to a Token Ring network?

    a. Translation

    b. Source-routing

    c. Transparent

    d. Brooklyn

24. Why don't repeaters and hubs segment the network?

    a. They only work at the Physical layer where there is nothing to filter.

    b. They are not considered devices.

    c. They operate at the Network layer where segmentation can't occur.

    d. They do segment the network.

25. Another name for IP address is _____ address, and another name for a MAC address is _____ address.

    a. Ethernet, logical

    b. physical, Ethernet

    c. logical, physical

    d. NIC, software

26. What device provides functions similar to a hub in wireless networks?

    a. Wireless local area network

    b. Optical repeater

    c. Virtual local area network

    d. Wireless access point

CASE PROJECTS

CASE PROJECTS

1. Winslow Networks wants to increase the performance of Sampson's network. As senior network administrator for Winslow, you assign Lisa to the job. That afternoon, while preparing to work on a lab assignment from her Cisco CCNA class, Lisa mentions that she would use a router to increase the performance of Sampson's network because routers are better than bridges. Explain to Lisa when and where a router would be the best choice. Under what circumstances would a router not be the best choice?

2. Another Winslow technician, Jennifer, overhears the discussion as she sits down to examine the lab materials spread out on Lisa's desk. Jennifer thinks Winslow should use a bridge to solve the problem. She reminds you that Sampson has a relatively small network and that a router would be more equipment than necessary. The Sampson network is running nonroutable protocols. What do you tell Jennifer?

3. Moe works at Winslow too. As a graduate of the Cisco CCNA course, he thinks that a brouter would be the best choice. He has read that a brouter performs as both a router and a bridge, but he isn't sure how this works. Explain to Moe how a brouter works. Is a brouter the best choice for Sampson? Are other devices worth consideration?

4. Moe and Lisa want you to settle an argument. Moe says a repeater is not the same as a hub. Lisa says it is. Moe argues that if you say a hub is a repeater, you might as well say that a bridge is a repeater too. Give Moe and Lisa your opinion and defend it.

5. Your colleague is preparing a presentation for new clients. She asks you to prepare a short part of the report, in which you describe the differences between segmentation with repeaters, routers, and bridges. Prepare this short report.

3

TCP/IP AND IP ADDRESSING

> **After reading this chapter and completing the exercises,**
> **you will be able to:**
> ♦ Discuss the origins of TCP/IP
> ♦ Understand the different classes of IP addresses
> ♦ Configure and verify IP addresses
> ♦ Subdivide an IP network
> ♦ Identify and discuss the different layer functions of TCP/IP
> ♦ Describe the functions performed by protocols in the TCP/IP protocol suite, including ICMP, UDP, TCP, ARP, and RARP
> ♦ Use ping and trace and describe their functions
> ♦ Understand advanced routing concepts such as CIDR, summarization, and VLSM

TCP/IP stands for Transmission Control Protocol/Internet Protocol, but this term has evolved to represent more than just these two protocols; TCP/IP is now a protocol suite that contains a variable number of protocols, depending on the specific manufacturer and network. In this chapter, you will learn about the most common and important protocols associated with TCP/IP networks.

ORIGINS OF TCP/IP

The invention and evolution of the **Transmission Control Protocol/Internet Protocol (TCP/IP)** protocol suite resulted from a coordinated effort by the United States Department of Defense (DOD). In the late 1960s, the DOD had a research branch named the **Advanced Research Projects Agency (ARPA)**. ARPA was charged with creating a wide area network (WAN) capable of surviving a nuclear attack. One of the results of the initial research was the TCP/IP protocol suite.

After completing the initial research and development, ARPA chose four university sites to help formulate the initial network: the University of California at Santa Barbara (UCSB), the University of California at Los Angeles (UCLA), the Stanford Research Institute (SRI), and the University of Utah. Initially, these sites were connected with 50-Kbps leased lines, which formed the **Advanced Research Projects Agency Network**. The name was later shortened to **ARPANET**.

NOTE

ARPA is now known as the Defense Advanced Research Projects Agency, although the agency's Web site is under *www.arpa.mil*.

Although the initial research was conducted for military purposes, academic researchers found the network to be a great way to communicate with one another. Because the U.S. government never classified or restricted the technology used to create the network, researchers at other organizations used the information gained from the project to create their own TCP/IP networks. This furthered the development of the protocol stack as various groups developed more protocols for the TCP/IP suite.

To further increase the popularity of TCP/IP, the DOD funded two projects. The first was the adaptation of TCP/IP to work with the UNIX operating system. The second was the inclusion of the TCP/IP protocol with Berkeley UNIX (Berkeley Software Distribution UNIX [BSD UNIX]). At the time, 90% of the university science departments in the United States used BSD UNIX, so TCP/IP quickly increased in popularity and use.

Eventually, this network interconnected so many different organizations and sites that it became known as the Internet. Because taxpayer money funded the project and the government did not classify it, it was considered to be in the public domain. This opened the Internet to everyone, organizations and individuals alike.

OVERVIEW OF THE TCP/IP PROTOCOL SUITE

The TCP/IP protocol suite is a network model with four layers: **Application**, **Transport**, **Internetwork**, and **Network Interface**. A series of documents called **Requests for Comments (RFCs)** define, describe, and standardize the implementation and configuration of the TCP/IP protocol suite.

Figure 3-1 compares the TCP/IP protocol suite to the OSI reference model. Notice that the Application layer and the Network Interface layer of the TCP/IP model support multiple functions that require five different layers in the OSI model.

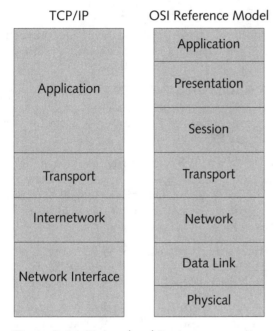

Figure 3-1   Protocol architecture comparison

- Application layer: The Application layer in the TCP/IP model maps to the OSI Application, Presentation, and Session layers. This layer defines the functionality of the upper layers, including support for data formatting, conversion, and encryption. Also, the layer provides an application interface while providing session establishment and control services.

- Transport layer: The Transport layer in both models determines the connectionless or connection-oriented services. Two main protocols—TCP and **UDP (User Datagram Protocol)**—operate at this layer.

- Internetwork layer: The Internetwork layer in the TCP/IP model is a direct equivalent to the Network layer in the OSI reference model. Logical addressing information, such as the IP address, occurs here.

- Network Interface layer: The Network Interface layer of the TCP/IP model maps to both the Data Link and Physical layers of the OSI reference model. Network functions at this level include hardware addressing, media access control, physical topology, and electrical and mechanical specifications.

Application Layer

The TCP/IP Application layer includes protocols for e-mail, remote logins, file transfers, Web browsing, network management, and name management. Specific protocols that exist at the TCP/IP Application layer include the following:

- FTP: The **File Transfer Protocol (FTP)** sends data over a reliable connection. This protocol can be used to send, delete, and move files to and from an FTP server and client.

- TFTP: The **Trivial File Transfer Protocol (TFTP)** sends data using an unreliable connection. This protocol functions similarly to FTP, but is faster and less reliable. A file transferred with TFTP is more likely to be corrupted than if it were transferred with FTP.

- NFS: The **Network File System (NFS)** is a distributed file system developed by Sun Microsystems that allows data to be shared across a network, regardless of the type of computer, operating system, network architecture, or protocol. This standard UNIX file system allows remote files to be manipulated as if they resided on the local computer.

- SMTP: The **Simple Mail Transfer Protocol (SMTP)** is the messaging or e-mail transfer protocol. This connection-oriented protocol allows mail to be transferred on TCP/IP networks and the Internet between e-mail servers.

- Telnet: A telnet client can use this **terminal emulation protocol (telnet)** to log on to a remote machine or telnet server. The telnet user can then run programs on the remote computer, using the remote computer's processor. Telnet is usually the first utility used when troubleshooting routers.

- rlogin: The **remote login application (rlogin)** allows you to gain access to TCP/IP hosts that support rlogin. This command-line utility allows you to navigate and manipulate a remote computer's directory structure.

- SNMP: You can install the **Simple Network Management Protocol (SNMP)** on TCP/IP hosts, including routers and other devices that support TCP/IP. SNMP is a connectionless protocol that permits remote tracking and management of TCP/IP hosts. For example, SNMP clients can report information such as hard drive space, network statistics, and various performance data. The SNMP manager can remotely monitor and control the SNMP clients.

- DNS: The **Domain Name System (DNS)** service provides TCP/IP host name to IP address resolution. For example, when you type *www.cisco.com* into a Web browser while connected to the Internet, the name must be resolved to an IP address before the communication can traverse the Internet. DNS servers on the Internet provide this name resolution so that you can establish a connection to the Cisco Web server.

- HTTP: The World Wide Web uses the **Hypertext Transfer Protocol (HTTP)**. This connection-oriented protocol allows you to connect your computer to other computers on the Internet and view Web page content.

Transport Layer

The TCP/IP Transport layer performs several functions, the most notable being end-to-end packet delivery, reliability, and flow control. Two protocols, TCP and UDP, reside in the Transport layer of the TCP/IP model. TCP provides reliable, connection-oriented communications between two hosts. UDP provides connectionless datagram services between two hosts. Of the two protocols, TCP requires more network overhead because data is acknowledged as it is received. UDP is faster, but less reliable, because the recipient does not acknowledge data as it is received. Applications and utilities are written (programmed) to use either UDP or TCP. With UDP, communication reliability is left to the Application layer.

Ports

Both TCP and UDP use port numbers for communications between hosts. Port numbers are similar to phone numbers in that Transport layer services can be "called" by their port number. For example, if you want to order a pizza delivery, you can look up the number of a pizza place and dial the correct digits on your phone to request delivery. A similar event happens when a computer wants service from the TCP/IP Transport layer. When a computer wants to transfer a file over FTP, it uses TCP port 21 to establish and control the connection and TCP port 20 to transfer the data. TCP ports 20 and 21 are called **Well Known Port numbers** because applications expect to find FTP services on TCP port 21 and to transfer their data on TCP port 20.

You should be familiar with the following Well Known TCP and UDP Port numbers from RFC 1700:

- TCP port 20 — FTP data transfer
- TCP port 21 — FTP control port
- TCP port 23 — Telnet
- TCP port 25 — SMTP
- TCP & UDP port 53 — DNS (also known as name or domain server)
- TCP port 80 — HTTP Web services
- TCP & UDP port 123 — Network Time Protocol (NTP)
- TCP port 110 — **Post Office Protocol version 3 (POP3)**

- TCP port 119 — Network News Transport Protocol (NNTP)
- UDP port 69 — TFTP
- UDP port 161 — SNMP

Each IP transport protocol has its own port numbers. This means that TCP has 65,535 ports available and UDP has another 65,535 ports available. Sometimes a service will exist on the same port number on both protocols. For example, DNS can use TCP port 53 or UDP port 53. Even if a Well Known Port number exists for a certain service, you do not have to use it for that service. For example, if you wanted to hide a Web server on the Internet, you might set its HTTP service port number to TCP 1055 (a randomly chosen number). Then, your Web clients would have to know the port number in order to contact your Web services. The port numbers are divided into three ranges: Well Known Ports, Registered Ports, and Dynamic/Private Ports.

- Well Known Ports are those from 0 through 1,023.
- Registered Ports are those from 1,024 through 49,151.
- Dynamic/Private Ports are those from 49,152 through 65,535.

To understand the use of ports in network communications, consider the diagram shown in Figure 3-2. The FTP client calls the FTP server on TCP port 21 to establish communication. Then the FTP server responds to the client. The client computer dynamically configures the client software to use a port above TCP 1023; in the figure, that TCP port is 1029. Then, the FTP data transfer port is established. Again, the client calls the server on the Well Known Port of TCP 20. After the necessary acknowledgments, the client computer sets the FTP client software to use a port above TCP 1023 (port 1030 in the figure) to conduct the actual data transfer.

TCP Three-way Handshake

To establish a reliable connection between two points, TCP uses a **three-way handshake**. To do this, TCP transmits three packets before the actual data transfer occurs between two hosts. In order to transfer data reliably, the hosts must synchronize their communications to ensure that no packets are missed during communication.

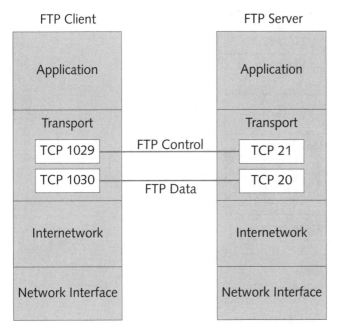

Figure 3-2   TCP port usage in FTP communications

As an analogy for the three-way handshake process, consider the following example: Assume that two pilots want to communicate with one another during a mission. The first pilot uses the call sign "Maverick" and the other pilot uses the call sign "Iceman." A call from Maverick to Iceman might be similar to the following:

Maverick: "Iceman, this is Maverick; do you copy?"

Iceman: "This is Iceman; I copy you, Maverick."

Maverick: "Roger, Iceman."

After this initial interaction, Maverick would begin sending information to Iceman. The major difference between the human interactions in the preceding example and how computers communicate via TCP is that the computers will use data packets with sequence numbers. Each host computer must acknowledge the sequence number of the sender and include its own sequence number in the following packet. This allows the computers to keep track of each packet and to ensure that none are lost during transmission. If a given packet does not arrive within a given time interval, the source computer will retransmit it. If the destination computer receives packets out of order, it can use the sequence numbers to reassemble those packets into the correct order.

Before investigating the three-way handshake process further, look at Figure 3-3, which illustrates a conceptual drawing of the TCP packet header structure. In the following text, you will be concerned with the sequence number field and the acknowledgment number field.

Source Port (16 bits)	Destination Port (16 bits)
Sequence Number (32 bits)	
Acknowledgment Number (32 bits)	
Offset, Reserved Bits, Flags (16 bits)	Receive Window Size (16 bits)
Checksum (16 bits)	Urgent Pointer (16 bits)
Options and Padding (32 bits)	
Data (variable length) Information for the next higher layer (Application layer)	

Figure 3-3   TCP packet header

NOTE

TCP is defined in RFC 793 *(www.faqs.org/rfcs/rfc793.html)*. The RFC describes all of the data fields in the TCP packet structure, as well as the other TCP concepts discussed in this chapter.

Before two computers can communicate over TCP, they must synchronize their **initial sequence numbers (ISN)**. These sequence numbers ensure that the communications are assembled in the proper order and that no missing packets exist. The synchronization process occurs when each host sends its own ISN and receives a confirmation and an ISN from the other host. When a synchronization request is sent, it is abbreviated SYN. When an acknowledgment is sent, the abbreviation is ACK. This process has four steps:

1. Host A sends a SYN packet to Host B, which indicates a sequence number represented here as ISN_A. The ACK field contains a zero in this first packet.

2. Host B composes an ACK packet for Host A, which acknowledges A's sequence number by adding one to the sequence number that Host A submitted (ISN_A+1). This is called an **expectational acknowledgment**.

3. Host B adds its SYN data for Host A, which indicates its sequence number ISN_B, and sends that information to Host A in the ACK packet composed in Step 2.

4. Host A submits an ACK packet to Host B. The packet includes a sequence number of ISN_A+1 (expected by Host B) and an acknowledgment number of $ISN_B +1$, which indicates that Host A received the last packet and now expects a sequence of $ISN_B +1$ from Host B.

Even with four steps, only three packets need to be exchanged because the SYN packet from Host B also serves as the acknowledgment to the SYN packet from Host A. This process is called the TCP three-way handshake because only three packets travel the network to negotiate and synchronize the TCP connection, as shown in Figure 3-4.

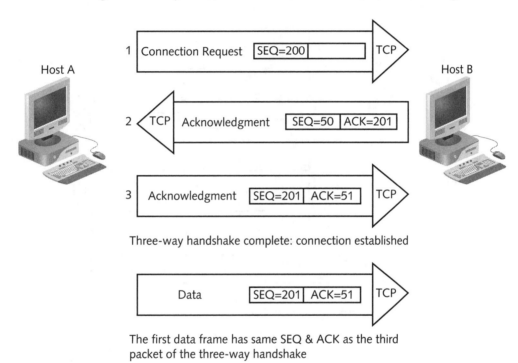

Figure 3-4 shows:

1. Connection Request | SEQ=200 | TCP (Host A → Host B)
2. TCP | Acknowledgment | SEQ=50 | ACK=201 (Host B → Host A)
3. Acknowledgment | SEQ=201 | ACK=51 | TCP (Host A → Host B)

Three-way handshake complete: connection established

Data | SEQ=201 | ACK=51 | TCP

The first data frame has same SEQ & ACK as the third packet of the three-way handshake

Figure 3-4   TCP three-way handshake

Notice in Figure 3-4 that the ACK number in the TCP packet from Host B is one number higher than the SYN number sent by Host A. This process shows that Host B expects to see SEQ number 201 next (ISN_A+1). The process is considered expectational (and not necessarily sequential because packets can get out of sequence). This allows hosts to detect and recover from failures or problems with TCP communications. RFC 793 states: "The principal reason for the three-way handshake is to prevent old duplicate connection initiations from causing confusion." A number of possible error conditions are described in the RFC. One example of how TCP recovers from old duplicate connections is illustrated in Figure 3-5.

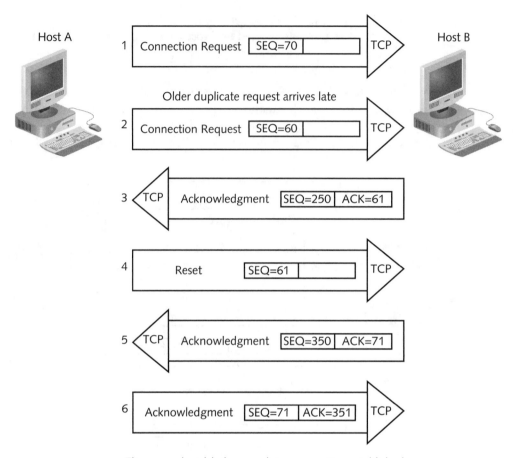

Three-way handshake complete: connection established

Figure 3-5 TCP connection recovery

In the example, the packets are numbered to help you follow what is happening. Packet 1 is a connection request that arrives before a previous connection request (shown as packet 2). Host B acknowledges the connection request with the lower sequence number first (packet 3). Host A realizes that Host B is acknowledging an old connection request and sends a reset packet (packet 4). A **reset packet (RST)** indicates that a TCP connection is to be terminated without further interaction. Host B then acknowledges the newer connection request from Host A with packet 5 (ACK=71, which is one higher than the SEQ in packet 1). Host A then completes the three-way handshake with Host B by sending data packet 6 with SEQ=71 and ACK=351 (which is one higher than packet 5). In this example, TCP packets 1, 5, and 6 complete the three-way handshake.

TCP Sliding Windows

Once the three-way handshake is complete and data transfer begins, TCP **sliding windows** control the flow and efficiency of communication. Sliding windows, also known as windowing, is a method of controlling packet flow between hosts. Windowing allows multiple packets to be sent and affirmed with a single acknowledgment packet. The size of the TCP sliding window determines the number of acknowledgments sent for a given data transfer because it constrains the amount of data that will be received before an acknowledgment is sent to the transmitting host. Essentially, once the window fills with data, the destination host sends an acknowledgment for all the packets received in that window. Then, the window slides over to accept new packets. It is important to note that the sender controls the sliding window's size.

Networks that perform large data transfers should use large window sizes. During a connection for a large data transfer on a network with few collisions, a large TCP sliding window would work well. Large window sizes can cause problems, however, on a network with lots of traffic or on one that does small data transfers. The large window may force the sending host to wait for an acknowledgment. If the sending host waits too long, it will retransmit data. Then, that sending host may receive an acknowledgment of both the original and the retransmitted data.

A small TCP window size produces frequent acknowledgments. Networks that transfer small amounts of data should use small window sizes; however, if the receiving computer is forced to acknowledge every data packet because of a small TCP sliding window, the increase in network traffic and the additional load placed on the hosts would be inefficient. Fortunately, TCP window sizes can adjust dynamically during the life of a connection, so that the window can be expanded or contracted as needed to make the communications more efficient.

TCP sliding windows is one of three methods used to control the flow of packets on a network. The other two are **buffering** and **congestion avoidance**. Buffering is a capability that most network devices have and use to keep up when packets are flowing in too quickly for them to process. The **buffer** is a portion of memory where the device stores incoming packets until they can be processed. Congestion avoidance is a communication method for network devices to reduce the flow of packets from their source. Devices implement congestion avoidance by sending a "slow down the transmission rate" request to the device that is sending packets too rapidly. The ICMP Source Quench (covered in the next section) is a type of congestion avoidance.

Internetwork Layer

The Internetwork layer in the TCP/IP model handles software, or logical, addressing. Four main protocols function at this layer:

- IP: The **Internet Protocol (IP)** provides a connectionless delivery service. The IP moves packets around the network, including through routers. IP is covered in greater detail later in the chapter.

- ICMP: The **Internet Control Message Protocol (ICMP)** controls and manages IP communications. This protocol, defined in RFC 792 (*www.faqs.org/rfcs/rfc792.html*), provides message control and error-reporting services between two TCP/IP hosts or between a host server and a gateway to the Internet. ICMP uses eight different message types to manage 11 different aspects of IP communications. The eight types of ICMP messages are **destination unreachable**, **time exceeded**, **parameter problem**, **source quench**, **redirect**, **echo request/reply**, **timestamp request/reply**, and **information request/reply**.

- ARP: The **Address Resolution Protocol (ARP)** resolves IP addresses to MAC addresses for source hosts that know the IP address of the destination host but not the MAC address. The source host issues an ARP broadcast requesting the MAC address for the corresponding IP address. Every station on the local subnet receives the ARP broadcast, but only the destination host responds.

- RARP: The **Reverse Address Resolution Protocol (RARP)** provides IP address to MAC address resolution in a manner similar to that of ARP, but does so under different circumstances. In the case of a **diskless workstation**, a source host will know its MAC address (because it is burned into the NIC) but not its IP address, because the IP address is implemented in software and a diskless workstation cannot store information locally. This host will get its IP address by issuing a RARP request to a RARP server.

ARP

IP, ARP, and RARP are all protocols associated with TCP/IP. IP is a **routed protocol**, which means that it contains enough information in its header to be routed through an internetwork. In order for data to be routed on an IP network, the packet must contain a source and destination IP address and a source and destination MAC address. ARP maps IP addresses to MAC addresses. In essence, the source of the network packet sends the information to the destination. Unique MAC addresses reference the endpoints in the exchange.

Many network devices maintain tables of the MAC and IP addresses of other devices on the network. These tables are called **ARP tables** and are maintained in volatile Random Access Memory (RAM). Many devices allow the network administrators to modify the ARP table (also known as ARP cache), but this is not a typical activity. Normally, devices automatically obtain and update their own ARP tables.

When a computer transmits a packet to a destination on the local network, it checks its ARP cache for an IP to MAC address mapping for the destination node. If the computer finds an appropriate IP to MAC address mapping, the source computer uses the IP and MAC addresses to encapsulate the data that it is ready to transmit. The source computer then sends the packet directly to the destination computer.

```
MS-DOS Prompt                                    _□✕
  10 x 18 ▾  □ 🖿 🖺  ⊞  🖺🖶  A
C:\>arp -a

Interface: 208.128.20.163 on Interface 0x1000002
  Internet Address      Physical Address    Type
  204.70.128.1          20-53-52-43-00-00   dynamic
  204.181.89.153        20-53-52-43-00-00   dynamic
  204.181.89.154        20-53-52-43-00-01   static

C:\>
```

Figure 3-6 IP host's ARP table

Figure 3-6 illustrates the ARP cache of a Windows 98 TCP/IP host attached to the Internet. Notice that the IP address is listed first, the MAC address next, followed by information about whether the entry is static or dynamic. Most entries are dynamic, which means that the system performed IP to MAC resolution as needed. Static entries, which are rarely used, provide semi-permanent IP to MAC address mappings that an administrator entered manually. Administrators make these manual mappings to reduce ARP traffic on the network only when they know that a specific hardware address and IP address combination will remain constant.

ARP Request

If a source computer cannot locate an IP to MAC address mapping in its ARP table, it must obtain the correct mapping because both an IP and MAC address for the source and destination are required to send data. To do this, the device initiates an **ARP request** to gain the destination's MAC address.

 NOTE This section focuses on obtaining the MAC address for a specific IP address and assumes that the device already knows the destination's IP address. If the source computer has only the destination computer's host name, the source must first obtain the IP address, which is beyond the scope of the address resolution discussed here.

A source computer broadcasts an ARP request to all hosts on the local segment. Each device determines whether the packet is destined for its IP address. The one device that discovers that the ARP request broadcast packet is destined for its IP address responds to the ARP request.

 NOTE Because it is a broadcast mechanism, ARP is only used on the local segment of a network. Routers will not pass ARP broadcasts. If the destination host is not on the same network segment as the source host, the source will send the packet to the **default gateway** (router) and will not ARP.

ARP Request Frame

As you have learned, the lower layers in the protocol configuration encapsulate data frames. With ARP, the computer is seeking an IP to MAC address resolution, so the ARP frame includes both the MAC and IP addresses. The frame header includes the MAC header and the IP header, followed by the ARP message. The MAC header contains the destination and source MAC addresses, and the IP header contains the destination and source IP addresses. Figure 3-7 represents the ARP request frame configuration.

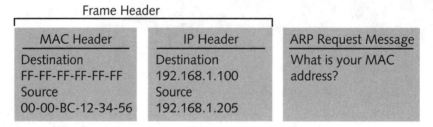

Frame Header

MAC Header	IP Header	ARP Request Message
Destination	Destination	What is your MAC
FF-FF-FF-FF-FF-FF	192.168.1.100	address?
Source	Source	
00-00-BC-12-34-56	192.168.1.205	

Figure 3-7   ARP request packet

The packets shown in the figure are simplified to illustrate a specific point. Real packets have 28 octets (28 sets of eight binary digits), which identify hardware types, protocol types, and message lengths. Because these components are not significant to the current discussion, they are not shown in the figure. RFC 826 (*www.faqs.org/rfcs/rfc826.html*) contains a detailed discussion of ARP.

Because the source host does not know the MAC address of the destination, the ARP request frame is a broadcast to all MAC addresses (FF-FF-FF-FF-FF-FF), and all devices on the local segment will investigate the frame to determine whether their IP addresses match that of the destination. The device that discovers its own IP address in the IP header reads the rest of the packet and returns an **ARP reply**. The rest of the devices on the segment discard the packet.

The ARP reply supplies the MAC address of the destination host in a unicast packet. When the computer that sent the ARP request receives the ARP reply from the host, it has the information necessary to properly address the data it wants to send to the destination computer. The source computer extracts the MAC address from the ARP reply and updates its ARP table. Then, the source computer creates and properly addresses its data packet and sends it with the MAC address of the destination computer.

NOTE   Devices on the network that receive and eventually discard an ARP request use the source information to update their own ARP tables. Recipients enter the source computer's MAC address from the ARP request packet into their local ARP tables.

ARP Cache Life

Because the source checks its local ARP cache prior to sending packets on the local network, the ARP cache must contain current information. If the ARP cache contains stale information, data packets could be routed to the wrong host. Because the ARP table directs data packets to a specific network card based on the mapping, it is important that the mappings are correct. Host IP addresses can change, so old ARP table mappings can cause misrouted packets. To ensure that old ARP table entries do not become a serious problem, network devices place a **time-to-live (TTL)** on ARP entries. For example, Microsoft operating systems use a two- to ten-minute TTL for their ARP cache, and initial mappings through ARP have a two-minute TTL. Any entry that is used twice within those first two minutes is automatically given a life of 10 minutes. After the 10 minutes, the ARP entry is removed from the ARP table.

By using TTLs, an operating system ensures that an ARP cache is never outdated for more than 10 minutes. The process of removing ARP entries from an ARP table is known as aging out the ARP table. In addition to aging out, devices on a network also replace ARP entries whenever new information is received. For example, if a computer receives a packet from a host that contains an IP and MAC address that are different from what it has listed in the ARP table, the computer updates its ARP table.

Even though the ARP tables are revised frequently, and their entries have short lives, they reduce network traffic. Without an ARP table, a device would have to perform an ARP for each packet, which could significantly increase network traffic on the local segment. As discussed earlier, increased traffic usually results in increased collisions and network delays.

RARP

The Reverse Address Resolution Protocol (RARP) is similar to ARP in that computers use it to bind MAC addresses to IP addresses. However, RARP is used primarily by diskless workstations, which have MAC addresses burned into their network cards but no IP addresses. Because these workstations have no disks, they have no hard drives to hold IP configuration information. Therefore, they must obtain their IP configuration information each time they boot on the network.

To do this, a client's IP configuration must be stored on a RARP server. The RARP server maintains a table of IP to MAC address mappings for RARP clients. During the boot process, RARP clients call the RARP server to obtain their IP configuration information.

RARP Request Frame

As mentioned earlier, a RARP packet has the same structure as an ARP packet. However, it contains different pieces of information. Figure 3-8 illustrates a RARP request frame.

Notice that the IP header does not have a specific destination or source IP address in the RARP frame. The source does not know which device is the RARP server, so it must broadcast to all devices on the segment.

RARP

Frame Header

MAC Header	IP Header	RARP Request Message
Destination FF-FF-FF-FF-FF-FF Source 00-00-8C-12-34-56	Destination 255.255.255.255 Source 0.0.0.0	What is my IP address?

ARP

Frame Header

MAC Header	IP Header	ARP Request Message
Destination FF-FF-FF-FF-FF-FF Source 00-00-8C-12-34-56	Destination 192.168.1.100 Source 192.168.1.205	What is your MAC address?

Figure 3-8   RARP request frame

RARP Client

Once a RARP client receives a RARP reply, it configures its IP networking components by copying its IP address configuration information into its local RAM. After the client receives the configuration settings, it can use the MAC and IP address to send packets on the network to other clients.

When the diskless workstation reboots or is shut down, the respective IP configuration information is lost. Consequently, each time the diskless workstation boots, it must obtain its IP configuration settings from a RARP server.

ARP and RARP Compared

The RARP process and the ARP process are both concerned with IP to MAC address mapping. In addition, they use the same packet format and use broadcast addresses to accomplish their tasks. Although they share similarities, they have certain differences as well:

- ARP is concerned with obtaining the MAC address of other clients by using an IP address, but RARP obtains the IP address of the local host by using the local host's MAC address. Computers broadcast ARP packets on the local network by using the broadcast MAC address, but RARP uses the broadcast IP address (255.255.255.255) as well as the broadcast MAC address.

- The local host maintains the ARP table. A RARP server maintains the RARP table.

- The local host uses an ARP reply to update its ARP table and to send packets to the destination. The RARP reply is used to configure the IP protocol on the local host.

BootP and DHCP are two other protocols that provide the same basic functionality as RARP. Although DHCP is the most advanced of the three, all of them provide IP configuration information to clients on bootup.

Routers and ARP

As you have learned, routers segment networks. Segmenting a network reduces network traffic because routers do not forward broadcast traffic from one segment (**subnet**) to another by default. (Although you can configure most routers to forward broadcasts, such an action would increase network traffic unnecessarily.)

Because hosts rely on ARP requests to determine MAC addresses, and ARP requests use broadcasts, hosts must create broadcast traffic to determine the MAC address of other hosts. However, routers filter broadcast traffic, which means that ARP requests can go no further than the local segment (subnet). What happens when the source computer needs to send a message to a host on a remote segment? In such a case, the source must forward the packet to the router. This section explains how routers use their routing tables and ARP to correctly route packets across a network.

ARP Tables

Like other network devices, routers maintain ARP tables to assist in transmitting packets from one network to another. If the destination IP address of a packet is on a segment to which a router is attached, the router will forward the packet directly to the destination. To do this, the router must obtain the MAC address for that destination. If the router has the MAC to IP mapping in its ARP table, the router can forward the packet directly. However, if the router does not have that mapping in its ARP table, the router must issue an ARP request.

A router uses ARP just as other hosts use ARP. However, the router is bound to have a larger ARP table because it typically deals with more hosts. It connects to multiple networks; a typical TCP/IP host only connects to and receives ARP mappings for its local segment. Of course, the actual number of ARP table entries depends on the amount of traffic sent between and within the various segments. Routers have multiple network interfaces and therefore also include the port numbers of their NICs in the ARP table. Thus, routers can make routing decisions for incoming packets quickly by forwarding the packets to the appropriate interface.

The Ping Utility

Network administrators and support personnel commonly use the **Packet Internet Groper (ping)** utility to verify connectivity between two points. The ping utility uses ICMP echo request/reply messages to verify connectivity at the Internetwork layer of the TCP/IP model, which is one reason that ICMP echo request/reply messages are the most commonly used ICMP message. When you issue the ping command, the source node sends out ICMP echo request packets to the specified destination node. The destination node, if it is up and running correctly, replies with ICMP echo reply packets. A simple ping request can be issued by typing the ping [ip address] command. Figure 3-9 shows the output of the ping command on a Cisco router.

```
RouterB>ping 172.22.5.1
Type escape sequence to abort.
Sending 5, 100-byte ICMP Echoes to 172.22.5.1, timeout is 2 seconds:
!!!!!

Success rate is 100 percent (5/5), round-trip min/avg/max = 68/70/76 ms
RouterB>
```

Five exclamation points represent five successful ping replies

Figure 3-9   Ping example

The reply of five exclamation points means that all five echo request packets were responded to with echo reply packets. The following table shows a list of possible replies:

Table 3-1   Ping responses

Ping Response	Result
!	Echo request successfully replied to with echo reply
.	Time-out (no response from destination)
U	Destination unreachable
?	Unknown packet type
&	Time-to-live exceeded
C	Packet experienced congestion

Cisco routers include two ping commands: standard ping and extended ping. Figure 3-10 shows the proper syntax for the extended ping command. The extended ping allows you to specify more echo request packets and larger packets. You can also use this command to ping IPX nodes with the IPX protocol. Overall, the standard and extended ping commands give you an excellent tool for determining the status of remote hosts on your network.

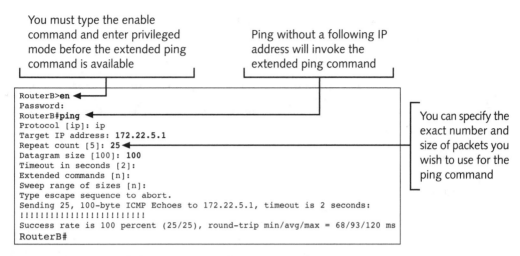

You must type the enable command and enter privileged mode before the extended ping command is available

Ping without a following IP address will invoke the extended ping command

You can specify the exact number and size of packets you wish to use for the ping command

```
RouterB>en
Password:
RouterB#ping
Protocol [ip]: ip
Target IP address: 172.22.5.1
Repeat count [5]: 25
Datagram size [100]: 100
Timeout in seconds [2]:
Extended commands [n]:
Sweep range of sizes [n]:
Type escape sequence to abort.
Sending 25, 100-byte ICMP Echoes to 172.22.5.1, timeout is 2 seconds:
!!!!!!!!!!!!!!!!!!!!!!!!!
Success rate is 100 percent (25/25), round-trip min/avg/max = 68/93/120 ms
RouterB#
```

Figure 3-10   Extended ping commands

The Trace Utility

The **trace** utility also uses ICMP echo request/reply messages. Trace shows the exact path a packet takes from the source to the destination. This is accomplished through the use of the TTL counter. The packet is sent out first with a time-to-live of one. Once it finds the first hop (router) on the path to the destination, the packet is returned with a destination unreachable message. The TTL is incremented to two and the packet is resent. This process continues until the packet reaches the destination or times out. The net effect is that you see the hops (transitions from one device to another) that a packet takes as it travels the network. Figure 3-11 shows a trace to a router port with IP address 172.22.5.1. You can use the trace utility to determine where communications are breaking down along a particular path.

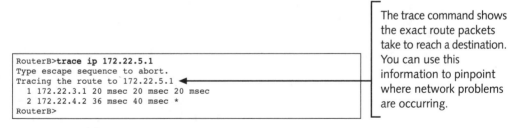

The trace command shows the exact route packets take to reach a destination. You can use this information to pinpoint where network problems are occurring.

```
RouterB>trace ip 172.22.5.1
Type escape sequence to abort.
Tracing the route to 172.22.5.1
  1 172.22.3.1 20 msec 20 msec 20 msec
  2 172.22.4.2 36 msec 40 msec *
RouterB>
```

Figure 3-11   Trace command example

Be aware that some routers can be configured to discard ICMP echo requests and therefore become invisible to the trace command. This feature is often used as a security measure because some network administrators do not want all of their network devices and IP addresses exposed to people who decide to run a trace. Several different malicious network attacks have also been created using ICMP messages; one in particular is called an **ICMP flood**. An ICMP flood is caused by a malicious user or program that sends a large quantity of ICMP echo requests (pings) to a target device in an attempt to crash or greatly reduce the performance of the target device. This is another reason network administrators may choose to turn off ICMP support on key devices, such as routers.

Using ping and trace on a PC workstation is slightly different than on a Cisco router.

NOTE

Network Interface Layer

The TCP/IP Network Interface layer plays the same role as the Data Link and Physical layers of the OSI model. The MAC address, network card drivers, and specific interfaces for the network card function at this level of the TCP/IP protocol stack. No specific IP functions exist at this layer because the layer's focus is on communication with the network card and other networking hardware such as cable, hubs, and repeaters.

IP ADDRESSING

An IP address has 32 bits divided into four octets (four sets of eight binary digits). To make the address easier to read, people use decimal numbers to represent the binary digits. For example, the IP address 192.168.1.1 is 11000000.10101000.00000001.00000001 when written in binary. Notice that 32 binary digits create the address. The lowest number of any octet is 00000000, or zero, and the highest number of any octet is 11111111, or 255. When binary IP addresses are written in decimal format, it is often called dotted decimal notation.

To understand how eight binary ones are equal to the decimal 255, you must look at the places for each of the binary values. Table 3-2 illustrates the places of the binary digits 128, 64, 32, 16, 8, 4, 2, and 1. Notice that the number 192 is created when the first two binary digits are ones and the following six digits are zeros. To determine the decimal equivalent, you add the binary places that are identified by ones. In the first row of Table 3-2, the 128 and 64 places have ones, which creates the decimal number 192 (i.e., 128 + 64 = 192).

Table 3-2   Binary to decimal conversion

	128	64	32	16	8	4	2	1
192	1	1	0	0	0	0	0	0
168	1	0	1	0	1	0	0	0
1	0	0	0	0	0	0	0	1
255	1	1	1	1	1	1	1	1
0	0	0	0	0	0	0	0	0

MAC to IP Address Translation

The MAC address identifies a specific computer on a network, so each MAC address is unique. TCP/IP networks can use MAC addresses in communication. However, network devices could not efficiently route traffic on a large internetwork or on the Internet with MAC addresses; MAC addresses are not grouped logically, they cannot be modified, and they don't give information about physical or logical network configuration. Therefore, another addressing scheme called **IP addressing** was devised for use on large networks. Unlike MAC addresses, IP addresses have a hierarchical structure and do provide logical groupings. The structure of the IP address makes packet routing possible on large networks.

You can compare driver's license numbers to MAC addresses. The driver's license allows you to drive a car, and it uniquely identifies you as a vehicle operator. However, when people want to talk with you, they don't call your driver's license number. Instead, they call your phone number. Phone numbers identify your location with an area code and other digits specific to you. Similarly, IP addresses identify the specific network on which you reside and your computer on that network. For example, if your IP address is 192.168.1.3, your computer is host 3 on network 192.168.1.0.

Because the IP address identifies both a network and a host, you can route communications through large networks, including the Internet. Routers can send communications in a more efficient manner by using the hierarchical IP address. If the Internet used MAC addresses, huge tables would have to be maintained containing not only the MAC addresses of each and every computer, but also each device along the path to that computer. Clearly, that would be unmanageable, especially given that network cards can malfunction. Every time someone replaced a network card, the giant MAC table would have to be updated!

IP Classes

The **Internet Assigned Numbers Authority (IANA)** devised the hierarchical IP addressing structure, and the **American Registry of Internet Numbers (ARIN)** manages IP addresses in the United States. These organizations work in conjunction with the **Internet Corporation for Assigned Names and Numbers (ICANN)**, which is a global, government-independent entity with overall responsibility for the Internet. ICANN has effectively replaced IANA. Five different groups of IP addresses (labeled Class A through E) exist on the Internet. The first three classes, Classes A, B, and C, are assigned to governments, companies, schools, and public entities for use on the Internet. The other two classes (D and E) are reserved for **multicasting** and experimentation. Therefore, you will mainly be concerned with managing Class A, B, and C addresses.

Class A

ARIN reserves Class A IP addresses for governments and large corporations throughout the world. Class A addresses, when written in binary format, will always begin with a zero. You can tell what class an Internet address belongs to by looking at its first octet.

For example, Class A addresses in decimal notation will have 1 to 126 as their first octet. Figure 3-12 displays the binary digits associated with these decimal numbers.

Binary Place Values   Decimal   Description
                                                      Equivalent

128	64	32	16	8	4	2	1
0	0	0	0	0	0	0	0	= 0	Subnet identifier
0	0	0	0	0	0	0	1	= 1	Bottom of Class A range
0	1	1	1	1	1	1	0	= 126	Top of Class A range
0	1	1	1	1	1	1	1	= 127	Loopback address

Figure 3-12   Class A addresses

Notice that all zeros identify the subnet, which is not a usable IP address. The first Class A address that can be assigned is 1.0.0.0 (decimal) or 00000001.00000000.00000000.00000000 (binary). The last Class A address that can be assigned is 126.0.0.0 in decimal notation, which is 01111110.00000000.00000000.00000000 in binary format.

It seems that 127.0.0.1 (decimal) is the highest assignable Class A address, but that particular address range is reserved as the **loopback** address. The loopback address is widely known as 127.0.0.1, but all addresses with 127 as their first octet are part of the loopback range. You can use the loopback address range for diagnostics, such as ping. If you ping 127.0.0.1 or any other IP address on the 127.0.0.0 network, your internal IP configuration should respond. This response verifies a properly installed TCP/IP protocol suite. Because the entire 127 Class A address is reserved for diagnostics, the highest Class A address that can be assigned is 126. (It is important to note that a successful loopback test does not mean the device can communicate with other devices. You can get a successful loopback response from a computer with no network cable attached to the NIC card.)

Notice that you cannot create a decimal number higher than 127 with eight binary digits if the first digit must be zero. The IANA specified that the first binary digit in a class A address would be zero to separate it from the other four categories (B, C, D, and E).

For Class A addresses, the ARIN only assigns the first octet. However, the same is not true for Class B and Class C addresses. Class B addresses are assigned with the first two octets set. Class C addresses are assigned with the first three octets set. This means that there is a difference between the number of hosts that you can assign based on the type of address you are assigned:

- Class A: Each Class A address supports 16,777,214 hosts.
- Class B: Each Class B address supports 65,534 hosts.
- Class C: Each Class C address supports 254 hosts.

Why is there such a difference in the number of hosts supported? When you are assigned a Class A network, you can use the last three octets for your network hosts. When you use a Class B network, only the last two octets can be used. A Class C address only has a single octet for you to modify.

Class B

Class B IP addresses are assigned to large- and medium-sized companies. The IANA specifies that Class B addresses will lead with 10 when written in binary format. This means that the range in decimal notation for the first octet of Class B addresses is 128 through 191. Figure 3-13 illustrates the binary to decimal calculations that specify this range.

Binary Place Values   Decimal   Description
                                                       Equivalent

128	64	32	16	8	4	2	1		
1	0	0	0	0	0	0	0	= 128	First Class B address
1	0	1	1	1	1	1	1	= 191	Last Class B address

Figure 3-13   Class B addresses

With the first two binary digits of the first octet in the Class B category defined, the address range is limited. When the last six configurable bits of the first octet are set to zero, the lowest configurable number is obtained (128). When those same six digits are set to one, the highest configurable number is set (191).

Class C

Class C IP addresses are assigned to groups that do not meet the qualifications to obtain Class A or B addresses. The IANA specified that the first three binary digits of a Class C address must be 110, which means that Class C addresses can range from 192 through 223 in decimal notation. Figure 3-14 illustrates the binary to decimal equivalents for the Class C addresses.

Binary Place Values   Decimal   Description
                                                       Equivalent

128	64	32	16	8	4	2	1		
1	1	0	0	0	0	0	0	= 192	First Class C address
1	1	0	1	1	1	1	1	= 223	Last Class C address

Figure 3-14   Class C addresses

In Class C addresses, the last five digits are configurable. The graphic shows that when the last five digits are set to all zeros, the decimal equivalent is 192. When those same five digits are set to binary ones, the decimal equivalent is 223.

Class D

Class D addresses (also known as **multicast addresses**) are reserved for multicasting. Multicasting is the sending of a stream of data (usually audio and video) to multiple computers simultaneously. Compared to broadcasting, this saves bandwidth. Many routers forward multicasts, and computers configured to receive the multicast information accept the packets and can receive the data stream. Because Class D addresses must have 1110 as their first four binary digits, the range for Class D starts with decimal 224 and ends at 239 in the first octet. Figure 3-15 illustrates the binary and decimal range for Class D addresses.

Binary Place Values   Decimal   Description
                                                           Equivalent

128	64	32	16	8	4	2	1
1	1	1	0	0	0	0	0	= 224 First Class D address
1	1	1	0	1	1	1	1	= 239 Last Class D address

Figure 3-15 Class D addresses

Class E

The IANA reserved Class E addresses for research, testing, and experimentation. The Class E range starts where Class D leaves off. Notice that Figure 3-16 illustrates the first address in the "experimental" range as 240. No top range is listed because Class E is the final range defined. Therefore, Class E is everything above and including 240 (decimal) as the first octet.

Binary Place Values   Decimal   Description
                                                           Equivalent

128	64	32	16	8	4	2	1
1	1	1	1	0	0	0	0	= 240 First Class E address

Figure 3-16 Class E addresses

Private IP Ranges

Many companies today use private IP addresses for their internal networks. This prevents the organizations from having to obtain official IP addresses from their ISP every time they add a host to the network. Class A, B, and C private address ranges have been defined by RFC 1918 (*www.faqs.org/rfcs/rfc1918.html*). Table 3-3 illustrates the private IP address ranges that network administrators can use. If these private ranges are used for an internal network, they will not be routable on the Internet. This is fine for most organizations because they have one or more gateway devices (such as routers, firewalls, or proxy servers) that provide connectivity to the Internet. These gateway devices have network interface connections to both the internal network and the Internet and route packets between them (thereby providing Internet connectivity to internal clients). The company will simply have to obtain one or more official IP addresses if it chooses to provide services (like an organizational Web site) to people using the Internet.

Table 3-3   The private IP ranges

Class	Private Address Range
A	10.x.x.x
B	172.16.x.x – 172.31.x.x
C	192.168.x.x

Subnet Addressing

As previously mentioned, IP addresses identify both the network and the host. However, the division between the two is not specific to a certain number of octets. In an earlier example, the IP address 192.168.1.3 was used to illustrate that 192.168.1.0 was the network and 3 was the host identifier on that network. This suggests that the first three octets comprise the network identifier and the last octet is the host identifier, but that is not always true. In fact, the network portion can be as small as the first octet or as large as 30 of the 32 binary digits of the IP address.

How do you determine how many digits are used for the network identifier? You must look at the **subnet mask**, which is a required component for all IP hosts. On every TCP/IP network, hosts must have both an IP address and a subnet mask. The subnet mask indicates how much of the IP address represents the network or subnetwork. Standard (default) subnet masks are as follows:

- Class A subnet mask is 255.0.0.0 or
  11111111.00000000.00000000.00000000

- Class B subnet mask is 255.255.0.0 or
  11111111.11111111.00000000.00000000

- Class C subnet mask is 255.255.255.0 or
  11111111.11111111.11111111.00000000

Notice that Class A addresses come with the first octet masked, Class B addresses have the first two octets masked, and Class C addresses have the first three octets masked.

The mask is essentially a continuous string of binary one digits. TCP/IP hosts use the combination of the IP address and the subnet mask to determine if other addresses are local or remote. The binary AND operation is used to perform the calculation. The binary AND operation is simple—each of the 32 binary digits in the IP address is compared with the corresponding digit on the subnet mask to arrive at the ANDing result. One and one results in one, and all other combinations result in zero. When devices AND the IP address with the corresponding subnet mask, the network (or subnetwork) number is the result. Computers and routers use the AND computation to determine the subnet identifier for each IP address. If the subnet identifier for the local IP address is the same as that of the IP address to which it wants to communicate, then the packet is sent on the local subnet (ARP is used, as necessary, to locate the destination MAC address on the local subnet). However, if the subnet identifiers are different, then the packet is sent to the default gateway (usually the local router) to be routed to the remote subnet. Figure 3-17 illustrates ANDing.

Source IP:	64.168.1.1	01000000.10101000.00000001.00000001
Subnet mask:	255.255.255.0	11111111.11111111.11111111.00000000
ANDing result:	64.168.1.0	01000000.10101000.00000001.00000000
Destination IP :	64.168.5.7	01000000.10101000.00000101.00000111
Subnet mask:	255.255.255.0	11111111.11111111.11111111.00000000
ANDing result:	64.168.5.0	01000000.10101000.00000101.00000000

When the mask 255.255.255.0 is used the hosts are remote.

Source IP:	64.168.1.1	01000000.10101000.00000001.00000001
Subnet mask:	255.255.0.0	11111111.11111111.00000000.00000000
ANDing result:	64.168.0.0	01000000.10101000.00000000.00000000
Destination IP:	64.168.5.7	01000000.10101000.00000101.00000111
Subnet mask:	255.255.0.0	11111111.11111111.00000000.00000000
ANDing result:	64.168.0.0	01000000.10101000.00000000.00000000

When the mask 255.255.0.0 is used the hosts are local.

Figure 3-17   ANDing operations

In the figure, the first comparison uses the subnet mask 255.255.255.0, which defines the first three octets as the network identifier. A quick look will tell you that these hosts are on two different subnets. Notice that the first three octets from the ANDing result of the source host are 64.168.1, while those of the destination host are 64.168.5. This means that the source is on subnetwork 64.168.1.0 and the destination is on subnet 64.168.5.0. The source host will have to send communications for 64.168.5.7 through its default gateway.

Now consider the calculations shown on the bottom half of Figure 3-17. The subnet mask has been changed to 255.255.0.0. Given this configuration, the two hosts are on the same subnet because the network identifier in this case is 64.168.0.0 for both. This means that the source host would use ARP, if necessary, to determine the MAC address of host 64.168.5.7 and then transmit its data to that MAC address. Notice that in both of these examples, the default mask is not used. The 64 in the first octet identifies this as a Class A address, which would have a default subnet mask of 255.0.0.0. This means the network administrator has manipulated the mask to get more network numbers. This is called **subnetting** and is discussed later in this chapter.

Subnet Address

If you look at the preceding network and host number divisions, you will notice that the network is identified by the first, or first few, octets. Notice that after the masked portion of the subnet mask, the network identifier changes to zero(s). For example, the network identifier of a host that has IP address 192.168.23.45 with subnet mask 255.255.255.0 is 192.168.23.0.

One of the IP networking rules stipulates that a TCP/IP host must have a nonzero host identifier. From this information, you can determine that on a subnet using mask 255.255.255.0, the IP address 222.12.150.4 is a valid host IP address. However, the address 222.12.150.0 is not a host address, but a network identifier. In other words, you could not assign 222.12.150.0 to a computer.

NOTE
Do not expect all subnetwork identifiers to end in a decimal zero. It is true that subnetworks are identified by all the binary digits in the host portion being zero, but that does not mean that the entire last octet will be zero. For example, 199.192.65.32 could be a subnetwork identifier using subnet mask 255.255.255.224. In this case, the host identifier will be the last five binary digits of the last octet. Because 32 is 00100000 in binary, the final five digits are all zero, which indicates the subnetwork. This concept is described in greater detail as the chapter progresses.

Broadcast Address

IP addressing has another rule that you must commit to memory. On any subnet, when the entire host portion of an IP address is all binary ones, it is a broadcast to all of the computers on that segment. For example, on subnet 192.168.1.0, the IP address 192.168.1.255 is a broadcast. This also can apply to larger subnetworks such as 190.55.0.0; the IP address 190.55.255.255 is a broadcast on that network.

Converting these addresses into binary digits can quickly show if an IP address is a broadcast. If all the binary digits in the host identifier are ones, the address is a broadcast. Figure 3–18 illustrates a broadcast address for a subnet.

Subnet ID:	199.192.65.0	11000111.11000000.01000001.00000000
Subnet Mask:	255.255.255.0	11111111.11111111.11111111.00000000
Broadcast:	199.192.65.255	11000111.11000000.01000001.11111111

Figure 3-18   Broadcast addresses

By looking at Figure 3–18, you can quickly determine the broadcast address (199.192.65.255) because the decimal 255 represents eight binary ones. The binary calculation is not necessary if you know that all bits in the octet that represents the host portion are ones. However, the determination is not so easy when an octet is partially masked, as shown in Figure 3-19.

Subnet ID:	199.192.65.32	11000111.11000000.01000001.00100000
Subnet Mask:	255.255.255.224	11111111.11111111.11111111.11100000
Broadcast:	199.192.65.63	11000111.11000000.01000001.00111111

Figure 3-19   Broadcasts on partially masked octets

In Figure 3-19, you can see that subnetwork identifiers don't always end in a zero decimal value. In this case, the last octet has been partially masked (three binary places), leaving the last five binary digits of the last octet to represent the host identifier. In decimal format, it may be difficult to determine that 199.192.65.63 is a broadcast address for the subnet 199.192.65.32, but in binary format, it is much easier. You can see quickly that the last five binary digits are all ones, which indicates a broadcast on the local subnet.

Notice how important the subnet mask is in determining the logical subdivision of the network. For example, if the subnet mask in Figure 3-19 were 255.255.255.0 instead of 255.255.255.224, the broadcast address would not be 199.192.65.63. Instead, 199.192.65.255 would be the correct broadcast address.

Broadcast Types

There are two different types of broadcasts: flooded and directed. **Flooded broadcasts** are broadcasts for any subnet and use the IP address 255.255.255.255. A router does not propagate flooded broadcasts because they are considered local. When a host sends a packet to the IP address 255.255.255.255, the packet remains on the local subnet.

On the other hand, **directed broadcasts** are for a specific subnet. Routers can forward directed broadcasts. For example, a packet sent to the Class B address 129.30.255.255 would be a broadcast for network 129.30.0.0. The router would forward that packet to the identified network. For security purposes, directed broadcasting is often disabled on a router.

SUBDIVIDING IP CLASSES

By now, you know that ARIN assigns Class A, B, and C addresses. You have also seen how these address groups can be further subdivided into subnetworks. Organizations that are not connected to the Internet can define their own subnets in any way they desire. In this section, we will look closer at how networks can be logically segmented using IP subnets.

When a private organization decides to subnet its network identifier, the outside world does not see a difference in the organization; only the internal structure of the organization's network changes. An organization may decide to subnet for various reasons:

occupies a six-story building with 30 hosts per floor, the network administrator may create six different subnets, one for each floor.

- To match the administrative structure of the organization: Some organizations may choose to divide their network by administrative structure. For example, the administrator might subdivide the network by department. Each department could have its own subnetwork.

- To plan for future growth: A network administrator who foresees and plans for organizational growth may decide to subnet the network based on that expectation.

- To reduce network traffic: This is one of the most common reasons to divide an IP network into smaller subnetworks. Because routers are required for each network division, the number of routers on the network must increase when subnetting occurs. Typically, routers do not forward broadcast traffic, which means that there will be less broadcast traffic on the network. Routers, as their name implies, also route packets along a path instead of broadcasting them to all hosts on a segment. Overall, this equates to a more efficient use of the network and a corresponding reduction in network traffic.

As an example, assume that a private organization had the Class B address 190.45.0.0; the network manager of this organization might decide to subnet the Class B address to mirror the internal administrative structure of the organization. This decision would not affect the external network (Internet); it would only influence the structure of the network inside the private organization. The organization's internal routers would be responsible for handling inbound communications for that Class B address.

You can divide the 190.45.0.0 address by adding 255 to the third octet of the subnet mask. By default, the subnet mask for a Class B address is 255.255.0.0, but the network administrator might decide to use 255.255.255.0. Figure 3-20 illustrates what the subnetting does to the Class B address.

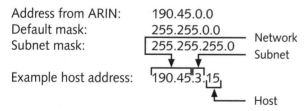

Figure 3-20   Dividing a Class B network

The example address in the figure shows how the different octets can be broken out. Notice that the third octet now defines the subnet. By masking the third octet, the administrator can create 254 different subnetworks, each of which can contain 254 hosts.

Subnet Masking

When network administrators create subnets, they borrow bits from the original host field to make a set of subnetworks. The number of borrowed bits determines how many subnetworks and hosts will be available. Whenever you subnet a network address, you lose some of the host addresses that you could have had without the subnetting. For instance, in the example from the previous section, the network administrator divided the Class B address 190.45.0.0 by masking the third octet. You know from the previous section that Class B addresses support 65,534 hosts. However, when the third octet is masked, there is only room for 254 subnetworks, each containing 254 hosts. This means that the number of addresses is reduced to 64,516 (254 x 254). Table 3-4 illustrates the types of subnet masks that can be used and how these masks affect the number of hosts available per subnet.

Table 3-4   Class B subnet masks

Subnet mask	Subnets on network	Hosts per subnet
255.255.192.0	2	16,382
255.255.224.0	6	8,190
255.255.240.0	14	4,094
255.255.248.0	30	2,046
255.255.252.0	62	1,022
255.255.254.0	126	510
255.255.255.0	254	254
255.255.255.128	510	126
255.255.255.192	1,022	62
255.255.255.224	2,046	30
255.255.255.240	4,094	14
255.255.255.248	8,190	6
255.255.255.252	16,382	2

When the host portion of an IP address is all binary zeros, that address is the subnetwork identifier. When the host portion of an IP address is all binary ones, that address is a broadcast address.

TIP

The network administrator can use up to 14 bits to subnet a Class B address. Two bits must be left for host numbers.

NOTE

Class C addresses also can be subdivided, but not as many options or available masks exist because only the last octet can be manipulated with this class. Table 3-5 illustrates the five available subnet masking options for Class C addresses.

Table 3-5 Class C subnet masks

Subnet mask	Subnets on network	Hosts per subnet
255.255.255.192	2	62
255.255.255.224	6	30
255.255.255.240	14	14
255.255.255.248	30	6
255.255.255.252	62	2

NOTE

The network administrator can use up to six bits of the last octet to subnet the Class C address. Two bits must be left for host numbers.

Each example in Table 3-5 follows a pattern in the last octet. If you refer to Table 3-4, you will see the same numbers in the last masking octet in those examples. This pattern exists because subnet masks must have continuous binary one digits from the left side. Figure 3-21 illustrates the possible binary combinations that can be used as subnet masks.

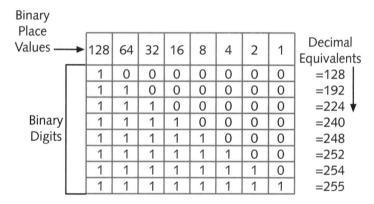

Figure 3-21 Subnet mask values

The subnet masks have a clear binary pattern. They must have a continuous string of ones from the left side of the octet. Such a table would be easy to recreate, if you remember the binary places at the top. Then, you need only to add up the binary places to get their decimal equivalents. For example, the mask 11000000 can be calculated by adding binary places 128 and 64 (128 + 64 = 192).

Learning to Subnet

The best way to learn to subnet a network is to use a Class C address. A Class C address only allows the administrator to subnet the last octet. Also, as Table 3-5 shows, you can use only five different numeric masks on the last octet of a Class C address.

Suppose you had a network with five different segments and somewhere between 15 and 20 TCP/IP hosts on each network segment. You just received your Class C address from ARIN (199.1.10.0). Refer to Table 3-5 to decide which subnet mask you will use. Notice that only one subnet mask can handle your network configuration: 255.255.255.224. This subnet mask will allow you to create six subnetworks and to place up to 30 hosts per network. The other subnet masks will give you either too few subnetworks or too few hosts.

Deciding on the subnet mask is fairly straightforward. You just select the mask that meets your needs. Your next task is to assign the addresses to your network. You must find the IP address of each subnet identifier and a valid range of IP addresses for each subnet. A quick way to determine the subnet identifiers (IP addresses) is to write the last masking octet as a binary number. Then, you can determine the binary place of the last masking digit, as shown in Figure 3-22.

Class C Address: 199.1.10.0
Standard Mask: 255.255.255.0
Selected Mask: 255.255.255.224

	128	64	32	16	8	4	2	1
224	1	1	1	0	0	0	0	0

Figure 3-22   Subnet masking example

Notice that the last masking digit in this example occupies the binary place of 32. To calculate the subnets, begin with the major network number and increment by 32. Stop counting when you reach the value of the mask (224):

- 0 (binary 00000000) — unusable
- 32 (binary 00100000)
- 64 (binary 01000000)
- 96 (binary 01100000)
- 128 (binary 10000000)
- 160 (binary 10100000)
- 192 (binary 11000000)
- 224 (binary 11100000) — unusable

Now you have determined the different subnet identifiers. You cannot use the first subnet because the resulting IP address would be the same as the major network number (the network number with no subnetting). It is also known as "subnet zero." You also cannot use 224 because it is the mask, so you have six numbers left. These six numbers will be the last octets of the IP addresses identifying your six subnets. You can quickly determine that they are subnet identifiers because the host portions (last five binary digits in this case) are all zero.

NOTE RFC 1878 (*www.faqs.org/rfcs/rfc1878.html*) discusses the inclusion and exclusion of all zero and one subnets. Subnet zero can be used in special circumstances, which are beyond the scope of the CCNA exam.

3

Next, you must determine the valid ranges for your hosts on each subnet. These are IP addresses that can be configured on the computers on your network. For this operation, you need only take the ranges between each subnet identifier. In doing this, you must remember to remove the broadcast address for each subnet from the list of valid ranges. Each subnet has a broadcast address, and it is the last number before the start of each new subnet, because the last number is equivalent to placing all binary ones in the host portion of the IP address. Table 3-6 illustrates the subnet identifier, valid host range, and broadcast address for each subnet.

Table 3-6 Class C address 199.1.10.0 masking 255.255.255.224

Subnet identifier	Valid host range	Broadcast address for subnet
199.1.10.32	199.1.10.33 – 199.1.10.62	199.1.10.63
199.1.10.64	199.1.10.65 – 199.1.10.94	199.1.10.95
199.1.10.96	199.1.10.97 – 199.1.10.126	199.1.10.127
199.1.10.128	199.1.10.129 – 199.1.10.158	199.1.10.159
199.1.10.160	199.1.10.161 – 199.1.10.190	199.1.10.191
199.1.10.192	199.1.10.193 – 199.1.10.222	199.1.10.223

As first described in Table 3-5 and shown in Table 3-6, there are six available networks with 30 available hosts per network. One address on each subnet is the subnetwork identifier, and one is the broadcast address for that subnet. You also lose the addresses below the first network identifier (199.1.10.32, in this case) and the addresses that are greater or equal to the last masking octet (224 in this example).

Notice that the masking digits in the last octet cover the first three binary digits, as shown in Figure 3-23. Each valid subnet in the list has a different combination of the first three binary digits. However, all zeros or all ones in the first three places (the network identifier) are not allowed. If three zeros lead the octet, the address is equivalent to the assigned IP network address (199.1.10.0). If three ones lead the octet, the address is equivalent to a broadcast for the entire Class C address.

NOTE Automated subnet calculators on the Internet are quite useful for determining the number of subnets versus the number of hosts. One example is the IP Subnet Calculator from WildPackets (*www.wildpackets.com*).

Binary				Binary		
Decimal	32	00100000	Decimal	128	10000000
Mask	224	11100000	Mask	224	11100000
Decimal	64	01000000	Decimal	160	10100000
Mask	224	11100000	Mask	224	11100000
Decimal	96	01100000	Decimal	192	11000000
Mask	224	11100000	Mask	224	11100000

Figure 3-23   A binary look at the mask

Subnetting Formulas

If you take an exam on IP subnetting, you probably will not be permitted to use a subnet calculator. Although you can write the numbers out in binary format and create tables to determine the subnet identifiers and ranges, you can also use formulas to solve these problems. Consider memorizing the following two formulas:

- $2^y - 2$ = # of usable subnets (where y is the number of bits borrowed)
- $2^x - 2$ = # of usable hosts per subnet (where x is the number of bits remaining in the host field after borrowing)

To demonstrate how these formulas can be used, assume that you have the subnet mask 255.255.255.240 on your Class C network address of 199.4.10.0. To determine the number of subnets, you would figure out how many masked bits (borrowed bits) exist in the final octet, as shown in Figure 3-24.

```
C Address          199.4.10.0        11000111.11000000.01000001.00000000
Standard mask      255.255.255.0     11111111.11111111.11111111.00000000
Mask               255.255.255.240   11111111.11111111.11111111.11110000

y = 4 (borrowed bits)
x = 4 (bits left in host field after borrowing)

Formulas:
2^y - 2 = # of usable subnets
2^x - 2 = # of usable hosts per subnet
2^4 - 2 = 14 usable subnets
2^4 - 2 = 14 usable hosts per subnet
```

Figure 3-24   Sample calculation using formulas

3

Figure 3-25 illustrates the subnets created when the Class C address 199.4.10.0 is used with the subnet mask 255.255.255.240. Notice that the last octet of the subnet increments by the decimal value of the right-most significant binary digit in the mask, which in this case is 16. The zero subnet range is invalid because when any of those IP addresses are ANDed with the subnet mask 255.255.255.240, they are identical to the network identifier (subnet zero). The 15th subnet range is invalid because when any of those IP addresses are ANDed with the subnet mask 255.255.255.240, they are identical to the broadcast range for the Class C IP address.

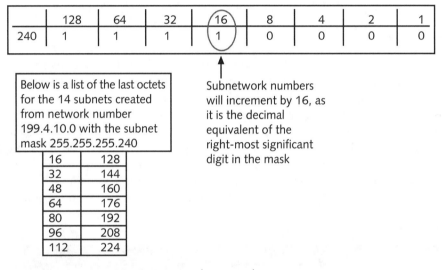

	128	64	32	16	8	4	2	1
240	1	1	1	1	0	0	0	0

Below is a list of the last octets for the 14 subnets created from network number 199.4.10.0 with the subnet mask 255.255.255.240

Subnetwork numbers will increment by 16, as it is the decimal equivalent of the right-most significant digit in the mask

16	128
32	144
48	160
64	176
80	192
96	208
112	224

Figure 3-25   255.255.255.240 subnet mask

NOTE   Refer back to Figure 3-17 for an illustration of ANDing.

CIDR

Classless Inter-Domain Routing (CIDR) was developed to slow the exhaustion of IP addresses. It is based on assigning IP addresses on criteria other than octet boundaries. It became apparent in the mid-1990s that this address space was becoming depleted, mostly because IP addresses were being wasted. For example, a Class C address provides 254 host addresses, which is clearly not enough for many large businesses. On the other hand, an unsubnetted Class B address provides over 65,000 IP addresses, which is usually far more than necessary on any one network, so the unused addresses are wasted. The CIDR addressing method allows the use of a **prefix** to designate the number of network bits in the mask. The prefixes allow a more flexible assignment of IP network numbers. For example, a company may be assigned the IP network of 200.16.1.48 /25. The prefix of 25 means that the first 25 bits in the mask are network bits, in other words, '1's''. In binary, the mask is 11111111.11111111.11111111.10000000. In decimal, the mask is 255.255.255.128. It is much easier to express the mask as a prefix, which is the CIDR notation. CIDR notation is also known as bit-count notation because the number of "1's" in the mask are counted and displayed. The prefix can be longer than the default subnet mask (subnetting) or it can be shorter than the default mask (**supernetting**).

The allocation of network numbers based on CIDR has helped slow the depletion of addresses. CIDR is now used by all backbone routers and most ISPs. However, knowledge of the original class system is essential to understand subnetting and CIDR.

Summarization

Summarization is also known as route aggregation. It is also sometimes called supernetting. This is because the network/node boundary in the subnet mask moves to the left with supernetting, rather than to the right as with subnetting. The purpose of summarization is to allow many IP subnets to be advertised as one. This reduces the number of entries in the router's routing table. Large routing tables are a concern because they negatively affect router performance. Deciding how to summarize a group of subnets is relatively straightforward. You simply count the number of bits that are common to all of the networks you want to advertise, and then you use the prefix that identifies the number of common bits. For example, Table 3-7 shows four subnets in both decimal and binary that can be summarized.

Table 3-7   Example summarization

Decimal	Binary Equivalent
213.64.132.0 /24	11010101.01000000.10000100.00000000
213.64.133.0 /24	11010101.01000000.10000101.00000000
213.64.134.0 /24	11010101.01000000.10000110.00000000
213.64.135.0 /24	11010101.01000000.10000111.00000000

Rather than advertising the Class C addresses as four separate networks, the router on the edge of this internetwork could be configured to advertise network 213.64.132.0 with a shorter prefix that includes all four networks. Notice that the first 22 bits of the four network addresses are the same. This means all four of these networks can be advertised in the summary route 213.64.132.0 /22. Configuration of summary routes is considered an advanced routing concept, but it may be covered on the CCNA exam.

VARIABLE LENGTH SUBNET MASKS

Subnet masks tell the computer or router which part of an IP address is the network portion and which part is the host portion. Manipulating the mask via subnetting is a big improvement over using the traditional fixed-length mask because it allows a single major network number to be subdivided into smaller subnetworks. The problem with basic subnetting is that once the new mask is formulated, that same mask must be used on every one of the subnets. It is a "one-size-fits-all" design. For example, if you subnet to accommodate 254 hosts on each subnet, you will waste 252 of those IP addresses on a point-to-point WAN link where you only need two addresses.

Variable length subnet masking (VLSM) solves this problem by allowing different masks on the subnets. Essentially, this is done by subnetting the subnets. Basic routing protocols such as RIP version 1 and IGRP do not support VLSM because they do not carry subnet mask information in their routing table updates. More advanced routing protocols such as RIP version 2, OSPF, and EIGRP support VLSM because they carry subnet mask information inside their routing table updates.

Figure 3-26 shows an internetwork that would benefit from VLSM because of large variations in the number of host IP addresses necessary on each of the different subnetworks.

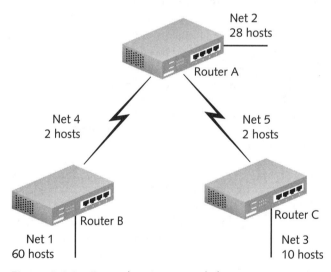

Figure 3-26   Example internetwork for VLSM

In this example we see that, assuming no growth, five subnetworks are necessary. The network requiring the most IP addresses is Net 1, with 60 hosts. On RIP version 1 and IGRP networks, which are **classful**, the major network number 192.168.59.0 is sized for 60 hosts, but there are problems. Although we have enough host bits to cover the maximum number of hosts on any of our subnetworks, there aren't enough bits to create the five subnetworks. Recall that the formula to calculate the number of subnets is

2^y-2, where y equals the number of bits borrowed. The two subnet numbers (2^2-2=2) will be 192.168.59.64 and 192.168.59.128 /26. Obviously, we are three subnets short. In addition, on the networks other than Net 1, far fewer IP addresses are necessary, thus many of the 62 available IP addresses per subnet will be wasted. This is especially true on Nets 4 and 5, which are point-to-point links. Only two host addresses per subnet are needed on these two networks so the other 60 IP addresses on each of these subnets will be wasted.

The problems are solved if a **classless** routing protocol such as RIP version 2, OSPF, or EIGRP is used instead of RIP version 1 or IGRP. In a classless world, the routing updates carry subnet mask information and allow different masks to be used on different subnets. Using VLSM with classless routing protocols will allow us to subnet our subnets. This will not only provide many more usable subnets, it will also enable us to more efficiently allocate the IP addresses.

We begin as we did previously by sizing for the subnet with the largest number of hosts— Net 1. The formula to calculate the number of hosts per subnet is 2^x-2, where x represents the number of host bits left in the host portion after bit borrowing has taken place. Two host IP addresses still must be reserved; one for the subnet number itself, and one for the broadcast address. So, x equals 6 and y, which is the number of bits borrowed, equals 2. The subnet numbers we create by borrowing two host bits for subnetting are 192.168.59.0, 192.168.59.64, 192.168.59.128, and 192.168.59.192 /26, and they will each support 62 hosts. Without VLSM, we have only two usable subnets of 62 hosts per subnet. This will not fit our needs in the network shown in Figure 3-26. After you figure the subnetting scheme for the maximum number of hosts, you can then take the remaining subnets and further subnet them to provide a subnet that supports the correct number of hosts.

NOTE   The use of subnet zero is on by default in all versions of the Cisco IOS 12.0 or later. On routers with earlier IOS versions, support for using subnet zero can be enabled with the ip subnet-zero command.

Using VLSM and making sure that our devices support the use of subnet zero, we assign the first subnet, 192.168.59.0, to Net 1, which needs almost all of the 62 available IP addresses. Next, the second available subnet will be further subnetted to accommodate Net 2 with 28 hosts and Net 3 with 10 hosts. The second subnet is 192.168.59.64. Net 2 must accommodate 28 hosts so 2^x-2 must equal at least 28. In this case, substituting 5 for x will produce 2^5-2=30 hosts on a subnet. Presently, there are six bits in the host portion from the first round of subnetting; now we need only five bits so we can give up one more bit for subnets—in other words, y=1. Therefore, we can create 2^1=2 new subnets from this second original subnet. The first new subnet will have the same starting value as the original, 192.168.59.64, and end at 192.168.59.95, but it will have a different mask, /27. Remember, originally two bits were borrowed, extending the mask from the default of /24 to /26. Now, we borrow one more bit, so the mask moves one more to the right to /27. This means our new second network will increment by 32 and not 64. The second subnet number is 192.168.59.96 /27. Each of these subnets provides 30 hosts, which is enough for Net 2 with 28 hosts and Net 3 with 10 hosts. So, Nets 1, 2, and 3 are taken care of and we have two of the original subnets left (192.168.59.128 and 192.168.59.192 /26). It would be more efficient to further subnet 192.168.59.128 /64 and assign the new subnets to Net 4 and Net 5. This will not only conserve IP addresses, it will leave the last original subnet (192.168.59.192 /26) unassigned so it can be used at a later date for growth if necessary.

So, we begin with the third original subnet, 192.168.59.128 /26. We need only two host addresses on each of the last two subnets (Net 4 and Net 5), so $2^x-2=2$, meaning x=2. Because only two bits are required in the host portion, we can move our mask to the right by four more bits, making it /30. Now, y=4 and we get $2^4=16$ more subnets, each with only two host IP addresses available.

The /30 mask is preferred on WAN links and is often referred to as the "serial mask."

NOTE

The first new subnet will be the same as the original 192.168.59.128 but with a different mask, /30. The new subnets will increment by four, as that is the value of the last bit borrowed. The new subnets are shown in Table 3-8.

Table 3-8 VLSM subnets created from 192.168.59.128 /26

192.168.59.128 /30	192.168.59.160 /30
192.168.59.132 /30	192.168.59.164 /30
192.168.59.136 /30	192.168.59.168 /30
192.168.59.140 /30	192.168.59.172 /30
192.168.59.144 /30	192.168.59.176 /30
192.168.59.148 /30	192.168.59.180 /30
192.168.59.152 /30	192.168.59.184 /30
192.168.59.156 /30	192.168.59.188 /30

Table 3-9 displays the entire IP scheme for Figure 3-26. It is important to note that the VLSM IP scheme presented in this example is just one of many ways VLSM could have been implemented to solve the problem presented by classful routing.

Classless routing protocols that support VLSM such as OSPF and EIGRP are explained in greater detail in Chapter 9.

REFERENCE

Table 3-9   VLSM IP scheme for 192.168.59.0

Major Network	Original Subnets	Subnetted Subnets Using VLSM	Subnet Assignments
192.168.59.0 /24	192.168.59.0 /26		Net 1
	192.168.59.64 /26	192.168.59.64 /27	Net 2
		192.168.59.96 /27	Net 3
	192.168.59.128 /26	192.168.59.128 /30	Net 4
		192.168.59.132 /30	Net 5
		192.168.59.136 through 192.168.59.188	Reserved
	192.168.59.192 /26		Reserved

IPv4 vs. IPv6

The version of IP currently being deployed on almost every system and the one described in this chapter is IP version 4 (**IPv4**). Waiting in the wings is IP version 6 (**IPv6**), which was designed primarily to address the eventual depletion of IPv4 addresses. IPv6 addresses are 128 bits compared with IPv4's 32-bit structure. This means there are approximately 2^{128} available addresses with IPv6, versus 2^{32} addresses with IPv4. Because of this significant increase in length, IPv6 addresses are expressed as hexadecimal numbers.

IP address conservation strategies such as CIDR have made the move to IPv6 less urgent; however, there are other reasons to upgrade, such as security and performance enhancements. Transition mechanisms built into IPv6 should make the upgrade relatively easy and will allow vendors and networkers to begin integrating IPv6 hardware and software on their own schedules.

UNDERSTANDING PACKET TRANSMISSION

As packets travel a given network segment, each host on the segment evaluates the packet to determine whether the destination MAC address listed in the packet matches its own or is a broadcast to all hosts. The host makes a copy of the packet and sends the original packet along the network path. If the copy of the packet is for the local host's MAC address, a broadcast, or a multicast for which the local host is configured to receive, the packet continues up the protocol stack. If the packet is not for the local host, the copy is discarded.

MAC address checking occurs at the Network Interface layer of the TCP/IP model, or the Data Link layer (layer 2) of the OSI model. In the TCP/IP networking model, if the data is destined for the local host's MAC address or is a broadcast, the Network Interface layer information is removed. Next, the protocol stack passes the packet to the Internetwork layer. There, the destination IP address contained in the packet is compared to the local host's IP address. If the IP address listed in the data packet matches the local host address, or is a broadcast, the protocol stack strips off the Internetwork layer information and moves the packet up the protocol stack again.

As you learned previously, the Internetwork layer of the TCP/IP protocol stack is equivalent to the Network layer of the OSI model. The Network Interface layer and the Internetwork layer of the TCP/IP protocol stack ensure that data gets from one host to another on a TCP/IP network. The MAC address, at the Network Interface layer, uniquely identifies a specific device on any network. The IP address, at the Internetwork layer, identifies a specific host on a specific network. For a packet to be routed on a TCP/IP internetwork, both an IP address and MAC address are required for both the source and destination hosts.

Routers on the Network

Routers connect two or more network segments. In doing so, a router must have a separate identity for each network it is connecting. A router requires an IP address for every network segment to which it is connected and a separate network interface or port for each network segment. For example, if a router connects four different network segments, it must have four different IP addresses and four different network interfaces. Figure 3-27 illustrates the configuration of a router that connects four segments.

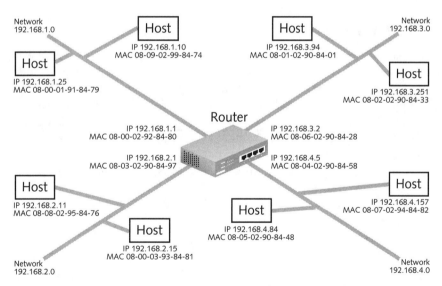

Figure 3-27   Configuration of a router with four segments

Notice that the router has an IP and MAC address for each of its ports that are valid for each of the network segments to which it is connected. Figure 3-27 also illustrates hosts configured on each network segment. Each device on the network has a unique IP address and MAC address.

NOTE   Serial interfaces—in other words, those attached to WAN links—typically do not have their own MAC addresses. The serial interfaces use MAC addresses assigned to LAN interfaces on the router.

When computers need to send packets to destinations not on their segment, they send the packets to the router (default gateway) instead. The router connected to the segment on which the packet originated recognizes that the destination host is on a different subnet. The router must determine which subnet should receive the packet. The router first removes the Network Interface information (OSI Data Link layer header), which contains the router's MAC address, because it was addressed to the router. (The sending computer obtained the router's MAC address either from looking in its ARP cache or by sending an ARP request if the address was not in its table.) Then, the router analyzes the Internetwork layer information—specifically, the destination IP address. The destination IP address will be the IP address of the final destination, not the IP address of the router. In fact, the source and destination IP addresses do not change throughout the journey of a packet from source to destination. Only the MAC address changes. The router references its **routing table** to determine which of its interfaces is connected to the destination network. Then the router rebuilds the Network Interface layer information with the appropriate format for the destination network and sends the packet out through the correct interface.

Network to Network

Routers maintain routing tables which they use to route packets from one network to another. When a network uses TCP/IP, each port on a router requires an IP address, which allows the router to correctly forward the packet to the appropriate network segment. For example, consider the router connections shown in Figure 3-28. Assume the router port 192.168.1.1 connects to network segment 192.168.1.0. If a packet comes in for a host computer that connects to 192.168.1.0, the router knows to forward this packet to the 192.168.1.1 port because that port attaches to the correct network. The router's routing table tells it that packets destined for 192.168.1.0 should be sent to the interface with IP address 192.168.1.1.

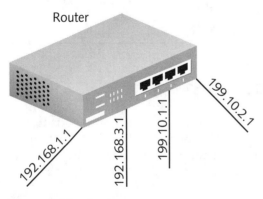

Figure 3-28   Router

On a TCP/IP network, the logical addresses on a certain segment must be matched. For example, if the network segment is 192.168.1.0, all the hosts on that segment must have addresses that start with 192.168.1. They will also have unique identifiers for the last octet. This means that if you move a computer from one segment to another, the IP address will have to be changed to make it a member of the new segment.

NOTE You only need to ensure that the logical address, such as the IP address, matches the network because MAC addresses are a permanent part of the NIC and do not change when the computer is moved to a new network.

Dynamic or Static Tables

Routing tables match network addresses with the addresses of the routers that handle those networks. The tables can be built statically or dynamically. A static routing table requires manual configuration by the network administrator. Each route must be entered by hand, and the router always uses the same route to send packets to a specific network address, even if that route is not the most efficient.

Dynamic updates are provided through **routing protocols**. Routing protocols allow the routers to be updated automatically. Routers automatically build dynamic routing tables; a router capable of dynamic routing can choose from among the various routes on a network without input from the administrator. The router communicates with other dynamic routers to determine the most efficient route from one point to another on the network. The routers can also track multiple paths to the same location so that alternate routes are available. Dynamic routers can use different methods to determine the best path across a network. One method is the distance-vector algorithm, which considers the number of hops between two points. A hop is a transition from one network segment to another. Each router along a network path is considered one hop. The packet takes the path with the smallest number of hops. A second method used in dynamic routing is the **link-state** algorithm. Using the link-state algorithm, the router takes into consideration network traffic, connection speed, and other assigned costs.

Transmitting Packets to Remote Segments

When TCP/IP hosts transmit a packet to a remote segment, they cannot use ARP to obtain the correct MAC address because the router would filter the ARP request broadcast. In such a case, the TCP/IP host must use the services of the router. When TCP/IP hosts transmit packets to remote segments, they contact their default gateway, which is the network interface to which the client sends traffic that is destined for remote segments. The default gateway is usually a router connecting that local segment to other networks on the LAN or WAN. The TCP/IP host sends the data packet with the destination MAC address of the router. However, because the ultimate destination for the packet is a client on a remote network, the IP address listed as the destination is that of the remote host. When the router receives the packet, it pulls off the Network Interface information and analyzes the packet at the Internetwork layer.

The router checks its routing tables against the destination IP address to locate the appropriate network interface through which to forward the packet. If the router is directly connected to the network for which the packet is destined, it will readdress the packet at the Network Interface layer (OSI layer 2) with the MAC address of the destination host. It will get this MAC address from its ARP cache. If the information is not in its ARP table, the router will send an ARP request on the destination's segment and attempt to obtain the MAC address. If the router is not directly connected to the network in question, the router will send the packet to the next router in the path on the way to the destination. In this case, the destination IP address will stay the same but the destination MAC address will be that of the next router. The packet will be transferred around the internetwork until the destination is found or the TTL (hop count) reaches its maximum. Routers automatically discard packets that meet the packet's maximum hop count. This prevents packets from endlessly looping around the network or Internet. The process of moving a packet from one router to another in hopes of locating the correct IP address to MAC address mapping is known as indirect routing.

Routing Packets

This section discusses the journey of a packet across a network, from Host A to Host B, as shown in Figure 3-29.

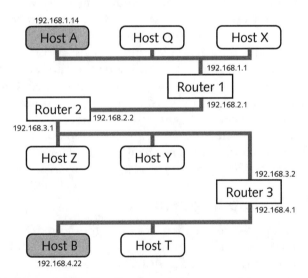

Figure 3-29   Routing a packet

Table 3-10 lists the IP address, network interface, and network identifier for each device. The assumed subnet mask for this network is 255.255.255.0.

Table 3-10   Information surrounding the journey of a packet

Device IP	Address	Interface	Network
Host A	192.168.1.14		192.168.1.0
Router 1	192.168.1.1	Ethernet 0	192.168.1.0
Router 1	192.168.2.1	Ethernet 1	192.168.2.0
Router 2	192.168.2.2	Ethernet 0	192.168.2.0
Router 2	192.168.3.1	Ethernet 1	192.168.3.0
Router 3	192.168.3.2	Ethernet 0	192.168.3.0
Router 3	192.168.4.1	Ethernet 1	192.168.4.0
Host B	192.168.4.22		192.168.4.1

Host A

Host A composes its data at the Application layer and then encapsulates that data in the appropriate Transport layer protocol. The data is then passed to the Internetwork layer. At the Internetwork layer of the TCP/IP protocol stack, the IP address (192.168.4.22) for the destination host (Host B) is added as well as Host A's own IP address. Because Host A is communicating with a remote host, it uses the MAC address of its default gateway (Router 1; 192.168.1.1) as well as its own MAC address when encapsulating the data at the Network Interface layer.

Once Host A has properly composed, formatted, and addressed the packet, it transmits the packet on the network. The other hosts on the network (Q and X) receive and discard the packet because the MAC address does not match theirs. Router 1 accepts the packet because the MAC address does match.

Router 1

Router 1 picks up the packet. After the router strips the Network Interface layer information off the packet, the router determines that the packet is destined for IP address 192.168.4.22. Given the subnet mask, the router determines that the network identifier is 192.168.4.0. Router 1 then consults its routing table to determine to which router port the packet should be sent. Table 3-11 contains essential information from the routing table of Router 1. To make the example simple, the routing table shown here has only two pieces of information, the network and interface addresses. In reality, routing tables contain several additional items, including subnet masks (or netmasks), default gateways, and cost metrics.

Table 3-11   Router 1 routing table

Network	Interface
192.168.1.0	192.168.1.1
192.168.2.0	192.168.2.1
192.168.3.0	192.168.2.2
192.168.4.0	192.168.2.2

When Router 1 consults its routing table, it sees that packets destined for network 192.168.4.0 must be sent to 192.168.2.2, which is the interface on the next hop in the path, Router 2.

Router 1 repackages the Network Interface part of the data packet and transmits the packet out interface 192.168.2.1 using the MAC address of Router 2. The destination IP address, 192.168.4.22, remains unchanged.

Router 2

Router 2 picks up the packet destined for its MAC address and strips off the Network Interface information. Router 2 analyzes the IP Header destination address and identifies that it is destined for network 192.168.4.0. Next, Router 2 checks its routing table, as shown in Table 3–12.

Table 3-12   Router 2 routing table

Network	Interface
192.168.1.0	192.168.2.1
192.168.2.0	192.168.2.2
192.168.3.0	192.168.3.1
192.168.4.0	192.168.3.2

According to its routing table, Router 2 must send the packet destined for network 192.168.4.0 to the next router interface, which is 192.168.3.2 on Router 3. Therefore, Router 2 repackages the Network Interface layer of the packet, adding the MAC address for Router 3 to the packet. The destination IP address remains 192.168.4.22, and the data packet is sent to Router 3.

Router 3

Router 3 receives the data packet destined for its MAC address and strips off the Network Interface layer information to reveal the IP address. Router 3 determines that the traffic is destined for network 192.168.4.0 and checks its routing table, as shown in Table 3–13.

Table 3-13   Router 3 routing table

Network	Interface
192.168.1.0	192.168.3.1
192.168.2.0	192.168.3.1
192.168.3.0	192.168.3.2
192.168.4.0	192.168.4.1

The routing table shows that one of Router 3's interfaces is directly connected to network 192.168.4.0. Because of this, Router 3 must then determine which host on the network has the IP address 192.168.4.22. Router 3 checks its ARP table to get a MAC address mapping for the client. If no mapping exists, Router 3 issues an ARP request on network 192.168.4.0 to get a mapping. Once the router has the correct MAC to IP mapping, it repackages the Network Interface layer using the MAC address of the destination. After the packet is properly addressed, Router 3 transmits it to Host B through interface 192.168.4.1.

Host B

Both Host B and Host T receive the traffic forwarded by the router. However, Host T discards the packet because it is not addressed to its MAC address. Host B accepts the packet at the Network Interface layer and continues to process the data frame. At the Internetwork layer, Host B confirms that the packet is intended for its IP address. Then, it passes the data packet up the protocol stack for further processing.

WORKING WITH HEXADECIMAL NUMBERS

The decimal number 192 expressed in binary is 11000000. It takes eight binary digits to express the three-digit decimal number 192. The reason is that decimal numbers can be expressed with up to 10 numerals (0–9), while binary numbers can only be expressed with two (0 and 1). The higher the quantity of numerals in a numbering system, the fewer it takes to express any given number. Decimal number systems have 10 numerals, which is why decimal is referred to as base 10. Binary number systems have two numerals and binary is referred to as base 2.

The **hexadecimal** numbering system is base 16; in other words, there are 16 numerals that can be used to express any given number. These numerals include 0 through 9 as well as A through F. Because more numerals are available in hexadecimal, it is logical that any given number can be expressed with fewer hexadecimal numerals than with either binary or decimal. For example, the decimal number 192 is C0 in hexadecimal.

Why should you care about hexadecimal numbering? Often you will come across hexadecimal numbers when working with computers and networking. For example, the MAC address described in this chapter is a 12-digit hexadecimal number. Another example is the color displayed on your TV and computer monitors. The colors are coded using two-digit hexadecimal numbers. Another common use of hexadecimal numbering occurs in packet sniffing. Sniffers placed on the network to capture packets usually display much of the capture information in hexadecimal. In addition, memory addresses are displayed in hexadecimal. Most importantly, computers typically process information in 8-bit chunks (bytes). It is easier to express those eight bits with two hex digits.

You have already learned how to convert binary numbers to decimal numbers and vice-versa. Now you must learn how to convert between hexadecimal and the other systems. The easiest way to convert a decimal number into a hexadecimal number is to convert the decimal number to binary first. This is because each group of four binary digits equals one hex digit and that hex digit will be between 1, which is 0001 in binary, and 15, which is 1111 in binary. Table 3-14 lists the 16 hexadecimal numerals and their binary and decimal equivalents.

NOTE   Four bits, which is half of a byte, is also called a **nibble**.

Table 3-14   Binary to hex to decimal conversion

Binary	Hexadecimal	Decimal
0000	0	0
0001	1	1
0010	2	2
0011	3	3
0100	4	4
0101	5	5
0110	6	6
0111	7	7
1000	8	8
1001	9	9
1010	A	10
1011	B	11
1100	C	12
1101	D	13
1110	E	14
1111	F	15

Let's look at a few conversion examples. As stated earlier, the decimal number 192 is equal to 11000000 in binary. We know that there are four binary digits for each hex digit, so let's group the eight binary digits above into two sets of four digits and write it as 1100 0000, two nibbles. Now all we have to do is treat each set of four binary digits as its own separate hex number. The first set of four binary digits equals 12 (8+4) and the second set of four digits equals 0. Table 3-14 indicates that a binary 1100, which is the same as a decimal 12, is equal to a hexadecimal C. A zero in binary is a zero in decimal as well as hexadecimal. We simply put the C and the 0 together to get C0, which is the hexadecimal equivalent of 192.

What if you are given a binary number for conversion that cannot be grouped by four digits (for example the binary number 100011, which has only six digits)? In this instance, you should add enough leading zeroes to the binary number to make even

3

groups of four digits. In this case you would express 100011 as 00100011. The value of the binary number does not change when you add leading zeroes. Now you can split the binary number into two groups of four digits: 0010 0011. The first four digits are equivalent to a hex 2 and the second four digits are equivalent to a hex 3. Therefore, the binary number 100011 is equal to the hex number 23. How do you know that the expressed number 23 is not a decimal number instead of a hex number? Often hex numbers are displayed with a small letter "h" after the number for clarity. Another way to explicitly indicate that a number is a hex number is to place a "0x" before the hex number. So the hex number 23 would be expressed as either 23h or 0x23.

When converting from hexadecimal to binary, we simply pull the hex digits apart and use four binary digits to represent each hexadecimal digit. For example, 3E9 is equivalent to 0011 1110 1001 in binary. To go directly from hexadecimal to decimal, recall that the hexadecimal numbering system is base 16. This means that each place value is a factor of 16. This means that 3E9 is equal to $3\times16^2 + 14\times16^1 + 9\times16^0$, which equals $3\times256 + 14\times16 + 9\times1$. That is equal to a decimal 1,001.

It has been said that humans use decimal, computers use binary, and humans use hexadecimal to understand binary. Although the base 16 numbering system seems foreign at first glance, largely due to the addition of letters, it really is an efficient way to express large numbers such as MAC and IPv6 addresses.

CHAPTER SUMMARY

- ❑ TCP/IP is more than just the Transmission Control Protocol/Internet Protocol; it is an entire suite of protocols that provides data transportation, management, and diagnostic capabilities for networks that use it.

- ❑ TCP/IP was started by the Defense Advanced Research Projects Agency (DARPA). That group was charged with developing a national communication system that could survive a nuclear war. Later, its network, ARPANET, was turned over to the public, especially universities. From there, the Internet grew into what it is today, a large worldwide commerce and communications network.

- ❑ TCP/IP maps to a four-layer network model: Application, Transport, Internetwork, and Network Interface. These layers map to equivalent functions in the OSI reference model.

- ❑ The Application layer in the TCP/IP model covers the Application, Presentation, and Session layers of the OSI reference model. The TCP/IP Transport layer maps directly to the OSI Transport layer. The Internetwork layer of the TCP/IP model maps directly to the Network layer of the OSI model. Finally, the Network Interface layer of the TCP/IP model is equivalent to the Data Link and Physical layers of the OSI model.

❏ The TCP and UDP protocols reside at the Transport layer of the TCP/IP networking model. UDP is an unreliable and connectionless communications protocol that does not guarantee packet delivery. TCP is a reliable and connection-oriented protocol that guarantees packet delivery. TCP uses a three-way handshake to establish a communications link between two points before data transfer. TCP also uses a sliding window to control the flow of packets and the number of acknowledgments between the two hosts.

❏ Both TCP and UDP use port numbers from 1 to 65,535 to establish their communications between two points. Ports with numbers 1023 and under are Well Known Port numbers, as defined in RFC 1700. These ports describe common Internet services that hosts can use to contact public servers for specific types of services, such as Web, FTP, and telnet.

❏ The Internet Protocol (IP) resides at the Internetwork layer. It provides the logical address that can be passed through a router. The subnet mask allows networks to be divided into subnetworks.

❏ You can use the ping utility with IP and ICMP to diagnose and troubleshoot network connections. Also, you can use the trace utility with IP to determine all the hops that a packet makes along its path to a remote TCP/IP host.

❏ Address Resolution Protocol (ARP) and Reverse ARP (RARP) reside in the Internetwork layer. These protocols allow the TCP/IP host to map the IP address to a MAC address.

❏ The MAC address is the final leg of communication between hosts. Packets are transmitted via the MAC address to the destination host once the packets arrive at the destination network or subnetwork.

❏ The Internet Corporation for Assigned Names and Numbers (ICANN) and the American Registry of Internet Numbers (ARIN) work together to subdivide and issue addresses for Internet clients. Three classes of addresses (A, B, and C) are available to organizations. Class A addresses are for governments worldwide. Class B addresses are assigned to medium to large companies and universities. Class C addresses are assigned to organizations and people who require an IP address but do not meet the criteria to have a Class A or B address. Addresses are now largely assigned without regard to classful boundaries using a system known as CIDR.

❏ Two other address categories, Class D and Class E, exist. Class D addresses are used for multicasting information. Multicasting allows anyone with the correct setup to broadcast a simultaneous transmission to multiple computers. Class E addresses are used for experimentation and research.

❏ You can subdivide assigned addresses. This process is called subnetting. The subnet mask divides the network portion of the IP address from the host portion of the address. The network or subnetwork IP address must always have zeros for the host identifier portion. IP addresses that identify TCP/IP hosts must be nonzero in the host portion. When the host portion of an IP address is all binary ones, the address is a broadcast address.

3

❑ Routing tables can be created manually and dynamically. Network administrators manually create static routing tables. A manual table requires more administrative overhead but gives the administrator greater control over the routing process. Dynamic updates are provided through routing protocols. The routing protocols allow the routers to be updated automatically.

❑ Advanced routing protocols such as RIP version 2, OSPF, and EIGRP support variable length subnet masking (VLSM). VLSM allows network administrators to better allocate their IP address space by using different subnet masks on their subnetworks. Classful routing protocols such as RIP version 1 and IGRP do not support VLSM. They require the same subnet mask on every subnet.

❑ IPv6 is the latest version of IP addressing. Unlike the 32-bit IPv4 addresses that are in use today on most networks, IPv6 addresses are 128 bits long and are expressed in hexadecimal. It is expected that vendors and networkers will slowly convert to IPv6 in the next several years.

❑ The hexadecimal numbering system is also known as base 16 because there are 16 available numerals. The numerals include all of the numbers 0–9 as well as the letters A–F. For example, the letter A represents the decimal number 10 and the letter F represents the decimal number 15. Hexadecimal numbers are found in MAC addresses and IPv6 addresses, and are often used in computer and networking applications.

KEY TERMS

Address Resolution Protocol (ARP) — A protocol that works at the Internetwork layer of the TCP/IP networking model; resolves a known IP address to an unknown MAC address, which is the final leg of communication between the source and destination.

Advanced Research Projects Agency (ARPA) — The government organization operating in the Department of Defense (DOD) that was responsible for the creation and proliferation of the Internet and the TCP/IP protocol suite.

Advanced Research Projects Agency Network (ARPANET) — The original name of the Internet.

American Registry of Internet Numbers (ARIN) — Manages IP address allocation in the United States.

Application layer — The TCP/IP layer that corresponds to the Application, Presentation, and Session layers of the OSI model.

ARP reply — A reply sent by the device that discovers its own IP address in the IP header of the ARP request frame and includes the requested MAC address.

ARP request — A process used to obtain the correct mapping when a source computer cannot locate a destination MAC address for a known IP address in its ARP table.

ARP table — A table used by a network device that contains MAC to IP address mappings.

buffer — A portion of memory used to store information that is being sent or created too fast for a system to process.

buffering — A way in which devices on a network are able to handle packet flows that exceed their processing capabilities. Packets are stored in a buffer until the system can process them.

classful — A routing process that involves using subnet masks with traditional octet boundaries.

classless — A routing process that allows subnet masks to partition the network and the node portions on any bit boundary.

Classless Inter-Domain Routing (CIDR) — A system of allocating IP network numbers based on arbitrary subnet mask boundaries. CIDR notation uses a prefix to designate the network portion of the subnet mask.

congestion avoidance — A method by which a system on the network can reduce the flow of packets on a network by sending a message request to the sender to reduce the rate at which packets are being transmitted.

default gateway — The address to which a host or IP device sends a packet when the destination host is not on its subnet. The default gateway is usually an interface on a router.

destination unreachable — An ICMP message sent back to the source host when a gateway cannot deliver an IP datagram.

directed broadcasts — Broadcasts sent to specific segments. For example, a broadcast on segment 192.168.1.0 would be 192.168.1.255.

diskless workstation — Workstations configured to download their operating systems from a central server. These workstations typically do not have a hard drive.

Domain Name System (DNS) — A hierarchical naming service that is used on the Internet and IP networks to provide host name to IP address resolution.

echo request/reply — The most commonly used ICMP message. ICMP echo request/reply messages are used to check the availability of a remote host, the devices along a network path (intermediate gateways), and to verify the installation of the TCP/IP protocol on the local source host.

expectational acknowledgment — A TCP acknowledgment process in which the acknowledgment number refers to the sequence number expected next. If the expected sequence is not received within an expected time interval, a retransmission is requested.

File Transfer Protocol (FTP) — A part of the TCP/IP protocol suite that provides reliable file transfers across the Internet or other TCP/IP networks. FTP uses TCP to transfer files.

flooded broadcasts — A broadcast for any subnet that uses the IP address 255.255.255.255. Routers do not pass flooded broadcasts.

hexadecimal — A base 16 numbering system that uses numerals 0 through 9 and the letters A through F to represent numbers. MAC addresses and IPv6 addresses are displayed in hexadecimal.

Hypertext Transfer Protocol (HTTP) — A protocol used for communications on the World Wide Web. Web servers are HTTP servers.

ICMP flood — A large quantity of ICMP echo requests sent to a target device by a malicious person or program in an attempt to crash or greatly reduce the performance of the target device.

information request/reply — ICMP messages that are typically used to determine the subnet mask used by the destination. This message allows a host to determine the number of the network it is on.

initial sequence number (ISN) — Sequence numbers that allow communicating hosts to synchronize their communications in a TCP three-way handshake. When the communication is initiated, two hosts communicating over TCP will synchronize their initial sequence numbers.

Internet Assigned Numbers Authority (IANA) — The regulatory agency originally responsible for subdividing and administering the address hierarchy used on the Internet. IANA has been replaced by ICANN.

Internet Control Message Protocol (ICMP) — A protocol in the TCP/IP protocol suite at the Internetwork layer. ICMP messages control and manage IP protocol communications.

Internet Corporation for Assigned Names and Numbers (ICANN) — The global government-independent entity responsible for the Internet.

Internet Protocol (IP) — The Network layer (Internetwork layer) protocol that is responsible for addressing which allows IP to be routed.

Internetwork layer — The layer of TCP/IP that is equivalent to the Network layer of the OSI model.

IP addressing — The act of assigning (unique) IP addresses to devices on the network.

IPv4 — The currently deployed system of IP addressing involving 32-bit numbers expressed as decimal numbers in four octets.

IPv6 — The newest version of IP addressing that involves 128-bit addresses expressed as hexadecimal numbers.

link-state — A routing protocol that uses cost when calculating the best path between two points. It considers items such as network traffic, router congestion, bandwidth, reliability, and other factors that could affect network performance.

loopback — The TCP/IP Class A address 127.x.x.x that is reserved for diagnostic purposes. Any address on this network allows you to check if TCP/IP has been properly installed on the system. (Specifically, the IP address 127.0.0.1 is the address usually given as the loopback.)

multicast address — A special subdivision of IP categories reserved for data streaming. Multicast addresses are used to send information to groups of computers. The range for multicasting addresses is 224.0.0.0 to 239.255.255.255.

multicasting — The sending of a stream of data to multiple computers simultaneously.

Network File System (NFS) — A file system associated with the UNIX operating system that allows for network communications between hosts.

Network Interface layer — In TCP/IP, the layer that is equivalent to the Physical and Data Link layers of the OSI model.

nibble — Equal to four bits. There is one hexadecimal digit in a nibble.

Packet Internet Groper (ping) — A troubleshooting utility that uses ICMP to verify that a remote host is currently running and accessible.

parameter problem — An ICMP message sent whenever incorrect datagram header information is received. The message identifies the octet in the datagram that caused the problem.

Post Office Protocol version 3 (POP3) — A protocol used by client machines, which allows users to download their e-mail from an e-mail server.

prefix — A way of designating the subnet mask that involves a forward slash followed by the number of binary ones in the mask; in other words, the network portion.

redirect — An ICMP message sent to source hosts requesting that they change routes because the one they chose was not optimal. This packet is used to update a source host's internal routing table.

remote login application (rlogin) — A utility that allows remote computers to connect to other computers or devices.

Requests for Comments (RFC) — A group of Internet-related documents that specify Internet protocols and standards.

reset packet (RST) — A packet indicating that the receiver should delete the TCP connection without further interaction.

Reverse Address Resolution Protocol (RARP) — A protocol used to resolve the client's unknown IP address to the client's MAC address for the final leg of communication between an IP source and destination. RARP clients broadcast a request for their IP address. A RARP server has a table of IP to MAC mappings and responds to the client with a RARP reply.

routed protocol — A protocol that contains enough OSI Network layer information that its packets can be routed from a source to a remote destination on an internetwork.

routing protocols — Used to dynamically create routing tables so that routed protocols can route the data.

routing table — A table used by a router to determine which of its interfaces is connected to the destination network.

Simple Mail Transfer Protocol (SMTP) — The main protocol that transfers electronic mail on the Internet between e-mail servers.

Simple Network Management Protocol (SNMP) — A protocol that provides network administrators the ability to centrally control and monitor the network.

sliding windows — A feature of TCP used to control the flow of communications between two hosts. The size of the TCP sliding window regulates how often acknowledgments will be sent to the transmitting host from the receiving host.

source quench — An ICMP message request to reduce the rate at which the sender is transmitting packets to the destination. This message is used for flow control, when packets arrive too fast (the receiving host runs out of buffer space for the message), or if the system is near capacity (network is congested).

subnet — A portion of a network that has been separated from the main network by using a different subnet mask.

subnet mask — A required component for all IP hosts used in combination with an IP address to determine to which subnet the local host belongs. The local host uses this information to determine if the destination is local or remote to the source. Based on this information, the source will either broadcast information on the local network or send its packet to the default gateway for delivery to a remote network.

subnetting — The act of subdividing a network logically with subnet masks.

summarization — The advertisement of many routes as a single route to reduce the total number of route table entries on a router.

supernetting — Also known as summarization or route aggregation. Done by moving the network/node boundary in the subnet mask to the left to include more than one network in an advertisement.

TCP/IP — *See* **Transmission Control Protocol (TCP)** and **Internet Protocol (IP)**.

terminal emulation protocol (telnet) — A connection-oriented, Application layer utility that allows TCP/IP clients to log in to a remote system and operate on that system as if the connection between the two were local.

three-way handshake — The method used by TCP to negotiate a reliable connection between two hosts on a network. This process involves the exchange of three data packets before the communication process begins.

time exceeded — An ICMP message sent whenever a packet's time-to-live (hop count) reaches zero and the datagram is dropped.

time-to-live (TTL) — The number of hops (routers) that a packet can make before it is discarded. The router discards a packet when its TTL is zero, which prevents a packet from looping endlessly around the network. Routers normally decrement the packet TTL by one before passing the packet to the next router.

timestamp request/reply — ICMP messages that are used to synchronize clocks by requesting the destination machine's current time of day value, which is given in milliseconds since midnight Universal Time.

trace — A utility that uses ICMP messages to determine the path between a source and destination host. Trace can discover all of the hops (routers) along the path between two points.

Transmission Control Protocol (TCP) — The protocol that guarantees the delivery of a packet by sending an acknowledgment for each window of data received. This protocol operates at the Transport layer and sends its data encapsulated in the IP protocol. TCP communications are also known as connection-oriented because TCP negotiates a communication path between hosts on the network.

Transport layer — The TCP/IP layer that maps directly to the OSI model Transport layer.

Trivial File Transfer Protocol (TFTP) — A file transfer utility used on the Internet. TFTP uses UDP to transfer files and is therefore less reliable than FTP, which uses TCP in transferring files.

User Datagram Protocol (UDP) — The protocol that operates at the Transport layer and transports data unreliably over IP. This is sometimes known as connectionless communication because the messages are sent without expectation of acknowledgment. There is no connection negotiation process as in TCP. The packets that are sent by UDP are also known as datagrams. Because UDP does not negotiate a connection, it is faster than TCP.

variable length subnet masking (VLSM) — The use of different masks on different subnets, which allows for more efficient IP address allocation. Supported by advanced routing protocols such as RIP version 2, OSPF, and EIGRP.

Well Known Port numbers — TCP and UDP ports from 0 through 1023 on which client applications expect to find common Internet services.

REVIEW QUESTIONS

1. Which of the following is a reliable communications protocol?

    a. UDP

    b. TCP

    c. IP

    d. ICMP

2. Which of the following is used by the TFTP protocol?

    a. UDP

    b. TCP

    c. ICMP

    d. Telnet

3. Which of the following is a layer in the TCP/IP protocol stack? (Choose all that apply.)

    a. Application

    b. Presentation

    c. Physical

    d. Data Link

    e. Internetwork

4. Which of the following is a TCP/IP Application layer protocol? (Choose all that apply.)

    a. DNS

    b. FTP

c. UDP

d. IP

e. ICMP

5. Which of the following is a TCP/IP Internetwork layer protocol? (Choose all that apply.)

a. ICMP

b. FTP

c. DNS

d. ARP

e. IP

6. Which of the following is a TCP/IP Transport layer protocol? (Choose all that apply.)

a. ARP

b. RARP

c. IP

d. UDP

e. TCP

7. If your Class C address has a three-bit subnet mask, which of the following would be a subnetwork identifier?

a. 203.16.34.33

b. 203.16.34.135

c. 203.16.34.32

d. 203.16.34.240

8. Which of the following would be a broadcast address for a Class C network?

a. 190.15.23.255

b. 190.42.25.255

c. 221.21.23.255

d. 129.21.15.255

9. Which of the following Class C IP addresses is a broadcast (assuming the subnet mask is 255.255.255.224)?

a. 219.129.32.5

b. 219.129.32.63

c. 219.129.32.97

d. 219.129.32.161

10. For a Class B broadcast, which octets will be completely binary ones?

    a. 2nd

    b. 2nd and 3rd

    c. 1st and 2nd

    d. 3rd and 4th

11. Which of the following is a Class A broadcast?

    a. 11.255.255.255

    b. 127.75.255.255

    c. 193.255.255.255

    d. 14.25.255.255

12. What is the purpose of the reserved numbers in a Class D address?

    a. Unicast

    b. Experimental

    c. Broadcast

    d. Multicast

13. What is the purpose of the reserved numbers in a Class E address?

    a. Unicast

    b. Broadcast

    c. Multicast

    d. Experimental

14. In a Class C address, which octets identify the network?

    a. All of them

    b. The first octet only

    c. The first and second octet

    d. The last octet

    e. The first three octets

15. Class B addresses allow you to configure how many octets on your network for host IP addresses?

    a. One

    b. Two

    c. Three

    d. Four

16. Which of the following are valid network identifiers for Class A addresses?

    a. 1–127

    b. 1–126

    c. 192–223

    d. 224–240

    e. 128–191

17. What would the value of the first octet of the subnet mask be if the CIDR notation for an address is 192.168.1.16/27?

    a. 224

    b. 254

    c. 255

    d. 265

18. What would the value of the last octet of the subnet mask be if the CIDR notation for an address is 192.168.1.16/28?

    a. 192

    b. 224

    c. 240

    d. 248

    e. 252

19. Assuming that the address 165.24.3.6 uses the correct default mask, what is the host identifier?

    a. 165.24

    b. 24.3.6

    c. 3

    d. 3.6

20. How many bits (maximum) can be used from the last octet of a Class C address to subnet your network?

    a. 2

    b. 4

    c. 6

    d. 8

21. Which of the following address classes allows you to borrow a maximum of 14 bits to create a subnet mask?

    a. Class A

    b. Class B

    c. Class C

    d. None of the above

22. A subnet mask of 255.255.252.0 on a Class B network indicates that _____ bits have been borrowed from the host portion to subnet the network.

    a. 2

    b. 4

    c. 6

    d. 8

    e. 10

23. Given the following CIDR address and mask, which of the following is a broadcast on its subnetwork 162.17.12.125/24?

    a. 162.17.15.255

    b. 162.17.12.255

    c. 162.17.255.255

    d. 255.255.255.255

    e. None of the above

24. Given the address 190.14.20.255/20, which of the following statements is true?

    a. This is a broadcast address.

    b. This is a network address.

    c. This is a host address.

    d. This address is on network 190.14.20.0.

    e. This address is on network 190.14.16.0.

25. Given the address 190.14.20.0/22, which of the following statements is true?

    a. This is a broadcast address.

    b. This is a network address.

    c. This is a host address.

    d. This address is on network 190.14.20.0.

    e. This address is on network 190.14.16.0.

26. The TCP acknowledgment process is _____.

    a. expectational

    b. sequential

    c. exceptional

    d. sesquicentennial

27. Which of the following are NOT ICMP message types?

    a. Echo & destination unreachable

    b. Source quench & redirect

    c. Relay and reroute

    d. Parameter problem & information

    e. Timestamp & time exceeded

28. How does CIDR conserve IP addresses?

    a. By charging more for IP address assignments

    b. By allocating IP network numbers on criteria other than traditional bit boundaries

    c. By using traditional octet boundary subnet masks

    d. By aggregating routes

29. Which of the following routing protocols support VLSM? (Choose all that apply.)

    a. RIP version 1

    b. IGRP

    c. OSPF

    d. EIGRP

30. What is the purpose of summarization?

    a. To reduce the number of routing table entries

    b. To prevent route flapping

    c. To conserve IP addresses

    d. To reduce the cost of acquiring IP addresses

3

CASE PROJECTS

CASE PROJECTS

1. Moe is having a difficult time with IP subnetting. He knows the basics but has some specific questions. He wants to know why certain numbers are unavailable for use. For example, he was told that he cannot use 10 or 127 or any numbers over 223 in the first octet. Why are these numbers off limits? Explain your answer to Moe.

2. Moe wants to understand the concept of sliding windows. Explain their purpose to Moe. When should networks use large sliding windows? When should they use smaller sliding windows? What could happen if small data transfers occur in a large sliding window?

3. Moe and Jennifer want you to explain step by step what occurs when a host wants to send a message. Discuss where ARP fits in and how exactly ARP facilitates the communications.

4. Lisa does not understand the purpose of the RARP protocol or the RARP server. Explain to her how RARP works and why a computer might have a MAC address but no IP address.

4

NETWORK TOPOLOGY AND DESIGN

After reading this chapter and completing the exercises, you will be able to:

♦ Discuss the different physical topologies

♦ Describe various network architecture models

♦ Determine which types of network media to use given a set of requirements

♦ Understand horizontal cabling standards and wiring closets

♦ Consider performance requirements and improvements for given situations

♦ Install a telecommunications connector

♦ Wire a patch panel

♦ Test network cable

♦ Discuss LAN design

♦ Describe the function that network-management tools perform on a network

---

In this chapter, you will learn about the different physical topologies and types of cabling available for networks. In addition, this chapter explains standards and suggests ways to correctly and effectively design and implement the physical media and devices of a network. You will learn about wiring closets and performance considerations, how to wire a wall jack, and how to test cable for proper operation. You will also be introduced to the most common network architectures and their specifications. Finally, you will learn about the hierarchical network design models and network-management tools.

PHYSICAL TOPOLOGIES

A network's physical topology consists of the physical layout of the networking components. The three most common topologies are the bus, star, and ring. This section examines these network topologies and discusses the advantages and disadvantages of each.

Bus

A **bus** topology connects all stations in a linear fashion, which accounts for the name "linear bus." The wire on a bus network has two distinct endpoints, which are capped by terminators. Terminators absorb electronic signals so that they are not reflected on the network. Figure 4-1 illustrates this concept.

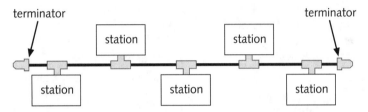

Figure 4-1   Bus topology

On a bus topology, all stations receive the signals transmitted by other stations. Network signals travel in both directions down the bus network, and each station checks the data frame as it passes by. If the receiving station identifies its own MAC address in the destination address of the data frame, it will accept the data. Otherwise, the frame is discarded, but the signal continues along the bus. Although the stations are all on one cable segment, the bus continues to work when stations are offline because the media do not actually pass through the individual stations.

The bus topology has several advantages:

- It is inexpensive.

- It is easy to design and implement because the stations are simply daisy-chained together.

The bus topology has disadvantages as well:

- It is difficult to troubleshoot. If a cable break occurs at any location on the bus, the entire bus fails and it can be difficult to locate the point of failure.

- It requires termination. If the last computers on the chain are not terminated correctly, stations cannot transmit.

Star

The **star** network configuration is the most popular physical topology. As Figure 4-2 shows, in a star configuration all computers or stations are wired directly to a central location, which is usually a **concentrator** (a.k.a. hub) or a **Multistation Access Unit (MAU)**. A data signal from any station goes directly to this central device, which transmits the signal according to the established **network access method** for the type of network.

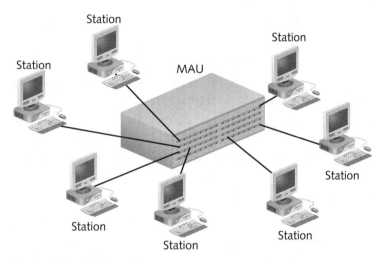

Figure 4-2   Star topology

The star topology has several advantages:

- A break in one cable does not affect all other stations as it does in bus technologies because there is only one station per segment, making the star generally more reliable.

- In a star, problems are easier to locate because symptoms often point to one station.

- The star is the second-easiest topology to design and install, after the bus.

- The star does not require manual termination. Instead, the media are terminated in the station at the **transceiver** on the network interface card (NIC) and in the hub or MAU.

The star topology has disadvantages as well:

- Hubs, which are required for a star topology, are more expensive than bus connectors.

- A failure at the hub can affect the entire configuration and all connected stations.

- Star topologies use more cable than bus topologies because separate wires run to each individual station.

Repeaters can extend the maximum usable distance of the bus or star topology. Typically, active hubs function as repeaters in a star configuration.

NOTE The bus and star topologies can be combined to form a **star/bus** or **bus/star** physical topology. Hubs that have connectors for coaxial cable as well as for twisted-pair wiring are used to form these types of networks. When different physical topologies are applied to a network, the result is often called a **mixed media** network.

Ring

Physical rings are most often seen in **Fiber Distributed Data Interface (FDDI)** networks. FDDI is a WAN technology and is discussed later in this chapter. Stations on a **ring** are wired to one another in a circle around the entire network.

A ring topology resembles a bus topology except that it has no termination points. Data is passed around the ring and, unlike a bus network, stations in a ring regenerate the signal before passing it along. This makes the ring topology active, as opposed to the passive bus topology.

The ring topology has these advantages:

- It prevents network collisions because of the **media access method** or architecture required.

- Each station functions as a repeater, so the topology does not require additional network hardware, such as hubs.

However, as with any topology, disadvantages exist:

- As in a bus network, a failure at one point can bring down the network.

- Because all stations are wired together, to add a station you must shut down the network temporarily.

- Maintenance on a ring is more difficult than on a star topology because an adjustment or reconfiguration affects the entire ring.

Influence of the 5-4-3 Rule on Topologies

The Institute of Electrical and Electronics Engineers (IEEE) identifies a maximum number of repeaters, segments, and populated segments that can be used on any given 10-Mbps (megabits per second) Ethernet network using repeaters and/or hubs. These maximums are known collectively as the **5-4-3 rule** because no more than five segments of cable and four repeaters can exist between any two stations on the network, and only three of the five segments can be populated with computers, bridges, or routers. The other two segments can only interconnect the repeaters and/or hubs. Typically, the 5-4-3 rule is represented graphically, as shown in Figure 4-3.

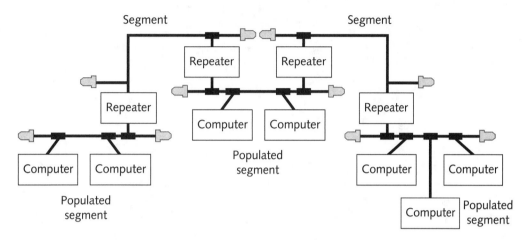

Figure 4-3 5-4-3 rule

The drawing illustrates a linear bus network. This network has five interconnected segments and four repeaters, and only three of the five segments are populated. It is easy to verify that this network complies with the 5-4-3 rule.

When networks employ different types of media, it can be difficult to verify compliance with the 5-4-3 rule. For example, bus networks (using coaxial cable) are easily identifiable as segments because they have one wire with many stations. However, when bus networks are combined with star networks (using twisted-pair cable), each cable running from the hub is a segment.

Evaluate the network configuration shown in Figure 4-4 for 5-4-3 rule violations. While doing so, remember that the hubs in this illustration function as multiport repeaters and that the terms station, host, terminal, server, and computer are used interchangeably to reflect industry use.

In the figure, one violation of the 5-4-3 rule exists: the separation between Station 3 and Server 1 and Host 2 because six segments and five repeaters exist between these stations. Either the hub and segment of Station 3 must be moved, or the hub and segments of Server 1 and Host 2 must be moved.

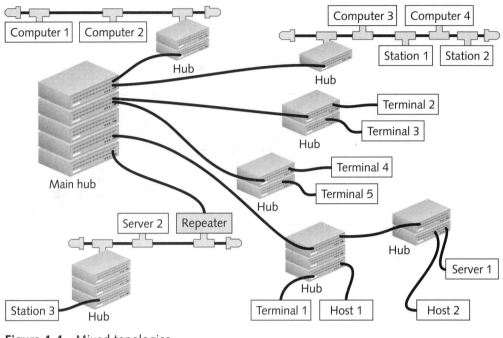

Figure 4-4   Mixed topologies

NETWORK ARCHITECTURE

The term network architecture refers to a network's physical and **logical topology**. This includes its physical structure or layout, the media used, the network access method, and the standards and protocols employed. The network access method, which is the same thing as logical topology, defines how the signal gains access to and travels on a wire. Logical topologies operate at the Data Link layer of the OSI model. The most common network architectures include Ethernet, Token Ring, FDDI, and AppleTalk.

Network architectures are defined primarily at the Physical and Data Link layers of the OSI model. The 802 standard defines these architectures.

IEEE 802

IEEE 802 covers issues concerning all types of networks—local area (LAN), metropolitan (MAN), wide area (WAN), and wireless. As originally written, IEEE 802 only addressed issues related to the first two layers of the OSI networking model—Physical and Data Link. Thus, by necessity, the standard is constantly evolving as committees research, discuss, and propose additions, revisions, and other modifications.

Several different specifications in the 802 standard are particularly interesting in basic networking architectures. This section covers the following specifications:

- 802.2 — Logical Link Control
- 802.3 — CSMA/CD
- 802.5 — Token Ring
- 802.11 — Wireless technologies

Logical Link Control (IEEE 802.2)

To better define and modularize the technologies used to transmit data on a network, the IEEE subdivided the Data Link layer of the OSI networking model. In the IEEE **802.2** specification, the Data Link layer is divided into the **Media Access Control (MAC) sublayer** and the **Logical Link Control (LLC) sublayer**, as shown in Figure 4-5.

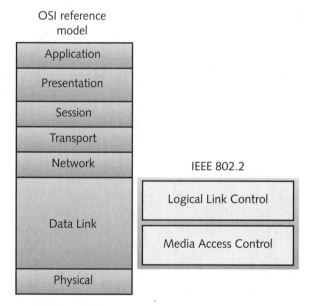

Figure 4-5   802.2 specification

The LLC sublayer is closer to the software components of the protocol stack because it controls data link communication and defines **Service Access Points (SAP)**, which are used to transfer information from the Logical Link Control layer to higher layers of the protocol stack.

The MAC sublayer is closer to the underlying hardware architecture because it is in direct contact with the network interface card (NIC). This sublayer is responsible for error-free data transmission and for providing electronic access to one or more NICs at the Physical layer. The MAC sublayer contains the hardware address for the NICs.

CSMA/CD (802.3)

IEEE **802.3** defines the **access method** used by most Ethernet networks (Ethernet being the most common LAN technology today). The network access method used by Ethernet was developed in the 1960s at the University of Hawaii. Xerox Corporation eventually adopted the access method in the 1970s. Xerox, Digital Equipment Corporation, and Intel furthered the development of Ethernet. The IEEE adopted the 802.3 standard in the early 1980s. Different types of Ethernet networks exist within the generic 802.3 specifications. These specifications call for different transmission rates, cable types, and minimum and maximum cable lengths.

Ethernet uses the Carrier Sense Multiple Access with Collision Detection (CSMA/CD) network access method. In fact, the 802.3 standard is typically referred to as CSMA/CD. To understand where the name originated, consider that on an Ethernet network, before transmitting, any device must listen to the wire for a carrier signal, which is present only when another station is transmitting. Listening to the wire is called carrier sense (CS). If no signal is detected, devices can send data. All devices have equal access to the wire, which is what the multiple access (MA) portion of CSMA/CD describes.

The last part of the name, CD, stands for collision detection, which means that the devices can detect collisions in the event that two individual transmissions collide on the network. Collisions occur when two hosts transmit data on the network at the same time. The area in which the collision originates and affects other stations is referred to as the collision domain. Because a collision of frames makes them unintelligible to the hosts on the network, such a situation is undesirable.

Although stations are required to listen to the wire before sending a transmission, two stations could listen to the wire simultaneously and not sense a carrier signal. In such a case, both stations might transmit their data at the same time. Shortly after the simultaneous transmissions, a collision would occur. Ethernet NICs can detect collisions on the wire. This ability further explains the collision detection (CD) piece of the CSMA/CD network access method.

Once the sending devices detect a collision, they transmit a 32-bit **jam signal** that tells all other devices except the collision parties that they are not to transmit for a brief period (9.6 microseconds or slightly longer). After the transmittal of the jam signal, the two stations that experienced the collision use an algorithm to enter a backoff period, which causes them not to transmit for a random interval. The backoff period ensures that those two stations do not immediately cause another collision.

The CSMA/CD access method uses a logical bus topology. This means that the signal will go out from the sending station in all directions to every host on the segment. The physical topology (or layout) may be a bus or a star. The five most well-known Ethernet specifications are 10BaseT, 10Base2, 10Base5, 100BaseT, and Gigabit Ethernet.

10BaseT describes an Ethernet network connected by twisted-pair cable that can support transmissions of 10 Mbps using **baseband** (digital) signals. The physical topology resembles a star, as each host is connected to a central device (in this case, a hub). Because each segment terminates in the workstation and the hub, there is only one host per segment. This is known as a star-bus topology. The minimum segment length is 2 meters, and the maximum length of any segment is 100 meters.

Another Ethernet specification, **10Base2**, describes a coaxial cable network that has a 10-Mbps baseband transmission rate over a maximum segment length of 185 meters. This specification is also known as **thin Ethernet**, or thinnet, because of the type of cabling used. Each end of a thinnet network must be terminated. This is because (unlike the 10BaseT specification) the wire does not terminate in the workstation and a hub. The physical topology of a thinnet network is a bus. Computers are daisy-chained together by segments of coaxial cable. There is a maximum of 30 hosts per segment.

A third Ethernet specification, **10Base5**, is a coaxial cable specification that indicates a 10-Mbps baseband transmission using a physical bus topology. 10Base5 networks allow segment runs of 500 meters. This specification is also known as Standard Ethernet, **thick Ethernet**, or thicknet, because of the type of cabling used. The longer allowable segment length is related to less attenuation on the wire because of the wider cable diameter. The maximum number of hosts on a thicknet segment is 100, and the computers on each end must be terminated.

A fourth specification, **Fast Ethernet**, is also known as **100BaseT** because it provides a 100-Mbps baseband transfer rate over twisted-pair wire. Fast Ethernet uses the same network access method (CSMA/CD) and the same topology as 10BaseT, which is star-bus, but provides 10 times the data transmission rate. Of course, different NICs and network devices are required to obtain the higher rate. IEEE defines Fast Ethernet as 802.3u. When converting to 100BaseT, existing 10BaseT network wiring can be used and the entire network does not have to be converted to 100BaseT, because the access method still employs CSMA/CD and other specifications are compatible with 10BaseT. Newer NICs support both 10- and 100-Mbps transmission rates.

The fifth specification, **Gigabit Ethernet**, is a more recent addition to the IEEE 802.3 specifications. It supports 1-Gbps baseband transmission. Gigabit Ethernet consists of two different IEEE standards. IEEE 802.3ab specifies Gigabit Ethernet over UTP or 1000BaseT. Gigabit Ethernet over UTP uses full duplex communication over all four wire pairs. Because 802.3ab is pushing UTP to its limits in terms of speed, it is much less tolerant of cable runs that exceed recommended maximums or of poor termination of cables. IEEE 802.3z is Gigabit Ethernet over fiber. Also known as 1000Base-X, it can use either single-mode or multimode fiber. The maximum cable segment for Gigabit Ethernet over single-mode fiber is 5 km.

Both of these standards employ the CSMA/CD access method and are backward-compatible with 100BaseT and 10BaseT technologies.

In 2002, the IEEE ratified yet another extension of the 802.3 standard. **10 Gigabit Ethernet**, or IEEE 802.3ae, allows Ethernet technologies to be used in the growing

MAN marketplace. It operates only over fiber and uses full duplex, so a method of collision detection is not needed. Still, the frame format remains the same as any other type of Ethernet in the 802.3 standard, making it backward-compatible with earlier versions. Multiple 10-Gb Base standards exist for running Gigabit Ethernet over single-mode and multimode fiber. Using single-mode fiber, cable runs of up to 40 km can be created.

Token Ring (802.5)

IBM developed Token Ring technology, and the IEEE updates the standard to keep current with changes by IBM. In the **802.5** specification, Token Ring networks use token-passing to keep track of which node is communicating. Although the specification does not mandate the physical topology of Token Ring, almost all Token Ring networks are connected in a physical star. The device at the center of the star is an MAU instead of a hub or switch. Token Ring networks typically use twisted-pair cable, and the transmission rates can be either 4 or 16 Mbps.

In the physical star configuration, the logical ring is implemented in the MAU. The token is passed from host to host through the MAU. So, although the physical layout of a Token Ring network is a star just as in the 10BaseT networks, the signal is traveling in a ring—thus, the term **star-ring**. Recall that in the 10BaseT star-bus network, the signal is sent through the hub to all hosts. This would be a logical bus instead of a logical ring. MAUs can be connected to other MAUs on the network. Up to 33 MAUs can be connected on a Token Ring network.

In the **token-passing** access method, a single token is passed from station to station. From the perspective of any given station, the token is received from the **nearest active upstream neighbor (NAUN)** and passed to the **nearest active downstream neighbor (NADN)**. The token is, in fact, a small data frame. Stations may transmit on the network only when they have received the token. Each station requires the token in order to transmit. Thus, no two stations transmit at the same time, which prevents collisions. Because the token is passed from one station to another, a break in the cable or a loss of a host can interrupt the flow of the token.

As stations are powered on in a Token Ring network, the first station turned on becomes the **active monitor**. It ensures that the network continues to function by periodically sending a packet around the ring to ensure ring integrity. Any Token Ring NIC can detect a failure on the ring. If a NIC does detect a failure, it starts **beaconing**. Beaconing means that the NIC sends frames to all other NICs on the wire. The frame includes the address of the NIC originating the frame and its NAUN. The NAUN should recognize its own address in the beacon frame and remove itself from the network to run self-diagnostics. If the diagnostics pass, the NIC will reinsert itself on the wire; otherwise, it will remain disconnected from the ring. Once the failure point is detected, the ring is automatically reconfigured around the failed NIC. Token Ring technology provides for traffic prioritization, is more reliable than Ethernet technologies, and works in industrial environments where interference from EMI sources makes many Ethernet installations untenable.

Wireless Technologies (802.11)

Wireless LANs connect users over the air using electromagnetic waves, and are usually used where there are limitations to installing cable. The IEEE **802.11** standard for wireless LANs specifies parameters at both the Physical and Data Link layers of the OSI model. At the Physical layer, infrared or spread spectrum technologies are supported.

Infrared (IR) transmission requires line-of-sight between the transmitter and receiver. If you use a remote control to change the channels on your TV, you are most likely using an IR transmitter. Infrared transmissions cannot go through walls and can be degraded by sunlight, but they are relatively secure because they are highly directional (point-to-point).

Spread spectrum, which is a form of radio frequency (RF) transmission, involves the deliberate spreading of the transmitted signal over many different frequencies, or over a wide bandwidth, and does not require line-of-sight. This technology requires greater bandwidth than standard RF transmission. There are two flavors of spread spectrum transmission: frequency-hopping spread spectrum (FHSS) and direct-sequence spread spectrum (DSSS). In FHSS, a relatively high-power signal is continually switched between different frequencies. With DSSS, the transmission is spread across a wide signal bandwidth at low power levels. FHSS and DSSS provide some degree of security from unauthorized interception.

At the Data Link layer, 802.11 specifies **Carrier Sense Multiple Access/Collision Avoidance (CSMA/CA)** as the network access method. This is similar to CSMA/CD where the node first listens to see if the channel is clear. However, in the case of CSMA/CA, if the channel is not clear, the node chooses a random backoff time to determine how long to wait until it can transmit. When it is time to transmit, the node first sends out a ready-to-send (RTS) packet. If the destination node gets the RTS, it sends a clear-to-send (CTS) packet, and subsequently the data is sent. The 802.11 standard is still being reviewed and reworked. Wireless LAN implementations are expected to increase exponentially as the technology develops and improves.

FDDI

The Fiber Distributed Data Interface (FDDI) standard is the responsibility of the **American National Standards Institute (ANSI)**. The standard describes a network that can span up to 100 km (62 miles) over single-mode fiber-optic cabling. The transmission rate on an FDDI network is 100 Mbps, and FDDI allows up to 500 devices per network. The FDDI access method is based on the Token Ring (802.5) specification but does not have the same limitations. FDDI is a physical and logical ring.

The FDDI network has two rings, the primary ring and the secondary ring. Data travels on the primary ring. The secondary ring is used as a backup, in case the primary ring fails. However, if the secondary ring is not used for backup, it can increase the effective transmission rate to 200 Mbps. Although regular Token Ring networks are limited to one token on the ring at a time, FDDI networks can circulate more than one token. Thus, data can be transmitted more quickly on the network.

MEDIA

Modern networks can use several types of network media. Most networks use some type of cable for the connection medium; however, radio waves are also considered a medium when used in wireless networks. Wireless technologies, such as infrared and satellite communications, will become increasingly important in the future. This section covers twisted-pair, coaxial, and fiber-optic cabling.

Twisted-Pair Cabling

Most networks are connected with twisted-pair cabling. The cable that runs from your telephone to the wall is probably twisted-pair. Different types and categories of twisted-pair cable exist, but they all have some things in common:

- The wires are copper.

- The wires come in pairs.

- The pairs of wires are twisted around each other.

- The pairs of wires are usually enclosed in a cable sheath individually and as a group of wires.

The twisting of network wires inside the cable sheath reduces **crosstalk**—the bleeding of a signal from one network wire to another, which can corrupt signals and cause network errors. Transmitting cables have a naturally created magnetic field around them. When two networking wires are twisted around one another (inside the same cable sheath), their electronically created magnetic fields cancel each other out. This **cancellation** insulates the signal from the effects of signal bleeding. The twisting of the wires not only protects the signal inside from internal crosstalk, but also guards against other external forms of signal interference (bleeding of energy or signals from other wires or appliances that may be near the twisted wires).

Unshielded Twisted-Pair (UTP)

Unshielded twisted-pair (UTP) cabling is used for a variety of electronic communications. UTP cable supports data transmissions of 4, 10, 16, 100, and 1000 Mbps. The maximum segment length for UTP is 100 meters. Although additional categories of UTP are being developed and are expected to reach speeds greater than 100 Mbps, currently there are five accepted categories of UTP that you should know about. Table 4-1 shows these five categories of UTP wiring.

Table 4-1   Categories of UTP

Type	Description
CAT 1	Voice-grade communications only; CAT 1 twisted-pair does not support data transmission.
CAT 2	Data-grade 4 Mbps; CAT 2 is an older, rarely used specification of UTP.

Table 4-1   Categories of UTP (continued)

Type	Description
CAT 3	Data-grade 10 Mbps; CAT 3 cable meets the minimum transmission rate for 10BaseT networking.
CAT 4	Data-grade 16 Mbps; CAT 4 is an intermediate UTP specification that has largely been replaced by CAT 5 cable.
CAT 5	Data-grade 100 Mbps; CAT 5 is the most widely implemented cabling in networks today. Some recent network specifications outline using CAT 5 cable for up to 1000-Mbps transmission rates.

NOTE   Most building codes require that **plenum**-grade cable be used when installing networking cable in ceilings or walls. The jackets of certain types of network cable give off a toxic gas when burned, which is unacceptable for most fire codes. Plenum-grade cable does not give off a toxic gas when burned and is often required by fire codes. Plenum cabling is typically about twice as expensive as normal PVC CAT 5 cabling.

The advantages of UTP cable include:

- It is a thin, flexible cable that is easy to string between walls.
- Most modern buildings come with CAT 5 UTP already wired into the wall outlets or at least run between the floors.
- Because UTP is small, it does not quickly fill up wiring ducts.
- UTP costs less per foot than any other type of LAN cable.

Using UTP also has disadvantages:

- It is more susceptible to interference than most other types of cabling. The pair twisting does help, but it does not make the cable impervious to electrical noise.
- Its unrepeated length limit is 100 meters.

RJ-45 Connectors

Twisted-pair wiring is fitted with a plastic connector and inserted into a transceiver on a NIC at the computer end and a hub, switch, or wall connector at the other end. These connectors are known as **Registered Jacks (RJ)**. Typically, RJ-45 connectors connect UTP networks. The RJ-45 connectors resemble the typical RJ-11 connectors that connect your phone to the wall. The difference between the RJ-45 connectors and the RJ-11 connectors is that the former has eight wire traces (four-pair) and the latter has only four (two-pair). These extra wire traces result in the RJ-45 connector being larger than the RJ-11 connector.

Some RJ-11 connectors are used with three-pair (six-wire) UTP.

NOTE

Shielded Twisted-Pair (STP)

Shielded twisted-pair (STP) cabling is often seen in Token Ring networks and is similar to UTP in that the wire pairs are twisted around each other inside the cable. However, STP also has metal shielding around the cable to further protect it from external interference and crosstalk. Some types of STP have additional shielding around each individual pair as well as the bundle of pairs. Of course, shielding the individual wire pairs increases the overall diameter and weight of the cable. The maximum segment length of STP cable is 100 meters. The maximum bandwidth of STP is 155 Mbps.

The advantage of STP over UTP is that it has greater protection from interference and crosstalk due to the shielding.

The disadvantages to STP include the following:

- STP has a higher cost per foot.
- The STP shield must be grounded at one end; if grounded improperly, it can cause serious interference.
- STP is heavier and less flexible, and is more difficult to install.
- Because of its thickness, STP may not fit down narrow cable ducts.

Coaxial Cabling

Coaxial cable consists of either a solid inner core (often made of copper) or a wire strand **conductor** that is surrounded by insulation. Just outside of the insulation is a shield, which is a foil or copper braid that protects the inner conductor. A protective jacket (external coating) surrounds the outside of the cable. Coaxial cable is installed using a physical bus topology. It is a dated technology, however, and should not be used for new cable installations.

Coaxial cable supports data transmission rates of 10 Mbps. The two most commonly used types of coaxial cable are **thicknet** and **thinnet**. Thicknet is simply a thicker form of coaxial cable than thinnet. Thicknet segments can be up to 500 meters long, whereas thinnet segments are limited to 185 meters. Figure 4-6 shows coaxial cable.

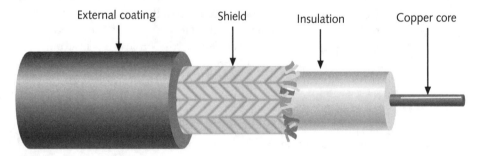

External coating   Shield   Insulation   Copper core

Figure 4-6   Coaxial cable

4

The advantages of using coaxial cabling on a LAN include the following:

- The segment lengths are longer than UTP or STP.
- Coaxial cable has greater interference immunity than UTP.
- Hubs between stations are not required.

Coaxial cable has disadvantages as well:

- It is not as easy to install as UTP because it is not as flexible or thin.
- It is more expensive than UTP.
- It supports a maximum bandwidth of only 10 Mbps.
- It requires more room in wiring ducts than UTP.
- It is relatively difficult to troubleshoot thinnet and thicknet networks.

Table 4-2 lists several types of coaxial cable you might encounter.

Table 4-2 Coaxial cable types

Cable type	Description
RG-8	50-ohm thicknet (10Base5) cabling
RG-58	50-ohm thinnet (10Base2) cabling RG-58/U — solid copper core RG-58 A/U — wire strand center conductor RG-58 C/U — military specification for thinnet
RG-59	75-ohm broadband cable (cable TV)
RG-62	93-ohm ARCNet

Thinnet is sometimes referred to as **cheapernet**.

TIP

Thinnet and Thicknet Connectors

The most common connectors for **RG-58** cabling on thinnet networks are **barrel connectors**, **T-connectors**, and **terminators**. These connectors are known as **BNC** connectors. Terminators are placed on the T-connectors that are on the computers at the end of a thinnet segment. These devices absorb signals as they reach the end of the wire. This absorption keeps the signals from reflecting (signal bounce) and preventing other stations from transmitting. Barrel connectors are used to connect two cable segments, and T-connectors are used to connect two cable segments to a NIC. Figure 4-7 shows these connectors.

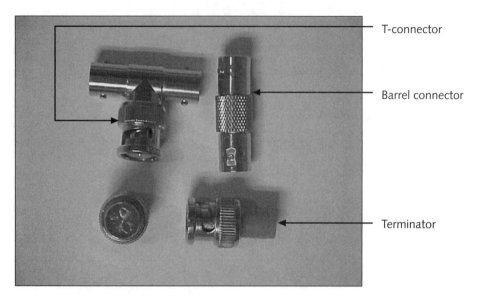

T-connector

Barrel connector

Terminator

Figure 4-7   Thinnet connectors

Although a thicknet network also uses coaxial cabling, the connectors can be different. Thicknet cable can be attached directly to computers using larger BNC-style connectors that are similar to thinnet connectors, but thicknet is extremely difficult to manipulate and usually is connected indirectly.

In this indirect method, a small device called a vampire tap pierces the thicknet cable to make a connection with the copper core. The tap is then attached to a transceiver external to the NIC. A drop cable, no more than 50 feet long, connects the transceiver to an **attachment unit interface (AUI) port** on the NIC. Unlike a BNC attachment or an RJ-45 attachment, the AUI attachment on the NIC is not a transceiver. The AUI interface is typically 15-pin and female.

NOTE

Thicknet is rarely seen on modern LANs. The most common use of thicknet today is as backbone cable running in elevator shafts and other areas where electrical interference is an issue. This is because of thicknet's good interference immunity.

Fiber-Optic Cable

Fiber-optic cable carries light pulses rather than electrical signals along its fibers. This cable is made of glass or plastic fibers, rather than copper wire like most other network cabling. The core of the cable is usually pure glass. Surrounding the glass is a layer of cladding made of glass or plastic, which traps the light in the core. The cladding is usually wrapped with an insulating layer. This is then surrounded with Kevlar fibers, which is the strong substance used in bulletproof vests. Finally, a protective outer sheath made of either PVC or Teflon (plenum grade) is added. See Figure 4-8.

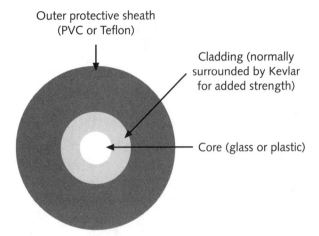

Outer protective sheath
(PVC or Teflon)

Cladding (normally
surrounded by Kevlar
for added strength)

Core (glass or plastic)

Figure 4-8   Fiber-optic cable

The light pulses carrying the signals in fiber-optic cable originate from a light-emitting diode (LED) for multimode cable or a laser for single-mode cable. Multimode cable can support transmissions up to 100 Mbps, over segments up to 2 km (1.2 miles). Single-mode cable can transmit up to 2 Gbps with segments that span up to 62 miles. Fiber-optic cable is the media of choice for connections between LANs, between buildings, across MANs, and where there is excessive electromagnetic interference or security issues.

Fiber-optic cabling has several advantages:

- It can transmit over long distances, farther than any other network media.
- It is not susceptible to electromagnetic interference or crosstalk.
- It supports extremely high transmission rates.
- The cable has a small diameter and can be used in narrow wiring ducts.
- It is not susceptible to eavesdropping.

There are disadvantages to fiber-optic cable as well:

- It is more expensive than other types of networking media.
- It is more difficult and expensive to install than other types of network media. The ends of each cable must be polished perfectly flat and scratch-free before they are inserted into the connection devices.
- Because it is fragile, fiber-optic cable must be installed carefully and protected after installation.

Fiber-optic cables use two main types of connectors. ST connectors, shown in Figure 4-9, are connected via a "twist-on/twist-off" method similar to the method used for thinnet BNC connectors. These connectors are in widespread use, but due to problems with the need to allow enough space on fiber-optic panels to twist the connectors, they are no longer recognized for new fiber installations. Instead, the SC connector shown in Figure 4-10 has replaced the ST connector. SC connectors use a "click-in" method for connection. New installations of fiber-optic cable should use some form of SC connector.

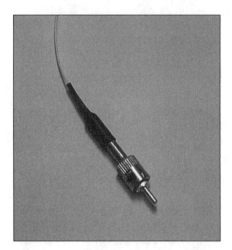

Figure 4-9   ST connector

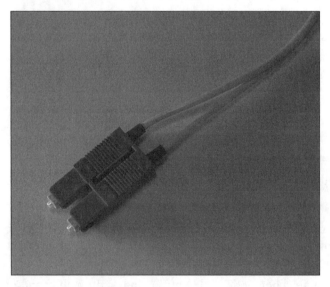

Figure 4-10   SC connector

NOTE An easy way to remember these connectors is to think of the ST as "single twist" and SC as "single click."

Signal Degradation

Most media are susceptible to signal degradation. The sources of the degradation can be internal or external. When signals degrade over distance, attenuation results. Three internal factors can cause attenuation:

- **Resistance**: Opposition to the flow of electrons in a wire

- **Inductive reactance**: Opposition to the changes of electrical current in a wire

- **Capacitive reactance**: Opposition to voltage changes in a wire

When these internal opposition forces are combined and measured, the measure is called **impedance**. Each type of cabling has its own impedance rating, which is part of its specification. If all cabling on a network does not have the same impedance, the network can suffer from transmission errors or a reduction in the total usable segment length. For example, a 50-ohm coaxial cable should not be wired directly to a 93-ohm cable.

Internal signal degradations are naturally occurring and dictate the limitations on network cable lengths. In addition to the internal opposition of a wire to a signal, external forces can act on network signals. These external forces come in two main categories:

- **Electromagnetic interference (EMI)**

- **Radio frequency interference (RFI)**

Both types of interference can degrade and corrupt network signals as they travel through a wire. Electrical lighting (particularly fluorescent lighting), generators, elevators, machinery, and other electromagnetic equipment can be sources of EMI. Crosstalk is a form of EMI. Radio-transmitting devices cause RFI.

To reduce EMI/RFI on network cabling, you can do the following:

- Keep network media away from sources of EMI, such as lights, generators, and high-voltage electrical wiring.

- Ensure that network media are installed properly. Crosstalk is often the result of shoddy installation techniques.

- Use shielded cabling, which is more resistant to external interference. Token Ring STP even has shielding around each individual wire pair to protect from internal crosstalk.

- Use repeaters, which amplify and clean up networking signals. Of course, a repeater next to a noise source repeats the noise (if it appears to be valid data), which could cause more problems on the network. Repeaters are best used in the battle against attenuation.

- Ensure that you install high-quality cabling.

HORIZONTAL CABLING STANDARDS

Horizontal cabling is the twisted-pair or fiber-optic network media that connects workstations and **wiring closets**. The **Electronic Industries Alliance** and **Telecommunications Industry Association (EIA/TIA)** define a set of specifications, **EIA/TIA-568**, which covers the outlets near the workstation, mechanical terminations in the wiring closets, and all the cable that runs along the horizontal pathway between the wiring closet and the workstation. The standards also specify the names given to cabling and devices on the network, as shown in Figure 4-11.

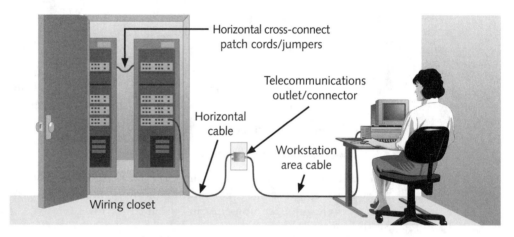

Figure 4-11   Horizontal cabling

The figure shows the following items:

- Workstation area cable: Connects the workstation to the wall outlet
- Telecommunications connector: Found at the wall outlet
- Horizontal cable: Runs between the wiring closet and the wall outlet
- Horizontal cross-connect patch cord: Connects devices in the wiring closet

Although EIA/TIA-568 specifies twisted-pair or fiber-optic cabling for horizontal cabling, the standard still recognizes 50-ohm coaxial cabling. However, this cable type is not recommended and will likely be removed from the standard at the next revision.

EIA/TIA-568B specifies that the maximum distance for a UTP horizontal cable run is 90 meters (295 feet). In addition, the **patch cords** (a.k.a. **patch cables**) located at any horizontal cross-connection cannot exceed six meters (20 feet), and those used to connect workstations in the work area can be a maximum of three meters (9.8 feet). Therefore, the total length of any unrepeated segment should not exceed the 100-meter limitation for UTP.

In addition to UTP, the following cable types may be used for horizontal pathways:

- Shielded twisted-pair (STP): Two pairs of 150-ohm cabling
- Fiber-optic cabling: A two-fiber 62.5/125-micron multimode cable

WIRING CLOSETS

Wiring closets serve as the center of a star topology. They contain the wiring and wiring equipment for connecting network devices, such as routers, bridges, switches, patch panels, and hubs. Because wiring closets are so significant to the physical cabling scheme of the network, their configuration and layout have been standardized by EIA/TIA.

EIA/TIA-568 and **EIA/TIA-569** standards apply to the physical layout of media and wiring closets, with the latter stating that there must be a minimum of one wiring closet per floor. Further, when a given floor area (**catchment area**) exceeds 1000 square meters, or the horizontal cabling is in excess of 90 meters, additional wiring closets are required. In configurations in which more than one wiring closet is needed, a single wiring closet is designated the **main distribution facility (MDF)**. The MDF is the central junction point for the wiring of a star topology. The additional closets are called **intermediate distribution facilities (IDFs)**. The IDFs are dependent on the single MDF. IDFs are required when:

- The catchment area of the MDF is not large enough to capture all nodes.
- The LAN is in a multistory facility.
- The LAN encompasses multiple buildings.

If you are working with multistory buildings, you should place the MDF as close to the middle as feasible. For example, if there are three floors, place the MDF on the second floor, if possible.

Proximity to the POP

You should ensure that your main wiring closet is close to the **point of presence (POP)** to the Internet. Broadly defined, a POP is where two communications systems meet. In this context, the POP is the location of the telecommunications for a given building. It is where a LAN connects to the Internet via the telecommunications company's dial-up or leased lines. Placing the MDF near the POP facilitates your network's connection to the Internet. If you plan to have multiple wiring closets in support of a larger network, then your MDF should be located in the POP room if possible. Figure 4-12 illustrates the relationship of the MDF, IDF, and POP for a typical LAN that spans multiple buildings.

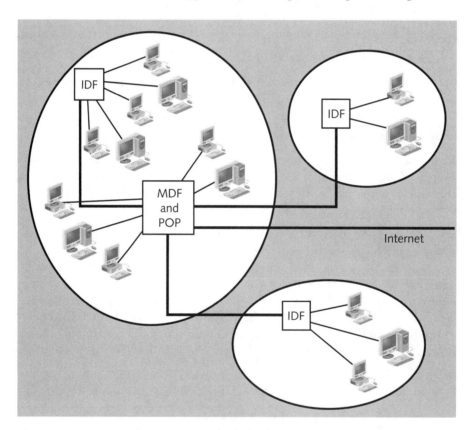

Figure 4-12   Network spanning multiple buildings

In the case of a multistory building, the POP will usually be on the ground floor, and the MDF should be on the middle floor. In this case, you cannot place the MDF and the POP in close proximity to each other.

Figure 4-13 illustrates the relationship of the MDF, IDF, and POP for a typical multistory LAN.

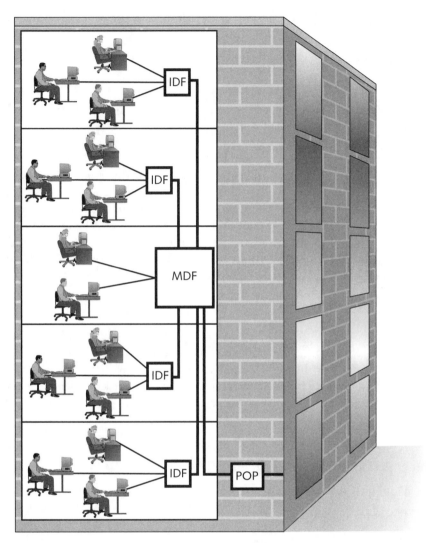

Figure 4-13   Network spanning multiple floors

Backbone

When two or more wiring closets are implemented on a network, they must be connected to each other via **backbone** cable. Backbone cable connects wiring closets to each other in an extended star topology. Backbone cabling also connects wiring closets to the POP and wiring closets between buildings. It does not connect workstations, and is therefore sometimes called **vertical cabling** to distinguish it from horizontal cabling, which does connect hubs to workstations. EIA/TIA-568 specifies four different options for backbone cabling:

- 100-ohm UTP
- 150-ohm STP
- 62.5/125-micron optical fiber (most popular for new installations)
- Single-mode optical fiber

Because the vertical cabling carries the data traffic between the wiring closets, it is best for this cabling to be the fastest link on a network. For this reason, network administrators using 100-Mbps networks often choose to make their vertical (backbone) cabling 1000 Mbps. This allows them to increase performance and often increase the usable length of their vertical cabling. The length of the vertical cable depends on the type of cable that is used. As discussed previously, the maximum unrepeated distance for UTP is 100 meters. The maximum vertical cable distance for multimode and single-mode fiber is 2000 and 3000 meters, respectively.

PERFORMANCE CONSIDERATIONS

When designing a network, you must keep in mind the network performance needs of the customer. Sometimes these are somewhat difficult to predict, especially if there isn't an existing network in place. However, it is still important to consider a customer's performance needs and, where possible, optimize the performance of the network. Items that you should consider when reviewing the performance needs of your customer include:

- Connection speeds
- Utilization and broadcast traffic
- Collisions and contention
- Resource placement

In the following sections, each of the preceding items is discussed. You will learn a technique for analyzing the bandwidth requirements of an organization. In addition, you will review several of the factors that influence how a network performs.

Connection Speeds

The complexity of the data being transferred affects bandwidth. For example, it takes more bandwidth to download a graphic in one second than it takes to download a text file in the same amount of time. Although your network may have a theoretical bandwidth of 100 Mbps, what you experience in terms of network capacity at any given time may be far less than 100 Mbps. The real capacity of a network is sometimes referred to as **throughput**. Factors that affect throughput include the type of network devices being used on the network, the number of nodes, power issues, **network architecture**, and other variables. The bandwidth calculations most commonly required involve determining either the time to download a file under best conditions or the actual rate of a file transfer.

Utilization

Network utilization is an important factor that influences the performance of a network. The higher the utilization is, the greater the impact on performance. The typical rule of thumb for an Ethernet network is that more than 40% utilization for a sustained period should be investigated. Many factors influence the overall utilization of a network. However, when investigating causes (or potential causes) of high utilization, be sure to consider the following items:

- Video or audio streaming/teleconferencing

- Client/server applications

- Host/terminal applications

- Routing protocols

- Routine maintenance tasks (file backup and database copying)

- Broadcast traffic

- Ethernet collisions

You must be aware of the type of information that will be passed on the network. In most cases, it is best to find a network similar to the one you are designing, so that you can estimate the performance requirements. If this is not possible, you should attempt to get calculations from application vendors and equipment manufacturers concerning performance. You want to ensure that the average and peak requirements of applications do not exceed your available bandwidth. In the next section, you will learn a way to estimate bandwidth and throughput.

The most common solution for reducing network utilization is to segment a network with a connectivity device such as a bridge, switch, or router. Other solutions may include the following:

- Reducing the number of services provided on the segment

- Reducing the number of protocols in use on the segment

- Disabling bandwidth-intensive applications or protocols, such as those that support audio or video streaming

- Relocating the systems consuming the most bandwidth on the segment

Calculating Bandwidth and Throughput

As you consider the bandwidth that is required by an organization, you should attempt to discover the types of bandwidth-intensive communications that will be conducted on its network. You can then use that information to calculate the bandwidth requirements. For example, assume that you know that a 300-MB file must be transferred across a WAN link that runs at 56 Kbps every night. You want to estimate the time that it will take the file to transfer and see if the performance is acceptable to your client. The time that it takes a file to transfer from one location to another is called **transmission time**. You can calculate the transmission time by dividing the file size by the bandwidth, as shown in the following formula:

Transmission Time = File Size/Bandwidth   (T = Fs/Bw)

As an example of the use of this formula, consider the different units of measure for the file size 300 megabytes and the transmission speed 56 kilobits per second. The first task is to obtain a common unit of measurement, which in this case is bits. 300 megabytes equals 300,000,000 bytes, which must then be multiplied by eight to convert to bits (eight bits in a byte). That is 2,400,000,000 bits that must be transferred over the link. Because a kilobit is 1000 bits, 56 Kbps means that the transfer rate is actually 56,000 bits per second. Now, plug those numbers into the formula and you will see how long it takes to transfer the file:

2,400,000,000/56,000 = 42,857 seconds

Convert the number of seconds into hours and minutes to make it more recognizable: 42,857 seconds is 11 hours, 54 minutes, and 17 seconds. Assuming that the client wants to complete the file download in eight hours, this performance would be unacceptable, and a faster link would have to be considered.

If you have an existing connection, you can time a file transfer and determine your actual throughput for the link. Throughput is a more realistic measure of transmission time because it is based on the observed transfer rate. Throughput equals the size of the file divided by the actual download time. Consider this formula:

Throughput = File Size/Download Time   (Tp = Fs/Dt)

If you send actual data across your network connection, you can time the transfer and calculate the throughput. For example, assume that you transfer four gigabytes of data across your network connection and it takes six minutes. First, you convert the numbers to a common format. (Four gigabytes is four billion bytes, which is 32 billion bits. Six minutes is 360 seconds.)

Then, plug the numbers into the formula:

32,000,000,000/360 = 88,888,889 bits per second

To make the throughput figure more recognizable, convert it into megabits per second by dividing by one million. When you do this, you discover the throughput is roughly 89 Mbps.

You may find a throughput of 89 Mbps on a network that has a 100-Mbps connection and wonder why you didn't get the full 100 Mbps of bandwidth. This is because bandwidth and actual throughput aren't equal. Throughput is affected by variables other than the connection speed, including other traffic on the wire, the latency of connectivity devices, and the capabilities of the source and destination to receive packets. If you were calculating the speed of the file transfer based on your 100-Mbps connection speed, you would expect the 4-GB transfer to complete in about 5 minutes and 20 seconds, as shown in the following:

32,000,000,000 bits/100,000,000 bits per second = 320 seconds

4

NOTE

Keep in mind that you may need to factor in additional bandwidth to account for the variables affecting actual throughput.

By performing these calculations, you can ensure that your proposed network design and equipment will be able to meet the needs of your client.

Collisions and Contention

All stations on an Ethernet segment must share the available connection with each other. This means that the stations contend with one another for the opportunity to transmit on the wire. Two stations cannot transmit at the same time, or a collision will occur. Collisions cause delays because, for a short period, all transmissions cease on the wire, and the stations that caused the collision must reset and wait to transmit again.

When you are considering upgrading an existing network, you can check the rate of collisions on the network using a **protocol analyzer** or other network performance-monitoring tools. Although collisions are expected to occur on Ethernet networks, a high rate of collisions can cause serious performance problems. As a rule of thumb, collision rates of 5% or more should be investigated. If no errors, such as faulty adapters, are detected when you investigate the collision rate, the collisions may be caused by too many stations trying to contend for the same bandwidth on the segment. In such a case, one course of action may be to segment the network with a bridge, router, or switch.

Resource Placement

One important item that can improve the performance of a network is the proper placement of resources. When possible, network users should be on the same network segment as the resources they need to access. When resources that are frequently accessed by users are not placed on the same segment as the user, increased traffic across the network results. For example, consider the placement of the accounting database in Figure 4-14.

Assume that the most frequent users of the accounting database are in the Accounting Department. Because the file server is located in a segment that is mostly used by the Marketing Department, traffic between the marketing and accounting segments is higher than necessary. If the Accounting Department is using the accounting database server more than the Marketing Department, then the database server should be part of the Accounting Department's segment.

Deciding where to place resources on a network is a very important part of configuring the most efficient communication paths. Of course, the need for security and centralized control may sometimes outweigh the need for increased performance.

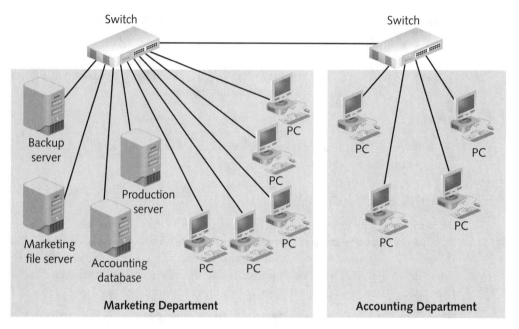

Figure 4-14 Resource placement

INSTALLING TELECOMMUNICATIONS CONNECTORS

Once you have run the horizontal cable from the closets to the various locations to be networked, you must attach it to the telecommunications connectors. If you have decided to use surface mounting, then the connection can be made quickly outside the wall by simply wiring the cable to the box and jack. However, if you have selected a flush mounting, you must fish the cable from the interior of the wall and run it outside the hole you previously cut for the connection box or bracket.

If you are using a box connector, cut or snap out a portion of the back of the box and bring the wire through it. Then, insert the box into the hole in the wall. You can secure the box by turning the screws in the corners, which extends tabs behind the wall. If a bracket is used, then push out the side flanges to attach it to the hole.

As previously discussed, the type of wall jack that is specified in the 568B standard for connecting Category 5 UTP is RJ-45. The RJ-45 connector, as shown in Figure 4-15, is similar in design to a standard (RJ-11) telephone jack, but it is larger and has more pins (eight, instead of two to six).

The side of the RJ-45 jack that faces out from the wall has a female plug where the male connector of the workstation area cable connects. The portion of the plug inside the wall must be wired. In order to connect the wire from the wall to the RJ-45 jack, you must strip back the cable's jacket to expose the eight individual wires, as shown in Figure 4-16.

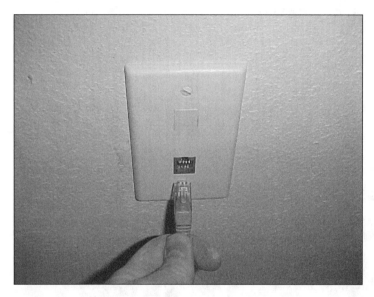

Figure 4-15   RJ-45 connector

Figure 4-16   UTP wires

Be sure to strip back only about one to two inches of the jacket. If you strip too much of the jacket, the connection may be degraded. Be careful not to untwist the wire too much; the EIA/TIA-568 standard allows for CAT 5 untwisting of up to a half-inch.

The individual wires should be placed according to their corresponding color-coded pins into the back of the RJ-45 jack. If the back of the jack does not have color-coded pins, you should place the wires in the **EIA/TIA-568A** or 568B order. Note that a mixture of 568A and 568B should not be used. Figure 4-17 shows the 568B wiring scheme.

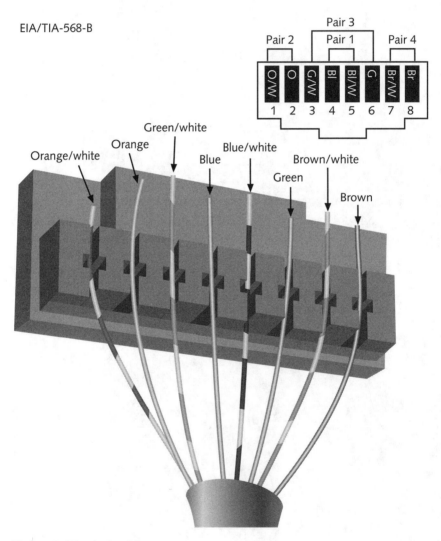

Figure 4-17 Jack wiring

Once the wire is inserted into the pins on the back of the plug, use a **punch tool** to punch down the wire into the back of the plug. Do this carefully; skewed wires can negatively affect the transmission rate. The punch tool should simultaneously complete the connection and remove the excess wire. If any excess wire remains, be sure to remove it. If the wires do not make a good connection, the network performance may degrade or transmission may even stop altogether. Be sure that there are no wire shorts (one wire touching another) at the connector. Try to keep the wire jacket within ⅛ inch from the connector (the shorter the distance of the exposed wire, the better).

Once all of the wires have been properly punched into the connector, place the clips on the jack. Ensure that they are tight so that they will properly protect the wiring. Place any excess cable inside the wall (flush mounting) or inside the connector box (surface mounting). Next, snap or screw the faceplate into the box or bracket that you installed earlier.

PATCH PANEL

The **patch panel** is a device with rows of pins and ports that connects the horizontal cabling to the patch cables inside the wiring closets. The side with the ports is considered the front of the patch panel. The side with the pins is considered the back side. Patch panels are located at the center of a star or extended star topology and serve as a switchboard interconnecting the devices on a network. Figure 4-18 shows the pins side of a patch panel.

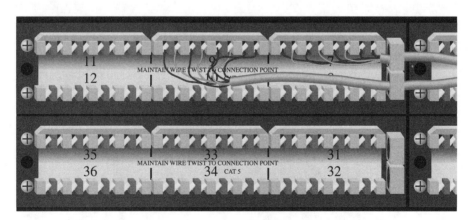

Figure 4-18 Patch panel pins

Figure 4-19 shows the ports side of a patch panel.

The horizontal cables coming in from other parts of the network are punched into the exposed groups of pins on the patch panel. Each group of pins represents a connection for one cable and directly corresponds to a port on the opposite side of the patch panel.

The pins are color-coded to facilitate wiring. The process for punching these wires into the panel is similar to that of wiring an RJ-45 telecommunications connector:

Step 1   Strip back 1½ to 2 inches of UTP cable.

Step 2   Untwist the individual wires no more than ½ inch for Category 5 UTP.

Step 3   Match the wires with the corresponding colors on the patch panel pins.

Step 4   Punch down the cables with the appropriate punch tool—Krone or 110.

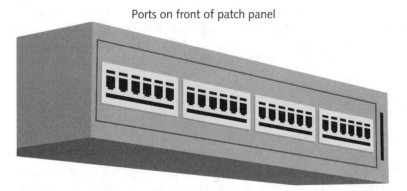

Ports on front of patch panel

Figure 4-19   Patch panel ports

The punch tool should simultaneously connect and cut the cable. The specific type of tool that you use depends on the type of patch panel in use. Figure 4-20 shows a 110 punch tool. Be sure to check in the documentation or with the manufacturer to determine which type of tool is appropriate.

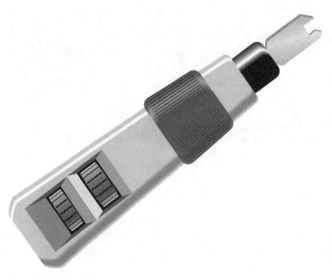

Figure 4-20   110 Punch tool

With any punch tool, you must hold it with the cutting edge away from the connectors you are punching down or the wires will not be cut when they are punched down.

On the opposite side of the patch panel, patch cables are used to connect the patch panel ports to other devices inside the wiring closet, such as hubs, routers, and switches. The patch panel ports accept RJ-45 connectors, so no punching down of cable is necessary for this side. However, the patch cable itself must be fitted with RJ-45 connectors on both ends so that it can connect from the port on the patch panel to the intended network device (i.e., hub, switch, or router).

4

TESTING CABLE

Once cabling is installed, be sure to test it. There are several types of tests you can run on your network cable to ensure that it will perform optimally. All cable testing devices can be used to check basic connectivity. More advanced cable testers can be used to check cable performance characteristics in addition to connectivity. In this section, you will learn about the common cable connectivity tests and performance measures.

Cable Testers

There are many different cable testers available with a wide variety of features. Cable testers with limited features can be as inexpensive as $50 to $100. More advanced models can be priced above $5000. Important measurements that cable testers can make are:

- Wire map

- Attenuation

- Noise

- Near end crosstalk (NEXT). Only the very high-end cable testers have this capability.

- Distance measure

EIA/TIA and IEEE specify standards for these measurements, which gives a reference point for acceptable measurements. To ensure that the network is performing optimally, take periodic measurements and compare them with EIA/TIA and IEEE specifications. In the following sections, the preceding measurements are explained, and tips for correcting and minimizing cable problems are presented.

Wire Map

A **wire map** is an important measurement that a cable tester makes to check the wiring sequence. Regardless of which wiring method you use, EIA/TIA-568A or EIA/TIA-568B, wire pairings will always be the same, as follows: 1+2, 3+6, 4+5, and 7+8. An incorrectly wired cable can prevent or degrade signal transmission. The test shows whether the installer properly or improperly connected the wires to the jack or plug. Table 4-3 illustrates and defines the various cabling problems that a wire map can detect.

Table 4-3 Wire map error detection

Condition	Visual	Description
Crossed wires		A wire from pair 1 and 2 is crossed with a wire in the 3 and 6 pair.
Reversed pairs		The wires 1 and 2 are crossed.
Crossed pairs		Pair 1 and 2 is crossed with pair 3 and 6.
Short		Wires 1 and 3 are shorted.
Open		Wire 2 is open and does not complete the circuit.

Crossed wires, reversed pairs, and crossed pairs all indicate incorrect wire placement at the jack, connector, or patch panel. Figure 4-21 illustrates the condition known as crossed pairs.

Figure 4-21 Crossed pairs

Shorts are caused when two wires make contact with each other at some point, which usually means that the cable was bent or creased more than 90 degrees. A short can also occur if cable is pierced, any open wire is broken at some point inside the wire, or a wire is not properly connected.

There is another condition—a split pair—that only very high-end cable testers can detect. A simple wire map cannot detect a split pair because there are no incomplete circuits, as shown in Figure 4-22.

Figure 4-22   Split pairs

A split pair usually results from poor wiring at the jack and the patch panel. The sequence must be incorrectly wired in both places for the pair to be split. This problem can result in crosstalk because the actual twisted wires are carrying two different signals. Normally, one pair is used to send and the other to receive, but in this configuration, the wire pair is twisted incorrectly, which increases the likelihood of crosstalk during signal transmission. Although wire maps cannot detect this problem, a NEXT test or visual inspection can detect a split pair.

Attenuation

Attenuation is the loss of signal power over the distance of a cable. To measure attenuation on a cable, the cable tester must be assisted by a second test unit called a **signal injector**. The signal injector sends electric pulses down the wire from one end, and the cable tester picks them up at the other end. In this way, the loss in pulse strength is measured and the level of attenuation can be calculated.

Often, the cable tester is preprogrammed with the level of attenuation allowed according to the EIA/TIA-568A specification; otherwise, you must check the specification to see what an acceptable attenuation is at various frequencies. The pulse from the signal injector for Category 5 cable should be set at 100 MHz to test the cable fully. The lower the attenuation, the better; for example, attenuation of 10 decibels is better than 20 decibels.

Noise

Noise consists of unwanted electrical signals that alter the shape of the transmitted signals on a network. Noise on a cable can be produced by many different sources, such as other wire pairs, fluorescent lights, radios, electronic devices, heaters, and air-conditioning units. When the wiring in a wall is too long, it can act as an antenna for noise by picking up EMI and RFI from other devices and sending the noise along with the electrical signals that it is meant to transmit between devices on the network.

Alternating current (AC) signal noises are called **oscillations** and can alter the digital signal that computers receive on the wire. Network signals are typically digital transmissions, which means they have two states—on and off. Network devices interpret the on state as a digital "one" and the off state as a digital "zero." The network card samples the wire continuously as it receives transmissions bit by bit. If oscillations mask the transmission, the network card may incorrectly interpret the data or discard the data frames as corrupt.

Improper grounding can also cause noise. The motherboard and other internal integrated **circuits** of a computer use the chassis as their ground (zero reference). However, the chassis is also the ground for the incoming power. If there is a wiring error, it could not only electrify the chassis but cause internal component errors as well. Faulty AC wiring can also cause problems with transmissions because the **signal reference ground** is the computer chassis and grounding plate. If the ground is wired incorrectly, the reference voltage may be something other than zero. When the computer attempts to interpret a signal from the wire with a skewed signal reference ground, the data could be misinterpreted.

NOTE   Keep only one **transformer** on a LAN to reduce problems caused by faulty wiring, overloaded circuits, different grounds, and long AC wiring runs acting as antennas.

Cable testers can listen for noise on a wire. To perform a test for cable noise, the horizontal cable should be unplugged from the network jacks and patch panel. The cable tester then listens for noise on the cable. If noise is found on the cable, the path of the wire should be traced to determine if there is any possible noise source in the area. Unplug devices where possible to see if the noise disappears. You can eliminate oscillations by rewiring electrical connections.

NEXT

Near end crosstalk (NEXT) is a measure of interference from other wire pairs. A signal may bleed from one set of wires to another, causing crosstalk. The NEXT measure seeks to determine how much signal bleed is occurring. The cable tester measures NEXT by placing a series of different frequency signals on the wire (usually up to 100 MHz for Category 5 cable). A good cable tester displays the NEXT readings against the acceptable limits put forth in the EIA/TIA standard. For example, Figure 4-23 illustrates a cable tester displaying NEXT results against the standard.

The test for NEXT should be done at both ends of a cable. This is because the crosstalk can be affected by attenuation. Typically, a cable tester measuring NEXT sends a signal out on a pair of wires. The NEXT measurement represents the effect of the test signal on another pair of wires. Higher NEXT values correspond to less crosstalk and better network performance. If the signal experiences significant attenuation, the crosstalk may be seen as insignificant. Therefore, both ends of the cable should be tested for NEXT. Causes of NEXT include:

- Split pairs

- Too much wire untwisted at the patch panel, jack, or connectors

- Bends, kinks, or stretches in the cabling

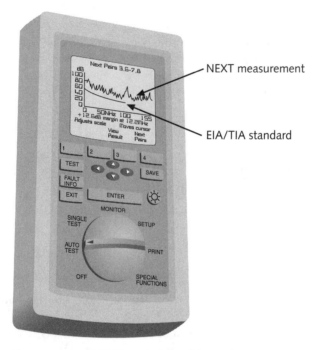

Figure 4-23   NEXT test on a cable analyzer

To minimize NEXT, be sure to handle cable carefully. Never apply more than 25 pounds of pressure when stringing or fishing cable. (Some vendors sell 10-pound-rated pulling string that will break before too much tension is placed on the wire.) Be sure not to step on, cut, crush, or twist the wire during installation. Finally, ensure that jacks and patch panels are wired correctly to avoid split pairs.

Visually check the horizontal cables if NEXT is detected; look for untwisted wires, stretched areas, or kinks in the cable.

Distance Measure

EIA/TIA-568A specifies maximum cable lengths for network media. Cables that are too long can cause delays in transmission and network errors. Cable testers use time-domain reflectometry to find the distance of a cable. Time-domain reflectometry is similar to radar in that a signal is sent, it bounces off an object, and it is reflected back to the emitting device. The time it takes for the signal to travel between the two points indicates the distance to the object.

A cable tester that uses time-domain reflectometry is called a **time-domain reflectometer (TDR)**. TDR measurements can detect the overall length of a cable or the distance to a cable break or opening. This is because the signal is reflected anytime that the wiring is open.

Good TDRs can even show various levels of signal change along the way. These measurements can tell the efficiency of the wiring at a connector or patch panel. If the measurement is made through a wall jack or patch panel, tiny spikes may appear at the connector showing the signal transition. A large spike could indicate a wiring problem or faulty connection. The accuracy of the measurement is fairly high, usually within two feet or less.

Baseline

After a network is up and running, it is important to take a baseline measurement to tell you how well the network is performing at a given moment. The baseline measurements can then be compared with future measurements. Baseline measurements can include the following:

- Error rates
- Collision rates
- Network utilization

When the network is in full operation, you can determine the utilization, number of collisions, and network errors. This helps you determine how efficiently the network is running. Then, periodically, you can take measurements of the network to see how it compares to the baseline. If the network seems generally slow, you can check the statistics at that moment against the baseline.

When you compare the two measurements, you may see immediately why the network seems to be running slowly. If the network utilization is above 40% (for Ethernet), then you might consider segmenting the network. You may also find a higher number of network errors, which could indicate a bad network card tying up the bandwidth.

LAN DESIGN MODELS

You can choose many different network design models to implement on your network. However, there are two basic design strategies that are typically followed: **mesh design** and **hierarchical design**. Mesh designs are less structured than hierarchical designs. In a mesh design, there is typically no clear definition of where certain network functions are performed. Routers in a mesh design act as peer devices and perform essentially the same functions. As shown in Figure 4-24, the mesh is a flat structure in which expansion of the network is done laterally.

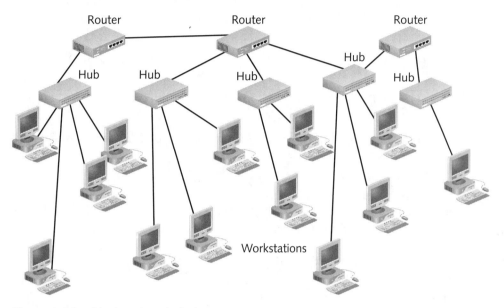

Figure 4-24   Mesh network design

Hierarchical designs, on the other hand, are more structured and defined. These types of designs separate different equipment and network media by their connectivity functions. Compared with a mesh design, a hierarchical design:

- Is easier to manage: Mesh designs are not as organized as hierarchical networks, so they can be considerably more difficult to manage.

- Is easier to troubleshoot: The defined structure of the hierarchical design makes it easier to identify, locate, and isolate network problems.

- Has improved scalability: A well-defined hierarchical design can be modified and redefined to support a larger organization more easily than a mesh design. The more organized the network, the easier it is to expand. Furthermore, the structure allows for additional users, equipment, and media to be added without extensive investigations into the distance between nodes and the number of nodes per segment.

- Allows easier analysis: Measurements of performance are easier to obtain when a network has a defined structure. The measurements are also easily applied to future expansion plans for the network.

In the following sections you will learn more about three hierarchical network models: the three-layer network model, the two-layer network model, and the one-layer network model.

Three-Layer Network Model

The **three-layer network model** is the most complex of the three models. It consists of a **core layer**, a **distribution layer**, and an **access layer**. The following list describes each in turn:

- Core layer: Provides WAN connectivity between sites located in different geographic areas
- Distribution layer: Used to interconnect buildings with separate LANs on a campus network
- Access layer: Identifies a LAN or a group of LANs that provides users with access to network services

Figure 4-25 illustrates how each layer would be categorized in a large network environment. As you can see, the core layer connects networks in different cities, the distribution layer connects several LANs within the same part of the city, and the access layer is where each group of users gains access to the greater network.

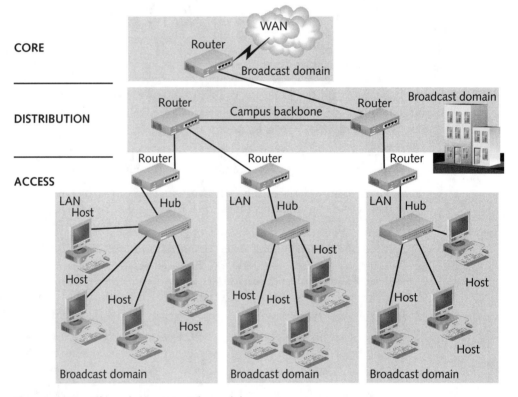

Figure 4-25   Three-layer network model

Each layer is separated into its own broadcast domain because the layers are separated by routers. Notice that within the access layer, there are several broadcast domains, each providing users with access to the network. Therefore, the separation between the layers in the three-layer network model is mostly due to function. However, there is also a separation of broadcast domains between the layers because of the connectivity equipment used to create the configuration.

Core Layer

4

The core layer provides WAN connections between the various locations of the network. Because the core layer mostly consists of point-to-point WAN connections, hosts are not typically part of this layer. Organizations usually lease the connections used for the core layer from a telecommunications company. Organizations use the core layer to provide a fast connection path between remote sites. Therefore, efficient use of the available bandwidth is a concern for those negotiating, designing, and administering the core layer connections. Often, network administrators establish multiple connections at the core layer to ensure that connectivity is maintained between each remote site and the main site.

Distribution Layer

The distribution layer consists of all the equipment necessary to make the connection between different LANs in a single geographic area or campus. This includes the backbone connection and all the routers used to form the connections to each LAN. At this level of the network, network administrators usually implement **policy-based connectivity**. This means that the network administrator determines the type of traffic (such as Web or FTP) to allow on the backbone and the type of traffic that the router will filter. The network administrator can use routers to filter the traffic from the incoming WAN connection and between the various LAN connections. This allows the network administrator to control users' access to services and broadcast traffic between LANs.

The administrator of the distribution layer can also control the LAN interconnections by establishing path metrics between the LANs. This allows the network administrator to predict and control the path a network packet should traverse between two points. By doing this, the network administrator may reserve certain network communication paths for certain types of traffic. For example, the network administrator could choose a specific path on the network to filter all traffic except that which is related to e-mail communications. Because e-mail is transferred over TCP port 25, the administrator could configure the router to allow only TCP port 25 traffic. This would mean that no matter how congested the rest of the network became, e-mail communications would have a dedicated path across the wire.

The best practice is not to place any end stations at the distribution layer, because those stations will have access to traffic traversing the LANs. Sitting a user at an end station at the distribution layer would essentially allow that user access to all traffic flowing between the LANs, which could become a security threat. Placing a server at the distribution layer would mean that traffic would be originating and terminating at the distribution layer, which compromises the separation of the layers. Controlling traffic and troubleshooting would be more complex because the traffic filters, which apply to servers at the access layer, could not apply to a server placed at the distribution layer. For example, if you place a Web server at the distribution layer, users will only have access to it if you allow Web traffic through the routers that separate the distribution and access layers. This means that you can no longer filter Web traffic between the LANs.

Access Layer

In the three-layer model, the end systems should be located in the access layer. The access layer provides a logical grouping of users by function. This results in a logical segmentation of the network. This segmentation is typically based on boundaries defined by the organization. For example, the Marketing, Accounting, and Human Resources Departments in a company are typically segmented from one another. These departments may share some common information, but for the most part, their daily functions are separate. While each would be part of the access layer, connectivity devices such as bridges, switches, or routers would typically separate their domains. The main goal at this layer is to isolate the traffic between the individual workgroups, segments, or LANs.

The three-layer network model works well for large network environments. However, network administrators find that the two-layer or one-layer model works best for smaller network environments. These two models are discussed in the following sections.

Two-Layer Network Model

The difference between the **two-layer network model** and the three-layer network model is that the distribution layer or campus backbone is not defined or implemented in the former. Network administrators use WAN connections to interconnect separate LANs, as shown in Figure 4-26.

Notice that each broadcast domain is still separated by access-layer routers, yet the domains may be further subdivided by switching equipment. The structure is still in place so that the network administrator can add a distribution layer and implement a three-layer model at a later date.

One-Layer Network Model

Smaller networks can employ a one-layer network model design strategy. The one-layer network model has less need for routing and access-layer separation than the two-layer or three-layer models. Typically, the **one-layer network model** includes a LAN with a few remote sites. In the one-layer network model, servers may be distributed across the LAN or placed in one central location. Figure 4-27 illustrates a one-layer network configuration.

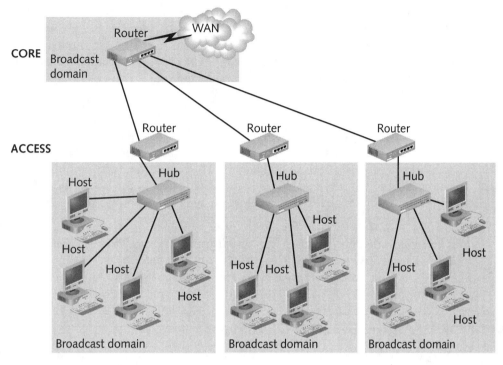

Figure 4-26   Two-layer network model

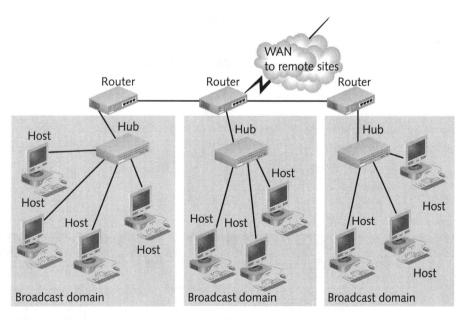

Figure 4-27   One-layer network model

Most of the traffic in the one-layer network will be concentrated on the LAN. The WAN should only have a light traffic load, because the remote sites will not be generating much traffic. The network users gain access to the rest of the network via routers that may connect other segments of the LAN or parts of the WAN. Network administrators can change the one-layer design model into a two- or three-layer structure as the network grows.

As you can see by reviewing the illustrations of the one-layer, two-layer, and three-layer network models, the main difference among these hierarchical models is the number of routers deployed in each configuration. In the three-layer model, there are three levels of routers: one at the core layer for the WAN, one at the distribution layer for the campus backbone, and one at each site in the access layer. In the two-layer network, two levels of routers divide the structure. The one-layer model only has one layer of routers, all of which operate at a peer level.

The main difference between the one-layer design model and the mesh design is the definition of structure. With a mesh network, the chances of having to restructure the entire network configuration as the network increases in size are greater.

NETWORK-MANAGEMENT TOOLS

Network-management tools allow you to perform management functions, such as monitoring network traffic levels, finding bottlenecks, and monitoring software usage. The most common tools are cable testers, **network monitors**, and **network analyzers**. Because you have previously learned about cable testers, this section discusses only network monitors and analyzers.

The differences between a network monitor and a network analyzer can be small. Usually a network monitor is implemented in software while a network analyzer is implemented in hardware. In fact, in many situations, the term analyzer is more of a marketing slogan than a distinction of service. In reality, however, the network analyzer (or protocol analyzer) provides a more sophisticated level of service than a monitor.

To illustrate the differences between network monitors and network analyzers, Table 4-4 compares some of the features of the Microsoft Network Monitor and the Fluke LANMeter, which is a network analyzer.

Table 4-4 Monitor and analyzer

Feature	Microsoft Network Monitor	Fluke LANMeter
Collects network statistics	Yes	Yes
Stores and opens network packets	Yes	No
Uses Simple Network Management Protocol (SNMP) to query devices	No	Yes

Table 4-4 Monitor and analyzer (continued)

Feature	Microsoft Network Monitor	Fluke LANMeter
Analyzes network statistics	No	Yes
Troubleshoots network devices	No	Yes
Provides diagnostic tools	Yes	Yes
Generates traffic for the analysis	No	Yes
Analyzes types of devices on network	No	Yes
Analyzes types of collisions	No	Yes
Analyzes types of errors	No	Yes
Ranks top broadcasting hosts	No	Yes

4

In addition to the tools presented in the table, other sophisticated tools can be used for daily network management and control. These management tools typically have three components:

- **Agent**: The agent is the client software part of the management tool. It collects information for use by the management system. The agent resides on each network device.

- **Manager**: The manager is a centralized software component that manages the network. The management software stores the information in a standardized database.

- **Administration system**: The administration system is the centralized management component that collects and analyzes the information from the managers. Most administration systems provide information, alerts, and automatic modifications. Often, the administration system is coupled with the management application.

There are two main management protocols used with network-management systems: SNMP and CMIP. The following sections discuss these protocols and their basic operations.

SNMP

The Simple Network Management Protocol (SNMP) is a TCP/IP standard protocol included in all major TCP/IP protocol suites. SNMP is a connectionless protocol that operates at layer 7 of the OSI model and port number 161. The U.S. Department of Defense and TCP/IP developers released SNMP in 1988; today, it is the most widely implemented network-management tool.

SNMP allows SNMP agents (client devices on a network that use SNMP agent software) to collect information and statistics for SNMP management software. An SNMP manager can then query a device to obtain the information that the agent has trapped, as shown in Figure 4-28.

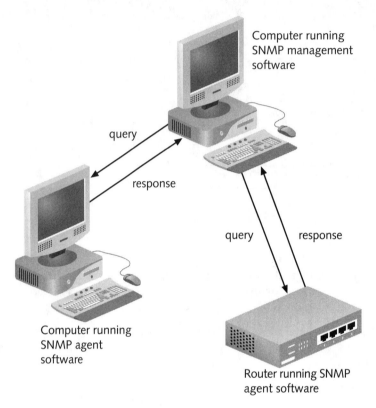

Figure 4-28   SNMP in action

A **Management Information Base (MIB)** is a database that maintains the statistics and information that the SNMP reports and uses. Typically stored measurement items include disk space available, network packets transmitted/received, network errors, and system-utilization statistics. Because a network administrator can edit the MIB and insert additional measurement items, any number of statistics can be tracked. The only requirement is that the MIB on both the SNMP management software and the SNMP agent software be configured to track and retrieve the new measurement items.

Network administrators commonly use SNMP to manage hubs and routers. Management tasks include:

- Network traffic monitoring
- Automatic disconnection of problem nodes
- Connection or disconnection of nodes based on time and/or date

- Port isolation for testing purposes
- Remote management capabilities

SNMP managers can also provide network topology maps, historical management information, alerts, and traffic monitoring throughout a network. Examples of SNMP management systems include OpenView, by Hewlett-Packard; NetView, by Tivoli Systems and IBM; and SunNet Manager, from Sun Microsystems.

4

Although SNMP is an extremely popular management tool, it is not the only one available. Another well-known management protocol is CMIP.

CMIP

The **Common Management Information Protocol (CMIP)** is similar to SNMP in that it uses the MIB to monitor the network. Although this protocol has not been as widely implemented as SNMP, it is more efficient because the clients report the information to the management device. This means less network traffic because the management device doesn't have to call for the information, as is the case with SNMP.

In summary, in SNMP, continuous calls must be exchanged to keep the management device updated, even if those calls only determine if a component has reached a certain threshold. In CMIP, the client makes one call to notify the management tool when a particular threshold is reached. A threshold is set manually to alert the administrator when a certain criterion is met, such as 80% capacity on a hard drive.

CHAPTER SUMMARY

- There are three basic physical LAN topologies: bus, star, and ring.

- These topologies, or layouts, typically involve cable, such as UTP, STP, coaxial, or fiber. The network architecture used on a LAN defines the physical topology, the media used, and the network access method. The most popular architectures are 10BaseT and Token Ring.

- The IEEE has defined many standards that have influenced the way networks are designed and implemented. It has also defined different network access methods, which include CSMA/CD, token-passing, and CSMA/CA.

- One of the largest contributions from the IEEE is the 802 standard, which has subsets that define Ethernet (802.3), Token Ring (802.5), and wireless (802.11) network architectures.

- The 802.2 standard from the IEEE subdivided the OSI Data Link layer into two parts to make functional distinctions between the Media Access Control (MAC) sublayer and the Logical Link Control (LLC) sublayer.

- Ethernet is also known by its access method, CSMA/CD (Carrier Sense Multiple Access with Collision Detection).

❏ Token Ring uses an entirely different access method that is governed by token-passing. The token, a small data frame, is passed from station to station around the ring, and a station can transmit only when it has the token.

❏ FDDI uses token-passing like Token Ring networks, but it is not subject to the same limitations.

❏ CSMA/CA is a network access method specified by the wireless LAN standard—802.11. This standard supports spread spectrum and infrared technologies for use on wireless LANs. CSMA/CA nodes listen before sending but determine when to send based on a random backoff factor. Before transmitting, CSMA/CA nodes send a notification that they are going to transmit.

❏ Installing media on a network is a multifaceted project. The layout of the network should be determined and documented. The number of wiring closets necessary, as well as their locations, must be determined. Standards for wiring closets, cable runs, distances, and cable must be considered when the routes are established.

❏ Obstructions and EMI/RFI must be overcome. After you install cable, you should test it for wiring, performance, and configuration problems. Cable testers can be used to determine if cables are wired correctly, if they meet length standards, and if they have attenuation or noise problems.

❏ When implementing a network, you can choose one of three hierarchical network models: one-layer, two-layer, or three-layer.

❏ The one-layer network model is the least complex, and is a flat structure where all components function at essentially the same level. The two-layer model separates the WAN from the rest of the internal network, which is usually done by adding routers with packet filters. In the three-layer model, the internal LANs are further divided by backbone cabling, which has additional routers with packet filters. In this model, the WAN connection is called the core layer, the backbone cabling and routers form the distribution layer, and the individual LANs function at the access layer.

❏ Network administrators use network monitors and network analyzers to manage a network on a daily basis. These tools can also be used to troubleshoot abnormal situations.

❏ The main difference between a network monitor and network analyzer is the level of service provided. The network analyzer typically offers more advanced features, such as SNMP querying, remote administration, and even automatic problem correction.

KEY TERMS

100BaseT — An Ethernet standard that provides a 100-Mbps baseband transfer rate over twisted-pair cabling. Also called Fast Ethernet. Known as IEEE standard 802.3u.

10Base2 — An Ethernet standard that specifies a 10-Mbps baseband transmission over thin Ethernet (RG-58); the maximum transmission distance of any single segment is 185 meters.

10Base5 — An Ethernet standard that indicates a 10-Mbps baseband transmission over a maximum segment length of 500 meters; the type of cable used in this standard is called thick Ethernet, or thicknet, and uses RG-8 coaxial cable.

10BaseT — An Ethernet standard that specifies a 10-Mbps baseband transmission over twisted-pair cabling; the maximum segment length is 100 meters.

10 Gigabit Ethernet — IEEE 802.3ae standard that uses Ethernet frames in full duplex mode over fiber only. Used extensively in MANs for distances up to 40 km over single-mode fiber.

5-4-3 rule — The rule that stipulates that between stations on a LAN, there can be no more than five network segments connected, the maximum number of repeaters between the segments is four, and the maximum number of segments with stations on them is three.

802.2 — A standard of the IEEE that specifies the subdivision of the Logical Link Control sublayer from the Media Access Control (MAC) sublayer. These sublayers are part of the OSI Data Link layer.

802.3 — The IEEE standard that defines CSMA/CD or Ethernet networking.

802.5 — The IEEE standard that defines Token Ring networking.

802.11 — The IEEE standard that defines wireless LANs.

access layer — The layer in the three-layer network model that provides users access to the network. This is the layer in which end systems are connected to the network.

access method — The rules that determine which station can send data and how collisions are managed. The two most popular access methods are CSMA/CD and token-passing. Access method is also known as logical topology.

active monitor — The computer in a Token Ring network that is powered on first and manages the beaconing process.

administration system — The centralized management component that collects and analyzes the information from the managers in a network-management system, such as SNMP or CMIP.

agent — The client software part of the management tool in a network-management system, such as SNMP or CMIP; responsible for collecting the information that is used by the management system; resides on each network device.

alternating current (AC) — Type of current that is delivered to homes and office buildings. It changes polarity cyclically as it is manufactured by power plants.

American National Standards Institute (ANSI) — The organization that guides the process of standardization by ensuring that consensus, openness, and due process are maintained during the development process. ANSI is responsible for the FDDI standard.

attachment unit interface (AUI) port — A 15-pin physical connector interface between a computer's network interface card (NIC) and an Ethernet network that uses 10Base5 (thicknet) coaxial cable. On 10Base5 Ethernet, the NIC uses the AUI to connect to a transceiver cable that in turn taps into the main cable.

4

backbone — Cabling used to connect wiring hubs in an extended star topology; typically, 62.5/125-micron multimode cable is used for this connection. However, 100-ohm UTP, 150-ohm STP, and single-mode fiber can also be used to connect wiring closets to wiring closets, wiring closets to the POP, and wiring closets between buildings; sometimes called vertical cable.

barrel connector — Used in coaxial networks; connects one coaxial cable segment to another, effectively forming a single cable.

baseband — A digital signal used in network transmissions where a single carrier frequency is used to transmit the signal.

beaconing — A fault-detection method implemented in Token Ring networks where stations broadcast packets to other stations on the ring in an attempt to find a break in the wire or a faulty interface.

BNC — A hardware connector for coaxial cable that has a cylindrical shell with two small knobs that allow it to be locked into place when twisted. Depending on the source, the letters BNC are said to stand for Bayonet Navy Connector, British Naval Connector, Bayonet Neill Concelman, or Bayonet Nut Connection. *See also* **barrel connector**.

bus — In the physical sense, a network topology where computers are daisy-chained together on the same coaxial cable segment; in the logical sense, refers to the CSMA/CD access method that sends data frames to all other stations simultaneously.

bus/star — A physical bus and physical star can be combined to form a star/bus or bus/star physical topology; hubs that have connectors for coaxial cable as well as twisted-pair wiring are used to form these types of networks. When different topologies are applied to a network, it is often called a mixed-media network.

cancellation — The desirable situation in which magnetic fields generated by two different wires carrying electronic signals cancel out each other; cancellation provides limited protection from crosstalk and external interference.

capacitive reactance — A naturally occurring opposition to voltage changes in a wire used for electronic signal transmission.

Carrier Sense Multiple Access/Collision Avoidance (CSMA/CA) — The network access method used by wireless LANs as outlined in IEEE 802.11. Nodes must first listen to a channel before transmitting. If the channel is busy, nodes configure a random backoff time to wait before transmitting.

CAT 1 — Category 1 unshielded twisted-pair (CAT 1 UTP) is a voice-grade only communication medium that should not be used as network media.

CAT 2 — Category 2 unshielded twisted-pair (CAT 2 UTP) is a voice- or data-grade medium that is rarely used in modern networks but does have the rating to transmit up to 4 Mbps.

CAT 3 — Category 3 unshielded twisted-pair (CAT 3 UTP) is a voice- or data-grade medium that can transmit at 10 Mbps and supports 10BaseT networking.

CAT 4 — Category 4 unshielded twisted-pair (CAT 4 UTP) supports voice or data and is capable of a 16-Mbps transmission rate.

CAT 5 — Category 5 unshielded twisted-pair (CAT 5 UTP) is the most popular installation medium today; this media type supports 100-Mbps transmission rates, but new standards attempt to achieve 1000 Mbps over CAT 5 cabling.

catchment area — The area serviced; for example, the area serviced by a wiring closet is the catchment area of that wiring closet.

cheapernet — A reference to RG-58 thin Ethernet cable.

circuit — Path in which electrical current can flow.

Common Management Information Protocol (CMIP) — A standard developed by the International Organization for Standardization (ISO) to provide a method for monitoring and managing network resources.

concentrator — A term used to describe a hub.

conductor — Material with low resistance to electron flow.

core layer — The layer that provides fast WAN connectivity for large network designs using the three-layer network model.

crosstalk — Signal bleed from one cable to another; this type of error usually occurs in poorly wired media.

distribution layer — Provides the backbone for a network; this layer is used in the three-layer network model to allow for access and protocol control and to increase security on the network.

EIA/TIA — *See* **Electronic Industries Alliance** and **Telecommunications Industry Association**.

EIA/TIA-568 — Defines and describes operational parameters for various grades of unshielded twisted-pair cabling.

EIA/TIA-568A — A wiring method used to indicate which colors are assigned to which pin for UTP cable.

EIA/TIA-568B — A wiring method used to indicate which colors are assigned to which pin for UTP cable.

EIA/TIA-569 — Describes various network media configurations, such as those for horizontal pathways, entrance facilities, wiring closets, equipment rooms, and workstations.

electromagnetic interference (EMI) — A form of interference that can degrade and corrupt network signals. Fluorescent lighting, generators, elevators, and other machinery can be sources of EMI.

Electronic Industries Alliance (EIA) — The organization that provides standards that define how cabling should be configured on a network; often, these standards are done as a joint operation with the TIA.

Fast Ethernet — *See* **100BaseT**.

Fiber Distributed Data Interface (FDDI) — Describes the general specifications for the use, installation, configuration, and limitations of fiber-optic networking; pronounced "fiddy;" this standard is the responsibility of ANSI.

Gigabit Ethernet — New 802.3 standard that allows 1-Gbps transmission, usually across fiber-optic cable. Known as IEEE 802.3z.

hierarchical design — In network design methodology, a network that is structured in a layered hierarchical fashion, such as the one-layer, two-layer, and three-layer network models; the opposite would be a mesh design.

horizontal cabling — Media that connect workstations and wiring closets.

IEEE 802 — Standard that focuses on the Physical and Data Link layers of the OSI model; developed in 1980.

impedance — Measure of the total opposition to electron flow, changes in current, and changes in voltage in cable; causes attenuation.

inductive reactance — Opposition to the changes of electrical current in a wire.

infrared (IR) — One of the wireless technologies defined in IEEE 802.11. This technology requires line-of-sight between the transmitter and receiver. It is low power but cannot be intercepted.

intermediate distribution facility (IDF) — Dependent upon the MDF in a star topology; another wiring closet used to support devices on a network.

jam signal — A 32-bit message to all computers on an Ethernet network that tells all stations not to transmit.

Logical Link Control (LLC) sublayer — A networking sublayer defined by the IEEE to further modularize the software functions versus the hardware functions (defined by the MAC sublayer) of the OSI Data Link layer.

logical topology — Describes the way a signal travels in a network, which is a function of the access method; the logical topology is usually a bus or a ring.

main distribution facility (MDF) — The central wiring closet in an extended star topology; typically, an MDF houses the POP, patch panel, and network-interconnection devices (bridges, routers, switches, repeaters, and concentrators).

Management Information Base (MIB) — A central repository of network statistics used by SNMP and CMIP; allows management protocols to maintain network statistics; can be modified to control workstations and other network devices.

manager — A centralized software component that is used to manage the network in a network-management system, such as SNMP or CMIP.

Media Access Control (MAC) sublayer — A networking sublayer defined by the IEEE to further modularize the hardware functions versus the software functions (defined by the LLC sublayer) of the OSI Data Link layer.

media access method — *See* **access method**.

mesh design — In network design methodology, a network that has no organized structure; the opposite would be a hierarchical design.

mixed media — When different physical topologies are applied to a network, it is often called a mixed media network; for example, the bus and star topologies can be combined to form a star/bus or bus/star physical topology.

Multistation Access Unit (MAU) — The central device in a Token Ring architecture; forces the signal to be transmitted in a logical ring topology.

near end crosstalk (NEXT) — A measure of crosstalk performed at the location nearest the cable tester; the cable tester injects a signal of varying frequencies on a wire and measures signal bleed between other pairs of wires.

nearest active downstream neighbor (NADN) — The station on a Token Ring network that, during normal operations, receives the token from its nearest active upstream neighbor (NAUN).

nearest active upstream neighbor (NAUN) — The station on a Token Ring network that, during normal operations, passes the token to its NADN.

network access method — *See* **access method**.

network analyzer — A device that can collect and analyze information obtained by monitoring network traffic; may be able to query and manage network devices; also called protocol analyzer.

network architecture — A network's physical and logical topology, including its physical structure or layout, the media used, the network access method, and the standards and protocols employed.

network monitor — A program that collects information by monitoring network traffic; typically, does not have the advanced features of analysis and device management common to network analyzers.

one-layer network model — Includes WAN connectivity equipment and organizes a network so that it can be easily adapted to the two- and three-layer design models in the future.

oscillations — Undesirable, irregular signals (noise) riding on top of the desired signal.

patch cable — *See* **patch cord**.

patch cord — Cables used to terminate communication circuits in a wiring closet or between a workstation and a telecommunications outlet. *See also* **cross-connect jumpers**.

patch panel — A device that includes ports and pin locations used to connect devices in a wiring closet to devices on the network; acts as a switchboard for the network.

physical ring — *See* **ring**.

plenum — A space or enclosure in which air or gas is at a higher pressure than that of the outside atmosphere; a rating for network cable that specifies that the cable does not give off a toxic gas when burned.

point of presence (POP) — The point of interconnection between the telephone company and the building, floor, or company.

policy-based connectivity — A method that the network administrator uses to control access. The network administrator creates policies, such as "no video streaming is allowed at site 1," then implements them on the network, using equipment such as routers and switches.

protocol analyzer — *See* **network analyzer**.

punch tool — Used to punch down cable at the patch panel or RJ-45 wall jack; completes the connection while simultaneously removing excess wire.

radio frequency interference (RFI) — Electronic signal interference caused by radio transmissions.

Registered Jack (RJ) — A type of telecommunications connector that is used for twisted-pair cabling.

resistance — Opposition to the flow of electrons in a wire.

RG-58 — A type of thin coaxial cable that meets the 10Base2 Ethernet specification.

RG-8 — A type of thick coaxial cable that meets the 10Base5 Ethernet specification.

ring — A physical topology in which computers or other devices are connected in a circle or ring.

Service Access Point (SAP) — A protocol located in the Logical Link Control layer; defines how data can be passed up to higher layers.

shielded twisted-pair (STP) — Describes a type of cabling in which pairs of wires are twisted around one another inside a wire bundle; the wire bundle is then shielded by a foil coating, which protects it from external interference.

signal injector — Puts traffic on a wire so that a cable tester can measure attenuation and crosstalk.

signal reference ground — Zero-volt reference point on a computer cabinet or chassis; incoming signals are measured against this ground to determine if they are a "one" or a "zero."

spread spectrum — One of the wireless technologies defined in IEEE 802.11. This technology involves radio frequency transmission with the deliberate spreading of the signal over different frequencies.

star — Most popular physical topology in which computers are connected to a central device, usually a hub or a MAU.

star-bus — A network architecture that uses a physical star topology with a logical bus topology.

star-ring — A network architecture that uses a physical star topology with a logical ring topology.

T-connector — Used with coaxial cabling to connect a workstation NIC to a coaxial network.

Telecommunications Industry Association (TIA) — Provides standards that define how cabling should be configured on a network; often, these standards are done as a joint operation with the EIA.

terminator — A device used at the end of a coaxial segment to absorb a signal and prevent it from reflecting back along the wire.

thick Ethernet — *See* **thicknet**.

thicknet — An Ethernet networking standard that employs RG-8 coaxial cabling; a thicknet network can have segments of up to 500 meters and provides a 10-Mbps baseband transmission rate.

thin Ethernet — *See* **thinnet**.

thinnet — An Ethernet networking standard that employs RG-58 coaxial cabling; the specification includes a 10-Mbps baseband transmission rate and up to 185-meter segments.

three-layer network model — Divides a network into three connectivity layers: core, distribution, and access.

throughput — The observed transfer rate of a network; transfer rate is affected by device latency, network traffic, and capacity of source and destination to send and receive traffic.

time-domain reflectometer (TDR) — Cable tester that can detect the overall length of a cable or the distance to a cable break or opening by measuring the distance to where the signal is reflected anytime the wiring is open.

token-passing — A network access method that employs a data token to enable a computer to transmit information.

transceiver — A device that converts a data signal into an electronic signal for transmission; designed to attach to a specific type of wiring or network media; transceivers for thinnet and UTP are on the NIC; transceivers for thicknet are usually attached to a vampire tap on the cable itself.

transformer — Device that steps voltage up or down where the hot lead originates and the neutral wire is grounded.

transmission time — Time that it takes a file to transfer from one location to another.

two-layer network model — Divides a network into two connectivity layers: core and access.

unshielded twisted-pair (UTP) — A type of cabling in which pairs of wires are twisted around one another inside a wire bundle.

vertical cabling — *See* **backbone**.

wire map — A function that displays the connections of UTP wiring from point to point; used to see if the connectors were properly wired.

wiring closet — A central junction point, usually located in a separate room, used for interconnecting various network devices.

REVIEW QUESTIONS

1. Which of the following UTP cable types are not rated for at least 10-Mbps transmissions? (Choose all that apply.)

   a. Category 1

   b. Category 2

   c. Category 3

   d. Category 4

   e. Category 5

2. Which of the following are true statements about Ethernet? (Choose all that apply.)

   a. Stations must have a token before they can transmit.

   b. Stations can transmit anytime.

   c. Stations can detect collisions.

   d. Stations beacon during error conditions.

3. Which of the following devices extends the network at the Physical layer while serving as a central connection point?

   a. Active hub

   b. Router

   c. Gateway

   d. Passive hub

4. Which of the following are benefits to installing fiber-optic cable? (Choose all that apply.)

   a. Impervious to EMI

   b. Small diameter

   c. Easy to install

   d. Low cost

5. Which of the following is the correct specification for wireless technologies?

   a. 802.3

   b. 802.4

   c. 802.5

   d. 802.11

6. Which of the following is an advantage to using the bus topology?

   a. Centralized connection point

   b. Low implementation cost

   c. Ease of troubleshooting

   d. Fault tolerance

7. Which of the following specifications defines Token Ring?

   a. 568B

   b. 802.2

   c. 802.5

   d. 802.3

8. Which of the following can cause the complete failure of a star network?

   a. Failure of one station

   b. Break in a cable

   c. Failure of the hub

   d. Bad port on the hub

9. What does an active hub do that a passive hub does not?

   a. Connect media

   b. Route traffic

c. Segment a network

d. Repeat network signals

10. Which of the following is desirable as it relates to network media?

a. High-voltage lines in close proximity

b. Attenuation

c. Cancellation

d. Crosstalk

11. Which type of cable is usually required by fire codes?

a. Voice-grade

b. Plenum-grade

c. CAT 1

d. CAT 5

12. Which of the following is the most expensive type of cabling?

a. Thinnet

b. Coaxial

c. Twisted-pair

d. Fiber-optic

13. Which type of connector is used with twisted-pair cabling?

a. BNC

b. Barrel

c. T-connectors

d. RJ-45

14. Which of the following cables have shielding that protects them from EMI? (Choose all that apply.)

a. Fiber-optic

b. RG-58

c. STP

d. UTP

15. Which media should be installed if there is significant concern for the security of the data carried within?

a. Thicknet

b. Thinnet

c. Fiber

d. UTP

e. STP

16. Which wireless technology requires line-of-sight between the transmitter and the receiver?

    a. Spread spectrum

    b. Direct sequencing

    c. Frequency–hopping

    d. Infrared

17. Which of the following describes a loss of signal strength over the length of a wire?

    a. Crosstalk

    b. Split pair

    c. Attenuation

    d. EMI

18. Which of the following are true of star topology cables? (Choose all that apply.)

    a. Patch cables connect the telecommunications outlet to the patch panel.

    b. The horizontal cable is terminated at the patch panel.

    c. The horizontal cable is terminated at the RJ-45 jack.

    d. The horizontal cable runs between hubs.

19. What is the main purpose of monitoring a network when there are no known problems on the network?

    a. Helps to pinpoint the location of a network bottleneck

    b. Allows you to establish a baseline for normal operations

    c. Increases network security

    d. Makes people more cautious

20. Which of the following devices can actually increase network traffic but do nothing to decrease it?

    a. Bridge

    b. Router

    c. Repeater

    d. Switch

21. At which layer of the three-layer network model should users connect to the network?

    a. Core

    b. Central

    c. Access

    d. Distribution

    e. Campus

22. Which of the following is also known as vertical cabling?

    a. Horizontal

    b. Parallel

    c. Backbone

    d. Serial

23. What is another name for the MDF and IDF?

    a. Backbone

    b. Vertical cabling

    c. Wiring closets

    d. Bandwidth

24. In a three-layer network model, each layer is part of a separate _____.

    a. LAN

    b. WAN

    c. organization

    d. broadcast domain

    e. area of responsibility

25. The cable that connects a workstation to a wall outlet is called a _____.

    a. telecommunications connector

    b. vertical cable

    c. horizontal cable

    d. patch cable

26. In an organization in which multiple wiring closets are required, the central junction point for the wiring of the star topology will be located in the _____.

    a. MDF

    b. IDF

    c. workstation area

    d. catchment area

27. When the distance between wiring closets exceeds 500 meters, which of the following cable types could be used to traverse the distance without the use of intermediate wiring closets or connectivity devices?

    a. UTP

    b. STP

    c. Copper

    d. Fiber-optic cabling

28. When possible, the POP should be located near the _____.

   a. IDF

   b. workstation area

   c. MDF

   d. bathroom

29. The usable distance of the UTP cable between the MDF and IDF is _____.

   a. 90 meters

   b. 200 meters

   c. 150 meters

   d. 100 meters

30. If single-mode fiber-optic cable is used between the MDF and IDF, what is the maximum usable distance?

   a. 100 meters

   b. 1000 yards

   c. 3000 meters

   d. 2000 meters

CASE PROJECTS

CASE PROJECTS

1. Your company is sending you and your team to the Americanus Corporation to set up a 100BaseT network. Jennifer wants to know why 100BaseT and other star configurations are referred to as "star-bus" networks. Explain to her where "bus" comes from and how the CSMA/CD access method works to manage collisions.

2. Moe mentions that the token-passing access method can also look like a star. This topology is known as a "star-ring." Moe wants to know how "star-ring" networks differ from "star-bus" networks and how collisions are managed in the "star-ring" configuration.

3. Lisa has learned that determining the networking media is the most important network design decision. She wants to know which factors led the Americanus Corporation to choose Category 5 UTP cable and the 100BaseT architecture. Discuss the advantages of using Category 5 UTP cable and the 100BaseT architecture.

4. You have just learned that the Americanus Corporation may decide to connect its new 100BaseT LAN to another LAN in a different building several miles away. What cable type can be used for this connection? Can you think of any other alternatives?

5. Jennifer has been asked to do a presentation for a Winslow Network client. The focus of the presentation is the different media included in the EIA/TIA-568 standards for backbone cabling. Tell her what cables to include, the distance limitations, and when and where to use these different cable types.

WAN CONCEPTS

> **After reading this chapter and completing the exercises, you will be able to:**
>
> ♦ Describe WAN standards
> ♦ Explain the WAN connection methods
> ♦ Discuss WAN data link protocols
> ♦ Understand the WAN Physical layer
> ♦ Recognize the various WAN physical topologies
> ♦ Emerging WAN connection methods

The information in previous chapters was oriented toward local area networks (LANs). This chapter focuses on wide area networks (WANs) and the standards and devices specific to WAN communications. Throughout the chapter, the differences between LANs and WANs are highlighted.

WAN STANDARDIZATION

Wide area networks (WANs) differ from local area networks (LANs) in several ways. First, WANs connect geographically separate LANs. Second, WANs historically used low-speed connections over serial interfaces. This has changed in recent years as new WAN technologies have reached speeds in the gigabit-per-second range. Third, WAN standards differ from LAN standards at the Physical and Data Link layers of the OSI reference model. Fourth, WANs often carry more than just data. Other traffic types seen on WAN links include audio, video, and voice.

Several organizations contributed to the standardization of WAN technologies. These organizations created standards that applied to both the Physical and Data Link layers of WAN implementations:

- International Organization for Standardization (ISO)

- American National Standards Institute (ANSI)

- Electronic Industries Alliance (EIA)

- **Internet Engineering Task Force (IETF)**

- International Telecommunication Union-Telecommunication Standardization Sector (ITU-T)

 ITU-T was formerly the Consultative Committee for International Telegraph and Telephone (CCITT).

NOTE

These organizations concentrated on standardizing the equipment and Data Link layer protocols used to transfer data over WAN connections. The standards applied to WANs are based on the type of facilities in which the WAN is expected to operate.

WAN Connection Methods

You can configure WAN connections in different ways. As the following section discusses, the type of connection partially determines the appropriate data link protocol for the connection. Networking standards recognize three different connection methods for WANs.

The first method is the dedicated point-to-point connection. Dedicated lines are also known as leased lines. The connection is made between two points and used only to transfer data between those two points. One office LAN connecting to another office LAN in a geographically separate location is an example of a dedicated point-to-point connection, as shown in Figure 5-1.

The second type of connection is a variation of the dedicated point-to-point connection. The only difference is that more than one dedicated point-to-point connection exists. This type of connection is called a multipoint facility connection, which is based on dedicated facilities, as shown in Figure 5-2.

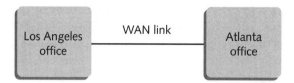

Figure 5-1   Dedicated point-to-point facilities

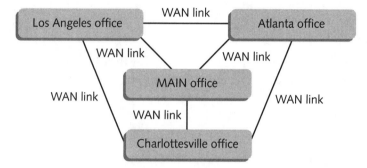

Figure 5-2   Multipoint facility based on dedicated facilities

Dedicated lines provide service 24 hours a day, seven days a week. They can typically carry data, voice, and video. These different traffic streams are **multiplexed** onto a single physical line using **Time Division Multiplexing (TDM)**. Multiplexing refers to the combining of different traffic streams onto a single physical medium. Because this kind of service is expensive, it should be used when bandwidth is used in a constant and steady pattern, because you pay for the service even when no traffic is being transmitted. The most common dedicated service is a T1 line. T1s provide point-to-point connectivity at 1.544 Mbps.

The third connection type uses a circuit-switched WAN connection between facilities. This means that the communication path between the points is not necessarily the same each time. This type of connection is called a multiaccess switched service because none of the lines is dedicated. Instead, the service switches the lines as necessary, as shown in Figure 5-3.

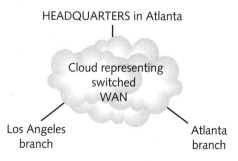

Figure 5-3   Multiaccess switched services

NOTE   The cloud that appears in Figure 5-3 represents a switched network, as it is labeled in the figure. The cloud illustrates that the network uses switched or unknown paths between connection points. This cloud also could represent the Internet because specific paths across the Internet are not defined.

A fourth type of WAN connection is **packet-switched**, in which data is broken into packets that can travel via different paths to the destination. Each packet in a single WAN communication could theoretically travel across a different path when using a packet-switched connection. Frame Relay is one type of WAN connection that uses a packet-switched connection.

The standards organizations also defined several types of data link protocols to be used with the WAN connections listed previously. These protocols are discussed next.

WAN Data Link Protocols

The data link protocols available for WAN communications define how networks will carry the data frames on a given data link. The data link protocols used for WANs come in three categories:

- Interface to IBM enterprise data centers: Synchronous Data Link Control (SDLC)

- WAN connections using peer devices: High-level Data Link Control (HDLC) and Point-to-Point Protocol (PPP)

- Switched or relayed services: X.25/Link Access Procedure Balanced (LAPB), Frame Relay, Integrated Services Digital Network (ISDN)/Link Access Procedure D-channel (LAPD), and Asynchronous Transfer Mode (ATM)

Some of these protocols provide functionality as high as in the Network layer of the OSI reference model, and all of these protocols transfer data over a WAN data link.

SDLC

IBM developed the **Synchronous Data Link Control (SDLC)** protocol in the 1970s to allow IBM host systems to communicate over WAN connections. IBM systems can use the SDLC protocol for point-to-point or point-to-multipoint connections between remote devices and a central mainframe computer. In SDLC, the network has one primary station and one or more secondary stations. SDLC networks always make connections between the primary station and one of the SDLC secondary stations because secondary stations cannot communicate with each other directly.

Cisco routers can interface with the IBM mainframe systems and pass native SDLC traffic via point-to-point serial links; also, other protocol traffic can be multiplexed with SDLC over those links. In addition, Cisco routers can encapsulate SDLC data frames into IP datagrams so that SDLC communications can traverse non-SDLC networks.

Communications over SDLC are **synchronous**, which means that the clock or timing mechanism between the source and destination must be synchronized. The synchronization is maintained by a bit pattern encoded into the **bit stream**. **Asynchronous**, the opposite of synchronous, means that timing devices are not required for transmission. In asynchronous communication, the bit stream is interpreted by start and stop bits. The destination uses the start and stop bits to ascertain where the transmission begins and ends. Because synchronous communication does not require start and stop bits, it is more efficient than asynchronous communication.

Other WAN protocols have been derived from the SDLC protocol. For example, the ISO developed HDLC from SDLC. HDLC is the default protocol on WAN links.

5

HDLC

The **High-level Data Link Control (HDLC)** protocol is a superset of the SDLC protocol. Another name for HDLC is **Advanced Data Communication Control Procedures (ADCCP)**, which came from the American National Standards Institute (ANSI). However, the most widely accepted name for this protocol remains HDLC.

Devices can use HDLC for both point-to-point and multipoint connections. The protocol also supports **full-duplex** communication, which means that information can be transmitted and received simultaneously. HDLC also permits both synchronous and asynchronous communications. In **half-duplex** communication, devices can send data in both directions, but not simultaneously. With **simplex** transmissions, devices can send data in one direction only.

HDLC does not support multiple protocols (by default) because its packet structure does not have a field for indicating higher-layer protocols. However, Cisco's proprietary HDLC frame has a field that allows for the specification of a protocol type. The **Point-to-Point Protocol (PPP)** further extends the typical HDLC data frame by providing a protocol field.

Figure 5-4 illustrates the frame formats of HDLC, Cisco modified HDLC, and PPP.

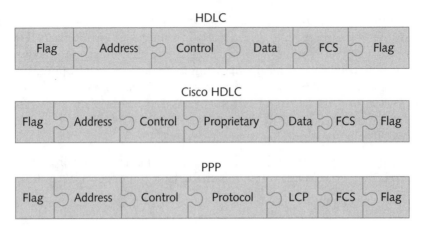

Figure 5-4   HDLC and PPP

The following list details the common fields among these frame formats:

- **Flag**: Placed at the beginning and end of a frame to mark the start and finish of that frame.

- **Address**: Indicates the destination address.

- **Control**: The sequence number that ensures the data is handled and reassembled in correct order.

- **Frame Check Sequence (FCS)**: A field that calculates a checksum for the frame, which is used for error checking.

In the HDLC frame, the data field contains the information that is to be passed to the Network layer. In a PPP frame, the area occupied by data in HDLC identifies the encapsulated protocol and holds the Link Control protocol (LCP).

LCP is similar to the Logical Link Control (LLC) in the IEEE 802.2 definition for LAN protocols. PPP uses LCP to establish, configure, maintain, and terminate point-to-point connections. The data for the Network layer is also located inside the LCP.

PPP

As mentioned earlier, PPP extends the functionality of the HDLC protocol by providing Network layer protocol encapsulation. WAN devices commonly use PPP over dial-up or leased lines to provide connections to IP networks. However, because PPP makes use of **Network Control Protocols (NCPs)**, WAN devices can use it to transfer IP, IPX, AppleTalk, and other Network layer protocols over PPP connections.

The **Serial Line Internet Protocol (SLIP)** was the predecessor to PPP; it only supported IP connections. PPP replaced SLIP because PPP is more efficient and because it supports more protocols and interfaces.

NOTE

PPP is an Internet standard protocol defined in RFCs 2153 and 1661. The Internet Engineering Task Force (IETF) defined PPP to provide router-to-router, host-to-router, and host-to-host connections. You can use PPP over several different physical interfaces, including:

- Asynchronous serial

- ISDN/Synchronous serial

- High-Speed Serial Interface (HSSI)

Asynchronous serial connections are used with analog modems, which connect directly to existing phone lines and outlets in residential areas throughout the United States. ISDN/**Synchronous serial** connections require special modem (**ISDN modem**) equipment to interface with the **Integrated Services Digital Network (ISDN)** provided by many public carriers. HSSI is a serial device that was developed by Cisco and T3Plus Networking. It defines a serial connection that operates at speeds of up to 52 Mbps over distances of up to 15 meters (50 feet), and is typically used to connect a router to a T3 line.

PPP and HDLC are both methods for accessing the services of WAN providers by using protocols that connect peer devices. In this context, "peer" means devices on the same level. The final group of protocols to discuss are those that provide switched or relayed services, such as X.25, ISDN, Frame Relay, and ATM.

REFERENCE

PPP configuration details are discussed in Chapter 11.

X.25/LAPB

X.25 is a CCITT (ITU-T) specification that describes the connection of PCs and terminals through packet-switching networks. Packet switching is a technology whereby individual packets, each with source and destination addresses, are routed through the network based on the best path. The packets may not necessarily take the same route. They are put back in order, if necessary, at the destination.

X.25 is one of the most widely implemented techniques for international communications because almost every country with a telephone system has an X.25 addressable network. In the United States, AT&T, Sprint, CompuServe, the Regional Bell Operating Companies (RBOCs), and others provide X.25 services.

X.25 provides communication between two points over **virtual circuits**. A virtual circuit is a logical circuit and not a dedicated physical link. The virtual circuit is a point-to-point connection across the WAN. Because the communication can travel any path inside the WAN switched network, the WAN is often indicated by a cloud.

Originally, X.25 was created to function over existing and unreliable analog telecommunications lines, so error correction and flow were built into the protocol. Although this provides a reliable transmission, it also negatively affects the performance of the protocol. X.25 originally had a throughput of 56 Kbps, but the CCITT revised the standard and boosted the throughput to 2 Mbps. Even so, up to 70 percent of the throughput is used for error checking.

The X.25 specification is older than the OSI model, so its terminology does not directly translate. However, the X.25 standard defines three layers that are similar to the lower three layers of the OSI model.

- Physical layer: Defines the physical and electrical interface from the computer or terminal to the attachment of the X.25 packet-switching network. The Physical layer is also known by its interface, either X.21 or RS-232-C (described later in this chapter). This layer is equivalent to the OSI Physical layer.

- Link Access layer: Defines the data-transmission and framing sequence. The actual name of the protocol used with X.25 communications is **Link Access Procedure Balanced (LAPB)**. This protocol was derived from HDLC. This layer is similar to the OSI Data Link layer.

- Packet layer: Is the virtual-circuit transmission through packet-switched networks. This layer describes a point-to-point connection as opposed to a point-to-multipoint connection. This layer is roughly equivalent to the OSI Network layer.

Figure 5-5 compares these X.25 layers with the OSI model.

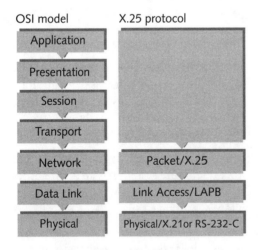

Figure 5-5   OSI and X.25 layer comparison

Although X.25 is similar to the Frame Relay protocol, Frame Relay provides speed advantages over X.25, as the following section describes.

Frame Relay

Frame Relay is a Data Link layer protocol that the telecommunications companies created to improve upon the X.25 standard. Frame Relay is also a service. This protocol/service operates between 56 Kbps and 45 Mbps over a WAN connection, and relies on higher-layer protocols to provide error checking and flow control. Like X.25, Frame Relay is a packet-switching technology. Unlike X.25, which was created in the 1970s, Frame Relay assumes a more reliable connection provided by modern fiber and digital networks. Frame Relay shares bandwidth with other Frame Relay subscribers. In this sense, Frame Relay is not a dedicated service. Because it is not dedicated, it is less expensive than a leased line.

5

TIP

Frame Relay uses high-quality digital connections and is the fastest WAN-only protocol described in this chapter.

Frame Relay defines the connection between the **customer premises equipment (CPE)**, usually a router, and the service provider's local access switching equipment, or Frame Relay switch. Frame Relay services are available in the United States from telecommunications carriers such as MCI, Sprint, AT&T, and the RBOCs. Because Frame Relay is a Layer 2 protocol, it can operate over virtually any Physical layer interface. However, it is most often implemented between a router and a Frame Relay switch. The Frame Relay service provider supplies the Frame Relay switches.

NOTE

CPE is defined as both customer premises equipment and customer-provided equipment. Both definitions indicate equipment under the customer's control.

Two types of virtual circuits, **switched virtual circuits (SVC)** and **permanent virtual circuits (PVC)**, connect Frame Relay ports. SVCs are controlled by software and are active only while a connection to the WAN is active. The software dials the WAN as required, establishes an SVC, and terminates the SVC that has the connection to the WAN when the communication ends. More often, Frame Relay connections are configured with PVCs, which (as their name implies) remain connected to the WAN. The PVC is defined manually by the network administrator and exists until it is manually removed. Frame Relay uses **statistical multiplexing** to allocate bandwidth to the virtual circuits. Statistical multiplexing is a method for transmitting several types of data simultaneously across a single line, in which bandwidth is dynamically allocated to the virtual circuits on a packet-by-packet basis.

The network administrator and the telecommunications company (telco) define the following information when setting up a Frame Relay connection between a router and a Frame Relay switch.

- **Local Access Rate**: The speed of the line that indicates transfer rate. Common U.S. access rates are 64 Kbps and 128 Kbps, which are provided by ISDN connections, and 1.544 Mbps, which are provided by **T1** connections.

- **Committed Information Rate (CIR)**: The minimum average transfer rate of the Frame Relay circuit. This is usually lower than the access rate because the transfer rate may exceed the CIR during short bursts. This is the most important parameter.

- **Committed Burst Size (CBS)**: The maximum amount of data bits that the service provider agrees to transfer in a set period under normal conditions.

- **Excess Burst Size (EBS)**: The amount of excess traffic (over the CBS) that the network will attempt to transfer during a set period. The network can discard EBS data, if necessary.

- **Data Link Connection Identifier (DLCI)**: Pronounced *dell-see*, this is configured on the router and used to identify the PVCs and SVCs. In this way, DLCI identifies which path leads to a specific Network layer address (i.e., IP address). The DLCI is not a network-wide unique address, as is a MAC address; instead, the DLCI is only locally significant, meaning that it can, and usually does, change on each physical link.

- **Local Management Interface (LMI)**: A standard signaling mechanism between the CPE and the Frame Relay connection. The LMI can provide the network server with a local DLCI and give DLCI global (network wide) significance rather than merely local significance. In addition, it can provide keep-alive and status information to the end user (router) regarding the connections. The LMI also uses inverse ARP to automatically determine the protocol address of remote devices.

- **Discard–Eligible (DE)**: Certain frames can be configured at the router as discard-eligible; thus, during times of congestion, DE frames are discarded to provide a more reliable service to frames that are not discard-eligible.

Frame Relay switches attempt to control congestion on the network. When congestion is recognized, the Frame Relay switch sends a **Forward Explicit Congestion Notification (FECN)** message to the destination. This message tells a router that congestion was experienced on the virtual circuit. In addition, the switch sends a **Backward Explicit Congestion Notification (BECN)** message to the transmitting or source router. In response to the BECN, the router should reduce the amount of traffic it is sending.

When the sum of the data arriving over all virtual circuits exceeds the access rate, the situation is called oversubscription. This can occur when the CIR is exceeded by burst traffic from the virtual circuits. Oversubscription results in dropped packets. In such a case, the dropped packets must be retransmitted.

Frame Relay configuration details are discussed in Chapter 12.

As mentioned, Frame Relay can be connected over ISDN connections. Although ISDN can host Frame Relay, it can be used for WAN connections without Frame Relay as well. The following section describes ISDN.

ISDN/LAPD

ISDN is a circuit switching technology. This means there is a dedicated circuit for the length of the transmission. All data takes the same path. Regular phone calls are circuit switched. Circuit switching is usually preferred for data that must be received in real time, such as video streaming. Network devices can use ISDN over existing digital telephone lines to transmit both voice and data. **B-channels (bearer channels)** transmit the data and **D-channels (data channels)** maintain ISDN connections. ISDN service is available from most communication providers in the United States, including Sprint, MCI, AT&T, and the RBOCs.

There are two basic service levels for ISDN connections: **Primary Rate Interface (PRI)** and **Basic Rate Interface (BRI)**. PRI provides a throughput of up to 1.544 Mbps over its 23 B-channels and single 64-Kbps D-channel, whereas BRI provides two B-channels at 64 Kbps each and one D-channel at 16 Kbps. This means that BRI provides a throughput of 128 Kbps because the 16-Kbps line is used to control the connection. The **Link Access Procedure D-channel (LAPD)** protocol specification developed by the CCITT (ITU-T) defines the method of using the D-channel to control communications. The CCITT derived this protocol from the HDLC protocol.

ISDN connections can also provide X.25 and Frame Relay connections. ISDN configuration is discussed in Chapter 11.

Another protocol used to connect LANs is considered both a WAN and a LAN protocol. This technology is called ATM.

ATM

Asynchronous Transfer Mode (ATM) is a communications protocol that is used within and between LAN connections. Telecommunications companies based the ATM on the foundations of Frame Relay, although ATM is circuit-oriented in the sense that ATM cells follow the same path for the duration of the connection. ATM provides high-speed data transmission rates for voice, data, video, audio, and imaging. Public carriers such as Sprint and AT&T offer ATM.

ATM requires devices capable of ATM communications. Cisco 4000, 7000, and 7500 router families support ATM communications. ATM communications can be conducted over T1, **fractional T1**, and **T3** lines. ATM can be used between LANs as a WAN connection, within LANs as a backbone, and/or wired directly to desktops using ATM NICs and hubs.

ATM is similar to Frame Relay and X.25 in that it runs over a switched service. Also, like Frame Relay, ATM does not provide the redundant error checking that X.25 uses. Unlike both Frame Relay and X.25, the ATM packets (called cells) have a fixed length of 53 bytes. The fixed length of each cell allows ATM to efficiently plan and disperse packets quickly. (Variable-length packets can introduce traffic delays.) ATM switching is implemented in the hardware, making it much faster than the other switching techniques covered in this section. Currently, ATM can reach speeds of 10 Gbps.

TIP

Because ATM can be used both between LANs and inside LANs, it is not just a WAN protocol. The fastest WAN-only protocol presented in this chapter is Frame Relay.

WAN PHYSICAL LAYER

Thus far, you have learned about Data Link layer components and standards that apply to WAN connections. However, WAN standards apply to both the Data Link and Physical layers of the OSI model. In this section, you learn more about the connections, equipment, and standards in the physical connections of the WAN.

As described, WAN connections usually require service from a telecommunications provider, such as AT&T, MCI, or Sprint, over their **Public Switched Telephone Network (PSTN)**. Connections to the PSTN involve several pieces of equipment both at the customer location and the phone company locations.

WAN Connections

WANs provide connections between two LANs. The WAN moves data and packets between routers at each end of the LANs that are supported by the WAN connection. RBOCs, or other telecommunications providers such as AT&T, MCI, and Sprint, provide these WAN connections.

Figure 5-6 illustrates the equipment commonly used to create a connection between two LANs.

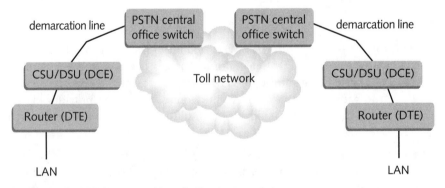

Figure 5-6   WAN connection devices

Typically, two devices reside at the customer location—the **channel service unit/data service unit (CSU/DSU)** and the router. The CSU/DSU provides the connection from the customer site to the telecommunications company network. The CSU/DSU is the provider's side of the WAN link. The router provides the connection between the LAN and the CSU/DSU. The router is the subscriber's side of the WAN link.

As shown in the graphic, the router is also called **data terminal equipment (DTE)**. A DTE can also be a computer or some other type of terminal; in all cases, it is a device at the user end of the network. The CSU/DSU is also called **data circuit-terminating equipment (DCE)**. A DCE can be a modem or a **terminal adapter (TA)**. In all cases, the DCE is a physical connection at the end of the WAN connection.

The CSU/DSU is the interface between the DTE and the DCE. In some cases, the CSU/DSU is built into the router. DTE devices must use some type of DCE to access the WAN connection. The DCE provides clocking and formatting for information to go out on the WAN connection.

The **demarc**, or **demarcation**, is the next link in the chain from the DCE to the WAN. The demarc is the point at which the telecommunications company facility (Point of Presence, or POP) connects to the DCE. The POP is the room or area where the telecommunications company terminates its wires on the customer's premises. It is the point where the telecommunications company's equipment ends and the customer's begins. The connection between the demarc and the telephone company (WAN service provider) office is called the **local loop** or last mile.

The **Central Office (CO) switch** is the telecommunications company location that is the point of entry into the **toll network**. The toll network consists of the PSTN, including all the switches and trunks that comprise it. The toll network is so named because the telecommunications company bills the client to use the network. Billing can either be a flat fee or a rate based on usage.

Most of the connections between two LANs over a PSTN are the responsibility of the telecommunications company. Typically, the network administrator is responsible for the WAN connection from the router (DTE) up to the CSU/DSU (DCE). These connections are defined in the Physical layer standards for WAN connections.

WAN Physical Standards

As you have learned, WAN standards describe communications at both the Physical layer and Data Link layer of the OSI model. The standards that focus on the Physical layer WAN connection center around the interface between the DTE and DCE—usually a serial interface.

The following is a list of the telecommunication standards that apply to the Physical layer WAN serial interface between the DTE and DCE devices:

- EIA/TIA-232: Also known as RS-232. Version numbers, such as RS-232-C and EIA/TIA-232-E, can follow both of these. This specification defines the interface for the connection between DTE and DCE data-communications devices.

RS-232 can transfer data at up to 56 Kbps. RS-232 connections are made with 25-pin or 9-pin, D-shaped connectors. These connectors are known as DB-25 and DB-9, respectively. Most personal computers have an RS-232 interface.

■ EIA/TIA-449: Also known as RS-449. This standard defines a faster serial inter-face version of RS-232. RS-449 can transfer data at up to 2 Mbps. RS-449 con-nections are made by DB-37 connectors.

■ EIA-530: The successor to RS-449. It is also known as the RS-530 specifica-tion. RS-530 defines the connection between DTEs and DCEs. Like EIA/TIA-449, this specification allows for up to 2-Mbps connection rates over the same DB-25 connectors that are used for RS-232 connections. However, RS-232 and RS-530 are not compatible standards.

■ High-Speed Serial Interface (HSSI): Cisco and T3Plus Networking developed the HSSI standard. It operates at speeds of up to 52 Mbps over distances of up to 15 meters (50 feet). The cable is typically shielded twisted-pair and the interface is a 50-pin connector.

■ V.24: A list of definitions for interfaces between DTE and DCE to PSTNs.

■ V.35: Used to define the trunk interface between a packet network and a network access device. The specification provides data-transfer rates of up to 4 Mbps for DTE-to-DCE communication equipment that interfaces high-speed digital carriers.

■ X.21: Defines the interface between the DTE and DCE for synchronous communication.

■ G.703: The ITU-T recommended the G.703 standard to define European con-nections of 2.048 Mbps. It also includes specifications for the U.S. 1.544-Mbps transmission rates. This 1984 standard defines the physical and logical transfer of information over digital networks.

WAN TOPOLOGIES

You can use different topologies to create WAN connections. These topologies are the peer, the star, the partial mesh, and the full mesh (see Figure 5-7).

The peer topology is like the bus LAN topology. Nodes are just strung along in a daisy-chained fashion. Very often, there will only be two routers connected. This is the sim-plest WAN topology. It is the least expensive and is easy to configure. The disadvantage to the peer WAN topology is that a failure between nodes will affect the WAN because there is no redundancy.

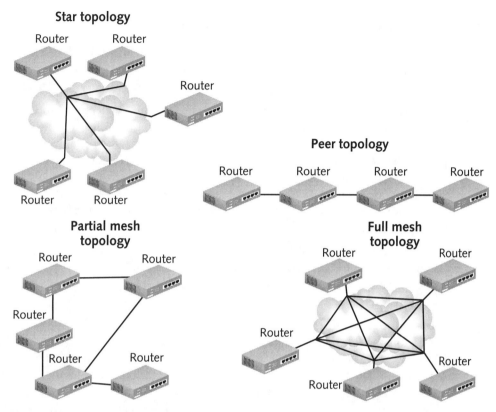

Figure 5-7 WAN topologies

The star is the most popular WAN topology. This configuration is also called the hub-and-spoke topology because one router functions as a central point, or hub, in a simple hierarchical configuration. All other devices are connected to the central router as spokes would connect to a hub. Typically the network administrator will configure the central router with a single interface that makes a multipoint connection to all other routers.

The full mesh is the most expensive topology to implement because each router has a direct connection to every other router. However, this topology is the most fault-tolerant because there are always at least two routes to every router on the network. The more routers you add to the full mesh, the more expensive the topology becomes, because multiple routes are required for each router.

The partial mesh is a compromise between the hierarchy of the star and the expense of the full mesh. A partial mesh is not as expensive as a full mesh because the principle of connecting every router to every other router is not required. Instead, connections are made according to need and traffic flow. If there is heavy traffic flow to one router, multiple circuits may be established between that router and the routers sending the most traffic to it. The partial mesh does not follow the hierarchical structure of the star, in that all routers do not have to be connected to a single central router.

EMERGING WAN CONNECTION METHODS

In the search for faster and cheaper Internet access, service providers have created two new WAN connection methods. **Digital Subscriber Lines (DSL)** and cable modems use existing wiring facilities to provide broadband access, mostly to consumers.

DSL modulates both voice and data over the existing copper telephone lines in a residence. DSL download speeds can vary from 256K to faster than T1 speeds (1.544 Mbps). Upload speeds for nearly all DSL technologies are substantially slower than download speeds. The vast difference in the types of available DSL is one of its limiting factors. What one service provider calls DSL may be very different from another. In general, two basic types of DSL exist: asymmetric and symmetric. **Asymmetric DSL** provides greater download speeds than upload speeds. **Symmetric DSL** provides the same download and upload speeds.

Another problem with DSL stems from the need to be close to the provider's DSL switch. This distance limitation forces many homes outside the range of DSL service. On the other hand, the main advantages of DSL service are speed and costs. DSL offers fast, always-on Internet access for a nominal cost.

Cable modems use existing cable TV infrastructure to provide high-speed Internet access along with cable TV access (although you can get just Internet access if you do not want cable TV). Cable modem speeds vary, but most companies offering the service match or exceed DSL speeds. The problem with cable modems come from the shared aspect of bandwidth. In most implementations, subscribers share the link back to the cable companies' main switch. As a result, available bandwidth can decrease as the number of subscribers increases. Otherwise, cable modems do not suffer as badly from the distance limitations of DSL and offer an excellent high-speed, always-on Internet solution.

Both of these new technologies have introduced new ways for business users to connect to the corporate network. In the past, companies had to maintain large modem banks to allow remote users to connect back to the main office. With the advent of DSL and cable modems, remote home users have the speed necessary to use Virtual Private Networks (VPNs) to access the main office.

CHAPTER SUMMARY

- ❏ WANs connect LANs in geographically separate areas.

- ❏ WAN connections typically function at the Physical and Data Link layers of the OSI reference model, and are made over serial connections.

- ❏ WAN connections operate at a lower speed than LAN connections, and can be made as point-to-point, point-to-multipoint, and switched WAN connections.

❏ You can use several different data link protocols for WAN connections. The different types of WAN connections are: (1) interfaces to IBM mainframes provided by SDLC; (2) WAN connections using peer devices with HDLC and PPP; and (3) switched or relayed services including X.25, Frame Relay, ATM, and ISDN.

❏ X.25 is the oldest of the switched or relayed services and provides the least efficient service because of its excessive error checking.

❏ Frame Relay is an enhancement over X.25 because it is faster and does not provide redundant error checking.

❏ ATM is similar to Frame Relay, except that it uses fixed-length cells instead of variable-length packets. In addition, the ATM protocol can be used on LANs as well as WANs.

❏ ISDN is a leased digital line that can support X.25 and Frame Relay connections, among others.

❏ ISDN comes in PRI and BRI levels. BRI only provides 128-Kbps throughput over two B-channels, and 16 Kbps over one D-channel that is used for controlling the connection. PRI provides 23 B-channels of 64 Kbps each and one 64-Kbps D-channel for controlling the connection. This allows PRI to offer 1.544-Mbps throughput.

❏ The Physical layer WAN connections concern the interface between the DTE and DCE.

❏ The DTE is the endpoint of the user's network, which connects to the WAN interface. This is typically a router, computer, or terminal of some type. The WAN service provider usually provides the DCE, which is often a CSU/DSU, modem, or terminal adapter. The DCE is then connected to a demarc, which is a communications facility owned by the WAN service provider. The local loop is the connection (usually copper cable) that links the demarcation to the WAN service provider's CO switch, which is actually part of the toll network or PSTN.

❏ The physical WAN topologies are: the peer, which is simply customer facilities connected in a daisy-chained fashion; the star, which involves connecting remote customer facilities to a central facility; the full mesh, which connects every location to every other location; and the partial mesh, which provides redundancy only where necessary.

5

Key Terms

address — A field that indicates the destination address of the frame.

Advanced Data Communication Control Procedures (ADCCP) — The ANSI standard for HDLC.

asymmetric DSL — A DSL service that provides faster download than upload speeds.

asynchronous — Asynchronous communications rely on start and stop bits to define the endpoints of a transmission; timing mechanisms are not needed to maintain clock synchronization between the source and destination.

asynchronous serial — Serial connections that are employed in most modems connected to residential phone lines.

Asynchronous Transfer Mode (ATM) — A networking implementation for both high-speed LAN and WAN connectivity.

B-channel (bearer channel) — An ISDN channel used to carry data; two or more B-channels, each supporting 64 Kbps, are provided with ISDN service.

Backward Explicit Congestion Notification (BECN) — When congestion is recognized, the Frame Relay switch sends a BECN message to the source router; should reduce the amount of traffic that is sent by the router.

Basic Rate Interface (BRI) — An ISDN service that provides two B-channels for data transfers up to 128 Kbps and one D-channel to control the communications.

bit stream — The stream of bits, or data, that flows between a source (transmitter) and a destination (receiver); can be communicated by synchronous or asynchronous methods.

cable modem — Broadband technology that provides cable TV and high-speed Internet access over existing coaxial TV cable.

Central Office (CO) switch — The telecommunications company location that is part of the PSTN or toll network; point of entry to the toll network from the demarc.

channel service unit/data service unit (CSU/DSU) — A telecommunications company device that provides connectivity between the WAN service provider network and the customer's LAN.

Committed Burst Size (CBS) — The maximum amount of data bits that the service provider agrees to transfer in a set period under normal conditions.

Committed Information Rate (CIR) — The minimum average transfer rate of the Frame Relay circuit; usually lower than the access rate because the transfer rate may exceed the CIR during short bursts.

control — A sequence number that ensures the data is handled and reassembled properly.

customer premises equipment (CPE) — Equipment under the customer's control; also known as customer-provided equipment, depending on the publication.

D-channel (data channel) — The control channel used in ISDN communications; can be 16 to 64 Kbps.

data circuit-terminating equipment (DCE) — Typically, the telecommunications-provided device on the customer side that allows the customer to connect to the WAN; often, a CSU/DSU, but can also be a modem or TA.

Data Link Connection Identifier (DLCI) — Pronounced *dell-see*, information in a Frame Relay connection that is configured on the router and used to identify which path leads to a specific Network layer address (i.e., IP address). The DLCI is only locally significant, meaning that it can, and usually does, change on each physical link.

data terminal equipment (DTE) — A customer device that is used to connect to the telecommunications company equipment. This device is typically a router, but it can also be a computer or other type of terminal.

demarc — Location that is the responsibility of the telecommunications provider and that connects to the nearest telephone company office.

demarcation — *See* **demarc**.

Digital Subscriber Lines (DSL) — Broadband technology that provides high-speed Internet access and simultaneous voice service over existing copper telephone lines.

discard-eligible (DE) — During times of congestion, DE frames are discarded to provide a more reliable service to frames that are not discard-eligible.

Excess Burst Size (EBS) — The amount of excess traffic (over the CBS) that the network will attempt to transfer during a set period; can be discarded by the network, if necessary.

flag — A field placed at the beginning and end of an HDLC and PPP frame to mark the beginning and end of the frame.

Forward Explicit Congestion Notification (FECN) — Message sent to the destination router on a Frame Relay circuit that tells the router that congestion was experienced on the virtual circuit.

fractional T1 — Instead of leasing a full T1 connection, customers may decide to lease the less-expensive fractional T1 connections. Connections range from one 64-Kbps channel up to the full T1 connection of 24 channels.

Frame Check Sequence (FCS) — A field in a frame that calculates a checksum for the frame, which is used for error checking.

Frame Relay — A Data Link layer protocol that relies on high-speed, reliable connections; can operate between 56 Kbps and 45 Mbps over a WAN connection.

full-duplex — A connection that allows communication in two directions simultaneously.

half-duplex — A connection that allows communication in two directions, but not simultaneously.

High-level Data Link Control (HDLC) — A superset of the SDLC protocol; a WAN protocol that can be used for both point-to-point and multipoint connections.

Integrated Services Digital Network (ISDN) — A service provided by most major telecommunication carriers, such as AT&T, Sprint, and the RBOCs; operates over existing phone lines and transfers both voice and data.

Internet Engineering Task Force (IETF) — Organization that defines Internet operating protocols; defines the serial line protocols PPP and SLIP.

ISDN modem — A modem used in ISDN communications that must be installed at ISDN subscriber locations.

Link Access Procedure Balanced (LAPB) — A derivative of the HDLC WAN protocol; adapted to provide WAN services over X.25 networks.

Link Access Procedure D-channel (LAPD) — A WAN protocol adapted from HDLC; used in communications over ISDN lines.

local access rate — The speed of the line that indicates transfer rate; common U.S. access rates are 64 Kbps and 128 Kbps, provided by ISDN connections, and 1.544 Mbps, provided by T1 connections.

local loop — The connection between the demarcation and the telephone company (WAN service provider) office.

Local Management Interface (LMI) — A standard signaling mechanism between the CPE and the Frame Relay connection; can provide the network server with a local or global DLCI; can provide keep-alive and status information to the Frame Relay connection.

multiplexed — Combining different traffic streams onto a single physical medium. The traffic is separated (demultiplexed) at the receiving end.

Network Control Protocol (NCP) — A functional field that contains codes, which indicate the type of protocol that is encapsulated; allows PPP to encapsulate multiple protocols including IP, IPX, and AppleTalk.

packet-switched — A WAN connection in which data is broken into smaller packets and then routed to the destination over multiple paths.

permanent virtual circuit (PVC) — A connection to the WAN that is established by the network administrator at the customer location; not expected to be terminated and therefore remains active.

Point-to-Point Protocol (PPP) — An Internet standard WAN protocol defined in RFCs 2153 and 1661; used to provide router-to-router, host-to-router, and host-to-host WAN connections.

Primary Rate Interface (PRI) — An ISDN service that provides 23 B-channels for data transfers up to 1.544 Mbps and one D-channel for controlling communications.

Public Switched Telephone Network (PSTN) — A telecommunications network that connects telephones around the country.

Serial Line Internet Protocol (SLIP) — A protocol that was originally used for IP connections over serial lines. It was replaced by the more efficient and versatile PPP.

simplex — A circuit that is unidirectional is called simplex because data can only be transmitted in one direction.

statistical multiplexing — A method for transmitting several types of data simultaneously across a single line; bandwidth is dynamically allocated to the virtual circuits on a packet-by-packet basis.

switched virtual circuit (SVC) — A temporary virtual circuit created when a network device calls the WAN to establish a connection; is terminated when the connection is terminated.

symmetric DSL — A DSL service that provides equal upload and download speeds.

synchronous — Communications that rely on a clock. The clocks of the source and destination must be synchronized so that the destination can pick up and interpret the transmitted frames correctly.

Synchronous Data Link Control (SDLC) — A protocol that was developed by IBM in the 1970s to allow IBM host systems to communicate over WAN connections; can be used for point-to-point or point-to-multipoint connections between remote devices and a central mainframe.

synchronous serial — The type of serial connection used with ISDN lines.

T1 — A leased line from a telecommunications carrier capable of carrying both voice and data with a 1.544-Mbps bandwidth.

T3 — A leased line from a telecommunications carrier that provides the bandwidth of 28 T1 connections, which equals 44.736 Mbps.

terminal adapter (TA) — An adapter that allows non-ISDN terminals to operate on ISDN lines.

Time Division Multiplexing (TDM) — A method for transmitting several types of data simultaneously across a single line; each path (circuit) has dedicated bandwidth allocated to it for the duration of the call; less efficient than statistical division multiplexing.

toll network — A section of a WAN that is owned by a telecommunications provider; a monthly billed connection or a per-minute billed connection for the customer.

virtual circuit — Point-to-point connections through a switched network.

5

REVIEW QUESTIONS

1. Which of the following WAN services operates over existing telephone lines to provide voice and data communications?

   a. SDLC

   b. Frame Relay

   c. ISDN

   d. ATM

2. Which of the following is true about Frame Relay communication? (Choose all that apply.)

   a. Provides faster communications over WAN links than X.25

   b. Is slightly less efficient than X.25

   c. Uses highly reliable digital facilities

   d. Provides host-to-router and router-to-router communications

3. Which of the following is the provider's end of the WAN link?

   a. DTE

   b. Computer

   c. DCE

   d. Dumb terminal

4. Which two devices would be considered part of the Physical layer for WAN equipment?

   a. Routers and hubs

   b. DTE and DCE

   c. Gateways and hubs

   d. Hubs and switches

5. Which of the following connection types can PPP support? (Choose all that apply.)

   a. Router-to-router

   b. Host-to-router

   c. Host-to-host

   d. Asynchronous

   e. Synchronous

6. Which of the following can HDLC support? (Choose all that apply.)

   a. Point-to-point

   b. Multipoint

   c. Synchronous

   d. Asynchronous

   e. Full-duplex

   f. Half-duplex

7. Which of the following is a data link protocol used for connecting LANs in geographically separate areas? (Choose all that apply.)

   a. TCP

   b. PPP

   c. OSPF

   d. Frame Relay

8. Which of the following data link protocols is most closely associated with the X.25 specification?

   a. LAPB

   b. LAPD

   c. PPP

   d. Frame Relay

9. Which of the following defines how frames are formatted and transmitted between systems on a single WAN link?

    a. Physical layer WAN standards

    b. Data Link layer WAN standards

    c. Network layer WAN standards

    d. Application layer WAN standards

10. In WAN communications, which of the following identifies the device that is located at the user's end of the WAN?

    a. DTE

    b. DCE

    c. CSU/DSU

    d. TA

11. A modem is an example of a DCE in a WAN connection. True or False?

12. Which of the following data link protocols is most closely associated with the ISDN specification?

    a. LAPB

    b. LAPD

    c. PPP

    d. Frame Relay

13. A computer is an example of a DTE in a WAN connection. True or False?

14. Which of the following can make use of ISDN lines? (Choose all that apply.)

    a. Frame Relay

    b. LAPD

    c. X.25

    d. SDLC

15. Which of the following WAN protocols was developed specifically to connect mainframe computers?

    a. PPP

    b. SDLC

    c. Frame Relay

    d. ISDN

16. WAN standards typically provide definitions for which two layers of the OSI model? (Choose all that apply.)

    a. Physical

    b. Data Link

    c. Application

    d. Presentation

    e. Transport

17. Which of the following defines communications that can flow in two directions, but not simultaneously?

    a. Full-duplex

    b. Simplex

    c. Half-duplex

    d. Quarter duplex

18. Which of the following communication methods relies on a timing device?

    a. Synchronous

    b. Asynchronous

    c. Full-duplex

    d. Half-duplex

19. Which of the following organizations was formerly known as CCITT?

    a. Internet Engineering Task Force

    b. International Organization for Standardization

    c. International Telecommunication Union

    d. Electronic Industries Alliance

20. Which of the following standards organizations has defined the RS-232, RS-449, and RS-530 standards?

    a. IETF

    b. ITU-T

    c. ISO

    d. EIA

21. What is the purpose of multiplexing?

   a. To split up a signal into discrete chunks so it can be transported across the WAN

   b. To combine multiple signals onto a single medium

   c. To put packets back in order after they become disorganized during transport

   d. To acknowledge the receipt of packets

22. Which WAN technology can also be used on LANs?

   a. Frame Relay

   b. ISDN

   c. PPP

   d. ATM

5

CASE PROJECTS

**CASE
PROJECTS**

1. It is obvious to Moe that WANs cover a larger area than LANs. He is not sure about the finer differences. Compare the characteristics of WANs and LANs for Moe.

2. The Americanus Corporation is ready to connect its network to the Internet. Jennifer helped set up this 100BaseT network and feels comfortable with the LAN devices. She has no idea how to interface with the Internet. Who usually provides Physical layer connectivity for WAN services? What WAN devices operate at the Physical layer? Who usually owns this equipment? What is the difference between a DTE, a DCE, a CSU/DSU, and a terminal adapter?

3. Lisa thinks that the same protocols operating on LANs are also operating on WANs. Describe some of the WAN protocols operating at the Data Link layer to Lisa. What do these protocols describe?

4. Moe is curious. He dials into his Internet Service Provider (ISP) from home using regular phone lines. His friend has BRI service on an ISDN line. Explain to Moe the differences between these two methods of Internet access. Specifically, what kind of signal is being transmitted, what are the speed limitations, and what constitutes the DCE in each case? Would either of these connections be considered dedicated? What WAN protocols might be in play during a typical Internet session?

6

ROUTER AND IOS BASICS

> **After reading this chapter and completing the exercises, you will be able to:**
>
> ♦ Describe the benefits of network segmentation with routers
>
> ♦ Understand the elements of the Cisco router user interface
>
> ♦ Configure the HyperTerminal program to interface with the Cisco router
>
> ♦ Describe the various router configuration modes
>
> ♦ Describe the various router passwords
>
> ♦ Understand the enhanced editing features of the Cisco IOS
>
> ♦ Understand the elements of the Cisco switch user interface
>
> ♦ Compare router components to typical PC components

This chapter revisits the benefits of routing. You will learn about the elements of the Cisco user interface, including the system configuration dialog, various configuration modes, and the many Cisco router passwords. You will also configure the Windows program HyperTerminal for use with the router. In addition, the enhanced editing features of the Cisco IOS and router components will be explored.

BENEFITS OF ROUTING

As previous chapters explained, network administrators use routers in large networks to provide packet filtering, connections between local networks, traffic control, and wide area network (WAN) connections. Routers operate at the Network layer of the OSI reference model and because of Network layer addressing, routers can direct packets to both local and remote segments.

One of the main benefits of using a router is that it filters traffic. When a device sends a packet on the local segment, all other devices on that segment must receive or discard the packet. Bridges can segment the network at the Data Link layer, but broadcast traffic from one segment to another must still pass through the bridge because the bridge cannot distinguish addresses above layer 2. In a large network composed of one giant segment, this broadcast traffic could seriously affect performance. Routers solve the problem by filtering traffic and forwarding only packets that are addressed to hosts on other networks. In this way, routers reduce traffic by segmenting the network and filtering broadcasts. Said another way, routers create collision domains as well as broadcast domains.

When network administrators add routers to a network, they must configure those routers to operate within the network. To perform routine maintenance and troubleshooting, network operators and administrators must be able to check the status of the router and its components. This necessary interaction with the router requires an interface through which the routers can be configured.

CISCO ROUTER USER INTERFACE

Network administrators commonly configure and interact with a Cisco router via the **Cisco Internetwork Operating System (IOS)**. The Cisco IOS provides a command-line interface (CLI), which allows network operators to check the status of the router and network administrators to manage and configure the router. The software that interprets the commands is called the **command executive**, or **EXEC**.

A router can be accessed in several different ways. Each of these methods involves access through one of three lines. Network administrators typically access the router directly through the **console port** (also known as the **console**) located on the back of the router. The console port connects directly to a PC through an **RJ-45 to RJ-45 rollover cable** with an **RJ-45 to DB-9** or **RJ-45 to DB-25** connector included with the router. Whether you select the DB-9 or DB-25 connector will depend on the type of port on the back of the PC. The second line used to access the router is through the **auxiliary port (AUX)**, which is also on the back of the router. The auxiliary port allows a remote administrator to dial into the router through an external modem, which gets attached to the auxiliary port. The remote PC must also have a modem to use this method.

Figure 6-1 shows a laptop connected to a Cisco 2500 series router via the console port using the RJ-45 to RJ-45 rollover cable and RJ-45 to DB-9 connector. The DB-9 is attached to the COM1 port of the laptop in the picture.

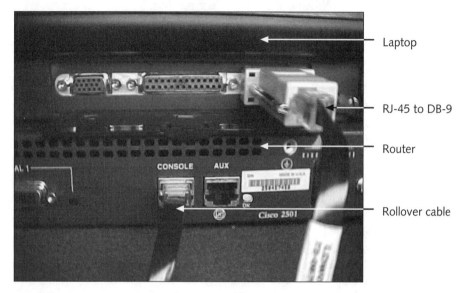

Figure 6-1   Connecting a PC to the console

In addition to the AUX and the console ports, five **virtual terminals (VTY)** can be used to configure the router. When you access the router through VTY lines, you are using telnet. The virtual terminals are numbered from zero to four. You can reference the virtual terminals by their abbreviation and numeric indicators: VTY 0, VTY 1, VTY 2, VTY 3, and VTY 4. Network administrators access the virtual terminals through a telnet session.

In addition to configuration through access via the AUX, console, or virtual terminals, the router can obtain configuration information from a **Trivial File Transfer Protocol (TFTP) server**. The router configuration information can be stored as a file on a TFTP server and can be downloaded to configure the router. (The process is described later in this chapter.) Also, network administrators can use network management software such as HP OpenView or CiscoWorks to manage Cisco routers. Figure 6-2 illustrates different methods for accessing a router for configuration purposes.

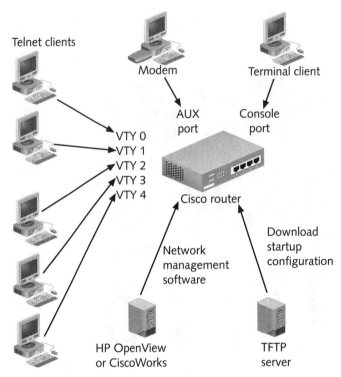

Figure 6-2 Methods for configuring a Cisco router

Connecting via Terminal Programs

When configuring the router through the console or AUX ports, you must first make the physical connection. Then, you can access the router through a terminal program. There are many different terminal programs that you can use, including HyperTerminal, MicroPhone Pro, ProComm Plus, Telix, Teraterm, and Terminal on Microsoft DOS and Windows systems; Kermit and Tip on Sun Workstations; Z-terminal on Apple Macintosh computers; and Minicom on Linux systems. For example, if the connection from the router to the PC attaches at the COM1 port on the PC, you would configure your terminal program to use COM1. HyperTerminal is available in Windows operating systems from Windows 95 and later.

You can use the following steps to configure HyperTerminal:

1. Open the HyperTerminal application. In Microsoft Windows XP and Windows 2000, you should find HyperTerminal in the Programs/ Accessories/Communications group in the Start menu. If you cannot find HyperTerminal, you may have to install additional Accessories programs from the Add/Remove Programs icon in the Control Panel of your Microsoft Windows system. In Microsoft Windows XP, click **Start** and navigate to **All Programs**, **Accessories**, **Communications**, and **HyperTerminal**.

2. Create a new connection. If the New Connection Wizard does not appear automatically, click **File** on the menu bar, and then click **New Connection**.

3. Enter a name for the connection. The name is for user reference only, so you can use any name that describes the connection. Click **OK** to continue.

4. You must then configure how you will connect to the router via the Connect To dialog box (you may be prompted to install a modem). You will see a field to enter a phone number. If you are connecting to the router through the AUX port, you would provide the router phone number here. If connecting to the router through the console port, click the "Connect using" list box and choose the COM port to which the RJ-45 to DB-9 or DB-25 connector is attached. Click **OK** to continue.

5. Configure the following settings for the COM port: Bits per second, **9600**; Data bits, **8**; Stop bits, **1**; Parity, **None**; Flow control, **None**. Click **OK** to complete the configuration. Click **File** on the menu bar, and then click **Properties**. Under Settings, make sure the keys are set to act as "Terminal" keys.

When the HyperTerminal configuration is complete, the program will attempt to connect to the router. At this point, you would turn on the router. On the screen, you should then see the router boot routine. Sometimes it is necessary to press Enter a few times to get a response from the router.

NOTE
If you see a series of miscellaneous characters after you turn on the router, you probably have incorrectly set the bits per second (also known as baud rate). Click File on the menu bar, click Properties, and reconfigure your connection as described previously.

When the router boots, it should eventually show a prompt, such as **router>**, or you may be prompted to enter the **system configuration dialog** (also known as the initial configuration dialog), which is an automated setup routine described next.

System Configuration Dialog

If the router hasn't been configured previously, or if the startup file has been erased, the Cisco IOS will prompt you to run the initial configuration dialog after the router boots. You can also access the system configuration dialog by typing the setup command at the privileged EXEC prompt. The system configuration dialog presents a series of prompts that guide you through the initial configuration for the router. Each question is followed by a default option in brackets. If you decide to accept the default option, you can press the Enter key. Beginning with version 12.0 of the IOS, there are two different levels of setup: basic management setup and extended setup. Basic management setup only configures enough connectivity for management of the system. Extended setup prompts you for configuration of all interfaces and provides enough configuration information to make the router operational.

The first question you are asked by the system configuration dialog is whether you want to enter the initial configuration dialog. If you type "y", you will begin the router configuration process. The next question is, "Would you like to enter basic management setup?" If you press "y" you will enter basic management setup. If you answer "n" you will enter extended setup mode. Figure 6-3 illustrates use of the setup command.

After the system configuration dialog program completes, the router will run through its typical startup process (which is described in greater detail later in this chapter). After this initialization process, you can begin to view and configure the router settings.

```
lab-a#setup


        --- System Configuration Dialog ---

Continue with configuration dialog? [yes/no]: y

At any point you may enter a question mark '?' for help.
Use ctrl-c to abort configuration dialog at any prompt.
Default settings are in square brackets '[]'.


Basic management setup configures only enough connectivity
for management of the system, extended setup will ask you
to configure each interface on the system.

Would you like to enter basic management setup? [yes/no]: y
Configuring global parameters:

  Enter host name [lab-a]:
```

Figure 6-3   Output from the setup command

User Interface

When the router completes its initialization process, you must press the Return or Enter key to reach the prompt. The initial prompt consists of two parts: the host name of the router followed by the greater than symbol (>). By default, the router's host name is router, so the default prompt is router>.

When the prompt displayed is the greater than symbol, the router is in **user EXEC mode** (or **user mode**). In this mode the network operator can check router status to see if the interfaces are operational, and review several of the router settings. From any prompt, you can see a list of possible commands at that prompt by typing a question mark (?), as shown in Figure 6-4. You do not need to press Enter after typing the question mark.

The question mark activates **context-sensitive Help** on the Cisco router. The term context-sensitive means that the router evaluates the command mode that you are in, and any command strings you have entered on the line prior to the question mark, before providing the Help screen. For example, when you are in user mode and type the question mark, the Help that follows will be commands available from user mode. However, if you type "ping ?", you will get a list of options you can use with the ping command.

NOTE   When the list of Help screen options does not fit on one screen, Help displays only the first screen of options. You can view additional commands line-by-line by pressing the Enter or Return key for each line. You can page through the list of commands by pressing the space bar. Pressing a letter on the keyboard will take you immediately back to the prompt.

```
RouterB(config)#?
Configure commands:
aaa                      Authentication, Authorization and Accounting.
access-list              Add an access list entry
alias                    Create command alias
arp                      Set a static ARP entry
async-bootp              Modify system bootp parameters
banner                   Define a login banner
boot                     Modify system boot parameters
bridge                   Bridging Group.
buffers                  Adjust system buffer pool parameters
busy-message             Display message when connection to host fails
cdp                      Global CDP configuration subcommands
chat-script              Define a modem chat script
clock                    Configure time-of-day clock
config-register          Define the configuration register
default-value            Default character-bits values
dialer-list              Create a dialer list entry
dnsix-dmdp               Provide DMDP service for DNSIX
dnsix-nat                Provide DNSIX service for audit trails
downward-compatible-config Generate a configuration compatible with older
                         software
enable                   Modify enable password parameters
end                      Exit from configure mode
exit                     Exit from configure mode
frame-relay              global frame relay configuration commands
help                     Description of the interactive help system
hostname                 Set system's network name
interface                Select an interface to configure
ip                       Global IP configuration subcommands
ipx                      Novell/IPX global configuration commands
key                      Key management
line                     Configure a terminal line
logging                  Modify message logging facilities
login-string             Define a host-specific login string
map-class                Configure static map class
map-list                 Configure static map list
menu                     Define a user-interface menu
modemcap                 Modem Capabilities database
netbios                  NETBIOS access control filtering
no                       Negate a command or set its defaults
ntp                      Configure NTP
partition                Partition device
priority-list            Build a priority list
privilege                Command privilege parameters
prompt                   Set system's prompt
queue-list               Build a custom queue list
resume-string            Define a host-specific resume string
rlogin                   Rlogin configuration commands
rmon                     Remote Monitoring
route-map                Create route-map or enter route-map command mode
router                   Enable a routing process
scheduler                Scheduler parameters
service                  Modify use of network based services
snmp-server              Modify SNMP parameters
state-machine            Define a TCP dispatch state machine
tacacs-server            Modify TACACS query parameters
terminal-queue           Terminal queue commands
tftp-server              Provide TFTP service for netload requests
username                 Establish User Name Authentication
x25                      X.25 Level 3
x29                      X29 commands

RouterB(config)#
```

Typing a ? invokes the Help system of the IOS. In this case, all commands available in global configuration mode are displayed.

6

Figure 6-4 Output from the ? command

User mode does not allow you to configure the router. To do this, you must go into the **privileged EXEC mode**. To enter privileged EXEC, you can type the enable command at the user mode prompt. Next, you may be prompted for a password. If an enable password has been configured, you must enter it. As you type, the password will not be displayed on the terminal screen. If an enable secret password has been configured, then you will type the enable secret password. The different types of passwords are described in greater detail later in this chapter.

After you enter the enable password or the enable secret password, the greater than symbol (>) changes to a pound sign (#) to indicate that you are in privileged EXEC mode (**router#**). Most router configuration takes place in router modes beyond privileged EXEC mode; however, you can do a few things at this prompt to substantially affect router operations:

- Setup—The setup command will cause the router to enter the system configuration dialog, which allows the router to be completely reconfigured.

- Copy—Configurations can be copied from TFTP servers to the router and therefore change the router configuration.

- Erase—Configuration files as well as the entire IOS can be erased.

Privileged EXEC mode is called **enable mode** because you must enter the enable command to access it.

Configuration Modes

Several configuration modes are accessible only through the privileged EXEC mode. This section discusses some of these basic **router configuration modes** and their respective options.

After you have placed the router into enable mode, you will be able to choose from various router configuration options. From the **enable mode prompt** (router#), you can view the router's configuration and access several other configuration modes. You access the basic configuration mode, called **global configuration mode**, by typing "configure terminal" at the enable mode prompt.

From the global configuration mode, you can access several other configuration modes. For example, **interface configuration mode** allows you to configure the Ethernet and serial interfaces on your router. With **line configuration mode**, you can configure the virtual terminals, console, and AUX lines that let you access the router. Router configuration mode permits you to enable routing protocols such as RIP and IGRP. Table 6-1 lists these modes, the associated prompt, the method for entry and exit, and a brief description of what you can accomplish in each mode.

Table 6-1   Common configuration modes

Mode	Prompt	To enter	To exit	Used for
User EXEC	Router>	If there is a line password, enter it. Otherwise, press the Return or Enter key.	Logout or Exit	Shows the status of the router and allows network operators to manage connections
Privileged EXEC	Router#	Type enable at the prompt.	Disable Exit Logout	Copies, erases, sets up, and shows router settings
Global configuration	Router (config)#	Configure	Exit End	Allows you to configure various items, including clock, host name, enable password, and enable secret password
Interface configuration	Router (config-if)#	Interface Ethernet0/0 or Interface Serial0/0	Exit End	Allows you to configure the settings, such as IP, for a specific interface
Line configuration	Router (config-line)#	Line console 0 or Line vty 0 4 or Line aux 0	Exit End	Configures lines, such as the console, virtual terminal, or auxiliary
Router configuration	Router (config-router)#	Router rip or Router igrp	Exit End	Adds or configures RIP, IGRP, or other routing protocols

6

Typing "exit" will take you back one level. For example, if your prompt shows "router(config-router)#" and you type "exit", your prompt will change to "router(config)#". Typing "end" or pressing the Ctrl+Z keys will take you all the way back to the enable prompt. For example, if you see "router(config-line)#" and you type "end", your prompt will revert to "router#", not "router(config)#". Note that if you are typing commands and you see the dollar sign "$", it means that the line is continued from a previous line.

NOTE   All the commands shown in the table can be abbreviated. Usually, the abbreviation for a command is the fewest number of characters that can be used to uniquely identify the command. For example, to enter the enable mode, you can type "enable", or "en". (You can also type "enab" and "enabl".) On simulation questions on the CCNA exam, make sure to type the entire command, without abbreviations.

Often, you can discover abbreviated commands by simply trying them. If the command does not work, the router will tell you that the command is invalid. If you get part of the command correct, the router will show you the point at which you entered an incorrect character by pointing to the character with a caret symbol (^). For example, to show the current running configuration of the router, you can type "show running-config". However, if you accidentally type "show runing-config", the router will indicate that the command is incorrect by pointing to the first incorrect character. In Figure 6-5, the first incorrect character is the letter "i".

```
router#show runing-config
                 ^
% Invalid input detected at '^' marker.

router#
```

Figure 6-5   Command error checking

 Using the shortcut for the show running-config command, which is "sh ru", reduces the chance of making a typo.

NOTE

Once you have a basic understanding of the commands presented in Table 6-1, you are ready to start practicing basic router configuration tasks. One of the first areas that you might want to investigate is password configuration.

Plethora of Passwords

Five passwords can be set on a Cisco router. If you configure the router using the system configuration dialog (setup), you will be prompted for three of these five: the enable password, the enable secret password, and the **virtual terminal password**. You can add a **console password**, an **AUX line password**, and an individual password for each virtual terminal.

Table 6-2 lists and describes these router passwords.

Table 6-2   Router passwords

Enable	Used only when the enable secret password is not present. This password is not encrypted, but it does restrict access to enable mode if the enable secret password is removed.
Enable Secret	This is the primary password used to access enable mode because it supersedes the enable password. When the enable secret password is configured, only the enable secret password (not the enable password) allows you to access enable mode. This enable secret password is encrypted with the **MD5 algorithm**, which has no known method of reversal.

Table 6-2   Router passwords (continued)

Console	Protects the router from console access. When this password is set, someone attempting to access the router from the console connection will have to enter a password before he or she can enter any other commands. This password is not configured by default during setup.
AUX	The AUX line can also have a password configured. This password is requested whenever someone attempts to access the router by a modem through the AUX port. This password is not configured by default during setup.
Virtual Terminal	The router identifies each telnet session as a virtual terminal. You can configure a password for any number of virtual terminals or each one individually. Usually, a five-session limit is put on the router. If you type VTY 0 4 when configuring the password, you will be setting a single password for the five virtual terminals. To configure a password for a single virtual terminal, type VTY followed by the terminal number.

If you have an enable secret password set, you may see it as a string of miscellaneous characters when viewing your router configuration. Do not mistake those characters for the actual password; they are just a representation of an encrypted password.

If you want to configure encryption for all of your router passwords, type "service password-encryption" at the global configuration prompt.

TIP

In the following sections, you will learn how to configure each of the passwords shown in Table 6-2.

Enable Password and Enable Secret Password Configuration

Both the **enable password** and **enable secret password** can be set from the global configuration mode prompt, which is router(config)#. To add or change the enable password or enable secret password, simply type the name of the password you want to configure and follow it with the password you want to set.

Figure 6-6 illustrates the steps to configure the enable password and enable secret password from the terminal.

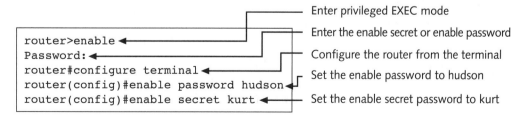

```
router>enable ◄──────────────────────┐
Password: ◄───────────────────────┐
router#configure terminal ◄────────┐
router(config)#enable password hudson◄┘
router(config)#enable secret kurt ◄───
```

— Enter privileged EXEC mode
— Enter the enable secret or enable password
— Configure the router from the terminal
— Set the enable password to hudson
— Set the enable secret password to kurt

Figure 6-6   Setting enable password and enable secret password

Because it is encrypted, the enable secret password is more secure than the enable password. The enable password can be viewed from the configuration file, but the encrypted enable secret password cannot. To see the difference, type "show running-config" or "show run" at the enable mode prompt and read the configuration file, as shown in Figure 6-7.

```
RouterB#show run
Building configuration...
Current configuration:
!
version 11.1
service udp-small-servers
service tcp-small-servers
!
hostname RouterB
!
enable secret 5 $1$RHhg$ngXce3OBeC7GprpPjtqsP1

enable password stuff

!
ipx routing 0060.474f.6506
!
interface Ethernet0
 ip address 172.22.2.1 255.255.255.0
 ipx access-group 800 out
 ipx network 300
!
interface Serial0
 no ip address
!
interface Serial1
 ip address 172.22.3.2 255.255.255.0
!
router rip
 network 172.22.0.0
!
no ip classless
access-list 800 deny 300 500
access-list 800 permit FFFFFFFF FFFFFFFF
!
!
!
!
line con 0
 password cisco
 login
line vty 0 4
 password password
 login
!
end

RouterB#
```

The enable secret password is stored in an encrypted form for increased security

The enable password is stored as plain text and can pose a security risk

Figure 6-7 The enable password and enable secret password

If you want to remove the enable secret password, you can type "no enable secret" at the global configuration mode prompt. You can also type "no enable password" to remove the enable password. Of course, if you remove both the enable secret and enable password, the router can be configured by anyone who can log on.

To configure the console line, AUX line, and virtual terminal passwords, you must be in a line configuration mode, as the next section discusses.

Setting Line Passwords

Line passwords are the first line of defense against unauthorized intrusion into the router. You can set passwords for each line used to configure the router. As mentioned previously, these lines are the console line, the AUX line, and each of the five virtual terminal lines. By default, the virtual terminal passwords can be configured if you use the initial router setup process, but all virtual terminals are set for the same password.

One of the first passwords you might want to configure is the console line password. To configure a console password, you must enter line configuration mode. Figure 6-8 illustrates the process for configuring a console line password.

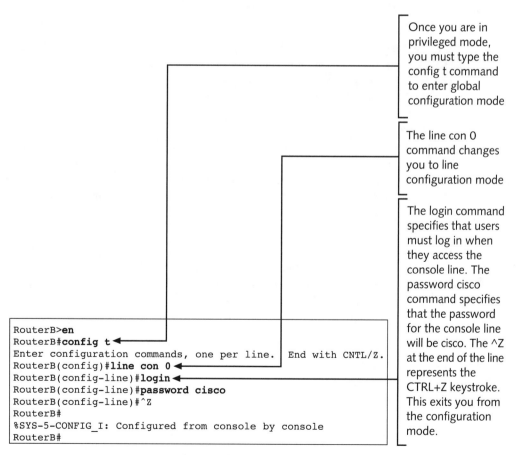

Once you are in privileged mode, you must type the config t command to enter global configuration mode

The line con 0 command changes you to line configuration mode

The login command specifies that users must log in when they access the console line. The password cisco command specifies that the password for the console line will be cisco. The ^Z at the end of the line represents the CTRL+Z keystroke. This exits you from the configuration mode.

```
RouterB>en
RouterB#config t
Enter configuration commands, one per line.   End with CNTL/Z.
RouterB(config)#line con 0
RouterB(config-line)#login
RouterB(config-line)#password cisco
RouterB(config-line)#^Z
RouterB#
%SYS-5-CONFIG_I: Configured from console by console
RouterB#
```

Figure 6-8   Applying a console password

After you have added the password to the console, you can check it by exiting line configuration mode and logging off the terminal. When you then attempt to log on to the terminal, you will be prompted for a password, as shown in Figure 6-9.

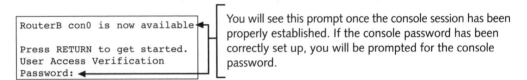

```
RouterB con0 is now available

Press RETURN to get started.
User Access Verification
Password:
```

You will see this prompt once the console session has been properly established. If the console password has been correctly set up, you will be prompted for the console password.

Figure 6-9   Console password example

You can also configure passwords on the five virtual terminal lines that exist on every router, in much the same way as on the console port. In fact, you must configure a VTY password if you want to enable access via telnet. This is a safety precaution; without it, anyone with the IP address of the router will be able to access it. To configure the VTY password, go into line configuration mode on the router for the VTY lines and add the login and password commands. Figure 6-10 shows the process of applying a VTY password.

If you just wanted to set an individual VTY password for VTY line 0, you would have typed "line vty 0" instead of "line vty 0 4" at the RouterB(config)# prompt shown in Figure 6-10. The same is true for any other VTY port; they are individually numbered 0, 1, 2, 3, and 4 (five lines total).

NOTE

Passwords can be placed on auxiliary ports in the same way they are placed on console or vty ports. Using all three of these passwords will at least slow down someone trying to enter your routers. If they happen to get through these passwords, the single most important password, the enable or enable secret password (depending on which one is in use) can stop them from actually modifying the router's configuration.

Enhanced Editing

By default, the router supports enhanced editing features that allow you to modify lengthy commands. The enhanced editing commands let you jump to the beginning or end of a command line. You can also jump ahead or behind, character by character, or word by word. Table 6-3 shows the shortcuts and the definitions.

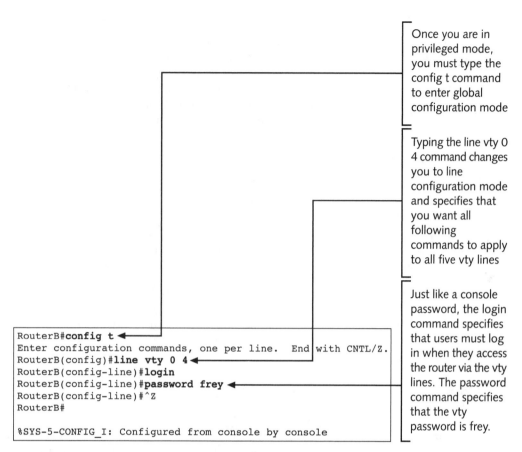

Figure 6-10 Applying a VTY password

Table 6-3 Editing commands

Key combination	Description
Ctrl+A	Moves the cursor to the beginning of the current line.
Ctrl+E	Moves the cursor to the end of the current line.
Ctrl+F	Moves the cursor one character to the right. You can also accomplish this by pressing the right arrow key.
Ctrl+B	Moves the cursor one character to the left. You can also accomplish this by pressing the left arrow key.
Esc+F	Moves the cursor one word forward.
Esc+B	Moves the cursor one word back.

You can turn off the enhanced editing features by typing "terminal no editing" at either the user EXEC or the privileged EXEC prompts. You can turn on terminal editing by typing "terminal editing".

When you type an incorrect command, the bogus command might be mistaken for a host name. If this happens, the router will, by default, attempt to look up the host name and give you the corresponding IP address. If you want to prevent the router from doing this, type "no ip domain-lookup" from the global configuration prompt. To cancel any command or process, press the Ctrl, Shift, and 6 keys simultaneously. You may also have to let go of those keys and then press the X key to initiate the escape sequence on some routers.

Command History

The command history allows you to retrieve previously typed commands. You can see up to 10 previously typed commands by typing "show history" from either the user EXEC or privileged EXEC mode. You can use the up arrow (or press Ctrl+P) to retrieve previous commands. The down arrow (or Ctrl+N) will retrieve recent commands, assuming that you are viewing previous commands. If you type part of a command, you can press the Tab key to complete the command.

To modify the number of commands stored by the router, you can use the terminal command. You can set the history buffer to zero so that it won't store commands, or you can set it to store up to 256 previous commands. For example, to decrease the number of commands stored from the default of 10 to three, you would type "terminal history size 3" at the enable prompt.

Configuring Router Identification

You can identify your router in several ways. The most obvious is the router host name. The default host name is simply "router", which is displayed at the beginning of every prompt. The command for configuring the host name for the router must be typed in global configuration mode. If you want to set the router host name, type "hostname" followed by the name that you want to set. For example, to set the router's name to router57, type "hostname router57".

Another way to configure identification for the router is to configure a banner. A banner is a message that you can configure to display each time someone attempts to log in to the router. To configure the banner, you must first enter global configuration mode by typing "router(config#)"; then type "banner motd", followed by a space and a delimiting character. Note that "motd" stands for "message of the day", and the delimiting character can be any keyboard letter or symbol.

When you type the delimiting character in a banner configuration, the router will interpret the character as the end of the banner; therefore, it is best to use a delimiting character that won't be typed in your banner message. A typical character used for delimiting the banner message is the pound symbol (#).

Banner motd is typically used as a legal means of warning anyone who accesses the banner that they will be held accountable.

Figure 6-11 illustrates the configuration process for a banner page.

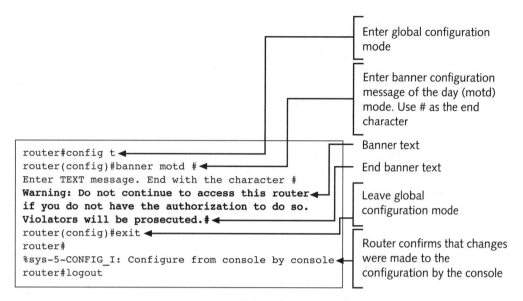

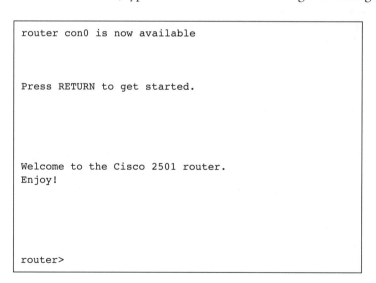

Figure 6-11   Configuring a banner message

Notice that once the delimiting character is typed, the router assumes that the banner message is complete. To see the banner message, log out and attempt to log on to the router. Figure 6-12 illustrates how the banner message in this section's example would look. To remove the banner, type "no banner motd" at the global configuration prompt.

```
router con0 is now available


Press RETURN to get started.




Welcome to the Cisco 2501 router.
Enjoy!



router>
```

Figure 6-12   Banner message displayed

Another method of identifying router components is to configure an interface description. You can configure a description for each of the interfaces physically attached to your router by using the description command. The interface description helps you remember which network the interface services. For example, if you wanted to configure a description for the Ethernet0 interface to remind you that it is connected to the Department A LAN, you would type commands similar to those shown in Figure 6-13.

```
router#config t
router(config)#interface e0/0
router(config-if)#description Attached to Dept A LAN
```

Figure 6-13   Configuring an interface description

After you have configured the description for the interface, return to the basic privileged EXEC prompt (router#) and type "show interfaces" to check your work. The description for Ethernet0 should now have the text you typed.

Configuring the Time and Date

Another basic configuration task is to configure the router's time clock and time zone. Use the clock set command in enable mode to configure the time. You must be in global configuration mode to configure the time zone. The commands in Figure 6-14 show how to configure the time zone, the time, and the date.

```
router#config t
router(config)#clock timezone pacific -8
router(config)#exit
%SYS-5-CONFIG_I: Configured from console by console
router#clock set 02:46:10 29 August 2003
```

Figure 6-14   Configuring the time and date

When entering the time zone, you must include the name of the time zone and the offset from the **Universal Time Code (UTC)**. The UTC is based on the time in Greenwich, a city in the United Kingdom. All other time zones are either plus or minus a certain number of hours. For example, Eastern Standard Time is minus five, or five hours earlier than in Greenwich. After you have configured the time zone, you can configure the clock. If you configure the time zone and clock in the opposite order, your clock will change after you configure the time zone. To confirm your settings, type "show clock" at the privileged EXEC prompt.

SWITCH USER INTERFACE

Two types of operating systems are in use on Cisco switches: IOS-based and set-based. Switches that use IOS-based commands are Cisco Catalyst 1900, 2820, and 2900 switches. A set-based system is older and uses "set" commands at the command line interface. Cisco 1984G, 2926, 4000, 5000, and 6000 series switches employ the set-based configuration commands. In this book, the focus is on commands specific to the Catalyst IOS-based operating system because that is the switch type that appears on the CCNA exam. Basic IOS-based configuration is covered in this section. If your 1900 switch has the Standard edition of the IOS, you do not have the option of using commands at the command line interface. You will have to upgrade to the Enterprise version of the software or use the menu-driven interface to configure the switch.

You will receive additional configuration instructions for the Catalyst 1900 in future chapters, as appropriate.

REFERENCE

You can connect to a Cisco switch in the same way you connect to a Cisco router, as shown earlier in Figure 6-1. The Cisco switch has a console port to which you can connect your laptop or PC. Once you power on the switch, a menu appears on your terminal program. The Catalyst 1900 menu includes the following options:

    [M] Menus

    [K] Command Line

    [I] IP Configuration

You simply press the appropriate key (M, K, or I) on the keyboard to begin configuring the switch. In the following sections and in other chapters, you'll learn the command line configuration methods for the Catalyst 1900. The command line interface is the focus because you can configure anything from it, and the CCNA exam focuses on it.

Modes and Passwords

You've already learned that enable mode is how you can actually make configuration changes on a Cisco router. The same is true for a Cisco switch with an IOS-based operating system. To enter enable mode, you can simply type enable at the command line prompt > and then press Enter. The prompt then changes to the pound (#) symbol and you are in enable mode (assuming a password hasn't been set yet). As a matter of fact, the next thing you should do is configure a password. To do so you must enter configuration mode by typing "configure terminal" (or an abbreviated version of the command such as config term or conf t), which is the same command to enter global configuration mode on a router. Once there you can set the enable password, which is different from doing so on a Cisco router.

You can set the user mode password or enable mode password from the (config)# prompt. For example, if you type "enable password level ?", you will see that you can enter 1 through 15 to pick your password level. The level chosen dictates what commands can be used. Level 1 is for the user mode password and 15 is for the enable mode password (each must be four to eight characters). These passwords are all encrypted. Just like the router, you can also set an enable secret password, which usurps the enable password. The enable secret password also provides for levels 1 through 15. In addition, you can choose to use an encrypted or unencrypted secret password. To illustrate the configuration of passwords on a Catalyst 1900 switch, assume that you want a user-level password to be *viewonly,* the enable password to be *ccnafix,* and an encrypted enable secret password to be *ccnasafe.*

> (config)#**enable password level 1 viewonly**

> (config)#**enable password level 15 ccnafix**

> (config)#**enable secret ccnasafe**

Setting the Host Name

The actual task of setting the host name on the Cisco Catalyst 1900 is identical to setting the host name on a Cisco router. As with the router, the host name is only locally significant, so the function of the name is to identify the switch, not to provide any sort of Internet name resolution. The best idea is to set the name to identify the location of the switch. For example, if you worked for a company named HudLogic, Inc. and its switch was on the fourth floor of Room 410, you might name the switch Rm410HL, which stands for Room 410 HudLogic. To configure this, you would type:

> (config)#**hostname Rm410HL**

> Rm410HL(config)#

Once the host name is set, the prompt will change to reflect the name of the switch, as shown above.

ROUTER COMPONENTS

A router is a computer and has many of the same hardware components that a typical PC does. This section discusses the hardware elements of the router, including:

- ROM
- Flash memory
- NVRAM
- RAM/DRAM
- Interfaces

6

ROM

Read-only memory (ROM) loads the **bootstrap** program that initializes the router's basic hardware components. ROM is not modified during normal operations, but it can be upgraded with special plug-in chips. The content of ROM is maintained even when the router is rebooted, which is similar to how ROM operates on a PC.

The ROM monitor firmware runs when the router is turned on or rebooted. You can configure new passwords with ROM monitor if password recovery is necessary. You can also download new software to the router using ROM monitor. You know that you are in **ROM monitor mode** when the prompt is just the greater than sign (>) or the greater than sign preceded by rommon 1 or something similar (rommon 1>).

Flash Memory

Flash memory is erasable, programmable, read-only memory (EPROM). This means that flash memory is not typically modified during normal operations; however, it can be upgraded or erased when necessary. The content of flash memory is maintained even when the router is rebooted.

Flash memory contains the working copy of the current Cisco IOS and is the component that initializes the IOS for normal router operations. Flash memory on certain series of Cisco routers can store multiple versions of the IOS, which can make upgrading the IOS easier and safer. For example, if an upgrade to the IOS is implemented, but later found undesirable or difficult to use, the router can be configured to use the original copy of the IOS. The show version command displayed in Figure 6-15 provides a summary of IOS information.

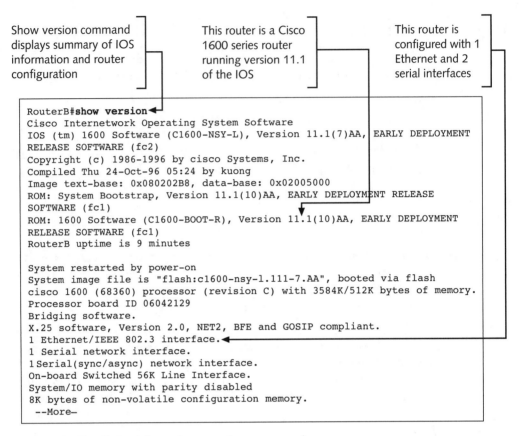

Show version command displays summary of IOS information and router configuration

This router is a Cisco 1600 series router running version 11.1 of the IOS

This router is configured with 1 Ethernet and 2 serial interfaces

```
RouterB#show version
Cisco Internetwork Operating System Software
IOS (tm) 1600 Software (C1600-NSY-L), Version 11.1(7)AA, EARLY DEPLOYMENT
RELEASE SOFTWARE (fc2)
Copyright (c) 1986-1996 by cisco Systems, Inc.
Compiled Thu 24-Oct-96 05:24 by kuong
Image text-base: 0x080202B8, data-base: 0x02005000
ROM: System Bootstrap, Version 11.1(10)AA, EARLY DEPLOYMENT RELEASE
SOFTWARE (fc1)
ROM: 1600 Software (C1600-BOOT-R), Version 11.1(10)AA, EARLY DEPLOYMENT
RELEASE SOFTWARE (fc1)
RouterB uptime is 9 minutes

System restarted by power-on
System image file is "flash:c1600-nsy-1.111-7.AA", booted via flash
cisco 1600 (68360) processor (revision C) with 3584K/512K bytes of memory.
Processor board ID 06042129
Bridging software.
X.25 software, Version 2.0, NET2, BFE and GOSIP compliant.
1 Ethernet/IEEE 802.3 interface.
1 Serial network interface.
1 Serial(sync/async) network interface.
On-board Switched 56K Line Interface.
System/IO memory with parity disabled
8K bytes of non-volatile configuration memory.
 --More-
```

Figure 6-15   Output from show version command

NVRAM

Nonvolatile random access memory (NVRAM) is a special type of RAM that is not cleared when the router is rebooted. The startup configuration file for the router is stored in NVRAM by default. When the router is first shipped, the configuration file is not present. This is the first file created by the person who sets up the router.

NVRAM stores all the user-defined configuration information for the router, which can include the host name of the router, the protocol configurations, and the cache configurations.

The Cisco IOS uses the configuration file in NVRAM during the router boot process, which is explained in the next chapter. Whenever the configuration of the router is updated, the administrator copies the running configuration, which is the one that has just been updated, to the startup configuration. The startup configuration is maintained in NVRAM, whereas the running configuration is maintained in RAM/DRAM.

RAM/DRAM

Random access memory (RAM), also known as **dynamic random access memory (DRAM),** is a **volatile** hardware component because its information is not maintained in the event of a router reboot. This is similar to how RAM operates in a PC. RAM/DRAM contains the working or running copy of the configuration file. During normal operations, changes to the router's running configuration take place in RAM/DRAM.

The IOS contains commands to view each of the router's components. To view the contents of RAM, you can issue one of several commands (because several components reside in RAM). One of the most common commands is the show running-config command. With this command, you can view the current configuration that is running in RAM, as illustrated in Figure 6-16. Two other common commands that can show the contents of RAM are the show memory and show buffers commands. Because they produce long, detailed output, their output has not been included in this text.

Another very useful command is the show startup-config command. With this command you can display the current startup configuration file on the router, which is stored in NVRAM. An administrator who wants to ensure that changes are maintained, even if the system is rebooted, must copy the running configuration to the startup configuration. The command to do this is as follows:

Copy running-config startup-config

This command can be abbreviated as follows:

Cop ru st

These commands copy the configuration changes from RAM/DRAM to NVRAM. When the router is rebooted, the IOS will implement these changes through the startup-configuration file. If you want to combine your running configuration with the startup configuration stored in NVRAM, you can type "copy startup-config running-config" at the privileged EXEC mode prompt.

Interfaces

A router can ship with a variety of configurable interfaces. A common interface is Ethernet0, which is used to connect the router to an Ethernet LAN. Although this chapter focuses on the Ethernet, serial, console, and auxiliary interfaces, the router can have other types of interfaces, including:

- Token Ring
- Basic Rate Interface (BRI)
- Asynchronous Transfer Mode (ATM)
- Fiber Distributed Data Interface (FDDI)
- Channel Interface Processor (CIP) for System Network Architecture (SNA)
- High-Speed Serial Interface (HSSI)

```
RouterB#show running-config
Building configuration...

Current configuration:
!
version 11.1
service udp-small-servers
service tcp-small-servers
!
hostname RouterB
!
enable secret 5 $1$RHhg$ngXce3OBeC7GprpPjtqsP1
!
ipx routing 0060.474f.6506
!
interface Ethernet0
 ip address 172.22.2.1 255.255.255.0
 ipx access-group 800 out
 ipx network 300
!
interface Serial0
 no ip address
!
interface Serial1
 ip address 172.22.3.2 255.255.255.0
!
router rip
 network 172.22.0.0
!
no ip classless
access-list 800 deny 300 500
access-list 800 permit FFFFFFFF FFFFFFFF
!
!
!
!
line con 0
line vty 0 4
 password password
 login
!
end

RouterB#
```

Show running-config command shows the configuration currently running in RAM on a router

This router is configured to route both IPX and IP traffic

This router is using the RIP routing protocol. RIP is discussed further in Chapter 8.

Figure 6-16 Output from show running-config command

You can view all of the configured interfaces for your router with the show interfaces command, as shown in Figure 6–17.

Configuration options for the Ethernet and serial interfaces are covered in Chapter 7. The configuration options for the other interfaces are beyond the scope of this text.

REFERENCE

```
RouterB#show interfaces

Ethernet0 is up, line protocol is up
   Hardware is QUICC Ethernet, address is 0060.474f.6506 (bia 0060.474f.6506)
   Internet address is 172.22.2.1/24
   MTU 1500 bytes, BW 10000  Kbit, DLY 1000 usec, rely 255/255, load 1/255
   Encapsulation ARPA, loopback not set, keepalive set (10 sec)
   ARP type: ARPA, ARP Timeout 04:00:00
   Last input 00:00:10, output 00:00:00, output hang never
   Last clearing of "show interface" counters never
   Queueing strategy: fifo
   Output queue 0/40, 0 drops; input queue 0/75, 0 drops
   5 minute input rate 0 bits/sec, 0 packets/sec
   5 minute output rate 0 bits/sec, 0 packets/sec
      171 packets input, 25815 bytes, 0 no buffer
      Received 171 broadcasts, 0 runts, 0 giants
      0 input errors, 0 CRC, 0 frame, 0 overrun, 0 ignored, 0 abort
      0 input packets with dribble condition detected
      368 packets output, 37244 bytes, 0 underruns
      0 output errors, 0 collisions, 3 interface resets
      0 babbles, 0 late collision, 0 deferred
      0 lost carrier, 0 no carrier
      0 output buffer failures, 0 output buffers swapped out
Serial0 is down, line protocol is down
   Hardware is QUICC Serial (with onboard CSU/DSU)
   MTU 1500 bytes, BW 1544 Kbit, DLY 20000 usec, rely 255/255, load 1/255
   Encapsulation HDLC, loopback not set, keepalive set (10 sec)
   Last input never, output never, output hang never
   Last clearing of "show interface" counters never
   Input queue: 0/75/0 (size/max/drops); Total output drops: 0
   Queueing strategy: weighted fair
   Output queue: 0/64/0 (size/threshold/drops)
   Conversations  0/0 (active/max active)
      Reserved Conversations 0/0 (allocated/max allocated)
   5 minute input rate 0 bits/sec, 0 packets/sec
   5 minute output rate 0 bits/sec, 0 packets/sec
      0 packets input, 0 bytes, 0 no buffer
      Received 0 broadcasts, 0 runts, 0 giants
      0 input errors, 0 CRC, 0 frame, 0 overrun, 0 ignored, 0 abort
      0 packets output, 0 bytes, 0 underruns
      0 output errors, 0 collisions, 84 interface resets
      0 output buffer failures, 0 output buffers swapped out
      0 carrier transitions
      DCD=down  DSR=down  DTR=up  RTS=up  CTS=down

Serial1 is up, line protocol is up
   Hardware is QUICC Serial
   Internet address is 172.22.3.2/24
   MTU 1500 bytes, BW 1544  Kbit, DLY 20000 usec, rely 255/255, load 1/255
   Encapsulation HDLC, loopback not set, keepalive set (10 sec)
   Last input 00:00:02, output 00:00:04, output hang never
   Last clearing of "show interface" counters never
   Input queue: 0/75/0 (size/max/drops); Total output drops: 0
   Queueing strategy: weighted fair
   Output queue: 0/64/0 (size/threshold/drops)
      Conversations  0/1 (active/max active)
      Reserved Conversations 0/0 (allocated/max allocated)
   5 minute input rate 0 bits/sec, 0 packets/sec
   5 minute output rate 0 bits/sec, 0 packets/sec
      355 packets input, 22240 bytes, 0 no buffer
      Received 354 broadcasts, 0 runts, 0 giants
      2 input errors, 0 CRC, 2 frame, 0 overrun, 0 ignored, 0 abort
      359 packets output, 22790 bytes, 0 underruns
      0 output errors, 0 collisions, 7 interface resets
      0 output buffer failures, 0 output buffers swapped out
      0 carrier transitions
      DCD=up  DSR=up  DTR=up  RTS=up  CTS=up
```

The show interfaces command lists a summary of the status of each interface. If the Physical layer and Data Link layer protocols are up and running, the interface will be listed as Interface is up, line protocol up.

The configured Network layer address is displayed with this command. A /24 after the IP address denotes a 24-bit subnet mask or a mask of 255.255.255.0.

This interface is listed as Serial0 is down, line protocol is down because neither a Physical layer or Data Link layer connection is active. In this case, the interface is not sensing a signal.

Figure 6-17   Output from show interfaces command

CHAPTER SUMMARY

❑ Cisco routers use the Cisco IOS to provide an interface for network operators and administrators.

❑ The first mode entered is user EXEC (router> prompt) and the next mode is privileged EXEC (router# prompt).

❑ In user EXEC, you can accomplish basic tasks such as checking the router status, checking connectivity, and viewing some configuration information.

❑ To actually configure the router, privileged EXEC mode must be accessed, as this mode leads to the two most common modes for router configuration: global configuration mode and interface configuration mode.

❑ The privileged EXEC mode is often called enable mode because it is entered using the enable command.

❑ The enable, enable secret, and VTY passwords are set during initial configuration if the system configuration dialog is used, but they can also be added and changed in global configuration mode (router(config)# prompt).

❑ When configured, the enable secret password supersedes the enable password. This is because the enable secret is an encrypted password that is not viewable in the configuration file, which means that it has less chance of being compromised. For this reason, it should be different from the enable password.

❑ The Cisco 1900 switch allows configuration from a command line just like a Cisco router. Host names and passwords, as well as other parameters, are configured on the Cisco 1900 switch in much the same way as they are configured on a router.

❑ The components of a router include ROM, flash memory, NVRAM, RAM/DRAM, and interfaces.

❑ ROM stores a limited version of the Cisco IOS and routines for checking the hardware during system boot. It is responsible for initializing the router.

❑ Flash memory stores the Cisco IOS that is loaded by default during system boot.

❑ NVRAM stores the startup copy of the router configuration file that is loaded by default during system boot.

❑ RAM/DRAM stores the working copy (running configuration) of the router configuration. This configuration is loaded into RAM from NVRAM by default during bootup. It is erased if the router is rebooted, unless it is saved to the startup configuration.

❑ Interfaces provide connectivity to various types of LANs and WANs.

KEY TERMS

AUX line password — A password used to access the router through the AUX port.

AUX port — *See* **auxiliary port (AUX)**.

auxiliary port (AUX) — A secondary port that allows connection to a modem that will be used for direct access to the router for configuration.

bootstrap — A small program used to load a much larger program. In the case of a router or switch, the bootstrap program loads the IOS.

Cisco Internetwork Operating System (IOS) — A router operating system that provides a command-line interface, which allows network operators to check the status of the router and allows network administrators to manage and configure the router.

command executive — The user interface that interprets commands and is provided by the Cisco IOS (also known as the EXEC).

console — A physical connection on the back of the router to which you can connect a rollover cable to attach to a PC for router configuration (also known as a console port).

console password — The password that is used to access the router through the console port.

console port — *See* **console**.

context-sensitive Help — Help with the syntax of commands for the router that is based on the current router mode and prompt, as well as any part of a command that is typed.

dynamic random access memory (DRAM) — *See* **random access memory (RAM)**.

enable mode — Another name for the privileged EXEC mode. The enable or enable secret password must be entered in order to access this mode.

enable mode prompt — The prompt that indicates operation in privileged EXEC or enable mode. It has two elements: the host name of the router and the pound (#) symbol.

enable password — The password that protects enable mode in the event that the enable secret password has been removed.

enable secret password — An MD5-encrypted password that is not visible when viewing the system configuration; supersedes the enable password.

EXEC — *See* **command executive**.

flash memory — Erasable, programmable, read-only memory (EPROM). The content of flash memory is maintained when the router is rebooted. Flash memory contains the working copy of the Cisco IOS and it is the component that initializes the IOS for normal router operations.

global configuration mode — A router mode that allows manipulation of most of the router's generic settings. The prompt for global configuration mode is router(config)#.

6

interface configuration mode — A router mode that allows you to configure the Ethernet and serial interfaces. The prompt for this mode is router(config-if)#.

line configuration mode — A router mode that allows you to configure the virtual terminals, console, and AUX lines that let you access the router. The prompt for this mode is router(config-line)#.

MD5 algorithm — An algorithm used to encrypt an enable secret password. It has no known reversal.

nonvolatile random access memory (NVRAM) — A special type of RAM that is not cleared when the router is rebooted. NVRAM is where the startup configuration file for the router is stored.

privileged EXEC mode — A router mode used to configure the router.

random access memory (RAM) — Memory that stores the working copy of the router configuration. This configuration is erased if the router is rebooted, unless it is saved to the startup configuration.

read-only memory (ROM) — Memory that contains the necessary routines to boot the system and check its hardware. It also contains a limited version of the Cisco IOS for use only when the primary copies of the IOS in flash memory or on a TFTP server are accidentally lost.

RJ-45 to DB-9 — A connector that ships with the router to enable connection to a PC with a DB-9 COM port to the router console port.

RJ-45 to DB-25 — A connector that ships with the router to enable connection to a PC with a DB-25 COM port to the router console port.

RJ-45 to RJ-45 rollover cable — A cable that connects the console port on the back of the router to an RJ-45 to DB-9 or RJ-45 to DB-25 connector on the back of a PC. This cable ships with the router.

ROM monitor mode — A router mode that allows you to configure your router in the event that there is no valid IOS file in your flash memory.

router configuration mode — A router mode that allows you to enable routing protocols such as RIP and IGRP. The prompt for router configuration mode is router(config-router)#.

router# — *See* **enable mode prompt**.

router> — *See* **user EXEC mode**.

system configuration dialog — An automated setup routine that runs if you type "setup" from privileged EXEC mode or if the router is started/restarted without a configuration file.

Trivial File Transfer Protocol (TFTP) server — A computer that provides TFTP services and can be used to maintain the IOS and configuration file of a Cisco router.

Universal Time Code (UTC) — Based on the time in the city of Greenwich in the United Kingdom. All other time zones are either plus or minus hours of the clocks in Greenwich.

user EXEC mode — A router mode that allows a network operator to check router status, see if the interfaces are operational, and review several of the router settings.

user mode — *See* **user EXEC mode**.

virtual terminal password — A password that is used to access the router over a telnet connection.

virtual terminals (VTY) — Terminals provided with each Cisco router that can be used by telnet sessions to configure the router.

volatile — Contents of memory that are lost when the power is turned off. RAM is an example of volatile memory.

VTY — A Cisco IOS abbreviation for virtual terminal used in commands to reference virtual terminals.

6

REVIEW QUESTIONS

1. From which of the following prompts can you change the enable secret password?

    a. router(config)#

    b. router#

    c. router>

    d. router(config)>

2. If you type "show ?" at the router> prompt, what is the result of the command?

    a. You will see a list of usable show commands at the user mode prompt.

    b. You will see a list of connected users.

    c. You will see the current mode displayed.

    d. You will see the configuration register settings.

3. If you need to abort a command in the middle of execution, which key sequence will you press simultaneously?

    a. Ctrl+Esc

    b. Ctrl+X

    c. Ctrl+Shift+6

    d. Ctrl+Alt+Del

4. Which of the following commands will allow you to type a banner for your router?

    a. router(config-if)# banner message $

    b. router(config)# banner motd @

    c. router(config)# banner msg #

    d. router# banner config !

    e. router# banner motd #

5. By default, which of the router's components stores configuration files set up by the administrator?

   a. ROM

   b. Flash

   c. IOS

   d. NVRAM

6. If you are in global configuration mode, which router prompt will you see?

   a. global#

   b. router(config)#

   c. router(config-if)#

   d. router#

   e. router(config-gl)#

7. By default (during normal boot operations), where does the router look first for a working version of the Cisco IOS?

   a. NVRAM

   b. TFTP

   c. Flash

   d. ROM

8. What three commands can be used in privileged EXEC mode to alter the router configuration?

   a. setup, erase, and copy

   b. enable, setup, and tftp

   c. setup, show version, and show buffers

   d. erase, copy, and show run

9. ROM in a router is nothing like ROM in a PC. True or False?

10. Which of the following are routing protocols? (Choose all that apply.)

   a. RIP

   b. IGRP

   c. IP route

   d. Cisco IOS

   e. TCP

11. From which of the following prompts can you modify the terminal VTY password?

    a. router(config-line)#

    b. router#

    c. router>

    d. router(config)>

12. What does VTY 1 stand for?

    a. The first virtual Y connector

    b. Virtual terminal one

    c. Virtual test connection yes on 1

    d. v-modem terminal 1

13. How do network administrators access a VTY?

    a. ftp

    b. smtp

    c. telnet

    d. http

14. If, after connecting to the router via HyperTerminal, you see only illegible characters in the terminal window, what should you try?

    a. Adjust the baud rate.

    b. Change connectors.

    c. Use a telnet session.

    d. Turn on parity.

15. If you enter a VTY password during the automated setup routine, to which VTY will it apply? (Choose all that apply.)

    a. VTY 0

    b. VTY 1

    c. VTY 2

    d. VTY 3

    e. VTY 4

16. What are the two different levels of setup when using the system configuration dialog?

    a. Initial and basic

    b. Enable and enable secret

    c. Basic and extended

    d. None of the above

6

17. How do you save your changes to the configuration file to NVRAM?

    a. copy start run

    b. copy run start

    c. copy start flash

    d. copy run flash

18. From the router# prompt and the terminal, what must you type to enter global configuration mode?

    a. CON 0

    b. term gf

    c. conf t

    d. global conf

19. If you are at the router(config-if)# prompt and you press the Ctrl+Z keys simultaneously, which prompt will you see next?

    a. router>

    b. router#

    c. router(config)#

    d. Press Return to continue

20. Which of the following commands will allow you to enter privileged EXEC mode from the router> prompt? (Choose all that apply.)

    a. en

    b. ena

    c. enable

    d. enab

    e. enabl

21. What does the sh ru command show you?

    a. Remote users

    b. Running configuration

    c. Startup configuration

    d. Remote boot procedure

22. Which password can be used instead of the enable password?

    a. VTY 0

    b. console

    c. AUX

    d. enable secret

    e. login

23. Which password is encrypted by default?

   a. login

   b. MD5

   c. enable

   d. enable secret

   e. console

   f. VTY 0

24. If no host name has been configured on a 1900 series switch, which of the following illustrates how the prompt will display in global configuration mode?

   a. router(config)#

   b. switch(config)#

   c. (config)#

   d. (switch)#

25. Which of the following best describes the operating system of the Cisco 1900 series switch?

   a. Set-based

   b. IOS-based

   c. Switch-based

   d. IP-based

CASE PROJECTS

CASE
PROJECTS

1. Jennifer and Moe brought a client's router to the office to configure but they aren't sure how to make the physical connections. They want to use an older PC in Brad's office to configure the router. The COM2 port is available on this PC, and it has a DB-25 connector. How would you suggest the router be accessed? What hardware will you need? Where will you get this hardware?

2. You have helped Moe and Jennifer connect the router to the PC. Now, it is time to access the router and configure it. The old PC has the Windows 95 operating system on it. What program will you use to access the router? What are the important parameters to configure in this program, and what will the initial settings be?

3. Moe and Jennifer have accessed the router successfully. Explain to them which passwords the system configuration dialog will prompt them for during the initial configuration. Describe any particulars regarding those passwords. What other passwords are available to them? When and why might they want to implement these additional passwords?

4. Moe is a terrible typist. Lisa tells him to stop wasting time retyping router commands and use the command history and enhanced editing features of the Cisco IOS. When Moe asks her how to do this, she says that she read about it but doesn't remember exactly how these features work. Help Moe and Lisa by explaining to them the easy way to edit router commands. How do you retrieve previously typed commands? How do you move the cursor forward and back along the command line?

5. Lisa is planning to take a CCNA practice exam on the Internet. She is having a difficult time memorizing the components of the Cisco router. List the router components for her and give a brief description of the purpose of each component. How do similar components in a typical PC compare to the router components you have listed?

ROUTER STARTUP AND CONFIGURATION

After reading this chapter and completing the exercises, you will be able to:

♦ Understand router startup

♦ Describe and use the Cisco Discovery Protocol

♦ Understand configuration management commands for Cisco routers and the 1900 series switch

♦ Configure IP on the Cisco router and the 1900 series switch

♦ Troubleshoot router connectivity problems

In this chapter, you will learn about the various configurable components of the Cisco router and how to manipulate them. The chapter describes basic router configuration and administrative tasks, and introduces the CDP protocol and its configuration. In addition, you will learn how to configure and test IP. Finally, you will understand the steps involved in troubleshooting a Cisco router when there are connectivity problems.

ROUTER STARTUP

A router follows a specific boot process, but processes can vary. This section discusses the variety of startup options available during the boot process. In general, the boot process follows these steps:

1. Test hardware (POST).

2. Load the bootstrap program.

3. Locate and load the Cisco IOS.

4. Locate and load the router configuration file.

Figure 7-1 illustrates a simplified version of the basic flow of the boot process. The steps in the flow chart are discussed in greater detail in the following subsections.

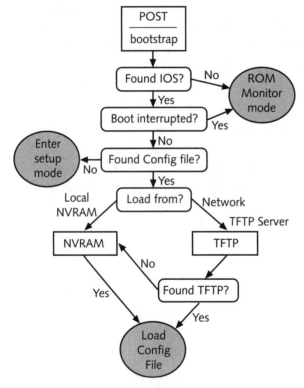

Figure 7-1   The boot process

POST

Read-only memory (ROM) in a router typically contains the **power-on self-test (POST)**, the bootstrap program, and often a version of the operating system. Most types of computer equipment perform some type of POST immediately after being turned on. POST is a diagnostic test that determines if the hardware is operating correctly. During the POST, the bootstrap program, also called the **ROM Monitor**, checks basic operations of the attached hardware, including CPU, memory, and interfaces. The ROM Monitor checks the **configuration register** for instructions regarding how to load the Cisco IOS. Every Cisco router has a 16-bit configuration register, which is stored in NVRAM. This register allows you to control several boot functions, including:

- Forcing the system into the bootstrap program
- Enabling or disabling the console Break function
- Setting the console terminal baud rate
- Loading the IOS from ROM
- Loading the IOS from a TFTP server

You can examine the configuration register by typing "show version" at either the enable mode or user mode prompt. The default is to load the IOS from flash memory. Figure 7-2 displays the output of the show version command.

7

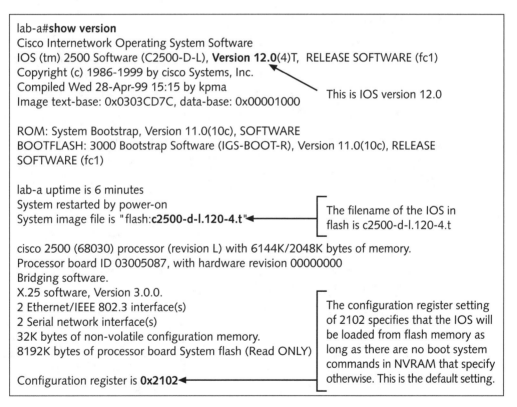

Figure 7-2 Output from the show version command

The last line of this output should read "Configuration register is" followed by a hexadecimal code. The last four digits of the code specify system boot instructions. The very last hexadecimal digit determines from where the IOS will load. The first three hex digits of the last four control other aspects of how the router will operate after it boots. Table 7-1 describes the various IOS boot locations and the corresponding value of the last hexadecimal digit in the configuration register.

Table 7-1   Configuration register codes

Last Hex Digit in Configuration Register	Description
0	Boot into ROM Monitor mode
1	Boot helper image from ROM (RxBoot mode)
2	Check the startup configuration file in NVRAM for boot system commands; load IOS from flash if nothing else is specified

ROM Monitor Mode

You can set the router to enter **ROM Monitor mode** during the boot process by modifying the configuration register. The router will also enter ROM Monitor mode if it cannot find an IOS image during the boot process. The prompt for ROM Monitor mode is the greater than (>) symbol; on the Cisco 1003, 1600, 2600, 3600, 4500, 7200, and 7500, the prompt is rommon>.

NOTE

On Cisco 2000, 2500, 3000, and 4000 series routers, you can press the Ctrl+Break keys within the first 60 seconds of the boot process to enter ROM Monitor mode.

You can use ROM Monitor mode to configure your router manually. You must provide each command in the correct syntax to configure the router. Also, you can initiate the interactive startup process by typing "setup" at the prompt.

To configure your system to enter ROM Monitor mode, you can enter the following command at the global configuration prompt:

```
config-register 0x2100
```

The 0x2100 is just one example of a hexadecimal register setting that would boot the router into ROM Monitor mode. The important factor is that the last number is 0. To configure your system to boot a smaller IOS image from ROM and enter RxBoot mode, you must enter the following command at the global configuration prompt:

```
config-register 0x2101
```

Once again, it is the last hexadecimal digit that forces the router to boot into RxBoot mode. RxBoot mode is described in the next section. To confirm your changes, go to the enable mode or user mode prompt, and then type "show version". The last line, depending on your previous actions, should have "(will be 0x2100 at next reload)" or "(will be 0x2101 at next reload)." You can reboot using the reload command. When the router reboots, the ROM Monitor will load the IOS as specified in the configuration register.

Be careful when modifying the configuration register. Using ROM Monitor mode will not cause problems, but entering random hexadecimal commands above 0x0002 may present a variety of problems. Modifying your configuration in this manner is only advisable when there is no other course of action.

If you see a series of seemingly random characters when you boot your router, change the baud rate on your terminal. Typically, the correct setting is 9600; however, when troubleshooting the system startup, you should try 2400 and other baud settings if 9600 does not work.

RxBoot Mode

RxBoot mode is another configuration mode that you can enter when changes to your system make it impossible to boot from the flash memory and you cannot locate a valid IOS image. The prompt from RxBoot mode is the host name of your router followed by "boot" in parentheses. For example, if your router's name is router2, the prompt would be router2(boot). RxBoot mode provides a limited set of the Cisco IOS commands from ROM to allow you to configure the router. The commands that are accepted are a subset of those used in the normal user EXEC and privileged EXEC mode.

Cisco IOS

As mentioned, the Cisco IOS is usually loaded from flash memory. Figure 7-3 displays the output from a Cisco 2500 series router during bootup under this default condition.

If you want to see information about your router's flash memory, type "show flash" from the enable mode prompt. Figure 7-4 displays the output from the show flash command.

System Bootstrap, Version 11.0(10c), SOFTWARE
Copyright (c) 1986-1996 by cisco Systems
2500 processor with 6144 Kbytes of main memory

%SYS-4-CONFIG_NEWER: Configurations from version 12.0 may not be correctly understood.
F3: 7379840+96124+568408 at 0x3000060

       Restricted Rights Legend

Use, duplication, or disclosure by the Government is
subject to restrictions as set forth in subparagraph
(c) of the Commercial Computer Software - Restricted
Rights clause at FAR sec. 52.227-19 and subparagraph
(c) (1) (ii) of the Rights in Technical Data and Computer
Software clause at DFARS sec. 252.227-7013.

      cisco Systems, Inc.
      170 West Tasman Drive
      San Jose, California 95134-1706

Cisco Internetwork Operating System Software
IOS (tm) 2500 Software (C2500-D-L), **Version 12.0**(4)T, RELEASE SOFTWARE (fc1)
Copyright (c) 1986-1999 by cisco Systems, Inc.
Compiled Wed 28-Apr-99 15:15 by kpma
Image text-base: 0x0303CD7C, data-base: 0x00001000   This is IOS version 12.0

cisco 2500 (68030) processor (revision L) with 6144K/2048K bytes of memory.
Processor board ID 03005087, with hardware revision 00000000
Bridging software.
X.25 software, Version 3.0.0.
2 Ethernet/IEEE 802.3 interface(s)   There are 2 Ethernet
2 Serial network interface(s)   interfaces and 2 Serial
32K bytes of non-volatile configuration memory.   interfaces on this router
8192K bytes of processor board System flash (Read ONLY)

Press RETURN to get started!

Figure 7-3 Output from the Cisco 2500 series router on bootup

lab-a#**show flash**

System flash directory: The IOS filename in flash
File Length Name/status   is c2500-d-l.120-4.t
  1 7475996 **c2500-d-l.120-4.t**
[7476060 bytes used, 912548 available, 8388608 total]
8192K bytes of processor board System flash (Read ONLY)   There is 8 MB of
                                          flash memory

Figure 7-4 Output from the show flash command

Cisco routers support the following fallback options for loading the IOS:

- If the IOS is configured to load from a TFTP server, but that server cannot be located, the IOS is loaded from flash memory.

- If the IOS cannot be found in flash or on a TFTP server, a minimal version of the IOS is loaded from ROM. The version of the IOS in ROM may be an older version than the one currently running.

The default fallback sequence for the router to locate the IOS is:

1. Flash

2. TFTP server

3. ROM

You may want to alter the default sequence for loading the IOS. For example, routers are sometimes configured to boot their IOS image from a TFTP server. You can alter the default sequence by configuring boot system commands.

NOTE

A **Trivial File Transfer Protocol (TFTP) server** is a computer, such as a PC, UNIX workstation, or laptop, that is running TFTP server services. A Cisco router can also operate as a TFTP server. TFTP software allows the Cisco router to transfer the IOS image, as well as other files, to the TFTP server via TFTP, a simple connectionless protocol that is less complex than FTP.

Boot System Commands

You can force the router to load its IOS from a TFTP server by putting boot system commands into the configuration file. As long as the configuration register is configured with a "2" as the final hexadecimal digit, the ROM Monitor will look for boot system commands in NVRAM during the bootup process.

A typical IOS filename might look like this: igs-j-l.111-5. The default filename for the destination file is the same as the name of the source file. If you want to enable your system to boot the flash file from the TFTP server, issue the following command from **global configuration mode**:

```
boot system tftp igs-j-l.111-5
```

NOTE

The boot system flash bootflash command will force the router to boot into ROM.

This command assumes that the IOS filename is igs-j-l.111-5. This command will be broadcast so that a computer running TFTP software will respond. After you have inserted this command, you can type "show running-config" to see that the line has been entered in your configuration file. You should see "boot system tftp igs-j-l.111-5 255.255.255.255" on the terminal screen. To use the TFTP server, your system must have IP correctly configured for one of its interfaces, because TFTP is one of the many protocols associated with the TCP/IP suite.

You can enter as many boot system tftp commands as you want for redundancy. This ensures that your system can boot from a TFTP server, even if the primary server is not available. When you view your configuration after entering multiple boot system tftp commands, you will see multiple boot system lines in the configuration. To remove any given line, type "no boot system tftp", followed by the IOS filename at the global configuration prompt. Remember, if you want these modifications to be applied to your startup configuration, you must type the following at the privileged EXEC mode prompt to ensure that your changes are applied to the startup configuration in NVRAM:

```
copy running-config startup-config
```

NOTE

If you want to clear the Cisco IOS in your flash memory, you can type "erase flash" at the privileged EXEC mode prompt. Be extremely careful with this command, as it wipes out the working IOS on the router. Be sure to back up your configuration to a TFTP server before using this command.

Upgrading the IOS

Before you load a flash file to your router, use the show flash command to ensure that there is enough free memory to load the new Cisco IOS software. The system will tell you how much memory is used and how much is free. You may have to erase the existing flash memory before writing onto it due to space limitations.

NOTE

If you abort the copying process in the middle of copying a new flash memory, your existing flash memory will still be active, assuming that you have not erased it already.

Any time you are planning to upgrade or modify the IOS, you should back up your current IOS to a TFTP server. You can use the show flash or show version commands to learn the name of the flash file that you are using and then copy that file to the TFTP server. TFTP software is available for a variety of platforms such as UNIX, Windows NT, Windows 95/98, and MS-DOS/Windows. You can download TFTP server software from the Cisco Web site at *www.cisco.com*.

Cisco Catalyst 1900 IOS and Configuration Management

If you want to upgrade or restore the IOS via TFTP, the command syntax is **copy tftp://tftp_server_address/IOS_file/ opcode**. The opcode command tells the device to load the file into flash memory. For example, assume that you had a backup of your switch configuration saved as cat1900en_9_01.bin on the TFTP server 192.168.1.220. You would use the following command from the enable mode prompt (assuming your switch is named Rm410HL):

```
Rm410HL#copy tftp://192.168.1.220/cat1900en_9_01.bin opcode
```

To back up the configuration settings for your Catalyst 1900 switch, you copy the contents of NVRAM to a TFTP server. The command syntax is **copy nvram tftp://tftp_server_ address/config_file_name**. Therefore, if you want to make a backup copy of your switch configuration and you want to name it "rm410HLconfig", you would enter the following command on a TFTP server:

```
Rm410HL#copy nvram tftp://192.168.1.220/rm410HLconfig
```

If you later need to restore the configuration of your switch from the TFTP server, you would change the order of the command slightly to show that the file was to be copied into NVRAM. To restore the configuration file that was backed up in the previous command, enter this command:

```
Rm410HL#copy tftp://192.168.1.220/rm410HLconfig nvram
```

If you decide that you don't want the configuration file, you can delete it with this command:

```
Rm410HL#delete nvram
```

That command will reset your switch to its factory default settings and you will be asked to confirm the change.

Router Configuration Files

The router configuration file that is used during the boot process is called the *startup-config*. Sometimes this file is referred to as the backup configuration because it is the saved version of the configuration file. Any time you want to revert to the settings in your startup-config, you can reboot the system by powering the router off and back on again, or by issuing the reload command. As long as you haven't saved the running configuration on top of the startup configuration, the running configuration in RAM will be dumped when you reload, and the saved version in NVRAM will be loaded into RAM. It is important to note that when you copy over the startup configuration in NVRAM, that file is replaced. However, when you copy to the running configuration in RAM, either from NVRAM or from a TFTP server, the configuration files are blended. In other words, the resulting working configuration will be a combination of the startup configuration file in NVRAM (or the one on the TFTP server) and the current working configuration in RAM. In addition, there is no erase run command. If you want to get rid of the running configuration, you must reload either by command or by turning the router off and on.

If you want to view the contents of the startup-config, you can type "show startup-config" or just "sh star" at the enable prompt. If you want to see your working or running configuration, type "show running-config" or just "sh ru" at the enable prompt. The important copy commands as well as some other configuration commands are shown in Table 7-2.

This table lists the most important commands. If you are curious about additional commands, type "copy ?" at the enable prompt.

Table 7-2   Important router copy commands

Command from Enable Mode	Description
copy running-config tftp	Copies the running configuration located in RAM to a TFTP server.
copy startup-config tftp	Copies the startup configuration located in NVRAM to a TFTP server.
copy tftp running-config	Copies the configuration from the TFTP server to the running configuration. The reconfiguration of the router is immediate when this command is issued. The running-config is not replaced. The files are blended.
copy tftp startup-config	Copies the configuration from the TFTP server to the startup configuration. The startup-config is replaced with the one from the TFTP server.
copy run start	Copies the working configuration file in RAM to the startup configuration file in NVRAM. Replaces the startup configuration file.
copy start run	Copies the startup configuration file in NVRAM to the running configuration in RAM. Does not replace the file in RAM; the files are blended.
copy flash tftp	Copies the IOS in flash memory to a TFTP server.
copy tftp flash	Copies the IOS from a TFTP server to flash memory.
configure terminal	Used to specify that you want to configure your settings manually from the console terminal.
configure memory	Used to specify that you want to pull your configuration information from NVRAM.
configure network	Indicates that you want to load your working configuration from a TFTP server.
configure overwrite-network	Indicates that you want to overwrite the existing NVRAM with the configuration information stored on the TFTP server.
erase startup-config	Erases the current startup configuration. When you reboot the router, you will be prompted to enter the automated setup program.

NOTE

Notice there is no copy command that copies between flash and a running or startup configuration file. It is important to think of the IOS and configuration files as separate. The IOS is a relatively large file that is the entire operating system, whereas the configuration files are very small and modify the operation of the router.

Methods for Making Changes

When changes to the router's configuration or boot process are required, the administrator should follow a logical process for making those changes. Remember that changes usually can be implemented and tested without saving them to the startup configuration. This is because changes to the running configuration take place immediately. Almost everything can be done in RAM (running-config). When you are satisfied that the changes are correct, you can copy the running configuration to the startup configuration. These basic steps can be used for implementing changes:

1. Make changes as desired to the configuration.

2. Examine those changes.

3. Determine if the changes meet the desired result.

4. Remove the changes if they do not meet the desired result, or simply reboot the router.

5. Copy the changes from the running configuration to the startup configuration when they do meet the desired result.

If the administrator makes changes that should be tested by rebooting the router, then he or she can copy the Cisco IOS and startup configuration to a TFTP server first. This way, if the changes do not meet the desired result, those files can be copied back to the router from the TFTP server.

CDP

The **Cisco Discovery Protocol (CDP)** is a Cisco proprietary Data Link layer protocol that shares configuration information between Cisco devices that are connected directly to each other. All Cisco devices, including routers, switches, and access servers, can use CDP to discover each other and learn about the configurations of other devices. Using CDP can help you quickly determine the network topology.

With CDP, you can discover other devices on the same LAN segment and those connected over a serial interface. Figure 7-5 illustrates the CDP feedback after the show cdp neighbor command has been issued.

```
route#show cdp neighbor
Capability codes:   R- Router, T - Tran bridge, B - Source Route Bridge
                    S - Switch, H - Host, I - IGMP, r - Repeater

Device ID          Local Interface   Holdtme   Capability   Platform   Port ID
ROUTER1                Ser 1           170          R          2500      Ser 1
ROUTER2                Ser 0           170          R          4000      Ser 0
```

Figure 7-5   Show cdp neighbor command

The show cdp neighbor command supports the following options:

- Ethernet: To learn more about Ethernet interfaces attached to neighbors

- Null: To learn more about interfaces of a neighbor that does not have an address assigned

- Serial: More information about neighbors connected to serial interfaces

- Detail: Detailed information about the CDP neighbor and all attached devices. This detailed information includes device identification, remote interface type, and remote IP address.

CDP was designed to be a low-overhead protocol. CDP broadcasts information every 60 seconds by default. You can modify the length of time between updates by using the cdp timer command. The CDP command is the same for routers and Cisco IOS enabled switches. For example, to change CDP to update every 120 seconds, type:

```
router(config)#cdp timer 120
```

The CDP information is only held for a set length of time, which is 180 seconds by default. You can modify the length of time that the CDP information is held by issuing the cdp holdtime command. For example, to configure CDP packets to be discarded after one minute, type:

```
router(config)#cdp holdtime 60
```

After 60 seconds, the CDP information is discarded, given the preceding example. By default, CDP is enabled on all Cisco devices, but you modify CDP broadcasts on the network. To turn off CDP on the entire router, use the no cdp run command at the global configuration prompt. If you want to disable CDP information from being sent on a given interface, change to the interface configuration mode prompt, and then issue the no cdp enable command. For example, to remove CDP broadcasts from your Ethernet0 interface, enter the following from enable mode:

```
router#config  t
```

```
router(config)#interface Ethernet0
```

```
router(config-if)#no cdp enable
```

You can use the show cdp interface command in enable mode to retrieve the statistics that CDP will report on the local router's interfaces.

NOTE   As an administrator, you can learn about a network's topology by using the telnet command in combination with the show cdp neighbor or show cdp neighbor detail command. Simply telnet into one of the virtual terminals and issue the cdp commands that you would use locally to determine attached Cisco devices.

IP ON THE ROUTER

If the router is initially configured using the extended setup program, you will be asked if you want to enable IP on your router. If you answer yes, you will be prompted to configure IP on each of the interfaces that you want to set up. If you answer no, you can either run setup again later, or you can configure the interfaces manually.

To manually configure IP on an interface, you must first change to interface configuration mode. Then, you can use the ip address command to configure an IP address for your specific interface. For example, if you want to configure the IP address 192.168.1.1 with the default Class C subnet mask for the Ethernet interface, type the following from enable mode:

```
Router#config t

Router(config)#int E0/0

Router(config-if)#ip address 192.168.1.1 255.255.255.0

Router(config-if)#no shutdown
```

NOTE
Depending on the router type, the interface may be expressed in two different ways. In the example in the previous section on CDP, the Ethernet interface was expressed as "Ethernet0". Alternatively, "e0" could have been used. The "0" means this is the first Ethernet port. This notation is for a router such as the Cisco 2500 series that has a fixed number of interfaces. In this section, the Ethernet interface was expressed as E0/0. Alternatively, Ethernet0/0 could have been used. This notation is for a router such as the 2600 series that has a slotted chassis allowing for multiple interfaces on multiple cards. The first number indicates the slot in which the card is inserted. If there is only one card, it will be in slot 0. The second number indicates the port number. In this example, the interface being configured for IP is the first Ethernet interface on the first card (slot). Fast Ethernet interfaces will usually be expressed as F0/0 or F0/1.

Notice that the subnet mask was included in the IP address command. The command would be incomplete without the subnet mask. You can also add the command secondary to an ip address command and configure the address as a second IP address for the interface. Also notice the addition of the no shutdown command. This command will enable the interface. In the event you are configuring a serial interface as a **DCE (data communication equipment)**, you will also need to add the clockrate (bandwidth in bits per second) command.

NOTE
If you want to change the way the subnet mask is shown when you view statistics about an interface, type "term ip netmask-format" at the enable mode prompt. You will have to choose decimal, bit-count, or hexadecimal to complete the command; the default is decimal. If you choose bit-count, the mask is displayed in CIDR format.

IP ON THE SWITCH

An IP address is not necessary on a switch like the Catalyst 1900 because switches, as you know from previous discussions, operate mainly on Layer 2 (MAC addresses). However, you may want to configure an IP address for your switch so that you can manage it over the network via telnet or some other management software. Also, you may need to configure an IP address for your switch if you want to implement VLANs on your network (a concept covered in a later chapter).

By default, Cisco switches are not configured with IP addresses. In order to set an IP address, you must enter global configuration mode by typing "configure terminal" (or one of its abbreviations). Then, you can configure the IP address and default gateway using these commands:

```
Rm410HL(config)#ip address 192.168.1.204 255.255.255.0

Rm410HL(config)#ip default-gateway 192.168.1.1
```

IP CONNECTIVITY

Once you configure the router for IP, you should test for connectivity. There are several commands that can help you verify this connectivity. These commands apply to various layers of the OSI model, as described in Table 7-3.

Table 7-3   Testing connectivity by layer

Command	OSI Layer	TCP/IP Layer
Telnet	Application layer	Application layer
Ping	Network layer	Internetwork layer
Trace	Network layer	Internetwork layer
Show ip route	Network layer	Internetwork layer
Show interfaces	Data Link and Physical layers	Network Interface layer

When testing connectivity, if you cannot get a connection at a higher layer, check the connectivity of a lower layer. For example, if you cannot get a telnet connection, you should attempt to ping the host to which you are trying to connect.

Telnet

Telnet is a utility that connects at the highest layer of the OSI model and provides remote access to other devices. Cisco routers allow telnet connections via their virtual terminal ports. If you can establish telnet connectivity to a router, you have established that it is available on the network and that you have connectivity at all layers. After you establish telnet connectivity, you can learn more about the configuration of the remote router by executing commands as if you were connected to the router locally.

NOTE If you accidentally initiate a connection with another router from your locally attached router, you can stop the process by pressing Ctrl+Shift+6. This key combination can be used to stop any command from running. You can also use the logout command at the user EXEC or privileged EXEC mode prompt. This will log you out of the remote router but maintain the connection with your local router.

IP Host Names

When telnetting to a remote router or host, the IP address of the host must follow the telnet command. Rather than using IP addresses, it is easier to refer to a remote host or router using a name. Sometimes, you cannot gain connectivity because the host name that you are trying to connect with is entered in a table incorrectly. For example, suppose you are trying to telnet into router15, but the address for router15 is configured incorrectly on your system. To determine the address to name mapping on your router, check the name table by issuing the following command:

```
router#show hosts
```

You will then see a list of the names configured on your router. If you want to add an entry to your hosts file for name resolution, you must go to global configuration mode. For example, if you want to add an entry telling your router that router15 is at IP address 192.168.5.1, type:

```
router(config)#ip host router15 192.168.5.1
```

If you want to later remove that entry, type:

```
router(config)#no ip host router15 192.168.5.1
```

If you find that one of the entries in your host table is incorrect, you can remove it and enter the correct mapping. You can also allow a name server to handle the IP address to name resolution. For example, if you want to specify that a name server with IP address 172.33.44.1 be used by the router for name resolution, enter the command:

```
router(config)#ip name-server 172.33.44.1
```

Then, when a friendly name is used, the name server will be consulted to provide name resolution for the router. In this example, if you type "ping router3", the router will ping the IP address of router3 based on the name resolution in the table located on the device with the IP address 172.33.44.1. Using a name server provides name resolution from one location, making a table configuration on each device unnecessary.

Ping and Trace

If you can't get connectivity at the Application layer, try connectivity at the Internetwork layer. Ping and trace are available from the user EXEC and privileged EXEC mode. Ping and trace verify connectivity at the Internetwork layer of the TCP/IP model. Both commands use ICMP messages to verify that the destination host is reachable, and if not, give possible reasons for the problem. Ping sends an echo request packet to the destination and waits for an echo reply. By default, the ping utility with Cisco routers is configured to send five packets to the target. Ping can return the following replies:

- !: Successful receipt of the ICMP echo
- .: Request timed out
- U: Destination was unreachable
- C: Congestion experienced
- I: Ping interrupted
- ?: Packet type unknown
- &: Packet TTL exceeded

Additional information returned from ping includes the quantity of ICMP packets sent, the timeout duration, the transfer success rate, and the minimum, average, and maximum roundtrip times for the ICMP packets sent.

If you simply type "ping" and then press the Return key at the enable mode prompt, you will be able to enter your ping command step by step. You also will be able to control the protocol type (for example, IPX rather than IP), the size of the ping packet, the number of packets sent, and other options. Using the ping command alone is referred to as **extended mode ping**. Extended mode ping can only be accessed from the privileged mode prompt.

Ping is a quick way to determine if there is network layer connectivity. If ping indicates a problem with connectivity, using trace may provide a better clue as to the source of the connectivity problem. The trace command is similar to the ping command, except that the replies are requested at each hop along the way to the destination. Trace sends multiple ICMP packets with progressively higher time-to-live counters (TTL) until the packet reaches the destination. If there are three routers between the destination and the source of the trace, there will be four replies to the message—one for each hop along the way and one when the trace reaches the final destination. The trace command is useful for determining where in the process the communication is breaking down. The following responses can be returned by a trace:

- !H: Indicates that a router received, but didn't forward, the ICMP echo request
- P: Protocol unreachable
- N: Network unreachable
- U: Port unreachable
- *: Request timed out

IP Route

If you cannot get connectivity using ping or trace, you should check your routing table. If the routing table is sending communications out of the wrong interface, or if there is no entry in the routing table that will handle routing to the target network, it will cause your higher-level connectivity to fail. You can issue the show ip route command from the enable mode prompt. This command displays the routing table. Typically, routing tables are dynamically created when routing protocols are configured on the router. If you want, you can use the ip route command from the global configuration mode to statically enter routes in the routing table. Very often a routing table will consist of routes learned both through dynamic and static means.

Routing is covered in more detail in Chapter 8.

REFERENCE

Checking the Interface

One of the biggest mistakes made when troubleshooting is not checking the interfaces on the router. If the interfaces are down, packets cannot be delivered. Router interfaces go down for a variety of reasons, including incorrect IP configuration and cable problems. You can use the show ip interface command to view the configuration of IP on your interfaces and to check the status of the interface.

You can check the configuration of a specific interface from the enable mode prompt with the show interfaces command. For example, if you want to check the statistics for Serial0/0, type:

```
router#show int s0/0
```

The first line reports the status of the interface. There are two elements to the first line: The first reports the physical status of the interface, and the next reports the status of the line protocol. If the interface and protocol are fully functional, you will see the following information:

```
Serial0/0 is up, line protocol is up
```

That report means that both the interface and line protocol are functioning properly. In other words, the interface is functioning at both the Physical and Data Link layers. You may also see one of the following replies:

- Serial0/0 is up, line protocol is down: The interface is not receiving any network data or **keepalive frames**, but the physical interface is up and operational. This typically indicates a problem with the configuration of the router. Check the running configuration using the show run command. Make sure routing protocols and static routing commands have been properly configured. Also make sure that the IP address for the interface was entered correctly. On serial interfaces, you will also get this report if the router to which your router is connected through this interface is down. In other words, the remote attached router can push your router interface down.

- Serial0/0 is administratively down, line protocol is down: This indicates that the interface is disabled on the router. This usually occurs when you are not using the interface and there is no cable attached to it.

- Serial0/0 is up, line protocol is administratively down: This indicates that you need to use the no shutdown command on this interface to bring the interface back up. This typically happens when configurations are copied to the router from a file or TFTP server.

- Serial0/0 is down, line protocol is down: This indicates a physical problem with the serial interface on the router. Check the cable.

 Different types of interfaces can show different types of reports. For example, a Token Ring interface reports down when there is no electrical carrier signal present.

NOTE

Figure 7-6 displays the output from the show interfaces command. Some of the less important output is not shown for space considerations.

Clear Counters

The router keeps detailed statistics regarding data passing across its interfaces. Before using the show interfaces command, you may want to clear the existing interface information. You can clear these statistics **(counters)** on the interface by using the clear interface or clear counters command. To clear the counters for interface E0, type the following:

```
router#clear interface E0
```

If you want to clear the counters on all attached interfaces, use the clear counters command.

Debug

One of the most powerful tools you can use to obtain information from your router is the debug command. This tool is only available from privileged EXEC mode. Debug has numerous subcommands that allow you to troubleshoot particular protocols. If you want to see all of the debugging counters available, you can use the debug all command. However, the debug all command will seriously affect router performance, so you should avoid experimenting with debug on a production router. Output from the debug all command is displayed in Figure 7-7.

With debug, you can also check for specific types of traffic on the wire. For example, if you want to perform general IP packet debugging, type the following:

```
router#debug ip packet
```

Details regarding IP packets received by the router will display. Again, the debug command is powerful, but also resource-intensive and should not be run for extended periods of time due to its negative impact on router performance. Use the debug command only when necessary to check network traffic; use the no debug command to disable debugging when you are finished. For example, to turn off debugging for broadcast traffic, you would type:

```
router#no debug ip packet
```

You can also type "no debug all" or "undebug all". Additional debug commands are introduced in later chapters.

```
lab-a#show interfaces
Ethernet0 is up, line protocol is up
  Hardware is Lance, address is 0000.0c8e.b490 (bia 0000.0c8e.b490)
  Internet address is 192.5.5.1/24
  MTU 1500 bytes, BW 10000 Kbit, DLY 1000 usec,
    reliability 255/255, txload 1/255, rxload 1/255
  Encapsulation ARPA, loopback not set
  Keepalive set (10 sec)
  ARP type: ARPA, ARP Timeout 04:00:00
  Last input never, output 00:00:03, output hang never
  Last clearing of "show interface" counters never
  Queueing strategy: fifo
  Output queue 0/40, 0 drops; input queue 0/75, 0 drops
  5 minute input rate 0 bits/sec, 0 packets/sec
  5 minute output rate 0 bits/sec, 0 packets/sec
Serial0 is down, line protocol is down
  Hardware is HD64570
  Internet address is 201.100.11.1/24
  MTU 1500 bytes, BW 1544 Kbit, DLY 20000 usec,
    reliability 255/255, txload 1/255, rxload 1/255
  Encapsulation HDLC, loopback not set
  Keepalive set (10 sec)
  Last input never, output never, output hang never
  Last clearing of "show interface" counters never
  Queueing strategy: fifo
  Output queue 0/40, 0 drops; input queue 0/75, 0 drops
  5 minute input rate 0 bits/sec, 0 packets/sec
  5 minute output rate 0 bits/sec, 0 packets/sec
    0 packets input, 0 bytes, 0 no buffer
    Received 0 broadcasts, 0 runts, 0 giants, 0 throttles
    0 input errors, 0 CRC, 0 frame, 0 overrun, 0 ignored, 0 abort
    15 packets output, 3198 bytes, 0 underruns
    0 output errors, 0 collisions, 2 interface resets
    0 output buffer failures, 0 output buffers swapped out
    0 carrier transitions
    DCD=up  DSR=up  DTR=down  RTS=down  CTS=up
Serial1 is administratively down, line protocol is down
  Hardware is HD64570
  MTU 1500 bytes, BW 1544 Kbit, DLY 20000 usec,
    reliability 255/255, txload 1/255, rxload 1/255
  Encapsulation HDLC, loopback not set
  Keepalive set (10 sec)
  Last input never, output never, output hang never
```

Interface E0 is fully functional. Frames can be sent and received on this interface.

S0 is not functional.

The S1 interface is not functional. In this case, there is no cable attached to S1 as it is not being used.

Figure 7-6 Output from the show interfaces command

```
RouterB#debug all
This may severely impact network performance. Continue? [confirm]

All possible debugging has been turned on
RouterB#
IP: s=172.22.3.1 (Serial1), d=255.255.255.255, len 76, rcvd 2
UDP: rcvd src=172.22.3.1(520), dst=255.255.255.255(520), length=52
RIP: received v1 update from 172.22.3.1 on Serial1
      172.22.4.0 in 1 hops
      172.22.5.0 in 2 hops
RIP: Update contains 2 routes
SERVICE_MODULE(0): lxt441 interrupt 1 status A7 loop 0
SERVICE_MODULE(0): lxt441 interrupt 1 status 87 loop 0
SERVICE_MODULE(0): lxt441 interrupt 1 status A7 loop 0
SERVICE_MODULE(0): lxt441 interrupt 1 status 87 loop 0
Serial1: HDLC myseq 6631, mineseen 6631, yourseen 6580, line up
SERVICE_MODULE(0): lxt441 interrupt 1 status A7 loop 0
SERVICE_MODULE(0): lxt441 interrupt 1 status 87 loop 0
SERVICE_MODULE(0): lxt441 interrupt 1 status A7 loop 0
SERVICE_MODULE(0): lxt441 interrupt 1 status 87 loop 0
RIP: sending v1 update to 255.255.255.255 via Ethernet0 (172.22.2.1)
      subnet  172.22.3.0, metric 1
      subnet  172.22.4.0, metric 2
      subnet  172.22.5.0, metric 3
RIP: Update contains 3 routes
IP: s=172.22.2.1 (local), d=255.255.255.255 (Ethernet0), len 55, sending broad/m
ulticast
RIP: sending v1 update to 255.255.255.255 via Serial1 (172.22.3.2)
      subnet  172.22.2.0, metric 1
RIP: Update contains 1 routes
IP: s=172.22.3.2 (local), d=255.255.255.255 (Serial1), len 67, sending broad/mul
ticast
SERVICE_MODULE(0): lxt441 interrupt 1 status A7 loop 0
SERVICE_MODULE(0): lxt441 interrupt 1 status 87 loop 0
Serial0: attempting to restart
Serial1: HDLC myseq 6632, mineseen 6632, yourseen 6581, line up
IP: s=172.22.5.1 (Ethernet0), d=255.255.255.255, len 106, rcvd 2
UDP: rcvd src=172.22.5.1(520), dst=255.255.255.255(520), length=72
RIP: ignored v1 update from bad source 172.22.5.1 on Ethernet0
SERVICE_MODULE(0): lxt441 interrupt 1 status A7 loop 0
SERVICE_MODULE(0): lxt441 interrupt 1 status 87 loop 0
SERVICE_MODULE(0): lxt441 interrupt 1 status A7 loop 0
SERVICE_MODULE(0): lxt441 interrupt 1 status 87 loop 0
SERVICE_MODULE(0): lxt441 interrupt 1 status A7 loop 0
SERVICE_MODULE(0): lxt441 interrupt 1 status 87 loop 0
Serial1: HDLC myseq 6633, mineseen 6633, yourseen 6582, line up
All possible debugging has been turned off
RouterB#
```

The debug all command warns you that issuing this command could cause severe network congestion. This command should only be used for a short period of time as a troubleshooting tool.

Figure 7-7   Debug all command output

ROUTER PASSWORD RECOVERY

Sometimes a password is forgotten or compromised. A procedure called password recovery on Cisco routers allows you to get into the router without the necessary passwords. For security reasons, you cannot perform the password recovery procedure through telnet or other remote means. The procedure differs slightly depending on the router series. The password recovery instructions for all router series are on the Cisco Web site at *www.cisco.com*. The steps to perform password recovery on the Cisco 2600 series are:

1. Connect to the router from a PC using the console port and the HyperTerminal program, as described in Chapter 6.

2. If you have access, enter the show version command and record the value of the configuration register (e.g., 0x2102 or 0x102). If you can't access the router configuration, you should assume that the configuration register is 0x2102.

3. Turn the router off and on using the power switch.

4. Press the Break key within the first 60 seconds of bootup to break out of the normal boot routine and enter ROM Monitor (rommon) mode. If the break-out routine doesn't work, try Ctrl+Break.

5. At the rommon 1> prompt, type confreg 0x2142 and press Enter. This will boot the IOS from flash without loading the configuration from NVRAM.

6. Enter the reset command at the rommon 2> prompt. The router will reboot.

7. Press Ctrl+C or enter No after each setup question.

8. When you get to the Router> prompt, enter enable to get to privileged mode.

9. Enter the copy start run command to load the saved configuration file from NVRAM into RAM.

10. Enter the show run command to view the configuration. You will be able to see all unencrypted passwords. Any encrypted passwords will have to be reconfigured. To change the enable secret command, enter the following commands:

    ```
    Router# config t
    Router(config)# enable secret [secret password]
    ```

11. Enter config-register 0x2102 (or the configuration register value you recorded in Step 2) at the global configuration mode prompt to make sure the router reboots in the default manner.

12. Enter the copy run start command to save your changes.

7

CHAPTER SUMMARY

- When the router boots, it follows a set routine.

- Although the router's boot process can vary, the typical boot process follows this sequence: First, the router checks all of its internal hardware components during a process called the POST (power-on self-test). Next, the router loads the basic configuration routine known as the bootstrap program. Then, the bootstrap attempts to locate the Cisco IOS, which in turn loads the router configuration file.

- If the Cisco IOS is set to load from a TFTP server, but the TFTP server cannot be located, then the IOS will boot from flash memory.

- If the IOS cannot be found in flash memory or on the TFTP server, then a limited version will boot from ROM.

- If the Cisco IOS is set to load a configuration file from a TFTP server, but the file or server is not available, the configuration file will be loaded from NVRAM. However, if a configuration file is not available in NVRAM or on a TFTP server, then the automated setup routine will be initialized.

- The Cisco Discovery Protocol (CDP) is proprietary to Cisco devices. This protocol shares information between Cisco devices about other local Cisco devices.

- CDP uses broadcasts to update neighbors every 60 seconds by default (the update time interval is configurable).

- Devices share information about their interface configurations and connections to other devices.

- IP configuration on Cisco switches and routers is similar: the command syntax is ip address [IP address] [subnet mask].

- When you configure an address for a router interface, you must be in interface configuration mode (config-if).

- When you configure an IP address for a Catalyst 1900 switch, you need only be in global configuration mode. These switches don't require IP addresses; you need only configure one if you intend to remotely manage the switch.

- You can verify router connectivity to other systems by using telnet to determine if there is Application layer connectivity.

- If you cannot get connectivity at the Application layer, try trace and ping. Then, check your routing table with the show ip route command to determine if there is a problem with the Network layer.

- One of the most important troubleshooting commands is the show interfaces command. If your interfaces are not up, you cannot route packets.

KEY TERMS

Cisco Discovery Protocol (CDP) — A Cisco proprietary Data Link layer protocol that shares configuration information between Cisco devices that are locally connected.

configuration register — A feature in Cisco routers that is stored in NVRAM and allows the administrator to control several boot functions.

counters — Detailed statistics kept by a router about data passing across its interface.

DCE (data communication equipment) — Equipment that performs some type of signal conversion between the terminal device and the transmission facility. Usually the DCE is part of the telco provider's equipment.

extended mode ping — When you type the word "ping" at the privileged EXEC prompt, and then press the Return or Enter key, you will be presented with ping options. Extended mode ping options include the destination address of the ping, the protocol, repeat count, and datagram size.

global configuration mode — A router mode that allows you to manipulate most of the router's generic settings. The prompt for global configuration mode is router(config)#.

keepalive frames — Data frames sent between two hosts to ensure that the connection between those hosts remains open.

power-on self-test (POST) — A diagnostic program in ROM that runs when the router is powered on. POST checks hardware availability.

ROM Monitor — A bootstrap program that runs during the power-on self-test and checks basic operations of hardware, including CPU, memory, and interfaces.

ROM Monitor mode — A router mode in which you can configure the router manually.

RxBoot mode — A configuration mode that can be entered when changes to a system make it impossible to boot from the flash memory and a valid IOS image cannot be located.

Trivial File Transfer Protocol (TFTP) server — A Computer, such as a PC, laptop, or UNIX workstation, that can be used to maintain Cisco IOS versions and Cisco router configuration files. TFTP is a protocol that is used to copy files back and forth from a computer running TFTP server services.

REVIEW QUESTIONS

1. If you want to see the hexadecimal boot setting for the configuration register, which command would you use? (Choose all that apply.)

   a. router> sh int

   b. router> sh ver

   c. router#sh ver

   d. router#sh int

2. When the trace command is used, multiple packets are sent to a remote destination with:

   a. Progressively higher TTL values until a packet reaches the destination

   b. Progressively lower TTL values until a packet is returned from the destination

   c. Progressively smaller hop counts

   d. Full routing tables

3. If you want to configure the values that ping uses and have access to extended mode ping options, which of the following represents the appropriate prompt and the command you would type before pressing the Return key?

   a. router#ping

   b. router#ping ex md

   c. router#ping motd

   d. router> ping

   e. router#ping –e

   f. router> ping –e

4. What is usually stored in NVRAM? (Choose all that apply.)

   a. Configuration register

   b. Backup copy of the IOS

   c. Limited version of the IOS

   d. Configuration file

5. Which of the following connectivity utilities use ICMP messages for troubleshooting the connection? (Choose all that apply.)

   a. Ping

   b. Telnet

   c. Trace

   d. IP route

   e. Show version

6. Which layer of the OSI model contains the telnet utility?

   a. Application

   b. Network

   c. Data Link

   d. Physical

   e. Transport

7. Which of the following information is *not* visible after you issue a ping?

    a. Quantity of ICMP packets sent

    b. Timeout duration

    c. Success rate

    d. MAC address

    e. Roundtrip times

8. If the packet type is unknown, what does ping report?

    a. !

    b. .

    c. ?

    d. U

9. Which of the following commands are considered incomplete or will not be recognized by the router's IOS? Assume that the Return key is pressed immediately after the command. (Choose all that apply.)

    a. router> ping 192.168.1.1

    b. router#ping

    c. router> ping

    d. router#config

    e. router> config

10. Which of the following maps the route from HostA to HostB across the Internet?

    a. show ip route command

    b. Ping

    c. Trace

    d. Finger

11. If the configuration register is set to 0x2102, where will the system look for boot instructions?

    a. Flash

    b. NVRAM

    c. RAM

    d. ROM

12. If there are no specific instructions to the contrary, from where does the system attempt to load the IOS?

    a. ROM

    b. RAM

    c. NVRAM

    d. Flash

13. If you want to see information about other Cisco devices attached to your router, which of the following commands would you use?

    a. show cisco neighbor

    b. show cdp neighbor

    c. show cdp config

    d. initiate cdp scan

14. CDP is enabled by default on Cisco devices. True or False?

15. Which of the following is the first step in the router boot process?

    a. Locate and load Cisco IOS

    b. Load bootstrap

    c. Locate and load router configuration file

    d. POST

16. Which of the following occurs after the loading of the bootstrap?

    a. Test hardware

    b. Configuration register is examined to determine from where to load the IOS

    c. Locate and load router configuration file

    d. POST

17. What is another name for the privileged EXEC mode?

    a. Enable secret mode

    b. Enable mode

    c. Login mode

    d. User mode

18. By default, what will happen if the IOS cannot be found in flash memory?

    a. The router attempts to load a minimal copy from ROM.

    b. The router uses CDP.

    c. The router contacts an HTTP server.

    d. The router automatically shuts down.

19. If the router is configured to load the IOS from a TFTP server, where will the router look next for the IOS?

    a. ROM

    b. Flash

    c. FTP server

    d. HTTP server

    e. CDP

20. Which command could you use to back up the IOS to a TFTP server?

    a. copy IOS tftp

    b. copy flash tftp

    c. copy rom tftp

    d. copy running-config tftp

21. If you want to see information about other Cisco devices attached to your router, including their IP addresses, which of the following commands would you use?

    a. show cisco neighbor

    b. show cdp neighbor

    c. show cdp neighbor detail

    d. show cdp neighbor Ethernet

22. What is the command to erase the configuration file on a Cisco 1900 series switch?

    a. erase start

    b. delete start

    c. disable nvram

    d. delete nvram

23. The show interfaces command displays the following output: Ethernet0 is up, line protocol is administratively down. What do you infer?

    a. There is no cable attached to the Ethernet0 interface on the router.

    b. The no shutdown command needs to be configured on the Ethernet0 interface.

    c. Incompatible routing protocols have been configured on the router.

    d. There is a physical problem with the Ethernet0 interface on the router.

24. What is the purpose of a hosts file on a router?

    a. To allow you to use host names instead of IP addresses when referring to network devices

    b. To facilitate ARP on the router

    c. To allow routers to see other devices on the network

    d. To block unwanted hosts from using the router

25. Which of the following commands will display the routing table for a Cisco router?

    a. show route

    b. show ip route

    c. show routing table

    d. show table

CASE PROJECTS

1. Lisa and Moe are discussing the CDP protocol. They know it was developed by Cisco and is not part of any protocol suite with which they are familiar. What can you tell them about CDP? Specifically, what is the purpose of this protocol? With which OSI layer is it associated? Is it enabled by default? What is the update interval? How do you turn it on and off of a router? How do you turn it on and off of a single interface on a router? Why might you want to turn it off?

2. Moe and Jennifer have configured a router for a client. With the network administrator's help, they have connected it to the client's network. Unfortunately, it isn't working. They have called you for guidance. What troubleshooting steps do you recommend?

3. While configuring a client's router, Moe types the erase flash command. What are the consequences of this action? What steps will the router go through when it boots if the router is not configured to boot from a TFTP server?

4. Moe is embarrassed about erasing the router's flash memory. Lisa thinks the company has a backup flash file on a TFTP server. They've got you on the phone, and they want you to step them through the procedure to recover the router's operating system. The IOS filename is igs-j-l.111-5.

8

ROUTING PROTOCOLS AND NETWORK ADDRESS TRANSLATION

After reading this chapter and completing the exercises, you will be able to:

♦ Understand the purpose and operation of network address translation (NAT)

♦ Configure static NAT, dynamic NAT, and dynamic NAT with overload

♦ Understand and configure port address translation (PAT)

♦ Differentiate between nonroutable, routed, and routing protocols

♦ Define Interior Gateway Protocols, Exterior Gateway Protocols, distance-vector routing protocols, and link-state routing protocols

♦ Explain the concepts of count-to-infinity, split horizon, split horizon with poison reverse, and hold-down timers

♦ Describe, configure, and monitor the interior routing protocols RIP and IGRP

♦ Explain static routing and administrative distance

♦ Configure static routing and default routes

This chapter explains the concepts of nonroutable, routed, and routing protocols, with a discussion of major protocols in each category. The distinction between distance-vector and link-state routing protocols is also examined. In addition, you learn the proper way to configure and monitor the Routing Information Protocol (RIPv1) and Interior Gateway Routing Protocol (IGRP) on Cisco routers. The concepts and techniques needed to configure static routing and default routes are presented, along with discussions and configuration examples of network address translation and port address translation.

Network Address Translation

Network address translation (NAT) allows many home users, corporations, and organizations around the world to connect far more computers to the Internet than they would otherwise be able to connect. NAT is defined in RFC 3022, which describes methods for connecting private (internal) IP addresses to the Internet. In Chapter 3 you learned that the private IP addresses specified in RFC 1918 could not be routed on the Internet. However, NAT uses a one-to-one mapping or one-to-many mapping method to allow one or more private IP clients to gain access to the Internet by mapping the private IP addresses to public IP addresses. The private addresses are shown in Table 8-1.

Table 8-1   RFC 1918 private address ranges

Class	Private Address Range
A	10.x.x.x
B	172.16.x.x – 172.31.x.x
C	192.168.x.x

NAT has several advantages. First, it conserves public IP addresses. Networks can make use of the private IP address ranges and NAT to either a single external public IP or a smaller pool of public IP addresses. It also hides your internal IP addressing scheme from the outside world. This greatly enhances network security. Finally, it allows for easy renumbering of your IP addresses. For example, if you use all public IP addresses and suddenly decide to change ISPs, you must change all of your internal IP addressing. Using NAT, the internal network uses private IP addresses, which need not change. You would only need to change your outside NAT address(es) if you decided to change ISPs.

There are disadvantages with NAT, however. NAT does introduce a small amount of delay into your network. This delay comes from the NAT router having to create and maintain the NAT table, which is a table of inside addresses and the associated outside addresses. In addition, due to the translation of the source IP address, end-to-end IP traceability is lost. While it is still possible to track a packet back to the NAT device, finding the actual original host is difficult. Finally, some applications fail due to NAT, although this was more of a problem when NAT was first implemented. Today, most modern applications expect NAT to be present on a network.

Cisco developed NAT, and today the technology is used by routers, firewalls, and even individual computers with multiple network connections. Four forms of NAT are available:

- Static NAT
- Dynamic NAT
- Dynamic NAT with overload
- Port address translation

Static NAT

Static NAT is the simplest form of NAT, in which a single private IP address is mapped to a single public IP address. For example, a router could be configured to translate all communications from the internal 192.168.0.1 address to the address 209.86.192.197. In this way, when the host 192.168.0.1 accesses the Internet, the router will translate its IP address to 209.86.192.197. The router will then translate communications between that host and any system on the Internet. Therefore, all Internet devices will communicate with host 209.86.192.197, but the actual packets will be forwarded by the NAT router to host 192.168.0.1 on the local network. In order for the NAT router to translate communications between the internal and external network, it must maintain a table in memory that maps internal IP addresses to addresses presented to the Internet (external addresses). With static NAT, the mapping is one-to-one. For example, internal address 192.168.0.1 maps to 209.86.192.197 and 192.168.0.2 maps to 209.86.192.198, and so on. Figure 8-1 shows a network with static NAT between the internal IP address of an FTP and Web server and a defined public address. Static NAT must be used if you want clients outside your network to access services on your servers.

8

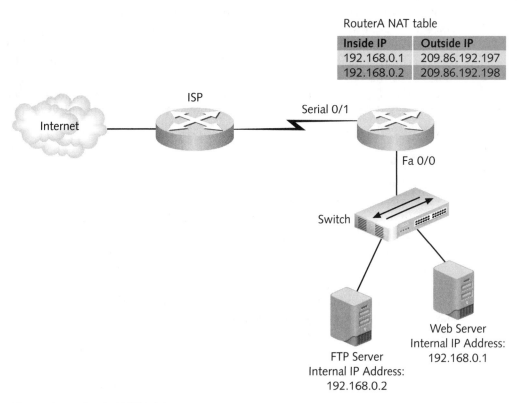

RouterA NAT table

Inside IP	Outside IP
192.168.0.1	209.86.192.197
192.168.0.2	209.86.192.198

Figure 8-1 Static NAT table

The network configuration for NAT is quite simple in a small network because the NAT router will be the default gateway for all clients. In a larger network, the NAT router might be one of many routers. Routers would have to be configured to use the NAT router for Internet communications. NAT should be configured on the border router of a large network. In other words, as shown in Figure 8-1, NAT is needed on the router that connects directly to the ISP.

When the local host 192.168.0.1 communicates with other hosts on the internal network (intranet), NAT will not be involved. For example, when host 192.168.0.1 sends packets to host 192.168.0.2, the packets will not go through the router. This is also true if the local host communicates with other hosts on different networks or subnetworks within the intranet. The router, even if enabled with NAT, will act as a router, sending packets to the appropriate internal network.

Dynamic NAT

Dynamic NAT means that the NAT router automatically maps a group of valid local IP addresses to a group of Internet IP addresses, as needed. This means that the network administrator really doesn't care which IP address the internal clients use, just that they can get an address. The network administrator also doesn't have to spend any time defining specific one-to-one mappings between the private and public IP addresses. Any private IP address will automatically be translated to one of the available Internet IP addresses by the NAT router. Addresses for dynamic NAT are pulled out of a predefined pool of public addresses. The administrator must define the pool and then state which internal private addresses can use the pool. Actual NAT configuration is covered later in this chapter.

Overloading

Overloading is a form of dynamic NAT that uses **port address translation (PAT)**. PAT allows multiple internal, unregistered IP addresses to use a single external registered address. To differentiate between the connections, PAT uses multiple public TCP and UDP ports to create unique sockets that map to internal IP addresses. The socket, as you learned earlier, is a combination of the IP address and port. For example, you may communicate with a Web server with IP address 209.120.178.205 over TCP port 80. The socket for that communication is 209.120.178.205:80, representing the IP address and port. When that Web server contacts your hosts, it will call your local IP address and the TCP socket you indicated in your three-way handshake, as you learned in Chapter 3. Now, assume that you have five clients on your LAN, all communicating with different Web servers, but your NAT router only has one valid Internet IP address. How can the NAT router keep track of where the packets should be sent? The simple answer is by using PAT, which maps internal addresses and ports to the same external address but with different communication ports.

Consider the following example while referring to the sample NAT mapping table (see Table 8-2). Assume an organization has five internal clients—Hosts A–E with IP address ranges 192.168.0.1–192.168.0.5. The organization also has a Web server at 192.168.0.100 hosting connections from Internet clients. The NAT server uses **port forwarding** to send connections from external clients to the Web server on the internal network. Hosts A, B, and C are communicating with a Web server that has the address 209.120.178.205 over port 80, which is socket 209.120.178.205:80. Host D is communicating with an FTP server with IP address 64.247.37.221 over TCP ports 21 and 20. Host E is connected to a Web server at 64.46.108.24. Each internal host had to supply one or more ports when it established communications. The organization only has one Internet IP available: 209.86.192.198.

Table 8-2 NAT mapping table

Host	Source Local Socket	Source Translated Socket	Destination Remote Socket
A	192.168.0.1:1025	209.86.192.198:1025	209.120.178.205:80
B	192.168.0.2:1027	209.86.192.198:1026	209.120.178.205:80
C	192.168.0.3:1025	209.86.192.198:1027	209.120.178.205:80
D	192.168.0.4:1512	209.86.192.198:1049	64.247.37.221:21
D	192.168.0.4:1513	209.86.192.198:1050	64.247.37.221:20
E	192.168.0.5:1025	209.86.192.198:1029	64.46.108.24:80
Internal Web server	192.168.0.100:80	209.86.192.198:80	72.13.15.24:1099

8

In Table 8-2, you can see how the NAT router would keep track of these individual connections uniquely. The local sockets will always be unique because the local hosts have unique IP addresses, even though they may end up using similar port numbers. Remote sockets may be the same because multiple internal hosts can call the same external host. The only item that the NAT router has to make unique is the translated socket. The NAT router does this by not duplicating a port number for the unique IP addresses that it is configured to use. In the preceding example, the NAT router is configured to use a single IP address, making sure there is no port number duplication in the translated sockets. However, many NAT routers can be configured to use multiple public addresses and would therefore just have to ensure that the translated sockets were unique. For example, if the NAT router had IP addresses 209.86.192.198 and 209.86.192.199 as public addresses, it could use dynamic port 1027 twice: once in socket 209.86.192.198:1027, and again in socket 209.86.192.199:1027.

Overlapping

Overlapping occurs when the internal network has been incorrectly configured for an IP range that actually exists on the Internet (registered to another entity) or when two companies merge and each company was using the same private IP address range. This problem usually occurs only when uninformed network engineers configure a network using arbitrary addresses. Sometimes the thought is that a connection to the Internet will never be required. In this case, the organization cannot connect directly to the Internet because it has an IP range registered to someone else. This overlapping problem can be solved using NAT because NAT hides the incorrectly configured internal IP scheme. The NAT router must be configured to translate the internal IP addresses to a valid external address or address range. This is really no different than previous forms of NAT except that the organization's internal IP address range really belongs to someone else. The "someone else" just doesn't know about it because those addresses are never exposed to the Internet, thanks to NAT. Most companies don't run into this problem because their network engineers and designers know to use one of the private IP address ranges (10.x.x.x, 172.16.x.x.–172.31.x.x, and 192.168.x.x.) when configuring a private internal TCP/IP network.

CONFIGURING NETWORK ADDRESS TRANSLATION

You can configure NAT as static NAT or dynamic NAT. Both methods are described in the following sections.

Configuring Static NAT

As mentioned previously, static NAT is a one-to-one mapping of private IP addresses to public IP addresses. Configuring static NAT is a two-step process:

- Define the static mapping between the inside address and the outside address
- Define the NAT router's interfaces as inside or outside

The static mapping is defined with the following command:

```
ip nat inside source static [inside ip] [outside ip]
```

In the example network shown in Figure 8-1, the commands to map the Web server's internal IP to the public IP address 209.86.192.197 would be:

```
RouterA(config)#ip nat inside source static 192.168.0.1 209.86.192.197
```

The only other necessary commands are the definition of interfaces as either inside or outside. In this example, the private addresses are located on Fa 0/0 and the public addresses on Serial 0/1. So, Fa 0/0 must be defined as inside and Serial 0/1 as outside. The syntax for identifying interfaces as inside or outside is:

```
ip nat [inside | outside]
```

The commands to correctly identify the interface for the network in Figure 8-1 are as follows:

```
RouterA(config)#int fa 0/0
RouterA(config-if)#ip nat inside
RouterA(config-if)#int serial 0/1
RouterA(config-if)ip nat outside
```

After these commands are configured, the NAT router has a static one-to-one mapping of 192.168.0.1 to 209.86.192.197. The show IP nat translations command will now display the static NAT mapping.

Configuring Dynamic NAT

Configuring dynamic NAT is a more involved process than static NAT. Still, it can be broken down into four easy-to-remember steps:

- Configure a standard access control list to define what internal traffic will be translated.

- Define a pool of addresses to be used for dynamic NAT allocation.

- Link the access list to the NAT pool.

- Define interfaces as either inside or outside.

REFERENCE

This section shows only the syntax necessary to configure a standard access list for use with NAT. The entire definition and syntax for access lists are in Chapter 10.

To define the standard access list, you must use the following syntax:

```
RouterA(config)#access-list [1-99] permit [inside IP
network(s)] [wildcard mask]
```

Continuing to use Figure 8-1 as an example, assume that the network administrator adds 10 hosts to the network and wants to use dynamic NAT to support them. The access list to allow those 10 clients (and any others who are not defined by static NAT) to use NAT is:

```
RouterA(config)#access-list 1 permit 192.168.0.0 0.0.0.255
```

The administrator also obtains the public address range of 209.86.192.200 to 209.86.192.240 for use as his dynamic NAT pool. Step two defines the NAT pool. The syntax for this command is:

```
ip nat pool [pool name] [start ip] [end ip] netmask [netmask]
```

Because the administrator has a range of addresses to use, the pool can be defined as follows:

```
RouterA(config)#ip nat pool PoolExample 209.86.192.200
209.86.192.240 netmask 255.255.255.0
```

The pool must then be mapped or linked to the access list. This step essentially states what is being defined as needing to be translated and what it can be translated to. The syntax for the command is:

```
ip nat inside source list [access list number] pool [pool name]
```

The command necessary to link the access list and NAT pool in our example is as follows:

```
RouterA(config)#ip nat inside source list 1 pool PoolExample
```

Two very important items must match in this command. First, the access list number you place in the command must match the list number you created in the first step. Second, the pool name must match the pool you create exactly. Cisco routers are case sensitive, so placing poolexample instead of PoolExample in the command would result in NAT not functioning correctly. This command states that all 192.168.0.0 internal IP addresses (as defined in access list 1) must be translated to the addresses found in pool, PoolExample, 209.86.192.200-209.86.192.240.

Finally, you must define the interfaces as either inside or outside. These commands are exactly the same as those shown in the static NAT example:

```
RouterA(config)#int fa 0/0
RouterA(config-if)#ip nat inside
RouterA(config-if)#int serial 0/1
RouterA(config-if)ip nat outside
```

Configuring Dynamic NAT with Overload

Configuring dynamic NAT with overload involves the same four basic steps as dynamic NAT. Dynamic NAT with overload tells your NAT router to keep up with both the internal IP and internal source port number. In short, it allows multiple internal IP addresses to share a single external IP address. Changing from dynamic NAT to dynamic NAT with overload requires a slight change in the syntax for linking the access list to the NAT pool. To perform overload on the dynamic NAT example shown earlier, you would change the command to read:

```
RouterA(config)#ip nat inside source list 1 pool
PoolExample overload
```

The addition of the overload keyword forces the NAT router to translate based on IP address and port numbers; in other words, sockets. In addition, the command requires only a single IP address in the range. Therefore, the command to configure a pool with a single address for use with dynamic NAT with overload is:

```
RouterA(config)#ip nat pool PoolExample 209.86.192.200
209.86.192.200 netmask 255.255.255.0
```

Theoretically, 64,511 translations can occur to a single IP address. However, Cisco recommends configuring at least one NAT overload IP address per 8,000 hosts.

Configuring Port Address Translation to an Outside Interface

On smaller networks, connections originating from the outside to inside addresses may not be needed. In addition, the ISP may be unwilling to give multiple IP addresses to be used for NAT, or the company may not want to pay for additional IP addresses. When these situations occur, port address translation can be configured to allow an outside interface's IP address to be used for translation. Figure 8-2 shows a network where the single outside IP address that is assigned to Serial 0/1, 172.16.0.6/30, is also used for PAT. As the clients on the inside attempt to reach the Internet via the ISP, the internal source IP and source port are translated to the external IP address and an external source port. The PAT router attempts to use the same external source port as the original inside port number. The example in Figure 8-2 shows this occurring with the first two PAT table entries. If, however, the original inside source port number is already in use, as is the case in the third entry in the table, the PAT router will use the next unassigned outside port number.

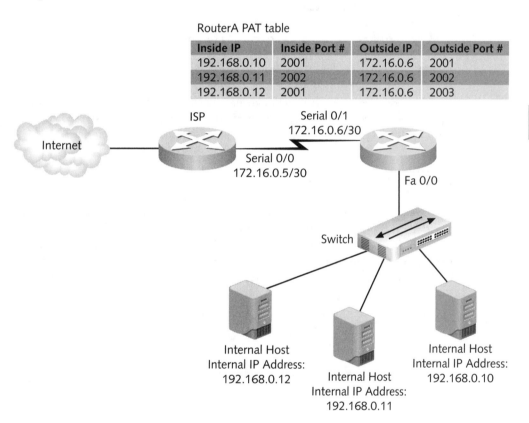

RouterA PAT table

Inside IP	Inside Port #	Outside IP	Outside Port #
192.168.0.10	2001	172.16.0.6	2001
192.168.0.11	2002	172.16.0.6	2002
192.168.0.12	2001	172.16.0.6	2003

Figure 8-2   Port address translation example

Configuring PAT is a three-step process.

- Configure a standard access list to define what internal traffic will be translated.

- Link the access list to the interface to be used for PAT.

- Define interfaces as either inside or outside.

In the example from Figure 8-2, a standard access list must be configured that permits 192.168.0.0/24 networks to be translated. Then, this list must be linked to interface serial 0/1. Finally, serial 0/1 must be defined as outside and fa 0/0 as inside. The commands to accomplish all of these tasks are:

```
RouterA(config)#access-list 1 permit 192.168.0.0 0.0.0.255
RouterA(config)#ip nat inside source list 1 interface
serial 0/1 overload
RouterA(config)#interface serial 0/1
RouterA(config-if)#ip nat outside
RouterA(config-if)#interface fa 0/0
RouterA(config-if)ip nat inside
```

NOTE Dynamic NAT with overload is essentially the same as port address translation. The main difference between the two is the IP address used for translation. In dynamic NAT with overload, the IP address used for PAT is not shared with any external physical interface. With PAT, the address used for overloading is the same one assigned to the outside physical interface.

NONROUTABLE PROTOCOLS

In the early days of networking, networks were small collections of computers tied together for the purpose of sharing expensive peripherals such as high-end laser printers. Few companies could afford to link all their computers together on a local area network (LAN). Instead, using coaxial cable, computers were hooked together in workgroups. Figure 8-3 shows a typical early network.

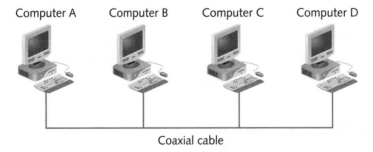

Figure 8-3   Early network model using coaxial cable

Early networks were sometimes configured as **peer-to-peer networks**, in which computers communicate with and provide services to their "peers." Peer-to-peer networks do not pass packets between multiple networks. All communication occurs on the one network segment where the peer-to-peer network exists.

Due to the localized nature of traffic on a peer-to-peer network, network source and destination information is not needed and would produce unnecessary overhead. Instead, peer-to-peer networks can use small and efficient nonroutable protocols.

Several **nonroutable protocols** exist in today's networking world, but NetBEUI, short for NetBIOS Enhanced User Interface, is the most common. NetBEUI ships with all Microsoft Windows operating systems. In small, peer-to-peer networks, NetBEUI is easy to configure and use. Because it is very small, it is fast and efficient.

Unfortunately, NetBEUI cannot scale into large internetworks because it cannot hold Network layer information in its network header. Without this information, packets cannot be routed between multiple network segments. Therefore, if you try to use NetBEUI—or any nonroutable protocol—in a network with multiple networks, communication between the networks will fail.

ROUTED PROTOCOLS

Routed protocols have packet headers that can contain Network layer addresses. Routed protocols were developed to support networks consisting of multiple networks or subnetworks. Figure 8-4 shows a typical **internetwork** within which routed protocols, such as TCP/IP or IPX/SPX, are used.

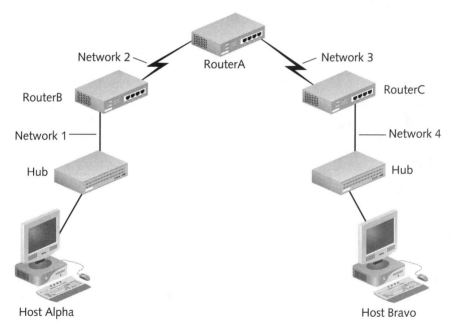

Figure 8-4 Common internetwork

In this sample internetwork, Host Alpha can communicate with Host Bravo only if Host Alpha uses a protocol that can add Network layer addressing to each packet header. With this Network layer addressing, information from Alpha can traverse the internetwork from Network 1 to Network 4. Without the Network layer information, all packets are only able to communicate within Network 1. **Transmission Control Protocol/Internet Protocol (TCP/IP)** and **Internetwork Packet Exchange/Sequence Packet Exchange (IPX/SPX)** are two protocols that can carry Network layer information. Thus, routers can route them through the internetwork.

For routed protocols to work on a network, every device (computer, printer, and router interface port) must be configured with a unique IP or IPX address. These Network layer **logical addresses** allow TCP/IP or IPX/SPX packets to be routed throughout the internetwork. Figure 8-5 shows the sample network with IP addresses assigned to each device.

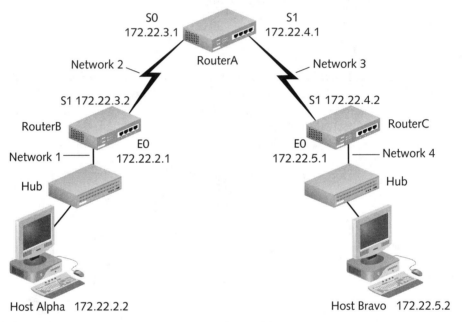

Figure 8-5 Common internetwork with IP addresses

ROUTING PROTOCOLS

For proper network connectivity, you need more than just routed protocols on large internetworks. In order for routers to find the correct path for routed protocols, they use routing protocols to build routing tables that specify where every network in the internetwork is located. The administrator can also build routing tables statically; static routing is described later in this chapter. **Routing protocols** are protocols used by routers to make path determination choices and to share those choices with other routers. Table 8-3 shows a conceptual routing table that RouterB in Figure 8-5 would use to route a TCP/IP packet from Network 1 to Network 4.

Table 8-3   Conceptual routing table

Network	Path	Distance
Network 2	Available via RouterB	directly connected
Network 3	Available via RouterA	1 hop
Network 4	Available via RouterC	2 hops

This table shows that RouterB can reach any of the networks in the internetwork. The Distance column refers to hop count as the single metric used in this routing table. **Hop count** is the number of routers a packet must pass through to reach a particular network. A **metric** is a value used to define the suitability of a particular route. In other words, routers use metrics to determine which routes are better than other routes.

NOTE   In the internetwork shown in Figure 8-5, routing metrics are simple because of the single-path nature of the internetwork. The route to Network 4 from RouterB will be via RouterA and RouterC; there is no better path available.

An **autonomous system (AS)**, which uses Interior Gateway Protocols as routing protocols, is a group of routers under the control of a single administration. Figure 8-6 shows Big Tin Inc.'s AS.

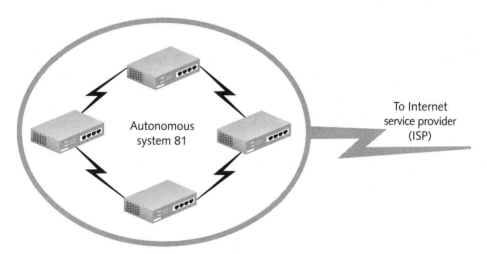

Figure 8-6   Big Tin Inc.'s AS

Big Tin Inc. has an autonomous system consisting of four routers under the control of local network engineers. In general, an AS runs a single routing protocol.

Routing protocols come in two major categories: **Interior Gateway Protocols (IGPs)** are the routing protocols used within an AS, and **Exterior Gateway Protocols (EGPs)** are routing protocols used to route information between multiple autonomous systems.

Routing Information Protocol (RIP), **Interior Gateway Routing Protocol (IGRP)**, **Enhanced Interior Gateway Routing Protocol (EIGRP)**, and **Open Shortest Path First (OSPF)** are examples of IGPs. RIP and IGRP are distance-vector routing protocols, and OSPF is a link-state routing protocol; these two categories are discussed in the following section. EIGRP is a hybrid routing protocol developed by Cisco to overcome some of the limitations associated with IGRP in particular and distance-vector routing protocols in general. As a hybrid routing protocol, EIGRP combines the best attributes of both distance-vector and link-state routing protocols. Additionally, EIGRP, when used with the no auto summary command, can support variable length subnet masking (VLSM). The use of VLSM within a single network number is beyond the scope of this book; it is covered in detail in studies for the CCNP Routing exam. EIGRP, like IGRP, is Cisco proprietary and can only be used between Cisco routers.

Border Gateway Protocol (BGP) is an example of an EGP. EGPs are the other category of routing protocols and are generally covered in depth in a CCNP Routing course. In this book, all discussions will focus on RIP and IGRP—both of which are basic IGPs.

Two Types of IGPs

IGPs are subdivided into two major types: **distance-vector** and **link-state**. These protocol types accomplish the same job—determining routes within an autonomous system—but they do so via different mechanisms.

Distance-Vector Routing Protocols

Distance-vector routing protocols broadcast their entire routing table to each neighbor router at predetermined intervals. The actual interval depends on the distance-vector routing protocol in use, but varies between 30 and 90 seconds. Figure 8-7 shows how this process occurs.

As the updates propagate throughout the network, RouterC will only receive information about RouterB's routing table via RouterA. This is sometimes referred to as **routing by rumor**. It is also one of the main problems with distance-vector routing protocols. If RouterB and RouterA have an update interval of 30 seconds, RouterC will not learn about network topology changes (changes in router interface states or route metrics) on RouterB for up to a minute. Figure 8-8 shows the types of problems this slow time to convergence can cause. **Convergence** is a state where all routers on the internetwork share a common view of the internetwork routes.

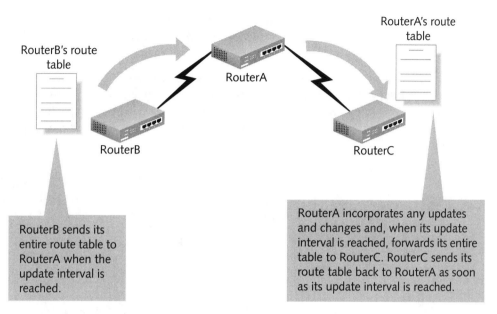

Figure 8-7 Distance-vector routing protocol process

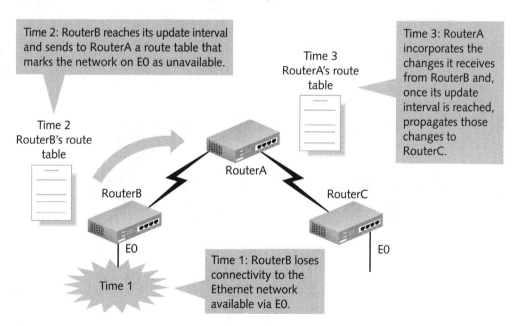

Figure 8-8 Distance-vector convergence example

Figure 8-8 shows that the time it will take the network to converge depends on the amount of time between update intervals on RouterB and RouterA. Given the small size of this sample network, the amount of time to converge would be fairly minimal.

Still, for a short amount of time, RouterC mistakenly believes the Ethernet network attached to RouterB is viable and continues routing packets addressed to hosts on that network.

Problems, such as routing loops, can occur with distance-vector protocols if control measures are not put in place. **Routing loops** are often referred to as **count-to-infinity** problems because loops, without preventive measures (described next), will cause packets to bounce around the internetwork infinitely. Figure 8-9 illustrates the types of problems that can occur with routing loops.

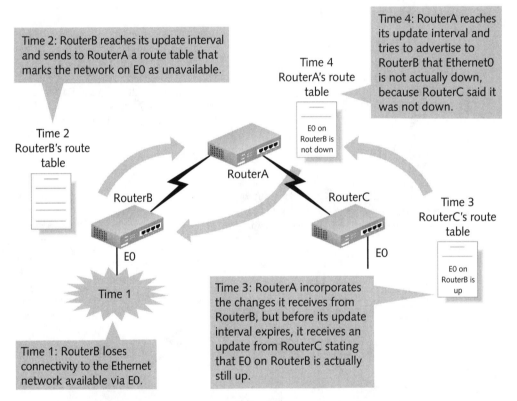

Figure 8-9   Distance-vector convergence problems

In this internetwork, true loops are not possible because of the linear nature of the network design. Still, the scenario presented in Figure 8-9 shows that the internetwork could, without proper precautions, readvertise a route that was actually not accessible. To prevent these problems, techniques such as defining a maximum, split horizon, split horizon with poison reverse, and hold-down timers are used to reduce the chances that incorrect routing table information will be propagated.

Defining a maximum is one of the easiest ways to limit count-to-infinity problems. If you assign a packet a maximum hop count, it cannot bounce infinitely around the internetwork. RIP, one of the most common distance-vector protocols, defines a maximum hop count of 15. Therefore, if a routing loop did occur on a RIP internetwork, the packet would only travel through 15 routers before the packet exceeded its TTL and was dropped. In other words, the 16th router that the packet tried to cross on a RIP internetwork would see that the packet had exceeded its TTL and would drop the packet. In the internetwork illustrated in Figure 8-9, packets could potentially bounce around infinitely. For the RIP (version 1) routing protocol, hop count is the sole metric used to determine the relative desirability of a particular path.

Split horizon and **split horizon with poison reverse** are two other common ways to prevent routing loops when using distance-vector routing protocols. Split horizon controls what information a router will send out through a particular interface. In short, a router will not send information back through an interface about a route that it originally learned about through that same interface. For example, if RouterA in Figure 8-9 uses split horizon, it will not accept the update regarding E0 on RouterB from RouterC at Time 4. (Time 4 in Figure 8-9 represents the time when RouterC's update interval expires and RouterC sends out its update table.) It won't accept the update because it would need to be sent out of the interface from which RouterA originally learned that E0 on RouterB was down. If RouterA uses split horizon with poison reverse, it not only refuses to accept RouterC's update regarding E0 on RouterB, but it also responds to RouterC's attempted update. RouterA will tell RouterC that the route to E0 on RouterB is no longer available by indicating that the hop count has been exceeded. In other words, it poisons the erroneous route advertised by RouterC so that no other router will see this as a viable route.

Another common technique used to stop routing loops is the **hold-down timer**. Hold-down timers allow a router to place a route in a state where it will not accept any changes to that route. If RouterA uses hold-down timers in Figure 8-9, the update from RouterC is ignored because the route would be in "hold-down" for a period of time after it was marked down. During this hold-down period, the router will not accept an update if it has a less favorable metric. It will accept an update and release the timer if the update has a more favorable metric. This prevents improper route information from being propagated throughout the internetwork. Hold-down timers are configurable by the network administrator.

Link-State Routing Protocols

Link-state routing protocols are the second type of routing protocols you can use to exchange route information between routers in an autonomous system. They behave very differently from distance-vector routing protocols. Routers configured with a link-state routing protocol use **link-state advertisements (LSAs)** to inform neighbor routers on the internetwork. However, instead of sending their entire routing tables, the LSAs contain only the local links for the advertised router. The **Shortest Path First (SPF) algorithm** uses the link information to compute the routes. So, router CPU resources are used instead of bandwidth.

Link-state packets (LSPs), packets used to send out LSAs, allow every router in the internetwork to share a common view of the **topology** of the internetwork. Figure 8-10 shows how a router configured with a link-state routing protocol **floods** or multicasts LSPs to the network so that every other router on the internetwork has a common view of its topology.

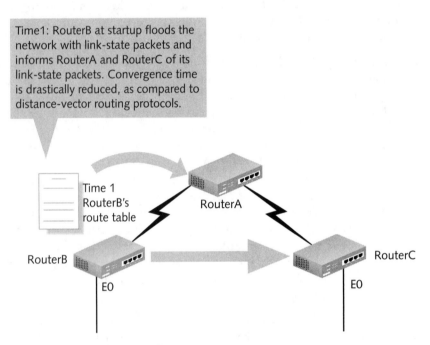

Time1: RouterB at startup floods the network with link-state packets and informs RouterA and RouterC of its link-state packets. Convergence time is drastically reduced, as compared to distance-vector routing protocols.

Time 1
RouterB's
route table

RouterA

RouterB

EO

RouterC

EO

Figure 8-10   Link-state advertisements

In the example in Figure 8-10, the network quickly reaches a state of convergence due to the flooding of link-state packets. This is one huge advantage that link-state routing protocols have over distance-vector routing protocols. Also, later updates by the routers in the internetwork will be **triggered updates**. These updates occur due to network topology changes, not periodic routing table advertisements. In other words, RouterB will flood the internetwork with LSPs if a change occurs to its routing table. This announcement contains only the changes in the routing table, not the entire routing table. This conserves bandwidth on the internetwork links.

There are some drawbacks to using link-state routing protocols. Due to the complexity of the Shortest Path First algorithm and the need to hold a view of the entire internetwork topology, routers using link-state protocols must be configured with more memory and processing power than those using distance-vector routing protocols. In addition, link-state routing protocols such as OSPF are much more complicated to configure on the routers. This is why, for smaller-scale internetworks, distance-vector routing protocols such as RIP and IGRP are typically used instead of OSPF.

Table 8-4 summarizes the key characteristics associated with distance-vector and link-state routing protocols.

Table 8-4   Major characteristics of distance-vector and link-state routing protocols

Distance-vector	Link-state
Periodically broadcasts entire routing table to neighbor routers	Multicasts links to all routers in the AS on startup; all other routing table updates contain only updated routes; updates occur when a network topology change occurs
Slow to converge	Fast to converge due to link-state advertisements
Prone to routing loops because of routing by rumor nature	Less prone to routing loops because all other routers share a common view of the network
Easy to configure and administer	Harder to configure; requires greater memory and processing power on each router
Consumes relatively more bandwidth	Consumes relatively less bandwidth

8

Now that you have been introduced to the theory behind routing protocols, you need to learn how to actually configure specific protocols on Cisco routers. RIP and IGRP, both distance-vector protocols, are the two main protocols covered on the CCNA exam. In the next two sections, you will learn how to configure each protocol.

ROUTING INFORMATION PROTOCOL

The first Interior Gateway Protocol you must know how to configure is RIPv1 (RIP version 1).

REFERENCE

There is another version of RIP called RIP version 2 (RIPv2), which is more sophisticated. RIPv2 is covered in Chapter 9. When discussing RIP in the context of the CCNA exam, you should assume RIPv1.

RIP is a distance-vector routing protocol that broadcasts entire routing tables to neighbors every 30 seconds, out of every interface. RIP uses hop count as its sole metric. As a result, RIP lacks the capability to factor in link speed or congestion between routers, which means that the shortest path chosen by RIP is not always the fastest. As previously mentioned, RIP has a maximum hop count of 15. As a result, RIP does not work in large internetworks. RIP has the following attributes:

- It is a distance-vector routing protocol.
- It has a maximum hop count of 15.
- 16 hops is considered infinity.
- Hop count is the only metric available for path selection.
- It broadcasts the entire routing table to neighbors every 30 seconds.

- It is capable of load balancing.
- It is easy to configure.

In addition, RIP is susceptible to all the problems normally associated with distance-vector routing protocols. It is slow to converge and forces routers to learn network information only from neighbors. Still, RIP is popular because it is easy to configure.

To install RIP on a Cisco router using TCP/IP, you must perform the following two tasks:

- Enable RIP.
- Configure RIP routing for each major network you want to advertise.

You need only configure major network numbers with RIP because RIP does not advertise subnet mask information. As you read the following text, remember that there are two versions of RIP. The CCNA exam focuses on RIP version 1, which does not pass subnet mask information with its routing table updates.

Enabling RIP Routing

For the following discussion of RIP, we will use the network in Figure 8-11. For brevity, we will only focus on enabling RIP on RouterB. You can assume that RIP has already been configured on RouterA and RouterC.

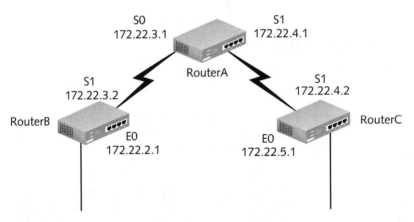

Figure 8-11   Sample IP network

To start configuring RIP, you must first enter privileged mode and then global configuration mode on your router. Once you type the enable command and config terminal command to enter global configuration mode, router output similar to that in Figure 8-12 should appear.

Once in global configuration mode, you must enable RIP with the router rip command. The command to enable RIP is displayed in Figure 8-13.

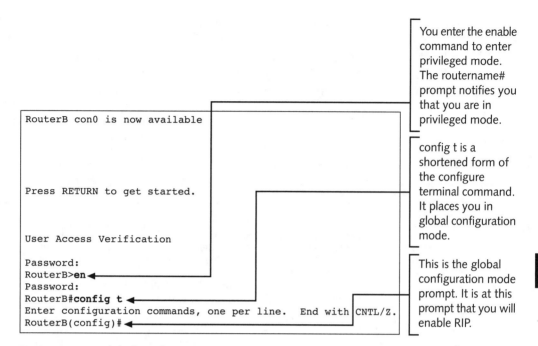

Figure 8-12   Global configuration mode

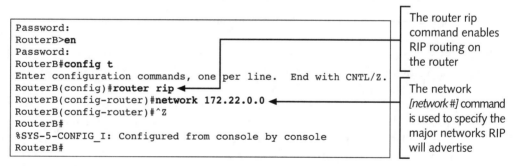

Figure 8-13   Configuring RIP

Configuring RIP Routing for Each Major Network

Figure 8-13 also displays the commands necessary to turn on RIP routing for a particular major network. The network *[network #]* command in Figure 8-13 turns on RIP routing for the major class B network 172.22.0.0. If you have multiple major networks
configured on a router, an individual network *[network #]* command must be issued for
each separate network.

After you have enabled RIP routing globally and configured each major network that the router will advertise with RIP updates, RIP is fully configured on the router. After the update interval of 30 seconds passes on each router, RouterB will eventually learn of all networks. You use the show ip route command to display the routing table. Figure 8-14 shows the output from the show ip route command on RouterB.

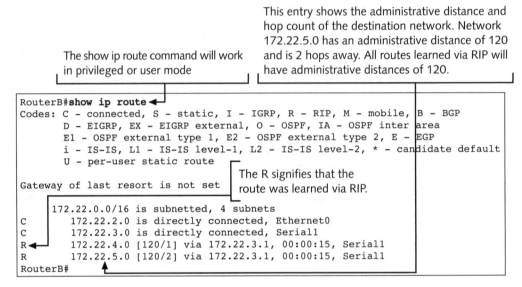

Figure 8-14   Output from the show ip route command

The output in Figure 8-14 illustrates an extremely important concept called administrative distance. **Administrative distance** is a value used to determine the reliability of the information regarding a particular route. Administrative distances range from 0–255. The larger the number, the less reliable the connection is considered to be. The more reliable connection will always be favored over the less reliable and will therefore be installed as a route in the IP routing table of the router. Table 8-5 shows common routing protocols and their administrative distances.

The value 120, shown in the routing table in Figure 8-14 after subnet 172.22.4.0 and 172.22.5.0, is the administrative distance for RIP. A metric of 1 (1 hop) is listed after the 120 for the 172.22.4.0 entry, and a metric of 2 (2 hops) is listed after the 120 for the 172.22.5.0 entry. Remember, RIP uses hops as its sole metric.

Table 8-5 Administrative distances

Route Learned via:	Administrative Distance
Directly connected network	0
Static route	1
EIGRP	90
IGRP	100
OSPF	110
RIP	120
Unknown	255

If a route is being discovered using both RIP and a directly connected interface, the route available via the directly connected interface will be the preferred route because it has a lower administrative distance. Likewise, if both IGRP and RIP advertise a route for a particular network, the IGRP route will be used because it is considered more reliable due to its lower administrative distance.

8

Show ip protocol and debug ip rip Commands

You can use the show ip protocol and debug ip rip commands to monitor RIP. You can type the show ip protocol command in either user mode or privileged mode. When you type this command, you will receive output similar to that shown in Figure 8-15.

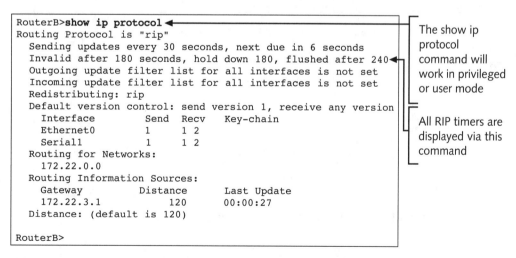

```
RouterB>show ip protocol
Routing Protocol is "rip"
  Sending updates every 30 seconds, next due in 6 seconds
  Invalid after 180 seconds, hold down 180, flushed after 240
  Outgoing update filter list for all interfaces is not set
  Incoming update filter list for all interfaces is not set
  Redistributing: rip
  Default version control: send version 1, receive any version
    Interface       Send  Recv   Key-chain
    Ethernet0         1    1 2
    Serial1           1    1 2
  Routing for Networks:
    172.22.0.0
  Routing Information Sources:
    Gateway         Distance      Last Update
    172.22.3.1           120      00:00:27
  Distance: (default is 120)

RouterB>
```

The show ip protocol command will work in privileged or user mode

All RIP timers are displayed via this command

Figure 8-15 Output from the show ip protocol command

In Figure 8-15, you can see the timers associated with RIP. RIP updates on TCP/IP networks, as stated previously, occur every 30 seconds. A route is considered invalid if six consecutive update intervals pass without an update from that route. The hold-down time of 180 seconds allows the router to stabilize its routing table to help prevent routing loops when a network path does go down. Finally, the **flush interval** is the time at which a route will be totally removed from the routing table if no updates are received.

The debug ip rip command, like all debug commands, should only be used when troubleshooting RIP. This command displays real-time rip updates being sent and received and places very high processing demands on your router, which could affect network performance. Figure 8-16 shows the output of the debug ip rip command.

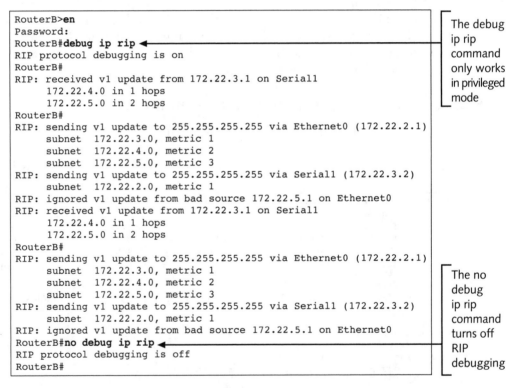

```
RouterB>en
Password:
RouterB#debug ip rip
RIP protocol debugging is on
RouterB#
RIP: received v1 update from 172.22.3.1 on Serial1
     172.22.4.0 in 1 hops
     172.22.5.0 in 2 hops
RouterB#
RIP: sending v1 update to 255.255.255.255 via Ethernet0 (172.22.2.1)
     subnet  172.22.3.0, metric 1
     subnet  172.22.4.0, metric 2
     subnet  172.22.5.0, metric 3
RIP: sending v1 update to 255.255.255.255 via Serial1 (172.22.3.2)
     subnet  172.22.2.0, metric 1
RIP: ignored v1 update from bad source 172.22.5.1 on Ethernet0
RIP: received v1 update from 172.22.3.1 on Serial1
     172.22.4.0 in 1 hops
     172.22.5.0 in 2 hops
RouterB#
RIP: sending v1 update to 255.255.255.255 via Ethernet0 (172.22.2.1)
     subnet  172.22.3.0, metric 1
     subnet  172.22.4.0, metric 2
     subnet  172.22.5.0, metric 3
RIP: sending v1 update to 255.255.255.255 via Serial1 (172.22.3.2)
     subnet  172.22.2.0, metric 1
RIP: ignored v1 update from bad source 172.22.5.1 on Ethernet0
RouterB#no debug ip rip
RIP protocol debugging is off
RouterB#
```

The debug ip rip command only works in privileged mode

The no debug ip rip command turns off RIP debugging

Figure 8-16   Output from the debug ip rip command

As previously mentioned, RIP is slow to converge, like most distance-vector routing protocols. If RouterC in Figure 8-11 loses its connection to subnet 172.22.5.0 on Ethernet0, RouterB will learn about the route status changing. However, it could take at least a minute for the changes to propagate throughout the network (30 seconds maximum for the update interval on RouterC and RouterA). Once RouterB learns of the change in status for network 172.22.5.0, it marks the route as possibly down and initiates a hold-down timer. You can type the show ip route command on RouterB to display this change in status. Figure 8-17 shows the results of the show ip route command after Ethernet0 on RouterC becomes inaccessible.

The route to subnet 172.22.5.0 is in hold-down and marked as possibly down

```
RouterB#show ip route
Codes: C - connected, S - static, I - IGRP, R - RIP, M - mobile, B - BGP
       D - EIGRP, EX - EIGRP external, O - OSPF, IA - OSPF inter area
       E1 - OSPF external type 1, E2 - OSPF external type 2, E - EGP
       i - IS-IS, L1 - IS-IS level-1, L2 - IS-IS level-2, * - candidate default
       U - per-user static route

Gateway of last resort is not set

     172.22.0.0/16 is subnetted, 4 subnets
C        172.22.2.0 is directly connected, Ethernet0
C        172.22.3.0 is directly connected, Serial1
R        172.22.4.0 [120/1] via 172.22.3.1, 00:00:19, Serial1
R        172.22.5.0/24 is possibly down,
            routing via 172.22.3.1, Serial1
```

Figure 8-17   Output from the show ip route command

Eventually, the route will be flushed from the routing table. Still, with a hold-down time of 180 seconds and a flush timer of 240 seconds, the time it takes for the internetwork to converge can become excessive. If you issue the show ip route command after the route has been flushed from the routing table, you will get the router output displayed in Figure 8-18.

The route to subnet 172.22.5.0 has been removed from the route table

```
RouterB#show ip route
Codes: C - connected, S - static, I - IGRP, R - RIP, M - mobile, B - BGP
       D - EIGRP, EX - EIGRP external, O - OSPF, IA - OSPF inter area
       E1 - OSPF external type 1, E2 - OSPF external type 2, E - EGP
       i - IS-IS, L1 - IS-IS level-1, L2 - IS-IS level-2, * - candidate default
       U - per-user static route

Gateway of last resort is not set

     172.22.0.0/16 is subnetted, 3 subnets
C        172.22.2.0 is directly connected, Ethernet0
C        172.22.3.0 is directly connected, Serial1
R        172.22.4.0 [120/1] via 172.22.3.1, 00:00:10, Serial1
RouterB#
```

Figure 8-18   New output from the show ip route command

> Note that RIP relies on hop count as its single metric. In the network in Figure 8-19, a router configured to use RIP would always route packets to the subnet 172.22.5.0 via the 56-Kbps link between RouterB and RouterC because of the hop count of one.

NOTE

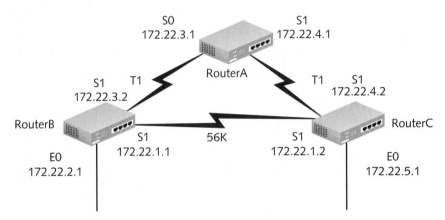

Figure 8-19   RIP problems caused by hop count reliance

As this network is configured, it may actually be faster to route packets along the T1 lines. This route, with a hop count of two, will not be used by RIP as the best route even though it may be faster. To combat this problem associated with distance-vector protocols such as RIP, Cisco developed its own proprietary distance-vector protocol: IGRP.

INTERIOR GATEWAY ROUTING PROTOCOL

IGRP is a proprietary distance-vector routing protocol created by Cisco to solve some of the problems associated with RIP. A larger hop count metric allows IGRP to be used on larger networks. In fact, IGRP supports a hop count of 255, although 100 is the default if hop count is configured to be used as a metric. If, for example, IGRP is configured to use hops as a metric and 255 hops is the value configured, on the 256th hop IGRP will return an ICMP destination network unreachable message. In some situations you may actually want to reduce IGRP's hop count to speed convergence and route processing. The metric maximum-hops command allows you to set the maximum hop count for IGRP. You should set the hop count to the maximum number of routers within your network if you are going to use hops with IGRP.

IGRP does not use hops as a metric by default. The default metrics for IGRP are bandwidth and delay only. IGRP can also be configured to use load and reliability metrics. The metrics that can be configured for IGRP are:

- Hops: Number of routers between source and destination networks
- Load: The load on a link in the path

- Bandwidth: The speed of the link (default)

- Reliability: Measures reliability with a scale of 0 to 255

- Delay: The delay on the medium (default)

- MTU: The size of the datagram

Remember, by default, IGRP computes the best available route using only bandwidth and delay, but it can be configured to use most of the metrics mentioned previously. The ability to use bandwidth as a factor in the route selection process, along with reliability and delay, allows IGRP to make more intelligent route choices than RIP. IGRP can also use multiple, different cost paths to allow for redundancy and load balancing. IGRP can support up to four cost paths.

Configuring IGRP on a Cisco router using TCP/IP is a simple process accomplished with the router igrp *[autonomous system #]* and network *[network #]* commands. Autonomous system numbers are public if the autonomous system exchanges routing information with other autonomous systems on the Internet. They are private if the routing is invisible to the Internet. The IANA (Internet Assigned Numbers Authority) assigns the numbers. The autonomous system number must be configured the same on all routers that need to share routing table information. IGRP routers will not share table information with other IGRP routers that are not in the same autonomous system. Figure 8-20 shows the router commands necessary to configure IGRP.

8

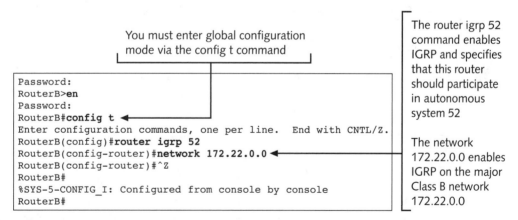

Figure 8-20   Commands used to configure IGRP

Once IGRP is configured throughout the internetwork, you can issue the show ip route command to monitor all available IGRP routes. Figure 8-21 shows the results of this command.

The Cisco IOS by default displays the subnet mask as a / (forward slash) followed by the number of bits in the mask. A /16 subnet mask indicates that a Class B network is being used.

```
RouterB#show ip route
Codes: C - connected, S - static, I - IGRP, R - RIP, M - mobile, B - BGP
       D - EIGRP, EX - EIGRP external, O - OSPF, IA - OSPF inter area
       E1 - OSPF external type 1, E2 - OSPF external type 2, E - EGP
       i - IS-IS, L1 - IS-IS level-1, L2 - IS-IS level-2, * - candidate default
       U - per-user static route

Gateway of last resort is not set

     172.22.0.0/16 is subnetted, 4 subnets
C       172.22.2.0 is directly connected, Ethernet0
C       172.22.3.0 is directly connected, Serial1
I       172.22.4.0 [100/10476] via 172.22.3.1, 00:00:20, Serial1
I       172.22.5.0 [100/10576] via 172.22.3.1, 00:00:20, Serial1
RouterB#
```

Routes learned via IGRP are displayed for each subnetwork.

The routes for RIP are no longer displayed because IGRP has a lower administrative distance and therefore a more reliable route.

In this example, the [100/10576] signifies the administrative distance and metric. The route to subnet 172.22.5.0 via 172.22.3.1 has an administrative distance of 100 (lower than RIP's 120 administrative distance) and a metric of 10576 (figured using the bandwidth and delay metrics by default).

Figure 8-21   The show ip route command with IGRP

If you want to see the IGRP timers, you can type the show ip protocol command. It will present output similar to that found in Figure 8-22.

IGRP sends out routing table updates every 90 seconds. Compared to RIP, this reduces the amount of broadcast traffic used to maintain routing tables. In Figure 8-22, you can see that the router is running multiple routing protocols, RIP and IGRP. In the real world, you would normally not configure your routers to run both RIP and IGRP on the same router on a permanent basis. Doing so would waste network bandwidth for RIP updates that would always be considered inferior to IGRP updates and therefore not be placed in the routing table. However, redistributing RIP routes in an IGRP network may be necessary on a temporary basis when companies or organizations merge and different communications facilities must be joined or interconnected.

IGRP sends updates every
90 seconds

```
RouterB#show ip protocol
Routing Protocol is "rip"
  Sending updates every 30 seconds, next due in 21 seconds
  Invalid after 180 seconds, hold down 180, flushed after 240
  Outgoing update filter list for all interfaces is not set
  Incoming update filter list for all interfaces is not set
  Redistributing: rip
  Default version control: send version 1, receive any version
    Interface        Send  Recv    Key-chain
    Ethernet0          1    1 2
    Serial1            1    1 2
  Routing for Networks:
    172.22.0.0
  Routing Information Sources:
    Gateway         Distance        Last Update
    172.22.3.1          120         00:00:12
  Distance: (default is 120)

Routing Protocol is "igrp 52"
  Sending updates every 90 seconds, next due in 68 seconds
  Invalid after 270 seconds, hold down 280, flushed after 630
  Outgoing update filter list for all interfaces is not set
  Incoming update filter list for all interfaces is not set
  Default networks flagged in outgoing updates
  Default networks accepted from incoming updates
  IGRP metric weight K1=1, K2=0, K3=1, K4=0, K5=0
  IGRP maximum hopcount 100
  IGRP maximum metric variance 1
  Redistributing: igrp 52
  Routing for Networks:
    172.22.0.0
  Routing Information Sources:
    Gateway         Distance        Last Update
    172.22.3.1          100         00:00:36
  Distance: (default is 100)

RouterB#
```

Figure 8-22   The show ip protocol command with IGRP

A final command available to monitor IGRP is the debug ip igrp command. Figure 8-23 shows the correct syntax for typing the command and some common router output from the command.

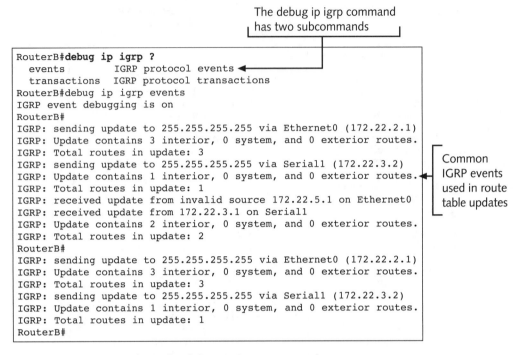

Figure 8-23   Output from the debug ip igrp command

STATIC ROUTING

Although routing protocols are easy to configure and maintain, many times they are unnecessary. Some networks are so small that using a routing protocol creates unnecessary traffic and an inefficient use of router processor resources. In addition, some networks may have only one route out and therefore can be configured with a single static route. Routers with only one route out are also known as **stub routers**. Stub routers are usually the last router in a chain. Networks with one route to the Internet are called **stub networks**. **Static routes** are configured by a network administrator using the ip route command, as shown in the next section.

Adding Static Routes

Figure 8-24 shows the routing table for RouterC. As previously mentioned, this table can be dynamically configured using routing protocols such as RIP and IGRP, or the table can be built statically using ip route commands. Although static routing gives the administrator full control as to how packets will be routed, the disadvantage of using static routing is the initial manual configuration and the possible reconfiguration if routes are changed. Notice that for all interfaces that are physically attached to RouterC, the route to the network is through a local interface on the router. However, for packets destined to network 172.32.1.0, RouterC must forward them to RouterD. As you can see, RouterC is configured to send the packets to the 172.32.2.1 interface on RouterD because that is the next hop for the packet from the perspective of RouterC.

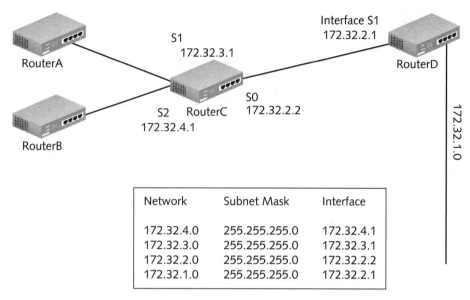

Figure 8-24   Routing table for RouterC

The commands that would be necessary to statically construct the proper routes for the routing table on RouterD to reach all the shown networks are shown below. To statically configure a route, you must type the destination network identifier, subnet mask, and the IP address of the interface of the next hop in the path. The syntax for the ip route command is **ip route** [*destination network address*] [*destination network mask*] [*ip address next hop interface*] [*administrative distance*]. The administrative distance is optional. You only have to add an administrative distance if you want to change the default administrative distance of 1 (see Table 8-5). The following entries for RouterD would allow it to route to all the networks in Figure 8-24:

- RouterD# config t
- RouterD(config)# ip route 172.32.3.0 255.255.255.0 172.32.2.2
- RouterD(config)# ip route 172.32.4.0 255.255.255.0 172.32.2.2

The two entries for networks attached to RouterC are headed for the same interface. RouterD must move those packets destined for networks on the remote side of RouterC to the interface on RouterC that is connected to RouterD. Static routes to 172.32.2.0 and 172.32.1.0 are unnecessary because RouterD has directly connected interfaces to those two networks.

Static routes are very powerful, as they allow administrators complete control over path selection. In addition, they use less bandwidth, less memory, and fewer CPU resources than routing protocols.

Changing Administrative Distance

The ip route command also allows you to configure an administrative distance, which, as discussed previously, is a value used by the router to select the best route to a destination when there are two or more different routes to the same destination being reported from more than one source—for example, from RIP, IGRP, and from a static entry. The default administrative distances were listed earlier in Table 8-5.

Static routes have a much lower default metric than routes learned by **dynamic routing protocols**, because a static route is considered to be a preferred route since someone took the trouble to enter it. Of course, if you want the static route to be used as a backup route to one learned via a dynamic routing protocol, be sure to set the administrative distance of the static route higher than that of the default dynamic routing protocol. Remember, unless you add an administrative distance value to the end of your ip route command, the administrative distance will be 1. For example, to set an administrative distance of 150 for the static entry to network 192.168.5.0, type:

```
router(config)#ip route 192.168.5.0 255.255.255.0
192.168.4.2. 150
```

If you want the static route entry to survive an interface shutdown, be sure to add the word "permanent" at the end of the line. For example, an interface such as E0 can be shut down by typing the shutdown command. The following commands could be used to shut down E0:

- `router#configure t`
- `router(config)#int E0`
- `router(config-if)#shutdown`

If you want your static route mappings to remain, even if an interface is shut down, you must add "permanent" to the end of the ip route command—otherwise the route will be deleted from the routing table when the interface is shut down.

Configuring a Default Route

When you connect a router to the Internet, as a practical matter, you cannot and would not want to enter all of the possible networks that are beyond your network. The table would be massive and difficult to maintain. Once you have the routing table set up to handle all of the networks that you care to configure and you want all other packets to go to a specific location (usually a router that connects to the Internet), you can enter a **default route** for your router. When you do, all packets that are not defined specifically in your routing table will go to the specified interface for the default route. A default route is a type of static route that the administrator configures. Without a default route, all packets addressed to destinations on networks not specifically listed in the routing table will not reach their destinations. This is why most network administrators use a combination of dynamic routing protocols and static routes to maintain the routing tables on their routers. In the case of stub networks, very often only static routing is used. When IP routing is enabled, you can use the ip default-network command or the ip route 0.0.0.0 0.0.0.0 command to configure a default route. The way in which routing protocols propagate the default route information varies for each protocol and is beyond the scope of this text and the CCNA exam.

The ip default-network command is typically configured on the routers that connect to a single router with a static default route. Look at Figure 8-24 again. This time, assume that RouterD connects to the Internet and that Routers A, B, and C are part of the internal network. If you are in charge of configuring Routers A, B, and C and you want to ensure that all packets destined for any external network are routed properly, enter the following command on Routers A, B, and C:

```
RouterA(config)# ip default-network 172.32.1.0
```

RouterA and RouterB would use RouterC interfaces as their default gateways. RouterC could use interface 172.32.2.1 as its default gateway. This means that it would be up to RouterD to route packets to the Internet for all internal hosts. To allow RouterD to route these packets, you would need to configure a default route as described below.

A default route uses the following format:

```
RouterD(config)# ip route 0.0.0.0 0.0.0.0 [next hop
router ip address] [administrative distance]
```

The zeroes in the command represent any destination network with any mask. Default routes are sometimes called **quad zero routes**. A default route is used only if no other route to a network exists in the routing table. In short, a router configured with a default route sends packets destined to a network for which it does not have a route to the next specified hop router. Figure 8-25 shows a network where a default route would be ideal.

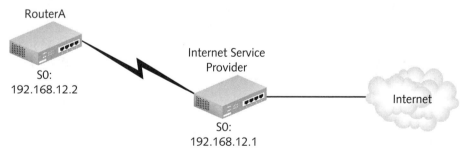

Figure 8-25   Default route example

As the figure shows, RouterA only has one way out to the Internet. The router of the Internet service provider (ISP) could therefore be set as the next hop router for all routes for which RouterA did not have a route. To accomplish this, the following command would be added to RouterA:

```
RouterA(config)# ip route 0.0.0.0 0.0.0.0 192.168.12.1
```

With the addition of this static default route, any packet destined for a network for which RouterA does not have an explicit route in its routing table will be forwarded to the ISP router.

CHAPTER SUMMARY

- ❏ NAT is a technology that allows organizations to map valid external addresses to private or unregistered internal addresses. This allows organizations to maintain a separation between the Internet and the intranet (internal network) while still providing access to the Internet.

- ❏ Organizations can use NAT to allow many more people to access the Internet by sharing one or more valid public addresses.

- ❏ PAT allows an organization to map more than one internal private IP address to a public IP address.

- ❏ Protocols vary in their functions. Some protocols are designed to be used in small networks without the need for Network layer addressing. These protocols are described as nonroutable protocols.

- ❏ The most common nonroutable protocol is NetBEUI.

- ❏ Other protocols were designed with the ability to move between multiple networks via Network layer addressing. These protocols are routed protocols.

- ❏ The most common routed protocol suite is TCP/IP.

- ❏ Protocols must be available that can find the best path throughout an internetwork and relay that information to routers. Routing protocols serve this function on modern networks.

- ❏ Routing protocols are classed in two major groups: Interior Gateway Protocols and Exterior Gateway Protocols.

- ❏ Interior Gateway Protocols are routing protocols that function within a single autonomous system. Exterior Gateway Protocols function as routing protocols between autonomous systems.

- ❏ Interior routing protocols are further divided into distance-vector and link-state routing protocols.

❑ These two types of Interior Gateway Protocols use very different methods to determine the best path in an internetwork.

❑ Distance-vector protocols periodically broadcast entire routing tables to neighbor routers.

❑ Link-state protocols multicast link updates to routers in their area upon startup and when network topology changes.

❑ Two common distance-vector IGPs are the Routing Information Protocol and the Interior Gateway Routing Protocol.

❑ RIP is an easy-to-configure routing protocol that uses hop count as its sole metric. RIP has a hop count limit of 15. RIP uses split horizon, split horizon with poison reverse, and hold-down timers to help limit routing loops. RIP can be used on Cisco and non-Cisco routers.

❑ IGRP is also a distance-vector routing protocol. IGRP has a maximum hop count of 255. IGRP is not limited to using hop count as its sole metric. IGRP can also use load, bandwidth, reliability, and delay when determining best path. IGRP uses only bandwidth and delay by default. IGRP is a Cisco proprietary protocol and can only be used on Cisco routers.

❑ Static routes are used to conserve bandwidth and lower memory and CPU load on a router while still allowing for correct routing table creation.

❑ Static routes give administrators control and flexibility in path selection in a network.

8

KEY TERMS

administrative distance — A value used to determine the reliability and desirability of a particular routing table update.

autonomous system (AS) — A group of routers under the control of a single administration.

Border Gateway Protocol (BGP) — An Exterior Gateway Protocol used to route between multiple autonomous systems.

convergence — The point at which all routers on a network share a similar view of the network.

count-to-infinity — A routing loop whereby packets bounce infinitely around an internetwork.

default route — A static route that directs all traffic not specified anywhere else in the routing table to a particular route. Same as quad zero route.

defining a maximum — A technique used with distance-vector routing protocols to prevent packets from bouncing infinitely throughout an internetwork by setting a maximum hop count.

distance-vector — A routing protocol that functions by broadcasting the entire routing table periodically to all connected neighbors; examples include RIP and IGRP.

dynamic NAT — A type of network address translation in which the valid external IP addresses to be mapped to internal addresses are floating or not fixed. The NAT router can then dynamically assign any of the available external addresses to any of the hosts on the internal network.

dynamic routing protocol — A protocol that builds the routing table automatically. Examples include RIP, IGRP, EIGRP, and OSPF.

Enhanced Interior Gateway Routing Protocol (EIGRP) — A proprietary Cisco routing protocol developed to overcome some of the limitations associated with distance-vector protocols. EIGRP is considered a hybrid routing protocol.

Exterior Gateway Protocol (EGP) — A gateway protocol used to route between multiple autonomous systems.

flood — The process of multicasting packets onto a network.

flush interval — The time at which a route is totally removed from the routing table.

hold-down timers — A technique used to stop routing loops in which updates from an inferior source are not allowed for a certain interval. Used by routers to stabilize routing tables and to prevent erroneous routing table updates.

hop count — A count of the number of routers a packet must pass through to reach a destination network.

Interior Gateway Protocol (IGP) — A gateway protocol used to route within one autonomous system.

Interior Gateway Routing Protocol (IGRP) — A proprietary Cisco distance-vector routing protocol that uses delay and bandwidth as its default metrics.

internetwork — Multiple networks connected by routers.

Internetwork Packet Exchange/Sequence Packet Exchange (IPX/SPX) — A routed protocol stack developed by Novell for use with the Netware network operating system.

link-state — Routing protocols that function via link-state advertisements using link-state packets to inform all routers on the internetwork of routing information. OSPF is the most common link-state routing protocol.

link-state advertisement (LSA) — A routing information packet used by link-state routing protocols to advertise their local network link information to neighbor routers in an internetwork.

link-state packets (LSP) — Packets used to send out link-state advertisements.

logical addresses — Layer 3 addresses (also referred to as Network layer addresses) that allow routing protocols to determine the best path to a particular host.

metric — A value used to define the suitability or desirability of a particular route.

network address translation (NAT) — A method for using a router to separate an internal network from an external network (usually the Internet), which is defined in RFC 3022. Internal hosts with private or unregistered IP addresses can effectively use one or more public registered IP addresses to communicate with external systems.

nonroutable protocols — Protocols that do not contain Network layer addressing and therefore cannot pass between multiple networks.

Open Shortest Path First (OSPF) — A link-state routing protocol based upon open (nonproprietary) standards.

overlapping — When an organization wants to connect to the Internet, but its internal addressing scheme is registered to another entity. Instead of renumbering the internal network, the organization uses NAT to translate its internal addressing scheme to the addresses that it was assigned by the ISP.

overloading — A type of NAT that allows multiple internal hosts to use one or more external IP addresses. The NAT router uses a table to keep track of the IP addresses and ports of each host, dynamically mapping each internal socket to a valid external socket.

peer-to-peer networks — Small networks, normally consisting of fewer than 10 computers, in which each computer can give and receive network services.

port address translation (PAT) — A process used in overloading that allows multiple internal, unregistered IP addresses to use a single external registered address.

port forwarding — A method for sending packets from an external host system through a firewall or NAT router to an internal device. In this way, the internal device IP address is hidden from the external network, yet the internal device can still service requests from the external network.

quad zero route — *See* **default route**.

routed protocols — Protocols that contain Network layer addressing and therefore can pass between multiple networks.

routing by rumor — The learning of routes through secondhand information, and not directly from the router experiencing the change. Routing by rumor is characteristic of distance-vector routing protocols.

Routing Information Protocol (RIP) — A distance-vector routing protocol that uses hop count as its only metric.

routing loops — A network state in which packets are continually forwarded from one router to another in an attempt to find the destination network.

routing protocols — Protocols used by routers to define and exchange routing table information in an internetwork.

Shortest Path First (SPF) algorithm — A complex algorithm used by link-state routing protocols to determine the best path in an internetwork.

split horizon — A technique used by routers to prevent routing loops. In short, a router will not send an update for a route via an interface from which it originally received knowledge of that route.

split horizon with poison reverse — A split horizon in which the router responds to attempts to update a route with an update that marks the route in contention as unreachable.

static NAT — A type of network address translation (NAT) that allows for a one-to-one mapping of internal to external addresses. One internal address is mapped to one specific external address.

8

static route — A route manually added by a network administrator to the routing table of a router.

stub network — A network with only one route to the Internet.

stub router — A router that is last in a chain of routers. There is only one path for all hosts connected to this router to get to the outside world.

topology — The physical or logical structure of a network.

Transmission Control Protocol/Internet Protocol (TCP/IP) — Routed protocol stack developed in the late 1960s for use on the precursor to the Internet; protocol stack of the modern-day Internet.

triggered updates — Updates that occur due to network topology changes, not periodic routing table advertisements.

REVIEW QUESTIONS

1. Which of the following commands is necessary to add IGRP to a router? (Choose all that apply.)

   a. router rip

   b. router igrp [*autonomous system #*]

   c. network [*major network #*]

   d. router network igrp

2. What is the administrative distance of RIP?

   a. 100

   b. 110

   c. 120

   d. 90

3. Link-state routing protocols _____. (Choose all that apply.)

   a. use link-state advertisements to notify routers of route changes

   b. send routing tables to neighbors

   c. reach convergence faster than distance-vector routing protocols

   d. determine the best path via the hop count algorithm

4. RIP has a maximum hop count of _____.

   a. 255

   b. 16

   c. 15

   d. 254

5. Which command enables RIP on a router?

    a. router network RIP

    b. router rip

    c. router igrp

    d. router ospf

6. Which command will show the IP routing table of a router?

    a. show ip route

    b. show ip protocol

    c. debug ip igrp events

    d. show run

7. Nonroutable protocols are able to pass packets among multiple networks. True or False?

8. IGRP can use which of the following as metrics? (Choose all that apply.)

    a. Hop count

    b. Bandwidth

    c. Delay

    d. Split horizon

9. Which of the following is a routed protocol? (Choose all that apply.)

    a. NetBEUI

    b. TCP/IP

    c. IPX/SPX

    d. RIP

10. Which of the following helps to prevent routing loops? (Choose all that apply.)

    a. Split horizon

    b. Count-to-infinity

    c. Hold-down timers

    d. Split horizon with poison reverse

11. At which router prompt can you use the router rip and router igrp [*autonomous system*] commands?

    a. routerB#

    b. routerB>

    c. routerB(config)#

    d. routerB(config-router)#

8

12. At which router prompt can you issue the network [*network #*] command?

    a. routerB#

    b. routerB>

    c. routerB(config)#

    d. routerB(config-router)#

13. The debug ip rip command can be used in user mode and privileged mode. True or False?

14. Which of the following routing protocols can route between autonomous systems? (Choose all that apply.)

    a. IGRP

    b. RIP

    c. BGP

    d. EGP

15. What type of routing protocol is used within autonomous systems?

    a. Exterior Gateway Protocols

    b. TCP/IP

    c. NetBEUI

    d. Interior Gateway Protocols

16. RIP and IGRP both advertise a route to a particular network. Which route will be added to the routing table?

    a. The RIP route

    b. The IGRP route

    c. Both RIP and IGRP routes

    d. BGP-enhanced IGRP

17. What command is used to display RIP timers?

    a. show ip route

    b. show run

    c. debug ip rip

    d. show ip protocol

18. What two commands are needed to configure RIP on a router? (Choose all that apply.)

    a. network rip

    b. router rip

    c. router network rip

    d. network [*network #*]

19. A metric is a variable used to determine the suitability of a route. True or False?

20. A major drawback of link-state routing protocols is:

    a. Routing by rumor

    b. Increased memory and processing required on routers

    c. Slow time to convergence

    d. Inability to adapt to network topology changes

21. Which of the following commands would enable a routing protocol that is only concerned with hop count?

    a. router# router igrp

    b. router(config)# router igrp

    c. router# router rip

    d. router(config)# router rip

    e. router# router ospf

22. Which of the following are true about administrative distance? (Choose all that apply.)

    a. The higher the administrative distance, the more desirable the route.

    b. Administrative distances are used with static routes.

    c. The default administrative distance for RIP is 120.

    d. The default administrative distance for static routes is higher than those for dynamic routes.

    e. The default administrative distance for a connected network is lower than that for the default route of IGRP.

23. What does the number 240 stand for in the following command?

    ```
    Router(config)# ip route 192.168.1.0 255.255.255.0 240
    ```

    a. Number of masked bits

    b. Decimal subnet mask

    c. Number of hops

    d. Administrative distance

    e. Autonomous network number

24. If you want to monitor real-time RIP traffic, which command would you type?

    a. router> router rip

    b. router# router rip

    c. router# show rip

    d. router(config)# show rip

    e. router# debug ip rip

8

25. Which of the following does RIP support? (Choose all that apply.)

    a. Load balancing

    b. Link reliability metric

    c. Bandwidth metric

    d. Delay metric

26. What is used on routers to hide intranet IP addresses from the Internet?

    a. PAP

    b. CHAP

    c. NAT

    d. FRAT

27. How does NAT deal with multiple internal IP addresses mapping to a single external address?

    a. PAP

    b. CHAP

    c. NAT

    d. PAT

28. How does overlapping occur?

    a. The network administrator doesn't plan for Internet connectivity.

    b. The network administrator uses registered IP addresses without getting permission.

    c. Both a and b

    d. None of the above

CASE PROJECTS

CASE PROJECTS

1. Winslow Networks has been hired by Big Tin Inc. to redesign Big Tin's network. Currently, the network consists of 14 routers with a potential growth of three routers in the next four months. Moe suggests that the company implement RIP for internetwork routing because it is so popular and easy to configure. Is this the best possible solution for Big Tin Inc.? Justify your answers.

2. Hogan's, an international food services conglomerate, wants to implement wide area network links between its 25 plants spread across 13 countries. You have been brought in as a consultant on the project. Hogan's wants convergence to be as quick as possible, and, due to slow WAN links in some undeveloped countries, it must reduce routing table updates to the absolute minimum to conserve bandwidth. Hogan's suggests using a distance-vector routing protocol because of its relative simplicity. Create a network design using the distance-vector protocol you feel will meet Hogan's needs. What metrics are used by default? Which metrics can and should be configured? Justify your answer.

3. Moe and Jennifer are configuring RIP on a client's router, and they want your help. The network number is 204.207.5.0. There are three interfaces on the router. The IP addresses for the interfaces are 204.207.5.97, 204.207.5.113, and 204.207.5.82. The subnet mask is 255.255.255.240. The host name for the router is "newyork." What mode should Moe and Jennifer be in to use the router rip command? What will the prompt look like? How will the prompt change after the router rip command is issued? Jennifer has written the following commands for entry next:

   network 204.207.5.96

   network 204.207.5.112

   network 204.207.5.80

   What do you tell her?

4. The Americanus Corporation wants to use RFC 1918 addresses on its LAN. They understand that NAT will have to be configured on the router but don't really understand how NAT works. Explain the four types of NAT to them.

8

9

ADVANCED ROUTING PROTOCOLS

> **After reading this chapter and completing the exercises, you will be able to:**
> ♦ Describe classful and classless routing protocols
> ♦ Describe and configure RIPv2
> ♦ Describe and configure EIGRP
> ♦ Describe and configure OSPF
> ♦ Control routing traffic

Routing protocols are an integral part of a functioning network. While distance-vector routing protocols such as RIP version 1 or Interior Gateway Routing Protocol (IGRP) suffice in simple networks, complex, modern networks demand more advanced protocols. This chapter begins with a discussion of classful and classless routing protocols. It continues with an examination of the classless routing protocols RIP version 2, EIGRP, and OSPF. By the end of the chapter, you should be able to describe and configure each of these protocols. The chapter concludes with a discussion of controlling routing traffic.

CLASSFUL AND CLASSLESS ROUTING PROTOCOLS

Routing protocols divide into the broad categories of interior or exterior gateway protocols and distance-vector protocols or link-state protocols. These broad definitions describe where each routing protocol is best used, either within the autonomous system or between autonomous systems. These definitions also describe how the routing protocols handle routing table updates and routing table creation. In general, distance-vector routing protocols send periodic updates of their entire routing table to their directly connected neighbors, while link-state protocols flood nonperiodic link-state advertisements of only changed routes throughout the entire internetwork.

While these characteristics generally define how routing protocols operate, another factor also helps to delineate them. Each routing protocol is defined as either classful or classless, terms that describe how the routing protocol handles subnet mask information in its routing table updates. **Classful routing protocols** summarize networks to their major network boundaries (Class A, B, or C) and do not carry subnet mask information in their routing table updates. These protocols cannot be used in networks with either discontiguous subnets or networks using variable length subnet masks (VLSM), because they summarize to the major network boundaries. RIPv1 and IGRP are classful routing protocols; they do not carry any subnet mask information in their routing table updates. Figure 9-1 shows the update message format for RIPv1.

Command (1)	Version (1)	must be zero (2)
Address Family Identifier (2)		must be zero (2)
IP Address (4)		
must be zero (4)		
must be zero (4)		
Metric (4)		

Figure 9-1 RIPv1 message format

The field of particular importance to a discussion of classful protocols is the IP address field. It is four bytes in size, just large enough for a 32-bit IP address. The message update format in RIPv1 does not have room for subnet mask information in the IP address field, and it does not contain a field dedicated to carrying subnet mask information. This is why RIPv1 uses major network numbers rather than subnet numbers.

Figure 9-2 shows an example of how different major networks separate two subnets from the same major network, 192.168.12.0/24. This is called discontiguous subnets.

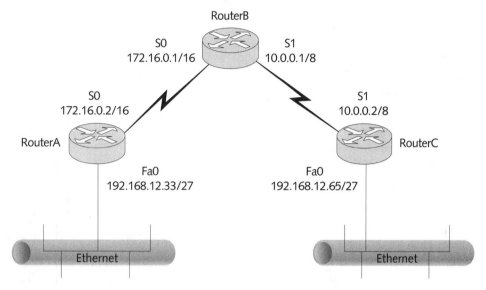

Figure 9-2   Network with discontiguous subnets

The command outputs in this chapter are taken from Cisco 1721 routers with a single WAN Interface Card (WIC) installed.

Figure 9-3 shows the configuration of RIPv1 on RouterA from the preceding illustration. As shown in the output of the show run command in the figure, RIPv1 summarizes the network entries to the major network. This will cause problems in the network in our example. Figure 9-4 shows the routing table of RouterB after RIPv1 has been configured on just RouterA and RouterB. RouterB believes the major network 192.168.12.0 is available via RouterA's S0 interface.

```
RouterA(config)#router rip
RouterA(config-router)#network 172.16.0.0
RouterA(config-router)#network 192.168.12.32◄

RouterA(config-router)# ^Z
RouterA#sh run
01:07:51: %SYS-5-CONFIG_I: Configured from console by console
Building configuration...

Current configuration :  519 bytes
!
version 12.2
service timestamps debug uptime
service timestamps log uptime
no service password-encryption
!
hostname RouterA
!
!
ip subnet-zero
!
!
!
!
interface FastEthernet0
 ip address 192.168.12.33 255.255.255.224
 no keepalive
 speed auto
!
interface Serial0
 ip address 172.16.0.2 255.255.0.0
 no fair-queue
!
interface Serial1
 no ip address
 shutdown
!
router rip
 network 172.16.0.0
 network 192.168.12.0◄
!
ip classless
no ip http server
!
!
!
line con 0
line aux 0
line vty 0 4
!
no scheduler allocate
end

RouterA#
```

Normally, you configure RIPv1 by putting in the major networks on each interface. The author intentionally put in the subnetwork address in this example to show that RIPv1 automatically summarizes to the major network number, even though the subnetwork address was entered in the command.

Figure 9-3 Configuring RIPv1 on RouterA

RouterB receives updates from RouterA stating that
the 192.168.12.0 network is available through it

```
RouterB#show ip route
Codes: C - connected, S - static, I - IGRP, R - RIP, M - mobile, B - BGP
   D - EIGRP, EX - EIGRP external, O - OSPF, IA - OSPF inter area
   N1 - OSPF NSSA external type 1, N2 - OSPF NSSA external type 2
   E1 - OSPF external type 1, E2 - OSPF external type 2, E - EGP
   i - IS-IS, L1 - IS-IS level-1, L2 - IS-IS level-2, ia - IS-IS inter area
   * - candidate default, U - per-user static route, o - ODR
   P - periodic downloaded static route

Gateway of last resort is not set

R   192.168.12.0/24 [120/1] via 172.16.0.2, 00:00:11, Serial0
C   172.16.0.0/16 is directly connected, Serial0
C   10.0.0.0/8 is directly connected, Serial1
RouterB#
```

Figure 9-4   RouterB's routing table—partial network configuration

After configuration of RouterC with RIPv1, however, RouterB's routing table changes quickly to include not one, but two equal cost routes to the 192.168.12.0 network. In this case, RouterB thinks it can load-balance over the two routes. Figure 9-5 shows the two equal cost routes in RouterB's routing table. Figure 9-6 shows a ping attempt by RouterB to the IP address 192.168.12.33 using the extended ping commands. As you can see, the ping works, but only intermittently. This is a result of the dual equal cost routes in RouterB's routing table.

After configuration of RouterC with RIPv1, RouterB erroneously
believes it has two equal cost routes to the 192.168.12.0 network

```
RouterB#show ip route
Codes: C - connected, S - static, I - IGRP, R - RIP, M - mobile, B - BGP
   D - EIGRP, EX - EIGRP external, O - OSPF, IA - OSPF inter area
   N1 - OSPF NSSA external type 1, N2 - OSPF NSSA external type 2
   E1 - OSPF external type 1, E2 - OSPF external type 2, E - EGP
   i - IS-IS, L1 - IS-IS level-1, L2 - IS-IS level-2, ia - IS-IS inter area
   * - candidate default, U - per-user static route, o - ODR
   P - periodic downloaded static route

Gateway of last resort is not set

R   192.168.12.0/24 [120/1] via 172.16.0.2, 00:00:01, Serial0
                    [120/1] via 10.0.0.2, 00:00:09, Serial1
C   172.16.0.0/16 is directly connected, Serial0
C   10.0.0.0/8 is directly connected, Serial1
RouterB#
```

Figure 9-5   RouterB's routing table—full network configuration

A long repeat count was used to show the effects of the dual routes

Only 50% of the pings reach RouterA's Fa0 interface. The other half are incorrectly routed to RouterC.

```
RouterB#ping
Protocol [ip]:
Target IP address: 192.168.12.33
Repeat count [5]: 100
Datagram size [100]:
Timeout in seconds [2]:
Extended commands [n]:
Sweep range of sizes [n]:
Type escape sequence to abort.
Sending 100, 100-byte ICMP Echos to 192.168.12.33, timeout is 2 seconds:
!U!.!U!.!U!.!U!.!U!.!U!.!U!.!U!.!U!.!U!.!U!.!U!.!U!.!U!.!U!.!U!.!U
!.!U!.!U!.!U!.!U!.!U!.!U!.!U!.
Success rate is 50 percent (50/100), round-trip min/avg/max = 28/28/28 ms
RouterB#
```

Figure 9-6   Ping example

Classful routing protocols cannot adapt to work in an environment where discontiguous networks or VLSM exist. Instead, to allow dynamic routing in these networks, a classless routing protocol must be used. In essence, the major improvement a **classless routing protocol** provides is the ability to carry subnet mask information in the routing table updates. RIPv2, EIGRP, OSPF, and BGP are classless routing protocols. Figure 9-7 shows RIPv2's route update message format.

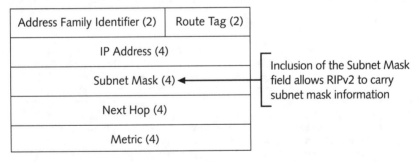

Address Family Identifier (2)	Route Tag (2)
IP Address (4)	
Subnet Mask (4)	
Next Hop (4)	
Metric (4)	

Inclusion of the Subnet Mask field allows RIPv2 to carry subnet mask information

Figure 9-7   RIPv2 update message format

The four bytes set aside for the Subnet Mask field allow RIPv2 to send the full 32-bit subnet mask for each network configured on the router's interfaces. Figure 9-8 shows the commands to convert RouterB to RIPv2.

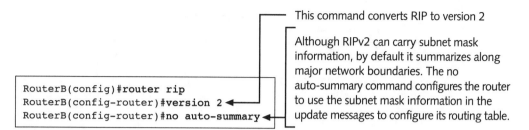

This command converts RIP to version 2

Although RIPv2 can carry subnet mask information, by default it summarizes along major network boundaries. The no auto-summary command configures the router to use the subnet mask information in the update messages to configure its routing table.

```
RouterB(config)#router rip
RouterB(config-router)#version 2
RouterB(config-router)#no auto-summary
```

Figure 9-8   Configuring RIPv2

Converting from RIPv1 to RIPv2 is very simple. The version 2 command switches RIP to version 2 while the no auto-summary command overrides RIPv2's default behavior of summarizing to major network boundaries. Once all the routers in the example are converted to RIPv2, RouterB's routing table looks drastically different than before.

Figure 9-9 shows RouterB's routing table after the conversion. Instead of two equal cost routes to the major network 192.168.12.0, a route for each subnet exists. As a result, the extended ping command in Figure 9-10 works correctly every time.

A separate route entry per subnet now exists

```
RouterB#sh ip route
Codes: C - connected, S - static, I - IGRP, R - RIP, M - mobile, B - BGP
       D - EIGRP, EX - EIGRP external, O - OSPF, IA - OSPF inter area
       N1 - OSPF NSSA external type 1, N2 - OSPF NSSA external type 2
       E1 - OSPF external type 1, E2 - OSPF external type 2, E - EGP
       i - IS-IS, L1 - IS-IS level-1, L2 - IS-IS level-2, ia - IS-IS inter area
       * - candidate default, U - per-user static route, o - ODR
       P - periodic downloaded static route

Gateway of last resort is not set

     192.168.12.0/27 is subnetted, 2 subnets
R       192.168.12.64 [120/1] via 10.0.0.2, 00:00:09, Serial1
R       192.168.12.32 [120/1] via 172.16.0.2, 00:00:07, Serial0
C    172.16.0.0/16 is directly connected, Serial0
C    10.0.0.0/8 is directly connected, Serial1
RouterB#
```

Figure 9-9   RouterB's routing table with RIPv2

Once the routing table has the correct entries, all pings are successfully sent

```
RouterB#ping
Protocol [ip]:
Target IP address: 192.168.12.33
Repeat count [5]: 100
Datagram size [100]:
Timeout in seconds [2]:
Extended commands [n]:
Sweep range of sizes [n]:
Type escape sequence to abort.
Sending 100, 100-byte ICMP Echos to 192.168.12.33, timeout is 2 seconds:
!!!!!!!!!!!!!!!!!!!!!!!!!!!!!!!!!!!!!!!!!!!!!!!!!!!!!!!!!!!!!!!!!!!!!!!!!!!
!!!!!!!!!!!!!!!!!!!!!!!!!!!!!!!!!!
Success rate is 100 percent (100/100), round-trip min/avg/max = 28/28/40 ms
RouterB#
```

Figure 9-10   Extended ping with RIPv2

In general, due to the complexity of modern networks and the use of VLSMs, which require subnet mask information to be sent with update messages, most networks use classless routing protocols.

ROUTING INFORMATION PROTOCOL VERSION 2

RIPv2 is not a totally new protocol. In reality, it is a set of extensions to RIPv1. As such, it is still a distance-vector routing protocol that uses the normal measures of hold-down timers and split horizon to prevent routing loops. It also suffers from RIPv1's major downfall, in that it only supports a maximum of 15 hops. The major change is RIPv2's ability to carry subnet mask information and a difference in the way it sends out its routing table updates. Unlike RIPv1, which broadcasts its routing table updates every 30 seconds, RIPv2 multicasts its updates using the multicast address of 224.0.0.9. This feature saves bandwidth on the network, as devices not running RIPv2 do not have to process unnecessary broadcast traffic. Additionally, RIPv2 provides a way to authenticate routing peers to provide enhanced security to a network.

Configuring RIPv2 is a simple process. Figure 9-11 shows a sample network in which two of the three routers are running RIPv2 while a third router is running RIPv1. Figure 9-12 shows the commands necessary to configure RIPv2 on RouterA. The commands are basically the same as those for RIPv1, except for the inclusion of the version 2 command and the no auto-summary command.

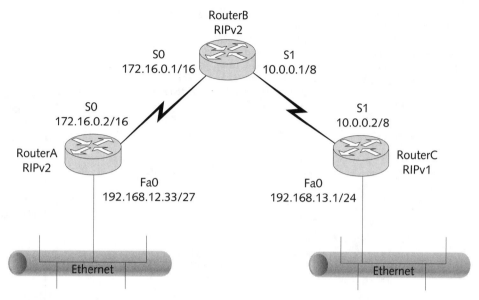

Figure 9-11   RIPv2 example network

9

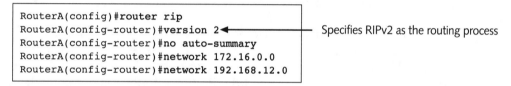

Specifies RIPv2 as the routing process

```
RouterA(config)#router rip
RouterA(config-router)#version 2
RouterA(config-router)#no auto-summary
RouterA(config-router)#network 172.16.0.0
RouterA(config-router)#network 192.168.12.0
```

Figure 9-12   RIPv2 configuration commands

Issuing the show ip protocols command displayed in Figure 9-13 shows that the current routing protocol is RIP and that routing updates for version 2 are being sent and received.

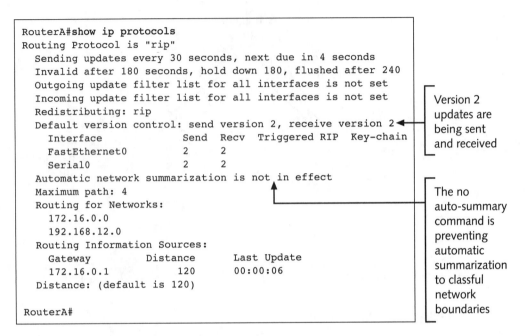

```
RouterA#show ip protocols
Routing Protocol is "rip"
  Sending updates every 30 seconds, next due in 4 seconds
  Invalid after 180 seconds, hold down 180, flushed after 240
  Outgoing update filter list for all interfaces is not set
  Incoming update filter list for all interfaces is not set
  Redistributing: rip
  Default version control: send version 2, receive version 2
    Interface           Send  Recv  Triggered RIP  Key-chain
    FastEthernet0        2     2
    Serial0              2     2
  Automatic network summarization is not in effect
  Maximum path: 4
  Routing for Networks:
    172.16.0.0
    192.168.12.0
  Routing Information Sources:
    Gateway         Distance      Last Update
    172.16.0.1          120       00:00:06
  Distance: (default is 120)

RouterA#
```

Version 2 updates are being sent and received

The no auto-summary command is preventing automatic summarization to classful network boundaries

Figure 9-13   Show IP protocols output with RIPv2

Additionally, RIPv2 maintains backward compatibility with RIPv1. Cisco routers running RIPv2 can be configured on a per-interface basis to either send or receive version 1 or 2 updates. Because of this per-interface basis, backward compatibility can be easily maintained as a network is migrated from RIPv1 to RIPv2. In our example network in Figure 9-11, RouterB must be configured to send and receive RIPv1 updates to RouterC. Figure 9-14 shows the commands necessary to correctly configure RouterB to share version 1 updates with RouterC. Once this configuration is complete, RouterA will learn via RIPv2 of the routes RouterC has advertised to RouterB. The result will be a network with proper routing throughout, even though all three routers are not running the same version of RIP.

```
RouterB#config t
Enter configuration commands, one per line.  End with CNTL/Z.
RouterB(config)#router rip
RouterB(config-router)#version 2
RouterB(config-router)#no auto-summary
RouterB(config-router)#network 10.0.0.0
RouterB(config-router)#network 172.16.0.0
RouterB(config-router)#int s1
RouterB(config-if)#ip rip send version 1
RouterB(config-if)#ip rip receive version 1
RouterB(config-if)#^z
RouterB#
```

By changing s1, the interface connected to the RIPv1 peer RouterC, to send and receive version 1 updates, all three routers can now share routing information

Figure 9-14   RouterB configuration for RIPv1 and RIPv2 support

If RouterB had not been configured to send and receive version 1 updates, the debug ip rip command would have displayed errors such as the one in Figure 9-15. In this example, RouterB, which has not yet been configured to receive version 1 updates, receives an illegal update from RouterC. Once RouterB has been correctly configured, it will accept the version 1 update from RouterC and pass it on to RouterA as a version 2 update.

9

If RouterB had not been configured to receive version 1 updates, this output would appear in the debug ip rip output. In this example, RouterB ignored a v1 update from RouterC.

```
RouterB#debug ip rip
RIP protocol debugging is on
RouterB#
3d00h: RIP: received v2 update from 172.16.0.2 on Serial0
3d00h:       192.168.12.32/27 via 0.0.0.0 in 1 hop
3d00h: RIP: sending v2 update to 224.0.0.9 via Serial0 (172.16.0.1)
3d00h: RIP: build update entries
3d00h:   10.0.0.0/8 via 0.0.0.0, metric 1, tag 0
3d00h: RIP: sending v2 update to 224.0.0.9 via Serial1 (10.0.0.1)
3d00h: RIP: build update entries
3d00h:   172.16.0.0/16 via 0.0.0.0, metric 1, tag 0
3d00h:   192.168.12.32/27 via 0.0.0.0, metric 2, tag 0
% Type "show ?" for a list of subcommands
RouterB#
3d00h: RIP: ignored v1 packet from 10.0.0.2 (illegal version)
RouterB#
RouterB#
RouterB#
```

Figure 9-15   Debug IP RIP output

Another enhancement of RIPv2 is its ability to authenticate routing peers. In the example network, authentication can be implemented between RouterA and RouterB because they are both running RIPv2. RIP authentication can occur either by passing the authentication keys in clear text or via **MD5** authentication. RFC 1321 defines MD5 as an "algorithm [that] takes as input a message of arbitrary length and produces as output a 128-bit 'fingerprint' or 'message digest' of the input." In short, using MD5 allows RIPv2 to authenticate a routing peer without sending the secret key (a text string) across the link between the two peers. Instead, it runs the MD5 algorithm against the secret key and sends the hash to the peer. A hash is a number generated by MD5 from the secret key. This number cannot be reverse-engineered easily enough for someone to guess the secret key. The hash is sent to the opposite peer, which runs MD5 against its configured secret key; if the two hashes match, then the two peers are considered authenticated.

Configuring RIPv2 authentication requires the following steps:

- Define a key chain.

- Define keys in the key chain.

- Enable authentication on the interface by specifying the key chain to be used.

- Enable either clear text or MD5 authentication.

- Manage the keys (optional key lifetimes).

Figure 9-16 shows authentication being configured on both RouterA and RouterB. If, by mistake, authentication was only configured on one of the two peers, the RIPv2 process would stop sharing routing updates between the peers and the error in Figure 9-17 would be displayed.

```
RouterB(config)#
RouterB(config)#key chain caudle
RouterB(config-keychain)#key 1
RouterB(config-keychain-key)#key-string ducks
RouterB(config-keychain-key)#interface s0
RouterB(config-if)#ip rip authentication key-chain caudle
RouterB(config-if)#ip rip authentication mode md5
RouterB(config-if)#


RouterA(config)#
RouterA(config)#key chain cannon
RouterA(config-keychain)#key 1
RouterA(config-keychain-key)#key-string ducks
RouterA(config-keychain-key)#interface s0
RouterA(config-if)#ip rip authentication key-chain cannon
RouterA(config-if)#ip rip authentication mode md5
RouterA(config-if)#
```

The two key-strings must match. In essence, this is the shared secret password between the two routers. Of course, because MD5 authentication has been specified, this key will not be sent between the two peers. Only a message digest of the two will be sent.

Figure 9-16   RIPv2 authentication commands

Because RouterB has been configured with MD5 authentication and RouterA has not, RouterB will not accept routing updates from RouterA

```
RouterB#debug ip rip
RIP protocol debugging is on
RouterB#
3d01h: RIP: ignored v2 packet from 172.16.0.2 (invalid authentication)
3d01h: RIP: sending v2 update to 224.0.0.9 via Serial0 (172.16.0.1)
3d01h: RIP: build update entries
3d01h: 10.0.0.0/8 via 0.0.0.0, metric 1, tag 0
3d01h: 192.168.13.0/24 via 0.0.0.0, metric 2, tag 0
3d01h: RIP: sending v1 update to 255.255.255.255 via Serial1 (10.0.0.1)
3d01h: RIP: build update entries
3d01h: network 172.16.0.0 metric 1
```

Figure 9-17   RIPv2 authentication failure

Once both routers have been configured with MD5 authentication, the debug ip rip command displays output similar to that in Figure 9-18. In this output, it is clearly visible that RouterB is accepting authenticated updates from RouterA via RIPv2 and unauthenticated updates from RouterC via RIPv1.

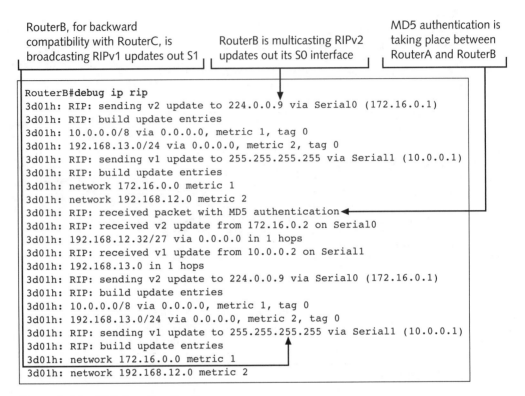

RouterB, for backward compatibility with RouterC, is broadcasting RIPv1 updates out S1

RouterB is multicasting RIPv2 updates out its S0 interface

MD5 authentication is taking place between RouterA and RouterB

```
RouterB#debug ip rip
3d01h: RIP: sending v2 update to 224.0.0.9 via Serial0 (172.16.0.1)
3d01h: RIP: build update entries
3d01h: 10.0.0.0/8 via 0.0.0.0, metric 1, tag 0
3d01h: 192.168.13.0/24 via 0.0.0.0, metric 2, tag 0
3d01h: RIP: sending v1 update to 255.255.255.255 via Serial1 (10.0.0.1)
3d01h: RIP: build update entries
3d01h: network 172.16.0.0 metric 1
3d01h: network 192.168.12.0 metric 2
3d01h: RIP: received packet with MD5 authentication
3d01h: RIP: received v2 update from 172.16.0.2 on Serial0
3d01h: 192.168.12.32/27 via 0.0.0.0 in 1 hops
3d01h: RIP: received v1 update from 10.0.0.2 on Serial1
3d01h: 192.168.13.0 in 1 hops
3d01h: RIP: sending v2 update to 224.0.0.9 via Serial0 (172.16.0.1)
3d01h: RIP: build update entries
3d01h: 10.0.0.0/8 via 0.0.0.0, metric 1, tag 0
3d01h: 192.168.13.0/24 via 0.0.0.0, metric 2, tag 0
3d01h: RIP: sending v1 update to 255.255.255.255 via Serial1 (10.0.0.1)
3d01h: RIP: build update entries
3d01h: network 172.16.0.0 metric 1
3d01h: network 192.168.12.0 metric 2
```

Figure 9-18   RIPv2 authentication success

Figure 9-18 also shows many of the features described in this section. It shows RouterB multicasting RIPv2 updates via 224.0.0.9 to RouterA. In addition, it shows RouterB broadcasting RIPv1 updates via 255.255.255.255. Finally, MD5 authentication is also shown.

Although RIPv2 has many enhancements, its 15-hop-count limit and distance-vector qualities limit its usefulness in large enterprise networks, where routing protocols such as Enhanced Interior Gateway Routing Protocol and Open Shortest Path First are better choices.

ENHANCED INTERIOR GATEWAY ROUTING PROTOCOL

Enhanced Interior Gateway Routing Protocol (EIGRP) is a Cisco proprietary protocol designed to overcome the limitations found in IGRP. Although it is often described as a hybrid protocol, one that contains the features of both distance-vector and link-state protocols, EIGRP is still a distance-vector routing protocol at its core, albeit an advanced one. EIGRP is classless whereas IGRP is classful. Therefore, EIGRP can support VLSM and complex internetworks. EIGRP can also route IP, IPX, and

AppleTalk. **Protocol Dependent Modules (PDMs)** allow EIGRP to carry these multiple routed protocols within their own native packet formats. Finally, EIGRP uses nonperiodic, partial, and bounded routing table updates. So, EIGRP does send route information to directly connected neighbors, but not on a periodic basis. Instead, updates are only sent when changes occur to the network. Also, the updates are not the entire routing table; they are partial, meaning that only routes that have changed are sent. Additionally, the updates are sent only to the routers that need to learn them, not to all directly connected routers. These updates are therefore considered bounded. Finally, because network security is paramount in today's world, EIGRP, like RIPv2, supports authentication of routing peers.

EIGRP is more than the addition of a few features to IGRP. In fact, while still backward-compatible with IGRP, EIGRP is a significantly better routing protocol for use in large enterprise networks. EIGRP uses the same metric as IGRP multiplied by 256. As a result, by simply multiplying or dividing metrics by 256, EIGRP can automatically share or redistribute routes between EIGRP and IGRP. This automatic redistribution of routes takes place between two routers if they are configured with the same autonomous system (AS) numbers. Figure 9-19 shows a network where EIGRP and IGRP automatic redistribution occurs. RouterB is configured with both EIGRP and IGRP using the autonomous system number of 52. As a result, the IGRP routes from RouterC are redistributed into EIGRP.

9

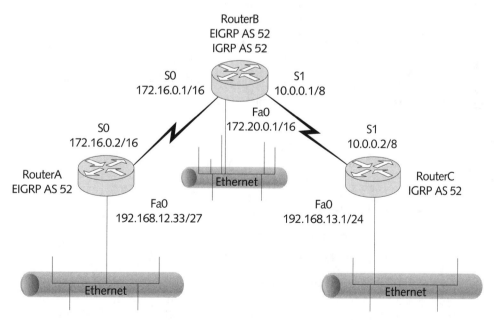

Figure 9-19   EIGRP example network

Figure 9-20 shows the routing table of RouterA. RouterA has a normal EIGRP route, flagged as "D" in the routing table, and external EIGRP routes, flagged as "D EX." The redistribution of the 10.0.0.0/8 and 192.168.13.0/24 networks to RouterA via EIGRP took no extra configuration, apart from enabling both EIGRP and IGRP with the same autonomous system number on RouterB. This is unique, as redistribution of routing protocols normally requires additional work.

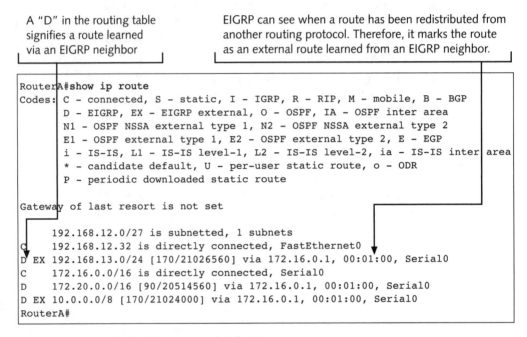

A "D" in the routing table signifies a route learned via an EIGRP neighbor

EIGRP can see when a route has been redistributed from another routing protocol. Therefore, it marks the route as an external route learned from an EIGRP neighbor.

```
RouterA#show ip route
Codes: C - connected, S - static, I - IGRP, R - RIP, M - mobile, B - BGP
       D - EIGRP, EX - EIGRP external, O - OSPF, IA - OSPF inter area
       N1 - OSPF NSSA external type 1, N2 - OSPF NSSA external type 2
       E1 - OSPF external type 1, E2 - OSPF external type 2, E - EGP
       i - IS-IS, L1 - IS-IS level-1, L2 - IS-IS level-2, ia - IS-IS inter area
       * - candidate default, U - per-user static route, o - ODR
       P - periodic downloaded static route

Gateway of last resort is not set

     192.168.12.0/27 is subnetted, 1 subnets
C    192.168.12.32 is directly connected, FastEthernet0
D EX 192.168.13.0/24 [170/21026560] via 172.16.0.1, 00:01:00, Serial0
C    172.16.0.0/16 is directly connected, Serial0
D    172.20.0.0/16 [90/20514560] via 172.16.0.1, 00:01:00, Serial0
D EX 10.0.0.0/8 [170/21024000] via 172.16.0.1, 00:01:00, Serial0
RouterA#
```

Figure 9-20 EIGRP/IGRP route redistribution

EIGRP Components

EIGRP is made up of four major components:

- Protocol Dependent Modules

- Neighbor discovery and maintenance

- Reliable Transport Protocol

- Diffusing Update Algorithm (DUAL)

As mentioned earlier, Protocol Dependent Modules allow EIGRP to support multiple Network layer routed protocols such as IP, IPX, and AppleTalk. Each PDM is designed to allow EIGRP to provide any protocol-specific needs, such as packet formats. This discussion of EIGRP focuses on IP environments and therefore relies on the IP-EIGRP PDM.

Unlike other distance-vector protocols such as RIP and IGRP, which broadcast their entire routing table out all interfaces, EIGRP must be able to keep updates bounded, sent only to those peers that need the information. To accomplish this task, EIGRP must build a neighbor table of directly connected peers. Neighbor discovery and maintenance allow EIGRP to discover neighbors and keep track of their status. EIGRP uses multicast address 224.0.0.10 to multicast Hello packets every five seconds on most networks of T1 speed or greater. On some slower WAN links (Frame Relay and multipoint links slower than T1 speed), Hello packets are sent as unicasts every 60 seconds to conserve bandwidth. The Hello packets allow EIGRP neighbors to determine if routing peers are still online and available. Once a Hello packet is received, a router determines a hold-down timer for its peer. By default, the hold-down timer is three times the Hello interval. So, on higher-speed connections such as Ethernet, the hold-down timer is 15 seconds. If a router does not hear a Hello from a neighbor before the expiration of the hold-down time, it marks the neighbor as unavailable and begins the process of recalculating routes. Unlike other routing protocols, EIGRP does not require all peer routers to have the same Hello and hold-down timers. As part of the Hello process, EIGRP neighbors inform one another of their currently configured timers. The timers are configurable on a per-interface basis. Still, unless a particular reason exists to change the default, the timers should be left at the defaults. Regardless of their interval, Hello packets use the Reliable Transport Protocol as their Transport layer protocol.

Because EIGRP is protocol-independent, it cannot use existing Transport layer protocols to carry its various packet types. Instead, Cisco developed an entirely new layer 4 protocol, the **Reliable Transport Protocol (RTP)**, for use by EIGRP. Reliable Transport Protocol is somewhat of a misnomer, as it can actually provide both reliable and unreliable delivery. For instance, the Hello packets are sent as unreliable multicasts. Having to acknowledge every Hello would be an enormous waste of bandwidth. Routing table updates are an example of an EIGRP packet type that uses reliable multicast via RTP. Reliable multicast is a feature of RTP that requests an acknowledgment via unicast to a multicast message. EIGRP uses reliable multicast to ensure that certain packets are acknowledged. In fact, EIGRP uses five packet types. Table 9-1 lists each packet type and its transport type:

Table 9-1   EIGRP packet types

Packet Type	Purpose	Transport Type
Hellos	Maintain neighbor status	Multicast, unreliable
Acknowledgments	Reply to reliable multicast request	Unicast, unreliable
Updates	Carry route information	Unicast for update to single router Multicast for update to group of routers Reliable delivery
Queries	Used by DUAL to compute best paths	Multicast or unicast, reliable delivery
Replies	Used by DUAL to compute best paths	Unicast, reliable delivery

The **Diffusing Update Algorithm (DUAL)** is the heart and soul of EIGRP, and is the reason that EIGRP can quickly recover from a link outage and route around network problems. In order to understand DUAL, you must understand several key terms associated with it:

- **Successor**: The best route to a destination; the next hop route to a network; stored in the EIGRP topology table and placed as the best route in the actual routing table
- **Feasible distance (FD)**: The lowest metric to a destination (determines which route becomes the successor)
- **Reported distance (RD)**: The distance a router advertises to a network; in other words, the distance from an advertising router to a network
- **Feasible successor**: A backup route to the successor route; must meet the feasibility condition for DUAL; stored as a backup in the topology table; does not get placed in the routing table until the successor fails
- **Feasibility condition**: Used to ensure that a backup route (i.e., a feasible successor) does not contain a loop; to become a feasible successor, a router's RD must be less than its neighbor's FD. The easiest way to remember the feasibility condition is:

    If RD < FD = feasible successor

- **Adjacency**: A relationship formed between EIGRP neighbors through the use of Hello packets

DUAL uses the EIGRP topology table to track the status of all links in a network. To better understand DUAL, it is best to observe it in action on a network. Figure 9-21 shows the network that will be used in this discussion. Each Cisco 1721 router is running EIGRP with an autonomous system number of 52. Each router creates a neighbor relationship with Hello packets. Figure 9-22 shows the output of the show ip eigrp neighbors command on RouterA. This command lists a router's EIGRP neighbors in the order they were discovered. Once neighbors have been discovered, EIGRP runs the DUAL algorithm to create the EIGRP topology table.

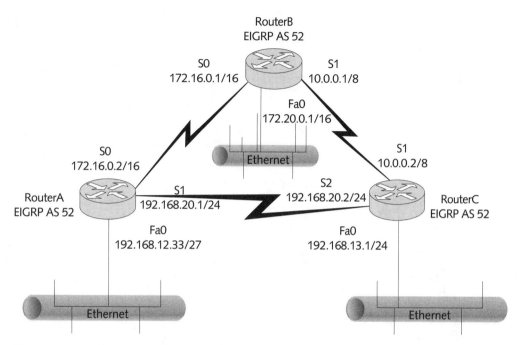

Figure 9-21 DUAL example network

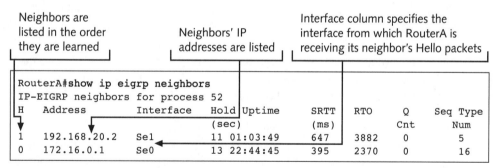

Figure 9-22 Show ip eigrp neighbors command output

The EIGRP topology table contains information about all the networks a router can reach. Using the show ip eigrp topology command shown in Figure 9-23, you can display information garnered from the DUAL process. Several items are of particular interest in the output. To begin, you can see that RouterA has two successors to the

10.0.0.0/8 network. This is possible because the routes are equal cost, which is apparent because the feasible distance (FD) via 192.168.20.2 and 172.16.0.1 is equal: 21024000.

```
RouterA#show ip eigrp topology
IP-EIGRP Topology Table for AS(52)/ID(192.168.12.33)
Codes: P - Passive, A - Active, U - Update, Q - Query, R - Reply,
       r - reply Status, s - sia Status
P 10.0.0.0/8, 2 successors, FD is 21024000
        via 192.168.20.2 (21024000/20512000), Serial1
        via 172.16.0.1 (21024000/20512000), Serial0
P 192.168.12.32/27, 1 successors, FD is 28160
        via Connected, FastEthernet0
P 192.168.13.0/24, 1 successors, FD is 20514560
        via 192.168.20.2 (20514560/28160), Serial1
P 192.168.20.0/24, 1 successors, FD is 20512000
        via Connected, Serial1
P 172.20.0.0/16, 1 successors, FD is 20514560
        via 172.16.0.1 (20514560/28160), Serial0
P 172.16.0.0/16, 1 successors, FD is 20512000
        via Connected, Serial0
RouterA#
```

Figure 9-23   Show ip eigrp topology command output

Another item of interest is the single successor to the 192.168.13.0/24 network, even though Figure 9-21 clearly shows that another route via RouterB is available. Why doesn't the second route show up as a feasible successor? The answer lies in the feasibility condition. In order for a route to be a feasible successor, the advertising router's reported distance (RD) must be less than the receiving router's FD. Figure 9-23 shows that RouterA's FD to 192.168.13.0/24 is 20514560. Figure 9-24 displays the show ip eigrp topology command on RouterB. RouterB's FD to the 192.168.13.0 network is 20514560. The feasibility condition states that, to become a feasible successor, the RD of the neighbor must be less than the FD. In this case, RouterA's FD is 20514560 and RouterB's RD is 20514560. Because the RD is not less than the FD, the feasibility condition is not met and no feasible successor exists in the EIGRP topology table for

RouterA. If the link between RouterA and RouterC failed, the DUAL algorithm would run and the route through RouterB would then be installed in the routing table. In truth, the topology table does contain the link via RouterB. To see it, you must use the show ip eigrp topology all-links command, as shown in Figure 9-25.

RouterB's feasible distance is the distance it will advertise to RouterA as its reported distance (RD). In short, the RD is the best path a neighboring router has to the destination network.

```
RouterB#show ip eigrp topology
IP-EIGRP Topology Table for AS(52)/ID(172.16.0.1)
Codes: P - Passive, A - Active, U - Update, Q - Query, R - Reply,
       r - reply Status, s - sia Status
P 10.0.0.0/8, 1 successors, FD is 20512000
        via Connected, Serial1
P 192.168.12.32/27, 1 successors, FD is 20514560
        via 172.16.0.2 (20514560/28160), Serial0
P 192.168.13.0/24, 1 successors, FD is 20514560
        via 10.0.0.2 (20514560/28160), Serial1
P 192.168.20.0/24, 2 successors, FD is 21024000
        via 172.16.0.2 (21024000/20512000), Serial0
        via 10.0.0.2 (21024000/20512000), Serial1
P 172.20.0.0/16, 1 successors, FD is 28160
        via Connected, FastEthernet0
P 172.16.0.0/16, 1 successors, FD is 20512000
        via Connected, Serial0
RouterB#
```

Figure 9-24   RouterB show ip eigrp topology command output

In all the outputs showing the topology table for EIGRP, the routes are tagged as "P" or Passive. In EIGRP, passive is a good state, as it means all DUAL computations have been completed and the route is stable. A route marked passive can be installed in the routing table and used to route packets. If a neighbor becomes unavailable for some reason, the table may list a route as "A" or Active. If marked as active, DUAL is sending queries and replies in an attempt to find the FD and the successor. Occasionally, due to hardware errors or configuration errors, a route may become "stuck in active." While in this state, the route cannot be passed for inclusion in the routing table and packets cannot be routed to that network via EIGRP.

Only one successor exists for the 192.168.13.0 network, but EIGRP still keeps the second route in the topology table in case the primary route fails. This is one reason convergence is so fast with EIGRP.

```
RouterA#show ip eigrp topology all-links
IP-EIGRP Topology Table for AS(52)/ID(192.168.12.33)
Codes: P - Passive, A - Active, U - Update, Q - Query, R - Reply,
       r - reply Status, s - sia Status
P 10.0.0.0/8, 2 successors, FD is 21024000, serno 15
        via 192.168.20.2 (21024000/20512000), Serial1
        via 172.16.0.1 (21024000/20512000), Serial0
P 192.168.12.32/27, 1 successors, FD is 28160, serno 1
        via Connected, FastEthernet0
P 192.168.13.0/24, 1 successors, FD is 20514560, serno 16
        via 192.168.20.2 (20514560/28160), Serial1
        via 172.16.0.1 (21026560/20514560), Serial0
P 192.168.20.0/24, 1 successors, FD is 20512000, serno 14
        via Connected, Serial1
P 172.20.0.0/16, 1 successors, FD is 20514560, serno 8
        via 172.16.0.1 (20514560/28160), Serial0
        via 192.168.20.2 (21026560/20514560), Serial1
P 172.16.0.0/16, 1 successors, FD is 20512000, serno 2
        via Connected, Serial0
```

Figure 9-25 Show ip eigrp topology all-links command output

Using the hold-down time in the neighbor table, EIGRP learns about down neighbors in as quickly as 15 seconds. The use of the topology table allows EIGRP to keep successors and feasible successors, or backup routes, that can be quickly installed in the event of a link failure. Ultimately, the routing table is the final destination for the information found via EIGRP's extensive route selection process. Via DUAL and the three tables—the neighbor table, topology table, and routing table—EIGRP can converge quickly in the event of most network problems. For this reason, EIGRP is a commonly used protocol in all-Cisco networks.

EIGRP Configuration

EIGRP configuration is nearly identical to IGRP configuration. Figure 9-26 shows the commands necessary to configure basic EIGRP on RouterA.

```
RouterA>enable
RouterA#config t
Enter configuration commands, one per line.  End with CNTL/Z.
RouterA(config)#router eigrp 52
RouterA(config-router)#no auto-summary
RouterA(config-router)#network 192.168.20.0
RouterA(config-router)#network 172.16.0.0
RouterA(config-router)#network 192.168.12.0
RouterA(config-router)#^Z
RouterA#
```

Figure 9-26   EIGRP configuration

Notice that the no auto-summary command is used once again. Like RIPv2, EIGRP is classless, but it summarizes to classful network boundaries by default. The no auto-summary command turns off this default behavior. EIGRP configuration requires turning on the EIGRP process with the router eigrp [as #] command. Each router will only share EIGRP information with other EIGRP routers configured in the same autonomous system. It is also highly recommended that you use the bandwidth command to set the actual bandwidth on serial links. Otherwise, EIGRP will make path selections based on the default link speed for an interface. Because serial links on Cisco routers default to 1.544 Mbps, not setting the bandwidth on a 56K link could cause strange routing behavior. Another helpful command to add to your EIGRP configuration is eigrp log-neighbor-changes. This command tracks neighbor state changes and will show you why neighbors have been reset. You must enter this command at the (config-router)# mode. Figure 9-27 shows EIGRP routes in the routing table of RouterA. All of the EIGRP routes in this table come from the EIGRP topology table.

9

The first number is the administrative distance and the second is the metric to the network. In this case, the two successors from the EIGRP topology table have been installed as equal cost paths in the routing table.

```
RouterA#show ip route
Codes: C - connected, S - static, I - IGRP, R - RIP, M - mobile, B - BGP
       D - EIGRP, EX - EIGRP external, O - OSPF, IA - OSPF inter area
       N1 - OSPF NSSA external type 1, N2 - OSPF NSSA external type 2
       E1 - OSPF external type 1, E2 - OSPF external type 2, E - EGP
       i - IS-IS, L1 - IS-IS level-1, L2 - IS-IS level-2, ia - IS-IS inter area
       * - candidate default, U - per-user static route, o - ODR
       P - periodic downloaded static route

Gateway of last resort is not set

     192.168.12.0/27 is subnetted, 1 subnets
C       192.168.12.32 is directly connected, FastEthernet0
D       192.168.13.0/24 [90/20514560] via 192.168.20.2, 00:00:03, Serial1
C       172.16.0.0/16 is directly connected, Serial0
D       172.20.0.0/16 [90/20514560] via 172.16.0.1, 00:00:03, Serial0
C       192.168.20.0/24 is directly connected, Serial1
D       10.0.0.0/8 [90/21024000] via 192.168.20.2, 00:00:03, Serial1
                   [90/21024000] via 172.16.0.1, 00:00:03, Serial0
```

Figure 9-27 EIGRP routing table

EIGRP supports optional authentication of routing peers. Unlike RIPv2, however, it only supports MD5 authentication. As clear text provides no real security, support only for MD5 is actually a good thing. Configuring EIGRP authentication requires the following steps:

- Define a key chain.
- Define keys in the key chain.
- Enable authentication on the interface by specifying the key chain to be used.
- Manage the keys (optional key lifetimes).

Figure 9-28 shows the commands necessary on RouterA and RouterB to configure authentication. The figure shows each router with matching key chain names. The key chain names do not have to match, but the routers must have a common key-string. In this case, both routers have a key-string of caudle and therefore will authenticate with one another. EIGRP is a powerful routing protocol that greatly enhances Cisco-only networks. However, because it is proprietary, many networks either will not or cannot use it. To provide robust routing services on multivendor networks, many system administrators turn to the open standards link-state protocol called Open Shortest Path First.

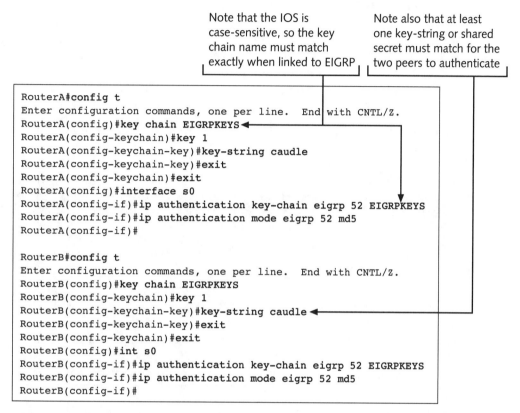

Note that the IOS is case-sensitive, so the key chain name must match exactly when linked to EIGRP

Note also that at least one key-string or shared secret must match for the two peers to authenticate

```
RouterA#config t
Enter configuration commands, one per line.  End with CNTL/Z.
RouterA(config)#key chain EIGRPKEYS
RouterA(config-keychain)#key 1
RouterA(config-keychain-key)#key-string caudle
RouterA(config-keychain-key)#exit
RouterA(config-keychain)#exit
RouterA(config)#interface s0
RouterA(config-if)#ip authentication key-chain eigrp 52 EIGRPKEYS
RouterA(config-if)#ip authentication mode eigrp 52 md5
RouterA(config-if)#

RouterB#config t
Enter configuration commands, one per line.  End with CNTL/Z.
RouterB(config)#key chain EIGRPKEYS
RouterB(config-keychain)#key 1
RouterB(config-keychain-key)#key-string caudle
RouterB(config-keychain-key)#exit
RouterB(config-keychain)#exit
RouterB(config)#int s0
RouterB(config-if)#ip authentication key-chain eigrp 52 EIGRPKEYS
RouterB(config-if)#ip authentication mode eigrp 52 md5
RouterB(config-if)#
```

Figure 9-28   EIGRP authentication

OPEN SHORTEST PATH FIRST

Large networks consisting of equipment from multiple vendors cannot use the advanced features of the Cisco proprietary protocol EIGRP. Moreover, many corporations make open standards protocols a requirement in their networks. **Open Shortest Path First (OSPF)** is an open standards, link-state routing protocol that supports classless routing, variable length subnet masks, and authentication.

Link-state routing protocols allow routers to share a common view of the entire network. Each router sends out link-state advertisements (LSAs) to all routers in an area describing its attached links. These LSAs are not periodic. Instead, they are sent only when a change occurs in the network. The nonperiodic nature of the updates saves network bandwidth. The downside of link-state routing protocols comes from the need for each router to hold a topological database of the entire area; this requirement increases CPU and memory demands on a router. Because OSPF creates an adjacencies database (basically a neighbor database similar to EIGRP), topological database, and a routing table, it requires more memory to run than a simple protocol such as RIP, which only creates a routing table. OSPF parameters are also much more complex to configure. However, for the CCNA, configuring OSPF in a single area is the only exam objective. Complex configurations of OSPF in a multi-area environment are part of CCNP study.

Table 9-2 summarizes the main differences between distance-vector and link-state routing protocols.

Table 9-2   Major characteristics of distance-vector and link-state routing protocols

Distance-vector	Link-state
Periodically broadcasts entire routing table to neighbor routers	Multicasts links to all neighbor routers in the AS on startup; all other routing table updates contain only updated routes; typically, updates only occur when a network topology change occurs
Slow to converge	Fast to converge due to link-state advertisements
Prone to routing loops because of routing by rumor nature	Less prone to routing loops because all other routers share a common view of the network
Easy to configure and administer	Harder to configure; requires greater memory and processing power on each router
Consumes relatively more bandwidth	Consumes relatively less bandwidth

OSPF is ideally suited for large networks, as it can use a concept known as areas to bound link-state advertisements. An **area** is the portion of a network within which LSAs are contained. All OSPF routers configured with the same area identification will accept LSAs from one another. Figure 9-29 shows an OSPF network that has been designed with two areas. Area 0 is the only required area in an OSPF network. In other words, all OSPF networks must have an area 0 configured. The significance of areas becomes apparent when you realize how LSAs are bounded within an area. In Figure 9-29, area 0 LSAs affect only routers A, B, and C. LSAs for area 1 only affect routers B, E, F, and D. Therefore, if a link on RouterA goes down, it will inform only RouterB and RouterC that the link has gone down. The ability to design OSPF in this bounded, hierarchical fashion is solely the result of the concept of areas. In the sample network, network administrators may have placed routers B, D, E, and F in a separate area because of a known problem with route flapping or because those routers did not contain the memory needed to hold a topological database of the entire network. They may also have created the area just as a way to logically group a set of routers in a geographical location. With OSPF, network designers have great flexibility. Still, as mentioned earlier, CCNAs only need to be able to configure single-area OSPF.

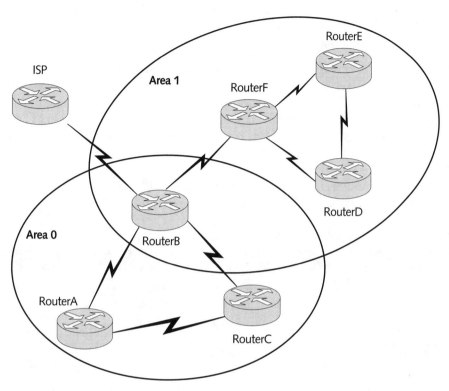

Figure 9-29   OSPF areas

OSPF Concepts

In order to configure OSPF, you must understand several main concepts associated with it:

- Link
- Link-state
- Area
- Cost
- Adjacencies database
- Topological database
- Designated router
- Backup designated router

A **link** in OSPF is a router's interface. So, a router has a link for each interface configured to run OSPF. **Link-state** is the status of a link on a router. An area defines the confines within which LSAs are contained. Areas, which were discussed in detail earlier, are responsible for allowing OSPF to use a hierarchical network design.

Cost is the default metric for OSPF. A link's cost is computed using the following formula:

Cost = (10^8 / bandwidth of the link)

Because the cost is computed using the bandwidth of the link, you must correctly set the bandwidth on serial interfaces (similar to why you must do the same on EIGRP networks). If you do not set the bandwidth, OSPF will use the default speed on serial links, which is 1.544 Mbps, and which may not be accurate. Table 9-3 shows Cisco's default OSPF costs for certain link types. As networks continue to increase in speed, OSPF will need to be modified to compute correct costs. Otherwise, Fast Ethernet, Gigabit Ethernet, and even 10-GB Ethernet will all have a cost of 1, even though their bandwidth specifications are different. This is because OSPF rounds off all fractions resulting from the cost formula to 1. Lower-cost routes are considered better in OSPF.

Table 9-3   Cisco's default OSPF costs for certain link types

Link Type	Cisco Default Cost
FDDI, Fast Ethernet	1
Ethernet	10
E1 (2.048 Mbps)	48
T1 (1.544 Mbps)	64
56 Kbps	1785

OSPF also shares the concept of a neighbor table with EIGRP. In OSPF, the **adjacencies database** contains information about all OSPF peers with which a router has successfully exchanged Hello packets. Once two neighboring routers establish bidirectional communication via Hello packets, they add one another to their respective adjacency databases. Hellos are multicast to a special multicast address of 224.0.0.5. This address is reserved for all OSPF routers, and they will accept anything sent to the address. Hello intervals for OSPF are different depending on the network in use. On broadcast or multiaccess networks such as Ethernet, Hellos are sent every 10 seconds by default. On nonbroadcast networks such as Frame Relay, Hellos are sent every 30 seconds by default.

OSPF also makes use of a dead interval, similar to an EIGRP hold-down timer. The default dead interval is four times the Hello interval. Therefore, the default dead interval is 40 seconds on broadcast networks and 120 seconds on nonbroadcast networks. Unlike EIGRP, which does not require neighbors to have their timers configured the same to become adjacent, OSPF requires that the Hello and dead interval timers match. This is a common problem when trying to implement OSPF. Many vendors set their default timers to different defaults for various reasons. To manually change the timers on a Cisco router, you can use the ip ospf hello-interval [*seconds*] and ip ospf dead-interval [*seconds*] commands. Both are interface commands (see Figure 9-30). Always be careful when changing timers. If RouterB's neighbors do not have their default timers changed, RouterB will not be able to form adjacencies or participate in OSPF LSA exchange.

```
RouterB#config t
Enter configuration commands, one per line.  End with CNTL/Z.
RouterB(config)#interface serial 0
RouterB(config-if)#ip ospf hello-interval 5
RouterB(config-if)#ip ospf dead-interval 20
RouterB(config-if)#
```

Figure 9-30   Configuring OSPF timers

OSPF also uses a **topological database**, which holds the common view of the network formed from the link-state advertisements that are received. The topological database allows the router to run the Shortest Path First algorithm and find the best path to a network.

The final OSPF concepts to cover are **designated routers (DRs)** and **backup designated routers (BDRs)**. On broadcast, multiaccess networks, OSPF elects a DR, which acts as a central point for LSAs. On multiaccess networks such as Ethernet, OSPF routers elect a DR and establish adjacencies with the DR only. This keeps each router from having to establish more adjacencies than necessary. In fact, the DR reduces the number of adjacencies and LSAs on a broadcast, multiaccess network. The reserved multicast address of 224.0.0.6 is used for all DRs and BDRs. In Figure 9-31, all the routers are connected to an Ethernet segment. A DR is elected on this network and each router forms an adjacency with it. So, assume that RouterB is elected the DR. RouterA would then form an adjacency with just RouterB, the DR. If DRs were not used on broadcast, multiaccess networks, RouterA would need to form an adjacency with Routers B, C, and D, its directly connected peers. DRs allow fewer adjacencies to be needed. Likewise, RouterA will send all LSAs to the DR, and the DR will redistribute them back out to all OSPF routers using the reserved multicast address of 224.0.0.5, an address for all OSPF routers. The backup designated router has one purpose: It takes over if the DR fails.

9

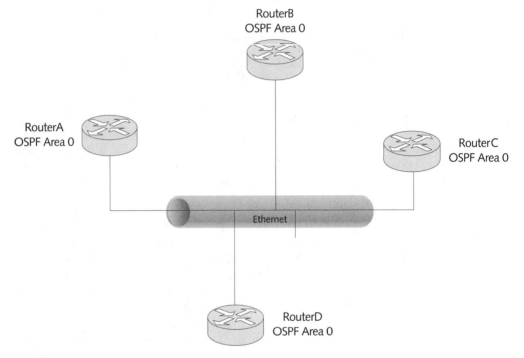

Figure 9-31   OSPF on a broadcast, multiaccess network

The DR election occurs via the Hello process. Hello packets contain an OSPF **router ID**. This ID can be one of two things: the highest IP address configured on a loopback interface or the highest IP address on a physical interface. By default, a loopback IP address will always become the ID if it is configured. The DR election looks first at the OSPF priority of a link. By default, all links have a priority of 1. Therefore, if you want to guarantee that a router will become the DR, you can assign it the highest OSPF priority. The ip ospf priority [*0-255*] interface command allows the priority to be set from 0 to 255. The router with the second-highest priority will become the BDR. In the example network in Figure 9-31, you could ensure that RouterC becomes the DR by using the following commands:

```
RouterC(config)#interface fa 0
RouterC(config-if)#ip ospf priority 100
```

If the priorities are equal, the router with the highest router ID will become the DR and the router with the second-highest will become the BDR. The router ID is the highest IP address on any active interface on the router unless a loopback address is configured. If a loopback address has been configured, the router ID will be the highest configured loopback address. Figure 9-32 displays the commands needed to configure a loopback address on RouterC.

```
RouterC#config t
Enter configuration commands, one per line.  End with CNTL/Z.
RouterC(config)#interface loopback 1
RouterC(config-if)#ip address 1.1.1.1 255.255.255.255
RouterC(config-if)#
```

The syntax for the loopback command is:
interface loopback [#]

Figure 9-32 Loopback address configuration

OSPF Operation

OSPF goes through a series of steps to get a router up and running. The first thing an OSPF router does is form adjacencies with neighbors. Routers exchange Hello packets and then place one another in their adjacency tables. Figure 9-33 shows the example network that will be used for the rest of this chapter. In this network, each router forms an adjacency with its neighbors. Figure 9-34 displays the show ip ospf neighbor command output from RouterB. It clearly shows that RouterB has RouterA and RouterC in its adjacency database.

9

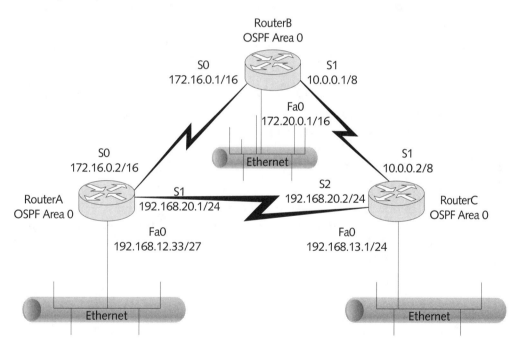

Figure 9-33 OSPF example network

The router ID is the highest IP address on an active interface on the neighbor router

Once neighbors are in a FULL state, they have correctly formed adjacency with one another

```
RouterB#show ip ospf neighbor
Neighbor ID     Pri   State      Dead Time    Address       Interface
192.168.20.2     1    FULL/  -   00:00:30     10.0.0.2      Serial1
192.168.20.1     1    FULL/  -   00:00:32     172.16.0.2    Serial0
RouterB#
```

Figure 9-34   Show ip ospf neighbor command output

The second thing that occurs in OSPF is the election of a DR and BDR. Of course, the network must be broadcast, multiaccess for this election to occur. In our example, all links are point-to-point links. Therefore, no DRs or BDRs exist on the network because no election takes place.

Finally, the routers will flood their link-state advertisements and go through the process of selecting the best route to each network. OSPF uses **Dijkstra's Shortest Path First Algorithm** to find the best path. In essence, each router sees itself as the central point from which a loop-free, best-cost path to each network is determined. The SPF algorithm allows each router to quickly find the best path to a destination network. It is a complicated algorithm, however, and uses a large amount of CPU processing and memory on a router.

After routes are installed, they must be maintained. If a link fails, OSPF routers send out link-state updates to notify the network, the SPF algorithm is run to find a new route, and the new route is advertised.

Single-Area OSPF Configuration

Just like EIGRP, OSPF concepts are much tougher than the actual configuration of simple, single-area OSPF. In the real world, OSPF offers a huge number of configuration options, including multiple areas of different types. For the CCNA exam, you only need to know how to configure single-area OSPF. The commands to configure single-area OSPF on RouterB are displayed in Figure 9-35.

```
RouterB#config t
Enter configuration commands, one per line.  End with CNTL/Z.
RouterB(config)#router ospf 1
RouterB(config-router)#network 172.20.0.0 0.0.255.255 area 0
RouterB(config-router)#network 172.16.0.0 0.0.255.255 area 0
RouterB(config-router)#network 10.0.0.0 0.255.255.255 area 0
RouterB(config-router)#exit
RouterB(config)#
```

OSPF is configured using the **router ospf [*process id*]** command.

Once OSPF is turned on, you must then specify which networks will be advertised. Note that OSPF does not use subnet masks. Instead, it uses wildcard masks. Also, each network must be associated with an area (in this case, area 0).

Figure 9-35   Single-area OSPF configuration

Two major commands are needed for OSPF. The first is router ospf [*process id*], which turns on OSPF. The process ID is not like the autonomous system number in EIGRP. Routers in the same area do not have to use the same process ID. The process ID is similar to a process on a server running Windows 2000 or Linux. The local router uses the process ID to keep up with the OSPF process running in memory. The other major command is the network command. OSPF uses wildcard masks in its network statements, which is dissimilar from all other protocols that have been discussed. Once these two commands are entered, the router begins the process of forming adjacencies and developing the topological database.

You may also want to configure default routing with OSPF. The default-information originate command allows injection of a default route into a network. This command must be used on the border router for the network. RouterB in Figure 9-29 would be considered a border router. The commands to configure and inject a default route into our example network are shown in Figure 9-36.

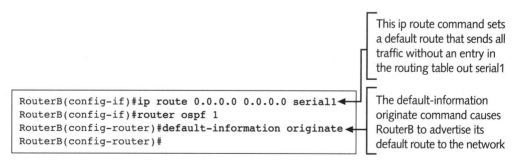

This ip route command sets a default route that sends all traffic without an entry in the routing table out serial1

```
RouterB(config-if)#ip route 0.0.0.0 0.0.0.0 serial1
RouterB(config-if)#router ospf 1
RouterB(config-router)#default-information originate
RouterB(config-router)#
```

The default-information originate command causes RouterB to advertise its default route to the network

Figure 9-36   Default route configuration in OSPF

CONTROLLING ROUTE TRAFFIC

The passive-interface command is an important entry-level command for controlling route traffic. In the network shown in Figure 9-37, RouterD may need to learn of the RIP routes on the rest of the network, but the network does not need to know its routes because RouterB is configured to route to it statically. In short, you need a way for RouterD to hear RIP updates, but not send out updates. The passive-interface command allows this. To make the serial interface on RouterD passive, you must use the following commands:

```
RouterD(config)#router rip
RouterD(config-router)#passive-interface s0
RouterD(config-router)#
```

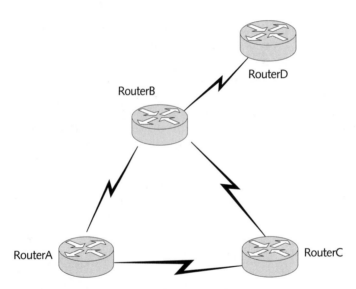

Figure 9-37   Passive-interface example

Unfortunately, this command disrupts the function of EIGRP and OSPF. The command causes a router to listen only on the passive interface. Therefore, if used with EIGRP or OSPF, the router will not send Hellos out the interface. The result is a link that is seen as having no neighbors on it. It will therefore not be used to form adjacencies. There are ways to control routing traffic in EIGRP and OSPF, but they are beyond the scope of the CCNA and this book.

CHAPTER SUMMARY

❑ Large, complex internetworks using variable length subnet masks require routing protocols that can handle the task. Several advanced routing protocols are in common use on networks today. These protocols are classless and carry subnet mask information in their routing table updates.

❑ RIPv2 is a classless routing protocol built as an extension to RIPv1. It supports modern networks' use of VLSM and authentication. In addition, it provides backward compatibility with RIPv1 when configured correctly. Still, RIPv2 suffers from all the pitfalls of distance-vector routing protocols.

❑ EIGRP is a Cisco proprietary protocol designed to incorporate some of the features of link-state routing protocols. It is, however, still a distance-vector routing protocol. EIGRP does support classless routing. Its use of neighbor, topological, and routing tables allows for quick convergence in the event of a link failure. In fact, for each destination network, EIGRP keeps a successor or best route, and if possible a feasible successor or backup route. Unfortunately, because it is proprietary, only all-Cisco networks can run EIGRP.

❑ The open standards protocol OSPF is the link-state protocol of choice in many networks; it supports VLSM, classless routing, and fast convergence. In OSPF, each router uses the Shortest Path First Algorithm to determine the best loop-free path to each network. Each router also uses an adjacency table, topological table, and routing table to pick the best route to a destination.

9

KEY TERMS

adjacencies database — The neighbor database in OSPF.

adjacency — Bidirectional communication formed by EIGRP neighbors.

area — An OSPF concept used to define the confines within which LSAs will propagate.

backup designated router (BDR) — An OSPF router on broadcast, multiaccess networks that takes over if the DR fails.

classful routing protocol — A dynamic routing protocol that does not carry subnet mask information in its routing table updates and consequently must summarize to major classful network boundaries.

classless routing protocol — A dynamic routing protocol that carries subnet mask information in its routing table updates; allows support for discontiguous subnets and VLSM.

cost — The default metric in OSPF, calculated with the following equation: Cost = $(10^8 / $ bandwidth of the link$)$.

designated router (DR) — Used on broadcast, multiaccess OSPF networks as a central point for adjacencies and LSAs.

Diffusing Update Algorithm (DUAL) — The algorithm used by EIGRP for path selection.

Dijkstra's Shortest Path First Algorithm — A complex algorithm used by OSPF routers to determine a loop-free, lowest-cost path to a destination network.

Enhanced Interior Gateway Routing Protocol (EIGRP) — A Cisco proprietary distance-vector protocol that uses some link-state features to improve performance.

feasibility condition — A condition (RD < FD) that allows a route to become a feasible successor.

feasible distance (FD) — The lowest-cost metric to a destination.

feasible successor — A backup route in the EIGRP topology table.

link — An OSPF router interface.

link-state — The status of an interface on an OSPF router.

MD5 — Message digest 5, an algorithm used to produce a secure hash of shared secret passwords.

Open Shortest Path First (OSPF) — A classless link-state routing protocol that uses areas to provide for hierarchical network design.

Protocol Dependent Modules (PDMs) — A component of EIGRP that allows it to support multiple routed protocols such as IP, IPX, and AppleTalk.

Reliable Transport Protocol (RTP) — A Transport layer protocol used by EIGRP.

reported distance (RD) — The distance an EIGRP router advertises to its neighbors for a network.

router ID — A router identifier used in OSPF Hellos and updates; normally the highest configured loopback or interface address.

successor — The best route to a destination in an EIGRP network.

topological database — A database that holds the common view of the network formed from the link-state advertisements that are received. It allows the router to run the Shortest Path First algorithm and find the best path to a network.

REVIEW QUESTIONS

1. What command injects a default route into an OSPF network?

   a. passive-interface

   b. loopback default

   c. router ospf

   d. default-information originate

2. Classless routing protocols carry _____ in their routing table updates.

3. The process ID must match on all routers in an OSPF network. True or False?

4. What command switches RIP to version 2?

    a. router rip 2

    b. version 2

    c. rip version 2

    d. ripv2 on

5. What command turns off automatic summarization to major network boundaries in both RIPv2 and EIGRP?

    a. summarization off

    b. no summary

    c. no auto-summary

    d. no ip classless

6. In what state are OSPF neighbors, when bidirectional communication has been established and adjacencies have been formed?

    a. Passive

    b. Up

    c. DR

    d. FULL

7. Which type of authentication sends only a hash across the link between two authenticating peers?

    a. MD5

    b. Clear text

    c. Signed secret keys

    d. Shared keys

8. What command places the 192.168.12.32/27 network into OSPF area 0?

    a. network 192.168.12.0 area 0

    b. network 192.168.12.32 area 0

    c. network 192.168.12.32 255.255.255.224 area 0

    d. network 192.168.12.32 0.0.0.31 area 0

9. EIGRP uses the same metric as IGRP multiplied by _____.

10. What feature of OSPF allows it to use a hierarchical design?

    a. Areas

    b. Auto summarization

    c. Wildcard masks

    d. Neighbor adjacencies

9

11. Cisco routers can be configured to send and receive RIPv1 updates on a per-interface basis. True or False?

12. The feasibility condition states _____.

13. What protocol is used by EIGRP to transport its routing protocol information?

    a. TCP

    b. UDP

    c. RTP

    d. DR/BDR

14. Which of the following commands enables EIGRP on a router with an autonomous system number of 101?

    a. router eigrp

    b. router eigrp 101

    c. router 101 eigrp

    d. as 101

15. What algorithm is used by OSPF for path selection?

    a. DUAL

    b. Open Path First

    c. Shortest Path First

    d. Default-information Originate

16. A backup route in EIGRP is a(n) _____.

17. OSPF timers must match for neighbors to form adjacencies. True or False?

18. EIGRP timers must match for neighbors to form adjacencies. True or False?

19. Which of the following commands would ensure that a router becomes the DR on a broadcast, multiaccess network?

    a. ip ospf priority 256

    b. ip ospf dr on

    c. ip ospf priority 0

    d. None of the above

20. What command displays the successors and feasible successors for EIGRP?

    a. show ip route

    b. show ip eigrp topology

    c. show ip ospf topology

    d. show ip topology

CASE PROJECTS

CASE PROJECTS

1. Hogan Enterprises needs to implement a new TCP/IP addressing scheme using VLSM. They are currently running RIPv1 on a network consisting of seven routers, four of which are Cisco routers. After being told by another contractor that they would have to abandon RIP to use VLSM, Hogan contacted you for a second opinion. You need to create a short paper discussing their network and recommendations concerning the move to VLSM. What protocol do you recommend, and how would you achieve the upgrade?

2. Conner, Inc., a large think tank, currently runs IGRP on its 50-router network. They are considering upgrading to a more robust routing protocol. You have been asked to create a short paper comparing and contrasting EIGRP and OSPF. In the end, you must recommend a protocol for the company. You must be able to defend your position.

9

10

ACCESS LISTS

After reading this chapter and completing the exercises, you will be able to:

♦ Describe the usage and rules of access lists

♦ Establish standard IP access lists

♦ Produce extended IP access lists

♦ Apply access lists to interfaces

♦ Monitor and verify access lists

In this chapter, you will learn how to create and apply access lists to control both traffic flow and network security. In the process, you will review the use and rules of access lists. Then, you will be introduced to the creation of standard and extended IP access lists. After learning the proper techniques for creating access lists, you will review how to apply such lists to router interfaces. Finally, you will learn how to monitor and verify access lists.

ACCESS LISTS: USAGE AND RULES

Network traffic flow and security influence the design and management of computer networks. Fortunately, access lists, which are built into the Cisco IOS, solve many of the problems associated with these two tasks. **Access lists** are permit or deny statements that filter traffic based on the source address, destination address, protocol type, and port number of a packet. They are available for IP, IPX, AppleTalk, and many other protocols.

Access List Usage

You can create a standard access list that examines a packet for the packet's source header information. For instance, RouterA can use an access list to deny access from Network 4 to Network 1; both networks are shown in Figure 10-1. If a packet from Network 4 arrives at the interface where you placed the access list, the router examines the packet and uses the access list to determine if it needs to discard the packet.

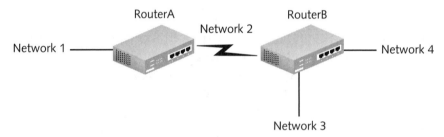

Figure 10-1   Sample network

With the following conceptual syntax, you create the standard access list to block access from Network 4 to Network 1:

```
access-list 1 deny Network 4

access-list 1 permit any
```

The access list ends with an **implicit deny any**, which blocks all packets that do not meet the requirements of the access list. Some administrators configure the deny any statement to make it more obvious, but this is unnecessary. Access list 1, if applied to the interface of RouterA connected to Network 1, blocks only the traffic coming from Network 4 to Network 1. If you wanted to deny traffic from Network 3 and Network 4, the conceptual access list syntax would then become the following:

```
access-list 1 deny Network 3

access-list 1 deny Network 4

access-list 1 permit any
```

The previous access-list statements are not the exact Cisco IOS syntax for the access list command. Actual IOS syntax will be covered later in the chapter.

The final permit any statement is necessary because all access lists in the Cisco IOS end with an implicit deny any. If you apply the access list to the interface of RouterA that is connected to Network 1, it blocks traffic from Networks 3 and 4, while allowing all other network traffic to access Network 1.

With careful planning, you can create access lists that control which traffic crosses particular links, and which segments of your network will have access to others. In other words, you can control traffic flow and security. Security is enhanced because you can permit or deny particular networks access to parts of your network. In the preceding example, Network 4 may be a student network, and Network 1 may be an administrative network. The first list stops students from Network 4 from accessing any resources in Network 1, the administrative network.

Although access lists can help with network security, they do not take the place of more advanced security measures, such as firewalls. Access lists, combined with dedicated firewalls at the edge of your network, provide the greatest security.

Problems with Access Lists

One of the most common problems associated with access lists is a lack of planning. Before you begin configuring access lists on your router, you must plan exactly what needs to be filtered and where it needs to be filtered. Careful planning prior to the configuration of lists can cut down on simple logic mistakes, which commonly occur when you do not think through the effects of your actions.

Another troublesome area is the sequential nature in which you must enter the list into the router. You cannot move individual statements once they are entered. When making changes, you must remove the list, using the no access-list [list number] command, and then retype the commands. Many network administrators simplify this time-consuming process by creating their access lists in a simple word processor, such as Notepad, and then copying and pasting the access list into the router configuration. Using this method, an administrator can create a perfect access list (free of typos) and then apply the list to any single router or a group of routers. This allows a type-once, use-many scenario that reduces errors and the time necessary to configure a router.

Finally, many new network administrators find themselves in trouble when they telnet into a router and begin applying an access list. Access lists begin working the second they are applied to an interface. It is very possible that many new administrators will find themselves inadvertently blocked from the very router on which they are applying an access list. While this is not a serious problem when the router is in the same building as the administrator, it is a serious problem when the router is in another city and thus physically inaccessible.

10

Fortunately, the reload command can save you from a long car ride or an embarrassing phone call to a local administrator to explain the problem. With the reload command, an administrator can schedule the router to reload in a certain number of minutes, hours, or even days. For access list configuration, you probably want to schedule the reload to the granularity of minutes or hours. The syntax for the reload command is reload in *[hh:]mm* (reloads in a certain number of hours or minutes) or reload at *hh:mm [month day | day month]* (reloads at a certain time on a certain date). For example, before modifying or adding access lists to a remote router, an administrator could type the following command:

```
RouterB#reload in 30
```

If an access list locks the administrator out, the router would reload in 30 minutes with a running-config that did not contain the access list that blocked the administrator's access. Note, however, that in this case, the reload command will only work if you do not copy the running-config to the startup-config while working with the access lists. If you create and apply the lists and they have the intended results, you can cancel the scheduled reload with the reload cancel command.

Access List Rules

Regardless of the type of access list you create, standard or extended, you must follow certain rules. For instance, you must create and apply access lists sequentially. Also, as stated earlier, access lists always end with an implicit deny.

The following example shows the structure of a standard IP access list. The router applies each line in the order in which you type it into the access list:

```
RouterA(config)#access-list 1 deny 172.22.5.2 0.0.0.0

RouterA(config)#access-list 1 deny 172.22.5.3 0.0.0.0

RouterA(config)# access-list 1 permit any
```

The previous example is a standard IP access list that denies the hosts 172.22.5.2 and 172.22.5.3, while allowing all other traffic. The list is applied sequentially from the top down as the router checks the packets arriving at the interface where this access list is applied, in order to check if the packets match the permit and deny statements.

In the process of applying access lists, the router first checks an arriving packet to determine if it matches the deny 172.22.5.2 0.0.0.0 statement. If it does, the router discards the packet. If it does not, the router applies the second statement, deny 172.22.5.3 0.0.0.0. If the packet matches the second statement, the router discards the packet. Once again, if the packet does not meet the rules of the first two lines, the router applies the final permit any statement, and the packet is forwarded through the interface.

If you want to add another deny line to this list, you can go back into global configuration mode and do so. Because all new lines are added to the end of the list, adding the line

RouterA(config)# access-list 1 deny 172.22.5.5 0.0.0.0 will produce the following list:

```
access-list 1 deny 172.22.5.2 0.0.0.0

access-list 1 deny 172.22.5.3 0.0.0.0

access-list 1 permit any

access-list 1 deny 172.22.5.5 0.0.0.0
```

The new line is appended to the end of access list 1. The router checks the packet against the first three statements. Once the packet matches one of the statements, the router discards or forwards it based on that match. Because the third statement says that all packets are permitted and can be forwarded, the existence of the fourth line has no effect; a packet from 172.22.5.5 would be forwarded before it ever reached the deny 172.22.5.5 0.0.0.0 statement. To fix this problem, you must remove the access list completely and recreate it using the correct sequence.

If you want to remove an access list, you use the no access-list *[list #]* command. For example, to remove the preceding list, you enter global configuration mode and type the no access-list 1 command. Figure 10-2 shows the correct procedure for typing this command.

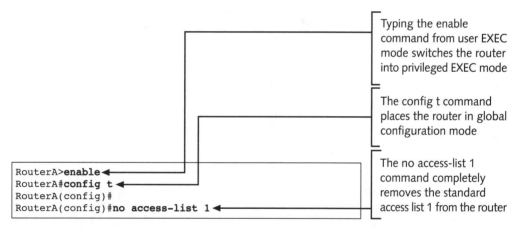

Figure 10-2   No access-list command

This command will remove the entire list. You cannot remove a particular line in an access list. As a general rule, the lines with the most potential matches should be first in the list so that packets will not undergo unnecessary processing. You should also avoid unnecessarily long access lists. A very long access list will consume large sums of CPU processing time and could cause your router to act as a bottleneck on your network.

As previously mentioned, to ease the administrative load associated with access lists, Cisco recommends using a text editor to create them. You can then easily make changes to the list and apply it to the router configuration using copy and paste. You should place a no access-list *[list #]* command as the first line of the text file. This command allows you to completely remove an access list from a router. If you don't use this command, the lines of the access list in the text file will be appended to the end of the existing list when you paste it into the configuration.

After you create access lists, you must apply them to interfaces so they can begin filtering traffic. You apply a list as either an outgoing or an incoming filter. To determine how to apply the list, you have to look through the eyes of "the man in the router." Traffic coming in to the man in the router, through any of the interfaces, is considered **inbound** and needs to be filtered using incoming traffic filters, as shown in Figure 10-3.

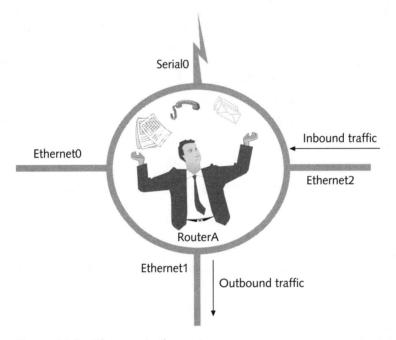

Figure 10-3   The man in the router

You would apply the access list to an interface with the following command:

```
ip access-group 1 in
(the one in this example represents the access list numbered 1)
```

Once traffic gets to "the man in the router," he must push it out to one of the interfaces. Access lists to block his outward delivery must be applied as **outbound** filters. You would use this command to set an outbound access list filter:

```
ip access-group 1 out
(again, the 1 specifies that you are applying access list 1 to the interface)
```

The final rule that access lists must follow states that an interface cannot have more than one inbound or outbound list, per protocol, assigned to it. This means that a router can have no more than one inbound IP access list and one outbound IP access list applied at the same time. Multiple lists are allowed only if the lists are different protocols.

In summary, all access lists follow these rules:

- Routers apply lists sequentially in the order in which you type them into the router.
- Routers apply lists to packets sequentially, from the top down, one line at a time.
- Packets are processed only until a match is made and then they are acted upon based on the access list criteria contained in access list statements.
- Lists always end with an implicit deny. Routers discard any packets that do not match any of the access list statements.
- Access lists must be applied to an interface as either inbound or outbound traffic filters.
- Only one list, per protocol, per direction can be applied to an interface.
- Access lists are effective as soon as they are applied; however, you must use the copy run start command to save your list after configuration if you want it to survive a router reload.

Now that you understand the basic rules of access lists, you need to understand specific types of access lists. The main types of access lists you will learn about are standard and extended IP lists.

STANDARD IP ACCESS LISTS

Standard IP access lists filter network traffic based on the source IP address only. Using a standard IP access list, you can filter traffic by a host IP, subnet, or a network address. To configure standard IP access lists, you must create the list and then apply it to an interface using the syntax following this paragraph. A detailed explanation of each item is contained in the subsequent bulleted list. The brackets in each command syntax are not part of the command; they group items that are replaced within each specific entry.

`access-list` *[list #] [permit|deny] [source address] [source wildcard mask]*

- *[list #]*: Standard IP access lists are represented by a number in the range of 1–99 (in IOS versions 11.2 and greater, they can also be represented by text names).
- *[permit|deny]*: Used to specify the nature of the access list line. It is either a permit or a deny statement.
- *[source address]*: The IP address of the source
- *[source wildcard mask]*: A **wildcard mask**, or **inverse mask**, applied to determine which bits of the source address are significant

Wildcard masks are one of the most important concepts in IP access lists. Routers use them to determine which bits in an address will be significant. Unlike subnet masks, 0s are placed in bit positions deemed significant, and 1s are placed in positions that are not significant. In other words, where there is a 0 in the mask, the corresponding bit in the incoming packet (either 0 or 1) must match the bit in the IP address in the access list. If there is no match, the packet passes to the next line in the access list. Consider the addresses and wildcard masks shown in Table 10-1.

Table 10-1 Wildcard mask examples

IP Address	Wildcard Mask	Result
172.22.5.2	0.0.0.0	All bit positions must match exactly. Therefore, the access list line will only be applied to host 172.22.5.2. For a match, the incoming packet must have an IP address of exactly 172.22.5.2.
172.22.5.0	0.0.0.255	Bit positions in the first three octets must match exactly, but the last octet can be any valid number. The access list line will apply to all hosts in the 172.22.5.0 subnet.
172.22.1.0	0.0.254.255	The first two octets must match exactly, as must the least significant bit position in the third octet, which in this case is a 1. The last octet can be any valid number. This mask would allow you to permit or deny odd-numbered subnets from the 172.22.0.0 major network because odd subnets will always have a 1 in the final bit position of the third octet. The example assumes a subnet mask of 255.255.255.0 for a Class B network.

To understand wildcard masking, you may find it helpful to examine the addresses in binary format. Consider the example in Figure 10-4, which shows a wildcard mask that forces the packet to match all four octets of the source address.

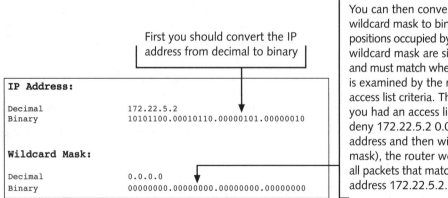

First you should convert the IP address from decimal to binary

You can then convert the wildcard mask to binary. All bit positions occupied by a 0 in the wildcard mask are significant and must match when a packet is examined by the router for access list criteria. Therefore, if you had an access list with a deny 172.22.5.2 0.0.0.0 (IP address and then wildcard mask), the router would deny all packets that matched the IP address 172.22.5.2.

```
IP Address:

Decimal        172.22.5.2
Binary         10101100.00010110.00000101.00000010

Wildcard Mask:

Decimal        0.0.0.0
Binary         00000000.00000000.00000000.00000000
```

Figure 10-4 Wildcard masking example matching a single host

Because 0s represent significant bits, you can see that in Figure 10-4, a wildcard mask of 0.0.0.0 requires that the source address match exactly. The second example, in Figure 10-5, shows how you permit or deny an entire subnet.

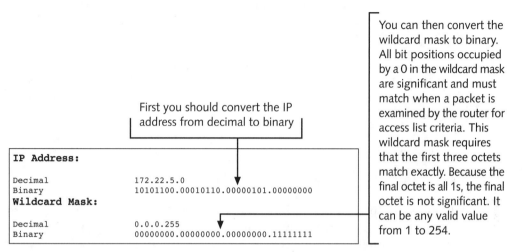

Figure 10-5 Wildcard masking example matching a complete subnet

Again, if you remember that 0s represent significant bits, you see that the first three octets must match. The final octet of the wildcard mask consists of 1s and signifies that the value of the fourth octet is not significant.

It is relatively easy to decipher wildcard masks when an entire octet is either all 0s (zero) or all 1s (255). It is more difficult when some bits in an octet are 0s and some bits are 1s. This mixing of 0s and 1s in an octet is called **partial masking**.

The final example of wildcard masking is a bit tougher and requires examining two IP addresses to fully understand it. Figure 10-6 illustrates the first address, an odd subnet.

In this example, the first two octets must match exactly. Also, the final bit place in the third octet must match; it must be a 1. Therefore, an access list that states access-list 1 permit 172.22.1.0 0.0.254.255 will allow traffic from any odd-numbered subnet to pass. Even-numbered subnets are blocked because their last bit position in the third octet is a 0.

This wildcard mask requires that the first two octets and the final bit position of the third octet match the IP address in the access list. The values in the last octet are not significant. Because the final bit positions in the third octet of the IP address in the access list are turned on (set to 1), all packets that the access list will permit or deny must have a 1 in the final bit position of the third octet.

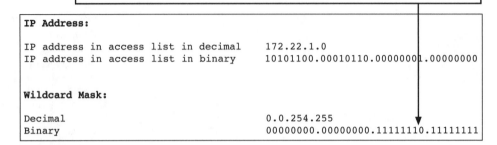

```
IP Address:

IP address in access list in decimal     172.22.1.0
IP address in access list in binary      10101100.00010110.00000001.00000000


Wildcard Mask:

Decimal                                  0.0.254.255
Binary                                   00000000.00000000.11111110.11111111
```

Figure 10-6   Wildcard masking example using partial masking

If you use a source of 172.22.1.0 and a wildcard mask of 0.0.254.255, any packet that the list will act upon must have a 1 in the least significant bit position of the third octet. If a packet with the IP address of 172.22.2.1 is examined by the access list in the previous paragraph, the router ignores it because the least significant bit of the third octet is a 0, not a 1. Figure 10-7 shows why this is true.

This wildcard mask requires that the first two octets and the final bit position of the third octet match the IP address in the access list. The values in the last octet are not significant. Because the final bit position in the third octet of the examined IP address and the IP address in the access list do not match (one is a 0 and the other is a 1), any line in an access list with a permit or deny 172.22.1.0 0.0.254.255 would not apply to the address 172.22.2.1. In fact, no even subnet could be affected because all even subnets would have a value of 0 in the last bit position of the third octet.

```
Decimal of examined IP address      172.22.2.1

Binary of examined IP address       10101100.00010110.00000010.00000001

IP address in access list:          10101100.00010110.00000001.00000000

Wildcard mask:                      00000000.00000000.11111110.11111111
```

Figure 10-7   Wildcard masking example without match

Because the least significant bit positions do not match, any address within the subnet 172.22.2.0 is out of the required range of the access list and is thus discarded (or ignored, depending on the function of the access list).

Standard IP Access List Examples

Standard IP access lists permit or deny packets based only on the source address. These addresses can be a single host address, a subnet address, or a full network address. Consider the IP network in Figure 10-8.

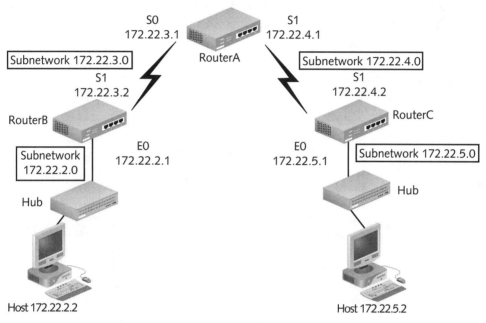

Figure 10-8   Sample IP network

Using the sample network in Figure 10-8, you can create a standard IP access list that blocks host 172.22.5.2 from accessing subnet 172.22.2.0. Figure 10-9 shows the commands you would enter on RouterB to accomplish this task.

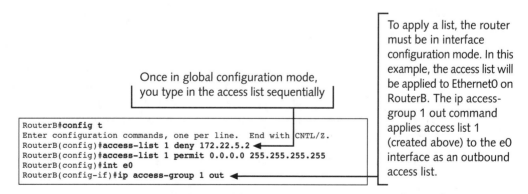

Figure 10-9   Creating a standard IP access list

In global configuration mode, you add each line of the access list sequentially and then apply it to an interface to cause it to take effect. In this example, the deny statement does not include a source wildcard mask because the default mask for standard IP access lists is 0.0.0.0, which is the exact mask needed in the example. It is also possible to replace the 0.0.0.0 255.255.255.255 entry, which represents all hosts and all networks, with the **any** keyword. Once the list is applied to RouterB's Ethernet0 interface, packets from 172.22.5.2 will be blocked from going out the interface.

Correct placement of a list is imperative. If the list were placed on RouterB's S1 interface as an inbound list, it would work with the sample network. However, if RouterB had another Ethernet interface, as shown in Figure 10-10, placing the access list on S1 would inadvertently block traffic to the second Ethernet interface, E1.

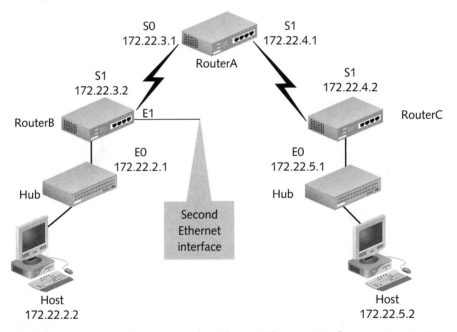

Figure 10-10   Sample IP network with two Ethernet interfaces on RouterB

Applying the previous list as an inbound access list on S1 blocks all traffic from host 172.22.5.2 to other ports on RouterB. Because you only want to block access to subnet 172.22.2.0, this is not the correct way to apply the list; you should apply the standard IP access list as close to the destination as possible. Otherwise, you will inadvertently block access to portions of your network.

To view the access lists defined on your router, use the show access-lists command. Because this is an IP access list, you could also use the show ip access-lists command. Figure 10-11 shows the correct procedures to type both commands.

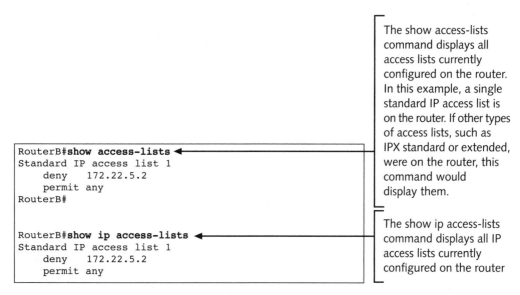

Figure 10-11 Show access-lists and show ip access-lists commands

RouterB has one standard IP access list defined on it. To view which interfaces have IP access lists set, use the show ip interface command. Your router will return a list of all interfaces and details about which access lists are applied, inbound and outbound. For the sake of brevity, only Ethernet0 is displayed in Figure 10-12.

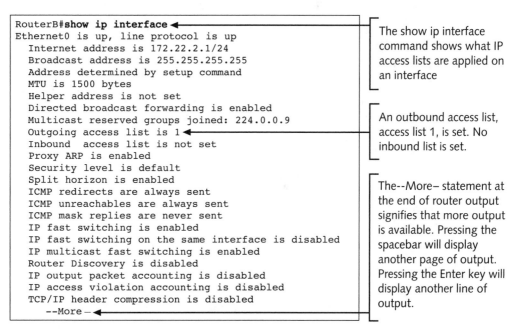

Figure 10-12 Show ip interface command

10

If you decide that an access list needs to be removed from an interface, you can remove it with the no ip access-group [*list #*] command, as shown in Figure 10-13.

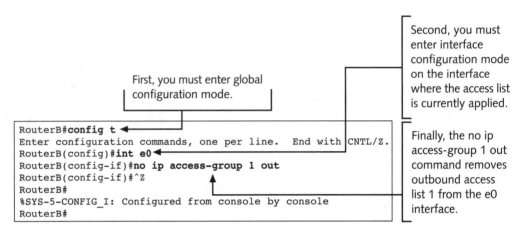

First, you must enter global configuration mode.

Second, you must enter interface configuration mode on the interface where the access list is currently applied.

```
RouterB#config t
Enter configuration commands, one per line.  End with CNTL/Z.
RouterB(config)#int e0
RouterB(config-if)#no ip access-group 1 out
RouterB(config-if)#^Z
RouterB#
%SYS-5-CONFIG_I: Configured from console by console
RouterB#
```

Finally, the no ip access-group 1 out command removes outbound access list 1 from the e0 interface.

Figure 10-13   Removing an IP access list from an interface

If you type the show ip interface command, it will show that access list 1 is no longer an outbound access list. Figure 10-14 displays the results of the show ip interface command after you type the no ip access-group 1 out command.

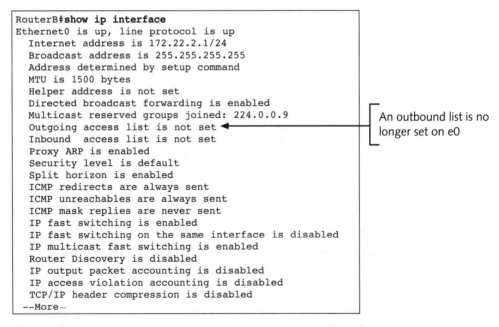

```
RouterB#show ip interface
Ethernet0 is up, line protocol is up
   Internet address is 172.22.2.1/24
   Broadcast address is 255.255.255.255
   Address determined by setup command
   MTU is 1500 bytes
   Helper address is not set
   Directed broadcast forwarding is enabled
   Multicast reserved groups joined: 224.0.0.9
   Outgoing access list is not set
   Inbound  access list is not set
   Proxy ARP is enabled
   Security level is default
   Split horizon is enabled
   ICMP redirects are always sent
   ICMP unreachables are always sent
   ICMP mask replies are never sent
   IP fast switching is enabled
   IP fast switching on the same interface is disabled
   IP multicast fast switching is enabled
   Router Discovery is disabled
   IP output packet accounting is disabled
   IP access violation accounting is disabled
   TCP/IP header compression is disabled
  --More—
```

An outbound list is no longer set on e0

Figure 10-14   Show ip interface after removal of access list 1 from e0

NOTE
Access lists are not effective until they are applied to an interface. If a list is created and not applied or if a list is applied and then the list itself is removed, the commands will be executed, but all traffic will be permitted in and out.

Now assume that instead of blocking a single host from subnet 172.22.5.0, you want to block all traffic from this subnet to subnet 172.22.2.0, using a standard IP access list. Once again, you need to create the access list in global configuration mode and apply the access list to an interface in interface configuration mode. In this example, you will apply the list as an outbound filter on RouterB's Ethernet0 interface, as this is closest to the destination as possible. (Recall that Figure 10-8 shows the network that contains RouterB.) Both parts of the task can be accomplished at the same time; the router output in Figure 10-15 shows both the creation of the list and the application of the list as an outbound filter on Ethernet0.

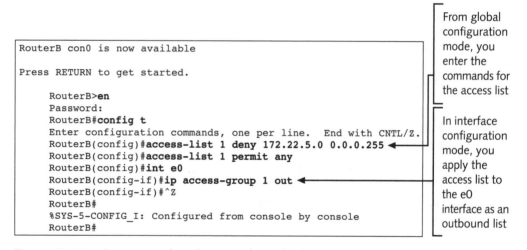

Figure 10-15   Creation and application of standard IP access list

You can use the show access-lists or show ip access-lists command and then the show ip interface command to verify that the list has been entered and applied correctly. Figure 10-16 shows the results of these two commands after the procedures in Figure 10-15 have been performed.

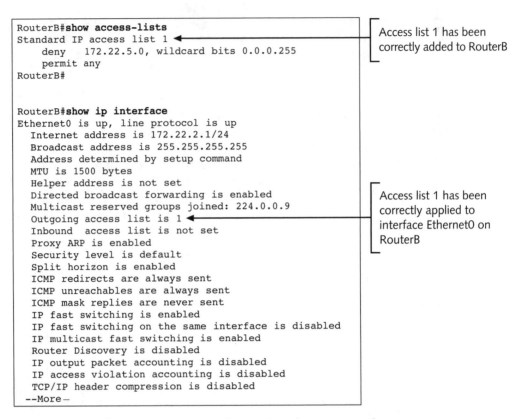

```
RouterB#show access-lists
Standard IP access list 1 ◄───────           Access list 1 has been
    deny   172.22.5.0, wildcard bits 0.0.0.255      correctly added to RouterB
    permit any
RouterB#


RouterB#show ip interface
Ethernet0 is up, line protocol is up
  Internet address is 172.22.2.1/24
  Broadcast address is 255.255.255.255
  Address determined by setup command
  MTU is 1500 bytes
  Helper address is not set
  Directed broadcast forwarding is enabled
  Multicast reserved groups joined: 224.0.0.9
  Outgoing access list is 1 ◄───────         Access list 1 has been
  Inbound  access list is not set            correctly applied to
  Proxy ARP is enabled                       interface Ethernet0 on
  Security level is default                  RouterB
  Split horizon is enabled
  ICMP redirects are always sent
  ICMP unreachables are always sent
  ICMP mask replies are never sent
  IP fast switching is enabled
  IP fast switching on the same interface is disabled
  IP multicast fast switching is enabled
  Router Discovery is disabled
  IP output packet accounting is disabled
  IP access violation accounting is disabled
  TCP/IP header compression is disabled
--More—
```

Figure 10-16   Show access-lists and show ip interface commands

Finally, assume that you want to block access to the 172.22.2.0 subnet from all hosts on subnets 172.22.4.0 and 172.22.5.0. You can accomplish this task by entering the commands shown in Figure 10-17.

Again, you can use the show ip access-lists or show access-lists commands to verify that the access list was entered correctly. The show ip interface command will show all IP interfaces. If you want to view a specific interface, you can use show ip interface *[interface#]*. For instance, throughout these examples, you could have used the show ip interface e0 command to view just the Ethernet0 interface.

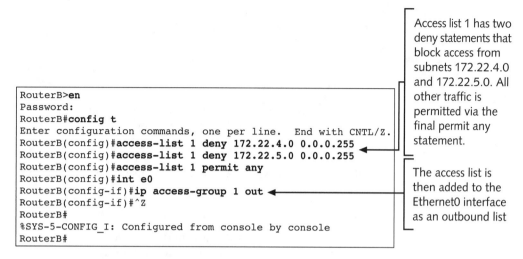

Access list 1 has two deny statements that block access from subnets 172.22.4.0 and 172.22.5.0. All other traffic is permitted via the final permit any statement.

The access list is then added to the Ethernet0 interface as an outbound list

```
RouterB>en
Password:
RouterB#config t
Enter configuration commands, one per line.  End with CNTL/Z.
RouterB(config)#access-list 1 deny 172.22.4.0 0.0.0.255
RouterB(config)#access-list 1 deny 172.22.5.0 0.0.0.255
RouterB(config)#access-list 1 permit any
RouterB(config)#int e0
RouterB(config-if)#ip access-group 1 out
RouterB(config-if)#^Z
RouterB#
%SYS-5-CONFIG_I: Configured from console by console
RouterB#
```

Figure 10-17   Access list that blocks multiple subnets

Monitoring Standard IP Access Lists

Three main commands are available for monitoring access lists on your router. The first two, show access-lists and show ip access-lists, display the exact syntax of all access lists and IP access lists, respectively. The show interfaces or show ip interface command is used to verify that an access list has been successfully applied to an interface. It is a good idea to run each of these commands after creating and applying access lists, to visually inspect and verify that statements were typed correctly and that the lists will function as entered. Use the no access-list *[list #]* command to remove the list and the no ip access-group *[list #] [direction]* command to remove the application of the list.1

EXTENDED IP ACCESS LISTS

As previously mentioned, standard IP access lists are limited to filtering by source IP addresses only. **Extended IP access lists**, on the other hand, can filter by source IP address, destination IP address, protocol type, and application port number. This granularity allows you to design extended IP access lists that permit or deny a single type of IP protocol, such as TCP, and then filter by a particular port of a particular protocol, port 21 or FTP, for example.

To configure extended IP access lists, you must create the list and then apply it to an interface using the following syntax. A detailed explanation of each item is contained in the subsequent bulleted list.

access-list *[list #] [permit|deny] [protocol] [source IP address]*
[source wildcard mask] [operator] [port] [destination IP address]
[destination wildcard mask] [operator] [port] [log]

10

- *[list #]*: Extended IP access lists are represented by a number in the range of 100–199 (in IOS versions 11.2 and greater, they can also be represented by text names).

- *[permit | deny]*: Used to specify the nature of the access list line. It is either a permit or a deny statement.

- *[protocol]*: The IP protocol to be filtered can be IP (which includes all protocols in the TCP/IP suite), TCP, UDP, ICMP, or others.

- *[source IP address]*: The IP address of the source

- *[source wildcard mask]*: A wildcard mask, or inverse mask, applied to determine which bits of the source address are significant

- *[destination IP address]*: The IP address of the destination

- *[destination wildcard mask]*: A wildcard mask, or inverse mask, applied to determine which bits of the destination address are significant

- *[operator]*: Can contain lt (less than), gt (greater than), eq (equal to), or neq (not equal to). It is used if an extended list filters by a specific port number.

- *[port]*: If necessary, the port number of the protocol to be filtered. Alternatively, a service using TCP such as www or ftp can be specified.

- *[log]*: Turns on logging of access list activity

Extended IP Access List Examples

Using Figure 10-18 as an example, this section discusses how to block host 172.22.5.2 from accessing Web services on server 172.22.2.2. The extended IP access list example shows how to block WWW access using the context-sensitive, built-in Help features in the Cisco IOS that display all available IOS options.

The configuration begins when you type the enable command to enter privileged mode on RouterC. Typing "?" at the privileged mode prompt shows all available commands. Figure 10-19 displays all the commands you must type to create the extended IP access list. The figure also displays the different access list groupings and their number ranges.

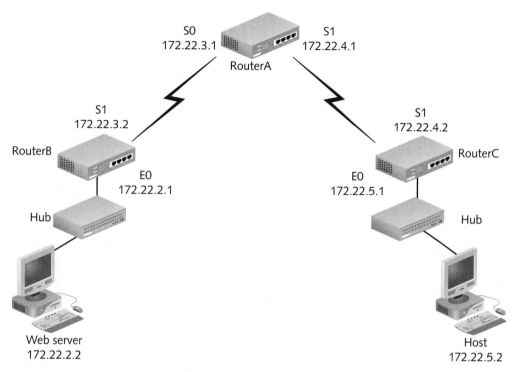

Figure 10-18   Sample IP network with a Web server

Unlike standard IP access lists, extended access lists do not have a default wildcard mask of 0.0.0.0. Therefore, you must specify the wildcard mask for the source IP address. You can use either the typical wildcard mask, as previously defined, or you can use short-cuts, as in the example in Figure 10-20. The **host** keyword is short for a wildcard mask of 0.0.0.0; in other words, the line will only be applied to packets that match the one source address specified with the host keyword. Figure 10-20 shows a continuation of the access list started in Figure 10-19; note the use of the host keyword. Notice also that the host keyword is placed before the IP address rather than after it like the wild-card mask would be.

10

Typing the ? command displays all commands available from this prompt. Notice that access-list is the second command on the list.

You then enter the access-list command to begin typing the access list. Again, the ? command reveals correct syntax for the command and possible number ranges for different access lists.

Because this list is an extended IP address, it will be designated with the number 100

```
RouterC>enable
Password:
RouterC#config t
Enter configuration commands, one per line.  End with CNTL/Z.
RouterC(config)#?
Configure commands:
  aaa                           Authentication, Authorization and Accounting.
  access-list                   Add an access list entry
  alias                         Create command alias
  arp                           Set a static ARP entry
  async-bootp                   Modify system bootp parameters
  banner                        Define a login banner
  boot                          Modify system boot parameters
  bridge                        Bridging Group.
  buffers                       Adjust system buffer pool parameters
  busy-message                  Display message when connection to host fails
  cdp                           Global CDP configuration subcommands
  chat-script                   Define a modem chat script
  clock                         Configure time-of-day clock
  config-register               Define the configuration register
  default-value                 Default character-bits values
  dialer-list                   Create a dialer list entry
  dnsix-dmdp                    Provide DMDP service for DNSIX
  dnsix-nat                     Provide DNSIX service for audit trails
  downward-compatible-config    Generate a configuration compatible with older
                                software
  enable                        Modify enable password parameters
 --More —


RouterC(config)#access-list ?
  <1-99>        IP standard access list
  <100-199>     IP extended access list
  <1000-1099>   IPX SAP access list
  <1100-1199>   Extended 48-bit MAC address access list
  <1200-1299>   IPX summary address access list
  <200-299>     Protocol type-code access list
  <700-799>     48-bit MAC address access list
  <800-899>     IPX standard access list
  <900-999>     IPX extended access list



RouterC(config)#access-list 100 ?
```

Figure 10-19   Extended IP access list example

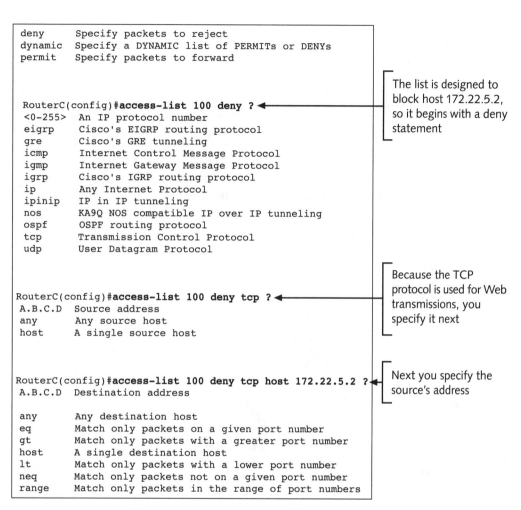

```
deny      Specify packets to reject
dynamic   Specify a DYNAMIC list of PERMITs or DENYs
permit    Specify packets to forward


RouterC(config)#access-list 100 deny ?
<0-255>   An IP protocol number
eigrp     Cisco's EIGRP routing protocol
gre       Cisco's GRE tunneling
icmp      Internet Control Message Protocol
igmp      Internet Gateway Message Protocol
igrp      Cisco's IGRP routing protocol
ip        Any Internet Protocol
ipinip    IP in IP tunneling
nos       KA9Q NOS compatible IP over IP tunneling
ospf      OSPF routing protocol
tcp       Transmission Control Protocol
udp       User Datagram Protocol



RouterC(config)#access-list 100 deny tcp ?
A.B.C.D   Source address
any       Any source host
host      A single source host



RouterC(config)#access-list 100 deny tcp host 172.22.5.2 ?
A.B.C.D   Destination address

any       Any destination host
eq        Match only packets on a given port number
gt        Match only packets with a greater port number
host      A single destination host
lt        Match only packets with a lower port number
neq       Match only packets not on a given port number
range     Match only packets in the range of port numbers
```

The list is designed to block host 172.22.5.2, so it begins with a deny statement

Because the TCP protocol is used for Web transmissions, you specify it next

10

Next you specify the source's address

Figure 10-19   Extended IP access list example (continued)

```
RouterC(config)#access-list 100 deny tcp host 172.22.5.2 host 172.22.2.2 ?
eq           Match only packets on a given port number
established  Match established connections
gt           Match only packets with a greater port number
log          Log matches against this entry
lt           Match only packets with a lower port number
neq          Match only packets not on a given port number
precedence   Match packets with given precedence value
range        Match only packets in the range of port numbers
tos          Match packets with given TOS value
<cr>
```

Figure 10-20   Extended IP access list example continued

At this point, you have specified your protocol and the source and destination addresses. You must now configure the operator and port. The example list should block WWW and therefore must contain an "equal to" operator and the WWW port number or name.

You place the port number or name and press Enter to add the line to the access list

The next line you must add is a line that will permit all other IP traffic. If you do not, the implicit deny any at the end of the access list will block all other traffic. Notice that the any keyword is used twice; the first instance corresponds to any source, and the second corresponds to any destination.

```
RouterC(config)#access-list 100 deny tcp host 172.22.5.2 host 172.22.2.2 eq ?
  <0-65535>   Port number
  bgp         Border Gateway Protocol (179)
  chargen     Character generator (19)
  cmd         Remote commands (rcmd, 514)
  daytime     Daytime (13)
  discard     Discard (9)
  domain      Domain Name Service (53)
  echo        Echo (7)
  exec        Exec (rsh, 512)
  finger      Finger (79)
  ftp         File Transfer Protocol (21)
  ftp-data    FTP data connections (used infrequently, 20)
  gopher      Gopher (70)
  hostname    NIC hostname server (101)
  ident       Ident Protocol (113)
  irc         Internet Relay Chat (194)
  klogin      Kerberos login (543)
  kshell      Kerberos shell (544)
  login       Login (rlogin, 513)
  lpd         Printer service (515)
  nntp        Network News Transport Protocol (119)
  pop2        Post Office Protocol v2 (109)
  pop3        Post Office Protocol v3 (110)
  smtp        Simple Mail Transport Protocol (25)
  sunrpc      Sun Remote Procedure Call (111)
  syslog      Syslog (514)
  tacacs      TAC Access Control System (49)
  talk        Talk (517)
  telnet      Telnet (23)
  time        Time (37)
  uucp        Unix-to-Unix Copy Program (540)
  whois       Nicname (43)
  www         World Wide Web (HTTP, 80)


RouterC(config)#access-list 100 deny tcp host 172.22.5.2 host 172.22.2.2 eq www
RouterC(config)#access-list 100 permit ip any any
RouterC(config)#
```

Figure 10-20   Extended IP access list example continued (continued)

Once an extended IP access list is created, it must be applied to an interface, just like a standard list. The difference is the placement of the list. Standard IP access lists examine the source address only. As a result, you must place them as close to the destination as possible to avoid blocking traffic bound for another interface or network. On the other hand, extended IP access lists are able to filter based on source and destination. Therefore, they are placed as close to the source as possible.

In our sample network, the list is best placed as an inbound filter on the Ethernet0 interface of RouterC. Traffic from host 172.22.5.2 destined for the Web server at 172.22.2.2 will be blocked before it has a chance to even enter the network. Because of their placement, extended access lists create less traffic across the internetwork. Figure 10-21 displays the proper commands for adding the extended access list as an inbound list on interface Ethernet0.

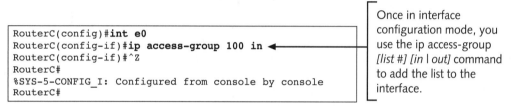

Once in interface configuration mode, you use the ip access-group *[list #] [in | out]* command to add the list to the interface.

Figure 10-21   Applying an extended IP access list to an interface

If you want to remove a list from an interface, you enter interface configuration mode and use the no ip access-group *[list #] [in | out]* command. Figure 10-22 shows this command.

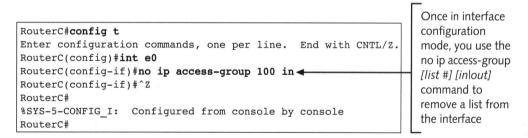

Once in interface configuration mode, you use the no ip access-group *[list #] [in|out]* command to remove a list from the interface

Figure 10-22   Removing an extended IP access list from an interface

The "Established" Parameter

Very often, network administrators want to block all TCP/IP traffic outside their network from coming into their network. However, if you use deny statements to deny all traffic coming in, no one will be able to browse the Web, get e-mail, ping, or perform other networking activities that involve a response to a request. For example, if you attempt to view the Web page at *www.cisco.com*, a DNS server somewhere has to resolve *www.cisco.com* to an IP address and provide that address to your computer. This usually requires traffic from outside your network coming into your network. If all traffic coming in were blocked by an access list, DNS and other network activities that we take for granted could not be accomplished. The easiest way to get around this problem is to use an extended IP access list with the **established** parameter. Review the following access list line:

```
access-list 100 permit tcp any 15.0.0.0 0.255.255.255 established
```

This command would permit traffic from any host on any network to any destination on the 15.0.0.0 network, as long as the traffic was in response to a request initiated inside network 15.0.0.0. In other words, a TCP connection must already be established in order for the outside traffic to be let in.

Monitoring Extended IP Access Lists

The same commands used to monitor standard IP access lists are used to monitor extended IP access lists. If you want to view the access lists configured on your router, you use the show access-lists or show ip access-lists command. To see if the list has been applied to an interface, use the show interfaces or show ip interface command. Figure 10-23 shows the show ip access-lists command.

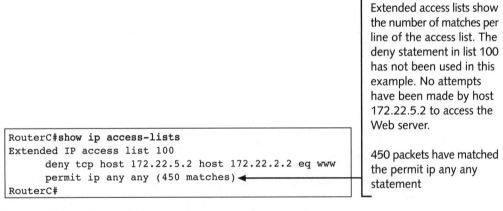

Figure 10-23   Show ip access-lists command

As shown in Figure 10-23, extended IP lists keep track of the number of packets that pass each line of an access list. These matches or counters can be reset to zero for troubleshooting purposes. To clear the counters, you issue the clear access-list counters *[list #]* command (see Figure 10-24). Use the no access-list *[list#]* command to remove the list and the no ip access-group *[list#] [direction]* command to remove the application of the list.

```
RouterC#clear access-list counters 100
RouterC#show ip access-list
Extended IP access list 100
     deny tcp host 172.22.5.2 host 172.22.2.2 eq www
     permit ip any any (9 matches) ◄
RouterC#
```

Notice that the number of matches on access list 100 has dropped from the previous 450 matches in Figure 10-23 to 9 because the counters were cleared to 0 (zero)

Figure 10-24   Clear access-list counters command

USING NAMED LISTS

In Cisco IOS versions 11.2 and above, you can use names instead of numbers to identify your lists. These are known as **named access lists**. You cannot use the same name for multiple access lists. Even different list types cannot have the same name. For example, you could not specify a standard list named Cannon if you already had an extended list named Cannon. To name a standard IP access list, use the following syntax:

> RouterC(config)#ip access-list standard *[name]*

To name an extended IP access list, use the following syntax:

> RouterC(config)#ip access-list extended *[name]*

Once the list is named, the permit or deny statement is entered. The commands follow the same syntax as unnamed lists, but the beginning part of the command is not included. For example, the syntax for a deny or permit statement for a standard IP named list would be:

> RouterC(config-std-nacl)#deny{*source [source-wildcard]* | *any*}

or

> RouterC(config-std-nacl)#permit{*source [source-wildcard]* | *any*}

To apply a standard IP named list to an interface, the syntax would be as follows:

> RouterC(config-if)#ip access-group *[name] [in | out]*

The naming feature allows you to maintain security by using an easily identifiable access list. It also removes the limit of 100 lists per filter type. In addition, with named access lists you can selectively delete lines in the ACL. This feature does not allow you to add lines to the ACL. Any lines added to a named ACL are applied to the end of the list. Named ACLs provide greater flexibility to network administrators who work in environments where large numbers of ACLs are needed (a large ISP, for example).

10

Controlling VTY Line Access

As previously discussed, access lists are used for both traffic flow and security. One useful security feature of access lists is restricting access to telnet on your router by controlling VTY line access. For example, imagine that you want to allow access to the VTY lines from a management station at the IP address 192.168.12.12/24 only. You must first create a standard IP access list that permits the management workstation. The access-list command to permit the workstation is:

```
RouterA(config)#access-list 12 permit 192.168.12.12 0.0.0.0
```

The access list can also be created using the host keyword instead of the 0.0.0.0 wildcard mask.

```
RouterA(config)#access-list 12 permit host 192.168.12.12
```

Because the single host wildcard mask is the default for standard IP access lists, the command could be written without either the 0.0.0.0 mask or the host keyword.

Once the access list is created, it must be applied to the VTY lines via the access-class command. The syntax for this command is:

```
access-class [acl #] in | out
```

To apply access list 12 to the VTY lines, you must use the following command:

```
RouterA(config)#line vty 0 4
RouterA(config-line)#access-class 12 in
```

While it is possible to restrict access to the VTY lines to a particular host as shown in the example, you can also restrict access to a subnet or network. To accomplish this, you must modify your access list to specify either a subnet or network. The commands to restrict access to the VTY lines to network 192.168.12.0/24 only are:

```
RouterA(config)#access-list 13 permit 192.168.12.0 0.0.0.255
RouterA(config)#line vty 0 4
RouterA(config-line)#access-class 13 in
```

This configuration allows VTY access from hosts on the 192.168.12.0/24 network only.

Chapter Summary

- ❑ Access lists are one of the most important IOS tools for controlling network traffic and security.

- ❑ Access lists are created in a two-step process. First, you create the list in global configuration mode, using the specific syntax of the type of list you want to create. Then, you apply the list to an interface in interface configuration mode to make it active.

❐ All access lists are created sequentially and applied sequentially to all packets that enter an interface where the list is applied.

❐ By default, access lists always end in an implicit deny any, which will drop any packet that does not meet an access list criterion.

❐ Only one access list per direction (inbound or outbound) per protocol can be applied to an interface.

❐ Standard IP access lists allow you to filter traffic based on the source IP address of a packet. They should be applied to an interface as close to the destination as possible to avoid accidentally blocking valid traffic.

❐ Extended IP access lists filter traffic based on source, destination, protocol type, and application type. They allow for more specific control over network traffic. They should be placed as close to the source as possible to keep unnecessary traffic from getting onto the internetwork.

❐ Access lists can be used to restrict telnet by controlling VTY line access. This is usually done using a single permit access list line. The list is applied using the access-class command. The list is placed on the device to which telnet is being restricted.

❐ Ranges of numbers represent all access lists. Table 10-2 summarizes the numbers associated with each type of list you need to be familiar with to pass the CCNA exam.

10

Table 10-2   Access list number ranges

Access List Type	Number
Standard IP access lists	1–99
Extended IP access lists	100–199

KEY TERMS

access lists — Permit or deny statements that filter traffic based on criteria such as source address, destination address, and protocol type.

any — A keyword used to represent all hosts or networks; replaces 0.0.0.0 255.255.255.255 in an access list.

established — A keyword that requires traffic to have originated inside the trusted network.

extended IP access lists — IP access lists that filter traffic by source IP address, destination IP address, protocol type, and port number.

host — A keyword for an extended IP list that specifies that an address should have a wildcard mask of 0.0.0.0.

implicit deny any — Blocks all packets that do not meet the requirements of the access list. Exists at the end of all lists.

inbound — A direction parameter used when applying an access list. Direction is into the router.

inverse mask — *See* **wildcard mask**.

named access list — An access list that uses names instead of number ranges.

outbound — A direction parameter used when applying an access list. Direction is out of the router.

partial masking — When an octet in a wildcard mask contains a mix of binary 1s and 0s.

standard IP access lists — Access lists that filter traffic based on source IP address.

wildcard mask — Applied to IP addresses to determine if an access list line will act upon a packet. Zeros are placed in positions deemed significant, and ones are placed in nonsignificant positions.

REVIEW QUESTIONS

1. Which wildcard mask would apply an access list line to all packets from network 175.25.0.0?

   a. 255.255.255.0

   b. 255.255.0.0

   c. 255.254.0.0

   d. 0.0.255.255

2. Standard IP access lists filter traffic based on which of the following? (Choose all that apply.)

   a. Destination IP address

   b. IP protocol

   c. Port number

   d. Source IP address

3. Wildcard masks use a _____ to signify which bits of an address are significant.

4. Which command shows only the IP access lists on a router?

   a. show access-lists

   b. show ipx access-lists

   c. show ip access-lists

   d. show interface

5. Which commands allow you to view the interfaces that have IP access lists applied to them? (Choose all that apply.)

    a. show interfaces

    b. show ip interface

    c. show ip traffic

    d. show ip counters

6. Which host and wildcard mask pair does the any keyword represent?

    a. 255.255.255.255   0.0.0.0

    b. 0.0.255.255   0.0.0.0

    c. 0.0.0.0   0.0.0.0

    d. 0.0.0.0   255.255.255.255

7. Which command is used to apply an IP access list to an interface?

    a. ip access-group *[list #] [in|out]*

    b. ip access-group permit 100

    c. ip access-group *[list #] [permit|deny]*

    d. show ip interface

8. Access lists are _____. (Choose all that apply.)

    a. used to filter traffic and control network security

    b. applied as either inbound or outbound filters

    c. sequential permit or deny statements

    d. built into the router's firmware

9. Standard IP access lists are represented by the _____ number range.

    a. 100–199

    b. 1–99

    c. 1000–1099

    d. 200–299

10. Which command could be used to remove an access list from your router?

    a. no ip access-group in

    b. no ip access-list 1 in

    c. no access-list 1

    d. no ip access-list one

10

11. Extended IP access lists are represented by the _____ number range.

    a. 100–199

    b. 200–299

    c. 1000–1099

    d. 1–99

12. The show access-lists command displays _____.

    a. access lists applied to interfaces

    b. all access lists on the router

    c. only IP access lists on the router

    d. only IPX access lists on the router

13. At which of the following prompts would you create an access list?

    a. routerC#

    b. routerC>

    c. routerC(config-if)#

    d. routerC(config)#

14. At which of the following prompts would you apply an access list to an interface?

    a. routerC#

    b. routerC>

    c. routerC(config-if)#

    d. routerC(config)

15. Which of the following host and corresponding wildcard mask pairs represent the same value as host 172.29.2.2?

    a. 0.0.0.0   255.255.255.255

    b. 172.29.2.2   0.0.0.0

    c. 255.255.255.255   0.0.0.0

    d. 0.0.0.0   172.29.2.2

16. A router can have one access list per protocol, per direction on each interface. True or False?

17. Which of the following is a benefit of using named lists?

    a. The syntax is identical to using numbered lists.

    b. There aren't as many lists allowed so it is easier to remember them.

    c. You are not constrained by the 100 lists per filter type limit.

    d. There are no benefits to using named lists.

18. What happens if a list is applied to an interface and then the list itself is removed?

    a. The commands will be executed and all traffic will be denied.

    b. The commands will be executed and all traffic will be permitted.

    c. The commands will not be executed and all traffic will be permitted.

    d. None of the above

19. What is true of the host keyword? (Choose all that apply.)

    a. It can only be used with extended IP lists.

    b. It can be used with standard and extended IP lists.

    c. It replaces the 0.0.0.255 wildcard mask.

    d. It replaces the 0.0.0.0 wildcard mask.

    e. It is placed before the IP address with which it is associated.

    f. It is placed after the IP address with which it is associated.

20. What is the purpose of the "established" parameter?

    a. To establish a connection between the sender and receiver

    b. To prevent any traffic into a network

    c. To prevent any traffic into a network that didn't originate from that network

    d. To permit all TCP traffic but not IP traffic into the established network

21. All access lists presented in this chapter, except standard IP lists, should be placed where?

    a. As close to the source as possible

    b. As close to the destination as possible

    c. As close to the serial interface as possible

    d. As close to the tftp server as possible

22. Which command links an access list to the VTY lines?

    a. ip access-group

    b. ip access-class

    c. vty access-class

    d. access-class

10

CASE PROJECTS

CASE PROJECTS

1. Freytech Industries has hired you and your team at Winslow Networks to help with an important network project. They want to block HTTP traffic from network 170.55.0.0 to their Web server at 164.106.105.3. Lisa suggests the following list:

    ```
    access-list 10 deny 170.55.0.0
    ```

    ```
    access-list 10 permit any
    ```

    What will Lisa's list do? Modify Lisa's list so that it will work for your client.

2. You have been asked to deliver a speech on the ability of access lists to control access to VTY lines. Describe how you would limit access to the VTY lines to a single management workstation at IP address 173.13.6.1/24. Also, describe how you would limit access to the 173.13.6.0 subnet only.

11

PPP AND ISDN

After reading this chapter and completing the exercises, you will be able to:

♦ Describe PPP encapsulation

♦ Configure PPP encapsulation and its options

♦ Describe and enable PPP multilink

♦ Explain how to implement ISDN BRI on Cisco routers

♦ Configure an ISDN BRI connection

In Chapter 5 you received an overview of WAN technologies such as Frame Relay, X.25, and Integrated Services Digital Network (ISDN). You also learned about WAN connectivity terminology such as channel service unit/data service unit (CSU/DSU), terminal adapter (TA), Central Office (CO), and Regional Bell Operating Companies (RBOC). WAN protocols, such as Point-to-Point Protocol (PPP) and High-level Data Link Control (HDLC), and WAN standards were also introduced. In this chapter, expanded coverage is given to PPP and ISDN. Finally, you learn how to configure a Cisco router to support PPP and ISDN.

PPP

PPP is an Internet standard protocol defined in RFCs 2153 and 1661. The IETF defined PPP to provide point-to-point, router-to-router, host-to-router, and host-to-host connections. Because of the point-to-point physical configuration, PPP is considered a peer technology. PPP is commonly used over dial-up or leased lines to provide connections into IP networks. PPP also supports other Network layer protocols such as Novell IPX and AppleTalk. Due to its flexibility, PPP is the most widely used WAN connection method today.

SLIP was the predecessor to PPP; it only supports TCP/IP connections. In addition, SLIP offers no encryption, compression, or error correction. It is an analog protocol limited to 56-Kbps transmission. PPP overcomes all of SLIP's limitations. Other advantages offered by PPP are the capability to handle asynchronous as well as synchronous communication. PPP is also more efficient and supports more protocols and interfaces. PPP can be used over several different physical interfaces, including:

- Asynchronous serial

- ISDN synchronous serial

- High-Speed Serial Interface (HSSI)

Asynchronous serial connections are typically used with analog modems, which connect directly to the existing phone lines and outlets that are wired in residential areas throughout the United States. ISDN synchronous serial connections require the use of ISDN modem equipment to interface with the Integrated Services Digital Network (ISDN) provided by many public carriers. (ISDN is described in greater detail later in this chapter.) **High-Speed Serial Interface (HSSI)** is a type of serial device that was developed by Cisco and T3Plus Networking. It defines a serial connection that operates at speeds of up to 52 Mbps over distances of up to 15 meters (50 feet).

PPP in the Protocol Stack

Most WAN protocols operate at the Data Link layer of the OSI model. As mentioned, you can use PPP over both asynchronous and synchronous connections at the Physical layer of the OSI reference model. The Link Control Protocol is used at the Data Link layer to establish, configure, and test the connection. PPP also relies on Network layer services called **Network Control Protocols (NCPs)** at layer 3 of the OSI model. NCPs allow the simultaneous use of multiple Network layer protocols and are required for each protocol that uses PPP. Examples of NCPs include **IP Control Protocol (IPCP)**, **IPX Control Protocol (IPXCP)**, and **AppleTalk Control Protocol (ATCP)**. Figure 11-1 illustrates the location of PPP in the protocol stack; notice that the NCPs function at the Network layer.

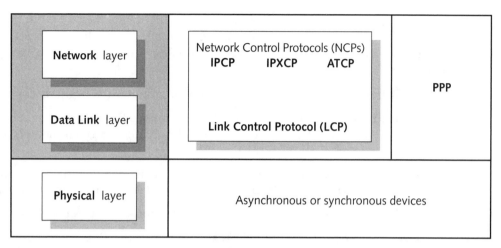

Figure 11-1   PPP in the protocol stack

Frame Format

PPP, like many WAN technologies, is based on the **High-level Data Link Control (HDLC)** protocol. The difference between PPP frames and HDLC frames is that PPP frames contain protocol and **Link Control Protocol (LCP)** fields, as shown in Figure 11-2. The Protocol field allows PPP to simultaneously support multiple protocols by allowing it to indicate which protocol it is encapsulating. PPP uses the LCP field to establish, configure, maintain, and terminate connections.

11

HDLC

Flag	Address	Control	Data	FCS	Flag

Cisco HDLC

Flag	Address	Control	Proprietary	Data	FCS	Flag

PPP

Flag	Address	Control	Protocol	LCP Data	FCS	Flag

LCP	Code	Identifier	Length	Data

Figure 11-2   HDLC and PPP packet structure

Figure 11-2 also shows the Cisco proprietary HDLC frame. Cisco HDLC has proprietary fields that support the encapsulation of multiple protocols. Cisco's HDLC is the default encapsulation type for serial interfaces on Cisco routers. The elements of the PPP frame are as follows:

- **Flag**: Binary sequence 01111110, which indicates the beginning of the frame

- **Address**: Binary sequence 11111111; because PPP is used to create a point-to-point connection, there is no need for PPP to assign an individual address for each host.

- **Control**: Binary sequence 00000011, which indicates that the transmission of user data will not be sequenced and is to be delivered over a connectionless link

- **Protocol**: Two bytes used to identify the protocol that is encapsulated

- LCP or **Data**: The LCP field is also known as the Data field. This location contains the LCP information and the data that has been encapsulated from the higher layers. The default size of this field is 1500 bytes, but PPP implementations can negotiate a larger size for this field. LCP is explained in greater detail in the following section.

- **Frame Check Sequence (FCS)**: Two bytes by default, but can be as large as four bytes; uses a cyclical redundancy check (CRC) to verify the integrity of the frame and ensure that it was not corrupted during transmission

- **Flag**: Binary sequence 01111110, which identifies the end of the data frame

LCP

LCP is described in RFCs 1548, 1570, 1661, 2153, and 2484. RFC 1661, which made RFC 1548 obsolete, describes PPP organization and methodology, including basic LCP extensions. RFC 1661 was later updated by RFC 2153, which explains PPP Vendor extensions. RFC 1570 and its update, RFC 2484, further expand the definition of LCP extensions. The LCP field of the PPP packet can contain many different pieces of information, including:

- **Asynchronous character map**: Allows PPP to encode its transmission properly for the recipient host

- **Maximum receive unit size**: Sets the receive buffer size for the LCP connection, typically 1500 bytes

- **Compression**: Data compression that can be performed on the PPP packet at the source and then uncompressed at the destination; typically improves the speed of data transfer over slow serial connections because less data has to traverse the connection

- **Authentication**: Can be enabled to require a password to establish the PPP connection. Two authentication protocols are available—**Password Authentication Protocol (PAP)** and **Challenge Handshake Authentication Protocol (CHAP)**. Authentication is described in greater detail in the following section.

- **Magic number**: Aids in detecting links that are in the looped-back condition. When interfaces are looped back, data that is sent out the interface is immediately received on that interface. Magic numbers are unique numbers added by the router to a packet, which allow it to detect a looped-back link. If the router receives a packet that contains its own unique magic number, it detects that the interface is looped back. Loopback is typically used for testing interfaces to ensure they are sending and receiving data. The **loopback command** can be run from the interface configuration prompt. Although good for testing, looped-back interfaces are undesirable in production environments. In a production environment, you can use the **down-when-looped** command from interface configuration mode, which will automatically shut down that interface when looping is detected.

- **Link Quality Monitoring (LQM)**: Checks the reliability of the link by monitoring the number of errors, latency between requests, connection retries, and connection failures on the PPP link

- **Multilink**: Allows multiple transmission devices to send data over separate physical connections. The benefit of multilink is that you can combine the bandwidth of two separate devices over one logical connection. For example, two 64-Kbps ISDN channels can be combined to provide an effective throughput of 128 Kbps. PPP will fragment, sequence, and reassemble these packets to provide faster throughput over multiple slow serial connections. Multilink is defined in RFC 1717; you can enable multilink with the ppp multilink command from the interface configuration mode.

11

LCP Link Configuration

The **LCP link configuration** process modifies and enhances the default characteristics of a PPP connection. This part of the link configuration process manages the link, controls the authentication, and can be used to set link quality. The LCP link configuration process includes the following actions:

- **Link establishment**: PPP must open and configure the PPP connection before any data can be transferred over the link.

- Authentication (optional): CHAP or PAP can be used to verify the identity of the devices that are establishing the connection. CHAP and PAP are discussed in greater detail later in this chapter.

- **Link-quality determination** (optional): Checks the quality of the link and monitors its reliability

- **Network layer protocol configuration negotiation**: Identifies the appropriate Network layer protocol for the connection; the devices negotiate to use a protocol that is common to both.

- **Link termination**: When the call is complete, or the specifications defining the call are no longer met, the call is terminated.

Establishing PPP Communications

Three of the five link configuration actions defined in the preceding list are involved in establishing PPP communications: link establishment, optional authentication, and Network layer protocol configuration negotiation. The link establishment phase involves the configuration and testing of the data link. As mentioned earlier, PPP connections may use the information contained in the LCP portion of the PPP packet to configure the link by passing requirements for maximum transmission units and compression.

The second phase of the establishing process is optional. The authentication process can use two authentication types with PPP connections: PAP and CHAP. Most network administrators configure their devices to use CHAP because it is the stronger authentication method of the two. RFC 1994 documents the PAP and CHAP authentication protocols.

PAP uses a simple two-way handshake method to establish the link. In this link, PPP transmits a clear text username and password across the link between hosts to establish the link. The device attempting to establish the link transmits the username and password, so that the destination host will allow the PPP session. PPP only conducts PAP authentication during initial link establishment.

Compared with PAP, CHAP provides a much more sophisticated authentication process. Like PAP, CHAP provides username and password authentication service during the initial link establishment. However, CHAP employs a three-way, rather than two-way handshake. Once the link is established, the local router queries the remote host with a packet known as a **challenge**. The challenge is in the form of a unique encryption key. The remote host uses the encryption key to encode the username and password. The router compares the decrypted username and password and looks for a match with its username and password. It then either accepts or drops the connection based on whether the comparison yields a matching username and password.

After the connection is made, CHAP can continue this query process, using a different encryption key each time and using unique and unpredictable intervals. This further ensures that connections are legitimate because it prevents someone from capturing the data packets that are exchanged during the initial authentication process between two authorized systems and then playing those data packets from an unauthorized system in an attempt to gain PPP access to the server.

TIP The router typically controls the authentication process, but a **Terminal Access Controller Access Control System (TACACS), RADIUS server,** or third-party authentication server can also be used to centralize management of CHAP authentication and other security features.

PPP is an encapsulation type for serial interface communications. Therefore, to configure a PPP connection, you must access the interface configuration mode for the specific interface you want to configure. For example, if you want to configure PPP on the first serial interface of the router (S0), you would use the commands shown in Figure 11-3 (assuming that the router was already in enable mode).

```
router#config t
router(config)#int s0
router(config-if)#encap ppp
```

Figure 11-3   Enabling PPP

The third phase of the establishing process is Network layer protocol configuration negotiation. After LCP has finished negotiating the configuration parameters, Network layer protocols can be configured individually by the appropriate NCP. At this point, packets can be sent over the link. The different protocols can be established and terminated at any time.

Configuring PPP Authentication

As mentioned previously, using authentication with PPP connections is optional. Therefore, you must specifically configure PPP authentication on each PPP host in order for the host to use it. You can choose to enable CHAP, PAP, or both on your PPP connection, in either order. For example, to set the router to first use CHAP, and then to go to PAP (assuming that CHAP is not available), you would type the command shown in Figure 11-4.

```
router(config-if)#ppp authentication chap pap
```

Figure 11-4   Enabling both CHAP and PAP authentication

If you entered that command, your local router would request CHAP authentication during the connection, but if the other device did not support CHAP or attempted PAP authentication instead, then PAP would be tried. You could also decide to use just CHAP or just PAP by omitting the undesired method from the command line.

Once you set the authentication type, you must still configure a username and password for the authentication. To do so, you must exit interface configuration mode and enter global configuration mode. Then, type "username" followed by the host name of the remote router; after that, type "password" followed by the password for that connection. Ensure that each router uses the same password, but uses the other router's host name after username. The link will go up and down (flapping) until both ends of the point-to-point link are configured correctly. Figure 11-5 illustrates a configuration and the commands required for that configuration to operate using CHAP authentication.

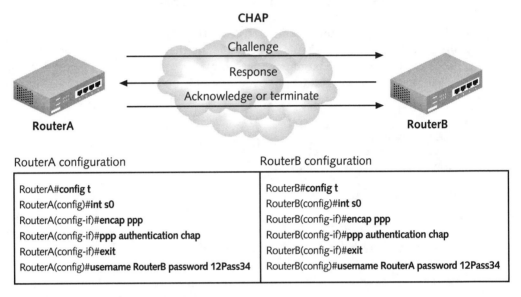

CHAP

RouterA configuration

RouterB configuration

RouterA#**config t**	RouterB#**config t**
RouterA(config)#**int s0**	RouterB(config)#**int s0**
RouterA(config-if)#**encap ppp**	RouterB(config-if)#**encap ppp**
RouterA(config-if)#**ppp authentication chap**	RouterB(config-if)#**ppp authentication chap**
RouterA(config-if)#**exit**	RouterB(config-if)#**exit**
RouterA(config)#**username RouterB password 12Pass34**	RouterB(config)#**username RouterA password 12Pass34**

Figure 11-5   Configuring CHAP

If you want to configure the same host name and password for CHAP authentication on several routers, you can do so via the interface configuration mode prompt. For example, if you wanted to configure the host name flagstaff and set the password to lumberjack for all routers, you would enter the commands in Figure 11-6 on all routers' PPP interfaces.

```
router(config-if)#ppp chap hostname flagstaff
router(config-if)#ppp chap password lumberjack
```

Figure 11-6   Configuring PPP and CHAP

In this example, the host name flagstaff sets the alternate CHAP host name to flagstaff. The password lumberjack part of the command sets the default CHAP password to lumberjack. This type of configuration is easier to implement than the one shown in Figure 11-5, in which you must configure each router with the same password, but with opposite host names.

TIP

If you are using PAP authentication with Cisco IOS Releases 11.1 or later, you must enable PAP on the interface of the router to receive the PAP request.

Confirming PPP Communications

Once you have completed configuring your PPP interface, you can verify your changes using the show interface command. You must be in privileged EXEC mode to view the interfaces. For example, if you want to view your configuration on the Serial 1 interface, type the following:

```
Router#show interface S1
```

ISDN

ISDN is a circuit-switched service from telecommunications providers to allow voice, data, video, and audio transmissions over existing digital telephone lines. Circuit switching is preferred for applications using streaming audio and video. This is because the data takes the same route from sender to receiver (unlike packet switching), so time is not required to reorder the packets at the destination. This makes for a smoother delivery of time-sensitive data. ISDN is often used as a lower-cost alternative to Frame Relay or T1 connections, while still offering a higher connection speed than an analog modem. The service is offered at two different levels: Basic Rate Interface (BRI) and Primary Rate Interface (PRI). BRI is typically used in small offices or for home connections, and PRI is used in larger environments because it provides higher bandwidth.

Telecommunications providers offer digital connections via ISDN as channels. BRI connections offer three channels: two at 64 Kbps and one at 16 Kbps. The 64-Kbps channels are known as bearer or B-channels, because they carry the data for the connection. ISDN BRI connections use the 16-Kbps signaling channel or data channel, which is also called a D-channel, to control the communications on the link. The two B-channels can be used together in a process called **bonding** to achieve 128 Kbps. If you are using voice with the service, data can be load-balanced across both lines or you can talk on the phone, which will use one B-channel, while the data uses the other B-channel. PRI connections offer 23 B-channels and one 64-Kbps D-channel for a total bandwidth of about 1.544 Mbps, which is the same as a T1 line.

TIP

European ISDN PRI service offers thirty 64-Kpbs B-channels and one 64-Kbps D-channel.

In both ISDN BRI and PRI, a single D-channel is used for signaling information, and the B-channels are used to carry the data. Because the control communications are conducted on a channel that is separate from the data transfer, ISDN is said to use **out of band signaling**. In some cases the D-channel can carry data as well as the signaling information. The Data Link layer protocol that manages the signaling exchange on the D-channel is **Link Access Procedure-D (LAPD)**.

11

ISDN Standards

The ITU maintains several standards on ISDN. These standards are organized into ITU-T groups, which are organized by three different letter designations: E, I, and Q. Each group is then subdivided into specific protocols, preceded by the group designator. For example, protocols I.430 and I.431 are part of the I-series protocol group. Protocols within each group define a related set of standards. Table 11-1 lists and describes the relationship between the protocol designators and the concepts they define.

Table 11-1   ISDN protocol series

Protocol Series	Description	Examples
E	Telephone and network standards	E.164 – International telecommunications numbering
I	Methods, terminology, concepts, and interfaces	I.100 – Terminology, structure, and concepts I.300 – Networking recommendations
Q	Signaling and switching standards	Q.921 – Data Link layer LAPD procedures (explained later in this chapter) Q.931 – Network layer functions

ISDN Operations

ISDN can use HDLC (default) or PPP as its WAN protocol. As previously mentioned, it uses the Link Access Procedure-D (LAPD) to pass the signaling messages between the router (or other terminal equipment) and the ISDN switch at the local telco central office. The data travels between routers on the B-channels via HDLC or PPP encapsulation, as shown in Figure 11-7.

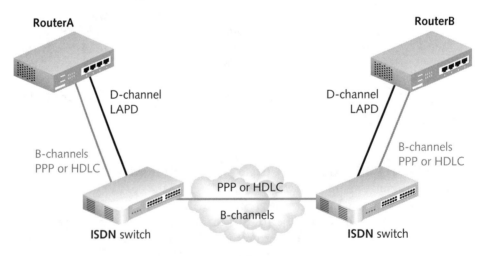

Figure 11-7   ISDN operations

Functions and References

ISDN standards use **function groups** and **reference points** to describe the various components that can be used in making an ISDN connection. Function groups describe a set of functions that are implemented by a device and software. For example, a terminal adapter (TA) converts network signals to a format appropriate for the ISDN connection. The TA is an example of a function group because it describes a device that provides a set of conversion functions to make ISDN communication possible. The connection between two function groups (including the cabling) is called a reference point. Not all function groups and reference points are required for each ISDN connection. Figure 11-8 shows the variety of different connection types that may exist. You are expected to memorize these components.

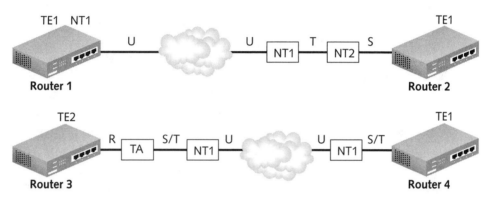

Figure 11-8   ISDN function groups and reference points

The function groups shown in the graphic are as follows:

- Terminal adapter: A converter device that allows non-ISDN devices to operate on an ISDN network. For a router that did not have a built-in ISDN interface (TE2), a TA would be a device that converts signals from a standard RS-232 or V.35 interface into ISDN signals.

- **Terminal Equipment 1 (TE1)**: A device that supports ISDN standards and that can be connected directly to an ISDN network connection. For example, ISDN telephones, personal computers, routers with ISDN interfaces, or videophones could function as TE1s.

- **Terminal Equipment 2 (TE2)**: A non-ISDN device, such as an analog phone or modem, or a PC, which requires a TA to connect to an ISDN network

- **Network Termination 1 (NT1)**: A small connection box that is attached to ISDN BRI lines. This device provides power for the ISDN service. It terminates the two-wire connection from the Central Office (CO) and connects to the four-wire customer network. In the graphic, the CO would be located inside the cloud, which represents the telephone company network.

- **Network Termination 2 (NT2)**: A device that multiplexes and switches signals between various network devices at the customer site. This type of interface is typically used with PRI lines when they need to be divided for several functions. For example, some channels may be used for WAN data communications and others for the telephone system or video teleconferencing. A multiplexer or PBX would be considered an NT2 device.

NOTE Some function groups can be combined into one device. For example, an NT1 may have a TE1 port and a TA port for non-ISDN devices (TE2s).

The reference points in Figure 11-8 include the following:

- **U**: The point that defines the demarcation between the user network and the telecommunications provider's ISDN facility. The **U-interface** is the actual two-wire cable, also called the local loop, which connects the customer's equipment to the telecommunications provider. In the U.S., the U-interface is supplied on a two-wire RJ-11 phone jack.

- **R**: The point between non-ISDN equipment (TE2) and the TA. The **R-interface** is the wire or circuit that connects TE2 to the TA.

- **S**: The point between the ISDN customer's TE1 or TA and the network termination (NT1 or NT2). The **S-interface** is a four-wire cable from TE1 or TA to the NT1 or NT2, which is a two-wire termination point.

- **T**: The point between NT1 and NT2, which is also the **T-interface**. This four-wire cable is used to divide the normal telephone company two-wire cable into four wires, which then allows the connection of up to eight ISDN devices.

- **S/T**: When NT2 is not used on a connection that uses NT1, the connection from the router or TA to the NT1 connection is typically called S/T. This is essentially the combination of the S and T reference points. The S/T interface is not typically used in the U.S.

SPID

Many telecommunications providers use ISDN switches, which require **Service Profile Identifiers (SPIDs)** for dial-in access. SPIDs are frequently referred to as **ISDN phone numbers** because their functions are similar. SPIDs provide a profile of your equipment to the ISDN switch.

An ISDN device can access each ISDN channel via its SPID number. You can configure the router to use single or multiple SPIDs when making a connection to the ISDN provider. The ISDN provider must assign the SPID numbers for each channel, which are normally 8- to 14-digit numbers. Then, you can use those numbers to configure your ISDN dialer connections. Most modern ISDN systems now have a feature called **AutoSPID**. This eliminates the need to configure SPID numbers on the router.

You must also define the type of switch that is used at the Central Office to which you are connecting. The commands shown in Figure 11-9 illustrate an ISDN configuration.

```
router(config)#isdn switch-type dms-100
router(config)#interface bri 0
router(config-if)#isdn spid1 52069145231010
router(config-if)#isdn spid2 52069145241010
```

Figure 11-9   ISDN switch configuration

In this figure, the commands illustrate the configuration for a BRI connection over two channels. The switch type will usually be a Northern Telecom DMS-100 or an AT&T 5ess or 4ess. Notice in the first line that the switch type is a DMS-100. You will have to obtain the switch type and the SPID numbers from the ISDN providers. Potential switch types include the following:

- dms-100: Northern Telecom DMS-100 (as previously described)

- ni1: National ISDN-1; used in North America

- net3: Net3 switch; used in Europe and the United Kingdom

- ntt: Switch from NTT; used in Japan

- 1tr6: 1TR6 switch; used in Germany

- ts013: TS013 Australian switch

- none: Used when a switch has not been specified

11

NOTE   In certain circumstances, the switch-type command can be configured in interface configuration mode as well as global configuration mode.

Multilink PPP

RFC 1717 defines multilink PPP, which allows you to combine the individual bandwidths of several modems and ISDN channels to increase the bandwidth of a single connection. Multilink provides load balancing, packet fragmentation and reassembly, and sequencing for packets sent across WAN links. Because multilink is available in PPP connections, it can function over synchronous or asynchronous serial connections, such as analog modems or ISDN channels. The command to enable multilink is:

```
router(config-if)#ppp multilink
```

NOTE   Each serial interface to be enabled with multilink must also be configured for PPP encapsulation and DDR.

DDR

The **dial-on-demand routing (DDR)** feature that is available on Cisco routers allows you to use bandwidth as needed. This feature can save organizations money on connections because DDR automatically connects and disconnects the line as needed. This is a more economical way to address the need for intermittent WAN access using circuit switching. With DDR, all traffic is classified as either interesting or uninteresting. **Interesting traffic** forces the router to connect to the remote router. Uninteresting traffic will not force the router to connect; however, uninteresting traffic is passed if the line is already active. The dialer-list commands, in conjunction with access-list commands, are used to define what is interesting and what is not.

There are many important commands to know for configuring a DDR connection. The following commands, shown in Figure 11-10, define the DDR connection parameters and the connection link.

```
router(config-if)#dial wait-for-carrier time 15
router(config-if)#dialer idle-timeout 300
router(config-if)#dialer load-threshold 50 either
router(config-if)#dialer map ip 192.168.52.1 name FLG speed 56 5205551212
```

Figure 11-10 ISDN settings

The first command tells the dialer to wait no longer than 15 seconds for the ISDN provider to answer during a DDR connection attempt. The second command tells the dialer to hang up the connection if it does not pass any interesting traffic for 300 seconds. The third command tells the dialer to only dial additional lines (assuming that you have configured multiple ISDN channels for the connection) when any channel is transferring at a load value of 50, either inbound or outbound. Load values can range from 1 (not loaded) to 255 (fully loaded), so a load value of 50 would indicate the line being about 20% loaded (50/255). In addition, load-threshold does allow you to specify a percentage load for inbound traffic, outbound traffic, or traffic in either direction. The fourth command maps the dialer to a specific host name (FLG), IP address (192.168.52.1), speed (56 Kbps), and phone number (5205551212). If you don't configure a speed, the default is assumed to be 64 Kbps.

As previously mentioned, you must use dialer-list commands to define what type of traffic is considered interesting. Sometimes access-list commands are used in conjunction with the dialer-list command. Dialer-group commands are used to associate dialer-list commands with the correct interface. The commands in Figure 11-11 illustrate how you can use dialer-list, dialer-group, and access-list commands to permit IP traffic on your link, but deny IGRP traffic.

```
router(config-if)#dialer-group 1
router(config-if)#exit
router(config)#dialer-list 1 protocol ip list 110
router(config)#access-list 110 deny igrp any any
router(config)#access-list 110 permit ip any any
```

Figure 11-11   ISDN and access lists

ISDN BRI Configuration Examples

Now that you have seen the configuration parameters individually in the preceding sections, it is useful to consider some sample configurations. Figure 11-12 shows two routers that will be used to create a temporary ISDN BRI connection. The group uses up to two channels for IP traffic. The routers will not use a routing protocol because link use is to be minimized for this DDR connection. (The point of DDR is to reduce the money spent on connection time.) In addition, routing updates are unimportant in this configuration because it is a point-to-point connection.

Note that the routers in the graphic are both using PPP with CHAP authentication. The username has been set for the opposite router in each configuration, and the password is the same so that CHAP will authenticate properly. Each router has the ability to dial the other router. The CLT router is located at the corporate network, which has other connections and uses IGRP to transfer routing tables on that network. However, IGRP is not desired on the ISDN connection, so the CLT router has an access list specifically denying IGRP on the ISDN link.

Further note that both routers do permit all IP traffic on the ISDN link and all IP traffic will be considered interesting or worthy of activating the ISDN link. Multilink is enabled on both routers, and they will dial their additional lines when there is 16% (40/255) or more utilization on the first channel. The link will be terminated if there is no interesting traffic for 600 seconds (10 minutes). The IP routes are configured such that all traffic destined from the corporate network to 192.168.24.0 will be sent to the FLG router. Because the FLG router is a remote branch with no other connections, all traffic that is not specifically destined for 192.168.24.0 will be sent to the CLT router. Notice that each router has its dialer mapped to the IP address of the other router.

11

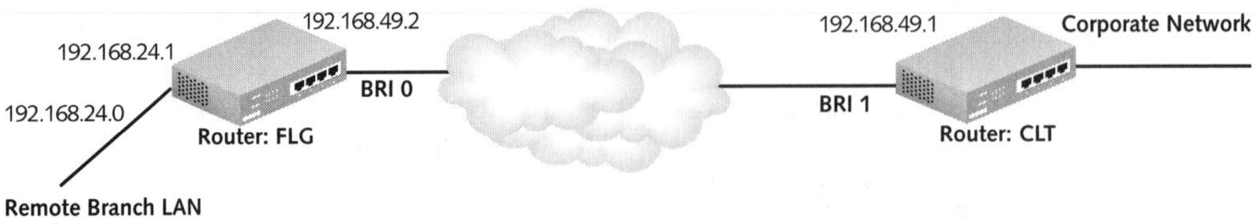


```
flg(config)#username clt pass lumberjack
flg(config)#isdn switch-type dms-100
flg(config)#int bri 0
flg(config-if)#encap ppp
flg(config-if)#ppp auth chap
flg(config-if)#isdn spid1 5208881111 5270936
flg(config-if)#isdn spid2 5208881212 5270956
flg(config-if)#ip address 192.168.49.2 255.255.255.0
flg(config-if)#dialer idle-timeout 600
flg(config-if)#dialer map ip 192.168.49.1 name clt 7045551212
flg(config-if)#dialer load-threshold 40 either
flg(config-if)#ppp multilink
flg(config-if)#dialer-group 1
flg(config-if)#exit
flg(config)#dialer-list 1 protocol ip permit
flg(config)#ip route 0.0.0.0 0.0.0.0 192.168.49.1
```

```
clt(config)#username flg pass lumberjack
clt(config)#isdn switch-type dms-100
clt(config)#int bri 1
clt(config-if)#encap ppp
clt(config-if)#ppp auth chap
clt(config-if)#isdn spid1 7047773333 5265933
clt(config-if)#isdn spid2 7047774444 5265944
clt(config-if)#ip address 192.168.49.1 255.255.255.0
clt(config-if)#dialer idle-timeout 600
clt(config-if)#dialer map ip 192.168.49.2 name
        flg 5205551212
clt(config-if)#dialer load-threshold 40 either
clt(config-if)#ppp multilink
clt(config-if)#dialer-group 1
clt(config-if)#exit
clt(config)#ip route
        192.168.24.0 255.255.255.0 192.168.49.2
clt(config)#dialer-list 1 prot ip list 101
clt(config)#access-list 101 deny igrp any any
clt(config)#access-list 101 permit ip any any
```

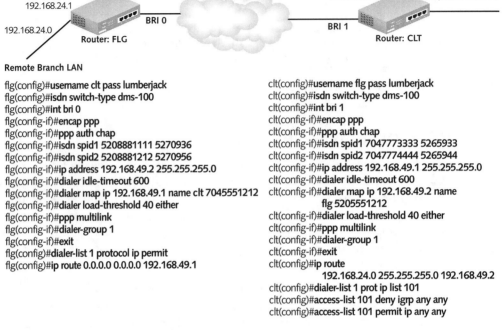

Figure 11-12 ISDN configuration sample

Dialer Profiles

The preceding implementation of DDR specifies that each ISDN BRI or PRI channel inherits the physical BRI or PRI interface's configuration. This implementation is also called **legacy DDR**. DDR can also be implemented using **dialer profiles**. Dialer profiles allow different DDR parameters to be set for each BRI or PRI channel. This is done by creating separate logical configurations that can be linked to the physical BRI or PRI interface on a per-call basis. All calls going to the same destination network will use the same dialer profile. Configuration of dialer profiles involves the following elements:

- Dialer interface: A logical configuration including a dial string for each destination subnet. A dial string operates like a phone number. The configuration includes all settings necessary to reach a particular destination network.
- Dialer map class: Optional commands that define characteristics for any call to a specified dial string. Multiple dial strings can be specified for the same dialer interface. Each dial string can be associated with a different dialer map class.
- Dialer pool: The physical interface that will be used by the dialer interface. A physical interface can be associated with one or many dialer pools, but a dialer interface uses only one pool. Figure 11-13 illustrates the relationships among dialer interfaces, dialer pools, and physical interfaces.

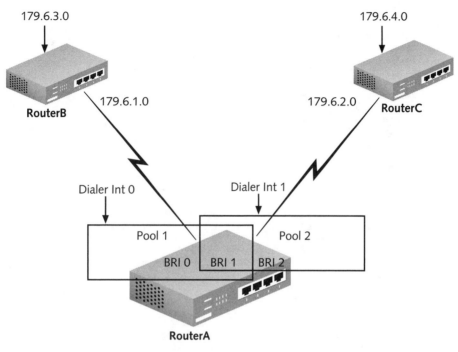

Figure 11-13   Dialer profile example

According to the example in Figure 11-13, dialer interface 0 is using dialer pool 1, which is associated with both the BRI 0 and BRI 1 physical interfaces. Dialer interface 1 is using dialer pool 2, which is associated with both the BRI 1 and BRI 2 interfaces. RouterA is connected to two remote offices; one through RouterB on subnetwork 179.6.1.0 and the other through RouterC on subnetwork 179.6.2.0. An example configuration for RouterA using dialer profiles is shown in Figure 11-14.

```
RouterA(config)# int dialer0
RouterA(config-if)# ip address 179.6.1.1 255.255.255.0          There are two dialer profiles
RouterA(config-if)# encap ppp                                   in this example.
RouterA(config-if)# dialer remote-name RouterB
RouterA(config-if)# dialer string 7749507 class mapclassAB
RouterA(config-if)# dialer pool 1
RouterA(config-if)# dialer-group 1
RouterA(config-if)# ppp auth chap
RouterA(config-if)# ppp multilink
RouterA(config-if)# exit
RouterA(config)# username RouterB password cannon
RouterA(config)# ip route 179.6.3.0 255.255.255.0 dialer0
RouterA(config)# map-class dialer mapclassAB
RouterA(config)# dialer idle-timeout 300
RouterA(config)# dialer-list 1 protocol ip permit

RouterA(config)# int dialer1
RouterA(config-if)# ip address 179.6.2.1 255.255.255.0
RouterA(config-if)# encap ppp
RouterA(config-if)# dialer remote-name RouterC
RouterA(config-if)# dialer string 7746972 mapclassAC
RouterA(config-if)# dialer pool 2
RouterA(config-if)# dialer-group 1
RouterA(config-if)# ppp auth chap
RouterA(config-if)# ppp multilink
RouterA(config-if)# exit
RouterA(config)# username RouterC password cannon
RouterA(config)# ip route 179.6.4.0 255.255.255.0 dialer1
RouterA(config)# map-class dialer mapclassAC
RouterA(config)# dialer idle-timeout 600
RouterA(config)# isdn speed 56
RouterA(config)# dialer-list 1 protocol ip permit

RouterA(config)# int bri0
RouterA(config-if)# no ip address
RouterA(config-if)# encap ppp
RouterA(config-if)# dialer pool-member 1              Dialer pool 1 includes both
                                                     BRI 0 and BRI 1. Dialer pool
RouterA(config)# int bri1                            2 includes both BRI1
RouterA(config-if)# no ip address                    and BRI2.
RouterA(config-if)# encap ppp
RouterA(config-if)# dialer pool-member 1
RouterA(config-if)# dialer pool-member 2

RouterA(config)# int bri2
RouterA(config-if)# no ip address
RouterA(config-if)# encap ppp
RouterA(config-if)# dialer pool-member 2
```

Figure 11-14   RouterA configuration using dialer profiles

Monitoring ISDN

Connection problems with ISDN are often related to PPP configuration. Before data transfer can occur, PPP must first negotiate the connection and then, if authentication has been configured, must authenticate using either PAP or CHAP. You can monitor these two important PPP phases using variations of the debug command. Figure 11-15 displays the output from the debug ppp negotiation command. In this example, PPP with CHAP is configured on both ends of the WAN link but no password is set on the lab-b router. The result is that a successful completion of connection establishment does not occur. The debug ppp authentication command shown in Figure 11-16 displays the command output when connected routers are both configured for PPP with CHAP correctly. As you can see, the debug ppp authentication command displays a subset of the information displayed with the previous debug ppp negotiation command. Only the authentication phase is displayed with the debug ppp authentication command.

```
lab-a#debug ppp negotiation
PPP protocol negotiation debugging is on
lab-a#
00:05:54: Se0 LCP: TIMEout: State TERMsent
00:05:54: Se0 LCP: State is Closed
00:05:54: Se0 PPP: Phase is DOWN
00:05:54: Se0 PPP: Phase is ESTABLISHING, Passive Open
00:05:54: Se0 LCP: State is Listen
00:05:54: Se0 LCP: I CONFREQ [Listen] id 200 len 15
00:05:54: Se0 LCP:    AuthProto CHAP (0x0305C22305)
00:05:54: Se0 LCP:    MagicNumber 0x309A512A (0x0506309A512A)
00:05:54: Se0 LCP: O CONFREQ [Listen] id 115 len 15
00:05:54: Se0 LCP:    AuthProto CHAP (0x0305C22305)
00:05:54: Se0 LCP:    MagicNumber 0x1080EAA9 (0x05061080EAA9)
00:05:54: Se0 LCP: O CONFACK [Listen] id 200 len 15
00:05:54: Se0 LCP:    AuthProto CHAP (0x0305C22305)
00:05:54: Se0 LCP:    MagicNumber 0x309A512A (0x0506309A512A)
00:05:54: Se0 LCP: I CONFACK [ACKsent] id 115 len 15
00:05:54: Se0 LCP:    AuthProto CHAP (0x0305C22305)
00:05:54: Se0 LCP:    MagicNumber 0x1080EAA9 (0x05061080EAA9)
00:05:54: Se0 LCP: State is Open
00:05:54: Se0 PPP: Phase is AUTHENTICATING, by both
00:05:54: Se0 CHAP: O CHALLENGE id 99 len 26 from "lab-a"
00:05:54: Se0 CHAP: I CHALLENGE id 5 len 26 from "lab-b"
00:05:54: Se0 CHAP: O RESPONSE id 5 len 26 from "lab-a"
00:05:54: Se0 LCP: I TERMREQ [Open] id 201 len 4
00:05:54: Se0 LCP: O TERMACK [Open] id 201 len 4
00:05:54: Se0 PPP: Phase is TERMINATING
00:05:56: Se0 LCP: TIMEout: State TERMsent
00:05:56: Se0 LCP: State is Closed
00:05:56: Se0 PPP: Phase is DOWN
```

Figure 11-15 Debug ppp negotiation command output

11

```
lab-a#debug ppp authentication
PPP authentication debugging is on
lab-a#
00:20:27: Se0 PPP: Phase is AUTHENTICATING, by both
00:20:27: Se0 CHAP: O CHALLENGE id 136 len 26 from "lab-a"
00:20:27: Se0 CHAP: I CHALLENGE id 232 len 26 from "lab-b"
00:20:27: Se0 CHAP: O RESPONSE id 232 len 26 from "lab-a"
00:20:27: Se0 CHAP: I RESPONSE id 136 len 26 from "lab-b"
00:20:27: Se0 CHAP: O SUCCESS id 136 len 4
00:20:27: Se0 CHAP: I SUCCESS id 232 len 4
00:20:28: %LINEPROTO-5-UPDOWN: Line protocol on Interface Serial0, changed state
to up
00:20:29: %LINK-3-UPDOWN: Interface Serial0, changed state to up
00:20:29: Se0 PPP: Treating connection as a dedicated line
```

Figure 11-16   Debug ppp authentication command output

In addition to the preceding debug ppp commands, you can use the following commands to view your ISDN configuration, manage the link, and view statistics. All the commands are available via the privileged EXEC mode (enable mode) prompt.

- clear interface: Disconnects all current connections. Use this command if you are having connection problems.

- show dialer: Shows the current dialer status, including the time that the link has been active

- debug dialer: Displays the configuration and operation of the dialer

- debug q921: Shows the call connection establishment and disconnection

- show isdn active: Displays the status of the ISDN connection while the call is in progress

- show isdn status: Gives status information for ISDN connections

- show int bri 0: Shows you the configuration statistics and speed of your ISDN BRI interface

You can also use the show ip route command to view the routing table and ensure that the IP packets are being routed properly on your system. If you have all IP traffic enabled on the link, you can use the ping or telnet command to test the link.

Digital Lines

ISDN is only one type of connection that you can obtain from a telecommunications provider. Other types of digital connections are available. The following list contains some currently available services:

- **T1**: North American, 24-channel digital line capable of supporting data transmissions of 1.544 Mbps

- **T1C**: North American, 48-channel digital line capable of supporting data transmissions of up to 3.152 Mbps

- **T2**: North American, 96-channel digital line capable of supporting data transmissions of up to 6.312 Mbps

- **T3**: North American, 672-channel digital line capable of supporting data transmissions of up to 44.376 Mbps

- **T4**: North American, 4032-channel digital line capable of supporting data transmissions of up to 274.176 Mbps

- **E1**: This European 30-channel digital line is capable of supporting data transmissions of up to 2.048 Mbps.

- **Fractional E1** and **fractional T1**: Some telecommunications providers allow organizations to order fractional T1 or E1 connections. A fractional T1 or E1 occurs when less than the full bandwidth is available. For example, a fractional T1 might be a 512-Kbps connection, instead of the full 1.544 Mbps.

- **Digital Subscriber Line (DSL)**: Services that offer high bandwidth over existing copper lines. DSL connections are generically referred to as **xDSL** because there are several different DSL technologies, such as **Asymmetric Digital Subscriber Line (ADSL)**, **High-bit-rate Digital Subscriber Line (HDSL)**, **ISDN Digital Subscriber Line (IDSL)**, **Symmetrical Digital Subscriber Line (SDSL)**, and **Very-high-data-rate Digital Subscriber Line (VDSL)**.

11

CHAPTER SUMMARY

- ❑ Many WAN connectivity options are available for modern networks, including digital lines, Frame Relay, and analog modems.

- ❑ WAN technologies typically define Data Link and Physical layer standards.

- ❑ The Point-to-Point Protocol (PPP) is the most widely used WAN protocol today.

- ❑ On Cisco routers, PPP is used mainly as a Data Link layer encapsulation method; however, it does provide an interface to the Network layer via specific Network Control Protocols (NCPs).

- ❑ PPP provides link establishment, quality determination, Network layer protocol encapsulation, and link termination services.

- ❑ PPP is often used over Integrated Services Digital Network (ISDN) connections.

- ❑ ISDN is a digital service provided by several telecommunications companies worldwide.

- ❑ ISDN was developed as a faster WAN connection to replace analog modems, and as a cheaper alternative to Frame Relay and full T1 connections.

❑ ISDN service comes in Basic Rate Interface (BRI) and Primary Rate Interface (PRI). BRI offers connections of up to 128 Kbps for data transfer, and PRI offers up to 24 channels in the United States, each with the ability to transfer data at 64 Kbps.

❑ Connections over ISDN can take advantage of dial-on-demand routing (DDR) and multilink services offered through PPP connections.

❑ DDR allows the router using an ISDN connection to dial only when there is interesting traffic and to add more channels as needed to support given traffic levels. DDR can be implemented using dialer profiles, which allow more flexibility regarding the calling parameters.

❑ Multilink allows ISDN to use multiple channels evenly by spreading the load across those channels.

KEY TERMS

address — The element of the PPP frame represented by the binary sequence 11111111; because PPP is used to create a point-to-point connection, there is no need for PPP to assign an individual address for each host.

AppleTalk Control Protocol (ATCP) — PPP interface protocol for AppleTalk; *see* **Network Control Protocol**.

Asymmetric Digital Subscriber Line (ADSL) — DSL service that provides from 1.536-Mbps to 6.144-Mbps connections in the United States. Outside the U.S. connections are either 2.048 or 4.096 Mbps.

asynchronous character map — The piece of information in the LCP field of the PPP packet that allows PPP to encode its transmission properly for the recipient host.

authentication — The process of verifying the right to complete a connection.

AutoSPID — A feature of modern ISDN systems whereby SPID numbers do not have to be configured on the router.

bonding — Load balancing across the two BRI B-channels to form a 128-Kbps single channel.

challenge — The query packet, or the action of sending the query packet over a CHAP connection, that is used to verify the participants of the PPP connection.

Challenge Handshake Authentication Protocol (CHAP) — PPP authentication protocol that provides better security than PAP in authenticating devices on PPP connections.

compression — Data compression that can be performed on the PPP packet at the source and then uncompressed at the destination.

control — The element of the PPP frame represented by the binary sequence 00000011, which indicates that the transmission of user data will not be sequenced and is to be delivered over a connectionless link.

data — The LCP field is also known as the Data field. This location contains the LCP information and the data that has been encapsulated from the higher layers. The default size of this field is 1500 bytes, but PPP implementations can negotiate a larger size for this field.

dial–on–demand routing (DDR) — A feature available on Cisco routers that allows you to use bandwidth as needed.

dialer profile — Allows multiple logical BRI or PRI configurations to be bound to a physical BRI or PRI interface on a per-call basis.

Digital Subscriber Line (DSL) — Telecommunications services that offer high bandwidth over existing copper lines. DSL connections are generically referred to as xDSL because there are several different DSL technologies.

down–when–looped — A Cisco router command that shuts down an interface when looping is detected; used to prevent testing scenarios from causing troubleshooting problems in a production environment.

E1 — European 30-channel digital line capable of supporting up to 2.048-Mbps data transmissions.

flag — Identifies the beginning and end of the PPP frame.

fractional E1 — A service that offers some number of channels less than the 30 (64-Kbps) digital channels provided by a full E1 connection.

fractional T1 — A service that offers some number of channels less than the 24 (64-Kbps) digital channels provided by a full T1 connection.

Frame Check Sequence (FCS) — A mathematical computation placed at the end of the frame, used to ensure that the frame was not corrupted during transmission.

function groups — Used in ISDN communication to describe a set of functions that are implemented by a device and its software; a terminal adapter (TA) is a function group.

High–bit-rate Digital Subscriber Line (HDSL) — Symmetric digital communication service capable of 1.536 Mbps in the United States and 2.048 Mbps in Europe.

High–level Data Link Control (HDLC) — A Data Link layer encapsulation protocol that is a superset of the SDLC protocol. HDLC is a WAN protocol that can be used for both point-to-point and multipoint connections.

High–Speed Serial Interface (HSSI) — A type of serial device developed by Cisco and T3Plus Networking that operates at speeds of up to 52 Mbps over distances of 15 meters.

interesting traffic — Network traffic for which you feel it is worth activating or maintaining an ISDN link that is configured with DDR.

IP Control Protocol (IPCP) — PPP interface protocol for IP; *see* **Network Control Protocol**.

IPX Control Protocol (IPXCP) — PPP interface protocol for IPX; *see* **Network Control Protocol**.

ISDN Digital Subscriber Line (IDSL) — A telecommunications service that makes an ISDN connection into a 128-Kbps DSL connection. Unlike ISDN, IDSL only supports data communications (not analog voice or video).

11

ISDN phone number — *See* **Service Profile Identifier (SPID)**.

LCP link configuration — A process that modifies and enhances the default characteristics of a PPP connection; includes the following actions: link establishment, authentication, link-quality determination, Network layer protocol configuration negotiation, and link termination.

legacy DDR — Each ISDN BRI or PRI channel inherits the physical BRI or PRI interface's configuration.

Link Access Procedure-D (LAPD) — A Data Link layer WAN protocol adapted from HDLC; used on D-channel over ISDN lines.

Link Control Protocol (LCP) — Used to establish, configure, maintain, and terminate PPP connections.

link establishment — The process of opening and configuring a PPP connection before any data can be transferred over the link.

link-quality determination — The process of checking the quality of a PPP link and monitoring its reliability.

Link Quality Monitoring (LQM) — PPP feature that checks the reliability of the link by monitoring the number of errors, latency between requests, connection retries, and connection failures on the PPP link.

link termination — The process of disconnecting a PPP connection when the call is complete, which is determined by the PPP hosts that made the connection.

loopback command — A Cisco router command that places an interface in a looped-back state, which means that all outgoing data will be redirected as incoming data without going out on the network; used for testing purposes.

magic number — Unique numbers added by the router to a packet, which allows it to detect a looped-back link.

maximum receive unit size — The piece of information in the LCP field of the PPP packet that sets the receive buffer size for the LCP connection, typically 1500 bytes.

multilink — Allows multiple transmission devices (such as two modems) to send data over separate physical connections; defined in RFC 1717.

Network Control Protocol (NCP) — Allows PPP to encapsulate multiple protocols including IP, IPX, and AppleTalk. NCPs are functional fields containing codes that indicate the type of protocol that is encapsulated.

Network layer protocol configuration negotiation — The process of determining a Network layer protocol to use over a PPP connection that is common to both PPP hosts.

Network Termination 1 (NT1) — A small connection box that is attached to ISDN BRI lines. This device terminates the connection from the Central Office (CO).

Network Termination 2 (NT2) — A device that provides switching services for the internal network.

out of band signaling — The practice of controlling an ISDN connection on a channel other than the channel(s) on which data is transferred.

Password Authentication Protocol (PAP) — PPP authentication protocol that provides some security in verifying the identity of devices using PPP connections.

protocol — The element of the PPP frame represented by two bytes used to identify the protocol that is encapsulated.

R — The point between non-ISDN equipment (TE2) and the TA.

RADIUS server — RADIUS is an authentication and accounting server.

R-interface — The wire or circuit that connects TE2 to the TA.

reference points — Used in ISDN communications to identify specific connection points along the ISDN connection, including the cables that form those connections; *see* **U** and **U-interface**.

S — The point between the ISDN customer's TE1 or TA and the network termination, NT1 or NT2.

S-interface — A four-wire cable from TE1 or TA to the NT1 or NT2, which is a two-wire termination point.

Service Profile Identifier (SPID) — A reference number assigned to ISDN channels; functions like a phone number.

S/T — When NT2 is not used on a connection that uses NT1, the connection from the router or TA to the NT1 connection is typically called S/T. This is essentially the combination of the S and T reference points.

Symmetrical Digital Subscriber Line (SDSL) — A symmetric digital communication service that uses a combination of HDSL and the regular telephone system.

T — The point between NT1 and NT2, which is also the T-interface; a four-wire cable that is used to divide the normal telephone company two-wire cable into four wires, which then allows you to connect up to eight ISDN devices.

T1 — North American 24-channel digital line capable of supporting up to 1.544-Mbps data transmissions.

T1C — North American 48-channel digital line capable of supporting up to 3.152-Mbps data transmissions.

T2 — North American 96-channel digital line capable of supporting up to 6.312-Mbps data transmissions.

T3 — North American 672-channel digital line capable of supporting up to 44.376-Mbps data transmissions.

T4 — North American 4032-channel digital line capable of supporting up to 274.176-Mbps data transmissions.

Terminal Access Controller Access Control System (TACACS) — An authentication protocol that allows Cisco routers to offload user administration to a central server. TACACS and Extended TACACS (XTACACS) are defined in RFC 1492.

Terminal Equipment 1 (TE1) — A device that supports ISDN standards and can be connected directly to an ISDN network connection.

Terminal Equipment 2 (TE2) — A non-ISDN device, such as an analog phone or modem, which requires a TA to connect to an ISDN network.

11

T-interface — *See* **T**.

U — The point that defines the demarcation between the user network and the telecommunications provider ISDN facility.

U-interface — The actual two-wire cable, also called the local loop, which connects the customer's equipment to the telecommunications provider.

Very-high-data-rate Digital Subscriber Line (VDSL) — A digital subscriber technology that supports 51.84-Mbps connections over unshielded twisted-pair cable.

xDSL — *See* **Digital Subscriber Line**.

REVIEW QUESTIONS

1. What do ISDN protocols that begin with E define?

   a. Methods, terminology, concepts, and interfaces

   b. Telephone and network standards

   c. Encapsulation

   d. Signaling and switching

2. The standards defined in the ISDN I.100 protocol cover which of the following?

   a. Signaling and switching

   b. Telephone and network standards

   c. ISDN addressing

   d. Methods, terminology, concepts, and interfaces

3. If you want to use CHAP authentication, which protocol would you employ?

   a. Multilink

   b. PAP

   c. Frame Relay

   d. PPP

4. Which of the following is the correct syntax to set the switch type to dms-100? (Choose all that apply.)

   a. router>isdn switch-type dms-100

   b. router#en switch-type dms-100

   c. router(config)#isdn switch-type dms-100

   d. router(config-if)#isdn switch-type dms-100

5. If you are configuring an ISDN connection and want to enable multilink, which of the following is the correct prompt and command?

   a. router(config)#ena multilink

   b. router(config-if)#ppp multilink

    c. router>ppp multilink

    d. router#enable multilink

6. Which of the following is typically used as a cheap alternative to Frame Relay or a T1 connection, but offers better performance than an analog modem?

    a. ISDN BRI

    b. T2

    c. E1

    d. DS5

7. What does the reference point R indicate in ISDN communications?

    a. A demarcation point between the user network and the telecommunications company

    b. A point between the non-ISDN equipment and the terminal adapter

    c. A point between the ISDN customer's TE1 or TA and the network termination NT1

    d. A point between NT1 and NT2

8. In ISDN communications, what does the functional group TE2 represent?

    a. A terminal adapter

    b. A non-ISDN device

    c. A device often used with ISDN PRI service

    d. A connection box attached to ISDN BRI lines, which terminates the connection from the CO

9. What is the ISDN indicator for a converter device that allows non-ISDN devices to operate on an ISDN network?

    a. TE2

    b. NT1

    c. U

    d. TA

10. What do ISDN protocols that begin with Q define?

    a. Methods, terminology, concepts, and interfaces

    b. Telephone and network standards

    c. Encapsulation

    d. Signaling and switching

11

11. What does the reference point U indicate in ISDN communications?

   a. A demarcation point between the user network and the telecommunications company

   b. A point between the non–ISDN equipment and the terminal adapter

   c. A point between the ISDN customer's TE1 or TA and the network termination NT1

   d. A point between NT1 and NT2

12. In ISDN communications, what does the functional group NT1 represent?

   a. A terminal adapter

   b. A small connection device attached to ISDN BRI lines, which terminates the connection from the CO

   c. A non-ISDN device

   d. A device often used with ISDN PRI service, which provides switching services for the internal network

13. What does the reference point S indicate in ISDN communications?

   a. A demarcation point between the user network and the telecommunications company

   b. A point between the non–ISDN equipment and the terminal adapter

   c. A point between the ISDN customer's TE1 or TA and the network termination NT1

   d. A point between NT1 and NT2

14. Which two of the following protocols could be used when establishing a connection over ISDN?

   a. HDLC

   b. PPP

   c. PAP

   d. CHAP

15. What does the reference point T indicate in ISDN communications?

   a. A demarcation point between the user network and the telecommunications company

   b. A point between the non–ISDN equipment and the terminal adapter

   c. A point between the ISDN customer's TE1 or TA and the network termination NT1

   d. A point between NT1 and NT2

16. Which portion of a PPP frame indicates the higher-layer encapsulated protocol?

   a. Protocol

   b. Address

   c. Control

   d. LCP

17. What is the Data Link layer protocol used on the ISDN D-channel?

   a. LAPD

   b. LAPP

   c. PPP

   d. HDLC

18. What is the default encapsulation type on serial interfaces of Cisco routers?

   a. PPP

   b. HDLC

   c. SDLC

   d. Frame Relay

19. Which of the following is an NCP? (Choose all that apply.)

   a. IPXCP

   b. HDLC

   c. SDLC

   d. ATCP

   e. IPCP

20. PPP was derived from _____.

   a. Frame Relay

   b. HDLC

   c. RBOC

   d. ISDN

21. What is a common reason for looping an interface?

   a. To achieve greater bandwidth

   b. To drop nonessential frames

   c. To increase packet size

   d. Testing

22. Which of the following is a unique number that helps devices discover looped interfaces?

   a. MAC

   b. LCP

   c. Magic number

   d. Bandwidth

11

23. Which of the following employs the strongest encryption technique?

    a. Plain text

    b. PAP

    c. CHAP

    d. Clear text

24. If you want your router to use CHAP and then PAP authentication, which of the following commands would be correct?

    a. router>ppp au chap pap

    b. router#ppp authentication chap pap

    c. router(config-if)#ppp au pap chap

    d. router(config-if)#ppp au chap pap

    e. router(config)#ppp authentication chap pap

25. Which WAN protocol did PPP replace?

    a. HDLC

    b. SDLC

    c. SLIP

    d. LAPD

26. What is the purpose of a dialer profile?

    a. To allow the BRI or PRI channel to inherit the physical BRI or PRI inter-face's configuration

    b. To allow different DDR parameters to be set for each BRI or PRI channel

    c. To allow multiple dialer pools for each dialer interface

    d. To allow multiple routers for each dialer pool

CASE PROJECTS

CASE PROJECTS

1. Lisa and Jennifer have been asked to handle the WAN setup for a company that has offices in Greensboro and Charlotte, North Carolina. Each office has a few users who must communicate with each other and across the WAN link. All network users use a database that is located in Charlotte. They need to connect the two offices via some type of WAN link. The link is not expected to get heavy use, but they need something better than the 56K modem they are using now. What kinds of questions should they ask about the company's connectivity requirements? What type of information will they need to collect? What equipment might be part of the connectivity solution? How should they configure the connectivity equipment?

2. Dave is an employee of a large dry goods manufacturer in Phoenix, Arizona, but he lives and works 140 miles north of Phoenix in Flagstaff. Currently, Dave uses an ISDN BRI connection to connect to the main intranet. Dave also uses one of the BRI channels to routinely transfer files to the main office in Phoenix. The information that Dave transfers to the main office is typically text-file order forms, not more than 30K each, and no more than 10 forms per day are usually submitted. However, Dave maintains the company's Web site, which is on his Web server in Flagstaff. Lately, some of the distributors have been complaining that the large product catalogs they require from the company's Web site are downloading quite slowly. In an attempt to keep the distributors happy, Dave is considering ordering a faster connection to the Internet from his telecommunications provider. Assume that you have been sent to help Dave investigate his connectivity options. What information would you collect? Which type of WAN connections would you consider? Is ISDN BRI an option?

3. Your network consulting team has been brought in by XYZ Corporation to solve a WAN connectivity problem. The customer has reported that the ISDN BRI connections it has in three different locations are not functioning properly. The remote office in Lexington, MO, won't connect at all. The router does dial, but the connection is dropped before it ever has a chance to connect. The main office in New York seems to maintain a connection all the time, even though it is supposed to be dial on demand. The branch office in Los Angeles doesn't seem to use both of its channels no matter how much data is being transmitted across the link. What type of information would you collect from each of these locations? What specific configuration parameters would you be interested in seeing for each location?

11

12

FRAME RELAY

> **After reading this chapter and completing the exercises, you will be able to:**
>
> ◆ Understand Frame Relay standards and equipment
> ◆ Describe the role of virtual circuits and performance parameters in Frame Relay
> ◆ Understand the Frame Relay topologies
> ◆ Understand the difference between multipoint and point-to-point configurations
> ◆ Configure and monitor Frame Relay

WAN technologies typically define the Physical and Data Link layer connections. Frame Relay is both a Data Link layer encapsulation type implemented on the router and a Physical layer service provided by a telecommunications company. In this chapter, you will learn about Frame Relay terms, specifications, and service types. In addition, you will see how to implement and configure Frame Relay connections on Cisco routers.

FRAME RELAY STANDARDS AND EQUIPMENT

Frame Relay is a packet switching and encapsulation technology that functions at the Physical and Data Link layers of the OSI reference model. Frame Relay is a communications technique for sending data over high-speed digital connections operating at anywhere from 56 Kbps to 44.736 Mbps or higher. A streamlined version of the older X.25 technology, Frame Relay is more efficient and faster because it does not perform the error checking that was present in X.25. Frame Relay also provides cost-effective access to remote facilities because one site can connect to multiple remote sites using a single connection. The **International Telecommunication Union–Telecommunication Standardization Sector (ITU-T)** and the American National Standards Institute (ANSI) define Frame Relay as a connection between the data terminal equipment (DTE) and the data communications equipment (DCE). DCE is switching equipment supplied by a telecommunications provider that serves as a connection to the **public data network (PDN)**. DTE is also known as customer premises equipment (CPE), because it is the equipment that belongs to, and is maintained by, the PDN customer. For example, if you connect your Cisco router to a **Frame Relay switch** (which is provided by the phone company), the Cisco router is the CPE and the Frame Relay switch is the DCE, as shown in Figure 12-1.

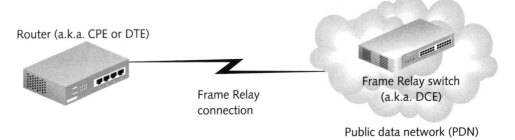

Figure 12-1   CPE to DCE connection

 The ITU-T was formerly known as the **Consultative Committee on International Telephony and Telegraphy (CCITT)**, which is the primary international organization for fostering cooperative standards for telecommunications equipment and systems.

The physical equipment that is used on a network may vary from one organization to another. For example, some networks may use a separate router and channel service unit/data service unit (CSU/DSU) to make their WAN connections. In Figure 12-2, you can see a CSU/DSU that is used with a Cisco 2501 router to make the connection. The CSU/DSU is at the customer location of the digital connection. The unit is used for encoding, filtering, and translating communications to and from the digital line.

Figure 12-2   CSU/DSU and router

Some routers have built-in cards that allow them to make WAN connections. For example, in Figure 12-3, you can see a T1 CSU/DSU card built into the router. The router in the picture is a Cisco 1600 series router. Notice that a T1 line connects directly to the CSU/DSU on the back of the router.

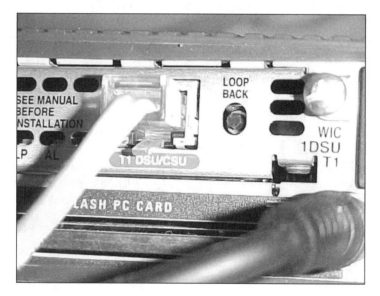

Figure 12-3   CSU/DSU connection

 The order of the term—CSU/DSU or DSU/CSU—is unimportant, because both forms refer to the same device. The ordering is a matter of personal preference.

TIP

In Frame Relay connections, the network device that connects to the Frame Relay switch is known as a **Frame Relay access device (FRAD)**; you may also see this defined as **Frame Relay assembler/disassembler**. The Frame Relay switch is also called the **Frame Relay network device (FRND)**, which is pronounced "friend." The network administrator typically handles the local connection up to the point that it enters the PDN. Items that are part of the PDN, including the Frame Relay switch, fall under the control and responsibility of the telecommunications provider.

VIRTUAL CIRCUITS

You can use Frame Relay with nearly any serial interface. It operates by multiplexing, which means that it combines multiple data streams onto one physical link. Frame Relay separates each data stream into logical (software-maintained) connections called virtual circuits, which carry the data transferred on the connection. These virtual circuits are multiplexed onto the physical channel. Two types of virtual circuits, switched virtual circuits (SVC) and permanent virtual circuits (PVC), connect Frame Relay ports. SVCs, which are the less common of the two, are controlled by software and are only active while a connection to the WAN is active. The SVC software automatically dials the WAN, establishing and terminating the connection as required to transfer data over the Frame Relay service. PVCs remain permanently connected to the WAN. The network administrator manually defines the PVC; it remains until the network administrator removes it.

DLCI

Frame Relay connections identify virtual circuits by Data Link Connection Identifier (DLCI) numbers. The DLCI (pronounced *dell-see*) numbers map virtual circuits to layer 3 protocol addresses. For example, a DLCI number associates an IP address with a specific virtual circuit. DLCI numbers do not specify a physical port and are not unique identifiers on the network; instead, they have only local significance, which means they are important only to the local router and Frame Relay switch. DLCI numbers are usually assigned by the Frame Relay provider and are most likely not the same on either side of the Frame Relay switch. This is what is meant by "local significance." The provider, which is usually the telco, controls how the DLCI switching occurs. Because DLCIs have only local significance, any available number can be selected for each end of a PVC at the time of subscription.

Frame Relay Map

DLCI numbers are mapped, or assigned, to a specific interface. Each router that supports Frame Relay will have a **Frame Relay map**, which is a table in RAM that defines the remote interface to which a specific DLCI number is mapped. The definition will contain a DLCI number and an interface identifier, which is typically a remote IP address. The Frame Relay map can be built automatically or statically depending on the Frame Relay topology. Various topologies are discussed later in the chapter.

Figure 12-4 shows a sample Frame Relay configuration. RouterA has two serial interfaces configured for Frame Relay. The first serial interface (S0) on RouterA is configured for DLCI 9, in order to form a virtual circuit between itself and RouterB. The second serial interface (S1) is configured for DLCI 12. It refers to a virtual circuit between RouterA and RouterC. The Frame Relay map shows which destination IP addresses are used with which DLCI numbers.

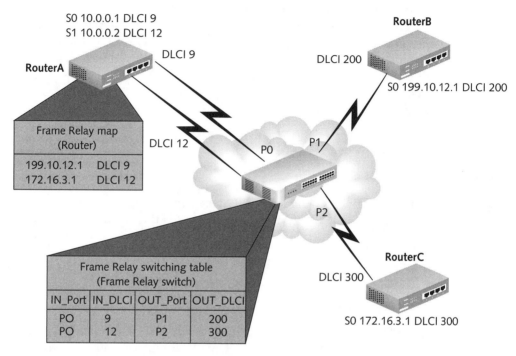

Figure 12-4   Sample Frame Relay configuration

Notice that the **Frame Relay switching table** is configured to map its ports (P0, P1, and P2) to the correct DLCI numbers for the virtual connection. Each switching table entry consists of four elements: the incoming port on the switch, the incoming DLCI number, the outgoing port on the switch, and the outgoing DLCI number. The switching table in this example is simplified; in reality, the switch would be more complex and involve additional Frame Relay switches.

In the example, only the mapping table for RouterA is shown. In reality, however, each router configured for Frame Relay will have its own mapping table. Remember that DLCI numbers are only locally significant, so it would be possible for RouterA and RouterB to use the same DLCI number to specify a virtual circuit.

Subinterfaces

In Figure 12-4, RouterA has two different serial interfaces, each configured for one virtual connection. In early implementations of Frame Relay, each PVC required its own dedicated serial interface. With current technology, however, a single router serial interface can now service multiple PVCs through a single physical serial interface. To allow a single serial interface to support multiple PVCs, the IOS divides the interface into logical **subinterfaces**.

Subinterfaces are created by referencing the physical interface followed by a period and a decimal number. For example, if Serial 0 (S0) had three subinterfaces, they would be referenced as S0.1, S0.2, and S0.3. Subinterfaces are not real physical interfaces; they are virtual interfaces associated with a physical interface. For the purposes of routing, however, subinterfaces are treated as physical interfaces. With subinterfaces, the cost of implementing multiple Frame Relay virtual circuits is reduced because only one port is required on the router. Also, the network administrator has to configure and maintain fewer physical connections. Sample subinterface configurations are shown later in this chapter.

LMI

Frame Relay engineers designed Local Management Interface (LMI) in 1990 to enhance standard Frame Relay. The LMI basically extended the functionality of Frame Relay by:

- Making the DLCIs globally significant rather than locally significant
- Creating a signaling mechanism between the router and the Frame Relay switch, which could report on the status of the link
- Supporting multicasting

Providing DLCI numbers that are globally significant rather than just locally significant makes automatic configuration of the Frame Relay map possible (as explained in the following section). Global significance means that each site is given a DLCI number and that number is then used as the DLCI at the far end of any PVC terminating at that site. In this manner, you can look at the DLCI numbers on the PVCs at one site and know the IP address of the destination router.

LMI uses **keepalive packets** (sent every 10 seconds by default) to verify the Frame Relay link and to ensure the flow of data. The Frame Relay switch in turn provides the status of all virtual circuits and their respective DLCI numbers to the Frame Relay connectivity device. Each virtual circuit, represented by its DLCI number, can have one of three connection states:

- Active: The connection is working and routers can use it to exchange data.
- Inactive: The connection from the local router to the switch is working, but the connection to the remote router is not available.
- Deleted: No LMI information is being received from the Frame Relay switch; this can indicate that the connection between the CPE and DCE is not functional.

The Frame Relay switch reports this status information to the Frame Relay map on the local router. The status information is used by the Frame Relay connectivity devices to determine whether data can be transmitted over the configured virtual circuits. Without LMI, the Frame Relay map must be built statically in the routers. However, by making the DLCIs globally significant, LMI facilitates dynamic Frame Relay map tables through the use of the Inverse ARP protocol, described in the next section.

Inverse ARP

As previously mentioned and illustrated in Figure 12-4, a Frame Relay map includes DLCIs and their corresponding remote IP addresses. In **multipoint** configurations, routers use the protocol Inverse ARP to send a query using the DLCI number to find a remote IP address. Multipoint and **point-to-point** configurations are discussed later in this chapter. As other routers respond to the Inverse ARP queries, the local router can build its Frame Relay map automatically. To maintain the Frame Relay map, routers exchange Inverse ARP messages every 60 seconds by default. Inverse ARP is on by default. LMI is required for Inverse ARP to work.

TIP
If the remote router does not support Inverse ARP, the Frame Relay map will have to be maintained statically (built and updated manually by the network administrator). Do not confuse Inverse ARP with Reverse Address Resolution Protocol (RARP); RARP is used primarily on LANs to provide hosts that only have MAC addresses with IP addresses.

12

Encapsulation Types

In the early days of Frame Relay, vendors and standards organizations worked separately to develop and define LMI. As a result, LMI has several different protocol encapsulation types that it can use for management communications. Different Frame Relay switches, CPE, and Frame Relay connectivity equipment employ or support different types of LMI encapsulation. Cisco routers, for example, support these types of LMI encapsulation:

- cisco: This LMI type was originally defined by four companies: DEC, Nortel, StrataCom, and Cisco. It allows for 992 virtual circuit addresses and uses DLCI 1023 as a management circuit, which transfers link and DLCI status messages. This is the default LMI encapsulation type on Cisco routers.

- ansi: ANSI standard T1.617 Annex-D provides for 976 virtual circuit addresses and uses DLCI 0 as the management circuit.

- q933a: ITU-T Q.933 Annex A, similar to ANSI T1.617 Annex-D, uses DLCI 0 as a management circuit.

Cisco routers (using IOS Release 11.2 or later) can "autosense" the LMI type used by the Frame Relay switch. If the Frame Relay responds with more than one LMI type, the Cisco router will automatically configure itself to use the last LMI type received. The network administrator can also manually configure the LMI type. This manual configuration is explained later in the chapter.

The basic LMI type has three information elements: report type, keepalive, and PVC status. The report type indicates whether the message is just a keepalive frame or a full status message. The Frame Relay devices send keepalive frames every 5 to 30 seconds (10 by default) to ensure that the link is still active. Full status messages contain DLCI status in addition to the keepalive information.

As stated, management circuits transfer DLCI status messages. Depending on your Frame Relay provider, these messages may contain all or some of the following information concerning the status of the virtual circuit:

- New: Used if a new DLCI connection has been configured

- Active: Used to indicate whether the virtual circuit is available for data transfer

- Receiver not ready: Used for flow control to indicate that the virtual circuit is congested; this option is not available in the q933a LMI type

- Minimum bandwidth: Indicates the minimum available bandwidth

- Global addressing: Used to give DLCI global significance, as described earlier

- Multicasting: Used to configure a group of destination addresses rather than a single address; the IEEE has reserved DLCI numbers 1019 through 1022 for this purpose. Frame Relay devices use multicasting to make DLCI numbers globally significant by advertising them across the Frame Relay network.

- Provider-Initiated Status Update: Normally, the Frame Relay switch obtains PVC status information only when the CPE sends a full status message and requests status information for the other DLCI connections; this option allows the provider to initiate a status inquiry.

Not all Frame Relay providers support every piece of link status information. All current implementations provide the New and Active information, but support for other information varies by provider.

TIP Frame Relay does not provide error checking, as do other network protocols such as Synchronous Data Link Control (SDLC). This makes Frame Relay connections more efficient, but it also means that Frame Relay must rely on the upper-layer protocols, such as TCP, to provide error correction.

Split Horizon

Split horizon is a routing technique that reduces the chance of routing loops on a network. A split horizon implementation prevents routing update information received on one physical interface from being rebroadcast to other devices through that same physical interface. People also refer to this rule as **nonbroadcast multiaccess (NBMA)**.

Although split horizon is useful for reducing routing loops, it can cause problems for Frame Relay routing updates. For example, consider a router (RouterA) that is connected to two other routers (RouterB and RouterC) through a single physical interface configured for different virtual circuits, as shown in Figure 12-5. This is a multipoint configuration, which is the default when configuring Frame Relay. Because of split horizon, RouterA would not be able to send router updates received from RouterB to RouterC, and vice versa.

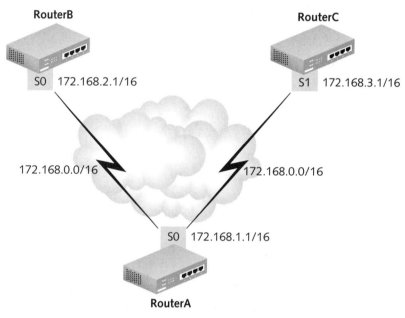

Figure 12-5   Split horizon problem

If the network is using IP, split horizon could be disabled on RouterA, which would solve the problem. However, disabling split horizon is not an option for IPX/SPX or AppleTalk. Furthermore, if the network administrator disables split horizon, the chance of getting routing loops on the network will be increased. The best solution is to configure separate point-to-point subinterfaces for each virtual connection, because the individual virtual circuits can be maintained and split horizon can remain on. Routing update information that is received through one subinterface can be propagated to other subinterfaces because they have different logical addresses.

As an example of this use of subinterfaces, examine Figure 12-6. It is the same as Figure 12-5, except that now the division of serial zero (S0) into subinterfaces S0.1 and S0.2 allows a different subnet identifier to be assigned to each virtual circuit. This allows router updates from RouterB to be transmitted to RouterC, and vice versa, because RouterA treats the subinterfaces as physically separate even though they are really only logically separate.

12

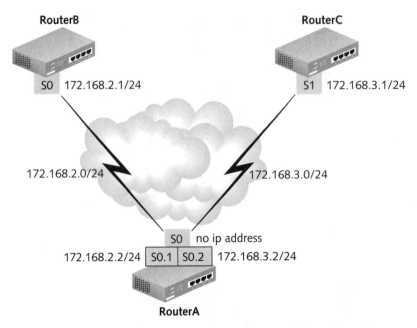

Figure 12-6   Subinterfaces in use in a point-to-point configuration

The network administrator can configure each subinterface as a point-to-point connection or a multipoint connection. Point-to-point connections allow you to divide a single serial interface into multiple subinterfaces, each supporting a separate virtual connection. The network administrator must configure each subinterface with its own subnet identifier in a point-to-point configuration, as shown in Figure 12-6. In a multipoint configuration, the network administrator can configure a single interface or subinterface to support multiple connections to physical or logical interfaces on other routers. A multipoint configuration is still subject to the split horizon rule, because multiple Frame Relay connections on the same network are connected to a single logical interface. The only benefit to the multipoint configuration is that it allows you to use a single network for all of your routers, as shown in Figure 12-7.

Notice that in Figure 12-7, the network uses the same subnet identifier for both virtual circuit connections. Note also that the routers all share the same subnet, identified by their first three octets.

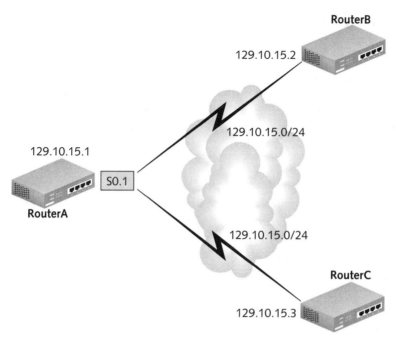

129.10.15.2 — **RouterB**

129.10.15.0/24

129.10.15.1

S0.1

RouterA

129.10.15.0/24

RouterC

129.10.15.3

Figure 12-7   Single subinterface configured for multipoint connection

PERFORMANCE PARAMETERS

12

When organizations contract Frame Relay services from a telecommunications provider such as MCI, Sprint, AT&T, or one of the Regional Bell Operating Companies (RBOCs), the contract specifies parameters by which the connection is expected to function. Terms that appear in the contract may include:

- Access rate: The speed of the line, which indicates transfer rate. Common U.S. access rates are 56 Kps, 64 Kbps, and 128 Kbps, which are provided by Integrated Services Digital Network (ISDN) connections; and 1.544 Mbps, which is provided by T1 connections. Access rate is also known as the local access rate.

- Committed Information Rate (CIR): The minimum transfer rate that the Frame Relay customer negotiates with the Frame Relay service provider. The service provider agrees to always allow the customer to transfer information at no less than the transfer rate specified by the CIR. This is usually lower than the access rate because the transfer rate may exceed the CIR during short bursts.

- Committed Burst Size (CBS): The maximum amount of data bits that the service provider agrees to transfer in a set time period under normal conditions.

- Excess Burst Size (EBS): The amount of excess traffic (over the CBS) that the network will attempt to transfer during a set time period. The network can discard EBS data, if necessary.

- **Oversubscription**: When the sum of the data arriving over all virtual circuits exceeds the access rate, the situation is called oversubscription. This can occur when the CIR is exceeded by burst traffic from the virtual circuits. Oversubscription results in dropped packets. In such a case, the dropped packets must be retransmitted.

Congestion

Frame Relay switches attempt to control congestion on the network. When the Frame Relay switch recognizes congestion, it sends a forward explicit congestion notification (FECN) message to the destination router. This message tells the router that congestion occurred on the virtual circuit. In addition, the switch sends a backward explicit congestion notification (BECN) message to the transmitting, or source, router. The router's reaction to the BECN should be to reduce the amount of traffic it is sending.

A network administrator can configure certain types of traffic at the router as discard eligible (DE). Thus, during times of congestion, the router can discard DE frames to provide a more reliable service to frames that are not discard eligible. DE lists can be configured on a Cisco router to identify the characteristics of frames eligible for discard. These lists are created based on the protocol or the interface, as well as on other characteristics.

FRAME FORMAT

Frame Relay devices can use different Frame Relay frame formats. Because this course is focused on Cisco devices, this section will focus on the Cisco proprietary Frame Relay frame format, its Frame Relay frame structure, and the Address field of the frame.

Figure 12-8 shows the Frame Relay frame format, the basic frame structure, and an expanded look at the Address field of that structure.

The Frame Relay frame format has these specific parts:

- Flag: An eight-bit binary sequence (01111110) that indicates the start of the data frame

- Address: Two to four bytes that contain several pieces of Frame Relay information

- Ethertype: Identifies the type of higher-layer protocol being encapsulated (IP, IPX, or AppleTalk); this data field is specific to the Cisco proprietary frame format

- Data: A variable-length field that contains the information from the higher layers encapsulated in the Frame Relay frame

- FCS: Frame check sequence (FCS) or cyclical redundancy check (CRC), a mathematical computation placed at the end of the frame and used to ensure that the frame was not corrupted during transmission

- Flag: An eight-bit binary sequence (01111110) that indicates the end of the data frame

Flag	Address	Ethertype	Data	Frame Check Sequence	Flag
1 byte	2–4 bytes	2 bytes	Variable	2 bytes	1 byte

	8	7	6	5	4	3	2	1
1st byte	DLCI, high-order bits						CR	EAO
2nd byte	DLCI, low-order bits				FECN	BECN	DE	EA1

Figure 12-8   Frame Relay frame format

Although the Address portion of the Frame Relay frame can contain up to four bytes, Figure 12-8 displays only two bytes because that is the most common format. Three- and four-byte addressing varies only slightly from the structure of two-byte addressing. Refer back to Figure 12-8 as you read the descriptions for the bits of the Address field.

- CR: A command or response bit that is used for sending connection management and frame acknowledgment information between stations

- FECN: Setting used to alert receiving devices if the frame experiences congestion

- BECN: Setting used on frames traveling away from the congested area to warn source devices that congestion has occurred on that path

- DE: Discard eligible bit that is used to identify frames that are first to be dropped when the CIR is exceeded; Cisco routers allow you to set the DE bit for a particular virtual connection by DLCI number

- EA: Extension address bits that are used to extend the Address field from two bytes to either three or four bytes; they allow you to create additional DLCI numbers. For each EA bit that is turned on, one byte is added to the Address field.

Although the Frame Relay frame formats vary slightly, the preceding information provides a thorough description. In addition to variety in Frame Relay formats, there is some variation in the topology that Frame Relay can use. In the next section you will explore different Frame Relay topologies.

FRAME RELAY TOPOLOGIES

Frame Relay can use all of the WAN topologies discussed in Chapter 5: peer (point-to-point), star (hub and spoke), partial mesh, or full mesh physical topology. Figure 12-9 depicts the four topologies again for your review.

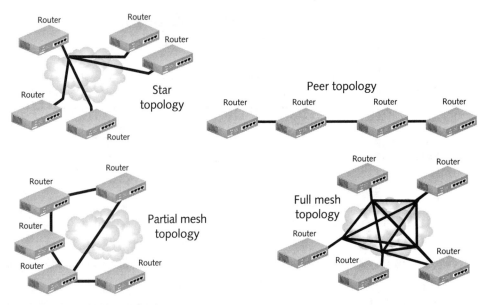

Figure 12-9   WAN topologies

The peer topology is like the bus LAN topology. Nodes are just strung along in a daisy-chained fashion. Very often, only two routers will be connected. This is the simplest WAN topology, and is the least expensive and easiest to configure. The disadvantage to the peer WAN topology is that a failure between nodes will affect the WAN. There is no redundancy.

The star is the most popular Frame Relay topology. One router functions as a central point, or hub, in a simple hierarchical configuration. All other devices are connected to the central router as spokes would connect to a hub. Typically the network administrator will configure the central router with a single interface that makes a multipoint connection to all other routers.

The full mesh is the most expensive topology to implement because each router has a direct connection to every other router. While this offers the most redundancy, it is extremely expensive to implement.

The partial mesh allows redundancy for critical connections while being less expensive than the full mesh. Essentially, any Frame Relay topology that isn't a star or a full mesh is a partial mesh.

FRAME RELAY CONFIGURATION

In this section, you will learn how to configure Frame Relay over serial interfaces using IP as the Network layer protocol. We will look at several examples, beginning with the simplest configuration and moving to successively more complex scenarios.

Basic Multipoint Configuration with Two Routers

We begin with the easiest Frame Relay configuration: a multipoint connection between two routers in which the local and remote routers support LMI and Inverse ARP. In this case, LMI will notify the router about the available DLCI numbers and Inverse ARP will build the Frame Relay map dynamically.

Look at Figure 12-10 and assume that you are responsible for configuring RouterA. RouterA is a Cisco router running IOS version 11.2, so it has the ability to autosense the LMI type. In addition, it automatically receives the DLCI information by querying the network. You only have to configure the serial interface for the correct IP address (129.10.15.1) and the subnet mask (255.255.255.0), and then configure it to support Frame Relay. Assume that the negotiated bandwidth of this connection is 56 Kbps and that you want to use the Routing Information Protocol (RIP) to pass the routing table updates between the routers.

12

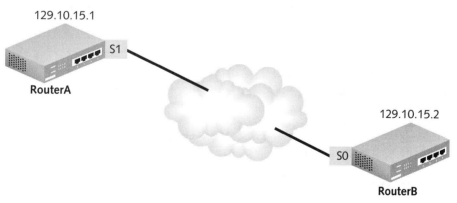

129.10.15.1

S1

RouterA

129.10.15.2

S0

RouterB

Figure 12-10   Simple Frame Relay configuration

Table 12-1 lists the Cisco router prompts and commands that you will need to complete this configuration.

Table 12-1 Basic router prompts and commands for configuring the multipoint
example shown in Figure 12-10

Router prompts this:	You type this:	Description
RouterA>	enable	Allows you to enter privileged EXEC (also called enable) mode. You will be prompted to enter the appropriate password after this command.
RouterA#	config terminal	Allows you to configure the router from the terminal line
RouterA(config)#	int s1	Tells the router to access interface serial 1 for configuration
RouterA(config-if)#	ip address 129.10.15.1 255.255.255.0	Maps the interface serial 1 to the IP address and subnet mask shown
RouterA(config-if)#	encapsulation frame-relay	Sets the encapsulation for this port to Frame Relay using Cisco (the default). The other option is ietf.
RouterA(config-if)#	ban 56	Sets the bandwidth for this port to 56 Kbps
RouterA(config-if)#	exit	Exits interface configuration mode
RouterA(config)#	router rip	Enables the RIP for routing table updates
RouterA(config-router)#	net 129.10.0.0	Enables RIP on the specified network address

The commands in Table 12-1 successfully configure RouterA for the connection shown
in Figure 12-10.

Now assume that you are the network administrator for RouterB and all the same information applies, except that your router is using IOS release version 11.0, which does not
support automatic LMI sensing. To accommodate this new fact, you would have to enter
the LMI type and, of course, different IP addresses. Also assume that the LMI type is
ansi. With these conditions, the configuration commands for RouterB are shown in
Figure 12-11.

```
RouterB#config t
RouterB(config)#int s0
RouterB(config-if)#ip address 129.10.15.2 255.255.255.0
RouterB(config-if)#encap fr
RouterB(config-if)#ban 56
RouterB(config-if)#frame-relay lmi-type ansi
RouterB(config-if)#ex
RouterB(config)# router rip
RouterB(config-router)# net 129.10.0.0
```

Figure 12-11 RouterB configuration

Multipoint Configuration Using a Subinterface

This example configuration requires more work than the last example because it has multiple routers and RouterA is using a subinterface rather than a physical interface. In this case the Frame Relay map will have to be built statically on RouterA. To configure a multipoint subinterface, you map it to multiple remote routers using the same subnet mask, but different DLCI numbers. For example, assume that you are the administrator for RouterA in Figure 12-12 and you want to configure subinterface S1.2, which has IP address 192.168.51.1 and subnet mask 255.255.255.0, to connect over three different virtual connections to the remote Routers B, C, and D.

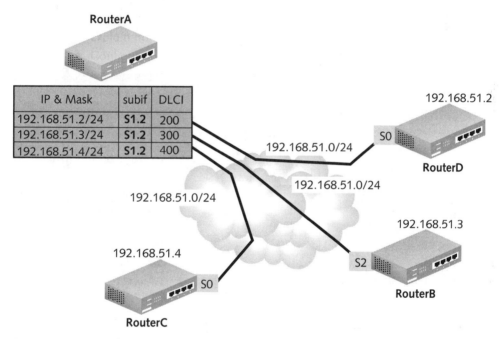

Figure 12-12   Multipoint subinterface configuration on S1.2

Table 12-2 outlines the steps to configure RouterA.

Table 12-2   Subinterface configuration prompts and commands for RouterA in Figure 12-12

Router prompts this:	You type this:	Description
RouterA#	config t	Allows you to configure the router from the terminal line
RouterA(config)#	int s1	Tells the router to access interface serial 1 for configuration

12

Table 12-2   Subinterface configuration prompts and commands for RouterA in Figure 12-12 (continued)

Router prompts this:	You type this:	Description
RouterA(config-if)#	no ip address	When you are configuring a subinterface, you do not want the main interface to have an IP address; this command removes any configured IP address for the S1 interface.
RouterA(config-if)#	encap fr	Sets the encapsulation for this port to Frame Relay using Cisco (the default). The other option is ietf.
RouterA(config-if)#	exit	Exits interface configuration mode
RouterA(config)#	int s1.2 multipoint	Configures subinterface S1.2 for a multipoint connection
RouterA(config-subif)#	ip ad 192.168.51.1 255.255.255.0	Sets S1.2 for the IP address shown
RouterA(config-subif)#	ban 64	Sets the bandwidth for this port to 64 Kbps
RouterA(config-subif)#	frame map ip 192.168.51.2 200 b	Maps subinterface to DLCI 200 and enables broadcast routing updates
RouterA(config-subif)#	frame map ip 192.168.51.3 300 b	Maps subinterface to DLCI 300 and enables broadcast routing updates
RouterA(config-subif)#	frame map ip 192.168.51.4 400 b	Maps subinterface to DLCI 400 and enables broadcast routing updates
RouterA(config-subif)#	exit	Leaves subinterface configuration mode
RouterA(config)#	router rip	Enables RIP
RouterA(config-router)#	network 192.168.51.0	Sets RIP to be used on the network

Point-to-Point Configuration Using Subinterfaces

The example shown in Figure 12-13 has the same physical star, but the "hub" router will be configured for three point-to-point connections to remote routers B, C, and D. Notice there is a different subinterface on RouterA for each remote router connection and the remote routers are all on different subnets. This is the definition of point-to-point. Point-to-point Frame Relay configurations do not support Inverse ARP. In this situation, you will have to configure each subnet separately and use the frame-relay interface-dlci command to associate the DLCI numbers with a specific subinterface. The configuration on the remote routers will be much simpler than the one on the hub router. These remote router configurations will resemble the earlier basic multipoint configuration example with two routers. If LMI and Inverse ARP are supported, the remote routers will build their Frame Relay map tables dynamically. The commands to configure RouterA for the point-to-point example shown in Figure 12-13 are shown in Figure 12-14.

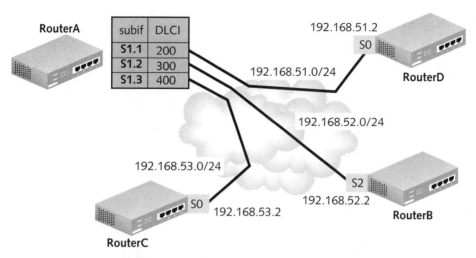

Figure 12-13   Point-to-point configuration sample using subinterfaces

```
RouterA(config)#int s1
RouterA(config-if)#no ip address
RouterA(config-if)#en fr
RouterA(config-if)#exit
RouterA(config)#int s1.1 point-to-point
RouterA(config-subif)#ip ad 192.168.51.1 255.255.255.0
RouterA(config-subif)#ban 64
RouterA(config-subif)#frame-relay interface-dlci 200 b
RouterA(config-if)#exit
RouterA(config)#int s1.2 point-to-point
RouterA(config-subif)#ip ad 192.168.52.1 255.255.255.0
RouterA(config-subif)#ban 64
RouterA(config-subif)#frame-relay interface-dlci 300 b
RouterA(config-if)#exit
RouterA(config)#int s1.3 point-to-point
RouterA(config-subif)#ip ad 192.168.53.1 255.255.255.0
RouterA(config-subif)#ban 64
RouterA(config-subif)#frame-relay interface-dlci 400 b
RouterA(config-subif)#exit
RouterA(config)#router rip
RouterA(config-router)#network 192.168.51.0
RouterA(config-router)#network 192.168.52.0
RouterA(config-router)#network 192.168.53.0
```

Figure 12-14   Point-to-point configuration commands

12

Frame Relay Static Mapping

As shown in Table 12-2 and Figure 12-14, you sometimes have to define the DLCI numbers manually. This is called making a **static address to DLCI Frame Relay map**. You statically configure your DLCI entries in the following situations:

- The remote router doesn't support Inverse ARP.

- You need to assign specific subinterfaces to specific DLCI connections.

- You want to reduce broadcast traffic.

- You are configuring Open Shortest Path First (OSPF) over Frame Relay.

Non-Cisco Routers

You have seen in the previous examples that the encapsulation frame-relay command is used to enable Frame Relay on a Cisco router. Non-Cisco routers use a different Frame Relay encapsulation than Cisco routers. If you are configuring Cisco routers to connect to other Cisco routers, they will automatically use the Cisco Frame Relay encapsulation. If, however, you are connecting a Cisco router to a non-Cisco router, you must specify "ietf" Frame Relay encapsulation using the following command:

```
RouterA(config-if)#encapsulation frame-relay ietf
```

Keepalive Configuration

By default, keepalive packets are sent out every 10 seconds to the Frame Relay switch. Keepalive packets, as previously described, are used to maintain the connection and inform the router of the connection status. You can change the keepalive period by typing "keepalive" followed by the time in seconds of the keepalive period at the router(config-if)# interface configuration prompt. The keepalive period can be set from as low as zero to as high as 30 seconds. For example, if you want to set the keepalive period to 15 seconds, type "keepalive 15" at the interface configuration prompt:

```
RouterA(config-if)#keepalive 15
```

MONITORING FRAME RELAY

You can check your Frame Relay configuration by using show commands. These commands allow you to verify that the commands you previously entered produced the desired effect on your router. The most common show commands for monitoring Frame Relay operation are show interface, show frame-relay pvc, show frame-relay map, and show frame-relay lmi. Figures 12-15, 12-16, 12-17, and 12-18 show these commands with their output.

The serial configuration for each serial interface is available by its interface number

The router gives a status report for the interface, the IP address and subnet mask, and DLCI and LMI statistics

```
router# show interface serial 0/0
Serial0/0 is up, line protocol is down
  Hardware is HD64570
  Internet address is 199.6.13.1/24
  MTU 1500 bytes, BW 56 Kbit, DLY 20000 usec, rely 255/255, load 1/255
  Encapsulation FRAME-RELAY, loopback not set, keepalive set (10 sec)
  LMI enq sent 19, LMI stat recvd 0, LMI upd recvd 0, DTE LMI down
  LMI enq recvd 11, LMI stat sent 0, LMI upd sent 0
  LMI DLCI 1023 LMI type is CISCO frame relay DTE
  Broadcast queue 0/64, broadcasts sent/dropped 0/0, interface broadcasts 0
  Last input 00:00:07, output 00:00:04, output hang never
  Last clearing of "show interface" counters never
  Queueing strategy: fifo
  Output queue 0/40, 0 drops; input queue 0/75, 0 drops
  5 minute input rate 0 bits/sec, 0 packets/sec
  5 minute output rate 0 bits/sec, 0 packets/sec
     354 packets input, 24860 bytes, 0 no buffer
     Received 290 broadcasts, 0 runts, 0 gaints
     0 input errors, 0 CRC, 0 frame, 0 overrun, 0 ignored, 0 abort
     303 packets output, 18589 bytes, 0 underruns
     0 output errors, 0 collisions, 26 interface resets
     0 output buffer failures, 0 output buffers swapped out
     19 carrier transitions
     DCD=up DSR=up DTR=up RTS=up CTS=up
```

Figure 12-15   Show interface command and output

The router tells you the DLCI number and whether the link is active. Other information includes total packet counts for the link and statistics for each FECN, BECN, and DE packet.

This command shows the PVC statistics for each serial interface

```
router# show frame-relay pvc
PVC Statistics for interface Serial0 (Frame Relay DTE)

DLCI = 200, DLCI USAGE = LOCAL, PVC STATUS = INACTIVE, INTERFACE = Serial0.1

  input pkts 0        output pkts 0       in bytes 0
  out bytes 0         dropped pkts 0       in FECN pkts 0
  in BECN pkts 0       out FECN pkts 0       out BECN pkts 0
  in DE pkts 0        out DE pkts 0
pvc create time 00:06:41, last time pvc status changed 00:06:41
```

Figure 12-16   Show Frame Relay permanent virtual circuit command and output

12

This command shows the DLCI-to-Network-layer address mapping for each remote router to which the local device is connected.

```
router# show frame-relay map
Serial0.1 (down): ip 199.6.13.2 dlci 200(0xC8,0x3080), static,
        broadcast,
        CISCO, status defined, inactive
```

Figure 12-17   Show Frame Relay map command and output

This command displays the amount and type of management information that is being transferred over the LMI DLCI connection. It also displays the LMI type used on the interface.

```
router# show frame-relay lmi
LMI Statistics for interface Serial0 (Frame Relay DTE) LMI TYPE = CISCO
 Invalid Unnumbered info 0            Invalid Prot Disc 0
 Invalid dummy Call Ref 0            Invalid Msg Type 0
 Invalid Status Message 0           Invalid Lock Shift 0
 Invalid Information ID 0           Invalid Report IE Len 0
 Invalid Report Request 0            Invalid Keep IE Len 0
 Num Status Enq. Sent 39             Num Status msgs Rcvd 0
 Num Update Status Rcvd 0            Num Status Timeouts 38
```

Figure 12-18   Show Frame Relay Local Management Interface command and output

CHAPTER SUMMARY

❑ Frame Relay is a flexible WAN technology that can be used to connect two geographically separate LANs.

❑ Frame Relay is both a service and type of encapsulation.

❑ The service parameters must be discussed with the Frame Relay provider (telecommunications company).

❑ Service parameters for Frame Relay include the access rate, Committed Information Rate (CIR), Committed Burst Size (CBS), and Excess Burst Size (EBS).

❑ Frame Relay connections employ virtual circuits that can be either permanent or switched.

❑ Virtual circuit connections across Frame Relay connections are defined by Data Link Connection Identifier (DLCI) numbers.

❑ The DLCI numbers can be associated with remote Network layer addresses; however, they are only locally significant unless the Local Management Interface (LMI) is available.

❑ Most Frame Relay providers support LMI, which allows Frame Relay maps to be dynamically created via Inverse ARP.

❑ Static mappings of DLCI numbers to remote IP addresses can be configured when routers do not support Inverse ARP.

❑ Inverse ARP is on by default for multipoint configurations.

❑ Inverse ARP is not enabled on point-to-point links because only one path is available.

❑ Frame Relay circuits can be established over serial interfaces or subinterfaces on Cisco routers.

KEY TERMS

Consultative Committee on International Telephony and Telegraphy (CCITT) — The former name of International Telecommunication Union-Telecommunication Standardization Sector (ITU-T).

Frame Relay access device (FRAD) — The device that the Frame Relay customer uses to connect to a Frame Relay network; also known as the Frame Relay assembler/disassembler.

Frame Relay assembler/disassembler — *See* **Frame Relay access device (FRAD)**.

Frame Relay map — A table that defines the interface to which a specific DLCI number is mapped.

Frame Relay network device (FRND) — The device that the Frame Relay provider supplies as the connection to the Frame Relay network; the acronym FRND is pronounced *friend*.

Frame Relay switch — A telecommunications company device that is used to support Frame Relay connections from customer locations; used to route Frame Relay traffic inside the public data network.

Frame Relay switching table — A table that is maintained on a Frame Relay switch; used to route Frame Relay traffic via virtual circuit DLCI numbers.

International Telecommunication Union–Telecommunication Standardization Sector (ITU-T) — A standards organization based in Europe, but with membership worldwide; involved in telecommunications standardization.

keepalive packets — Data packets sent between devices to confirm that a connection should be maintained between them.

multipoint — The configuration of a single interface or subinterface to use multiple virtual circuits.

nonbroadcast multiaccess (NBMA) — A rule used in Frame Relay that does not allow broadcasts to be sent to multiple locations from a single interface.

oversubscription — When the sum of the data arriving over all virtual circuits exceeds the access rate.

12

point-to-point — The configuration of one or more interfaces or subinterfaces to connect to multiple virtual circuits. Each circuit will be on its own subnet. Acts like a leased line.

public data network (PDN) — A telecommunications network that connects telephones around the country. These services can be provided by AT&T, Sprint, MCI, and RBOCs.

static address to DLCI Frame Relay map — A Frame Relay map that has been manually created by a network administrator.

subinterface — A logical division of an interface; for example, a single serial interface can be divided into multiple logical subinterfaces.

REVIEW QUESTIONS

1. Which protocol is used to automatically build the Frame Relay map along with LMI?

   a. ARP

   b. RARP

   c. Inverse ARP

   d. DLCI

2. To make DLCI numbers globally significant, LMI causes routers to issue _____ that advertise the DLCI numbers.

   a. unicasts

   b. keepalives

   c. broadcasts

   d. multicasts

3. When negotiating a data transfer rate for Frame Relay with a telecommunications provider, the rate agreed upon is the _____.

   a. keepalive rate

   b. CIR

   c. EBS

   d. DDR

4. The Address portion of the Frame Relay frame contains which of the following pieces of information? (Choose all that apply.)

   a. DLCI

   b. FECN

   c. Flag

   d. BECN

   e. FCS

5. The line speed of a Frame Relay connection is known as the _____.

   a. access rate

   b. CBS

   c. EBS

   d. CIR

6. _____ numbers are locally significant in Frame Relay connections and are used to identify specific virtual circuits.

   a. DLCI

   b. PDN

   c. ARP

   d. LMI

7. To prevent routing loops, Frame Relay uses _____.

   a. loopback attack

   b. split horizon

   c. event horizon

   d. DLCI numbers

8. Frame Relay is more efficient than older WAN encapsulation methods because error correction is handled by _____ in Frame Relay communications.

   a. lower layers

   b. DLCI

   c. LMI

   d. upper layers

9. Frame Relay uses _____ to combine multiple data streams on one connection.

   a. duplexing

   b. simplexing

   c. multiplexing

   d. encoding

10. What is the purpose of keepalive packets?

   a. To reduce data transfer rates

   b. To keep PVCs active

   c. To increase data transfer rates

   d. To negotiate connection speed

12

11. Which of the following layers do WAN specifications typically define? (Choose all that apply.)

    a. Physical

    b. Data Link

    c. Network

    d. Transport

    e. Presentation

12. In Frame Relay, what would be considered the DCE?

    a. Customer's router

    b. Terminal adapter

    c. PPP

    d. Frame Relay switch

13. Which of the following was formerly CCITT?

    a. ASCII

    b. ANSI

    c. ITU-T

    d. EBCDIC

14. What is another term used to describe a Frame Relay switch?

    a. FRND

    b. FRAD

    c. PDN

    d. PSTN

15. Which of the following would be a subinterface for Serial 1?

    a. S0.1

    b. S0.2

    c. S1.2

    d. S2.1

16. What does LMI stand for?

    a. Logical Management Interface

    b. Local Management Interface

    c. Logical Maintenance Interconnect

    d. Logical Maintenance Interface

17. What are the three possible connection states for a DLCI? (Choose all that apply.)

    a. Interactive

    b. Active

   c. Inactive

   d. Disconnected

   e. Deleted

18. Which of the following does not allow broadcasts to be sent to multiple destinations through a single interface?

   a. LMI

   b. Subinterfaces

   c. LCP

   d. MBA

   e. NBMA

19. Which of the following is a type of virtual circuit? (Choose all that apply.)

   a. MVC

   b. PVC

   c. SVC

   d. QVC

20. Which of the following are LMI encapsulation types supported by Cisco routers? (Choose all that apply.)

   a. LMI 2

   b. cisco

   c. ansi

   d. v923i

   e. q933a

21. Which of the following is the default LMI encapsulation type for a Cisco router?

   a. LMI 2

   b. cisco

   c. ansi

   d. v923i

   e. q933a

22. What does the router(config-if)#encap fr command do?

   a. Sets the enable mode prompt to FR

   b. Enables Frame Relay on the first serial interface

   c. Sets the encapsulation to Frame Relay

   d. Sets the language to French

12

23. Which of the following commands would show statistics for a virtual circuit?

    a. router>sh frame map

    b. router#sh frame map

    c. router#sh frame pvc

    d. router(config-if)#sh frame pvc

24. What Frame Relay encapsulation must be configured on Cisco routers that are attached to non-Cisco routers?

    a. ietf

    b. cisco

    c. ansi

    d. q933a

25. How often are Frame Relay keepalive packets sent by default?

    a. Every 30 seconds

    b. Every 10 seconds

    c. Once every hour on the half-hour

    d. Once every hour on the hour

    e. Once every 30 minutes

CASE PROJECTS

**CASE
PROJECTS**

1. Big Byte Consulting has hired your company to help it set up Frame Relay to connect several locations. Big Byte's headquarters are in Austin, Texas; it will be connecting PVCs to Dallas, San Antonio, and Houston. You and Jennifer are expected to have a conference call with the network administrators at the other locations to discuss the Frame Relay configuration. What type of information will have to be coordinated among the various locations? What type of information would you require to configure your Cisco 2500 series router to support your Frame Relay connection?

2. During the conference call with Big Byte, the subject of multipoint and point-to-point is raised. The Big Byte network team doesn't understand the differences between multipoint and point-to-point connections. How do you explain the differences to Big Byte using its own network as an example?

3. Big Byte has configured its Frame Relay network but there are problems. You have been informed that the Frame Relay connection between Austin and Houston is down. Someone has already contacted the phone company and determined that the Frame Relay switches are operating properly. You decide to verify the Frame Relay configuration between the two locations. What commands would you use to check the configuration? What type of configuration problems might you expect to find?

13

SWITCHING AND VLANS

After reading this chapter and completing the exercises, you will be able to:

♦ Explain the features and benefits of Fast Ethernet

♦ Describe the guidelines and distance limitations of Fast Ethernet

♦ Define full- and half-duplex Ethernet operations

♦ Distinguish between cut-through, fragment-free, and store-and-forward LAN switching

♦ Define the operation of the Spanning Tree Protocol and its benefits

♦ Describe the benefits of virtual LANs

♦ Understand the purpose of the VLAN trunking protocol (VTP)

In this chapter, you will revisit some of the concepts surrounding Ethernet operations. Specifically, you will learn about Ethernet performance and methods for improving it. Standard and Fast Ethernet will be part of this discussion, as will half- and full-duplex Ethernet operations. The concepts central to LAN switching, such as switch operations, forwarding techniques, and VLANs, will also be explained.

ETHERNET OPERATIONS

As you have learned, **Ethernet** is a **network access method** (or **media access method**) originated by the University of Hawaii, later adopted by Xerox Corporation, and standardized as IEEE 802.3 in the early 1980s. Today, Ethernet is the most pervasive network access method in use and continues to be the most commonly implemented media access method in new LANs. Many companies and individuals are continually working to improve the performance and increase the capabilities of Ethernet technology.

In the following sections, you will revisit the Ethernet access method, discuss Ethernet errors, investigate latency problems, and learn ways in which Ethernet performance can be improved. Becoming comfortable with these concepts will help you troubleshoot and improve the performance of your LAN.

CSMA/CD

Ethernet uses **Carrier Sense Multiple Access with Collision Detection (CSMA/CD)** as its **contention method**. This means that any station connected to a network can transmit anytime there is not already a transmission on the wire. After each transmitted signal, each station must wait a minimum of 9.6 microseconds before transmitting another packet. This is called the **interframe gap**, or **interpacket gap (IPG)**, which provides sufficient spacing between frames so that network interfaces have time to process a packet before receiving another.

Collisions

Even though stations must listen to the wire before sending a transmission, two stations could listen to the wire simultaneously and not sense a **carrier signal**. In such a case, both stations might begin to transmit their data simultaneously. Shortly after the simultaneous transmissions, a collision would occur on the network wire. The stations would detect the collision as their transmitted signals collided with one another.

Once a collision is detected, the first station to detect the collision transmits a 32-bit **jam signal** that tells all other stations not to transmit for a brief period (9.6 microseconds or slightly more). The jam signal is used to ensure that all stations are aware that a collision has occurred. After the first station to detect the collision transmits the jam signal, the two stations that caused the collision use an algorithm to enter a **backoff period**, which causes them not to transmit for a random interval. The backoff period is an attempt to ensure that the two stations do not immediately cause another collision.

Collision Domain

A **collision domain** is the physical area in which a packet collision might occur. You need to understand this concept in order to understand network segmentation, which is essentially the division of collision domains. Repeaters and hubs do not segment the network and therefore do not divide collision domains. Routers, switches, bridges, and **gateways** do segment networks and thus create separate collision domains.

If a station transmits at the same time as another station in the same collision domain, there will be a collision. The 32-bit jam signal that is transmitted when the collision is discovered prevents all stations on that collision domain from transmitting. If the network is segmented, the collision domain is also divided, and the jam signal will only affect those stations that operate within that collision domain. Stations that operate within remote segments (other collision domains) are not subject to the collisions or frame errors that occur on the local segment.

Latency

The time that a signal takes to travel from one point to another point on a network affects the performance of the network. **Latency**, or **propagation delay**, is the length of time that is required to forward, send, or otherwise propagate a data frame. Latency differs depending on the resistance offered by the transmission medium, the number of nodes, and in the case of a connectivity device, the amount of processing that must be done on the packet. For instance, sending a packet across a copper wire does not introduce as much latency as sending a packet across an Ethernet switch.

The amount of time it takes for a packet to be sent from one device and received at another device is called the **transmission time**. The latency of the devices and media between the two hosts affects the transmission time; the more processing a device must perform on a data packet, the higher the latency. The maximum latency for a repeater can be as high as 140 bit times. The maximum propagation delay for an electronic signal to traverse a 100-meter section of Category 5 unshielded twisted-pair (UTP) or shielded twisted-pair (STP) cable is 111.2 bit times.

NOTE A **bit time** is the duration of time to transmit one data bit on a network, which is 100 nanoseconds on a 10-Mbps Ethernet network and 10 nanoseconds on a 100-Mbps Ethernet network.

Table 13-1 illustrates the maximum propagation delays for various media and devices on an Ethernet network. The propagation delays shown illustrate the maximum allowable round-trip delays for cabling and devices on a 100-Mbps Ethernet network.

Table 13-1   Propagation delay for Ethernet media and devices

Media or Device	Maximum Propagation Delay (Bit Times)
Two Ethernet stations using two-pair UTP or fiber-optic cable	100
Two Ethernet stations using 100Base-T4	135
1-meter segment of Category 3 or 4 UTP cable	1.14
1-meter segment of Category 5 UTP or STP cable	1.112

13

Table 13-1   Propagation delay for Ethernet media and devices (continued)

Media or Device	Maximum Propagation Delay (Bit Times)
10-meter segment of fiber-optic cable	1.0
Class I repeater	140
Class II repeater	92

NOTE

Repeaters can take anywhere from less than 8 bit times up to 140 bit times to propagate a signal.

Slot time (512 bit times) is an important specification because it limits the physical size of each Ethernet collision domain. Slot time specifies that all collisions should be detected from anywhere in a network in less time than is required to place a 64-byte frame on the network. Slot time is the reason that the IEEE created the **5-4-3 rule**, which limits collision domains to five segments of wire, four repeaters and/or hubs, and three populated hubs between any two stations on a 10-Mbps network. Violating those design parameters could cause network errors. For example, if a station at one end of an Ethernet network didn't receive the jam signal before transmitting a frame on the network, another collision could occur as soon as the jam signal and newly transmitted frame crossed paths. Theoretically, this situation could occur repeatedly and prevent any useful data from being transmitted on the wire.

Ethernet Errors

Different errors and different causes for errors exist on Ethernet networks. Most errors are caused by defective or incorrectly configured equipment. Errors impede the performance of a network and the transmission of useful data. In this section, you will learn about several Ethernet packet errors and their potential causes.

Frame Size Errors

An Ethernet packet sent between two stations should be between 64 bytes and 1518 bytes. Frames that are shorter or longer are, according to Ethernet specifications, considered errors. The following list names and describes several frame size errors that occur on Ethernet networks:

- **Short frame** or **runt**: A frame that is shorter than 64 bytes. A collision, a faulty network adapter, corrupt NIC software drivers, or a repeater fault can cause this error.

- **Long frame**: Also known as a **giant**, a frame that is larger than 1518 bytes. Because 1518 is the largest legal frame size, a long frame is too large to be valid. A collision, a faulty network adapter, an illegal hardware configuration, a transceiver or cable fault, a termination problem, corrupt NIC software drivers, a repeater fault, or noise can cause this error.

- **Jabber:** This is another classification for giant or long frames. This frame is longer than Ethernet standards allow (1518 bytes) and has an incorrect **frame check sequence (FCS)**.

In addition to frame size errors, other packet errors might be seen on an Ethernet network. For example, a **frame check sequence (FCS) error**, which indicates that bits of a frame were corrupted during transmission, can be caused by any of the previously listed errors. An FCS error is detected when the calculation at the end of a packet doesn't conform correctly to the number and sequence of bits in the frame, which means there was some type of bit loss or corruption. An FCS error can be present even if the packet is within the accepted size parameters for Ethernet transmission. If a frame with an FCS error also has an octet missing, it is called an **alignment error**.

Collision Errors

Network administrators should expect collisions to occur on an Ethernet network. However, most administrators consider collision rates above 5% to be high. A large number of devices on a collision domain means a greater chance that there will be a significant number of collisions. Reducing the number of devices per collision domain will usually solve the problem. You can reduce the number of devices per collision domain by segmenting your network with a router, a bridge, or a switch.

A transmitting station will attempt to send its packet 16 times before discarding it as an **NIC error**. Thus, a network with a high rate of collisions, which prompts multiple retransmissions, may also have a high rate of NIC errors, and vice versa.

Another Ethernet error related to collisions is called a **late collision**. A late collision occurs when two stations transmit more than 64 bytes of their data frames before detecting a collision. This can occur when there are too many repeaters on a network or when the network cabling is too long. A late collision means that the slot time of 512 bits has been exceeded. The only way a station can distinguish between a late and normal collision is by determining that the collision occurred after the first 64 bytes of the frame were transmitted.

The solution for eliminating late collisions is to determine which part of the Ethernet configuration violates design standards by having too many repeaters or populated segments, or by exceeding maximum cable lengths. Occasionally, a network device malfunction may also cause late collisions. When such problems are located, they must be resolved.

Broadcasts

Stations on a network **broadcast** packets to other stations to make their presence known on the network and to carry out normal network tasks such as IP address-to-MAC address resolution. However, when there is too much broadcast traffic on a segment, utilization increases and network performance in general suffers. People may experience

13

slower file transfers, e-mail access delays, and slower Web access when broadcast traffic is above 10% of the available network bandwidth.

One simple way to reduce broadcast traffic is to reduce the number of services that servers provide on your network and to limit the number of protocols in use on your network. Limiting the number of services will help because each computer that provides a service, such as file sharing, broadcasts its service at a periodic interval over each protocol it has configured. Many operating systems allow you to bind the service selectively to only a specific protocol, which will reduce broadcast traffic on the network. You can also eliminate unnecessary protocols to eliminate broadcast traffic on the network. An example of an unnecessary protocol is the IPX protocol on a server in an IP-only network. In this case, services would be advertised on both IP and IPX, when other stations would only be communicating via IP. IPX advertisements and the use of the IPX protocol is unnecessary in this case because no other stations on the network would be using IPX.

NOTE   Network users who share files may be sharing them over multiple protocols. Broadcast messages typically advertise these file-sharing services on each network protocol configured. Therefore, limiting the number of protocols in use on stations that share files can reduce the amount of broadcast traffic on the network.

If a broadcast from one computer causes multiple stations to respond with additional broadcast traffic, it could result in a **broadcast storm**. Broadcast storms will slow down or completely stop network communications, because no other traffic will be able to transmit on the network. One of the most common causes of broadcast storms is a network loop. Loops are created when redundant links between switches and bridges exist in the network. The Spanning Tree Protocol, covered in detail later in this chapter, is used to combat the problems caused by these physical loops. A broadcast storm occurs on an Ethernet collision domain when there are 126 or more broadcast packets per second.

Software faults with network card drivers or computer operating systems are the typical causes of broadcast storms. You can use a **protocol analyzer** to locate the device causing the broadcast storm. Once the device is identified, you can correct the configuration error or apply an appropriate software driver update to correct the problem.

Fast Ethernet

When a 10BaseT network is experiencing congestion, upgrading to **Fast Ethernet** can reduce congestion considerably. Fast Ethernet uses the same network access method (CSMA/CD) as common 10BaseT Ethernet, but provides 10 times the data transmission rate—100 Mbps. That means that frames can be transmitted in 90% less time with Fast Ethernet than with standard Ethernet.

When you upgrade from 10BaseT to Fast Ethernet, all the network cards, hubs, and other connectivity devices that are now expected to operate at 100 Mbps must be upgraded. If the 10BaseT network is using Category 5 or higher cable, that cable can still be used for

Fast Ethernet operations. Also, a 10-Mbps Ethernet NIC can function on a Fast Ethernet network because the Fast Ethernet hub or switch to which the 10-Mbps device attaches will automatically negotiate a 10-Mbps connection. The Fast Ethernet hub will continue to operate at 100 Mbps with the other Fast Ethernet devices. Most modern NICs can operate at either 10 or 100 Mbps. Finally, Fast Ethernet devices are also capable of full-duplex operation, which allows them to obtain a transmission rate of 100 Mbps in each direction.

Fast Ethernet, which is defined under the **IEEE 802.3u** standard, has three defined implementations:

- **100Base-TX:** Uses two pairs of either Category 5 unshielded twisted-pair (UTP) or shielded twisted-pair (STP); one pair is used for transmit (TX), and the other is used for receive (RX). The maximum segment length is 100 meters; two Class II repeaters and a five-meter patch cable can be used to create a maximum distance of 205 meters between stations, for each collision domain.

- **100Base-T4:** Uses four pairs of either Category 3, 4, or 5 UTP cable; one pair is used for TX, one pair for RX, and two pairs are used as bidirectional data pairs. The maximum segment length is 100 meters; as with 100Base-TX, two Class II repeaters and a five-meter patch cable can be used to create a maximum distance of 205 meters between stations, for each collision domain. Because all four pairs are used, the T4 specification does not support full-duplexing, which is discussed in the next section.

- **100Base-FX:** Uses **multimode fiber-optic (MMF) cable** with one TX and one RX strand per link. The maximum segment length is 412 meters.

IEEE 802.3u specifies two types of repeaters: Class I and Class II. Class I repeaters have higher latency than Class II repeaters, as shown in Table 13-1. When two Class II repeaters are deployed on a twisted-pair network (100Base-TX or 100Base-T4), the specification allows for an additional five-meter patch cord to connect the repeaters. This patch cord is in addition to the normal 200-meter segment length. This means that the maximum distance between two stations can be up to 205 meters. When repeaters are used on networks with fiber-optic cable (e.g., 100Base-FX), the maximum segment lengths are actually reduced because the repeaters introduce latency. Latency increases the propagation delay, which means that the maximum distance possible between stations must be reduced to ensure that the slot time is maintained.

On a Cisco Catalyst 1900 switch, you can configure the 10BaseT and Fast Ethernet ports via interface configuration mode. The configuration commands follow a similar syntax: *interface Ethernet/fastethernet slot#/port#*. Catalyst 1900 switches only have one slot, which is 0. Also, the only ports that are capable of Fast Ethernet operations are 26 and 27. Ports 1–12 and 25 or 1–24 and 25 (depending on the specific model) are 10-Mbps ports. On a 2950 series switch, all ports are at least 10/100-Mbps and therefore can run as either standard Ethernet or Fast Ethernet ports. To enter interface configuration mode for one of the 10-Mbps ports of a switch named Rm410HL, you would use the following commands:

```
Rm410HL#configure terminal
Rm410HL(config)#interface ethernet 0/1
Rm410HL(config-if)#
```

However, if you want to configure one of the Fast Ethernet ports, ports 26 and 27 on a 1900 series switch, or any port on a 2950 series switch, you would use a slightly different command syntax; substitute the word fastethernet for ethernet:

```
Rm410HL#configure terminal
Rm410HL(config)#interface fastethernet 0/26
Rm410HL(config-if)#
```

To view the configuration of a port, use the show command. The following commands will display the configuration settings for port 1 and port 26:

```
Rm410HL#show interface e0/1
Rm410HL#show interface f0/26
```

Notice that "e" is used to specify 10-Mbps ports and "f" for 100-Mbps ports.

Half- and Full-Duplex Communications

In **half-duplex** communications, devices can send and receive signals, but not at the same time. In **full-duplex** communications, devices can send and receive signals simultaneously. As an analogy of these communication types, consider the walkie-talkie and the telephone. When two people use walkie-talkies, one person must finish speaking before the other can transmit. This is half-duplex communication. When two people communicate over the telephone, both people can speak simultaneously, and both transmissions will be heard at the opposite ends. This is full-duplex communication. Full-duplex is also known just as duplex.

10BaseT, 10Base-F, 100Base-FX, and 100Base-TX Ethernet networks can use equipment that supports half- and full-duplex communications. In half-duplex Ethernet communications, when a twisted-pair NIC sends a transmission, the card loops that transmission back from its transmit wire pair onto its receive pair (see Figure 13-1). The card stores the looped-back frame. The transmission is also sent out of the card. The card then compares the looped-back frame with the original frame. If the frame is the same, then there is no collision. If the looped-back frame is different from the original frame, then a collision is recorded.

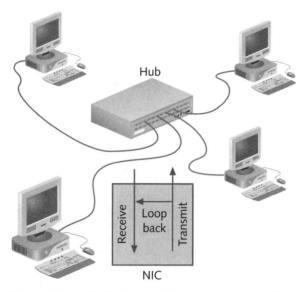

Hub

Receive | Loop back | Transmit

NIC

Figure 13-1 Half-duplex Ethernet communications

The transmitted frame travels along the network through the hub to all other stations on the collision domain. Half-duplex NICs cannot transmit and receive simultaneously, so all stations on the collision domain (including the transmitting station) listen to the transmission before sending another.

Full-duplex Ethernet components can send and receive signals at the same time. Full-duplex communications use one set of wires to send and a separate set to receive. Because full-duplex network devices conduct the transmit and receive functions on different wire pairs and do not loop back transmissions as they are sent, collisions cannot occur. Furthermore, full-duplex Ethernet increases the throughput capability between devices because there are two separate communication paths. This means that 10BaseT full-duplex network cards are capable of transferring data at a rate of 10 Mbps in each direction, as compared with half-duplex 10BaseT cards. The benefits of using full-duplex are:

- Time is not wasted retransmitting frames, because there are no collisions.

- The full bandwidth is available in both directions because the send and receive functions are separate.

- Stations do not have to wait until other stations complete their transmissions, because there is only one transmitter for each twisted pair.

On a Cisco Catalyst 1900 switch and 2950 switch, you can set the duplex capabilities port-by-port. To change the duplex of a switch port, you must enter the interface

13

configuration for the specific port you want to configure. The following list describes the four different duplex options:

- Auto: The default setting for 100-Mbps Ethernet ports. The switch port is set to determine whether the connected device is full- or half-duplex and configures itself to match.

- Full: This setting forces full-duplex mode on a 10- or 100-Mbps port. Use this if you know that the duplex should be full but auto-negotiate (auto) doesn't seem to be working.

- Full-flow control: This setting is used for 100Base-TX ports only. As its name implies, it uses flow control to ensure that switch buffers don't overflow.

- Half: The default setting for 10-Mbps Ethernet ports, which forces the port to communicate half-duplex.

Assume that you want to change port 26 on a Cisco 1900 switch or any port on a 2950 switch named Rm410HL to full duplex. The commands to complete this operation are as follows:

```
Rm410HL#configure terminal
Rm410HL(config)#interface fastethernet 0/26
Rm410HL(config-if)#duplex full
```

Networking tools, like the Fluke One-Touch, can determine whether your switch ports are set for full or half duplex. Some operating system tools, such as mii-daig in Linux, allow you to verify full- or half-duplex operations. Client network cards can be configured through the system BIOS, operating system, or manufacturer-provided software or hardware.

LAN SEGMENTATION

As mentioned, you can improve the performance of your Ethernet network by reducing the number of stations per collision domain. Typically, network administrators implement bridges, switches, or routers to segment the network and divide the collision domains.

In your previous studies, you learned about using bridges, switches, and routers to segment a network. In this section, you will review the concepts behind segmenting a LAN with bridges and routers.

Segmenting with Bridges

A **bridge** segments a network by filtering traffic at the Data Link layer. It divides a network into two or more segments and only forwards a frame from one segment to another if the frame is a broadcast or has the MAC address of a station on a different segment. Bridges learn MAC addresses by reading the source MAC addresses from frames as the frames are passed across the bridge. As you have already learned, the MAC addresses are contained in the header information inside each packet. If the bridge does not recognize a MAC address, it will forward the frame to all segments except the one it came in on.

The bridge maintains a **bridging table** to keep track of the different hardware addresses on each segment. The bridging table maps each MAC address learned to the port on the bridge that is connected to the segment where that MAC address is located. Bridges increase latency, but because they effectively divide the collision domain, this does not affect slot time.

When you segment a LAN with one or more bridges, remember these points:

- Bridges reduce collisions by segmenting the LAN and filtering traffic based on MAC addresses.

- A bridge does not reduce broadcast or **multicast** traffic.

- A bridge can extend the useful distance of the Ethernet LAN because distance limitations apply to collision domains, and a bridge separates collision domains.

- The bandwidth for the new individual segments is increased because they can operate separately at 10 Mbps or 100 Mbps, depending on the technology.

- Bridges can be used to limit traffic for security purposes by keeping traffic segregated; traffic between two hosts on one side of the bridge will not be propagated to the other side of the bridge.

Segmenting with Routers

A **router** operates at layer 3 of the OSI reference model. It interprets the Network layer protocol and makes forwarding decisions based on the layer 3 address. Routers typically do not propagate broadcast traffic; thus, they reduce network traffic even more than bridges do. Routers maintain routing tables that include the Network layer addresses of different segments. The router forwards packets to the correct router on another segment, based on those Network layer addresses. Because the router has to read the layer 3 address and determine the best path to the destination station, latency is higher than with a bridge or repeater/hub.

Keep in mind that when you segment a LAN with routers, they will:

- Decrease collisions by filtering traffic.

- Reduce broadcast and multicast traffic by blocking or selectively filtering packets.

- Support multiple paths and routes between them.

- Provide increased bandwidth for the newly created segments.

- Increase security by preventing packets between hosts on one side of the router from propagating to the other side of the router.

13

- Increase the effective distance of the network by creating new collision domains.

- Provide layer 3 routing, packet fragmentation and reassembly, and traffic flow control.

- Provide communications between different technologies such as Ethernet and Token Ring or Ethernet and Frame Relay.

- Have a higher latency than bridges, because routers have more to process; faster processors in the router can reduce some of this latency.

LAN SWITCHING

Although **switches** are similar to bridges in several ways, using a switch on a LAN has a different effect on the way network traffic is propagated. This difference happens because switches do quite a bit more than merely segment the LAN; they truly change the way in which communication is carried out on the LAN.

The remainder of this chapter focuses on the ways in which a switch can affect LAN communications. First, you will learn how a switch segments a LAN. The benefits and drawbacks of using a switch on the LAN are also described. Then, you will learn how a switch operates and the switching components that are involved. The final section of the chapter explains how you can use switches to create virtual LANs.

Segmentation with Switches

Bridges and switches are similar—so much so that switches are often called **multiport bridges**. The main difference between a switch and a bridge is that the switch typically connects multiple stations individually, thereby segmenting a LAN into separate ports. A bridge only separates two or more segments and is usually limited to 16 ports. In addition, switches are hardware-controlled, whereas bridges are controlled by software. Typically, hubs are connected to the bridge ports, so the workstations connected to the hubs are sharing the bandwidth on that segment. By connecting each port to an individual workstation, switches **microsegment** the network. The bandwidth is not shared as long as each workstation connects to its own switch port. This is called **switched bandwidth**, and it operates differently than the shared bandwidth through hubs.

Consider the illustration shown in Figure 13-2. When Host A sends a **unicast** to Host D, the switch (which operates at the Data Link layer of the OSI reference model) receives the unicast frame on the port to which Host A is attached, opens the data frame, reads the destination MAC address, and then passes the frame directly to the port to which Host D is attached. Unlike hub operations, the other hosts on the switch will not see the frame. However, when Host B sends a broadcast frame, the switch forwards the frame to all devices attached to the switch. This is similar to how a bridge handles broadcasts. Bridges and switches generally do not create broadcast domains. Figure 13-3 shows the inherent logic structure of this process.

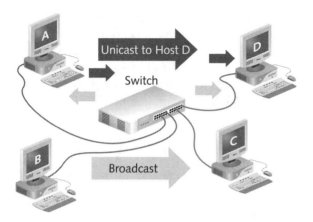

Figure 13-2 Switch packet forwarding actions

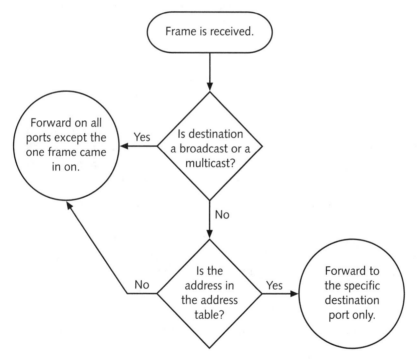

Figure 13-3 Packet forwarding decisions made by a switch

Given the number of steps that a switch must perform on each frame, its latency is typically higher than that of a repeater or hub. Although switches do slightly more work than bridges, faster processors and a variety of switching techniques make switches typically faster than bridges. In general, however, you can count on a switch adding approximately 21 microseconds of latency to network communications.

As previously mentioned, because switches microsegment most traffic, there is a better utilization of the available bandwidth. When one host is communicating directly with another host, the hosts can use the full bandwidth of the connection. For example, with a 10-Mbps switch on a 10BaseT LAN, the switch can often provide 10-Mbps connections for each host that is attached. If a hub were used instead of a switch, all devices on the collision domain would share the 10-Mbps connection.

Switches provide the following benefits:

- Reduction in network traffic and collisions
- Increase in available bandwidth per station, because stations can communicate in parallel
- Increase in the effective distance of a LAN by dividing it into multiple collision domains
- Increased security, because unicast traffic is sent directly to its destination and not to all other stations on the collision domain

Switch Operations

A switch learns the hardware address of devices to which it is attached by reading the source address of frames as they are transmitted across the switch. The switch matches the source MAC address with the port from which the frame was sent. The MAC-to-switch-port mapping is stored in the switch's **content-addressable memory (CAM)**. The switch refers to the CAM when it is forwarding frames, and it updates the CAM continuously. Each mapping receives a time stamp every time it is referenced. Old entries that are not referenced frequently enough are removed from the CAM.

The switch uses a memory buffer to store frames as it determines to which port(s) a frame will be forwarded. There are two different types of memory buffering that a switch can use: **port-based memory buffering** and **shared memory buffering**. In port-based memory buffering, each port has a certain amount of memory that it can use to store frames. If a port is inactive, then its memory buffer is idle. However, if a port is receiving a high volume of traffic (near network capacity), the traffic may overload its buffer, and other frames may be delayed or require retransmission.

Shared memory buffering offers an advantage over port-based memory buffering in that any port can store frames in the shared memory buffer. The amount of memory that each port uses in the shared memory buffer is dynamically allocated according to the port's activity level and the size of frames transmitted. Shared memory buffering works best when a few ports receive a majority of the traffic. This situation occurs in client/server environments, because the ports to which servers are attached will typically see more activity than the ports to which clients are attached.

Some switches can interconnect network interfaces of different speeds. For example, a switch might have a mix of 10-Mbps, 100-Mbps, and 1000-Mbps devices attached. These switches use **asymmetric switching** and, typically, a shared memory buffer. The shared memory buffer allows switches to store packets from the ports operating at higher speeds (100/1000 Mbps) when it is necessary to send that information to ports operating at lower speeds (10 Mbps). Asymmetric switching is also better for client/server environments when the server is configured with a network card that is faster than the network cards of the clients. The switch allows the server's NIC to operate at 100 Mbps or greater and all the clients' NICs to operate at 10/100 Mbps, if necessary. This allows the server to handle the clients' requests more quickly than if it was limited to 10 Mbps.

Switches that require all attached network interface devices to use the same transmit/receive speed are using **symmetric switching**. For example, a symmetric switch could require all ports to operate at 100 Mbps or maybe at 10 Mbps, but not at a mix of the two speeds.

Securing Switch Ports

There are several degrees of security that you might employ on a switch. First, you can configure a permanent MAC address for a specific port on your switch. This means that only the specified MAC address will not "age out" of the CAM table. Second, you could define a static MAC address entry into your switching table, which maps a restricted communication path between two ports. For example, port 7 might be configured to send frames only through port 2 via a specific hardware address. Finally, you can configure port security. This stops people from plugging hubs into network connections on your LAN by setting a limit on the number of MAC addresses that can use a specific port.

To configure a permanent MAC address on a switch port, the switch must be in global configuration mode. The command follows this syntax on a 1900 series switch: *mac-address-table permanent hwaddress slot#/port#*. Therefore, to set the MAC address 0080c8e81256 to communicate on switch port 7 of your Catalyst 1900, host name Rm410HL, you would enter the following commands:

```
Rm410HL(config)#mac-address-table permanent
0080.c8e8.1256 ethernet0/7
```

Notice that you must separate the MAC address into three groups using dots. Otherwise, the syntax is similar to all the previous switch configuration syntax you have seen.

To configure a static entry, the command follows a similar syntax, but uses *restricted static* in place of *permanent*. However, more information is required because you are telling the switch to allow communications from a specific port to another specific port with a specific hardware address. For example, to configure port 6 to communicate only with port 12 and specify that all communications should be going to MAC address 0080c8e81259, you would enter the following commands for a 1900 series switch:

```
Rm410HL(config)#mac-address-table restricted static
0080.c8e8.1259 e0/6 e0/12
```

13

If you want to configure port security, the command syntax is quite different. Remember, the purpose of port security is to limit the number of hosts on one switch port. Therefore, you need only set the maximum number of devices that should be allowed to use a port. For example, assume that you have a five-port hub attached to port 10 of your switch. You want to be sure that only those five hosts (already attached) are allowed to use switch port 10. In that case, you would enter the following on the 1900 series switch:

```
Rm410HL(config)#interface e0/10
Rm410HL(config-if)#port secure max-mac-count 5
```

The correct commands for a 2950 series switch are:

```
Rm410HL(config)#interface f0/10
Rm410HL(config-if)#switchport port-security
Rm410HL(config-if)#switchport port-security maximum 5
```

This would restrict the port to learning five connected MAC addresses. (Keep in mind that when you put a hub with multiple nodes connected to it in a switch port, those users are sharing bandwidth and cannot take advantage of the switch's switched bandwidth capability.) You can either let the switch learn the MAC addresses of those five hosts on its own (as they communicate) or you can configure the five MAC addresses statically, as shown earlier. If the switch learns the address on its own, it is termed a **sticky-learn** by Cisco. This means that the switch, when configured for a maximum limit, will learn that many addresses and configure them automatically as permanent.

On the 2950 series switch, you can also define the action that will be taken when a security violation occurs. The syntax for this configuration is switchport port-security violation [*protect* | *restrict* | *shutdown*]. The protect option stops forwarding of traffic from any host that connects after the maximum number of MAC addresses has been learned. In our example the maximum number of MAC addresses is five. If the port was set to protect, the sixth address and any subsequent new MAC addresses on the port would not be allowed to communicate. The restrict option also stops all traffic above the number of defined MAC addresses. In addition, it sends an alert that a security violation has occurred. The final option, shutdown, shuts the port down if a security violation occurs.

Switching Methods

All switches base frame-forwarding decisions on a frame's destination MAC address. However, all switches do not forward frames in the same way. There are three main methods for processing and forwarding frames: cut-through, store-and-forward, and fragment-free. One additional forwarding method was derived from cut-through and store-and-forward. It is called adaptive cut-through. Cisco switches come with a menu system that allows you to choose from the available switch modes, as shown in Figure 13-4.

```
Catalyst 2820 - System Configuration
System Revision: 0 Address Capacity: 2048
System UpTime: 2day(s) 21hour(s) 15 minute(s) 4second(s)
-----------Settings-----------
[N] Name of system
[C] Contact name
[L] Location
[S] Switching mode                        FragmentFree
[U] Use of store-and-forward for multicast   Disabled
[A] Action upon address violation          Suspend
[G] Generate alert on address violation     Enabled
[I] Address aging time                    300 seconds
[P] Network Port                            None
[H] Half duplex back pressure (10-mbps ports) Disabled
[E] Enhanced Congestion Control (10 Mbps Ports) Disabled
-------------Actions-------------
[R] Reset system              [F] Reset to factory defaults
-----------Related Menus-------------
[B] Broadcast storm control      [X] Exit to Main Menu
Enter Selection:
```

Figure 13-4   Catalyst 2820 switching menu

The figure illustrates the configuration menu for a Cisco Catalyst 2820 switch. Notice that the menu option [S] allows you to toggle switching modes and that the switch is currently set for fragment-free.

The four switching modes are based on varying levels of latency (delay) and error reduction in forwarding frames. For example, cut-through offers the least latency and least reduction in error propagation, whereas store-and-forward switching offers the best error reduction services, but also the highest latency. Each of these switching methods is described in greater detail in the following sections.

Cut-Through

Switches that use **cut-through** forwarding start sending a frame immediately after reading the destination MAC address into their buffers. The main benefit of forwarding the frame immediately is a reduction in latency, because the forwarding decision is made almost immediately after the frame is received. For example, the switching decision is made after receiving 14 bytes of a standard Ethernet frame, as shown in Figure 13-5.

Ethernet Frame

7 bytes	1 byte	6 bytes	6 bytes	2 bytes	variable	4 bytes
Preamble	SFD	Destination address	Source address	Length	Data	FCS

Read into switch buffer

Figure 13-5   Portion of packet read into buffer by a cut-through switch

Cisco routers use the term **fast forward** to indicate that a switch is in cut-through mode.

The drawback to forwarding the frame immediately is that there might be errors in the frame, and the switch would be unable to catch those errors because it only reads a small portion of the frame into its buffer. Of course, any errors that occur in the **preamble**, **start frame delimiter (SFD)**, or destination address fields will not be propagated by the switch, unless they are corrupted in such a way as to appear valid, which is highly unlikely.

Store-and-Forward

Store-and-forward switches read the entire frame, no matter how large, into their buffers before forwarding, as shown in Figure 13-6. Because the switch reads the entire frame, it will not forward frames with errors to other ports.

Ethernet Frame

7 bytes	1 byte	6 bytes	6 bytes	2 bytes	variable	4 bytes
Preamble	SFD	Destination address	Source address	Length	Data	FCS

Entire frame read into switch buffer

Figure 13-6   Entire packet read into buffer by a store-and-forward switch

However, because the entire frame is read into the buffer and checked for errors, the store-and-forward method has the highest latency.

Standard bridges typically use the store-and-forward technique.

Fragment-Free

Fragment-free switching represents an effort to provide more error-reducing benefits than cut-through switching, while keeping latency lower than does store-and-forward switching. A fragment-free switch reads the first 64 bytes of an Ethernet frame and then begins forwarding it to the appropriate port(s), as shown in Figure 13-7.

Ethernet Frame

7 bytes	1 byte	6 bytes	6 bytes	2 bytes		variable	4 bytes
Preamble	SFD	Destination address	Source address	Length		Data	FCS

|← 64 bytes read into switch buffer →|

Figure 13-7   Amount of packet read into buffer by a fragment-free switch

By reading the first 64 bytes, the switch will catch the vast majority of Ethernet errors and still provide lower latency than a store-and-forward switch. (Of course, for Ethernet frames that are 64 bytes long, the fragment-free switch is essentially a store-and-forward switch.)

NOTE   Fragment-free switches are also known as **modified cut-through** switches.

Adaptive Cut-Through

Another variation of the switching techniques described earlier is the **adaptive cut-through** switch (also known as **error sensing**). For the most part, the adaptive cut-through switch will act as a cut-through switch to provide the lowest latency. However, if a certain level of errors is detected, the switch will change forwarding techniques and act more as a store-and-forward switch. Switches that have this capability are usually the most expensive, but provide the best compromise between error reduction and frame-forwarding speed.

Changing the Switching Mode

If you want to see the type of switching method that your Cisco Catalyst 1900 switch is using, you can issue the show port system command from the enable mode prompt. The default switching type on the 1900 is fragment-free. To change the switching mode to store-and-forward, you would use the following command from global configuration mode:

```
Rm410HL(config)#switching-mode store-and-forward
```

The Catalyst 1900 supports two different modes: fragment-free and store-and-forward. When you change the switching type, you change it for all ports on the switch.

13

Spanning Tree Protocol

In networks that have several switches and bridges, there might be **physical path loops**. Physical path loops occur when network devices are connected to one another by two or more physical media links. The physical loops are desirable for network fault tolerance because if one path fails, another will be available. Consider the network shown in Figure 13-8; the four devices (two switches and two bridges) are configured in a physical as well as **logical loop**.

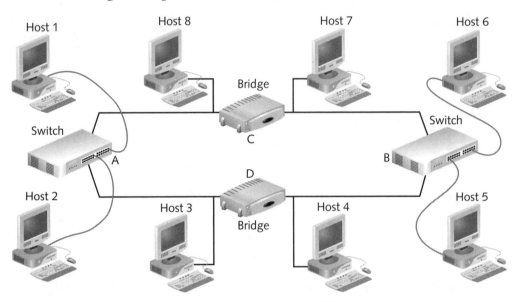

Figure 13-8   Physical loop created on LAN by switches and bridges

Assume that Host 1, which is attached to Switch A, sends out a frame with the destination MAC address of Host 5; there are actually two routes the packet can travel. The packet can be sent from Switch A to Bridge C or Bridge D. From there, it can be sent to Switch B, from which it can be forwarded to Host 5. The benefit of this configuration is that if either Bridge C or Bridge D fails, another path between Switch A and Switch B still exists.

NOTE   This sample network could have been configured with all switches, all bridges, or any combination thereof. The number of switches and bridges is not important; the important point is that when switches and bridges are interconnected, they might create a physical loop.

The drawback to the configuration is that endless packet looping can occur on this network, due to the existence of the physical loop. In other words, a frame can be sent continuously from one device to another, and the final destination might never be found. For example, assume that the MAC address for a station is not in any of the switching or bridging tables on the network. The packet could be forwarded endlessly around the network from bridge to switch to bridge.

The **Spanning Tree Protocol (STP)** was invented by Radia Perlman while she was with Digital Equipment Corporation (now Compaq) in the 1980s. It is a layer 2 link management protocol designed to prevent looping on bridges and switches. The specification for STP is IEEE 802.1d. STP uses the **Spanning Tree Algorithm (STA)** to interrupt the logical loop created by a physical loop in a bridged/switched environment. STP does this by ensuring that certain ports on some of the bridges and switches do not forward frames. In this way, a physical loop exists, but a logical loop does not. If a device fails, STP can be used to activate a new logical path over the physical network.

Building a Logical Path

With STP enabled, the switches and bridges on a network use an election process to configure a single logical path. First, a **root bridge (root device)** is selected. Then, the other switches and bridges configure their ports, using the root bridge as a point of reference. STP-enabled devices determine the root bridge via an administratively set priority number; the device with the lowest priority becomes the root bridge. If the priorities of two or more devices are the same, then the devices will make the decision based on the lowest MAC address.

NOTE When STP-enabled devices are first enabled on a LAN, they assume that they are the root device, which begins the election process.

Bridges use STP to transfer the information about each bridge's MAC address and priority number. The messages the devices send to one another are called **bridge protocol data units (BPDU)** or **configuration bridge protocol data units (CBPDU)**. Once the STP devices on the network select a root bridge, each bridge or switch determines which of its own ports offers the best path to the root bridge. The BPDU messages are sent between the root bridge and the best ports on the other devices, which are called **root ports**. The BPDUs transfer messages about the status of the network. If BPDUs are not received for a certain period of time, the non-root-bridge devices will assume that the root bridge has failed, and a new root bridge will be elected. The devices will then reconfigure their ports on the basis of the paths available to the new root bridge. During this period of reconfiguration, no data traffic is sent or received; only BPDUs are received on the ports.

13

Once the root bridge is determined and the switches and bridges have calculated their paths to the root bridge, the logical loop is removed by one of the switches or bridges. The switch or bridge will do this by blocking the port that creates the logical loop. This blocking is done by calculating costs for each port in relation to the root bridge and then disabling the port with the highest cost. For example, refer back to Figure 13-8 and assume that Switch A has been elected the root bridge. Switch B would have to block one of its ports to remove the logical loop from the network.

Port States

STP will cause the ports on a switch or bridge to settle into a stable state. **Stable states** are the normal operating states of ports when the root bridge is available and all paths are functioning as expected. STP devices use transitory states when the network configuration is undergoing some type of change, such as a root bridge failure. The **transitory states** prevent logical loops during a period of transition from one root bridge to another.

The stable states are as follows:

- **Blocking:** The port is sending and receiving the STP messages (BPDUs), but it is not receiving or forwarding data frames, in order to prevent logical loops in the network.

- **Forwarding:** The port is receiving and forwarding data frames, learning new MAC addresses, and sending and receiving BPDUs. All of the ports on a root bridge are configured for forwarding.

- **Disabled:** The port is disabled and is neither sending or receiving BPDUs nor forwarding or receiving frames.

The transitory states are as follows:

- **Listening:** The port is listening to frames so that a new root can be selected; it is not receiving or forwarding data frames, and it is not learning new MAC addresses.

- **Learning:** The port is learning new MAC addresses based on incoming frames, but it is not yet receiving or forwarding data frames.

STP devices use the transitory states on ports while a new root bridge is being elected. During the listening state, STP devices are configured to receive only the BPDUs that inform them of network status. STP devices use the learning state as a transition once the new root has been selected, but all the bridging or switching tables are still being updated. Because the routes may have changed, the old entries must either be timed out or replaced with new entries. Ports on STP-enabled devices move through the different states as indicated in the following list:

- From bridge/switch bootup to blocking

- From blocking to listening (or to disabled)

- From listening to learning (or to disabled)

- From learning to forwarding (or to disabled)

- From forwarding to disabled

In a completely configured and stable STP topology, all ports will be in either the forwarding or blocking state. There will only be one root device (bridge or switch) and all other devices will have one designated root port. All of the root ports on each device and all of the ports on the root bridge will be in the forwarding state.

Topology Changes

When the topology is changed, STP-enabled devices react automatically. If a device in an STP-enabled network stops receiving CBPDUs, then that device will claim to be the root bridge and will begin sending CBPDUs describing itself as such. This begins the rebuilding process, which is the same as the initial building of the STP topology. This event occurs when the root bridge fails or becomes separated from the other devices. Each device claims to be the root bridge for a short period until a new root bridge is elected.

VIRTUAL LANs

A **virtual LAN (VLAN)** is a grouping of network devices that is not restricted to a physical segment or switch. VLANs can be configured on most switches to restructure broadcast domains similarly to the way that bridges, switches, and routers divide collision domains. A **broadcast domain** is a group of network devices that will receive LAN broadcast traffic from each other.

NOTE

Because switches and bridges forward broadcast traffic to all ports, by default, they do not separate broadcast domains. Routers are the only devices previously mentioned that both segment the network and divide broadcast domains, because routers do not forward broadcasts by default.

By default, every port on a switch is in VLAN 1. This is the **management VLAN** (also known as the **default VLAN**), and it cannot be deleted. You can create multiple VLANs on a single switch or even create one VLAN across multiple switches; however, the most common configuration is to create multiple VLANs across multiple switches. With the latter configuration, routers must be used to move the traffic between the VLANs. Consider the network configuration shown in Figure 13-9, which does not employ VLANs. Notice that two broadcast domains are created, one on each side of the router.

13

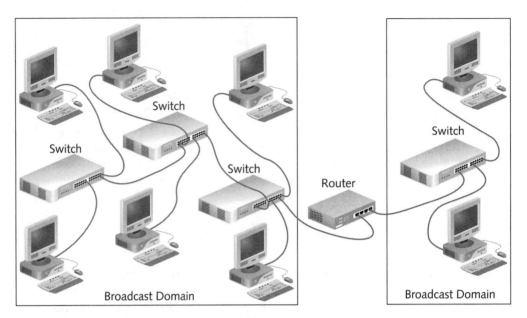

Figure 13-9   Broadcast domains on a LAN

Now consider the same network with VLANs implemented, as shown in Figure 13-10. The broadcast domains can now be further subdivided because of the VLAN configuration. This, of course, is only one way in which VLANs can be used to divide a broadcast domain.

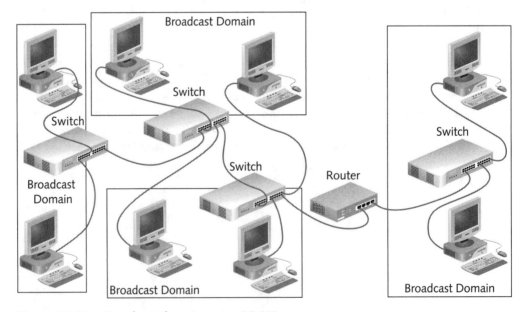

Figure 13-10   Broadcast domains using VLANs

Although VLANs can separate broadcast domains, as can routers, this does not mean that they segment at layer 3. A VLAN is a layer 2 implementation, and does not affect layer 3 logical addressing.

Benefits of VLANs

The benefits of using VLANs center on the idea that the administrator can divide a LAN logically without changing the actual physical configuration. This ability provides the administrator with several benefits:

- It is easier to add and move stations on the LAN.
- It is easier to reconfigure the LAN.
- There is better traffic control.
- There is increased security.

Cisco states that 20% to 40% of the workforce is moved every year. 3Com, another manufacturer of switching equipment, states that 23% of the cost of a network administration team is spent implementing changes and moves. VLANs help to reduce this cost because many changes can be made at the switch. In addition, physical moves do not necessitate the changing of IP addresses and subnets because the VLAN can be made to span multiple switches. Therefore, if a small group is moved to another office, a reconfiguration of the switch to include those ports in the previous VLAN may be all that is required.

In the same way that the VLAN can be used to accommodate a physical change, it can also be used to implement one. For example, assume that a department needs to be divided into two sections, each requiring a separate LAN. Without VLANs, the change may necessitate the physical rewiring of several stations. However, with VLANs available, the change can be made easily by dividing the ports on the switch that connect to the separate sections. Network reconfigurations of this nature are much easier to implement when VLANs are an option.

13

Because the administrator can set the size of the broadcast domain, the VLAN gives the administrator added control over network traffic. Implementing switching already reduces collision traffic immensely; dividing the broadcast domains further reduces traffic on the wire. In addition, the administrator can decide which stations should be sending broadcast traffic to each other.

Dividing the broadcast domains into logical groups increases security because it is much more difficult for someone to tap a network port and figure out the configuration of the LAN. Thus, the actual physical layout of the LAN is hidden from would-be network spies. Furthermore, the VLAN allows the administrator to make servers behave as if they were distributed throughout the LAN, when in fact they can all be locked up physically in a single central location.

As an example of this flexibility, consider Figure 13-11. All the servers are locked in the secured server room, yet they are servicing their individual clients. Notice that even the clients of the different VLANs are not located on the same switches. The figure illustrates the true flexibility of using VLANs, because the logical configuration of the network is quite different from the physical configuration.

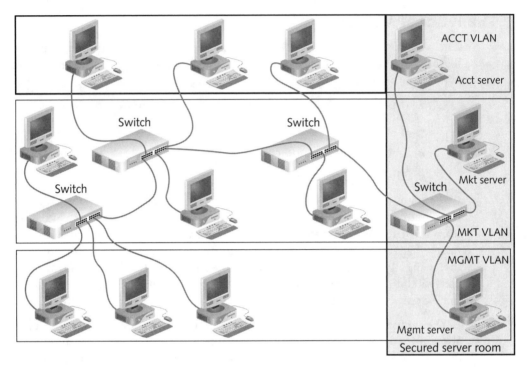

Figure 13-11   Securing servers with VLANs

In addition to allowing for the physical security of mission-critical servers, VLANs can be configured by network administrators to allow membership only for certain devices. Network administrators can do this with the management software included with the switch. The restrictions that can be used are similar to those of a firewall; unwanted users can be flagged or disabled, and administrative alerts can be sent if someone attempts to infiltrate a given VLAN. This type of security is typically implemented by grouping switch ports together according to the type of applications and access privileges required.

Dynamic vs. Static VLANs

Depending on the switch and switch management software, VLANs can be configured statically or dynamically. Static VLANs are configured port-by-port, with each port being associated with a particular VLAN. In a static VLAN, the network administrator manually types in the mapping for each port and VLAN.

Dynamic VLAN ports can automatically determine their VLAN configuration. Although they may seem easier to configure than static VLANs, given the description thus far, that is not quite the case. The dynamic VLAN uses a software database of MAC address-to-VLAN mappings that is created manually. This means that the MAC addresses and corresponding VLANs must be entered and maintained by the network administration team. Instead of saving administrative time, the dynamic VLAN could prove to be more time-consuming than the static VLAN. To its credit, however, the dynamic VLAN does allow the network administration team to keep the entire administrative database in one location. Furthermore, on a dynamic VLAN, it doesn't matter if a cable is moved from one switch port to another, because the VLAN will automatically reconfigure its ports on the basis of the attached workstation's MAC address. This is the real advantage of using dynamic VLAN systems.

VLAN Standardization

Before VLAN was an IEEE standard, early implementations depended on the switch vendor and on a method known as **frame filtering**. Frame filtering was a complex process that involved one table for each VLAN and a master table that was shared by all VLANs. This process allowed for a more sophisticated VLAN separation because frames could be separated into VLANs via MAC address, network-layer protocol type, or application type. The switches would then look up the information and make a forwarding decision based on the table entries.

When creating its VLAN standard, the IEEE did not choose the frame-filtering method. Instead, the **IEEE 802.1q** specification that defines VLANs recommends **frame tagging** (also known as **frame identification**). Frame tagging involves adding a four-byte field to the actual Ethernet frame to identify the VLAN and other pertinent information. The members of the IEEE considered this solution to be more scalable (able to accommodate larger networks) than frame filtering.

Frame tagging makes it easier and more efficient to ship VLAN frames across network backbones because switches on the other side of the backbone can simply read the frame instead of being required to refer back to a frame-filtering table. In this way, the frame-tagging method implemented at layer 2 is similar to routing layer 3 addressing because the identification for each frame is contained within the frame. A tagged frame can be as large as 1522 bytes, whereas a normal Ethernet frame is limited to 1518 bytes. Devices that are not VLAN-aware would see a 1522-byte frame as a long frame (a frame larger than normal size) or jabber.

The two most common types of frame tagging (encapsulation) are 802.1q and **Inter-Switch Link (ISL) protocol**. ISL is a Cisco proprietary frame-tagging method that uses a 26-byte header. It only works between Cisco devices. If you need a frame-tagging method that works between Cisco and another vendor, you will have to use 802.1q frame tagging. The Cisco 1900 series switch only supports ISL. The lowest-level Cisco router that supports ISL is the 2600 series. Other Cisco switches support additional types of frame tagging, such as **LAN emulation (LANE)** and **IEEE 802.10 (FDDI)**.

13

NOTE The additional header with the VLAN addressing information is typically stripped off the frame before it reaches the connected host stations. Otherwise, non-VLAN-aware host stations would see the additional information as a long frame or jabber.

Creating VLANs

Creating VLANs on the Cisco Catalyst 1900 switch using the command line interface is fairly straightforward. You name the VLANs individually via global configuration mode. For example, assume you want to create three VLANs on your switch (host name Rm410HL). The three VLANs are production, accounting, and marketing. (There will actually be four VLANs when you are finished, because the default VLAN, VLAN 1, is assumed.) Look at the following command sequence, which shows how to create and list VLANs on a Cisco Catalyst 1900:

```
Rm410HL>enable
Rm410HL#configure terminal
Rm410HL(config)#vlan 2 name production
Rm410HL(config)#vlan 3 name accounting
Rm410HL(config)#vlan 4 name marketing
Rm410HL(config)#exit
Rm410HL#show vlan
```

VLAN Name	Status	Ports
1 default	Enabled	1–12, AUI, A, B
2 production	Enabled	
3 accounting	Enabled	
4 marketing	Enabled	

[remaining output cut]

Here is the command sequence for the 2950 series switch configuration:

```
Rm410HL>enable
Rm410HL#vlan database
Rm410HL(vlan)#vlan 2 name production
Rm410HL(vlan)#vlan 3 name accounting
Rm410HL(vlan)#vlan 4 name marketing
Rm410HL(vlan)#exit
Rm410HL#show vlan
```

Notice that all ports are still assigned to the default VLAN. Notice also that the Fast Ethernet ports 26 and 27 are displayed as A and B, respectively. The next step is to assign switch ports to the new VLANs. Ports can be assigned as static or dynamic. Assigning dynamic VLANs is more complicated and is not a requirement for CCNA candidates. The commands to assign static ports to VLANs are shown next. The commands have to be entered port-by-port because there is no single command to assign multiple switch ports to a VLAN. Assume that you want to assign port 5 to VLAN 2, port 7 to VLAN 3, and port 9 to VLAN 4 on a 1900 series switch.

```
Rm410HL(config)#interface e0/5
Rm410HL(config-if)#vlan-membership static 2
Rm410HL(config-if)#exit
Rm410HL(config)#interface e0/7
Rm410HL(config-if)#vlan-membership static 3
Rm410HL(config-if)#exit
Rm410HL(config)#interface e0/9
Rm410HL(config-if)#vlan-membership static 4
Rm410HL(config-if)#exit
Rm410HL(config)#exit
Rm410HL#show vlan
```

To configure the same ports on the 2950, use the following commands:

```
Rm410HL(config)#interface f0/5
Rm410HL(config-if)#switchport access vlan 2
Rm410HL(config-if)#exit
Rm410HL(config)#interface f0/7
Rm410HL(config-if)#switchport access vlan 3
Rm410HL(config-if)#exit
Rm410HL(config)#interface f0/9
Rm410HL(config-if)#switchport access vlan 4
Rm410HL(config-if)#exit
Rm410HL(config)#exit
Rm410HL#show vlan
```

VLAN Name	Status	Ports
1 default	Enabled	1-4, 6, 8, 10-12
2 production	Enabled	5
3 accounting	Enabled	7
4 marketing	Enabled	9

[remaining output cut]

NOTE

You can use the show vlan [#] command to gather information about a specific VLAN (instead of listing all VLANs). The show vlan-membership command gives a variation of the same output as the show vlan command.

13

Link Types and Configuration

There are two types of links on Cisco switches: trunk links and access links. Trunk links are switch-to-switch or switch-to-router links that can carry traffic from multiple VLANs. Frame tagging is used to keep track of different VLANs between VLAN-aware connectivity devices. Access links are links to non-VLAN-aware devices such as hubs and individual workstations. These devices have no need to understand VLANs and they operate as if they were on a single broadcast domain.

Trunk links can only be applied to the 100-Mbps (Fast Ethernet) or greater Ethernet ports on a switch. 10-Mbps ports cannot be designated as trunk links. On a Catalyst 1900 switch, the Fast Ethernet ports 26 and 27 are capable of being trunk links. As previously mentioned, port 26 is known as Trunk A and port 27 is Trunk B.

There are five different states that you can set for a trunk link, as follows:

- Auto: Configure this interface for trunking only if the connected device is set to on or desirable.

- Desirable: The interface will become a trunk port if the connected device is on, desirable, or auto.

- Nonegotiate: The interface is a trunk interface and will not negotiate that status with any other device.

- Off: The interface is not a trunk interface and will attempt to disable trunking on attached devices.

- On: The interface is a trunk interface and will try to enable trunking on attached devices.

To configure a trunk link on a Catalyst 1900, you must be in the appropriate interface configuration mode. Remember, you only have two possible interfaces: 26 or 27. Assume you have port 26 of your Catalyst 1900 named Rm410HL connected to another switch. You decide that port 26 is your trunk link and you want it to encourage other devices to be trunk links. The commands to complete this operation on a 1900 series switch are as follows:

```
Rm410HL#config term
Rm410HL(config)#int f0/26
Rm410HL(config-if)#trunk on
```

To set a trunk port on a 2950 series switch:

```
Rm410HL#config term
Rm410HL(config)#int fastethernet 0/26
Rm410HL(config-if)#switchport mode trunk
```

By default, all VLANs are now enabled to be routed over this newly configured trunk link. There is no command to selectively enable VLANs for trunking. However, you can selectively clear a VLAN from a trunk link. For example, let's assume that you don't want packets from VLAN 7 to traverse this link. You would clear VLAN 7 from the trunk on a 1900 series switch using this command:

```
Rm410HL(config-if)#no trunk-vlan 7
```

To verify that this operation was completed successfully, you would use the show trunk command on trunk A with the allowed-vlans option:

```
Rm410HL#show trunk a allowed-vlans

1-6, 8-1004
```

Notice that every VLAN between 1 and 1004 is listed with the exception of VLAN 7. The VLANs not listed as allowed are excluded from using this trunk link. While the Cisco 1900 switch supports 1005 VLANs, STP can only be used on 64 VLANs simultaneously. By default, STP is enabled on VLANs 1 through 64.

 There is a switching table for each VLAN, and there is a root bridge (switch) for each VLAN.

NOTE

Trunking Protocol

Cisco created the **VLAN trunking protocol (VTP)** to manage all of the configured VLANs that traverse trunks between switches. VTP is a layer 2 messaging protocol that manages all the changes to the VLANs across networks. Any changes made to a VLAN by an administrator (e.g., add, rename, or delete) are automatically propagated by VTP to all VTP-enabled devices.

VTP Domains

VTP devices are organized into domains. Each switch can only be in one **VTP domain** at a time, and all devices that need to share information must be in the same VTP domain. To configure a Catalyst 1900 switch for a VTP domain named hudlogic, you would enter the name of the switch:

```
Rm410HL(config)#VTP domain hudlogic
```

For a 2950 series switch, you would enter:

```
Rm410HL#vlan database
Rm410HL(vlan)#VTP domain hudlogic
```

You would have to perform the same command on all the switches that you expect to share VLAN information. When you make changes to the VTP configuration on your 1900 series switches, you should verify them with the show vtp command from enable mode.

```
Rm410HL(config)#exit
Rm410HL#show VTP
```

For a 2950 series switch, you would enter:

```
Rm410HL(vlan)#exit
Rm410HL#show VTP status
```

If all of your switches are in the same VLAN, there is no need to configure a VTP domain.

NOTE

VTP Device Modes

There are three different modes for VTP-enabled devices: server, client, and transparent. Catalyst switches default to server mode, which means that they can add, rename, and delete VLANs and propagate those changes to the rest of the VTP devices. VTP servers save the VLAN configuration information in NVRAM. You must have at least one **VTP server** in your VTP domain. When a device is placed in **VTP client** mode, it is not allowed to make changes to the VLAN structure, but it can receive, interpret, and propagate changes made by a server. Clients do not save the VTP configuration in NVRAM. **VTP transparent** mode means that a device is not participating in VTP communications, other than to forward that information through its configured trunk links.

To configure a Catalyst 1900 switch as a server, client, or transparent mode device, you can enter the appropriate vtp command from global configuration mode. For example, to configure your 1900 series switch as a client, you would enter:

```
Rm410HL#config term
Rm410HL(config)#vtp client
```

To configure a 2950 series switch as a client requires the following commands:

```
Rm410HL#vlan database
Rm410HL(vlan)#vtp client
```

To set the switch back to server mode or to transparent mode, you would type "server" or "transparent" (respectively) instead of "client."

VTP Pruning

The **VTP pruning** option reduces the number of VTP updates that traverse a link. It is off by default on all switches. If you turn VTP pruning on, VTP message broadcasts are only sent through trunk links that must have the information. For example, if a Catalyst 1900 switch with two trunks receives an update concerning VLAN 7 on Trunk A (port 26), it will typically forward that update through Trunk B (port 27), assuming both ports are enabled for trunking.

However, assume that you have removed VLAN 7 from Trunk B. The update would still be forwarded out of Trunk B unless you enabled VTP pruning. VTP pruning can be enabled on a VTP device configured as a server. When you enable VTP pruning on a server, you enable it on every device in the entire domain. The command to enable and disable VTP pruning is straightforward: vtp pruning enable or vtp pruning disable from global configuration mode. For example, to enable VTP pruning on a Catalyst 1900 switch configured as a VTP server, you would use this command:

```
Rm410HL(config)#vtp pruning enable
```

To enable VTP pruning on the 2950 series switch:

```
Rm410HL(vlan)#vtp pruning
```

This will prune information as necessary for VLANs 2 through 1005. VLAN 1 is not eligible to be pruned because it is an administrative (and default) VLAN. Therefore, all updates for VLAN 1 will always traverse the switch.

When you add a new switch to a LAN, you should be sure to clear all VTP information, so as not to propagate it to the rest of the network. Use the following command on a 1900 series switch:

```
Rm410HL#delete vtp
```

To delete the VLAN information from a 2950 series switch:

```
Rm410HL#show flash
Rm410HL#delete flash:vlan.dat
```

Switch Interface Descriptions

You can configure a name for each port on a switch. This is useful when you begin to define roles for a switch port on a more global basis, such as when you configure VLANs. For example, perhaps you have dedicated port 1 on your switch to serve the production department's VLAN and port 26 on your switch to be a trunk to the next building (#777). You may decide to configure your switch interface descriptions on a 1900 series switch, as follows:

```
Rm410HL#configure terminal
Rm410HL(config)#int e0/1
Rm410HL(config-if)#description productionVLAN
Rm410HL(config-if)#int f0/26
Rm410HL(config-if)#description trunkBldg777
```

Descriptions can also be placed on a 2950 series switch:

```
Rm410HL#configure terminal
Rm410HL(config)#int f0/1
Rm410HL(config-if)#description productionVLAN
Rm410HL(config-if)#int f0/26
Rm410HL(config-if)#description trunkBldg777
```

13

Nonswitching Hubs and VLANs

When implementing hubs on a network that employs VLANs, you should keep a few important considerations in mind:

- If you insert a hub into a port on the switch and then connect several devices to the hub, all the systems attached to that hub will be in the same VLAN.

- If you must move a single workstation that is attached to a hub with several workstations, you will have to physically attach the device to another hub or switch port to change its VLAN assignment.

- The more hosts that are attached to individual switch ports, the greater the microsegmentation and flexibility the VLAN can offer.

Routers and VLANs

Routers can be used with VLANs to increase security and must be used to manage traffic between different VLANs. Typically a separate subinterface is configured on the router for each VLAN supported. In addition, the routers can implement **access lists**, which increase inter-VLAN security. Finally, the router allows restrictions to be placed on station addresses, application types, and protocol types. Figure 13-12 illustrates how a router might be implemented in a VLAN configuration.

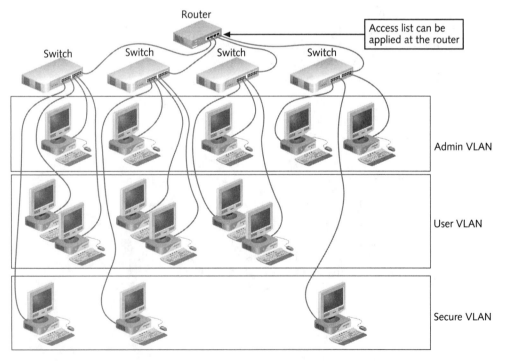

Figure 13-12   Router implemented in a VLAN configuration

The router in Figure 13-12 connects the four switches and routes communications among three different VLAN configurations. An access list on the router can restrict the communications between the separate VLANs. To configure a Cisco router for inter-VLAN communications, several steps are involved. First, enable ISL trunking on the switch port the router is connected to using the trunk on command. Next, assign an IP address to each subinterface on the router that will be associated with a VLAN. Finally, configure ISL encapsulation on the router subinterfaces. The following router commands illustrate how to enable inter-VLAN communications for VLANs 1 and 2 on a Cisco router that supports ISL.

```
Router(config)#interface e0.1
Router(config-subif)#ip address 164.106.1.1 255.255.255.0
Router(config-subif)#encapsulation isl 1
Router(config-if)#exit
Router(config)#interface e0.2
Router(config-subif)#ip address 164.106.2.1 255.255.255.0
Router(config-subif)#encapsulation isl 2
```

VLANs are created to logically segment hosts by function, application, or other common interest without regard to physical location. Grouping devices by VLANs will control the size of the broadcast domain and keep network traffic local. However, sometimes it is necessary to communicate with devices outside the VLAN. Because each VLAN is considered a different logical network, a router is required to move traffic between the two VLANs. The required router can either be an onboard **Route Switch Module (RSM)** or an external router. The router will accept the packet tagged by the sending VLAN and determine the best path to the destination address. The router will then switch the packet to the appropriate interface and forward it to the destination address. The router accomplishes the process of routing packets between two VLANs (two logical networks) in the same fashion as packets between two physical networks.

If a single link is used to connect an external router with the switch containing multiple VLANs, trunking is required for inter-VLAN routing. Trunking is the process of using either ISL or 802.1q to allow multiple VLAN traffic on the same link. For instance, an ISL trunk link would encapsulate each packet with the associated VLAN information and allow the router to route the packet accordingly. This scenario is often called a "router-on-a-stick" because of the process of pushing all the inter-VLAN traffic out a single switch port to the router and then having the traffic routed back to the same switch port to the destination VLAN.

13

You can see an example of routing between VLANS by configuring a 1700 router attached to a trunk link on a 2950XL switch. The configuration for each of these devices is:

The Router

```
Router>enable
Router#configure terminal
Router(config)#interface fastethernet0/0
Router(config-if)#full-duplex
Router(config-if)#no shutdown
Router(config-if)#exit
Router(config)#interface fastethernet0/0.1
Router(config-subif)#ip address 10.10.1.1 255.255.255.0
Router(config-subif)#encapsulation isl 1
Router(config-subif)#exit
Router(config)#interface fastethernet0/0.2
Router(config-subif)#ip address 10.10.2.1 255.255.255.0
Router(config-subif)#encapsulation isl 2
Router(config-subif)#exit
Router(config)#interface fastethernet0/0.3
Router(config-subif)#ip address 10.10.3.1 255.255.255.0
Router(config-subif)#encapsulation isl 3
Router(config-subif)#exit
Router(config)#interface fastethernet0/0.4
Router(config-subif)#ip address 10.10.4.1 255.255.255.0
Router(config-subif)#encapsulation isl 4
```

The Switch

```
Rm410HL>enable
Rm410HL#configure terminal
Rm410HL(config)#interface vlan 1
Rm410HL(config-if)#ip address 10.10.1.2 255.255.255.0
Rm410HL(config-if)#exit
Rm410HL(config)#ip default-gateway 10.10.1.1
Rm410HL(config)#exit
Rm410HL#vlan database
Rm410(vlan)#vtp domain hudlogic
Rm410(vlan)#vtp server
Rm410(vlan)#vlan 2 name production
Rm410(vlan)#vlan 3 name accounting
Rm410(vlan)#vlan 4 name marketing
Rm410(vlan)#exit
Rm410#configure terminal
Rm410(config)#interface f0/1
Rm410(config-if)#switchport mode trunk
Rm410(config-if)#exit
Rm410(config)#interface f0/2
Rm410(config-if)#switchport access vlan 1
Rm410(config-if)#exit
```

```
Rm410(config)#interface f0/3
Rm410(config-if)#switchport access vlan 2
Rm410(config-if)#exit
Rm410(config)#interface f0/4
Rm410(config-if)#switchport access vlan 3
Rm410(config-if)#exit
Rm410(config)#interface f0/5
Rm410(config-if)#switchport access vlan 4
```

CHAPTER SUMMARY

❑ Ethernet (CSMA/CD) is a media access method that was developed in the 1960s.

❑ Stations on an Ethernet LAN must listen to the network media before transmitting to ensure that no other station is currently transmitting.

❑ If two stations transmit simultaneously on the same collision domain, a collision will occur.

❑ The transmitting stations must be able to recognize the collision and ensure that other stations know about the collision by transmitting a jam signal. Once the jam signal has cleared the network, other stations can begin transmitting, but the stations that caused the collision must wait for a random backoff period before attempting to transmit again.

❑ The delays caused by collisions on a network can seriously affect performance when collisions exceed 5% of the traffic on the collision domain.

❑ One way to reduce the number of collisions on a network is to segment the network with a bridge, switch, or router.

❑ Switches do the most to divide the collision domain and reduce traffic without dividing the broadcast domain. This means that the LAN segment still appears to be a segment when it comes to broadcast and multicast traffic.

❑ However, a switch microsegments unicast traffic by routing frames directly from the incoming port to the destination port. This means that packets sent between two hosts on a LAN segment do not interrupt communication of other hosts on the segment. Switches are therefore able to increase the speed at which communications occur between multiple hosts on the segment.

❑ Another way to increase the speed at which a LAN operates is to upgrade from Ethernet to Fast Ethernet. This allows you to increase the speed at which frames are transferred on the wire, thereby increasing the performance of the network.

❑ To fully implement Fast Ethernet, you have to replace all the hubs, NICs, and any other network interfaces with interfaces that support Fast Ethernet. Several Fast Ethernet devices allow for compatibility between Fast Ethernet and standard Ethernet, but to take full advantage of Fast Ethernet, all components must be upgraded.

13

❑ Full duplex can also improve Ethernet performance over half-duplex operations because no collisions can occur on a full-duplex LAN.

❑ Full duplex also allows frames to be sent and received simultaneously, which makes a 10-Mbps full-duplex connection seem like two 10-Mbps half-duplex connections.

❑ As with Fast Ethernet, full-duplex operations are only supported by devices designed for this type of communication. This means that the half-duplex devices on a network will have to be completely replaced to take advantage of the speed offered by full-duplex operations.

❑ The Spanning Tree Protocol (STP), which is enabled by default on most bridges and switches, allows administrators to create physical loops between bridges and switches without creating logical loops that would pose a problem for packet delivery.

❑ Another way to increase the performance, flexibility, and security of a network is to implement VLANs via switches.

❑ VLANs are separate broadcast domains that are not limited by physical configurations. Instead, a VLAN is a logical broadcast domain implemented via one or more switches.

❑ Performance benefits associated with VLANs are derived from limiting the amount of broadcast traffic that would naturally pass through a switch without filtration. The enhanced flexibility to assign any port on any switch to a particular VLAN makes moving, adding, and changing network configurations easier.

❑ Because traffic on a VLAN broadcast can be limited to a specific group of computers, security is also enhanced by making it more difficult for eavesdropping systems to learn the configuration of a network. In addition, the microsegmentation of unicast traffic makes it even more difficult to intercept useful data passed between two hosts.

❑ VLAN information is communicated to switches using the VLAN trunking protocol (VTP).

KEY TERMS

100Base-FX — A Fast Ethernet implementation over multimode fiber-optic (MMF) cabling. The maximum segment length is 412 meters.

100Base-T4 — A 100-Mbps Fast Ethernet implementation that uses four pairs of either Category 3, 4, or 5 UTP cable. The maximum segment length is 100 meters.

100Base-TX — A Fast Ethernet implementation that uses two pairs of either Category 5 unshielded twisted-pair (UTP) or shielded twisted-pair (STP). 100Base-TX operates at 100 Mbps with a maximum segment distance of 100 meters.

5-4-3 rule — The networking rule that stipulates that between stations on a 10-Mbps half-duplex LAN, there can be no more than five wire segments connected, the maximum number of repeaters or hubs between the segments is four, and the maximum number of populated hubs is three.

access list — A list of criteria to which all packets are compared.

adaptive cut-through — A method of switching whereby the switch uses the cut-through technique unless network errors reach a certain threshold; then, it automatically switches to store-and-forward switching until the error rate returns to an acceptable level. Also known as **error sensing**.

alignment error — A frame that has both an FCS error and an entire octet missing from the frame.

asymmetric switching — A type of LAN switching that allows for multiple speeds of network communication; a switch that supports both 10-Mbps and 100-Mbps communications is an example of asymmetric switching.

backoff period — A random interval used by devices that have caused a collision on an Ethernet network, during which the devices cannot send, to prevent them from immediately causing another collision.

bit time — The duration of time to transmit one data bit on a network, which is 100 nanoseconds on a 10-Mbps Ethernet network or 10 nanoseconds on a 100-Mbps Ethernet network.

blocking — A port state on a switch that indicates the port is receiving and sending BPDUs, but is not receiving and forwarding data frames in order to prevent logical loops in the network.

bridge — A device that segments a network at the Data Link layer by filtering traffic based on the MAC address.

bridge protocol data unit (BPDU) — An STP management message used to transfer status information about the Spanning Tree configuration of a switched or bridged network. Also known as **configuration bridge protocol data unit (CBPDU)**.

bridging table — A table maintained on a bridge that maps MAC addresses to the bridge port through which they can be accessed.

broadcast — A frame that is addressed to all stations on the broadcast domain. The destination MAC address is set to FFFFFFFFFFFF so that all local stations will process the packet.

broadcast domain — A logical or physical group of devices that will receive broadcast traffic from each other on a LAN.

broadcast storm — An error condition in which broadcast traffic is above 126 packets per second and network communications are impeded. This is typically the result of a software configuration error or programming error.

Carrier Sense Multiple Access with Collision Detection (CSMA/CD) — An Ethernet networking method defined by IEEE standard 802.3, which states that an Ethernet station must first listen before transmitting on a network. Any station can transmit as long as there are no transmissions active on the network. If two stations transmit simultaneously, a collision will occur, and the stations must detect the collision and reset themselves.

carrier signal — A transmitted electromagnetic pulse or wave on the network wire that indicates a transmission is in progress.

13

collision domain — The area on a network in which collision can occur; a section of network that is not separated by routers, switches, or bridges.

configuration bridge protocol data unit (CBPDU) — *See* **bridge protocol data unit (BPDU)**.

content-addressable memory (CAM) — A memory location on a switch that contains the MAC address-to-switch port mapping information, which the switch uses to forward frames to the appropriate destination.

contention method — The method by which computers on a network must share the available capacity of the network wire with other computers.

cut-through — A switching technique in which an Ethernet frame is forwarded immediately after the destination address is deciphered. This method offers the lowest latency, but does not reduce packet errors.

default VLAN — The default configuration of every port on a switch. Same as VLAN 1.

disabled — A port state on a switch that indicates the port is neither receiving BPDUs nor forwarding frames.

error sensing — *See* **adaptive cut-through**.

Ethernet — *See* **Carrier Sense Multiple Access with Collision Detection (CSMA/CD)**.

Fast Ethernet — Defined in IEEE 802.3u, and includes any of the following 100-Mbps Ethernet LAN technologies: 100Base-T4, 100Base-TX, 100Base-FX.

fast forward — Indicates that a switch is in cut-through mode.

forwarding — The state of a port on a switch or bridge that indicates it will learn MAC addresses and forward frames out that port.

fragment-free — A method of switching whereby the switch reads the first 64 bytes of the incoming frame before forwarding it to the destination port(s).

frame check sequence (FCS) — A calculation based on the size of a transmitted data frame that verifies whether it was received intact.

frame check sequence (FCS) error — An error that occurs when the calculation in the FCS field indicates that a frame was not received intact.

frame filtering — A technique used on early VLAN implementations that employed the use of multiple switching tables.

frame identification — *See* **frame tagging**.

frame tagging — A method of VLAN identification endorsed by the IEEE 802.1q specification that calls for an additional four-byte field in the VLAN frame after the source and destination addresses in the data packet. Also known as **frame identification**.

full-duplex — A connection that allows communication in two directions at once; common telephone connections are typically full-duplex because people can talk and listen at the same time.

gateway — A combination of software and hardware that translates between different protocol suites.

giant — *See* **long frame**.

half-duplex — A connection that allows communication in two directions, but not simultaneously; the circuit can be used for sending or receiving bits in only one direction at a time.

IEEE 802.10 (FDDI) — A frame-tagging method used to identify VLANs trunked across Fiber Distributed Data Interfaces (FDDI).

IEEE 802.1q — The IEEE standard that defines VLAN implementations and recommends frame tagging as the way in which switches should identify VLANs. Used by Cisco switches for compatibility with non-Cisco switches.

IEEE 802.3u — The IEEE standard that defines Fast Ethernet implementations, including 100Base-T4, 100Base-TX, and 100Base-FX.

Inter-Switch Link (ISL) protocol — A frame-tagging method for VLANs proprietary to Cisco devices. Uses a 26-byte header.

interframe gap — The time required between the transmission of data frames on the network: 9.6 microseconds.

interpacket gap (IPG) — *See* **interframe gap**.

jabber — A frame that is longer than the 1518 bytes acceptable for transmission between stations and that also has an FCS error.

jam signal — A 32-bit signal that is sent by the first station to detect a collision on an Ethernet network; ensures that all other stations are aware of the collision.

LAN emulation (LANE) — A frame-tagging method used for VLANs on Asynchronous Transfer Mode (ATM) devices.

late collision — A situation that occurs when two stations transmit more than 64 bytes of their frames before detecting a collision.

latency — The lag or delay that a device or part of the network media causes; for example, fiber-optic cable delays a transmitted signal 1 bit time every 10 meters.

learning — A transitory state on a bridge or switch port that indicates it is trying to learn new MAC addresses and correct its bridge table before forwarding frames on the network; used to prevent loops during the election of a new root bridge.

listening — A transitory state on a bridge or switch port that is used during the election of a new root bridge; the port does not learn MAC addresses, nor does it forward data frames when in this state.

logical loop — A situation that occurs when a packet can be routed in an endless loop around a network, because bridging tables and routing tables reference each other as the destination for a given address.

long frame — An Ethernet frame that is over the 1518 bytes acceptable for transmission between stations.

management VLAN — The default configuration of every port on a switch. Same as VLAN 1.

media access method — *See* **network access method**.

microsegmentation — Increasing the number of collision domains without increasing the number of subnets.

modified cut-through — *See* **fragment-free**.

13

multicast — A frame that is addressed to a group of systems; typically used in radio- or television-style broadcasting on the network.

multimode fiber-optic (MMF) cable — Fiber-optic cabling that allows for multiple simultaneous light transmissions.

multiport bridge — Another name for a switch.

network access method — The process by which network interface cards and devices communicate data on a network; an example is CSMA/CD. Also known as **media access method**.

NIC error — An error that indicates a NIC is unable to transmit or receive a packet.

physical path loops — A loop that occurs when network devices are connected to one another by two or more physical media links.

port-based memory buffering — A memory buffer on a switch assigned by port, equally; doesn't allow for dynamic allocation of buffer space according to the activity level of a port.

preamble — Binary timing information that precedes an Ethernet frame; used by the receiving station to synchronize its clock circuits so the frame can be received correctly.

propagation delay — *See* **latency**.

protocol analyzer — A hardware or software device that can capture and analyze network packets, help you analyze traffic flow and packet errors, and track network problems.

root bridge — The bridge or switch that is designated the point of reference (point of origin) in STP operations. Also known as a root device.

root device — *See* **root bridge**.

root port — The communications port on a non-root bridge device that is used for BPDU communication between itself and the root bridge.

Route Switch Module (RSM) — A router placed on a switch blade; common with high-end Cisco switches such as the Catalyst 6500.

router — A device that segments a network at the Network layer by filtering on logical addresses. Creates networks or subnetworks.

runt — *See* **short frame**.

shared memory buffering — Dynamic memory buffer that is shared by all switch ports and allocated according to the needs of the ports; ports that have more activity and larger frames to process are allowed to use more memory buffer space.

short frame — A frame that is smaller than the 64-byte minimum frame transmission size required by Ethernet.

slot time — 512 bit times, which should be slightly longer than the time it takes to transmit a 64-byte frame on an Ethernet wire.

Spanning Tree Algorithm (STA) — The algorithm used by STP to ensure that logical loops are not created in the presence of physical loops on a network.

Spanning Tree Protocol (STP) — The Data Link layer protocol used by switches and bridges to prevent logical loops in a network, even though physical loops may exist.

stable state — The normal states of ports when the root bridge is available and all paths are functioning as expected.

start frame delimiter (SFD) — The one-octet binary pattern (10101011) that indicates the preamble is over and that the following information should be considered the actual data frame.

sticky-learn — A term used when a switch automatically learns MAC addresses during communications and configures them as permanent, due to a limit set by an administrator on the number of MAC addresses that can use a particular port.

store-and-forward — A switching method in which the entire transmitted frame is read into a switch's buffer before being forwarded by the switch. This method offers the greatest error reduction, but the highest latency. *See* **cut-through** and **adaptive cut-through**.

switch — A device that connects devices on a LAN and segments collision domains by port.

switched bandwidth — A switching technique whereby the total network bandwidth is dedicated to each unicast transmission, even if there are multiple unicast transmissions through the switch at the same time. Unicast traffic between devices on a switch do not share the total bandwidth of the network.

symmetric switching — A type of LAN switching that requires all devices to be operating at the same speed; it does not allow for a mix of 10-Mbps and 100-Mbps communications.

transitory state — The operating states of ports that prevent logical loops during a period of transition from one root bridge to another.

transmission time — The time it takes for a transmission to go from the source host to the destination host.

unicast — A frame that is sent or addressed to a single destination host; compare with multicast and broadcast.

virtual LAN (VLAN) — A logical broadcast domain on a LAN, created by one or more switches, that is not constrained by the physical configuration.

VLAN trunking protocol (VTP) — A Data Link layer protocol used to track VLAN membership changes across trunk links between VTP-enabled devices.

VTP client — A VTP device that receives and shares VTP information, but does not add, modify, or delete information and does not store the VTP database in NVRAM.

VTP domain — A group of VTP-enabled devices configured under one name to share VLAN information.

VTP pruning — An option configured for an entire VTP domain that prohibits the forwarding of VTP updates about VLANs disabled on specific trunk links.

VTP server — A VTP device that is capable of adding, modifying, sending, and deleting VTP configuration information.

VTP transparent — A device that does not participate in receiving or managing VTP domains, but will forward VTP information through its trunk ports.

13

REVIEW QUESTIONS

1. The IEEE standard 802.1q recommends which type of VLAN identification method?

   a. Frame filtering

   b. Frame tagging

   c. Frame segmenting

   d. Frame sequencing

2. Which of the following types of switching methods reads the first 64 bytes of a frame before forwarding it?

   a. Store-and-forward

   b. Cut-through

   c. Fragment-free

   d. Adaptive

3. The _____ provides sufficient spacing between frames so that network interfaces have time to process a packet before receiving another.

   a. interframe gap

   b. jam signal

   c. backoff period

   d. latency

4. Which devices look at a MAC address when making their forwarding decision? (Choose all that apply.)

   a. Switch

   b. Repeater

   c. Bridge

   d. Router

5. Which of the following network media provides the lowest latency?

   a. STP

   b. Category 3 UTP

   c. Category 4 UTP

   d. Category 5 UTP

   e. Fiber-optic cable

6. Which of the following correctly describes microsegmentation?

   a. Creating additional segments with passive hubs

   b. Creating additional segments with routers

   c. Creating additional segments with fewer users per segment via layer 2

   d. Limiting network segments to no more than 10 users

7. Which of the following Ethernet errors describes a packet that has a bad FCS and is over 1518 bytes?

   a. Runt

   b. Short

   c. Jabber

   d. Bad FCS frame

8. When two Ethernet stations can send more than 64 bytes of their data frames before detecting a collision, this is called a _____.

   a. jabber

   b. jam signal

   c. slot time

   d. late collision

9. The minimum size of an Ethernet frame should be _____ bytes.

   a. 32

   b. 64

   c. 512

   d. 1518

10. Collisions and Ethernet errors typically occur within the first _____ bytes of an Ethernet frame, which is why fragment-free switching catches most Ethernet errors.

    a. 64

    b. 512

    c. 1024

    d. 1518

13

11. Which of the following describes a method of Ethernet networking that does not have collisions?

    a. Fast Ethernet

    b. 100-Mbps Ethernet

    c. Full-duplex Ethernet

    d. Half-duplex Ethernet

12. Which of the following switching types has the highest latency?

    a. Store-and-forward

    b. Cut-through

    c. Adaptive

    d. Fragment-free

13. If a broadcast from one computer causes multiple stations to respond with additional broadcast traffic, and the level of broadcast traffic goes above 126 broadcasts per second, the situation is deemed a(n) _____.

    a. broadcast storm

    b. transmission overload

    c. excessive burst

    d. jabber

14. Which of the following fall under the heading of Fast Ethernet? (Choose all that apply.)

    a. 10BaseT

    b. 100Base–T4

    c. 10BaseF

    d. 100Base–TX

    e. 100Base–FX

15. Which of the following are reasons that a bridge port would be placed in the forwarding state? (Choose all that apply.)

    a. The port is on the root bridge.

    b. The port is connected to multiple bridges.

    c. The port is the root port.

    d. The port is not working.

16. Which of the following can divide a collision domain? (Choose all that apply.)

    a. Switch

    b. Bridge

    c. Router

    d. Hub

17. Which of the following allows you to reorganize broadcast domains no matter what the physical configuration dictates?

    a. Router

    b. VLAN

    c. Bridge

    d. Switch

18. If you attach a hub with five stations into a switch port that is configured for VLANs, how many different VLANs will the devices on the hubs be in?

    a. Five

    b. Three

    c. Two

    d. One

19. Which of the following are advantages of VLANs? (Choose all that apply.)

    a. VLANs make relocating devices easier.

    b. Separate VLANs do not require routers.

    c. VLANs increase effective bandwidth utilization.

    d. VLANs restructure broadcast domains.

20. Which of the following is a benefit that routers provide on the VLAN to increase security?

    a. Dividing broadcast domains

    b. Dividing collision domains

    c. Allowing for the creation of access lists

    d. Bridging the IP to IPX layer 3 protocol gap

21. When collisions are above 5%, you should consider _____.

    a. segmenting the LAN

    b. increasing traffic on the LAN

    c. monitoring traffic on the LAN

    d. adding hubs to the LAN

22. Which of the following advantages can Cisco switches provide over hubs? (Choose all that apply.)

    a. Separating collision domains

    b. Increased bandwidth for individual users

    c. Reduced latency

    d. Concurrent frame forwarding

23. Which of the following are true of half-duplex operation on a CSMA/CD network? (Choose all that apply.)

    a. The transmitting NIC loops back its transmission.

    b. The NIC listens to the media before transmitting.

    c. The transmitting NIC compares the original frame with the looped-back frame to determine whether there was a collision.

    d. Collisions are not possible in a half-duplex Ethernet.

24. The _____ switching method begins forwarding the incoming frame immediately after reading the destination address.

    a. cut-through

    b. store-and-forward

    c. adaptive

    d. fragment-free

13

25. Which of the following are VTP modes of operation? (Choose all that apply.)

   a. Client

   b. Server

   c. Transparent

   d. Blocking

CASE PROJECTS

**CASE
PROJECTS**

1. Your network administration consulting team at Winslow Networks has been assigned to a new project. Your client has requested that you optimize their LAN. Before you can begin making recommendations, what type of performance statistics should your team collect, at a minimum? What other information would be useful?

2. A local company has decided to upgrade its LAN configuration from five hubs and a single router to one that implements 10 switches. The switches the company is planning to buy have many more ports than necessary to support each segment. However, the company wants to divide the 10 departments into separate entities. The company is planning on using routers between each switch, thereby dividing the broadcast domains between the switches. What other options for configuring its network should the company consider? Moe has suggested foregoing the routers and using VLANs to divide the departments. What do you think?

3. The Flagstone Corporation has purchased a Cisco 1900 series switch and wants you to configure it. What kind of interface is available for configuration? What are the default settings on the switch? Does the switch support VLANs?

A

CCNA CERTIFICATION OBJECTIVES

> This appendix maps the Cisco CCNA certification objectives with the book chapter in which these objectives are covered. There are four categories of objectives assigned by Cisco:
>
> ♦ Planning and designing
> ♦ Implementation and operation
> ♦ Troubleshooting
> ♦ Technology

The following tables, A-1 through A-4, map the objectives of each category to a specific chapter.

Table A-1 Planning and designing

Objective	Chapter
Design a simple LAN using Cisco technology	4, 13
Design an IP addressing scheme to meet design requirements	3
Select an appropriate routing protocol based on user requirements	8, 9
Design a simple internetwork using Cisco technology	4, 13
Develop an access list to meet user specifications	10
Choose WAN services to meet customer requirements	5

Table A-2 Implementation and operation

Objective	Chapter
Configure routing protocols given user requirements	8, 9
Configure IP addresses, subnet masks, and gateway addresses on routers and hosts	7
Configure a router for additional administrative functionality	6, 7
Configure a switch with VLANs and inter-switch communication	13
Implement a LAN	4
Customize a switch configuration to meet specified network requirements	13
Manage system image and device configuration files	6, 7
Perform an initial configuration on a router	6, 7
Perform an initial configuration on a switch	13
Implement access lists	10
Implement simple WAN protocols	11, 12

Table A-3 Troubleshooting

Objective	Chapter
Use the OSI model as a guide for systematic network troubleshooting	1
Perform LAN and VLAN troubleshooting	2, 13
Troubleshoot routing protocols	8
Troubleshoot IP addressing and host configuration	3
Troubleshoot a device as part of a working network	2, 4, 5
Troubleshoot an access list	10
Perform simple WAN troubleshooting	5, 11, 12

Table A-4   Technology

Objective	Chapter
Describe network communications using layered models	1
Describe the Spanning Tree process	13
Compare and contrast key characteristics of LAN environments	4
Evaluate the characteristics of routing protocols	8
Evaluate the TCP/IP communication process and its associated protocols	3
Describe the components of network devices	2, 6
Evaluate rules for packet control	10
Evaluate key characteristics of WANs	5

A

ADDITIONAL RESOURCES

This appendix contains additional sources for information on subjects covered in this course.

INTERNET RESOURCES

Internet resources are invaluable for obtaining information on the latest news, technology, and standards. The Internet and Web resources listed in this section are divided into different categories, as follows:

- Standards organizations
- Technology reference
- Networking overviews and tutorials
- Technical forums
- Cisco routers
- Exam preparation resources

Standards Organizations

The following are sites for organizations that provide networking standards discussed in this course:

- American National Standards Institute: *http://www.ansi.org/*
- Electronic Industries Alliance: *http://www.eia.org*
- Telecommunications Industry Association: *http://www.tiaonline.org*
- Institute of Electrical and Electronics Engineers (IEEE): *http://www.ieee.org/*
- Internet Engineering Task Force (IETF): *http://www.ietf.org/*
- International Telecommunication Union (ITU): *http://www.itu.int/*
- International Organization for Standardization (ISO): *http://www.iso.ch/*
- International Electrotechnical Commission (IEC): *http://www.iec.ch/*
- Optimized Engineering Corporation Compendium: *http://www.optimized.com/COMPENDI/*
- World Wide Web Consortium (W3C): *http://www.w3.org/*

- RFC Editor: *http://www.rfc-editor.org/*

- Computer and Communications Standards: *http://www.cmpcmm.com/cc/ standards.html*

- Underwriters Laboratories (UL): *http://www.ul.com*

Technology Reference

These Web sites have online definitions for computer and networking terminology:

- Babel: Glossary of Computer Oriented Abbreviations and Acronyms: *http://www.geocities.com/ikind_babel/babel/babel.html*

- Federal Standard 1037C: Glossary of Telecommunications Terms: *http://glossary.its.bldrdoc.gov/fs-1037/*

- Webopedia: *http://www.pcwebopaedia.com/*

- Whatis.com: *http://www.whatis.com*

Networking Overviews and Tutorials

An introduction to various networking concepts is provided on the following Web sites:

- Alliance Datacom's Frame Relay tutorial list: *http://www.alliancedatacom.com/ frame-relay-tutorials.htm*

- Charles Spurgeon's Ethernet Web Site: *http://www.ethermanage.com/ethernet/ ethernet.html*

- Interoperability Lab Tutorials: *http://www.iol.unh.edu/training/*

- Optimized Engineering Corporation: *http://www.optimized.com/*

Technical Forums

The following sites contain technical information, discussions, and links to information covered in this course:

- Frame Relay Forum: *http://www.frforum.com/*

- Open Group: *http://www.opengroup.org/*

- Protocols.com: *http://www.protocols.com*

Cisco Routers

The following locations have information specific to Cisco routers:

- Cisco: *http://www.cisco.com*
  - Cisco product documentation list: *http://www.cisco.com/univercd/cc/td/doc/ product/*

- Cisco command reference documents by subject: *http://www.cisco.com/ univercd/cc/td/doc/product/software/ios100/rpcr/index.htm*

- Cisco routing tutorial: *http://www.alliancedatacom.com/cisco-routing-tutorial.htm*

Exam Preparation Resources

The following Web sites contain information and technical papers concerning the CCNA exam:

- CCPrep.com: *http://www.ccprep.com*

- CertNotes: *http://www.certnotes.com*

- CramSession: *http://www.cramsession.com*

- Transcender: *http://www.transcender.com*

- Boson Software: *http://www.boson.com*

C

A NETWORKING PROFESSIONAL'S TOOLKIT

Throughout this book, you have learned about the many tools you may use while implementing, analyzing, and troubleshooting a network. Although information on networking devices or software packages is readily available, it is not always easy to find details about the tools used by networking professionals. This appendix provides pictures of networking tools, some familiar and some probably unfamiliar, along with their proper names and uses. You can often find these tools together in toolkits with carrying cases. Toolkit providers include Aven Tools, Black Box, Curtis, Paladin, and Siemon.

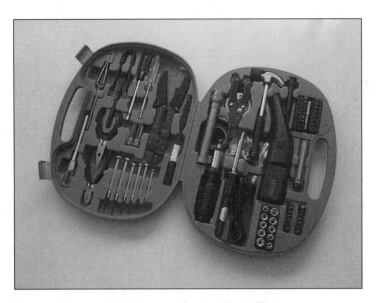

Figure C-1 A networking professional's toolkit

Many of the tools used by networking professionals are similar or identical to tools used by electricians. Tools pictured in the following figures fall into this category.

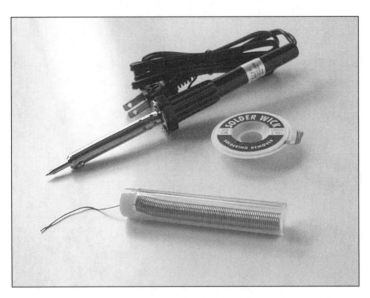

Figure C-2 Soldering iron, solder, and solder wick; used for repairing connections

C

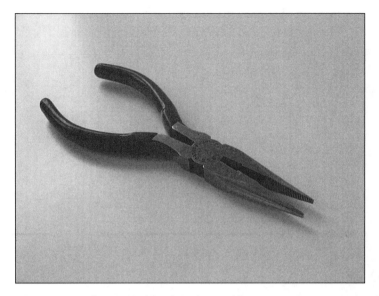

Figure C-3   Pliers; used for bending cable or components or working in tight spaces

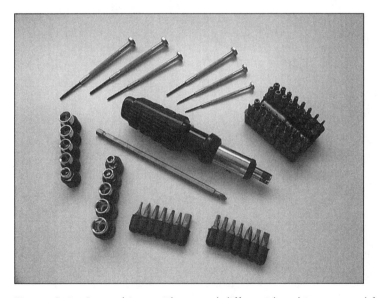

Figure C-4   Screwdriver with several different head types; used for installing and uninstalling components

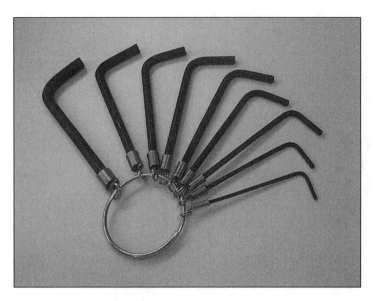

Figure C-5   Hex keyset; used for removing computer covers or components

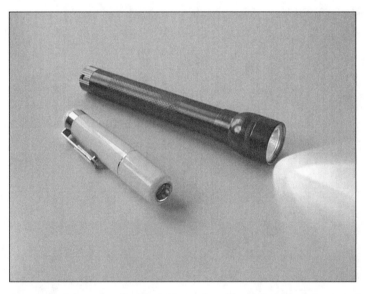

Figure C-6   Pocket flashlights; used to illuminate the interior of devices

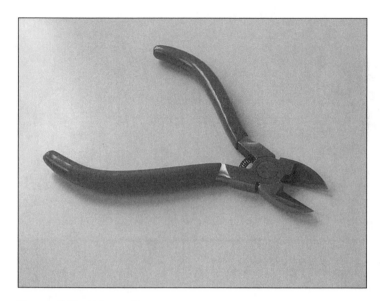

Figure C-7   Wire cutters

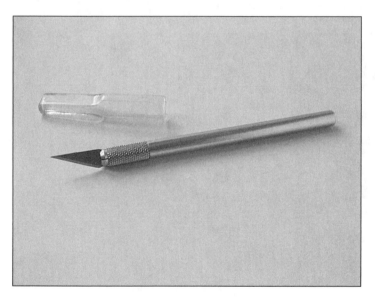

Figure C-8   Precision knife

Other tools used by networking professionals are unique to computer repair or telephony technicians. Tools pictured in the following figures fall into this category.

Figure C-9   Cable preparation tool, including wire stripper and cutter; used for preparing cable for termination

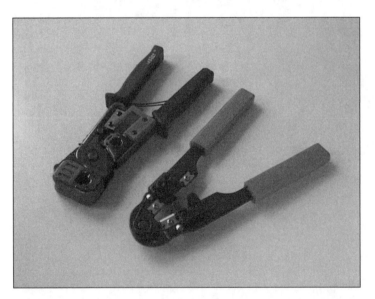

Figure C-10   Crimp tools; used for crimping wires into terminators

C

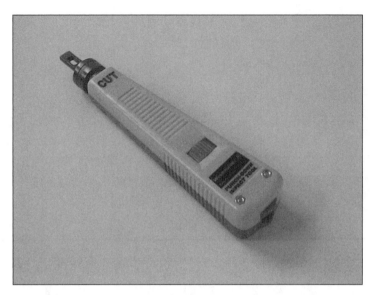

Figure C-11   Punch-down block tool; used for crimping wires into punch-down blocks

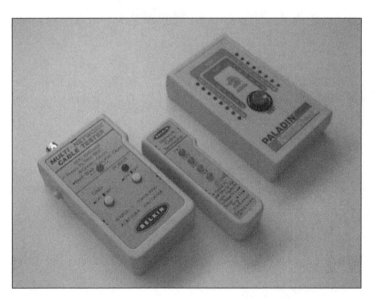

Figure C-12   Cable testing tools; used for verifying cable integrity

Figure C-13   Cable ties; used for holding bundles of cables together

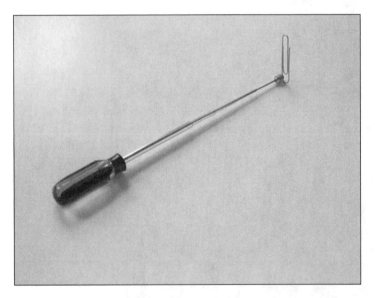

Figure C-14   Magnetic extractor; used for retrieving small components

C

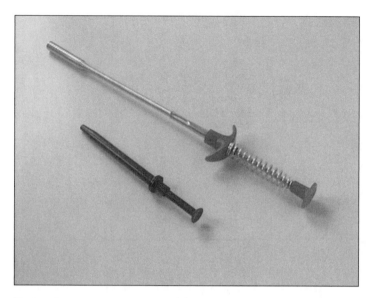

Figure C-15 Extractors; used for retrieving small components

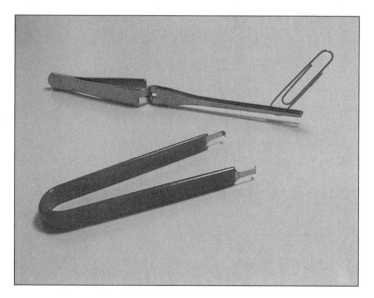

Figure C-16 Tweezers; used for holding and maneuvering small components

Figure C-17 Antistatic vacuum; used for cleaning electronic devices

D

COMMAND SUMMARY

This appendix lists the commands presented in this course. You should review these commands before you attempt the CCNA certification examination. The router commands in this appendix are organized into the following categories:

- ◆ Identification and navigation
- ◆ Passwords
- ◆ Router/switch general and startup configuration
- ◆ Examining the router and switch
- ◆ Interface configuration
- ◆ IP-related commands
- ◆ Access list configuration and status commands
- ◆ WAN configuration
- ◆ VLAN configuration

The tables in the following sections list the mode, command syntax, and description of each command. The mode column is abbreviated so you can see the router/switch configuration mode that you must be in to properly execute the command. The following list illustrates the symbols used in the command tables:

- >: Symbolizes user mode, in which the command prompt looks like hostname>

- #: Symbolizes privileged mode, or enable mode, in which the command prompt looks like hostname#

- GC: Indicates global configuration mode, in which the command prompt looks like hostname(config)#

- IF: Indicates interface configuration mode, in which the command prompt looks like hostname(config-if)#

- CL: Indicates line configuration mode, in which the command prompt looks like hostname(config-line)#

- CR: Indicates router configuration mode, in which the command prompt looks like hostname(config-router)#

- CS: Indicates subinterface mode, in which the command prompt looks like hostname(config-subif)#

- NA: Indicates that the mode is not significant for this command

If multiple symbols are listed in the mode field, the command will work with all modes listed.

NOTE This is not a comprehensive guide to all commands and options with which you can configure a router; such a guide would be too large for this appendix. This is an abridged guide that summarizes only the commands covered in this course. To see a larger list of Cisco commands, visit the Cisco Web site at *www.cisco.com/univercd/cc/td/doc/product/software/ios100/rpcr/index.htm.*

IDENTIFICATION AND NAVIGATION

The commands shown in Table D-1 are basic navigation commands for the router. These commands allow you to change the router into different configuration modes and even set the identity and clock of the router.

Table D-1   Identification and navigation commands

Mode	Command Syntax	Description
>	enable	Allows you to access privileged mode from user mode
#	disable	Returns prompt to user mode from privileged mode

Table D-1   Identification and navigation commands (continued)

Mode	Command Syntax	Description
#	configure terminal	Allows you to access global configuration mode
GC	line console 0	Allows you to configure the console line that is used to access the router; often used to set a console line password; see Table D-2
GC	line vty [#]	Allows you to access line configuration mode for virtual terminal lines; typing "line vty 0 4" affects all five virtual terminal lines at the same time; typing a single number (0–4) allows configuration of the virtual terminal number that you entered
GC	interface [interface type and number]	Allows you to access interface configuration mode; requires that you enter the type and number of the interface after the command; to configure the first Ethernet interface on your router, type "interface ethernet 0"
GC	interface [subinterface type and number]	Allows you to enter subinterface configuration mode; when creating an interface with Frame Relay with this command, add point-to-point or multipoint to the command
GC	router [routing protocol or static]	Allows you to enter router configuration mode; requires that you specify the name of a routing protocol or indicate static (to indicate a manually configured routing table); to enable RIP routing, for example, type "router rip"
GC	hostname [name]	Allows you to set the host name for your router; requires that you enter the name after the hostname command; for example, to name your router "clyde", you would type "hostname clyde"
GC	banner motd [banner end character]	Allows you to set the "message of the day" banner; to use this command, type "banner motd" followed by the single character that you want to end the message; for example, if you type banner motd @, the router prompt will move to the next line, and everything you type following that will be your banner message, until you enter the @ character, which indicates that you are finished typing your banner message; to see your message, reboot the router
NA	ctrl+z	Returns you to enable mode; do not press the plus key; press Ctrl+Z
#	clock set [hh:mm:ss month day year]	Used to set the time and date on the router

D

Table D-1   Identification and navigation commands (continued)

Mode	Command Syntax	Description
#	reload *[in hh:mm] [month day | day month]*	Reboots the router; setting a time delay or month and day for the reboot is optional
NA	exit	Logs you out from the > or # prompt; from other prompts, command takes you back one level; for example, typing exit at the router(config-if)# prompt takes you back to the router(config)# prompt
NA	CTRL ^	Allows you to abort a command in progress; executed by pressing Ctrl+Shift+6
> #	quit	Logs you out of the router

PASSWORDS

The commands shown in Table D-2 allow you to configure passwords for your router. Do not forget the passwords that you configure; you will need them when you want to access your router in the future.

Table D-2   Commands for configuring passwords

Mode	Command Syntax	Description
GC	enable password *[password]*	Allows you to set the privileged mode password, which is used to enter privileged mode
GC	enable secret *[password]*	Allows you to set the encrypted privileged mode password; overrides the enable password when configured
CL	login *[Enter]* password *[password]*	Allows you to set a line password; requires that you first type "login", press the Return or Enter key, then type "password" followed by the password you want to set

ROUTER/SWITCH GENERAL AND STARTUP CONFIGURATION

The commands listed in this section are vital to configuring and managing the configuration of the router or switch. These commands cover saving, copying, and replacing the contents of the IOS and the device's configuration file.

Table D-3   Startup and running configuration commands

Mode	Command Syntax	Description
#	hostname *[host name]*	Configures the host name of a router or switch
#	copy running-config startup-config	Copies the router running configuration to the NVRAM on the router; saves configuration changes you make while the router is running, so that they are implemented next time the router is restarted
#	copy startup-config running-config	Copies the router startup configuration from NVRAM to the running configuration. Does not replace the running configuration; instead, it merges the information.
#	copy tftp flash	Copies a router IOS file from a TFTP server to flash memory
#	copy flash tftp	Copies a router IOS file from flash memory to a TFTP server
#	copy tftp startup-config	Copies the router configuration file from a TFTP server to the startup configuration in NVRAM on the router
#	copy startup-config tftp	Copies the router startup configuration in NVRAM to a TFTP server
#	erase flash	Erases the flash memory on the router
#	erase startup-config	Erases the router startup configuration from NVRAM. This also works on certain switches.
#	delete nvram	Erases the switch configuration (depending on the switch model)
#	copy *tftp://tftp ip address/ IOS image/opcode*	Copies an IOS image to a switch from a TFTP server
#	copy nvram *tftp: //tftp ip address name*	Copies the configuration of a switch to a TFTP server
#	copy *tftp://tftp ip address/ name* nvram	Copies the configuration stored on a TFTP server to the switch
GC	mac-address-table permanent *[mac#] [slot/#]*	Maps a permanent MAC address to a switch port
GC	switching-mode *[mode]*	Configures the switching mode (fast forward, fragment-free, or store-and-forward)

D

EXAMINING THE ROUTER AND SWITCH

The following list of commands allows you to examine router and switch configuration, components, resources, and other statistics. These commands are useful for checking the device's performance and troubleshooting configuration problems.

Table D-4   Commands for examining components and configuration

Mode	Command Syntax	Description
> #	show clock	Displays the time and date
> #	show processes	Displays CPU utilization information
> #	show interface ethernet *[#]*	Shows statistics and configuration information for the Ethernet interface that is listed; requires that you enter the number of the interface after the command
> #	show interface serial *[#]*	Shows statistics and configuration information for the serial interface that is listed; requires that you enter the number of the interface after the command
> #	show interfaces	Lists configuration and statistics for all interfaces configured on the router
> #	show protocol	Shows the protocols configured on the system and indicates which interfaces are using them
> #	show history	Displays the last 10 commands executed
> #	show flash	Shows the flash file(s), size, name, and the amount of flash memory used, total, and available
> #	show cdp neighbor	Shows a list of Cisco devices that are directly attached to this device
> #	show cdp neighbor detail	Adds IP address information to output obtained from show cdp neighbor command
#	show running-config	Displays the currently running router configuration file
#	show startup-config	Displays the router startup configuration maintained in NVRAM
#	show mac-address-table	Displays the MAC address table of a switch
#	show port system	Displays the switching mode of a switch
> #	show version	Displays version information for the router/switch. On a router this includes the startup register setting, the router series number, how long the router has been up and running, and the IOS version number.

INTERFACE CONFIGURATION

Interfaces are an important part of the router, and Table D-5 lists commands that are specific to interface configuration. Table D-8 lists additional interface configuration commands related to WAN configuration.

Table D-5   Interface configuration commands

Mode	Command Syntax	Description
GC	interface serial *[#]*	Allows you to configure the specific serial interface that you identify
GC	interface ethernet *[#]*	Allows you to configure the specific Ethernet interface on a router that you specify
GC	interface ethernet *[slot/#]*	On a switch, you enter the slot number and the port number to configure an interface
GC	interface fastethernet *[slot/#]*	On a switch, Fast Ethernet interfaces and slots must be specified when configuring
IF	encapsulation *[encapsulation type]*	Allows you to set the encapsulation type for your interface
GC	cdp run	Allows you to enable the Cisco Discovery Protocol on a device
GC	no cdp run	Allows you to disable the Cisco Discovery Protocol on a device
IF	cdp enable	Allows you to enable the Cisco Discovery Protocol on an interface
IF	no cdp enable	Allows you to disable the Cisco Discovery Protocol on an interface
IF	description *[description]*	Allows you to configure a description for an interface
IF	duplex *[mode]*	Sets the duplex type on a 10-Mbps Ethernet interface (auto, full, full-flow-control, half)
IF	no shutdown	Tells the router or switch not to shut down the interface; leave enabled
IF	loopback	Allows you to configure the interface for loopback that is used for testing purposes; information transmitted out that interface will be immediately returned on the receive circuit of that same interface
GC	interface *[interface #.subinterface #]*	Creates and/or accesses a subinterface; for example, to create a subinterface #1 off S1, type "interface s1.1"

D

IP COMMANDS

The commands in Table D-6 are related to the configuration, control, and troubleshooting of TCP/IP. They cover configuring an IP address and subnet mask, in addition to configuring routing protocols.

Table D-6   IP-related commands

Mode	Command Syntax	Description
IF	ip address *[ip address] [mask]*	Sets the IP address and subnet mask for an interface on a router
GC	ip address *[ip address] [mask]*	Sets the IP address and the subnet mask for an interface on a switch
GC	ip default-gateway *[ip address]*	Sets the default gateway for an interface on a switch
#	show ip	Shows the IP address configuration of a switch
IF CS	ip unnumbered *[interface or logical interface]*	Allows you to establish that the interface is to support the IP protocol, but not be assigned an IP address
GC	router rip	Enables RIP routing and accesses router configuration mode
GC	router igrp *[autonomous system number]*	Enables IGRP routing and accesses router configuration mode; requires that you enter an autonomous system number
CR	network *[major network number]*	Used after router rip and router igrp to indicate network number
GC	router eigrp *[autonomous system number]*	Enables EIGRP routing and accesses router configuration mode; requires that you enter an autonomous system number
CR	network *[major network number]*	Used after router rip and router eigrp to indicate network number
GC	router ospf *[process id]*	Enables OSPF routing and accesses router configuration mode; requires a process ID number that is only relevant on the local router
CR	network *[ip address] [wildcard]*	Indicates the interface that participates in OSPF. The wildcard mask is a reversed subnet mask and is unique to identify interfaces for OSPF.
GC	no ip routing	Disables IP routing on the router
GC	ip routing	Enables IP routing on the router
CR	passive-interface	Enables the suppression of routing updates over some interfaces while allowing updates to be exchanged normally over other interfaces

Table D-6   IP-related commands (continued)

Mode	Command Syntax	Description
#	debug ip rip	Enables RIP debugging, which allows you to monitor RIP updates
#	debug ip igrp [transaction or events]	Enables IGRP transactions and/or event monitoring
#	no debug all	Disables all debugging activities
#	debug all	Enables all debugging options
#	undebug all	Disables all debugging activities
> #	show ip route	Displays the router's routing table
> #	ping [ip address	host name]	Allows you to verify that a host is reachable either by IP address or host name
> #	telnet [ip address]	Allows the user to start a telnet session with a telnet server
> #	show ip protocol	Shows statistics for the IP protocol, such as routing protocol information, timers, networks serviced, and gateway information
> #	show ip interface [interface type and number]	Shows statistics for interfaces configured for IP; adding the specific interface type and number is optional; if you only type "show ip interface", all interfaces configured with IP will be shown

D

ACCESS LISTS

Access lists allow you to control the types of packets that are allowed to traverse the router. Table D-7 illustrates the commands for IP access list creation and configuration.

Table D-7   Access list configuration and status commands

Mode	Command Syntax	Description
GC	access-list [list #] [permit	deny] [ip address] [mask]	Creates a standard IP access list
GC	access-list [list #] [permit	deny] [protocol] [source IP address] [source wildcard mask] [operator] [port] [destination IP address] [destination wildcard mask] [operator] [port] [log]	Creates an extended IP access list
GC	no access-list [list #]	Removes the access list indicated
GC	ip access-list [standard/extended] [name]	Creates a named access list (IOS 11.2 or higher)

Table D-7 Access list configuration and status commands (continued)

Mode	Command Syntax	Description
IF	ip access-group *[list number/name] [in | out]*	Applies an IP access list to the interface
IF	no ip access-group *[list #] [in | out]*	Removes an IP access list from the interface
CL	access-class *[access-list #] [in/out]*	Links an existing access list to VTY lines
#	show ip access-lists	Shows all IP access lists
#	show access-list *[list #]*	Allows you to review all access lists; you can enter the access list number you want to view instead of reviewing all of them

WAN CONFIGURATION

The following commands in Table D-8 cover the WAN configuration techniques mentioned in this course. These commands allow you to configure ISDN, PPP, and Frame Relay interfaces.

Table D-8 WAN configuration commands

Mode	Command Syntax	Description
IF CS	bandwidth *[bandwidth]*	Sets the bandwidth advertised on the serial interface in kilobits per second
IF	clock rate *[clock rate]*	Sets the clock rate in bits per second for a serial interface
IF CS	encapsulation *[WAN protocol]*	Sets the encapsulation type for a serial interface; common options are PPP, Frame Relay, and HDLC; for example, to set the interface to PPP encapsulation, type "encapsulation ppp"
IF CS	ppp authentication *[chap | pap]*	Sets the authentication type for ppp encapsulation; can be chap or pap; if both pap and chap are used, the order in which they are entered on the command line is the order in which they will be used
IF CS	frame-relay interface-dlci *[dlci #]*	Configures a DLCI number for a serial interface using Frame Relay encapsulation
IF CS	frame-relay lmi-type *[lmi-type]*	Sets the LMI type for a Frame Relay interface; options are cisco, q933i, and ansi
#	show frame-relay lmi	Allows you to view configuration and interface statistics concerning your Frame Relay interfaces using LMI; also shows LMI type
#	show frame-relay map	Displays the Frame Relay map

Table D-8 WAN configuration commands (continued)

Mode	Command Syntax	Description
GC	isdn switch-type *[switch identifier]*	Sets the ISDN switch type to which the router will be configured to communicate
GC	isdn spid *[spid channel designation] [SPID #]*	Sets the Service Profile Identifier (SPID) for each ISDN channel

D

VLAN CONFIGURATION

The following commands in Table D-9 cover the VLAN configuration techniques mentioned in this course. These commands work only on VLAN-enabled devices and assume configuration via a Cisco Catalyst 1900.

Table D-9 VLAN configuration commands

Mode	Command Syntax	Description
#	show vlan *[#]*	Shows the VLAN configuration of the switch. It can be specific to a particular VLAN number.
#	show vlan-membership	Shows VLAN assignments by port number
#	show trunk *[A/B]* allowed-vlans	Shows the allowed VLANs on the selected trunk
#	delete vtp	Deletes the VTP configuration on the selected device
GC	vtp password *[word]*	Sets the VTP password for a domain
GC	vtp server	Sets the current device as a VTP server
GC	vtp client	Configures the current device as a VTP client
GC	vtp transparent	Sets the current device in VTP transparent mode
GC	vtp domain	Sets the VTP domain name
GC	vtp pruning *[enable/disable]*	Enables or disables VTP pruning
GC	vlan *[#]* name *[name]*	Configures the name of the specified VLAN number
IF	no trunk-vlan *[#]*	Disables the VLAN number from being able to traverse the trunk port
IF	trunk on	Configures VLAN trunking on the selected port
IF	vlan-membership static *[#]*	Configures the VLAN membership for the selected port

E

TROUBLESHOOTING SUMMARY

This appendix lists router and switch commands that help you troubleshoot your network.

♦ Router troubleshooting commands

♦ Switch troubleshooting commands

The following tables list the mode, command syntax, and description of each troubleshooting command. The mode column indicates the configuration mode you must be in to properly execute the command. The following list illustrates the symbols used in the mode columns:

- >: Symbolizes user mode, in which the command prompt looks like hostname>

- #: Symbolizes privileged mode, or enable mode, in which the command prompt looks like hostname#

If both symbols are shown in the mode field, the command works with both modes.

NOTE This is not a comprehensive guide to all commands and options you can use to troubleshoot a router or switch; such a guide would be too large for this appendix. This abridged guide summarizes only the commands covered in this course. To see a larger list of Cisco commands, visit the Cisco Web site at *www.cisco.com/univercd/cc/td/doc/product/software/ios100/rpcr/index.htm.*

ROUTER TROUBLESHOOTING COMMANDS

The show and debug commands in Table E-1 are used on routers to help troubleshoot connectivity and correct operation.

Table E-1   Router troubleshooting commands

Mode	Command	Use	Corresponding Figure
>, #	ping [host/ip address]	Sends five ICMP echo requests to the specified host or IP address to ensure connectivity. If there are no replies, then your connection is not viable.	
#	ping	When a normal ping command is sent from a router, the source address of the ping is the IP address of the interface that the packet uses to exit the router. If an extended ping command is used, the source IP address can be changed to any IP address on the router. The extended ping is used to perform a more advanced check of host "reachability" and network connectivity. To use extended ping, simply enter the ping command in privileged mode with no parameters.	Figure E-1 (after this table)

Table E-1   Router troubleshooting commands (continued)

Mode	Command	Use	Corresponding Figure
#	telnet *[host/ip address]*	Creates a telnet connection to a host or IP address and allows you to remotely administer that device.	
#	show running-config	Shows the current running config-uration in RAM, which is useful for determining existing settings on your router.	Figure 6-7 Figure 6-16
#	show version	Shows the IOS version currently operating on your device. Also provides configuration register settings that can help in password recovery.	Figure 6-15 Figure 7-2
#	show interfaces *[type] [#]*	Provides details about the physical or logical interfaces on a router, including IP address, bandwidth settings, duplex settings (Eth), clock rate (serial), and more. It also shows the status of the interface, both Physical layer and Data Link layer.	Figure 6-17 Figure 7-6 Figure 12-15
#	show flash	Shows all current IOS images and configurations saved in flash memory, and indicates whether you have enough memory to store multiple copies of the IOS.	Figure 7-4
#	show cdp neighbor	Shows an overview of all directly connected Cisco devices, regardless of their Layer 3 address (e.g., IPX, IP, AppleTalk).	Figure 7-5
#	show cdp neighbor detail	Shows neighbor device ID, Layer 3 protocol information (for example, IP addresses), device platform, device capabilities, local interface type and outgoing remote port ID, hold-time value (in seconds), Cisco IOS software type, and release. The output from this command includes all the Layer 3 addresses of the neighbor device interfaces (up to one Layer 3 address per protocol).	

E

Table E-1 Router troubleshooting commands (continued)

Mode	Command	Use	Corresponding Figure
#	show ip protocol	Shows values about all routing protocols and routing protocol timer information associated with the router on which you issue this command (for example, which networks are being advertised by which protocols, such as RIP, IGRP, and OSPF).	Figure 8-15 Figure 8-22
#	show ip route	Displays the contents of the IP routing table.	Figure 8-17 Figure 8-18 Figure 8-21
#	show ip interface [type] [number]	Shows IP-related information about a particular interface, including the assigned IP address, whether any ACLs are set, whether the interface is up or down, and what type of IP switching is enabled.	Figure 10-12 Figure 10-16
#	show access-lists	Shows all standard and extended access lists, as well as the statements (in order) included in each list.	Figure 10-11 Figure 10-16
#	show ip access-lists	Shows only IP standard and extended access lists, as well as the statements (in order) included in each list.	Figure 10-11 Figure 10-23
#	show dialer [interface]	Shows dialer information on a particular interface.	
#	show isdn status	Gives status information for ISDN connections (requires BRI or PRI connection).	
#	show frame-relay pvc [dlci number]	Displays the status of all PVCs or a specified PVC. This command is useful for viewing the number of BECN and FECN packets received by the router. It also shows whether a PVC is active, inactive, or deleted.	Figure 12-16
#	show frame-relay map	Displays the current map entries and information about the connections. This command is useful for discovering a DLCI and its associated remote IP address. This is either discovered dynamically via inverse ARP or by a static entry.	Figure 12-17
#	show history	Shows all recent commands that have been issued in the IOS CLI. The default is to buffer 10 commands, but you can show up to 256.	

Table E-1   Router troubleshooting commands (continued)

Mode	Command	Use	Corresponding Figure
#	show starting-config	Shows the saved configuration in NVRAM. This configuration is loaded by default when a router restarts.	
#	show frame-relay lmi	Displays LMI traffic statistics and specifies which type of LMI is being used (Cisco, ANSI, or Q.933a).	Figure 12-18
#	debug all	Turns on debugging for all processes running on your router. (Warning: Never do this on a production router!)	Figure 7-7
#	debug ip igrp events	Turns on debugging for all IGRP routing events, such as updates sent and received from neighboring routers.	Figure 8-23
#	debug q921	Shows the call connection establishment and disconnection. This command is useful for seeing whether the ISDN call is made and established, or if it never connects.	
#	debug ip rip	Turns on debugging for all RIP events, such as periodic updates and triggered updates.	

E

```
Router A#ping
Protocol [ip]:
Target IP address: 192.168.40.1

!--- The address to ping.

Repeat count [5]:
Datagram size [100]:
Timeout in seconds [2]:
Extended commands [n]: y
Source address or interface: 172.16.23.2

!---Ping packets will be sourced from this address.

Type of service [0]:
Set DF bit in IP header? [no]:
Validate reply data? [no]:
Data pattern [0xABCD]:
Loose, Strict, Record, Timestamp, Verbose[none]:
Sweep range of sizes [n]:
Type escape sequence to abort.
Sending 5, 100-byte ICMP Echos to 162.108.21.8, timeout is 2 seconds:
!!!!!
Success rate is 100 percent (5/5), round-trip min/avg/max = 36/97/132 ms

!--- Ping is successful.

Router A#
```

Figure E-1   Ping command output

SWITCH TROUBLESHOOTING COMMANDS

The show commands in Table E-2 are used on switches to help troubleshoot connectivity and correct operation. Note that there are some differences from routers, as Access Catalyst switches from Cisco deal primarily with Layer 2 of the OSI model.

Table E-2   Switch troubleshooting commands

Mode	Command	Use	Corresponding Figure
#	show mac-address-table	Shows all currently learned MAC addresses in the CAM (content addressable memory) table. These are either learned dynamically by the switch or entered permanently with the "mac-address-table permanent" command in global configuration mode.	Figure E-2
#	show port system	Shows which frame switching mode the switch is using (e.g., cut-through, store-and-forward, fragment-free).	
#	show ip	Shows all IP information that is configured on the switch, including IP address, default gateway, subnet mask, and name servers.	
#	show vlan [number]	Shows information about VLANs that are configured on the switch. The command can also specify a particular VLAN.	Figure E-3
#	show vlan-membership	Shows all ports that are assigned to VLANs. This command is useful if you plug into a switch port that does not seem to be working.	
#	show trunk [a/b]	Shows the Fast Ethernet Port 0/26 or 0/27 on a Catalyst 1900 switch, and whether ISL trunking has been turned on.	
#	show spantree [number]	Shows whether Spanning Tree is enabled for a particular VLAN. If you do not specify a number, the command shows all the VLANs that Spanning Tree is running on. The command also shows the bridge ID of the switch and the bridge ID of the root bridge for that network segment.	Figure E-4

```
wg_sw_1900#show mac-address-table
Number of permanent addresses : 0
Number of restricted static addresses : 0
Number of dynamic addresses : 6

Address          Dest           Interface  Type     Source Interface List
------------------------------------------------------------------------
00E0.1E5D.AE2F   Ethernet       0/2        Dynamic  All
00D0.588F.B604   FastEthernet   0/26       Dynamic  All
00E0.1E5D.AE2B   FastEthernet   0/26       Dynamic  All
0090.273B.87A4   FastEthernet   0/26       Dynamic  All
00D0.588F.B600   FastEthernet   0/26       Dynamic  All
00D0.5892.38C4   FastEthernet   0/27       Dynamic  All
```

Figure E-2 Show mac-address-table command output

```
VLAN Name              Status      Ports
----------------------------------------------
1    default           Enabled     1-12, AUI, A, B
10   Engineering       Enabled
20   HR                Enabled
30   Sales             Enabled
40   Marketing         Enabled
1002 fddi-default      Suspended
1003 token-ring-defau  Suspended
1004 fddinet-default   Suspended
1005 trnet-default     Suspended

VLAN Type      SAID    MTU   Parent RingNo BridgeNo Stp  Trans1 Trans2
----------------------------------------------------------------------
1    Ethernet  100001  1500  0      0      0        Unkn 1002   1003
10   Ethernet  100010  1500  0      1      1        Unkn 0      0
20   Ethernet  100020  1500  0      1      1        Unkn 0      0
30   Ethernet  100030  1500  0      1      1        Unkn 0      0
40   Ethernet  100040  1500  0      1      1        Unkn 0      0

--More--
```

Figure E-3 Show vlan command output

```
VLAN1 is executing the IEEE compatible Spanning Tree Protocol
    Bridge Identifier has priority 32768, address 0001.961D.6B40
    Configured hello time 2, max age 20, forward delay 15
    Current root has priority 32768, address 0001.961D.6B40
    Root port is N/A, cost of root path is 0
    Topology change flag not set, detected flag not set
    Topology changes 0, last topology change occured 0d00h00m00s ago
    Times:   hold 1, topology change 8960
             hello 2, max age 20, forward delay 15
    Timers: hello 2, topology change 35, notification 2
Port Ethernet 0/1 of VLAN1 is Forwarding
    Port path cost 100, Port priority 128
    Designated root has priority 32768, address 0001.961D.6B40
    Designated bridge has priority 32768, address 0001.961D.6B40
    Designated port is 1, path cost 0
    Timers: message age 20, forward delay 15, hold 1
Port Ethernet 0/2 of VLAN1 is Forwarding
    Port path cost 100, Port priority 128
    Designated root has priority 32768, address 0001.961D.6B40
    Designated bridge has priority 32768, address 0001.961D.6B40
    Designated port is 2, path cost 0
    Timers: message age 20, forward delay 15, hold 1
--More--
-
```

Figure E-4 Show spantree command output

USING TROUBLESHOOTING COMMANDS

When using show and debug commands, it is important to know the difference between the two. Show commands are like a snapshot of a particular process or device configuration. Debug commands are like Web cameras that constantly monitor the processes and activities you specify.

Typically you use show commands on production routers and switches, as they are low in CPU and memory utilization. These commands usually provide information you need to know about a particular issue. On the other hand, if a problem is sporadic or only occurs at certain times during a process, then debug commands will serve you well; you can constantly monitor (and log) events as they occur.

You must be careful with debug commands. Because they use CPU and memory, having too many debug processes running at the same time can affect the performance of a router or switch. A good example is Network Address Translation (NAT) debugging. Because every packet that goes through the router must be translated if it goes outside the network interface, you will be processing a message for each packet. This can not only double your CPU utilization, it will also overwhelm a person monitoring these events. You could also overflow your memory if you have logging enabled.

Always remember to turn debugging off. For example, you can use the "no debug [process]" command, where [process] is the process you started. The best practice is to use the "no debug all" command or "u all", which is a shortcut for "undebug all". These commands turn off all possible debugging on a device.

TROUBLESHOOTING EXAMPLE

You receive a call at the Help desk from a user who can no longer access her file server. You walk to her desk and ask if she has changed anything on her computer. She says no. You open a command prompt and type "ping fileserver1". The computer says "Destination unreachable". You suspect a routing problem, because you added a new router on her floor over the weekend. You thank the user, walk into your router closet with your laptop, and plug into the new router.

Because you have a small network, you are using RIPv2 as your routing protocol. You log in to the router, go to the privileged mode prompt, and type "show ip protocols" to see the list of routing protocols running on the router. You notice that RIPv2 is running, but there are no networks being advertised. You then issue the "show ip route" command, which shows that you know only the directly connected routes.

You deduce that someone forgot to use the "network" command to identify the interfaces that would be advertising and using RIPv2. You quickly enter router configuration mode and type the two network statements that identify the two directly connected networks. You exit the configuration modes by typing "end".

Back in privileged mode, you type "show ip protocols" again and notice that the router is now advertising on those routes. You then type "show ip route" and notice that four new routes have appeared with R's next to them, identifying them as RIP learned routes. You call the user, who gives you the good news that she can now see the file server and download the files she needs.

E

INTRODUCING NETWORKS

CCNA Exam Objectives

Objective	Lab
Describe network communications using layered models	1.1, 1.4
Evaluate the TCP/IP communication process and its associated protocols	1.2
Troubleshoot IP addressing and host configuration	1.3

LAB 1.1 UNDERSTANDING THE OSI MODEL

Objectives

Within the networking world, the OSI seven-layer model has been widely adopted. This adoption has facilitated the teaching of networking principles and the development of networking software and hardware. The OSI seven-layer model is an open standard that has been accepted worldwide. The goal of this lab is to make sure you understand what happens at each of the seven layers so that you are successful as a network troubleshooter and as a CCNA candidate.

After completing this lab, you will be able to:

➤ Identify the OSI model layer associated with various network functions

➤ Describe the reasons for using the layered model

Materials Required

This lab requires the following:

➤ A pen or pencil

Estimated completion time: **30 minutes**

ACTIVITY

ACTIVITY

1. Relate the following networking descriptions to their correct OSI layer by placing them in the correct cell in the Description column of Table 1-1. There may be more than one term or phrase for each layer.

- Bits
- Where communications begin
- End-to-end transmission
- CSMA/CD
- Compression
- Logical address
- Signals
- Request for network services
- Duplex
- CRC
- LLC

- Frames
- Encoding

- NIC software functions
- Synchronization
- Voltage
- Services to applications
- Internetwork travel
- SQL

- Data segmentation
- Connectionless service

- Datagram
- Cable

- Best path selection
- MAC address
- Formatting
- ACK
- Hubs
- ASCII

- Encryption
- MTU

Table 1-1   OSI model layer functions

OSI Layer	Description
Application	
Presentation	
Session	
Transport	
Network	
Data Link	
Physical	

Certification Objectives

Objectives for the CCNA exam:

➤ Describe network communications using layered models

Review Questions

1. How does using the OSI model facilitate teaching and learning about networking?

2. How does using the OSI model facilitate the development of networking hardware and software?

3. How does using the OSI model provide compatibility and standardization between networking products?

4. How does the user fit into the OSI model?

5. What is the importance of the Network layer?

6. At which layer do the ultimate sender and receiver of data make contact?

7. If you are browsing the Web and the networking cable gets pulled out of the computer, the connection to the Web site can often be restored if you plug the cable back in. Which layer is responsible for maintaining the connection?

8. What are the two sublayers of the Data Link layer? Which one is closer to the Physical layer?

9. What is meant by "peer communication" with respect to the OSI model?

10. Is networking software more closely related to the upper layers or lower layers of the OSI model?

Lab 1.2 Understanding the Five Steps of Data Encapsulation

Objectives

During transport from the source node to the destination node, data makes its way down the protocol stack and is wrapped, or enclosed, at each layer by a header. This wrapping is called encapsulation.

There are five steps of data encapsulation during the data's journey from the Application layer through the Physical layer. The goal of this lab is to make sure you understand what happens at each of the five steps. Remember that this process begins with the user initiating network resources. This is at the top of the OSI model.

After completing this lab, you will be able to:

> ➤ Define encapsulation in terms of networking
> ➤ Describe the five steps of data encapsulation

Materials Required

This lab requires the following:

> ➤ A pen or pencil

Estimated completion time: **15 minutes**

ACTIVITY

1. The following bulleted list contains data encapsulation descriptions. Match these descriptions to their correct step numbers by placing them in the correct cell in the Description column of Table 1-2. There may be more than one term or phrase for each step.

   - Conversion to standard data format
   - Encoding
   - Frame
   - Datagram
   - Maximum transmission units
   - Logical address
   - Bit transmission
   - Upper layers
   - IP header
   - Trailer
   - Segments
   - Packet creation
   - Pulses
   - Physical address

2. For each step number in Table 1-2, give the associated OSI model layer(s).

Table 1-2   Data encapsulation

Step Number	Description	Associated OSI Model Layer(s)
1		
2		
3		
4		
5		

Certification Objectives

Objectives for the CCNA exam:

➤ Evaluate the TCP/IP communication process and its associated protocols

Review Questions

1. Which layers of the OSI model are involved in data encapsulation?

2. Which layers generally constitute the upper layers of the OSI model?

3. Encapsulation is often called "wrapping." Why?

4. During the encapsulation process, do upper layers provide services for the layers below them or do lower layers provide services for layers above them?

5. What is the most common logical address used in networking today?

6. What is another name for the physical address?

7. What is a maximum transmission unit?

8. What is the process of encoding?

9. What is a PDU?

10. How does the Network layer facilitate data encapsulation?

LAB 1.3 IDENTIFYING DATA LINK AND NETWORK LAYER ADDRESSES

Objectives

Networks use two different kinds of addresses: physical addresses at the Data Link layer and logical addresses at the Network layer. Typically, the physical address is a MAC address and the logical address is an IP address. The goal of this lab is finding and identifying these different addresses on a Windows computer and defining the purpose of a MAC address. The MAC address is also known as the physical address because it is burned onto the NIC during the manufacturing process. A NIC and a MAC address are shown in Figure 1-1.

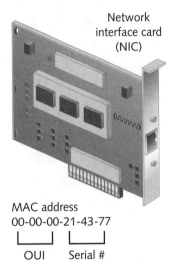

Figure 1-1   MAC address and NIC

After completing this lab, you will be able to:

➤ Describe Data Link and Network addresses and identify key differences between them

➤ Define and describe the function of the MAC address

Materials Required

This lab requires the following:

➤ A computer running Microsoft Windows 98, Windows NT, Windows 2000, Windows 2003, or Windows XP, with Internet access

Estimated completion time: **20 minutes**

ACTIVITY

1. Turn on the computer.

2. Click **Start**, then click **Run**, type **command**, and press **Enter**.

3. Type the command **ipconfig /all** at the DOS prompt, press **Enter**, and then answer the following questions:

   a. What type of NIC is in the computer?

1

    b. What is the MAC (adapter) address?

---

    c. Which part of the MAC address is the OUI?

---

    d. Which part of the MAC address is the serial number?

---

    e. What is the IP address?

---

    f. What is the subnet mask?

---

    g. What is the default gateway?

---

4. Close the DOS window.

5. Open a Web browser, type **http://standards.ieee.org/regauth/oui** in the Address box, and then press **Enter**.

6. In the OUI Search For: text box, type **Cisco**, and then press **Enter**.

7. What is one of the six-digit OUI codes for Cisco?

---

8. Repeat Step 6 and search for **3COM**.

9. What is one of the six-digit OUI codes for 3COM?

---

10. Close the browser window.

Certification Objectives

Objectives for the CCNA exam:

➤ Troubleshoot IP addressing and host configuration

Review Questions

1. Which layer of the OSI model is associated with the physical address?

2. Who assigns the first six digits of the MAC address?

3. Who assigns the second six digits of the MAC address?

4. What alphanumeric characters are acceptable in a MAC address?

5. What does an IP address look like?

6. Who assigns a logical address?

7. Which layer of the OSI model is associated with the logical address?

8. Which address is displayed as hexadecimal numbers?

9. Which address allows transport between networks?

10. Which address does every host on a LAN segment evaluate?

1

LAB 1.4 CONNECTION-ORIENTED VS. CONNECTIONLESS COMMUNICATIONS

Objectives

Protocols that reside at the Transport layer of the OSI model can be connection-oriented or connectionless. The type of transport is usually determined by the application being used. Some applications, such as e-mail, require connection-oriented transfer. Some, such as Internet gaming, are best used with connectionless transfer.

The objective of this lab is to make sure you understand the characteristics of connection-oriented and connectionless communications.

After completing this lab, you will be able to:

➤ Understand the differences between connection-oriented and connectionless communications

Materials Required

This lab requires the following:

➤ A pen or pencil

Estimated completion time: **15 minutes**

ACTIVITY

1. The first column of Table 1-3 contains terms relating to either connection-oriented or connectionless communications. Match these terms to their correct Transport method by adding either "connection-oriented" or "connectionless" in the second column of each row.

Table 1-3   Connection-oriented versus connectionless communications

Description	Transport Method
ACK	
Unreliable	
Regular mail is an example	
Reliable	
Datagram	
Return receipt for mail is an example	
Sessions	

Certification Objectives

Objectives for the CCNA exam:

➤ Describe network communications using layered models

Review Questions

1. Where do connection-oriented and connectionless communications fit into the OSI model?

2. What typically decides whether connection-oriented or connectionless communications are used during a data transfer?

3. Which type of communications (connection-oriented or connectionless) do you think is faster and why?

4. What is the benefit of using connection-oriented communications?

NETWORK DEVICES

Labs included in this chapter

➤ Lab 2.1 Simulating a Network by Connecting a CSU/DSU, Router, Bridge, Three Hubs, and Nine Computers

➤ Lab 2.2 Understanding Various Device Functions

➤ Lab 2.3 Understanding the Difference Between Bridges and Switches

---

CCNA Exam Objectives	
Objective	Lab
Design a simple LAN using Cisco technology	2.1
Design a simple internetwork using Cisco technology	2.1
Describe the components of network devices	2.1, 2.2, 2.3
Describe network communications using layered models	2.1, 2.2

# Chapter 2

LAB 2.1 SIMULATING A NETWORK BY CONNECTING A CSU/DSU, ROUTER, BRIDGE, THREE HUBS, AND NINE COMPUTERS

Objectives

As networks grow and become more complex, various devices such as hubs, bridges, and routers may need to be added. It is important to know how devices interconnect and operate on a LAN and WAN. It is also important to understand how these devices affect network traffic.

The objective of this lab is to provide you with the opportunity to connect a network using various WAN and LAN hardware. Although this is just a simulation, it gives you insight into the hardware connections required in a LAN/WAN relationship and how various devices affect network operations.

Figure 2-1 shows the configuration you will attempt to duplicate. In this lab, you will connect a CSU/DSU to a router with a standard serial cable. The router will then be connected to two hubs via Ethernet ports. On one side of the router there will be two hubs separated by a bridge. There is an additional hub on the other side of the router. (You will simulate the nine workstations in Figure 2-1 with old NICs.)

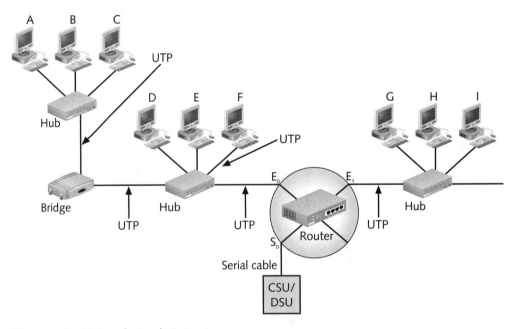

Figure 2-1   Network simulation setup

After completing this lab, you will be able to:

> ➤ Identify various WAN and LAN devices

> ➤ Connect the WAN and LAN devices, as shown in Figure 2-1

> ➤ Understand how various devices affect network communications

Materials Required

This lab requires the following:

> ➤ One CSU/DSU (may substitute a router if necessary)

> ➤ One Cisco router with two Ethernet ports and at least one serial port

> ➤ Transceivers for the router Ethernet ports if these Ethernet ports use an AUI connection instead of RJ-45

> ➤ Transceivers for the bridge connections if the bridge uses AUI connections instead of RJ-45

> ➤ Three hubs

> ➤ One bridge

> ➤ Nine NICs with RJ-45 transceivers for simulating the nine host computers in Figure 2-1

> ➤ Thirteen UTP patch cables

> ➤ One serial cable with a compatible connector for the serial interface on a router on one end and a v.35 connector on the other end to attach to the CSU/DSU. If another router is used instead of the CSU/DSU, the cable connector should match the serial interface on the additional router.

Estimated completion time: **30 minutes**

ACTIVITY

1. Lay out the devices on a table, as shown in Figure 2-1.

2. Connect the CSU/DSU to a serial interface on the router using the serial cable.

3. Connect an Ethernet port on the router to a hub using UTP cable.

4. Connect the other Ethernet port on the router to another hub using UTP cable.

5. Connect the hub on the left to the bridge using UTP cable. There may be a toggle switch on the bridge that needs to be configured, depending on the type of cable you have connected to it. Make sure the switch is in the correct position.

6. Connect the bridge to the next hub using UTP cable.

7. Connect three patch cables to a hub using UTP patch cables. Make sure none of the patch cables are connected to the uplink port of the hub. The uplink port is used for hub-to-hub connections when using a straight-through patch cable instead of a crossover cable. You cannot use this port for workstations. The uplink port is usually marked. Sometimes there is a switch that can be positioned to configure a regular port as an uplink port.

8. Connect the other end of the patch cables used in Step 7 to the NICs to simulate connecting workstations.

9. Repeat Steps 7 and 8 for the other hubs and NICs to complete your simulated network.

Certification Objectives

Objectives for the CCNA exam:

➤ Design a simple LAN using Cisco technology

➤ Design a simple internetwork using Cisco technology

➤ Describe network communications using layered models

➤ Describe the components of network devices

Review Questions

1. Which of the devices that you used in this lab are considered LAN equipment?

2. Which of the devices that you used in this lab are considered WAN equipment?

3. In Figure 2-1, are computers A, B, and C on the same network as D, E, and F?

4. In Figure 2-1, are computers A, B, and C on the same network as G, H, and I?

2

5. How does the bridge operate to filter traffic between the two attached segments in your network?

6. In Figure 2-1, how does the router operate to filter traffic between the segments off of E_0, E_1, and S_0?

7. What kind of domains do bridges create?

8. What kind of domains do routers create?

9. If the LANs in Figure 2-1 are 10-Mbps systems, which computers are sharing this bandwidth?

10. What kind of traffic is a bridge unable to filter?

LAB 2.2 UNDERSTANDING VARIOUS DEVICE FUNCTIONS

Objectives

It is important to understand how all devices operate on a network. These devices include repeaters, hubs, bridges, switches, brouters, routers, and gateways. The purpose of this lab is to make sure you understand the characteristics of all network devices.

After completing this lab, you will be able to:

➤ Identify characteristics of repeaters, hubs, bridges, switches, brouters, routers, and gateways

Materials Required

This lab requires the following:

➤ A pen or pencil

Estimated completion time: **20 minutes**

ACTIVITY

ACTIVITY

1. Fill in the Device(s) column of Table 2-1 with the device being described. You can fill in the table with **repeater**, **hub**, **bridge**, **switch**, **brouter**, **router**, or **gateway**. Note that more than one device might be appropriate for a characteristic.

Table 2-1   Network device characteristics

Characteristic	Device(s)
Operates at upper layers to translate between different protocol suites	
Filters traffic based on MAC address	
Introduces the most latency on a network	
Boosts the signal, but does not segment the network	
Operates differently depending on whether nonroutable or routable protocols are in use	
Creates broadcast domains	
Creates a virtual circuit between sender and receiver	
Forwards broadcast traffic	
Filters traffic based on logical address	
Associated with the term "microsegmentation"	
Creates subnetworks	
Connects computers in a physical star and uses "shared bandwidth"	
Creates collision domains	
Operates at layer 1 of the OSI model	
Operates at layer 2 of the OSI model	
Operates at layer 3 of the OSI model	

Certification Objectives

Objectives for the CCNA exam:

➤ Describe network communications using layered models

➤ Describe the components of network devices

Review Questions

1. When is it appropriate to introduce a router into your network?

2. What can bridges do that hubs and repeaters cannot do?

3. When would introducing a brouter on your network be appropriate?

4. What are the advantages and disadvantages of using a gateway on your network?

5. What is the benefit of replacing hubs on your network with switches?

LAB 2.3 UNDERSTANDING THE DIFFERENCE BETWEEN BRIDGES AND SWITCHES

Objectives

Bridges and switches operate at the Data Link layer of the OSI model and filter traffic using the MAC address; however, they operate somewhat differently. The goal of this lab is for you to understand exactly how bridges and switches operate on a network. You will use Figures 2-2 and 2-3 to learn about properties of both bridges and switches.

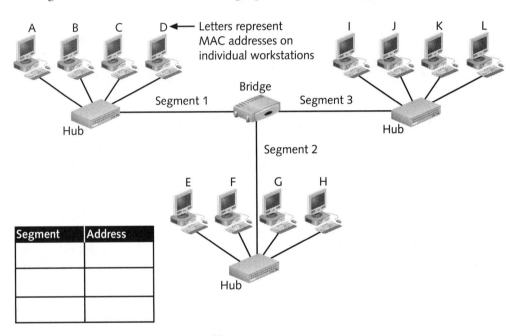

Segment	Address

Figure 2-2   Bridge with bridging table

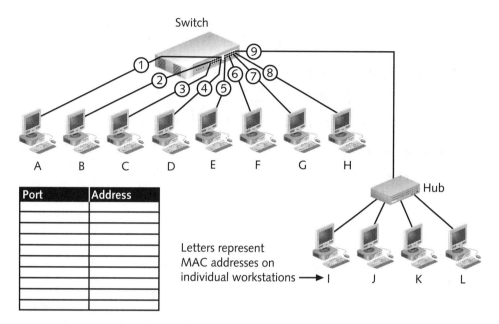

Figure 2-3   Switch with switching table

After completing this lab, you will be able to:

> Describe the tables, bridges, and switches used to filter traffic

> Explain why switches are the device of choice for enhancing network performance

Materials Required

This lab requires the following:

> A pen or pencil

Estimated completion time: **20 minutes**

ACTIVITY

1. Review Figure 2-2. In particular, note how the workstations, represented by letters, connect to the bridge.

2. Complete the bridging table shown in Figure 2-2 by filling in the columns in the table. Note that the letters in the figure represent MAC addresses on workstations.

3. Review Figure 2-3. In particular, note how the workstations, represented by letters, connect to the switch.

4. Complete the switching table shown in Figure 2-3 by filling in the columns in the table. The letters in the figure represent MAC addresses on workstations.

Certification Objectives

Objectives for the CCNA exam:

➤ Describe the components of network devices

Review Questions

1. How many collision domains are defined in Figure 2-2?

2. How many collision domains are defined in Figure 2-3?

3. Examine Figure 2-2. If a frame from computer A has a destination MAC address for computer D, which devices will see the layer 2 information?

4. Examine Figure 2-3. If a frame from computer A has a destination MAC address for computer D, which devices will see the layer 2 information?

5. Examine Figure 2-3. In terms of network performance, what is the difference between computers A through H and I through L?

6. What will a bridge and switch do with a frame for which it has no information about the destination in its table?

7. How do bridges and switches handle broadcast frames?

8. Why is a switch considered more effective than a bridge in terms of increasing network performance?

9. In general, how do bridges and switches dynamically create their tables?

10. What happens to tables when bridges and switches are turned off?

TCP/IP AND IP ADDRESSING

3

Labs included in this chapter

➤ Lab 3.1 Determine an IP Addressing Scheme for Network 192.3.2.0

➤ Lab 3.2 Decode the IP Address 172.16.31.255 /20

➤ Lab 3.3 Decode the IP Address 120.15.179.255 /18

➤ Lab 3.4 Design an Efficient IP Addressing Scheme for Network 176.10.0.0

➤ Lab 3.5 Determine IP and MAC Header Information in an ARP Request and ARP Reply

➤ Lab 3.6 Determine IP and MAC Header Information in a RARP Request

➤ Lab 3.7 Determine IP and MAC Header Information for a Data Packet

➤ Lab 3.8 Perform Binary/Decimal/Hexadecimal Conversions

CCNA Exam Objectives	
Objective	Lab
Design an IP addressing scheme to meet design requirements	3.1, 3.4
Configure IP addresses, subnet masks, and gateway addresses on routers and hosts	3.1, 3.2, 3.3, 3.4
Troubleshoot IP addressing and host configuration	3.1
Evaluate the TCP/IP communication process and its associated protocols	3.5, 3.6, 3.7

LAB 3.1 DETERMINE AN IP ADDRESSING SCHEME FOR NETWORK 192.3.2.0

Objectives

The objective of this lab is to demonstrate a logical way of determining an IP addressing scheme for the network shown in Figure 3-1. In this lab, you determine the subnet mask, the multiplier and usable subnetwork addresses, and the broadcast, interface, and host addresses. You will add labels to Figure 3-1 as you determine specific information.

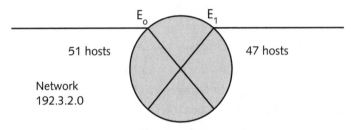

Figure 3-1   Example network

After completing this lab, you will be able to:

➤ Determine the minimum number of bits to borrow when subnetting a given network

➤ Determine and assign IP addresses to the router interfaces and the hosts

➤ Understand which IP addresses are reserved and why

Materials Required

This lab requires the following:

➤ A pen or pencil

Estimated completion time: **20 minutes**

ACTIVITY

1. Review Figure 3-1. In particular, note the number of networks and the structure of the network number.

_____

2. Determine the class of the network by examining the first octet of the network number given.

_____

3. Notice that there are two interfaces, E_0 and E_1. How many usable subnets do you need?

_____

4. Use the formula $2^y - 2 = \#$ of usable subnetworks to solve for y, where $y =$ the number of bits borrowed. Borrow just enough to cover the number of subnets you determined in Step 3.

_____

5. Use the formula $2^x - 2 = \#$ of usable host addresses (where x is the number of bits remaining in the host portion after borrowing) to make sure you have enough bits available for the hosts shown in Figure 3-1.

_____

6. Write the subnet mask in dotted decimal and in binary notation.

_____

7. Determine the multiplier by looking at the decimal value of the last bit borrowed as you move from left to right. The multiplier is either 128, 64, 32, 16, 8, 4, 2, or 1.

_____

8. Use the multiplier determined in Step 7 to determine the usable subnetwork addresses. The subnetwork addresses will increment by the value of the multiplier. Incrementing occurs in the octet in which borrowing broke off (the octet where the multiplier was determined).

_____

9. The last address on any subnet is always a broadcast address. Find this last possible IP address for each subnet. What are the broadcast addresses?

_____

10. Use the remaining addresses (all available addresses minus the subnet addresses and the broadcast addresses) for hosts. What is the range of hosts on each subnet?

_____

_____

_____

11. Assign the first host IP address in each subnet address to a router interface. This first address is available for hosts, but is traditionally used for the router interface connected to the subnet. What addresses did you assign?

_____

12. Write the subnet addresses in binary. How many bits are in the host portion? What does the host portion of these addresses look like?

_____

_____

13. Write the broadcast addresses in binary. What does the host portion of these addresses look like?

_____

Certification Objectives

Objectives for the CCNA exam:

➤ Design an IP addressing scheme to meet design requirements

➤ Configure IP addresses, subnet masks, and gateway addresses on routers and hosts

➤ Troubleshoot IP addressing and host configuration

Review Questions

1. When working with IP addresses and subnetting, why is it important to first identify the class of address and the default subnet mask for that class?

2. What values can a multiplier be?

3. How do you find the multiplier?

4. Why must you subtract 2 from 2^y when determining the number of usable subnets?

5. Why must you subtract 2 from 2^x when determining the number of hosts per subnet?

6. How do you know where to begin incrementing when determining subnet numbers?

7. When working with IP addresses, which addresses can never be assigned to a host?

8. How can you tell if an IP address is a network or subnetwork number if you write out the address in binary?

9. How can you tell that an IP address is a broadcast address if you write out the address in binary?

10. Must router interfaces be assigned the first available host address in a range?

LAB 3.2 DECODE THE IP ADDRESS 172.16.31.255 /20

Objectives

The objective of this lab is to help you become more familiar with subnetting and to expose you to the bit-count notation used to express the subnet mask. Instead of writing out the subnet mask in dotted decimal notation, the bit-count method simply uses a forward slash followed by the number of consecutive ones in the mask. In this lab you will decode the IP address 172.16.31.255 /20 and determine the subnet mask, the multiplier, the network number, and the usable subnetwork addresses and broadcast addresses.

After completing this lab, you will be able to:

➤ Recognize the subnet mask of an IP address given in bit-count format

➤ Determine the network number

➤ Determine subnetwork numbers and broadcast addresses

➤ Identify whether a given IP address is a broadcast, network, or host address

➤ Identify which subnetwork a given IP address is on

Materials Required

This lab requires the following:

➤ A pen or pencil

Estimated completion time: **20 minutes**

ACTIVITY

1. Determine the class of the network address given by examining the first octet.

_____

2. Determine the subnet mask by writing 1s for the first 20 bits of the address and 0s for the last 12 bits. How would you write this subnet mask in dotted decimal notation? How many bits have been borrowed?

_____

_____

_____

3. Use the formula 2^y-2 (where y is the number of bits borrowed from the default host portion) to calculate how many usable subnetworks can be created.

_____

4. Use the formula 2^x-2 (where x is the number of bits remaining in the host portion) to calculate how many usable hosts per subnetwork can be created.

_____

5. Determine the multiplier by looking at the decimal value of the last bit borrowed as you move from left to right. The multiplier is either 128, 64, 32, 16, 8, 4, 2, or 1.

_____

6. Determine the major network number in dotted decimal notation by substituting 0s for the default host portion of the given IP address.

_____

7. Use the multiplier determined in Step 5 to increment up through the first five usable subnetwork addresses. Incrementing occurs in the octet in which borrowing broke off.

_____

_____

_____

8. Determine the broadcast addresses on the five subnetworks listed in Step 7. The broadcast address on each subnetwork is the last possible address before the next subnet begins.

_____

_____

_____

9. What does the address 172.16.31.255 /20 represent?

_____

10. On what network is the given address in Step 9?

_____

Certification Objectives

Objectives for the CCNA exam:

➤ Configure IP addresses, subnet masks, and gateway addresses on routers and hosts

Review Questions

1. Where do you think the term "bit-count" comes from?

2. What is a benefit of using bit-count notation to express the subnet mask?

3. What would the bit-count notation of the IP address given in this lab have been if there were no subnetting?

4. If there were no subnetting in this lab, what would the given IP address have represented?

LAB 3.3 DECODE THE IP ADDRESS 120.15.179.255 /18

Objectives

The objective of this lab is to help you become familiar with subnetting and the bit-count notation used to express the subnet mask. In this lab you will decode the IP address 120.15.179.255 /18 and determine the subnet mask, the multiplier, the network number, and usable subnetwork addresses and broadcast addresses.

After completing this lab, you will be able to:

> ➤ Recognize the subnet mask of an IP address given in bit-count format

> ➤ Determine the network number

> ➤ Determine subnetwork numbers and broadcast addresses

> ➤ Identify whether a given IP address is a broadcast, network, or host address

> ➤ Identify which subnetwork a given IP address is on

Materials Required

This lab requires the following:

> ➤ A pen or pencil

Estimated completion time: **20 minutes**

ACTIVITY

ACTIVITY

1. Determine the class of the network by examining the first octet of the network address given. What is the default mask?

---

2. Determine the subnet mask by writing 1s for the first 18 bits of the address and 0s for the last 14 bits. How would you write this subnet mask in dotted decimal notation?

---

3. Use the formula 2^y-2 (where y is the number of bits borrowed from the default host portion) to calculate how many usable subnetworks can be created.

_____

4. Use the formula 2^x-2 (where x is the number of bits remaining in the host portion) to calculate how many usable hosts per subnetwork can be created.

_____

3

5. Determine the multiplier by looking at the decimal value of the last bit borrowed as you move from left to right. The multiplier is either 128, 64, 32, 16, 8, 4, 2, or 1.

_____

6. Determine the major network number in dotted decimal notation by substituting 0s for the default host portion of the given IP address.

_____

7. Use the multiplier determined in Step 5 to determine the first six usable subnetwork addresses. The incrementing occurs in the octet in which borrowing broke off.

_____

8. Determine the broadcast addresses on the usable subnetworks listed in Step 7. The broadcast address on each subnetwork is the last possible address before the next subnet begins.

_____

9. What does the address 120.15.179.255 /18 represent?

_____

10. On what network is the IP address given in Step 9?

_____

Certification Objectives

Objectives for the CCNA exam:

➤ Configure IP addresses, subnet masks, and gateway addresses on routers and hosts

Review Questions

1. What makes subnetting with Class A and Class B addresses more difficult than subnetting with Class C addresses?

2. What is the maximum number of bits that can be borrowed with a Class C address?

3. What is the maximum number of bits that can be borrowed with a Class B address?

4. What is the maximum number of bits that can be borrowed with a Class A address?

5. What would the subnet mask be in dotted decimal notation for a Class C address if there were 30 hosts per subnet?

LAB 3.4 DESIGN AN EFFICIENT IP ADDRESSING SCHEME FOR NETWORK 176.10.0.0

Objectives

The objective of this lab is to give you a chance to use the subnetting formulas demonstrated in Labs 3.1 through 3.3 and to do so without as much guidance. Use what you have learned to logically determine an efficient IP addressing scheme for network 176.10.0.0, shown in Figure 3-2, that allows 100% growth in the subnets.

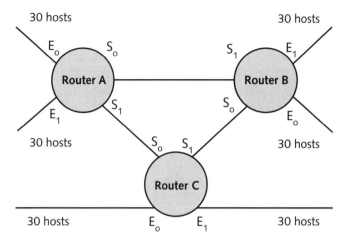

Figure 3-2   Network number 176.10.0.0

In this lab you will determine the subnet mask, the multiplier and usable subnetwork addresses, and the broadcast, interface, and host addresses. You will add labels to Figure 3-2 as you determine specific information.

NOTE

The "S_0" and "S_1" in Figure 3-2 represent serial links. Even though there are no hosts on these connections, they must be considered a subnet and the serial interfaces must be given IP addresses.

After completing this lab, you will be able to:

➤ Determine the minimum number of bits to borrow when subnetting a given network and allowing for 100% growth

➤ Determine and assign IP addresses to the router interfaces and the hosts

➤ Determine the subnet addresses and broadcast addresses on each subnet

Materials Required

This lab requires the following:

➤ A pen or pencil

Estimated completion time: **20 minutes**

ACTIVITY

ACTIVITY

1. Determine the class of the network by examining the first octet of the network address given.

2. Determine the number of subnets in Figure 3-2, and increase this number by 100% to allow for growth. For how many subnets do you allow?

_____

3. Determine how many bits must be borrowed in order to accommodate the number calculated in Step 2. How many usable subnets are available?

_____

4. Determine if borrowing the number of bits calculated in Step 3 leaves enough bits to accommodate the number of hosts per subnet, as indicated in Figure 3-2. How many usable hosts per subnetwork are available?

_____

5. Determine the new subnet mask in dotted decimal and in binary notation.

_____

6. Determine the subnet numbers of the nine existing subnets.

_____

_____

_____

_____

_____

7. Determine the broadcast addresses on each of the nine existing subnets.

_____

_____

_____

_____

_____

8. Determine the usable range of host addresses on each of the nine existing subnets.

_____

_____

_____

_____

_____

9. Assign IP addresses to the following router interfaces:
   - Router A: E_0, E_1, S_0, and S_1

   _____

   _____

   - Router B: E_0, E_1, S_0, and S_1

   _____

   _____

   - Router C: E_0, E_1, S_0, and S_1

   _____

   _____

10. Prove that 176.10.24.0 is a subnet number by using binary notation.

_____

_____

Certification Objectives

Objectives for the CCNA exam:

➤ Design an IP addressing scheme to meet design requirements

➤ Configure IP addresses, subnet masks, and gateway addresses on routers and hosts

Review Questions

1. True or False? Interfaces attached by point-to-point links such as the one between Router A's S_0 and Router B's S_1 in Figure 3-2 are on the same network (or subnetwork).

2. What kind of IP address is indicated by all binary ones in the host portion?

3. What kind of IP address is indicated by all binary zeroes in the host portion?

4. In every subnet created, why are two IP addresses unusable?

5. What is the purpose of a subnet mask?

6. What might you do if, when you borrowed enough bits for subnet numbers, you were not left with enough bits for host numbers?

LAB 3.5 DETERMINE IP AND MAC HEADER INFORMATION IN AN ARP REQUEST AND ARP REPLY

Objectives

The objective of this lab is to help you understand the information contained in the IP and MAC header of an ARP request and ARP reply. In this lab you will determine this IP and MAC information for an ARP request being issued by Computer A to determine the MAC address of Computer C, as illustrated in Figure 3-3.

Computer A

I want to send a message
to Computer C, but I don't
know C's MAC address.
C's IP address is 193.19.20.36.

My MAC: 05:61:8c:01:05:12
 My IP: 193.19.20.45

Figure 3-3 Computer A

After completing this lab, you will be able to:

➤ Determine the IP and MAC header for an ARP request, given the known addresses indicated in Figure 3-3

➤ Determine the IP and MAC header for an ARP reply, given the known addresses indicated in Figures 3-4 and 3-5

3

Materials Required

This lab requires the following:

➤ A pen or pencil

Estimated completion time: **10 minutes**

ACTIVITY

1. Record the destination and source IP addresses in the IP header in Figure 3-4.

2. Record the destination and source MAC addresses in the MAC header in Figure 3-4.

MAC header		IP header		ARP request
Dest	Source	Dest	Source	What is your MAC address?

Figure 3-4   ARP request frame

3. Examine Figure 3-5. Then, record the destination and source IP addresses in the IP header in Figure 3-6.

4. Record the destination and source MAC addresses in the MAC header in Figure 3-6.

Computer C

I'm the one you're looking for.
My MAC address is
09:01:02:98:91:80.

Figure 3-5   Computer C

MAC header		IP header		ARP reply
Dest	Source	Dest	Source	Here is my MAC address.

Figure 3-6   ARP reply frame

Certification Objectives

Objectives for the CCNA exam:

➤ Evaluate the TCP/IP communication process and its associated protocols

Review Questions

1. Explain your destination MAC address entry in Figure 3-4.

2. What will all hosts that see an ARP request do with the information?

3. How does a sending computer know a destination computer's IP address?

4. What type of frame is the ARP reply—unicast or broadcast?

5. Because ARP uses bandwidth by broadcasting, exactly how does ARP save bandwidth overall?

LAB 3.6 DETERMINE IP AND MAC HEADER INFORMATION IN AN RARP REQUEST

Objectives

The objective of this lab is to help you understand the information contained in the IP and MAC header of a Reverse ARP (RARP) request. In this lab you will determine this IP and MAC information for the RARP request issued by Computer D, as shown in Figure 3-7.

Computer D

I know my MAC address is
01:09:42:71:93:64, but I
don't know my IP address.

Figure 3-7   Computer D

After completing this lab, you will be able to:

➤ Determine the IP and MAC header for an RARP request, given the known
MAC address indicated in Figure 3-7

Materials Required

This lab requires the following:

➤ A pen or pencil

Estimated completion time: **10 minutes**

ACTIVITY

1. Examine Figure 3-7. Then, record the destination and source IP addresses in
Figure 3-8 using the information in Figure 3-7.

2. Record the destination and source MAC addresses in Figure 3-8.

MAC header		IP header		RARP request
Dest	Source	Dest	Source	What is my IP address?

Figure 3-8   RARP request frame

Certification Objectives

Objectives for the CCNA exam:

➤ Evaluate the TCP/IP communication process and its associated protocols

Review Questions

1. What kind of address is the destination MAC address in an RARP request?

2. How does a computer know its own MAC address?

3. Based on your lab activity, explain your entry for the source IP address in the RARP request.

4. What kind of address is the destination IP address in an RARP request?

5. How does the RARP server know which IP address to assign to an RARP client?

LAB 3.7 DETERMINE IP AND MAC HEADER INFORMATION FOR A DATA PACKET

Objectives

The objective of this lab is to help you understand the information contained in the IP and MAC header of a data packet as it travels from the source to the destination host through a router. In this lab, you will determine this IP and MAC information between computer A and router interface E_1 and again between router interface E_0 and computer B, as shown in Figure 3-9.

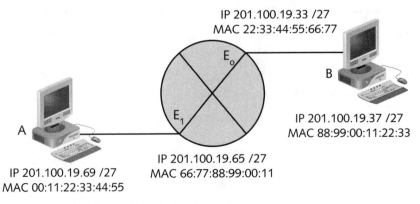

Figure 3-9   MAC and IP header information

After completing this lab, you will be able to:

➤ Determine the IP and MAC header for a data packet as it travels through a router, given the known MAC and IP information indicated in Figure 3-9

➤ Understand the concept of a default gateway

Materials Required

This lab requires the following:

➤ A pen or pencil

Estimated completion time: **10 minutes**

ACTIVITY

1. Record the destination and source IP addresses in Figure 3-10 for a frame transmitted from computer A to interface E_1 on the router that is destined for computer B.

MAC header		IP header		Data
Dest	Source	Dest	Source	

Figure 3-10   Frame from computer A to router interface E_1

2. Record the destination and source MAC address in Figure 3-10 for a frame transmitted from computer A to interface E_1 on the router that is destined for computer B.

3. Record the destination and source IP addresses in Figure 3-11 for a frame transmitted from the E_0 interface on the router to computer B during its journey from computer A to computer B.

4. Record the destination and source MAC address in Figure 3-11 for a frame transmitted from E_0 on the router to computer B during its journey from computer A to computer B.

MAC header		IP header		Data
Dest	Source	Dest	Source	

Figure 3-11 Frame from router interface E_0 to computer B

Certification Objectives

Objectives for the CCNA exam:

➤ Evaluate the TCP/IP communication process and its associated protocols

Review Questions

1. In Figure 3-9, what is the default gateway for computer A?

2. In Figure 3-9, what is the default gateway for computer B?

3. What can you say about the source and destination IP addresses in a frame as the data travels across routers in its journey from original sender to ultimate receiver?

4. What can you say about the source and destination MAC addresses in a frame as the data travels across routers in its journey from original sender to ultimate receiver?

5. Where do routers get the information necessary to make forwarding decisions?

6. Why do computers usually need a default gateway, and when is it used?

LAB 3.8 PERFORM BINARY/DECIMAL/HEXADECIMAL CONVERSIONS

Objectives

The objective of this lab is to help you understand the relationships between binary, decimal, and hexadecimal numbering systems and to teach you how to convert between them. In this lab you will convert a decimal number to binary and then to hexadecimal. Next, you will convert a hexadecimal number to binary and then to decimal.

After completing this lab, you will be able to:

➤ Convert from decimal to binary

➤ Convert from hexadecimal to binary to decimal

➤ Convert from binary to hexadecimal

Materials Required

This lab requires the following:

➤ A pen or pencil

Estimated completion time: **30 minutes**

ACTIVITY

1. The place values for the eight binary digits used in IPv4 addressing are as follows: 128, 64, 32, 16, 8, 4, 2, 1. Expand this range to include an additional four bits. Do this by recording the place values for 2^{11}, 2^{10}, 2^9, and 2^8.

   _____

2. Express the decimal value 2001 in binary by placing 1s in the binary positions requiring the addition of the corresponding place value. Place 0s in the binary positions where the corresponding place value should not be added. You should have 11 binary digits.

   _____

3. To express this binary number in hexadecimal, you must first group the 11 digits in sets of four. Because 11 is not evenly divisible by 4, begin by adding a leading zero to your binary number so that you have 12 binary digits. The decimal equivalent should still be 2001. It should not change because of the added leading zero. Record your binary 12-digit number below.

   _____

4. Group the 12 binary digits into three sets of four binary digits.

_____

5. Convert each group of binary digits to a hexadecimal digit using Table 3-1. The result should be a three-digit hex number.

_____

Table 3-1 Binary to hex to decimal conversion

Binary	Hexadecimal	Decimal
0000	0	0
0001	1	1
0010	2	2
0011	3	3
0100	4	4
0101	5	5
0110	6	6
0111	7	7
1000	8	8
1001	9	9
1010	A	10
1011	B	11
1100	C	12
1101	D	13
1110	E	14
1111	F	15

6. Check your answer by multiplying the hexadecimal digits in your answer by their corresponding place value to get the decimal equivalent. For example: (3rd hex digit * 16^2) + (2nd hex digit * 16^1) + (1st hex digit * 16^0). Your decimal equivalent should equal 2001. Did you get the correct result? If not, double-check your decimal to binary and binary to hexadecimal conversions.

7. Next, try converting a hexadecimal number (CD4) to binary and then to decimal. First, treat each hexadecimal digit as four binary digits, using Table 3-1 as necessary. Record your answer below. You should have 12 binary digits grouped in three sets of four.

_____

8. To convert the binary number recorded in Step 7, add the decimal place values of the 1's binary digits. Record your answer below.

_____

9. To double-check your answer, multiply the decimal value of each hexadecimal digit in CD4 with the corresponding place value, as you did in Step 6. Your answer should be 3284.

Certification Objectives

Objectives for the CCNA exam:

This lab does not map to a certification objective; however, it contains information that is covered on the CCNA exam.

Review Questions

1. For what purposes is the binary numbering system used in networking?

2. For what purposes is the hexadecimal numbering system used in networking?

3. Why does it require fewer hexadecimal numerals than binary numerals to express any given number?

4. True or False? Some numbers are too large to be expressed in binary.

NETWORK TOPOLOGY AND DESIGN

CCNA Exam Objectives

These labs do not map to certification objectives; however, they contain information that will be beneficial to your professional development.

LAB 4.1 MAKE AND TEST A STRAIGHT-THROUGH PATCH CABLE

Objectives

The objective of this lab is to teach you to make a typical unshielded twisted-pair (UTP) patch cable. Although you can readily purchase patch cables, making and testing one will give you insight to how UTP cable is made and how it operates. In addition, there are some instances where you will have to make a cable, so it is important to know how.

In this lab, you will make a straight-through cable according to the EIA/TIA 568B specifications shown in Figure 4-1. You will then test the cable using a simple continuity tester or other cable tester.

EIA/TIA 568B Ethernet-data	White/ orange	Orange	White/ green	Blue	White/ blue	Green	White/ brown	Brown
EIA/TIA 568A voice & data	White/ green	Green	White/ orange	Blue	White/ blue	Orange	White/ brown	Brown

Figure 4-1   EIA/TIA patch cable specifications

After completing this lab, you will be able to:

➤ Make a working patch cable per EIA/TIA 568B specifications

➤ Test the cable for continuity

Materials Required

This lab requires the following:

➤ A box or spool of CAT 5 UTP cable

➤ One UTP cable crimper and one pair of wire cutters for every four students

➤ Box of RJ-45 connectors

➤ One UTP continuity tester (or other cable tester) for every four students

Estimated completion time: **60 minutes**

ACTIVITY

1. Score (do not penetrate) the jacket of the cable with the wire cutters at about 1.5" down. Remove the outer jacket only, not the insulation on the individual wires.

2. Bend the cable gently at the score mark and try to snap off the jacket.

3. Untwist all the wires down to the jacket.

4. Moving from left to right, put the wires in order. Use the EIA/TIA 568B standard colors shown in Figure 4-1.

5. Use your thumb and third finger to flatten the wires.

6. Hold the wires flat and tightly together with the thumb and third finger of one hand, close to the base of the jacket.

7. Use the wire cutters to snip the wires all at once in a straight line to about 0.5" above the base of the jacket.

8. Keep your grip on the wires while you slide the RJ-45 connector onto the ends of the wires. Make sure you still have the wires in the correct order. The clip of the connector should be face down.

9. Slide the wires all the way in, and make sure the edge of the jacket slides just up under the edge of the connector about 0.25".

10. Slip the connector into the crimper tool. The clip of the connector should be face down.

11. Keep your hands free of the blade as you squeeze the handles of the tool together until they release again.

12. Repeat Steps 1 through 11 for the other end of the wire. Use the same EIA/TIA 568B standard for this opposite end.

13. Now test your cable by inserting both ends of the cable into the continuity tester. As you continually press the tester button, the indicator lights should light up to tell you that you have a good connection for each of the eight connections. If you have a more advanced type of tester, you may use that instead.

    The lights should match if you made a successful, straight-through EIA/TIA cable; that is, light one on the left side should match up with light one on the right side. If light one matches up with light two, for example, you have crossed pairs.

14. If your cables fail the test, visually inspect the connector and make sure the color coding is correct.

15. If the color coding is correct and the cable is still failing, try re-crimping the connectors.

16. If the color coding is incorrect or re-crimping doesn't work, you have to cut the wire and start over. You cannot reuse the connector after it has been crimped.

Certification Objectives

Objectives for the CCNA exam:

This lab does not map to a certification objective; however, it contains information that is beneficial to your professional development.

Review Questions

1. When might you have to make a patch cable?

2. What does a wire map tell you?

3. Why is it important to slide the jacket of the cable under the connector?

4. What kind of interference results from the bleeding of the signal from one wire pair onto another?

5. What are the two most popular LAN architectures using UTP?

LAB 4.2 MAKE AND TEST A CROSSOVER PATCH CABLE

Objectives

The objective of this lab is to teach you to make a crossover UTP patch cable. A crossover cable may be required when connecting a hub to a hub or other device-to-device connection. A crossover cable is also known as a cross-connect cable.

Although you can readily purchase crossover cables, making and testing one will give you insight about how UTP cable is made and how a crossover cable differs from a straight-through cable. In addition, you may find yourself in the position of having to make a crossover cable, so it is important that you know how.

In this lab, you will make a crossover cable according to the EIA/TIA 568A and 568B specifications shown in Figure 4-1. You will then test the cable using a simple continuity tester.

After completing this lab, you will be able to:

➤ Make a working crossover cable per EIA/TIA 568A and 568B specifications

➤ Test the cable for continuity

Materials Required

This lab requires the following:

➤ A box or spool of CAT 5 UTP cable

➤ One UTP cable crimper and one pair of wire cutters for every four students

➤ Box of RJ-45 connectors

➤ One UTP continuity tester (or other cable tester) for every four students

4

| Estimated completion time: **60 minutes** |

ACTIVITY

ACTIVITY

1. Score (do not penetrate) the jacket of the cable with the wire cutters at about 1.5" down. Remove the outer jacket only, not the insulation on the individual wires.

2. Bend the cable gently at the score mark and try to snap off the jacket.

3. Untwist all the wires down to the jacket.

4. Moving from left to right, put the wires in order. Use the EIA/TIA 568B standard colors shown in Figure 4-1.

5. Use your thumb and third finger to flatten the wires.

6. Hold the wires flat and tightly together with the thumb and third finger of one hand, close to the base.

7. Use the wire cutters to snip the wires to about 0.5" above the base of the jacket.

8. Keep your grip on the wires while you slide the RJ-45 connector onto the ends of the wires. Make sure you still have the wires in the correct order. The clip of the connector should be face down.

9. Slide the wires all the way in, and make sure the edge of the jacket slides just up under the edge of the connector about 0.25".

10. Slip the connector into the crimper tool. The clip of the connector should be face down.

11. Keep your hands free of the blade as you squeeze the handles of the tool together until they release again.

12. Repeat Steps 1 through 11 for the other end of the wire, but this time use the color configuration that corresponds to the EIA/TIA 568A standard in Figure 4-1. This will make the cable a crossover cable. Visually inspect your cable.

13. Now test your cable by inserting both ends of the cable into the continuity tester. As you continually press the tester button, the indicator lights should light up to tell you that you have a good connection for each of the eight connections.

If you made a successful crossover cable, the lights for one and three should match and the lights for two and six should match, as shown in Figure 4-2.

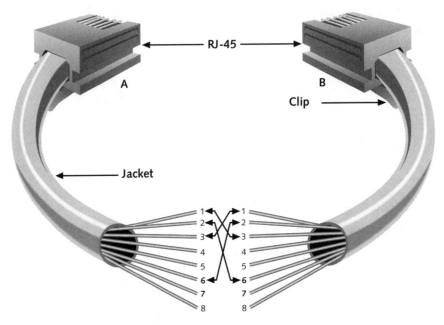

Figure 4-2   Crossover cable

14. If your cables fail the test, visually inspect the connector and make sure the color coding is correct.

15. If the color coding is correct and the cable still fails, try re-crimping the connectors.

16. If the color coding is not correct or re-crimping doesn't work, you will have to cut the wire and start over. You cannot reuse the connector after it has been crimped.

Certification Objectives

Objectives for the CCNA exam:

This lab does not map to a certification objective; however, it contains information that will be beneficial to your professional development.

Review Questions

1. In a UTP cable, which wires does Ethernet use?

2. When might you need a crossover cable?

3. If you have made a successful crossover cable, what does the wire map indicate?

4. What organizations control the specifications for UTP cable configuration on Ethernet networks?

5. What kind of tool is used to connect the RJ-45 connector to the wires when making a patch cable?

LAB 4.3 IDENTIFY VARIOUS CABLE TYPES AND CONNECTORS

Objectives

The objective of this lab is to help you become familiar with various cable types and connectors that might be part of a LAN or WAN. In this lab, your instructor will label examples of cable and connectors with the letters A through L. You will match the labeled hardware with the following descriptions.

After completing this lab, you will be able to:

➤ Identify various cable types and connectors that are part of typical LAN/WAN installations

Materials Required

This lab requires the following:

➤ Examples of cable and connectors, as listed in the Activity section in this lab, that are labeled from A through L

Estimated completion time: **30 minutes**

ACTIVITY

1. Match the labeled connectors and cable with the following descriptions. Put the appropriate letter next to the associated description.

- Thinnet   _____
- Thicknet   _____
- Category 6 UTP   _____
- Category 5 UTP   _____
- Category 3 UTP   _____
- Multimode fiber   _____
- Single-mode fiber   _____
- STP   _____
- T-connector   _____
- RJ-45 connector   _____
- RG-58 terminator   _____
- Plenum cable   _____

Certification Objectives

Objectives for the CCNA exam:

This lab does not map to a certification objective; however, it contains information that will be beneficial to your professional development.

Review Questions

1. What is the difference between multimode and single-mode fiber?

2. What purpose does the RG-58 terminator serve?

3. What is the difference between STP and UTP?

4. What is the difference between Category 3 and Category 5 UTP?

5. Why don't you see thinnet or thicknet in use on LANs much anymore?

4

LAB 4.4 PUNCH DOWN AND TEST UTP CABLE

Objectives

The purpose of this lab is to familiarize you with a patch panel and to teach you to punch down and test cable.

In this lab, you will use the EIA/TIA 568B specification to make one end of a patch cable. You will connect the other end to the pin side of the patch panel using the proper technique. You will finish by testing your connection for continuity.

After completing this lab, you will be able to:

➤ Punch down UTP cable into a patch panel

➤ Test the connection using a simple cable tester

Materials Required

This lab requires the following:

➤ One patch panel for every four students, preferably mounted on a rack to hold it steady

➤ One Krone tool or other punch-down tool for every four students

➤ Spool of Category 5 UTP cable

➤ A box of RJ-45 connectors

➤ One pair of wire cutters for every four students

➤ Several properly made UTP patch cables for testing

Estimated completion time: **60 minutes**

ACTIVITY

1. Make one end of an EIA/TIA 568B patch cable following the specifications in Figure 4-1.

2. At the opposite end of the cable connection you just made, score (do not penetrate) the jacket of the cable with the wire cutters at about 1.5" down. Remove the outer jacket only, not the insulation on the individual wires.

3. Bend the cable gently at the score mark and try to snap off the jacket.

4. Untwist the wires as little as possible.

5. Moving from left to right, line up wire colors with the punch-down block pin colors. The striped wires go to the left of the pin; the solid-color wires go to the right of the pin.

6. Push the wires between the pins, being careful to keep the correct color order. Only 0.25" of wire should be exposed between the cable jacket and the pins. Let the rest of the wire stick out above the pins.

7. Keep the cable centered about the pins. If the cable becomes skewed to the right or left, network performance will be affected.

8. Position the punch-down tool over the first wire. The cut side of the tool should face up.

9. Position the tool perpendicular to the block. Push into the wire with the tool.

10. The excess wire above the block should snap off. If it doesn't, you can twist it off with your fingers.

11. Continue punching down the rest of the wires.

12. When you finish, you should have a UTP cable attached at one end to the punch-down block. An RJ-45 connector should be at the other end.

13. To test the continuity of the connection, connect a regular EIA/TIA 568B patch cable to the port on the other side of the punch-down block that corresponds to the pin you have wired.

14. Plug the end of the patch cable that is connected to the port into a cable tester.

15. Plug the patch cable that is connected to the pin side of the block into the cable tester.

16. Each time you press the test button, the indicator lights should tell you that you have a good connection for that particular pair of wires.

17. If your cables fail the test, start troubleshooting with the help of your instructor.

Certification Objectives

Objectives for the CCNA exam:

This lab does not map to a certification objective; however, it contains information that will be beneficial to your professional development.

Review Questions

1. True or False? You should follow the color coding on the pins rather than the EIA/TIA 568A or 568B standard.

2. What is the opposite side of the pin side of the panel called?

3. What is the purpose of a patch panel?

4. What is the name of the tool used when attaching UTP cable wires to the pin side of the panel?

5. Does a patch panel repeat a signal?

LAB 4.5 CALCULATE BANDWIDTH

Objectives

The objective of this lab is to practice bandwidth and throughput calculations. Before you can design the topology of the network, you must discover the maximum bandwidth that will be demanded on the network. You should then factor in a growth allowance.

For the most part, bandwidth determines the media type, and the media type in turn dictates the physical and logical network topology. In this lab you will determine the bandwidth required for a hypothetical network based on the parameters given. You will then determine the type of topology that this bandwidth dictates.

After completing this lab, you will be able to:

➤ Calculate bandwidth given file size and transmission time

➤ Understand how and why bandwidth determines topology

Materials Required

This lab requires the following:

➤ Pencil or pen

➤ Calculator

Estimated completion time: **30 minutes**

ACTIVITY

ACTIVITY

1. Review the following scenario.

   Lowry A/V, Inc., is an emerging e-commerce and call center based in Charlottesville, Virginia, that sells and distributes high-end audio and video equipment via the Web and catalogs. Recently, they decided to build an additional facility in Malabar, Florida. This expansion requires a complete redesign of the company's network. On the LAN side they need to back up their database twice a day. The company's database is typically about 5 GB in size, but may increase over the next few years. This backup should not take more than 10 minutes. On the WAN side, the firm needs approximately 1.2 Mbps.

2. What formula do you use to calculate the necessary bandwidth for the LAN?

   _____

3. What is the LAN bandwidth required in Mbps? Do not adjust for growth at this time.

   _____

4. If the company wants a 40% growth factor built into the calculation, what will the new bandwidth requirement be?

   _____

5. Which cable type would you recommend for the LAN? Justify your answer.

   _____

6. Lowry A/V is considering a T1 connection for the WAN. Use the bandwidth formula to determine approximately how fast (in seconds) they will be able to transmit a 6-MB file across the T1 link. The bandwidth of a T1 is 1.54 Mbps.

   _____

Certification Objectives

Objectives for the CCNA exam:

This lab does not map to a certification objective; however, it contains information that will be beneficial to your professional development.

Review Questions

1. What is the difference between throughput and bandwidth?

2. What is the purpose of the growth factor?

4

3. What cable types, other than UTP, can be used on a LAN?

4. What are the benefits of using UTP?

# CHAPTER FIVE

WAN CONCEPTS

Labs included in this chapter

➤ Lab 5.1 Identify Connection Methods Used with WAN Data Link Layer Protocols

➤ Lab 5.2 Understand WAN Switching Terminology

➤ Lab 5.3 Associate WAN Technologies with the Appropriate Layer of the OSI Reference Model

CCNA Exam Objectives	
Objective	Lab
Evaluate key characteristics of WANs	5.1, 5.2, 5.3
Use the OSI model as a guide for systematic network troubleshooting	5.3
Describe network communications using layered models	5.3

LAB 5.1 IDENTIFY CONNECTION METHODS USED WITH WAN DATA LINK LAYER PROTOCOLS

Objectives

The objective of this lab is to clarify the relationship between WAN Data Link layer protocols and the connection methods with which they are typically used. In this lab you will define the protocol terms and indicate whether a particular WAN Data Link layer protocol is associated with point-to-point, multipoint, or switched connection methods.

After completing this lab you will:

➤ Understand the three connection methods used in WAN transmission

➤ Understand the various Data Link layer protocols associated with the WAN connection methods

Materials Required

This lab requires the following:

➤ Pencil or pen

Estimated completion time: **20 minutes**

ACTIVITY

ACTIVITY

1. For each protocol listed in Table 5-1, give the definition. Then, write in the WAN connection method—point-to-point, multipoint, or switched—that applies to each protocol. Note that a protocol can be associated with more than one connection method.

Table 5-1   WAN connection methods

WAN Protocol	Define the Term	Connection Method
LAPD		
SDLC		
PPP		
X.25		
ATM		
HDLC		
Frame Relay		

Certification Objectives

Objectives for the CCNA exam:

➤ Evaluate key characteristics of WANs

Review Questions

1. Why might you choose a point-to-point dedicated line rather than a switched service?

2. What is the advantage of Frame Relay as compared with X.25?

3. How is ATM different from X.25 and Frame Relay?

4. On which protocol is PPP based?

5. Which protocol did PPP replace?

LAB 5.2 UNDERSTAND WAN SWITCHING TERMINOLOGY

Objectives

The objective of this lab is to help you learn the terminology and definitions associated with switching technologies. In this lab, you will match the correct switching term with a definition.

After completing this lab you will:

➤ Understand characteristics of WAN switching technologies

➤ Relate WAN switching terms to the technology with which they are associated

Materials Required

This lab requires the following:

➤ Pencil or pen

Estimated completion time: **20 minutes**

ACTIVITY

1. Match each term in the following bulleted list with a definition in the numbered list.

- X.25
- LAPB
- Inverse ARP
- DLCI
- Frame Relay
- Multiplex
- PVC
- CIR
- LMI
- ISDN
- BRI
- ATM

- BECN
- FECN
- D-channel
- B-channel
- X.21
- LAPD
- Cell
- CSU/DSU
- Synchronous
- Asynchronous
- Terminal adapter
- Packet-switched

2. Type of network in which relatively small units of data are routed through the network based on the destination address. The data units may take different paths to the destination.

_____

3. LAN and WAN protocol that handles digital data transmission up to 622 Mbps. Requires dedicated hardware.

_____

4. ITU standard for dial-up, digital transmission over ordinary telephone wires, in addition to other media. Transmission speeds are up to 128 Kbps for home use.

_____

5. Hardware that converts digital data frames from a LAN into frames appropriate for a WAN and vice versa. Provider end of the WAN link.

_____

6. Cost-efficient data transmission protocol that uses a variable-size packet and leaves any necessary error correction to the upper-layer protocols.

_____

7. ISDN service consisting of two 64-Kbps B-channels and one 16-Kbps D-channel.

_____

8. Keepalive mechanism for Frame Relay that periodically sends the router status information regarding a transmission.

9. Allows Frame Relay router to discover the destination address of a node associated with the virtual circuit.

10. Carries control and signaling information for ISDN.

11. Underlying Data Link layer protocol for X.25.

12. Used to identify the PVC or SVC on a Frame Relay network.

13. Minimum bandwidth associated with a logical connection in a Frame Relay network.

14. Term used for the fixed-length packet associated with ATM transmission.

15. Should result in a router transmitting less traffic.

16. Relies on start and stop bits to define endpoints of a transmission.

17. Physical layer standard that defines the interface between the DTE and the DCE.

18. Warns the next router that congestion has occurred.

19. Underlying protocol for transmission over ISDN lines.

20. A Frame Relay connection that the network administrator sets up and that performs as if it were a dedicated line.

21. Used to transfer data over ISDN lines.

22. Combining different traffic streams onto a single physical line.

23. Interface between non–ISDN equipment and an ISDN line.

_____

24. Data Link layer WAN protocol originally developed to work over existing ana-log phone lines. Uses extensive error checking.

_____

25. Communications that rely on a clock.

_____

Certification Objectives

Objectives for the CCNA exam:

➤ Evaluate key characteristics of WANs

Review Questions

1. List all the terms in this lab that relate to Frame Relay.

2. List all the terms in this lab that relate to ISDN.

3. What are the two ISDN services and their corresponding bandwidths?

LAB 5.3 ASSOCIATE WAN TECHNOLOGIES WITH THE APPROPRIATE LAYER OF THE OSI REFERENCE MODEL

Objectives

The objective of this lab is to learn where WAN technologies fit into the OSI reference model. In this lab, you will indicate at which OSI layer(s) the listed WAN technology resides.

After completing this lab you will:

➤ Understand where various WAN technologies fit into the OSI reference model

Materials Required

This lab requires the following:

➤ Pencil or pen

➤ Computer with Internet access for help in answering the review questions

Estimated completion time: **20 minutes**

ACTIVITY

1. Next to each WAN technology listed in Table 5-2, write at which layer(s) of the OSI reference model the technology resides.

Table 5-2 WAN technologies in the OSI model

5

WAN Technology	Associated OSI Model Layer(s)
RS-232	
X.25	
LAPD	
HSSI	
Frame Relay	
SDLC	
X.21	
V.35	
PPP	
HDLC	
ATM	
EIA-530	

Certification Objectives

Objectives for the CCNA exam:

➤ Evaluate key characteristics of WANs

➤ Use the OSI model as a guide for systematic network troubleshooting

➤ Describe network communications using layered models

Review Questions

1. Define the RS-232 specification. In particular, indicate the connector type and the supported bandwidth.

2. Define the EIA-530 specification. In particular, indicate the connector type and the bandwidth supported.

3. Define the HSSI specification. In particular, indicate the connector type and the bandwidth supported.

4. Define the V.35 specification. In particular, indicate the bandwidth supported.

5. Define the X.21 specification. In particular, indicate the bandwidth supported.

ROUTER AND IOS BASICS

Labs included in this chapter

➤ Lab 6.1 Connect the Internetwork Lab

➤ Lab 6.2 Configure HyperTerminal to Access a Cisco Router

➤ Lab 6.3 Use the System Configuration Dialog to Configure a Cisco Router

➤ Lab 6.4 Configure Console and Aux Passwords

➤ Lab 6.5 Use Help, the Command History, Enhanced Editing Features, and the Show Command

---

CCNA Exam Objectives	
Objective	Lab
Design a simple internetwork using Cisco technology	6.1
Configure IP addresses, subnet masks, and gateway addresses on routers and hosts	6.3
Perform an initial configuration on a router	6.3
Configure a router for additional administrative functionality	6.4
Manage system image and device configuration files	6.5
Troubleshoot a device as part of a working network	6.5

Lab 6.1 Connect the Internetwork Lab

Objectives

The objective of this lab is to give you experience in making the hardware connections necessary to configure the Cisco router lab. This includes connecting computers, hubs, and routers to each other. In this lab you will connect five Cisco routers, five hubs, and five computers in preparation for router configuration.

After completing this lab, you will be able to:

➤ Identify routers, hubs, transceivers, DCE/DTE cables, rollover cables, DB-9 and/or DB-25 connectors, and the COM ports on the computers

➤ Correctly connect the hardware using the proper cables

Materials Required

This lab requires the following:

➤ Four 2501 series routers with power cables (could substitute a different series but must have two serial interfaces and one Ethernet interface)

➤ One 2514 series router with power cable (could substitute a different series but must have two serial interfaces and two Ethernet interfaces)

➤ Five hubs with power cables (can substitute switches)

➤ Three V.35 DTE cables (male) with serial ends to match serial interfaces on routers

➤ Three V.35 DCE cables (female) with serial ends to match serial interfaces on routers

➤ Six UTP patch cables

➤ Six Ethernet 10BaseT UTP-to-AUI transceivers (you will not need these if the Ethernet interfaces on the routers are RJ-45 transceivers)

➤ Five RJ-45 to RJ-45 rollover cables

➤ Five RJ-45 to DB-25 or DB-9 connectors

➤ Power strips

➤ Five Windows computers with a COM port available. Computers should be set up and labeled lab-a through lab-e, as shown in Figure 6-1. Routers and hubs can be placed in a rack.

➤ Routers labeled lab-a through lab-e. Router A should be the router with the two Ethernet interfaces.

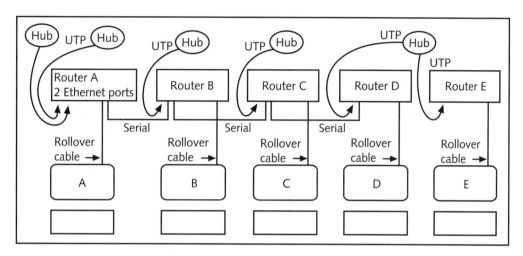

Figure 6-1 Standard internetwork lab configuration

Estimated completion time: **30 minutes**

ACTIVITY

1. Lay the five routers on the long table behind the computers with the routers' port sides facing the back of the computers. Alternatively, load the routers in a rack in order from the lab-a router at the top to the lab-e router at the bottom.

2. Place a hub behind or on top of each router.

3. Refer to Figure 6-2 for help with the next steps regarding cabling. The TFTP server will be connected in Lab 7.2.

4. Connect the lab-a router's first Ethernet interface to the hub behind it using a UTP patch cable. You may need a transceiver on the AUI0 port on the router to accept the RJ-45 connector. At the hub, make sure the UTP is not plugged into an uplink port. Ask your instructor for help if you cannot determine which port is the uplink port.

5. Connect the lab-a router to a second hub via its second Ethernet port or AUI1 port, as outlined in Step 4.

6. Connect the lab-b router to a third hub, as outlined in Step 4.

7. Connect the lab-c router to a fourth hub, as outlined in Step 4.

8. Connect both the lab-d and lab-e routers to the fifth hub, as outlined in Step 4 and shown in Figure 6-2.

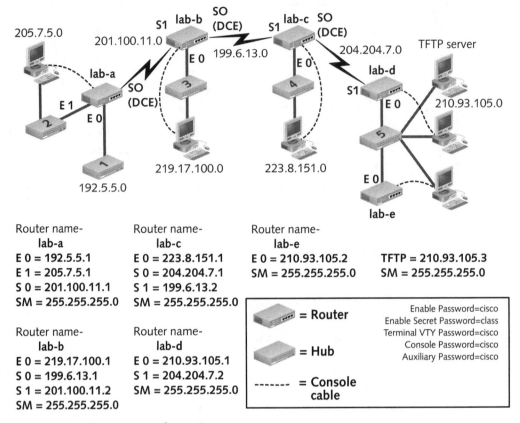

Figure 6-2 Connection information

9. Connect the console port of the lab-a router to a COM port on computer A using the router rollover cable and Figure 6-1 as your guide. At the COM port, you will need either a DB-25 or DB-9 connector between the RJ-45 rollover cable and the COM port.

10. Repeat Step 9 for the remaining routers and computers.

11. The DTE and DCE cables should be marked as such. Connect each V.35 end of a DTE cable to the V.35 end of a DCE cable. You should now have three cables, each with a DTE end and a DCE end.

12. The 60-pin ends (or other serial end types) of the DTE and DCE serial cables should be connected to the serial ports on the routers. Be extremely careful to line up the connections correctly. Pins can easily be damaged if a connection is forced. Connect the lab-a router to the lab-b router using Figure 6-2 as a reference. Notice that the DCE end goes in the lab-a router's S0 port, and the DTE end goes in the lab-b router's S1 port. In this lab setup, the DCE ends always go into the S0 ports.

13. Repeat Step 12 to connect the lab-b router to the lab-c router, and again to connect the lab-c router to the lab-d router.

14. Connect all devices to the power strips using the correct power cables.

15. Ask your instructor to check your lab setup.

Certification Objectives

Objectives for the CCNA exam:

➤ Design a simple internetwork using Cisco technology

Review Questions

1. For what is a transceiver used?

2. This lab connects routers directly to each other via serial cables. Is this a typical configuration? If not, to what equipment does the DCE end of the serial cable usually connect?

3. What does a rollover (console) cable look like?

4. What kind of port does the console cable attach to on the computer?

5. What kind of port does the UTP patch cable attach to on the router?

LAB 6.2 CONFIGURE HYPERTERMINAL TO ACCESS A CISCO ROUTER

Objectives

The objective of this lab is to give you experience configuring the Windows HyperTerminal program, which is frequently used to configure routers. In this lab you will configure HyperTerminal on a computer connected to a router via the console port. The computer was connected to the router in Lab 6.1.

After completing this lab, you will be able to:

➤ Configure HyperTerminal on a Windows computer for use in configuring Cisco routers

Materials Required

This lab requires the following:

> The internetworking lab setup in Lab 6.1 and shown in Figure 6-2, or a Windows computer connected to a Cisco router via the console port on the router

> HyperTerminal installed on a Windows computer

Estimated completion time: **30 minutes**

ACTIVITY

1. Make sure the router connected to the computer is turned off.

2. Turn on the Windows computer.

3. Click **Start**, point to **Programs**, point to **Accessories**, point to **Communications**, and then click **HyperTerminal**. This is the procedure for most Windows computers. The procedure, however, may be slightly different on your Windows computer.

4. Click **File** on the menu bar, and then click **New Connection** to open the New Connection window.

5. Enter an area code if prompted, and then click **No** if asked to install a modem.

6. In the Connection Description dialog box, enter the name **Cisco** for the connection. Click **OK** to continue.

7. You must now configure your connection to the router via the Connect To dialog box. In the **Connect Using** selection box, choose the COM port to which the RJ-45 to DB-9 or DB-25 connector is attached. Click **OK** to continue.

8. Configure these settings for the COM port: Bits per second: **9600**; Data bits: **8**; Parity: **None**; Stop bits: **1**; Flow control: **None**. Click **OK** to complete the configuration.

9. Click **File** on the menu bar, and then click **Save** to save the connection.

10. Close HyperTerminal, click **Yes** if prompted to confirm, and then double-click the connection to reopen it.

11. Turn on the connected router.

12. Watch for the router startup information. You may need to press **Enter** on the computer keyboard to initiate this process.

13. When you know HyperTerminal is correctly configured, you may turn off the router and exit HyperTerminal and Windows or continue with the next lab.

Certification Objectives

Objectives for the CCNA exam:

This lab does not map to a certification objective; however, it contains information that is beneficial to your professional development.

Review Questions

1. What program on a Windows computer is typically used for configuring a Cisco router?

2. What are the important settings to configure in HyperTerminal to access a Cisco router?

3. Where is the HyperTerminal program in most Windows computers?

4. Which port on a router do you use to connect the rollover cable when configuring the router with HyperTerminal?

5. You can use the auxiliary port on a router to access it with HyperTerminal. How would you be accessing the router if you used this port?

Lab 6.3 Use the System Configuration Dialog to Configure a Cisco Router

Objectives

The objective of this lab is to give you experience with the initial configuration of a Cisco router using the system configuration dialog. This dialog is a type of "wizard" that prompts you to enter the information that configures the router. This is easier than direct configuration using the command line.

Although most professionals do not use this method to configure Cisco routers, knowledge of the system configuration dialog is a CCNA objective. It is important to know how to use it and what it does. Remember that setting up the router using this method makes the router work; however, it may not be completely configured.

After completing this lab, you will be able to:

➤ Use the system configuration dialog to configure the routers in the internetworking lab shown in Figure 6-2

➤ Know how to access the system configuration dialog

➤ Understand the capabilities and limitations of the system configuration dialog

Materials Required

This lab requires the following:

➤ The internetworking lab setup, per Lab 6.2

➤ HyperTerminal configured to access the routers via the console port, per Lab 6.2

Estimated completion time: **45 minutes**

ACTIVITY

1. Refer to Figure 6-2. What will the host name of your router be?

   _____

2. Which interfaces is your router using?

   _____

3. What are the IP addresses and subnet masks for those interfaces?

   _____

4. What is the enable secret password?

   _____

5. What is the enable password?

   _____

6. What is the VTY password?

   _____

7. Turn the router off, if it is on. The router's startup configuration file should already be erased. Doing so makes the router prompt you to enter the initial configuration dialog. This is another term for the system configuration dialog.

8. Start the attached computer into Windows, if necessary. To open the HyperTerminal connection you created in Lab 6.2, click **Start**, point to **Programs**, point to **Accessories**, point to **Communications**, and then click **HyperTerminal**. Double-click the **Cisco** connection icon.

9. Turn on the router attached to your PC. If necessary, press **Enter** to get screen output. In a few seconds, you should see router activity display.

10. You may see a message that the NVRAM is invalid, possibly due to write erase. That is because your instructor has erased the startup configuration file or because the router is new and has never had a startup configuration.

11. Next, you are asked if you want to enter the initial configuration dialog. Press **y** for yes and press **Enter**. Notice that using the Ctrl+C key combination on the keyboard takes you out of the initial configuration dialog. This is sometimes necessary, as there is no way to go back and reenter an incorrect entry.

12. Next you are asked if you want to enter basic management setup. The basic management setup configures only enough connectivity to manage the router. The router will not be fully functional. You should press **n** for no and then press **Enter**. This puts you into extended setup.

13. When asked if you want to see the current interface summary, press **Enter** to accept the default answer shown in square brackets, which in this case is yes. The summary shows which interfaces are physically on the router. Remember that you will not necessarily configure all the displayed interfaces. Your configuration depends on the router you are configuring and the information in Figure 6-2.

14. Continue to configure your router, using the responses shown in Table 6-1 as your guide. The responses in the table are for the lab-c router. Tailor them to your router as shown in Figure 6-2 and the information you recorded in Steps 1 through 6 of this lab. As you move through the configuration process, note that valuable information is presented on the screen. Be sure to read everything that comes up. Eventually, your configuration is displayed and you are prompted to end the system configuration dialog by choosing option 0, 1, or 2. Choose **2** and press **Enter**. This saves your configuration to NVRAM and exits the system configuration dialog.

Table 6-1   Configuration responses

When You See This	Type or Press
Enter host name [Router]:	lab-c
Enter enable secret:	class
Enter enable password:	cisco
Enter virtual terminal password:	cisco
Configure SNMP Network Management? [yes]:	n
Configure bridging? [no]:	Enter
Configure DECnet? [no]:	Enter
Configure AppleTalk? [no]:	Enter
Configure IPX? [no]:	Enter
Configure IP? [yes]:	Enter
Configure IGRP routing? [yes]:	n
Configure RIP routing? [no]:	y
Do you want to configure Ethernet0 interface? [yes]:	Enter

Table 6-1   Configuration responses (continued)

When You See This	Type or Press
Configure IP on this interface? [yes]:	Enter
IP address for this interface:	223.8.151.1
Subnet Mask for this interface [255.255.255.0]:	Enter
Do you want to configure Serial0 interface? [yes]:	Enter
Configure IP on this interface? [yes]:	Enter
Configure IP unnumbered on this interface? [no]:	Enter
IP address for this interface:	204.204.7.1
Subnet Mask for this interface [255.255.255.0]:	Enter
Do you want to configure Serial1 interface? [yes]:	Enter
Configure IP on this interface? [yes]:	Enter
Configure IP unnumbered on this interface? [no]:	Enter
IP address for this interface:	199.6.13.2
Subnet Mask for this interface [255.255.255.0]:	Enter

15. There is another way to access the initial configuration dialog other than being prompted for it automatically as a consequence of having erased the contents of NVRAM. You can use the setup command at the privileged EXEC mode prompt. Press **Enter** if necessary to reach the user EXEC mode prompt. What does this prompt look like?

16. Type **enable** and press **Enter** to access privileged EXEC mode, which is also known as enable mode. You should be prompted for the enable secret password you configured in the system configuration dialog. How do you know you are being prompted for the enable secret password and not the enable password?

17. Type **class** and press **Enter**. How did the prompt change?

18. Enter the **setup** command to access the initial configuration dialog. When prompted to enter the initial configuration dialog, press **y** for yes and press **Enter**.

19. Press **Ctrl+C** to abort the configuration and exit the system configuration dialog.

20. Type **logout**, press **Enter**, close HyperTerminal, and then turn off the router.

Certification Objectives

Objectives for the CCNA exam:

➤ Configure IP addresses, subnet masks, and gateway addresses on routers and hosts

➤ Perform an initial configuration on a router

Review Questions

1. When configuring a router, when would you choose basic management setup rather than extended setup?

2. Which passwords are you prompted for when using the initial configuration dialog?

3. What does the current interface summary show you?

4. How can you break out of setup if you make a mistake?

5. What do square brackets [ ] in a prompt for input indicate?

6. Under what condition are you automatically prompted to enter the initial configuration dialog?

7. What command and prompt puts you into the initial configuration dialog?

8. Why is it important to configure an enable or enable secret password on a router?

6

LAB 6.4 CONFIGURE CONSOLE AND AUX PASSWORDS

Objectives

In Lab 6.3 you were prompted for the VTY (virtual terminal) password in addition to the enable and enable secret passwords when configuring the router using the system configuration dialog. The VTY password restricts access to the router via telnet. The VTY password is an example of a line password because you are getting a line into the router.

Besides VTY, there are two additional lines into the router. You can access the router through the console line and use a console password, which restricts access to the router through the console port. You can also access it through the auxiliary line by using the aux password, which restricts access through the aux port via a modem. Note that neither password is configured when using the system configuration dialog. Note also that a console password is not currently required when accessing your router via the console port.

In this lab, you will configure the console and aux passwords for the internetworking lab shown in Figure 6-2.

After completing this lab, you will be able to:

> Configure the console and aux passwords on a router

Materials Required

This lab requires the following:

> The internetworking lab setup in Lab 6.3

> HyperTerminal configured to access the routers via the console port, per Lab 6.2

Estimated completion time: **45 minutes**

ACTIVITY

ACTIVITY

1. If necessary, start the computer into Windows and begin the HyperTerminal session with the router.

2. Turn on the router if necessary. Press **Enter** to get the user EXEC mode prompt, which should be the name of the router (for example, lab-e) and the greater than sign (>).

3. Type **ena** and press **Enter** to access privileged EXEC mode. Why didn't you have to type the entire command?

_____

4. Type **class** and press **Enter** when prompted for the password. The prompt should change. For example, if the router name is lab-e, the prompt should change to lab-e#.

5. Type **configure terminal** and press **Enter** to enter global configuration mode. What did the prompt change to?

_____

6. Type **line console 0** and press **Enter**. This tells the router that you want to configure the console port. The prompt should change to indicate that you are in line configuration mode. What did the prompt change to?

   _____

7. Type **login** to require users to log in when accessing this port and press **Enter**.

8. Type **password cisco** and press **Enter**.

9. Type **exit** and press **Enter**. How many levels does the exit command take you back?

   _____

10. Type **line aux 0** and press **Enter**. This tells the router that you want to configure the aux port.

11. Type **login** to require users to log in when accessing this port and press **Enter**.

12. Type **password cisco** and press **Enter**.

13. Press **Ctrl+Z**. To what prompt does this key combination take you back?

    _____

14. Press **Enter** after you receive the message that the router has been configured by the console.

15. Type **show run** and press **Enter** to see the running configuration. Notice that the enable secret password is encrypted and looks nothing like "class," which is the password you entered during the system configuration dialog.

16. Press the **spacebar** to see more of the display.

17. Notice the console, aux, and VTY password information. Are these passwords encrypted?

    _____

18. Type **copy run start** and press **Enter**. Press **Enter** again to accept startup-config as the destination filename. What does the copy run start command do?

    _____

19. Is it really necessary to use this copy run start command, or are the configuration changes automatically saved?

    _____

20. Type **logout** and press **Enter** to exit the router.

Certification Objectives

Objectives for the CCNA exam:

➤ Configure a router for additional administrative functionality

Review Questions

1. Which passwords are you not prompted for when using the system configuration dialog?

2. Which mode must you be in to configure the VTY, console, and auxiliary passwords?

3. What does the prompt look like if you are in the mode that is the correct answer for Review Question 2?

4. What two commands are used to create the line passwords after you are at the prompt you specified in Review Question 3?

5. What is the only router password encrypted by default?

LAB 6.5 USE HELP, THE COMMAND HISTORY, ENHANCED EDITING FEATURES, AND THE SHOW COMMAND

Objectives

The objective of this lab is to give you experience in accessing command-line help, using the Cisco enhanced editing features and command history, and using the very important show commands to determine information about your router.

With a little experience, you can figure out how to do almost anything on a Cisco router or switch using command-line help. In addition, the enhanced editing features of the Cisco command executive allow you to move around commands quickly and avoid retyping previously used commands. You use show commands to monitor and verify what you have configured in the router. In this lab, you will use command-line help and various show commands, and you will edit the command line using the editing features of the Cisco command executive.

After completing this lab, you will be able to:

➤ Get help with commands

➤ Navigate the command line more efficiently

➤ Understand the kinds of information you can obtain using the most popular show commands

Materials Required

This lab requires the following:

➤ Completion of Labs 6.1, 6.3, and 6.4

➤ HyperTerminal configured to access the routers via the console port, per Lab 6.2

6

Estimated completion time: **60 minutes**

ACTIVITY

1. Start the computer into Windows if necessary, and begin the HyperTerminal session with the router.

2. Turn on the router if necessary. Press **Enter**. Which password are you being prompted for?

_____

3. Enter the password you configured in Lab 6.4.

_____

4. After the correct password is entered, your cursor should be at the user EXEC mode prompt, which should be the name of the router and the greater than sign (for example, lab-e>). Verify that this has occurred.

5. Type **?**. There is no need to press Enter. A list of commands should be displayed. Press the **spacebar** to scroll through the list. What do these commands represent?

_____

6. Type **show ?**. A list of commands should appear. What do these commands represent?

_____

Notice that the show start and show run commands cannot be used in user EXEC mode.

NOTE

7. Complete the show command by typing **hosts** and pressing **Enter**. Does your router know the names of any other routers? Why or why not?

_____

_____

8. Type **show version** and press **Enter**. What is the name of the IOS image file?

   _____

   _____

9. What version of the IOS is your router running?

   _____

10. Press the **spacebar** to scroll through the display.

11. Type **enable** and press **Enter** to access enable mode.

12. Type **class** and press **Enter** when prompted for the enable secret password. How did the prompt change?

    _____

13. Type **?**. Press the **spacebar** to scroll through the commands. What do these commands represent?

    _____

14. Type **show ?**. What do these commands represent? Why are there so many more commands in enable mode than in user mode?

    _____

    _____

15. Use the **show flash** command to display information about the flash. What is the IOS filename? Your answer should be the same as what you recorded in Step 8.

    _____

    _____

    How big is the file?

    _____

16. Type **show protocol** and press **Enter**. What protocol is enabled on your router?

    _____

17. What interface and address information appears?

    _____

18. Type **show arp** and press **Enter**. What information does this command display?

    _____

19. Type **clear ?** and look for the command to clear the contents of the ARP table. What do you think the command is?

    _____

20. Backspace over the word "clear" to erase it. Type **show start** and press **Enter**. What are you viewing the contents of?

    _____

21. What is the host name of the router?

_____

22. What interfaces are available for configuration on the router?

_____

23. What interfaces are actually configured on the router?

_____

24. Is a routing protocol configured on the router? If so, what is it?

_____

25. Type **show run** and press **Enter**. What are you viewing the contents of?

_____

26. Is the running configuration supposed to be the same as the startup configuration? Explain your answer.

_____

_____

_____

_____

27. Type **show history** and press **Enter**. What appears?

_____

28. Press the **up arrow** until you see the show start command. What does the up arrow do?

_____

29. Press the **down arrow** until you see the show history command. What does the down arrow do?

_____

30. Press **Ctrl+A**. What does this do?

_____

31. Press **Ctrl+E**. What does this do?

_____

32. Press **Esc+B**. What does this do?

_____

33. Press **Esc+F**. What does this do?

_____

34. Delete the command by pressing the **backspace** key. Type **terminal his** and press the **Tab** key. What does this do?

_____

_____

35. Use context-sensitive help to determine why the terminal history size command is used.

---

36. Change the history buffer size to 20 using the **terminal history size 20** command.

37. Enter the **show history** command again. You changed the buffer from the default of 10 to 20. Are there more than 10 entries in the buffer? Do you expect that an increased buffer size would require more router memory use?

---

38. Type **logout** and press **Enter** to exit the router. Close HyperTerminal and turn off the router.

Certification Objectives

Objectives for the CCNA exam:

➤ Manage system image and device configuration files

➤ Troubleshoot a device as part of a working network

Review Questions

1. Within the lab exercise, what exactly did the "?" show you?

2. Is the "?" prompt sensitive?

3. Which two commands display information about the IOS file?

4. What command increases the history size?

5. What is the key combination that has the same result as pressing the up arrow?

ROUTER STARTUP AND CONFIGURATION

Labs included in this chapter

➤ Lab 7.1 Configure IP Addresses and IP Hosts

➤ Lab 7.2 Install, Configure, and Use a TFTP Server

➤ Lab 7.3 Configure a Message and Interface Description

➤ Lab 7.4 Use the CDP, Ping, Trace, and Telnet Commands

➤ Lab 7.5 Copy and Paste Router Configurations

➤ Lab 7.6 Use Boot System Commands and the Configuration Register

---

CCNA Exam Objectives	
Objective	Lab
Configure IP addresses, subnet masks, and gateway addresses on routers and hosts	7.1, 7.2
Perform an initial configuration on a router	7.1
Troubleshoot IP addressing and host configuration	7.1, 7.4
Configure a router for additional administrative functionality	7.2, 7.3, 7.6
Manage system image and device configuration files	7.2, 7.5, 7.6
Troubleshoot a device as part of a working network	7.4

LAB 7.1 CONFIGURE IP ADDRESSES AND IP HOSTS

Objectives

The objective of this lab is to give you experience in configuring IP addresses without the aid of the system configuration dialog. In addition, you will make IP to host name mappings. These mappings can be configured using a name server, or in this case, the router. In this lab, you will use the IP address command to configure the router interfaces, and the IP host command to provide IP to host name mappings.

After completing this lab, you will be able to:

➤ Configure IP addresses for each interface on the router

➤ Configure IP to host name mappings using the IP host command

Materials Required

This lab requires the following:

➤ The internetworking lab setup shown in Figure 7–1

➤ Completion of all labs in Chapter 6

Estimated completion time: **45 minutes**

ACTIVITY

1. Start the computer into Windows, and begin the HyperTerminal session with the router.

2. Turn on the router and hubs if necessary. Press **Enter** to start, and type the console line password **cisco** to get to the user EXEC mode prompt.

3. Type **enable** and press **Enter** to access privileged EXEC mode.

4. Type **class** and press **Enter** when prompted for the enable secret password.

5. Type **conf t** and press **Enter**. What is the name of this mode?

   _____

6. Enter a name table into the router. Put all routers in the name table, including the one you are configuring. Refer to Figure 7–1 for router host name and IP addressing information. Type **ip host**, then the name of the first router in the lab, which is **lab–a**, and all IP addresses associated with the interfaces on this first router. Remote routers will attempt to access the named router via the IP addresses in the order you list them. Press **Enter**. The first lab router is the lab–a router, so you should have typed the following:
   ip host lab-a 192.5.5.1 205.7.5.1 201.100.11.1

   Note that the addresses in this example are the interfaces listed in the network diagram in Figure 7–1.

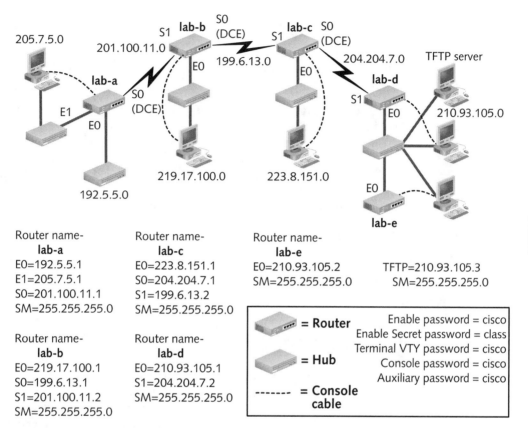

Router name-
lab-a
E0=192.5.5.1
E1=205.7.5.1
S0=201.100.11.1
SM=255.255.255.0

Router name-
lab-b
E0=219.17.100.1
S0=199.6.13.1
S1=201.100.11.2
SM=255.255.255.0

Router name-
lab-c
E0=223.8.151.1
S0=204.204.7.1
S1=199.6.13.2
SM=255.255.255.0

Router name-
lab-d
E0=210.93.105.1
S1=204.204.7.2
SM=255.255.255.0

Router name-
lab-e
E0=210.93.105.2
SM=255.255.255.0

TFTP=210.93.105.3
SM=255.255.255.0

= **Router**
= **Hub**
------ = **Console cable**

Enable password = cisco
Enable Secret password = class
Terminal VTY password = cisco
Console password = cisco
Auxiliary password = cisco

Figure 7-1   Connection information

7. Repeat Step 6 for all routers. Each router should eventually have the IP addresses of all router interfaces in the internetwork.

8. Press **Ctrl+Z** to exit global configuration mode. Press **Enter** to clear the message.

9. What is the value of the IP host command?

_____

10. Type **show host** and press **Enter**. What hosts does your router know about?

_____

11. Next, you will configure the active router interfaces for IP addresses. Type **conf t** and press **Enter**.

12. Type **int e0** (int e0/0 for 2600 series routers) and press **Enter**. What mode are you in, and what will the next commands you type affect?

_____

13. To configure the IP address of the Ethernet 0 interface, type the following:

ip address [*IP address of your router's e0 interface*] [*subnet mask*]
no shutdown

Use Figure 7-1 to determine the IP address of your router's E0 interface.

14. What does the first command line do in the example in Step 13?

_____

15. What does the second line do?

_____

16. Using Steps 12 and 13 as an example, configure the IP addresses of any additional interfaces that are to be configured on your router, per Figure 7-1. If you are configuring an S0 interface, you will need three commands instead of two. S0 has arbitrarily been chosen to perform the clocking function for the WAN links. Typically, the telco's CSU/DSU or other device does the clocking (DCE) outside of the lab environment. Make sure to add the following configuration command for S0 if you have an active S0 interface:

clock rate 56000

NOTE
Depending on the IOS version, the clock rate command can also be written as clockrate.

17. When finished configuring all interfaces on your router, as shown in Figure 7-1, press **Ctrl+Z** to return to the enable prompt.

18. Type **show run** to view the running configuration. There will be additional information in the running configuration that you did not configure. This consists of default router settings that are automatically configured and beyond the scope of the CCNA exam. Figure 7-2 displays the correct running configuration for the lab-c router.

```
lab-c#show run
Building configuration...

Current configuration:
!
version 12.0
service timestamps debug uptime
service timestamps log uptime        ┐  The host name for this
no service password-encryption        │  router is lab-c
!                                     ┘
hostname lab-c ◄─────────────────────
!                                    ┐  The enable secret
enable secret 5 $1$2m92$o55O17AYhrv9O7R9pgXEU/ ◄─  password, which is class,
enable password cisco                 │  is encrypted and
!                                     │  unrecognizable; the
ip subnet-zero                        │  enable password cisco
ip host lab-e 210.93.105.2            ┘  is in clear text
```

Figure 7-2   Output of the show run command

```
ip host lab-d 210.93.105.1 204.204.7.2
ip host lab-c 223.8.151.1 204.204.7.1 199.6.13.2
ip host lab-b 219.17.100.1 199.6.13.1 201.100.11.2
ip host lab-a 192.5.5.1 205.7.5.1 201.100.11.1
!
!
!
!
interface Ethernet0
 ip address 223.8.151.1 255.255.255.0
 no ip directed-broadcast
 no mop enabled
!
interface Serial0
 ip address 204.204.7.1 255.255.255.0
 no ip directed-broadcast
 no ip mroute-cache
 no fair-queue
 clockrate 56000
!
interface Serial1
 ip address 199.6.13.2 255.255.255.0
 no ip directed-broadcast
!
router rip
 redistribute connected
 network 199.6.13.0
 network 204.204.7.0
 network 223.8.151.0
!
no ip http server
ip classless
!
dialer-list 1 protocol ip permit
dialer-list 1 protocol ipx permit
!
line con 0
 password cisco
 login
 transport input none
line aux 0
 password cisco
 login
line vty 0 4
 password cisco
 login
!
end
```

The host name table allows you to use names rather than IP addresses when referring to the routers

Notice the clockrate command configured on the S0 interface

RIP is configured using major network numbers of connected networks

Console, auxiliary, and vty passwords are configured with the password cisco

7

Figure 7-2 Output of the show run command (continued)

19. Check all commands and IP addresses, router RIP network numbers, and IP host addresses. RIP was configured automatically via the system configuration dialog in Lab 6-3. The network numbers listed for RIP should be the networks directly connected to your router. If there are no mistakes, proceed to Step 24.

20. If there is a mistake in the interface configurations, return to Steps 11 through 18 and reconfigure the interfaces. Then go to Step 24.

21. If there is a mistake in the router RIP, type **conf t** and press **Enter** to enter global configuration mode. Then type **no router rip** and press **Enter** to remove the incorrect RIP information. Now type **router rip** to enter router configuration mode. Enter the correct numbers of the networks that are directly attached to your router, using this command as an example:

    network 210.93.105.0

22. Continue to use the network command until all networks attached to your router are listed. For example, the lab-a router will have three network command lines, because it is attached to three networks. Remember to use major network numbers, not interface addresses. When finished, press **Ctrl+Z** to return to enable mode.

23. If there is no mistake in the list of IP host names, go to Step 24. If there is a mistake in the list, type **conf t** and press **Enter**. Then type **no ip host** followed by the name of the router that has the error. Go to Steps 6 through 8, and reconfigure the IP to host name mappings. When you are sure they are correct, proceed to Step 24.

24. Type **copy run start** at the enable prompt, and press **Enter** to replace the startup configuration file. Press **Enter** again to accept the default destination filename.

25. Type **logout** to exit the router.

Certification Objectives

Objectives for the CCNA exam:

➤ Configure IP addresses, subnet masks, and gateway addresses on routers and hosts

➤ Perform an initial configuration on a router

➤ Troubleshoot IP addressing and host configuration

Review Questions

1. What mode must you be in to configure IP addresses on a Cisco router?

2. What is the purpose of a host name table?

3. What is the command to point to another router or server for host name resolution?

4. What is the clock rate command used for?

5. What does the no shutdown command do?

LAB 7.2 INSTALL, CONFIGURE, AND USE A TFTP SERVER

Objectives

The objective of this lab is to show you the benefit of having a TFTP server on your network to configure the routers in the event they lose their IOS or configuration information. If you completed the labs in Chapter 6 and Lab 7.1 properly, your routers are configured to match the internetworking lab setup shown in Figure 7-1. It is now appropriate to copy these configurations to a TFTP server.

There is more than one kind of TFTP software. One of the easiest to use is Cisco's own TFTPServ.exe. In this lab, you will add a computer to the internetworking lab on the hub between routers lab-d and lab-e. This corresponds to network 210.93.105.0, as shown in Figure 7-1. You will then install and configure the TFTP server software. Finally, you will copy the IOS and the router configuration files to the TFTP server.

After completing this lab, you will be able to:

➤ Install and configure TFTP server software

➤ Copy the Cisco IOS from the router to the TFTP server

➤ Copy router configurations to the TFTP server

Materials Required

This lab requires the following:

➤ Completion of all labs in Chapter 6

➤ Completion of Lab 7.1

➤ A Windows computer with a NIC configured and the TCP/IP protocol configured

➤ UTP patch cable

➤ TFTP server software on a floppy disk

Estimated completion time: **45 minutes**

ACTIVITY

1. Place the TFTP server in close proximity to the computer attached to the lab-e router, as shown in Figure 7-1.

2. Attach one end of the UTP patch cable to the NIC on the TFTP server.

3. Attach the other end of the UTP patch cable to the hub between router lab-d and router lab-e, as shown in Figure 7-1.

4. Turn on the computer and let it start into Windows.

5. Put the floppy disk containing the TFTP server software in drive A of the TFTP server.

6. Click **Start** and then click **Run**.

7. Click the **Browse** button to search for an executable file on drive A. Double-click the executable file and then click **OK** to install the TFTP server software. Accept any defaults presented during the installation.

8. Right-click **My Network Places** and click **Properties**.

9. Right-click **Local Connection** and click **Properties**.

10. Double-click **Internet Protocol**.

11. If the server patch cable has been attached to the hub between router lab-d and router lab-e, the network is 210.93.105.0, as shown in Figure 7-1. This figure shows that the E0 interfaces on routers lab-d and lab-e are using 210.93.105.1 and 210.93.105.2, respectively. Using this example, the next available host number for the TFTP server is 210.93.105.3. Assign the IP address **210.93.105.3** to the TFTP server.

12. You also need to provide the subnet mask for the TFTP server. It should be the same as the network to which it is attached, which in this example is **255.255.255.0**.

13. A gateway must be configured on the network hosts so that they can get to the rest of the internetwork or to the Internet. Typically, the gateway is the Ethernet interface on the router that is closest to the host being configured. In this example, the gateway is 210.93.105.1, which is the Ethernet interface on the lab-d router, as shown in Figure 7-1. Configure the correct gateway for the TFTP server.

14. Click **OK** twice. You will be prompted to restart the computer. Make sure there is no floppy disk in Drive A. Click **Yes** to restart.

15. After the computer restarts, open the TFTP program by clicking **Start**, pointing to **Programs**, and then clicking the name of the TFTP program; you can also double-click a desktop shortcut if one exists.

16. Move to a router terminal, and start the computer into Windows if necessary.

17. Begin the HyperTerminal session with a router.

18. Turn on the router and hubs if necessary. Press **Enter** to start, and then type **cisco** for the user EXEC mode password.

19. Type **enable** and press **Enter** to access privileged EXEC mode.

20. Type **class** and press **Enter** when prompted for the enable secret password.

21. What command will you type to look at the active configuration?

_____

Use the command you recorded in Step 21, and double-check to make sure it has been configured correctly, per Figure 7-1.

22. Ping the TFTP server to make sure you have connectivity to it. Type **ping** followed by **210.93.105.3**, which is the IP address you configured on the TFTP server. Press **Enter**. If your ping fails, use the **show interfaces** command to make sure all of your configured interfaces are up/up. Perhaps your team members are having problems that may be affecting your ping. Also, make sure you check all physical connections and the TCP/IP configuration on the TFTP server. When you can ping the TFTP server successfully, proceed to the next step.

23. Type **copy run tftp** and press **Enter** to begin the process of backing up the running configuration to the TFTP server. This command will eventually fail if the TFTP server software is not running.

24. Next you are prompted for the IP address of the TFTP server. Type **210.93.105.3** and press **Enter**.

25. You are prompted for the name of the configuration file. Type the host name of your router followed by **–config**. For example, the lab-e configuration file should be named lab-e-config. Press **Enter**. Look at the screen on the TFTP server for an indication of success.

26. Type **show flash** and press **Enter**. What is the name of the IOS image of the router? Look at the name carefully. Depending on the font style being used in HyperTerminal, it can be difficult to tell the difference between a lowercase L and the number one.

_____

27. Backing up the configuration files is typically fast, as these files are small. Conversely, the IOS file is relatively large and takes much more time to back up. Because the same IOS file is probably running on all the routers in the lab, only the person configuring the lab-e router should back up the IOS, which begins on Step 28. The other team members should observe the process.

28. Type **copy flash tftp** to begin backing up the router operating system (IOS) on the TFTP server.

29. You are prompted for the source filename. Type the name of the file you recorded in Step 26 and press **Enter**.

30. Next, you are prompted for the IP address of the TFTP server. Type **210.93.105.3**, and press **Enter**.

31. Finally, you are prompted for the destination filename. The default (indicated in square brackets) is the same name you typed for the source filename in Step 29. Press **Enter** to accept the default.

32. A series of exclamation marks on your screen indicates the IOS is copying to the TFTP server. The backup process can take 5 to 15 minutes.

33. When the process is finished, go to the TFTP server, and search for the backed-up files on the hard drive. When the router lab is completely backed up, you should have five configuration files and one IOS file on the TFTP server.

34. Log out of the router.

Certification Objectives

Objectives for the CCNA exam:

➤ Configure IP addresses, subnet masks, and gateway addresses on routers and hosts

➤ Configure a router for additional administrative functionality

➤ Manage system image and device configuration files

Review Questions

1. What is the purpose of a TFTP server?

2. What is the purpose of a default gateway?

3. What prompt and command are used to copy the active configuration to a TFTP server?

4. What prompt and command are used to copy the IOS to a TFTP server?

5. List two show commands that display the IOS image filename.

LAB 7.3 CONFIGURE A MESSAGE AND INTERFACE DESCRIPTION

Objectives

The objective of this lab is to show you how to customize your router further by configuring a message of the day and by assigning descriptions to interfaces. In this lab, you will use the banner motd command and the description command to customize your router.

After completing this lab, you will be able to:

➤ Use the banner motd command to provide a message for anyone accessing the router

➤ Use the description command to add a description to a configured interface

Materials Required

This lab requires the following:

➤ Completion of all labs in Chapter 6, as well as Lab 7.1

Estimated completion time: **20 minutes**

ACTIVITY

1. Start the computer into Windows, and begin a HyperTerminal session with the router.

2. Turn on the router and hubs if necessary. Press **Enter** to start, and type the password **cisco** to get to the user EXEC mode prompt.

3. Type **enable** and press **Enter** to access privileged EXEC mode.

4. Type **class** and press **Enter** when prompted for the enable secret password.

5. Type **conf t** and press **Enter** to enter global configuration mode.

6. Type **banner motd #** and press **Enter**. What message appears?

---

7. Type **Welcome to the Cisco 2500 series router**.

8. Type **#** and press **Enter** to signal the end of your message. Press **Ctrl+Z** to exit global configuration mode.

9. Type **exit** and press **Enter** to log out of the router.

10. When prompted by the router, press **Enter** to start. You should see the message of the day.

11. Enter the password **cisco** to get to the user EXEC mode prompt.

12. Type **enable** and press **Enter** to access enable mode.

13. Type **class** and press **Enter** when prompted for the enable secret password.

14. Type **conf t** and press **Enter** to enter global configuration mode.

15. Type **no banner motd** and press **Enter**. This removes the message of the day.

16. From the global configuration mode prompt, type **int e0** and press **Enter** to enter interface configuration mode.

17. Type **description Attached to Ethernet LAN lab-e** (substitute the name of your router if necessary) and press **Enter**.

18. Press **Ctrl+Z** to return to the enable prompt.

19. Type **show int e0**. Does the description configured for e0 appear?

_____

20. Copy the running configuration to the startup configuration.

21. Type **logout** to exit the router.

Certification Objectives

Objectives for the CCNA exam:

➤ Configure a router for additional administrative functionality

Review Questions

1. What is the purpose of the banner command?

2. What does MOTD stand for?

3. What is the purpose of the description command?

4. What mode must you be in to configure a banner?

5. What mode must you be in to configure a description?

LAB 7.4 USE THE CDP, PING, TRACE, AND TELNET COMMANDS

Objectives

The Cisco Discovery Protocol (CDP) shares configuration information between locally connected Cisco devices. The various show CDP commands tell you about routers and switches that are directly connected to your router. The ping and trace commands provide connectivity information at the Network layer of the OSI reference model and are used primarily for troubleshooting. Extended mode ping is a more sophisticated type of ping that you will also investigate. The telnet application provides Application layer connectivity information and lets you access remote routers.

The objective of this lab is to familiarize you with the displayed output of the various show cdp commands and other configured CDP commands. In addition, you will become familiar with the following troubleshooting commands: ping, extended mode ping, trace, and telnet.

After completing this lab, you will:

➤ Be familiar with the output generated by the various CDP commands

➤ Understand how to test for Network layer connectivity using the ping and trace commands

➤ Understand the difference between ping and extended mode ping

➤ Know how to use the telnet application to remotely access routers

Materials Required

This lab requires the following:

➤ Completion of all labs in Chapter 6, as well as Lab 7.1

Estimated completion time: **30 minutes**

ACTIVITY

1. Start the computer into Windows, and begin the HyperTerminal session with the router.

2. Turn on the router and hubs if necessary. Press **Enter** to start, and type the password **cisco** to get to the user EXEC mode prompt.

3. Type **enable** and press **Enter** to access enable mode.

4. Type **class** and press **Enter** when prompted for the enable secret password.

5. Type **show cdp neighbor** and press **Enter** to get information regarding your directly connected neighbors. If you are unable to see your neighbors, use the **show interfaces** command and make sure the status of each of your interfaces is up/up. What is one of your neighbors?

   _____

   What local interface is the neighbor on?

   _____

   What kind of device is it (capability)?

   _____

   What other information does this show command provide?

   _____

   _____

   _____

6. Press the **up arrow** until you get to the show cdp neighbor command. Press the **spacebar** once, and then type **detail**, and press **Enter**. What additional information do you get when you add "detail" to the show cdp neighbor command?

   _____

   _____

7. Type **show cdp interface** and press **Enter**. What is the default broadcast interval for CDP?

   _____

8. Type **conf t** and press **Enter** to enter global configuration mode.

9. Type **cdp timer 90** and press **Enter**. Exit to enable mode, and enter the **show cdp interface** command once again. Were you successful in changing the broadcast interval to 90 seconds?

   _____

   _____

10. Enter global configuration mode. Type **int e0** and press **Enter**.

11. Type **no cdp enable** and press **Enter**. What does this command do?

    _____

12. Press **Ctrl+Z** to return to enable mode, and enter the **show cdp interface** command. Has CDP been disabled on E0?

    _____

    How do you know?

    _____

13. Reenable CDP on the interface using the **cdp enable** command in interface configuration mode.

14. Press **Ctrl+Z** to return to enable mode. Can you confirm that CDP has been reenabled on the E0 interface?

_____

15. Type **ping** and then type an IP address of a remote router interface. For example, if you are on the lab-b router and want to check for connectivity to the lab-d, S1 interface, you would type **ping 204.204.7.2** and press **Enter**.

16. Was the ping successful?

_____

If not, attempt to ping several other interfaces. What symbol indicates a successful ping?

_____

If your ping succeeded, what were the minimum, average, and maximum roundtrip times?

_____

17. Type **ping** and press **Enter**. How does the extended mode ping command respond?

_____

18. Press **Enter** to accept the default protocol. Enter any remote IP address. Change the repeat count to 20. Change the datagram size to 1500. Continue to press **Enter** to accept the defaults for the remaining prompts. How does this output differ from the output from the ping command you issued in Step 15?

_____

_____

19. Type **trace** and then type the IP address of an interface on the farthest remote router from your location. For example, if you are on the lab-b router and want to check for connectivity to the E0 interface on the lab-e router, type **trace 210.93.105.2** and press **Enter**.

NOTE

If locked into an unsuccessful trace, break out by pressing **Ctrl+Shift+6**.

20. Was the trace successful?

_____

What information is obtained from the trace command?

_____

What is the advantage of using the trace command instead of the ping command?

_____

7

21. At which layer of the OSI reference model do ping and trace operate?

_____

22. At which layer of the TCP/IP reference model do ping and trace operate?

_____

23. What underlying protocol controls the messages from ping and trace as well as manages the work of IP in general?

_____

24. Type **telnet** and then type the IP address of an interface on a remote router. For example, if you are on the lab-b router and want to telnet to the lab-e router, type **telnet 210.93.105.2** and press **Enter**.

    Alternatively, you could just use the name of the router to which you want to connect. For example, you could type **lab-e** and press **Enter**.

    What makes it possible to use names instead of IP addresses when telnetting? (_Hint_: See Lab 7.1.)

_____

    Did the telnet succeed?

_____

25. If the telnet failed, try telnetting to a different router until you can telnet successfully. Ask your instructor for help if necessary.

26. You should be prompted for a password when you telnet successfully. Type **cisco** and press **Enter**. Is this the same kind of password you are prompted for when you log on to a router locally?

_____

    Exactly what kind of password is this?

_____

27. Type **enable** and press **Enter** to access enable mode.

28. Type **class** and press **Enter** when prompted for the enable secret password.

29. Type **show run** and press **Enter**. Exactly what is displayed?

_____

30. Type **show cdp neigh det** and press **Enter**. What is the advantage of using the telnet application in conjunction with the show cdp neighbor command?

_____

31. At which layer of the OSI reference model is telnet operating?

_____

32. At which layer of the TCP/IP reference model is telnet operating?

_____

33. As a troubleshooting tool, what advantages does telnet have over ping and trace?

_____

34. Type **logout** and press **Enter** to terminate your telnet session.

35. Type **logout** and press **Enter** to exit your router.

Certification Objectives

Objectives for the CCNA exam:

➤ Troubleshoot IP addressing and host configuration

➤ Troubleshoot a device as part of a working network

Review Questions

1. What is the purpose of the CDP protocol?

2. Is CDP enabled by default on all Cisco routers?

3. What is the difference between ping and extended mode ping?

4. What mode and command are used to disable CDP on an interface?

5. What mode and command are used to disable CDP on the entire router?

7

LAB 7.5 COPY AND PASTE ROUTER CONFIGURATIONS

Objectives

In Lab 7.2, you practiced backing up the IOS and configuration files to a TFTP server. Configuration files are small and can easily be stored on a floppy disk or a computer hard drive as simple text files. If you have local access to the router, it is faster to use the following method to save configuration files than using a TFTP server. The objective of this lab is to demonstrate how to save and retrieve your router configuration files locally.

In this lab, you will copy the running configuration of the router to a text file, using Notepad. Next, you will erase the startup configuration of the router and then reload and paste the saved router configuration back into the router.

After completing this lab, you will be able to:

➤ Save the router configuration locally using the Notepad application

➤ Erase the startup configuration of the router

➤ Re-create the running and startup configurations of the router by pasting the saved text file into the running configuration of the router

Materials Required

This lab requires the following:

➤ Completion of all labs in Chapter 6, as well as Lab 7.1

➤ The Notepad application

Estimated completion time: **30 minutes**

ACTIVITY

1. If necessary, turn on the workstation.

2. Create a folder on the desktop. Name it with your own last name.

3. Open the HyperTerminal program and create a session with the router.

4. If necessary, turn on the routers and hubs.

5. Press **Enter** to get started, and type the console password **cisco** to get to the user EXEC mode prompt.

6. Enter enable mode using **class** as the enable secret password.

7. Display the running configuration. Which command did you use?

_____

8. Press the **spacebar** until the entire configuration has been displayed.

9. Scroll up until you see the words "hostname lab-a." Your host name may differ, depending on the router you are configuring.

10. Use the mouse to highlight the entire configuration, beginning with the words **hostname lab-a** and ending with the word **end**.

11. Right-click the highlighted text, and click **Copy**.

12. Open the Notepad program by clicking **Start**, pointing to **Programs**, pointing to **Accessories**, and then clicking **Notepad**.

13. Maximize the window.

14. Right-click in the Notepad window, and then click **Paste**.

15. If Paste is not an option in the pop-up menu, return to the running configuration and attempt to copy it to the Clipboard again. If the words are running off the screen to the right, word wrap is not enabled. In this case, click **Edit** on the menu bar, and then click **Word Wrap** to enable it. (Depending on your version of Windows, word wrap may be an option in the Format menu.)

16. When you have successfully pasted the configuration into Notepad, save the file as **lab-a-config** (or substitute your router's host name) in the folder you created on the desktop.

17. **Minimize** the Notepad program and return to HyperTerminal.

18. At the enable prompt, type **erase start**, and then press **Enter**. Confirm the erase.

19. Type **show start** and press **Enter**. What does the erase start command do?

_____

20. Use the **reload** command to restart the router. If prompted to save the configuration, press **N** for no. **Confirm** the reload and let the router restart. The router may take a few minutes to reload. You should eventually get to the Router> prompt or a similar prompt that indicates your prior configuration has been erased.

21. If prompted to enter the initial configuration dialog, press **N** for no, and then press **Enter**.

22. If prompted to terminate autoinstall, press **Enter** to accept the default answer of Yes.

23. Enter privileged EXEC mode.

24. Enter global configuration mode.

25. Restore the Notepad window.

26. Click **Edit** on the menu bar of Notepad, and then click **Select All**.

27. Right-click the selection, and then click **Copy** from the menu.

28. Minimize Notepad, and right-click beside the router prompt.

29. Click **Paste to Host** from the pop-up menu.

30. When the router display stops scrolling, press **Enter** and display the running configuration on the router using the appropriate command. Does it appear to be correct?

_____

If it is not correct, get help from your teammates or instructor.

31. Type **show interfaces** and press **Enter**. What is the status of each of your interfaces?

_____

_____

_____

32. If any of your interfaces are administratively down, and you are using them, you should enter interface configuration mode for those interfaces and issue the **no shutdown** command. Interfaces often administratively go down when their configurations are obtained via pasting or from a TFTP server using the copy tftp run command.

33. Copy the running configuration to the startup configuration.

34. Log out of the router.

35. Close the Notepad program.

36. Delete the folder and file from the Windows desktop.

Certification Objectives

Objectives for the CCNA exam:

➤ Manage system image and device configuration files

Review Questions

1. Why is it a good idea to save your router configuration files to a hard drive or floppy disk?

2. Where does the startup configuration live and how do you erase it?

3. What do you think would happen if you used the erase flash command? (Note that this question is for discussion purposes only. Do _not_ use this command.)

4. What should you try if your interfaces administratively go down?

5. How can you erase the running configuration?

LAB 7.6 USE BOOT SYSTEM COMMANDS AND THE CONFIGURATION REGISTER

Objectives

When the router starts, it goes through a specified procedure outlined in Chapter 7 of your text. The IOS can be loaded from flash memory, ROM, or a TFTP server. By default, the configuration register is set to look to the startup configuration in NVRAM for boot instruction commands. If there are none, the IOS is loaded from flash by default. You can also affect the boot procedure by changing the configuration register.

The objective of this lab is to learn how to examine the configuration register and enter boot system commands into the router's configuration to force the router to boot from a TFTP server or to ROM. You will also learn how to change the configuration register and force the router to boot the IOS from ROM.

After completing this lab you will:

> Be familiar with the configuration register and its various settings

> Understand the various boot system commands and how to force the router to boot the IOS from a TFTP server or from ROM

Materials Required

This lab requires the following:

> Completion of all labs in Chapter 6, as well as Labs 7.1 and 7.2

Estimated completion time: **45 minutes**

ACTIVITY

1. Start the computer into Windows, and begin the HyperTerminal session with the router.

2. Turn on the router and hubs if necessary. Press **Enter** to start, and type the password **cisco** to get to the user EXEC mode prompt.

3. Type **enable** and press **Enter** to access enable mode.

4. Type **class** and press **Enter** when prompted for the enable secret password.

5. Type **ping 210.93.105.3** to make sure you have connectivity to the TFTP server. If you don't have connectivity, check the status of your interfaces by typing **show interfaces**. You can also trace to the TFTP server to pinpoint where the problem is.

6. Check to make sure the TFTP server software is running on the TFTP server.

7. Type **show version** and press **Enter**. Scroll to the bottom of the command output. What is the name of the IOS image file?

_____

What is the configuration register setting?

_____

From where does this register setting indicate the IOS will be loaded?

_____

8. Type **conf t** and press **Enter** to enter global configuration mode. Only the person configuring the lab-e router will perform Steps 9 through 19, which configure the lab-e router to boot from the TFTP server using the IOS that was previously copied to the server. The other team members should observe this process.

9. Type **boot system tftp [*filename*]**, where filename is the name of the IOS image file you recorded in Step 7.

10. Exit to enable mode.

11. Type **copy run start** and press **Enter**. Press **Enter** again to confirm.

12. Type **reload** and press **Enter**. Press **Enter** again to confirm.

13. When the router reloads, it will look to NVRAM for boot system commands. What tells it to do this?

_____

14. If your boot system command was correctly configured, your router will load the IOS from the TFTP server. It will take approximately 5 to 15 minutes and you will see a series of exclamation marks while it is loading. If it doesn't load correctly, you probably made a mistake when entering the filename. Make sure you recorded the filename correctly. Repeat Steps 8 through 12 if necessary.

15. Eventually you should be prompted to press **Return** to get started. Type the password **cisco** to get to the user EXEC mode prompt.

16. Type **enable** and press **Enter** to access enable mode.

17. Type **class** and press **Enter** when prompted for the enable secret password.

18. Type **conf t** and press **Enter** to enter global configuration mode.

19. Type **no boot system tftp [*filename*]**, where filename is the name of the IOS image file you recorded in Step 7.

20. All team members should configure their own routers, beginning with this step. Type **config-register 0x2100** and press **Enter**. Exit to enable mode.

21. Enter the **copy run start** command and confirm to save it as the default name.

22. Type **reload** and press **Enter**. Confirm if necessary.

23. When the router reloads, it will look to NVRAM for boot system commands. When it sees none, it will look at the configuration register. From where does the current configuration register tell the router to boot the IOS?

_____

24. What does the ROM Monitor mode prompt look like?

_____

_____

25. The commands in ROM Monitor mode are generally not the same as the commands from the command EXEC you have been using thus far in the labs. At this point, you must change the configuration register back to the value you recorded in Step 7 so that the IOS will once again be loaded from flash memory. Type **o/r 0x2102**. If your configuration register setting in Step 7 is not 0x2102, substitute the register setting you recorded. Press **Enter**.

26. Type **initialize** and press **Enter**.

27. At this point, the router should reload and the bootup procedure should appear as it has in previous labs. Enter the appropriate passwords to enter enable mode, then type **show version** and press **Enter**. Has the configuration register been reset to the default?

_____

28. Log out of the router.

Certification Objectives

Objectives for the CCNA exam:

➤ Configure a router for additional administrative functionality

➤ Manage system image and device configuration files

Review Questions

1. What are two ways to control the boot procedure for loading the IOS?

2. What would happen during bootup if the configuration register were set to 0x2101?

3. Why might you want to use a series of boot system commands in your configuration?

7

ROUTING PROTOCOLS AND NETWORK ADDRESS TRANSLATION

Labs included in this chapter

➤ Lab 8.1 Understand Terms and Concepts Related to Routing and NAT

➤ Lab 8.2 Configure Static Routes

➤ Lab 8.3 Configure RIP

➤ Lab 8.4 Configure IGRP

CCNA Exam Objectives	
Objective	Lab
Select an appropriate routing protocol based on user requirements	8.1
Configure routing protocols based on user requirements	8.1, 8.3, 8.4
Configure a router for additional administrative functionality	8.2
Troubleshoot routing protocols	8.3, 8.4

LAB 8.1 UNDERSTAND TERMS AND CONCEPTS RELATED TO ROUTING AND NAT

Objectives

Your router needs a routing table to route packets correctly and efficiently. Routing is an extremely important topic, and an entire Cisco CCNP exam is devoted to it. At your current level, however, you only need to understand the basic concepts and terminology involved with routing. Learning those concepts and terminology are the objectives of this lab. In addition, you will understand the basic functions of network address translation (NAT), a technology used often in routing but not specifically addressed on the CCNA exam. You will match the bulleted routing terms in the activity with the definitions in Table 8-1.

After completing this lab you will:

> ➤ Understand the terms and concepts related to routing and NAT

Materials Required

This lab requires the following:

> ➤ Pencil or pen

Estimated completion time: **20 minutes**

ACTIVITY

1. Relate the following bulleted terms to the descriptions in Table 8-1 by placing the terms in the correct cell in the second column. There may be more than one term or phrase for each description. Each term is used at least once.

- Link-state
- Metric
- EGP
- Hold-down timers
- BGP
- Static NAT

- Static route
- Split horizon
- RIP
- Direct connection
- IGP
- Dynamic NAT

- Administrative distance
- Distance-vector
- Convergence
- OSPF
- IGRP
- Overlapping

- NetBEUI
- IPX
- EIGRP
- Autonomous system
- IP
- Overloading

Table 8-1   Routing concepts and terminology

Routing Concept Description	Matching Term
Single private address mapped to a single public address	
Protocols that cannot be routed	
Protocols that broadcast their entire routing tables periodically	
Multiple private addresses mapped to a group of public addresses as needed	
A type of route used in a stub situation or as a backup	
The method a router uses to rank the reliability of routing information	
A group of routers that will share routing information and are under the control of one administrator	
Protocols that can be routed	
Used to combat the count-to-infinity problem	
Protocols that, after the initial flooding of routing information, update neighbors at triggered intervals and consume relatively low bandwidth	
A method of determining the suitability of a route	
Routing protocols used within an autonomous system or private internetwork	
Uses port address translation (PAT)	
A state where all routers in the internetwork have a common view of the topology	
Administrative distance of 100 or less	
Non-proprietary and commonly used routing protocol with a 15-hop limitation	
Routing protocols that can be used only between Cisco routers	
Use of an IP range registered to another entity	
Routing protocols used between autonomous systems or private internetworks	

8

Certification Objectives

Objectives for the CCNA exam:

➤ Select an appropriate routing protocol based on user requirements

➤ Configure routing protocols based on user requirements

Review Questions

1. A default route is a type of static route. What is it used for?

2. Why is it important to configure the same autonomous system number on all IGRP routers in your internetwork?

3. Rank IGRP, EIGRP, RIP, OSPF, static route, and direct connection in terms of administrative distance from lowest to highest. Record the administrative distance for each.

4. What is the difference between split horizon and split horizon with poison reverse?

LAB 8.2 CONFIGURE STATIC ROUTES

Objectives

The objective of this lab is to configure a static route on the router. To configure a router, you need to configure the interfaces and provide some way to find routes to other routers. The two methods for finding routes are (1) to let the routers update one another through dynamic routing protocols, and (2) to statically configure the routes using the IP route command.

In this lab you will configure the router for a static route to a remote network. In the process of configuring the router, you will also learn about the show commands that are useful for monitoring network routes.

After completing this lab you will:

➤ Understand the command syntax for configuring static routing

➤ Know how to check the router for routing table information

➤ Be familiar with the output from the show ip route command

Materials Required

This lab requires the following:

➤ The internetworking lab setup shown in Figure 8-1

➤ The successful completion of the labs in Chapter 6 and Lab 7.1

Estimated completion time: **30 minutes**

ACTIVITY

1. Start the Windows computer and begin the HyperTerminal session with the router.

2. Turn on the router and hubs, if necessary. Press **Enter**, type the password **cisco** to get to the user EXEC mode prompt, type **enable**, and then press **Enter** to access privileged EXEC mode.

3. Type **class**, and then press **Enter** when prompted for the enable secret password.

4. Enter the **show interfaces** command and make sure the status of all the participating interfaces is up/up.

5. Type **show ip route**, and then press **Enter** to see the routing table information on the router. Which networks are directly connected to your router?

_____

How do you know whether a network is directly connected?

_____

Are there any networks your router has learned about through the RIP routing protocol?

_____

How do you know whether a network has been learned about through RIP?

_____

6. To configure a static route on a router, you must know the destination network number, the subnet mask, and the IP address of the next router interface (hop) in the path to the destination network. Review the syntax for the ip route command, which is shown here:

ip route [*remote network*] [*subnet mask*] [*IP address of interface on next hop in the path*][*administrative distance* (optional)]

7. Examine the network in Figure 8-1. The following command configures a static route to network 205.7.5.0 from the lab-e router:

ip route 205.7.5.0 255.255.255.0 210.93.105.1 255

8

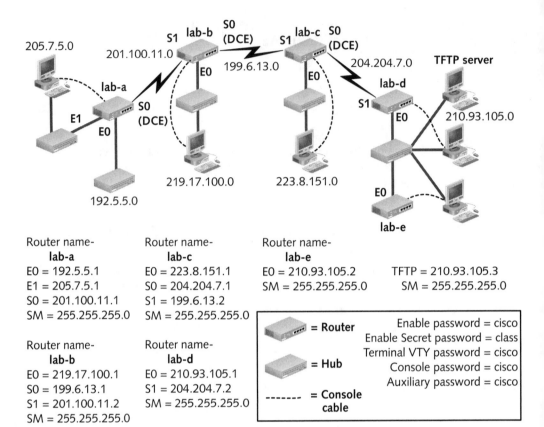

Figure 8-1 Connection information

8. The last IP address in the command in Step 7 is the E0 interface on the lab–d router. It corresponds to the next hop on the path to the destination network. The 255 at the end of the command is the optional administrative distance. If you don't put an administrative distance in the command, what is the default?

_____

9. Type **conf t**, and then press **Enter** to enter global configuration mode.

10. Use the **ip route** command to configure a static route on your router. Use an administrative distance of 255. Do not configure a static route to a network to which you are directly connected. Which router are you configuring?

_____

For which network are you configuring a static route?

_____

Which command did you enter?

_____

11. Use the **ip route** command to configure another static route on your router to a different remote network. Use an administrative distance of 255.

For which network are you configuring a static route?

_____

Which command did you enter?

_____

12. Press **Ctrl+Z** to return to the enable prompt, and then press **Enter** to clear the message.

13. Type **show ip route**, and then press **Enter** to see the routing table information on the router. Do you see your static routes? Why not?

_____

_____

14. Return to global configuration mode, and use the up arrow to find your static route commands. For each of them, remove the administrative distance, but leave the rest of the command intact.

15. Press **Ctrl+Z** to return to the enable prompt, and then press **Enter** to clear the message.

16. Type **show ip route**, and then press **Enter** to see the routing table information on the router.

You should see your static routes. What is the symbol that lets you know these are static routes?

_____

Why did removing the administrative distance of 255 from the static route commands change the routing table in this way?

_____

_____

17. Do not save the configuration. Type **logout**, and then press **Enter** to exit the router.

Certification Objectives

Objectives for the CCNA exam:

> ➤ Configure a router for additional administrative functionality

Review Questions

1. What is a stub router?

2. Why do you think the default administrative distance of a static route is only 1?

3. What is the purpose of changing the default administrative distance of a static route?

4. What is the only type of routing table entry that would have a default administrative distance less than the default administrative distance of a static route?

LAB 8.3 CONFIGURE RIP

Objectives

The objective of this lab is to demonstrate how to configure the router for RIP. RIP is the most common dynamic routing protocol in use on smaller internetworks. In this lab you will configure the router for the RIP dynamic routing protocol. In addition, you will change the timer information, including the update interval. You will also use the show commands and a debug command for monitoring network routes.

After completing this lab you will:

> Understand the difference between dynamic routing and static routing

> Understand the command syntax for configuring RIP routing

> Be familiar with the output from the show ip protocol, show ip route, and debug ip rip commands

Materials Required

This lab requires the following:

> The successful completion of the labs in Chapter 6 and Lab 7.1

> The internetworking lab setup shown in Figure 8-1

> Estimated completion time: **30 minutes**

ACTIVITY

1. Start the computer with Windows and begin the HyperTerminal session with the router.

2. Turn on the router, if necessary. Press **Enter**, type the password **cisco** to get to the user EXEC mode prompt, type **enable**, and then press **Enter** to access privileged EXEC mode.

3. Type **class**, and then press **Enter** when prompted for the enable secret password.

4. Enter global configuration mode.

5. Remove RIP from the router using the **no router rip** command.

6. Press **Ctrl+Z** to return to enable mode.

7. Wait a few minutes for the RIP routes to be flushed from the router.

8. Type **show ip route**, and then press **Enter**. Are all of your routes either directly connected or statically configured?

_____

_____

If the answer is "no" and RIP routes are still active, wait a few more seconds and try the **show ip route** command again. You should proceed to Step 9 only when you have confirmed that no RIP routes are active.

9. Enter global configuration mode.

10. Type **router rip** to enter router configuration mode.

11. Enter the networks to which your router is directly connected. Refer back to Figure 8-1, and use the **network** command to indicate which networks are directly connected to your router. For example, if you are configuring the lab-d router, you are directly connected to networks 204.204.7.0 and 210.93.105.0. In this case, you would type:

network 204.204.7.0 [Enter]

network 210.93.105.0 [Enter]

12. Press **Ctrl+Z** to return to the enable prompt, press **Enter** to clear the message, and then wait a minute to give the router a chance to update its routing table.

13. Type **show ip route**, and then press **Enter**. Has your router obtained any route information via RIP?

_____

14. Type **show ip protocol**, and then press **Enter**. What is the RIP update interval?

_____

What is the invalid interval?

_____

What is the hold-down timer interval?

_____

What is the flush interval?

_____

15. Enter global configuration mode, then type **router rip** and press **Enter** to enter router configuration mode.

16. The timers basic command allows you to change the default timers you recorded in Step 14. Review the format of the following command:

    timers basic [*update interval*] [*invalid interval*] [*hold–down timer*] [*flush interval*]

17. Type **timers basic 60 500 360 440** and press **Enter**.

18. Press **Ctrl+Z** to return to enable mode.

19. Type **show ip protocol** and review the timer information. Have the timers been reconfigured, as shown by the commands in Step 17?

    _____

20. Type **debug ip rip**, and then press **Enter**. Watch the screen for a minute or so to see the displayed information. What useful information can you obtain from this command?

    _____

21. Press **Enter** if necessary to get to the prompt, and then type **no debug all** and press **Enter** to disable all debugging.

22. Do not save the configuration. Type **logout**, and then press **Enter** to exit the router.

Certification Objectives

Objectives for the CCNA exam:

➤ Configure routing protocols based on user requirements

➤ Troubleshoot routing protocols

Review Questions

1. What is an advantage of increasing the update interval?

2. What is the purpose of the hold–down timer?

3. List three commands to turn off the debugging you configured using the debug ip rip command.

4. What is the purpose of the flush interval?

Lab 8.4 Configure IGRP

Objectives

The objective of this lab is to configure the router for IGRP. IGRP is Cisco's answer to RIP. This proprietary, dynamic routing protocol uses bandwidth and delay as its primary metrics. In this lab you will configure the router for the IGRP dynamic routing protocol. You will also use the show ip protocol command and a debug command for monitoring network routes.

After completing this lab you will:

➤ Understand the difference between dynamic routing and static routing

➤ Understand the command syntax for configuring IGRP routing

➤ Know how to check the router for routing table information

➤ Be familiar with the output from the show ip protocol and debug ip igrp events commands

Materials Required

This lab requires the following:

➤ The successful completion of the labs in Chapter 6 and Lab 7.1

➤ The internetworking lab setup shown in Figure 8-1

Estimated completion time: **30 minutes**

Activity

1. Start the Windows computer and begin the HyperTerminal session with the router.

2. Turn on the router, if necessary. Press **Enter**, type the password **cisco** to get to the user EXEC mode prompt, type **enable**, and then press **Enter** to access privileged EXEC mode.

3. Type **class**, and then press **Enter** when prompted for the enable secret password.

4. Enter global configuration mode.

5. Type **no router rip**, and then press **Enter** to disable RIP.

6. Type **router igrp 100**, and then press **Enter** to enable IGRP. To what did the prompt change?

_____

What does the number 100 represent?

_____

7. Refer back to Figure 8-1 and use the **network [*network #*]** command to enable IGRP routing for the networks that are directly connected to your router.

8. Press **Ctrl+Z** to return to enable mode.

9. Type **show ip protocol**, and then press **Enter**. Is IGRP configured on the router?

   _____

   What is the update interval?

   _____

   What is the invalid interval?

   _____

   What is the hold-down timer interval?

   _____

   What is the flush interval?

   _____

10. Type **show ip route** and press **Enter**. Are any IGRP routes indicated?

    _____

    If the answer is no, what is your explanation?

    _____

    _____

11. Type **debug ip igrp events**, and then press **Enter**. Watch the screen for a minute or so to see the displayed information. What useful information can you obtain from this command?

    _____

    _____

    _____

12. Type **no debug all**, and then press **Enter** to disable all debugging.

13. Do not save the configuration. Type **reload**, and then press **Enter** to reboot the router. Press **n** for no and then press **Enter** if you are asked to save the configuration. Confirm the reload if necessary.

Certification Objectives

Objectives for the CCNA exam:

➤ Configure routing protocols based on user requirements

➤ Troubleshoot routing protocols

Review Questions

1. Can IGRP be used on non–Cisco routers? Why or why not?

2. Why do routers running distance-vector routing protocols such as RIP and IGRP take a relatively long time to converge?

3. If debug is so informative, why not leave it on all the time for monitoring purposes?

4. What is the advantage of having a longer update interval?

8

ADVANCED ROUTING PROTOCOLS

Labs included in this chapter

➤ Lab 9.1 Identify the Characteristics of Various Routing Protocols

➤ Lab 9.2 Configure RIPv2

➤ Lab 9.3 Configure EIGRP

➤ Lab 9.4 Configure OSPF in a Single Area

CCNA Exam Objectives	
Objective	**Lab**
Select an appropriate routing protocol based on user requirements	9.1
Configure routing protocols given user requirements	9.2, 9.3, 9.4
Troubleshoot routing protocols	9.2, 9.3, 9.4
Evaluate the characteristics of routing protocols	9.1

LAB 9.1 IDENTIFY THE CHARACTERISTICS OF VARIOUS ROUTING PROTOCOLS

Objectives

While a complete understanding of only RIP and IGRP is expected of a CCNA, it is also important to understand the fundamentals of the more popular advanced routing protocols. The objective of this lab is to be able to identify the characteristics of RIPv2, EIGRP, and OSPF, as well as RIP and IGRP.

After completing this lab, you will be able to:

> ➤ Identify basic characteristics of RIP, IGRP, RIPv2, EIGRP, and OSPF

Materials Required

This lab requires the following:

> ➤ A pen or pencil

Estimated completion time: **20 minutes**

ACTIVITY

ACTIVITY

1. Fill in the Routing Protocol column of Table 9-1 with the protocol(s) being described. Possible answers are RIP, RIPv2, IGRP, EIGRP, and OSPF. Note that more than one routing protocol might be appropriate for a characteristic.

Table 9-1   Routing protocol characteristics

Characteristic	Routing Protocol
Broadcasts periodically	
Uses multicasting	
Uses multicast address 224.0.0.10	
Uses multicast address 224.0.0.9	
Uses multicast address 224.0.0.5	
May elect a DR	
Uses LSAs	
Is actually a hybrid routing protocol	
Limited to 15 hops	
Cisco proprietary	
Auto-summarizes at major network boundaries	
Calculates a feasible successor	
Uses the Dijkstra algorithm	

Table 9-1   Routing protocol characteristics (continued)

Characteristic	Routing Protocol
Uses the DUAL algorithm	
Classful	
Classless	
Has the ability to authenticate	
Uses PDMs to support multiple protocols such as IPX and AppleTalk	
Is backward-compatible with IGRP	
Uses Hello packets to establish adjacencies	
Open standard	
Uses cost as its only metric	

Certification Objectives

Objectives for the CCNA exam:

➤ Select an appropriate routing protocol based on user requirements

➤ Evaluate the characteristics of routing protocols

Review Questions

1. What can classless routing protocols do that classful routing protocols cannot?

2. What is an advantage of OSPF over EIGRP?

3. What is an advantage of EIGRP over OSPF?

4. Why might you have to turn off the auto-summarization feature?

5. Why is multicasting rather than broadcasting generally preferred for routing updates?

LAB 9.2 CONFIGURE RIPV2

Objectives

RIPv2 is a classless routing protocol, which means it can carry subnet masking information in its routing updates. RIPv2 configuration is only slightly more complicated than configuring basic RIP. The objective of this lab is to configure RIPv2 and compare it with the RIP you configured in Chapter 8. In addition, you will configure a router interface to be passive. Passive interfaces listen for updates from other routers but do not send routing updates.

After completing this lab, you will be able to:

➤ Configure RIPv2

➤ Configure passive interfaces

➤ Monitor RIPv2

Materials Required

This lab requires the following:

➤ The internetworking lab setup used in the labs in Chapters 6, 7, and 8

➤ The successful completion of the labs in Chapter 6 as well as Lab 7.1

Estimated completion time: **30 minutes**

ACTIVITY

1. If necessary, turn on the workstations.

2. Open the HyperTerminal program on each workstation that will connect to the routers.

3. If necessary, turn on the routers and hubs.

4. Press **Enter** on the workstations if you need to initiate a response from the router.

5. Enter enable mode using **cisco** as the console password and **class** as the enable password.

6. Enter global configuration mode.

7. Type **router rip**, and then press **Enter**.

8. Type **version 2** to change from basic RIP to RIPv2, and then press **Enter**.

9. Enter the networks to which your router is directly connected. Refer to Figure 9-1 and use the **network** command to indicate which networks are directly connected to your router. For example, if you are configuring the lab-d router, you are directly connected to networks 204.204.7.0 and 210.93.105.0. In this case, you would type:

network 204.204.7.0 [Enter]

network 210.93.105.0 [Enter]

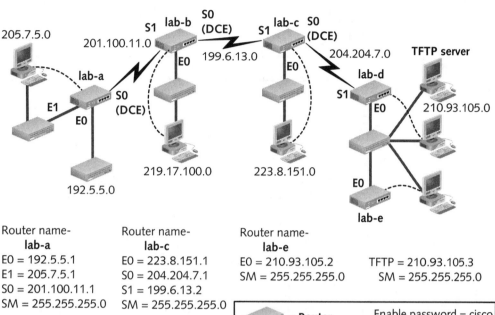

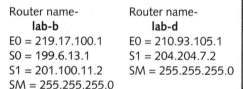

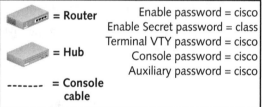

205.7.5.0

S1 lab-b
201.100.11.0

S0
(DCE)

lab-c S0
S1   (DCE)

199.6.13.0

204.204.7.0   **TFTP server**

lab-a

E1

E0

S0
(DCE)

EO

lab-d

S1

EO

210.93.105.0

192.5.5.0

219.17.100.0   223.8.151.0

EO

lab-e

Router name-
lab-a
E0 = 192.5.5.1
E1 = 205.7.5.1
S0 = 201.100.11.1
SM = 255.255.255.0

Router name-
lab-c
E0 = 223.8.151.1
S0 = 204.204.7.1
S1 = 199.6.13.2
SM = 255.255.255.0

Router name-
lab-e
E0 = 210.93.105.2
SM = 255.255.255.0

TFTP = 210.93.105.3
SM = 255.255.255.0

Router name-
lab-b
E0 = 219.17.100.1
S0 = 199.6.13.1
S1 = 201.100.11.2
SM = 255.255.255.0

Router name-
lab-d
E0 = 210.93.105.1
S1 = 204.204.7.2
SM = 255.255.255.0

= **Router**

= **Hub**

------- = **Console**
cable

Enable password = cisco
Enable Secret password = class
Terminal VTY password = cisco
Console password = cisco
Auxiliary password = cisco

Figure 9-1   Connection information

10. Press **Ctrl+Z** to return to enable mode.

11. Enter the **show ip protocol** command. Which routing protocol is listed?

_____

Which version of RIP updates is being sent and received?

_____

What is the update interval?

_____

What is the invalid interval?

_____

What is the hold–down timer interval?

_____

What is the flush interval?

_____

Are these default intervals the same or different from the ones recorded for RIP version 1 in Lab 8.3, Step 14?

_____

12. Type **show ip route** and press **Enter**. Can you tell by this command output which RIP version is running?

_____

13. What is the administrative distance of RIPv2?

_____

14. Type **debug ip rip** and press **Enter**. Wait for the output to display. Is RIPv2 sending and receiving updates to routers on all active interfaces?

_____

   If not, make sure RIPv2 is correctly configured on the routers.

15. Type **undebug all** and press **Enter**.

16. Enter global configuration mode.

17. Type **router rip** and press **Enter** to enter router configuration mode.

18. Type **passive-interface s[#]**, where [#] is an active serial interface on your router. The lab-e router has no active serial interfaces and should use e0. Which interface have you made active?

_____

19. Press **Ctrl+Z** to exit to enable mode.

20. Type **debug ip rip** and press **Enter**. Are you sending updates out of the passive interface you listed in Step 18?

_____

   If you are, you have incorrectly configured the passive interface.

21. Type **undebug all** and press **Enter** to disable all debugging.

22. Enter global configuration mode.

23. Type **router rip** and press **Enter**.

24. Use the **no passive-interface** command with the correct interface to reestablish normal routing updates in and out of all active router interfaces.

25. Log out of the router without saving your configuration.

Certification Objectives

Objectives for the CCNA exam:

➤ Configure routing protocols given user requirements

➤ Troubleshoot routing protocols

Review Questions

1. What command tells the router to listen for and advertise RIPv2 instead of RIPv1?

2. What is the advantage of RIPv2 over RIPv1?

3. What is the disadvantage of RIPv2?

4. What command tells an interface on a router to listen for but not send routing updates?

5. True or False? RIPv1 and RIPv2 default timers are identical.

LAB 9.3 CONFIGURE EIGRP

Objectives

EIGRP is based on distance-vector technology but is really a hybrid routing protocol because it also includes elements of link-state routing. Like most distance-vector routing protocols, EIGRP only needs to know about directly connected routers; in other words, neighbors. EIGRP uses the DUAL algorithm to calculate the best route to a destination. The objective of this lab is to configure and monitor EIGRP. In addition, you will disrupt the topology and watch as EIGRP runs DUAL in an attempt to find alternative routes.

After completing this lab, you will be able to:

➤ Configure EIGRP

➤ Monitor EIGRP

Materials Required

This lab requires the following:

➤ The internetworking lab setup used in the labs in Chapters 6, 7, and 8

➤ The successful completion of the labs in Chapter 6 and Lab 7.1

Estimated completion time: **30 minutes**

ACTIVITY

1. If necessary, turn on the workstations.

2. Open the HyperTerminal program on each workstation that will connect to the routers.

3. If necessary, turn on the routers and hubs.

4. Press **Enter** on the workstations if you need to initiate a response from the router.

5. Enter enable mode using **cisco** as the console password and **class** as the enable password.

6. Enter global configuration mode.

7. Type **router eigrp 65000** and press **Enter**.

8. Enter the networks to which your router is directly connected. Refer to Figure 9-1 and use the **network** command to indicate which networks are directly connected to your router. For example, if you are configuring the lab-d router, you are directly connected to networks 204.204.7.0 and 210.93.105.0. In this case, you would type:

network 204.204.7.0 [Enter]

network 210.93.105.0 [Enter]

9. Press **Ctrl+Z** to exit to enable mode.

10. Type **show ip route**. What is the letter code for EIGRP routes?

_____

What is the administrative distance of EIGRP?

_____

11. Type **show ip protocol** and press **Enter**. Does EIGRP auto-summarize by default?

_____

12. Type **show ip eigrp topology** and press **Enter**. What does this output display?

_____

How many entries are there in the table?

_____

13. Type **debug ip eigrp** and press **Enter**. Nothing will display if the network is stable. Now you will make the network unstable by shutting down an interface.

14. Type **conf t** and press **Enter** to change to global configuration mode.

15. Type **int s[#]**, where **[#]** is an active interface on your router that is connected to another active router interface. If you are configuring the lab-e router, you will need to use e0 as your interface. Press **Enter**.

16. Type **shutdown** and press **Enter**. Debug output immediately displays on all connected routers as they attempt to find alternate paths.

17. Press **Ctrl+Z** to return to enable mode.

18. Type **show ip eigrp topology** and press **Enter**. How many successors are now in the table?

_____

Compare this with your answer recorded in Step 12.

19. Enter global configuration mode.

20. Type **int s[#]** (or int e0 if you are configuring the lab-e router) and press **Enter**.

21. Type **no shutdown** and press **Enter**.

22. Press **Ctrl+Z** and press **Enter**.

23. Type **show ip eigrp topology** and press **Enter**. You should have the same number of entries in the table now as you did in Step 12.

24. Type **show ip route** and press **Enter**. All successors should be in your routing table.

25. Type **undebug all** and press **Enter** to disable all debugging.

26. Type **logout** and press **Enter**. Do not copy this configuration to NVRAM.

Certification Objectives

Objectives for the CCNA exam:

➤ Configure routing protocols given user requirements

➤ Troubleshoot routing protocols

Review Questions

1. Why didn't you need the no auto-summary command in this lab?

2. How is the EIGRP metric related to the IGRP metric?

3. What is in the EIGRP topology table?

4. True or False? EIGRP is a hybrid routing protocol based on link-state technology.

LAB 9.4 CONFIGURE OSPF IN A SINGLE AREA

Objectives

OSPF is a link-state routing protocol that is more complicated to configure than the routing protocols you have previously worked with in the labs. The CCNA exam requires you to know the basics about configuring OSPF in a single area. The objective of this lab is to configure and monitor OSPF.

After completing this lab, you will be able to:

➤ Configure OSPF

➤ Monitor OSPF

Materials Required

This lab requires the following:

➤ The internetworking lab setup used in the labs in Chapters 6, 7, and 8

➤ The successful completion of the labs in Chapter 6 and Lab 7.1

Estimated completion time: **45 minutes**

ACTIVITY

1. Turn off all routers and hubs.

2. Using Figure 9-1 for reference, disconnect the serial cable between the lab-b and lab-c routers. Using Figure 9-2 for reference, disconnect the serial cable between the lab-c and lab-d routers.

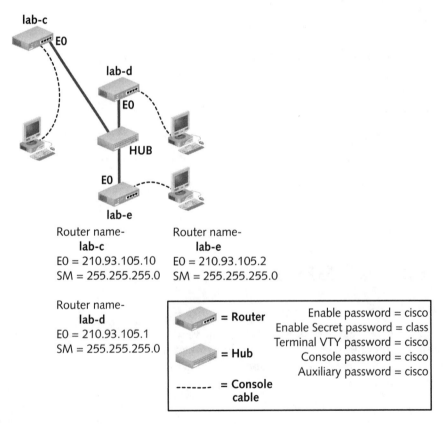

Router name-
lab-c
EO = 210.93.105.10
SM = 255.255.255.0

Router name-
lab-e
EO = 210.93.105.2
SM = 255.255.255.0

Router name-
lab-d
EO = 210.93.105.1
SM = 255.255.255.0

= Router
= Hub
------- = Console
cable

Enable password = cisco
Enable Secret password = class
Terminal VTY password = cisco
Console password = cisco
Auxiliary password = cisco

Figure 9-2   OSPF lab setup

3. Move the UTP cable from the lab-c router's hub to the hub shared by the lab-d and lab-e routers.

4. Turn on the lab-c, lab-d, and lab-e routers and the hub they share. Leave the rest of the lab equipment turned off.

5. Begin a HyperTerminal session with the routers.

6. Press **Enter** on the workstations if you need to initiate a response from the router.

7. Enter enable mode using **cisco** as the console password and **class** as the enable password.

8. On the lab-c router only, you need to change the IP address on the Ethernet interface. Using Figure 9-2 as a reference, change the IP address on the e0 interface of the lab-c router to **210.93.105.10**.

9. Make sure the routers can ping each other before continuing. The following steps apply to all routers unless otherwise mentioned.

10. Enter global configuration mode.

11. Type **router OSPF 1** and press **Enter**.

12. Type **network 210.93.105.0 0.0.0.255 area 0** and press **Enter**. Return to enable mode using **Ctrl+Z**.

13. Type **show ip ospf** and press **Enter**. What is your router ID?

_____

How many times has the SPF algorithm run?

_____

14. Type **show ip ospf database** and press **Enter**. All three participating OSPF interfaces should be listed under Router Link States.

15. Type **show ip ospf interface** and press **Enter**. What is the cost associated with this interface?

_____

Which router is the designated router (DR)?

_____

Which router is the backup designated router?

_____

What is the default priority?

_____

16. Type **debug ip ospf events** and press **Enter**. There will be no output if the network is stable. You will now destabilize the network and watch the SPF algorithm in action.

17. On the lab-d router only, enter global configuration mode and remove OSPF using the **no router ospf 1** command. Watch the debug output as OSPF adjusts to the new network topology.

18. On the lab-d router only, reconfigure OSPF using the commands from Steps 11 and 12. Watch the debug output as adjacencies are formed.

19. On all routers, type **undebug all** and press **Enter** to disable all debugging.

20. Log out of the routers. Do not copy this configuration to NVRAM.

Certification Objectives

Objectives for the CCNA exam:

➤ Configure routing protocols given user requirements

➤ Troubleshoot routing protocols

Review Questions

1. What extra parameters are necessary in the network command when using OSPF, as compared with RIP, IGRP, and EIGRP?

2. What is the purpose of areas in OSPF?

3. What is the purpose of the DR?

4. What determines which router will be the DR?

ACCESS LISTS

Labs included in this chapter

➤ Lab 10.1 Create and Apply a Standard IP Access List on the Lab-d Router

➤ Lab 10.2 Create and Apply an Extended IP Access List on the Lab-b Router

➤ Lab 10.3 Create and Apply a Named Access List on the Lab-c Router

---

CCNA Exam Objectives	
Objective	Lab
Develop an access list to meet user specifications	10.1, 10.2, 10.3
Implement access lists	10.1, 10.2, 10.3
Troubleshoot an access list	10.1, 10.2, 10.3
Evaluate rules for packet control	10.1, 10.2, 10.3

LAB 10.1 CREATE AND APPLY A STANDARD IP ACCESS LIST ON THE LAB-D ROUTER

Objectives

The objective of this lab is to configure a standard IP access list, which filters traffic based on source IP addresses. This process is carried out in two steps. First, the list is created using a text editor and configured in global configuration mode. Second, the list is applied to the appropriate interface as either an inbound list or an outbound list in interface configuration mode.

In this lab, you will create a standard IP access list that will deny access to network 210.93.105.0 from any host on network 205.7.5.0. You then will apply it to the appropriate interface on the lab-d router in the internetworking lab. Finally, you will monitor and test your list.

Note that you must complete the first six questions of this lab before attempting to configure the router. This will save time because designing the list is the most time-consuming part of access list configuration, and can be done in advance.

After completing this lab, you will be able to:

➤ Create a standard IP access list using Notepad

➤ Configure the standard IP access list and apply it to the appropriate interface

➤ Use the correct show commands to monitor the standard IP access list

➤ Test the standard IP access list

Materials Required

This lab requires the following:

➤ The internetworking lab setup used in the labs from Chapters 6 and 7

➤ The successful completion of the labs in Chapters 6 and 7

Estimated completion time: **45 minutes**

ACTIVITY

Before beginning, make sure the lab equipment is set up and configured as shown in Figure 10-1. Pay particular attention to the wiring and IP configuration changes that were made to the lab-c router during Lab 9.4. Do not skip the first six questions in this lab. Doing so will only slow down the configuration process.

1. Examine Figure 10-1. The access list to deny access to network 210.93.105.0 from any host on network 205.7.5.0 should be created and applied on the lab-d router. Why?

_____

_____

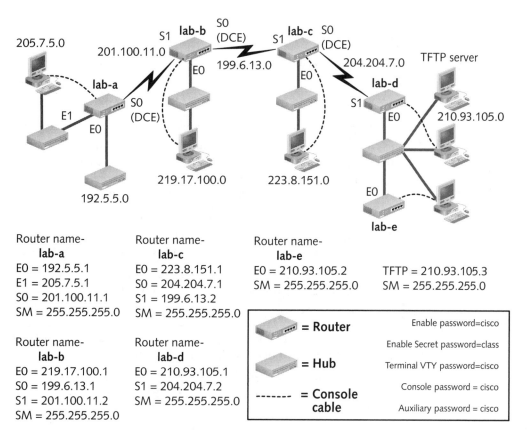

Router name-
lab-a
EO = 192.5.5.1
E1 = 205.7.5.1
SO = 201.100.11.1
SM = 255.255.255.0

Router name-
lab-c
EO = 223.8.151.1
SO = 204.204.7.1
S1 = 199.6.13.2
SM = 255.255.255.0

Router name-
lab-e
EO = 210.93.105.2
SM = 255.255.255.0

TFTP = 210.93.105.3
SM = 255.255.255.0

Router name-
lab-b
EO = 219.17.100.1
SO = 199.6.13.1
S1 = 201.100.11.2
SM = 255.255.255.0

Router name-
lab-d
EO = 210.93.105.1
S1 = 204.204.7.2
SM = 255.255.255.0

= Router	Enable password=cisco
	Enable Secret password=class
= Hub	Terminal VTY password=cisco
	Console password = cisco
------- = Console cable	Auxiliary password = cisco

Figure 10-1   Connection information

2. Write the access list to deny any traffic from network 205.7.5.0 from reaching any host on network 210.93.105.0. Don't forget the permit statement. Use Figure 10-1 for reference.

_____

_____

3. Why is the permit statement necessary?

_____

_____

4. Which list number did you use in the list?

_____

What is the acceptable range for a standard IP list?

_____

Correct your list number in Step 2, if necessary.

5. On which interface and in which direction will you apply the list you created in Step 2?

_____

Why?

_____

_____

6. Which command will you use to apply the access list?

_____

7. Turn on the Windows computers, routers, and hubs, if necessary. Attach a UTP patch cable between the NIC in the lab-a Windows computer and the hub connected to the E1 interface of the lab-a router. Make sure the NIC light on the computer and the corresponding port light on the hub are on.

8. Make sure the IP address and gateway configured on the lab-a Windows computer are 205.7.5.2 and 205.7.5.1, respectively. You may have to restart the computer if you make any IP configuration changes to the workstation.

9. Return to the lab-d computer, if necessary. Log in to the lab-d router using **cisco** as the console password. Enter enable mode using the password **class**.

10. Enter global configuration mode.

11. Click the Windows **Start** button, point to **Programs**, point to **Accessories**, and then click **Notepad** to open the Notepad program.

12. Type **no access-list [#]**, where # is the list number that you recorded in Step 4. Press **Enter**. Why should this statement be the first line in your text editor access list?

_____

_____

13. Type the access list commands created in Step 2 on separate lines under the no access-list command.

14. Highlight your list and copy it to the Clipboard.

15. Minimize Notepad, right-click beside the **lab-d (config)#** prompt, and then click **Paste to Host**. Your list should be entered into the router's running configuration. If it didn't work, try the copy-and-paste operation again.

16. When will the access list take effect?

_____

_____

17. Enter interface configuration mode for the interface you specified in Step 5.

18. Apply the list using the command you specified in Step 6.

19. Press **Ctrl+Z** to return to enable mode.

20. Use the **show access-lists** command to see the access list defined on the lab-d router. What information is provided by this command?

_____

21. In this case, which other command will give you identical information?

_____

22. Type **show ip interface**, and then press **Enter**. What kind of information do you get regarding the access list?

_____

23. Move to the computer attached to the lab-a router or ask your teammate configuring the lab-a router to do the next three steps for you. Make sure that it is turned on, and then close any open programs, if necessary.

24. Open a Windows command prompt window.

25. Type **ping 210.93.105.2**, and then press **Enter**.

26. What was the response?

_____

What does the response mean?

_____

_____

27. If you were able to ping successfully, your access list is incorrect or is applied incorrectly. Make any necessary corrections to your access list in Notepad, copy and paste to the host again, and then retest.

28. Close the command prompt window on the workstation connected to the lab-a router.

29. Return to the lab-d router, if necessary.

30. Enter global configuration mode and then interface configuration mode for the interface on which the list is applied.

31. Use the **no ip access-group [#] [direction]** command, where # is the list number and *direction* is either in or out, to remove the list from the interface.

32. Type **exit** to return to global configuration mode.

33. Type **no access-list [#]**, where # is the list number, to remove the list from the router.

34. Exit to enable mode and use the **show access-lists** command to verify that the list has been removed.

35. Log out of the lab-d router.

10

Certification Objectives

Objectives for the CCNA exam:

➤ Develop an access list to meet user specifications

➤ Implement access lists

➤ Troubleshoot an access list

➤ Evaluate rules for packet control

Review Questions

1. How does using Notepad facilitate creating access lists in the router?

2. Why must standard IP access lists be applied as close to the destination as possible?

3. What is the wildcard mask that filters any host on a class B network?

4. What is the wildcard mask that filters any host on a class A network?

LAB 10.2 CREATE AND APPLY AN EXTENDED IP ACCESS LIST ON THE LAB-B ROUTER

Objectives

The objective of this lab is to configure an extended IP access list. This process is the same as that for a standard IP access list. First, the list is created using a text editor and configured in global configuration mode. Second, it is applied to the appropriate interface as either an inbound list or an outbound list in interface configuration mode.

In this lab you will create an extended IP access list to deny the host with the IP address 219.17.100.2 from pinging the host with IP address 205.7.5.2. You will then apply the list to the appropriate interface on the lab-b router in the internetworking lab. Finally, you will monitor and test your list.

Note that you must complete the first six questions of this lab before attempting to configure the router. This will save time because designing the list is the most time-consuming part of access list configuration, and can be done in advance.

After completing this lab, you will be able to:

➤ Create an extended IP access list using Notepad

➤ Configure the extended IP access list and apply it to the appropriate interface

➤ Use the correct show commands to monitor the extended IP access list

➤ Test the extended IP access list

Materials Required

This lab requires the following:

➤ The internetworking lab setup used in the labs from Chapters 6 and 7

➤ The successful completion of the labs in Chapters 6 and 7

➤ Two extra UTP patch cables

10

Estimated completion time: **45 minutes**

ACTIVITY

Do not skip the first six questions in this lab. Doing so will only slow down the configuration process.

1. Examine Figure 10-1 again. The access list to deny the host with the IP address 219.17.100.2 from pinging the host with IP address 205.7.5.2 should be created and applied on the lab-b router. Why?

   _____

   _____

2. Write the access list to deny ping traffic from node 219.17.100.2 from reaching host 205.7.5.2. Do not forget the permit statement. Use Figure 10-1 for reference.

   _____

   _____

3. Why is the permit statement necessary?

   _____

   _____

4. Which list number did you use in the list?

   _____

What is the acceptable range for an extended IP list?

_____

Correct your list number in Step 2, if necessary.

5. On which interface and in which direction will you apply the list you created in Step 2?

_____

Why?

_____

_____

6. Which command will you use to apply the access list?

_____

7. Turn on the Windows computers, routers, and hubs, if necessary. Make sure a UTP patch cable is between the NIC in the lab-a Windows computer and the hub connected to the E1 interface of the lab-a router. Make sure the NIC light on the computer and the corresponding port light on the hub are on. The lab-b computer should be attached via UTP to the hub connected to the E0 interface on the lab-b router. Again, check lights to make sure you have Physical layer connectivity.

8. Make sure the IP address and gateway configured on the lab-a Windows computer are 205.7.5.2 and 205.7.5.1, respectively. You may have to restart the computer if you changed the IP configuration of the workstation.

9. Make sure the IP address and gateway configured on the lab-b Windows computer are 219.17.100.2 and 219.17.100.1, respectively. You may have to restart the computer if you changed the IP configuration of the workstation.

10. Return to the lab-b computer if necessary. Open a Windows command prompt window.

11. Type **ping 205.7.5.2**, and then press **Enter**.

What was the response?

_____

What does the response mean?

_____

_____

12. If you were unable to ping successfully, start troubleshooting with the help of your instructor. Make sure all of the interfaces between the lab-b router and the lab-a router have an up/up status. After you can ping successfully, continue with the next step.

13. Close the command prompt window on the workstation connected to the lab-b router.

14. Log in to the lab-b router using **cisco** as the console password. Enter enable mode using the password **class**.

15. Enter global configuration mode.

16. Click the Windows **Start** button, point to **Programs**, point to **Accessories**, and then click **Notepad** to open the Notepad program.

17. Type **no access-list [#]**, where # is the list number that you recorded in Step 4, and then press **Enter**. Why should this statement be the first line in your text editor access list?

_____

_____

18. Type the access list commands created in Step 2 on separate lines under the no access-list command.

19. Highlight your list and copy it to the Clipboard.

20. Minimize Notepad, right-click beside the **lab-b (config)#** prompt, and then click **Paste to Host**. Your list should be entered into the router's running configuration.

21. When will the access list take effect?

_____

_____

22. Enter interface configuration mode for the interface you specified in Step 5.

23. Apply the list using the command you specified in Step 6.

24. Press **Ctrl+Z** to return to enable mode.

25. Open a Windows command prompt window.

26. Type **ping 205.7.5.2**, and then press **Enter**.

27. What was the response?

_____

What does the response mean?

_____

_____

28. If you were able to ping successfully, your access list is incorrect or applied incorrectly. Make any necessary corrections to your access list in Notepad, copy and paste to the host again, and then retest.

29. Close the command prompt window on the workstation connected to the lab-b router.

30. Use the **show access-lists** command to see the access list defined on the lab-b router. What information is provided by this command?

_____

31. Compared to using this command with a standard IP list, what additional information do you receive for an extended IP list? (*Hint*: matches)

_____

_____

10

32. Type **clear access-list counters [#]**, where # is the list number, and then press **Enter**. What do you think this command does?

_____

33. Use the **show access-lists** command again. Were the counters (matches) cleared?

_____

34. Enter global configuration mode and then interface configuration mode for the interface on which the list is applied.

35. Use the **no ip access-group [#] [direction]** command, where # is the list number and _direction_ is either in or out, to remove the list from the interface.

36. Type **exit** to return to global configuration mode.

37. Type **no access-list [#]**, where # is the list number, to remove the list from the router.

38. Exit to enable mode and use the **show access-lists** command to verify that the list has been removed.

39. Log out of the lab-b router.

Certification Objectives

Objectives for the CCNA exam:

➤ Develop an access list to meet user specifications

➤ Implement access lists

➤ Troubleshoot an access list

➤ Evaluate rules for packet control

Review Questions

1. What does the host keyword represent?

2. What does the any keyword represent?

3. With standard IP lists, the 0.0.0.0 wildcard mask is assumed. Is it also assumed with extended IP lists?

LAB 10.3 CREATE AND APPLY A NAMED ACCESS LIST ON THE LAB-C ROUTER

Objectives

In Cisco IOS versions 11.2 and above, you can use names instead of numbers to identify your lists. The objective of this lab is to create an extended named list on the lab-c router that denies any Web or ICMP traffic to host 223.8.151.2.

After completing this lab, you will be able to:

➤ Create an extended named access list

➤ Apply the list to the appropriate interface

➤ Test the list

➤ Use the correct show commands to monitor the list

Materials Required

This lab requires the following:

➤ The internetworking lab setup used in the labs from Chapters 6 and 7

➤ The successful completion of the labs in Chapters 6 and 7

➤ One extra UTP patch cable

10

> Estimated completion time: **25 minutes**

ACTIVITY

1. Turn on the Windows computers, routers, and hubs, if necessary. Attach a UTP patch cable between the NIC in the lab-c Windows computer and the hub connected to the E0 interface of the lab-c router. Make sure the NIC light on the computer and the corresponding port light on the hub are on.

2. Make sure the IP address and gateway configured on the lab-c Windows computer are 223.8.151.2 and 223.8.151.1, respectively. You may have to restart the computer if you changed the IP configuration of the workstation.

3. Log in to the lab-c router using the HyperTerminal program. The console password is **cisco**. Enter enable mode using the password **class**.

4. Enter the **show interface** command and make sure that all of the active interfaces on the router are up. If any of the interfaces are administratively down, enter interface configuration mode for that interface and enter the **no shutdown** command.

5. Enter global configuration mode. Type **ip access-list extended cannon** and press **Enter**. To what does the prompt change?

_____

6. Type **deny tcp any host 223.8.151.2 eq www** and press **Enter**. What does this access list line do?

_____

7. Type **deny icmp any host 223.8.151.2** and press **Enter**. What does this access list line do?

_____

8. Type **permit ip any any** and press **Enter**.

9. Now apply the list. Type **int e0** and press **Enter**.

10. Type **ip access-group cannon out** and press **Enter**.

11. Press **Ctrl+Z** to return to enable mode.

12. Use the **show access-lists** command to see if your named list appears.

13. Use the **show ip interface** command to see if your named list was applied correctly. If your list has been configured and applied correctly, proceed to the next step. If it has not been configured or applied correctly, use the **no ip access-list extended cannon** command and the **no ip access-group cannon out** command to remove the list and then try again.

14. Now test the list. Move to the lab-b or lab-d computer and access the corresponding router. Type **ping 223.8.151.2** and press **Enter**. Alternatively, you could ask your teammate on the lab-b or lab-d router to ping that address. What was the response and what does it mean?

_____

15. Enter global configuration mode on the lab-c router.

16. Use the up arrow key on your keyboard to find the ip access-list extended cannon command you entered earlier.

17. Press **Ctrl+A** to move the cursor to the beginning of the line.

18. Type **no**, press the **spacebar** once, and then press **Enter** to remove the named access list.

19. Type **int e0** and press **Enter**.

20. Use the up arrow key on your keyboard to find the ip access-group cannon out command you entered earlier.

21. Press **Ctrl+A** to move the cursor to the beginning of the line.

22. Type **no**, press the **spacebar** once, and then press **Enter** to remove the application of the named access list.

23. Press **Ctrl+Z** to return to enable mode.

24. Use the **show access-lists** command to verify that the list has been removed.

25. Again attempt to ping 223.8.151.2 from the lab-b or lab-d router. This time the ping should be successful.

26. Log out of the lab-c router.

Certification Objectives

Objectives for the CCNA exam:

➤ Develop an access list to meet user specifications

➤ Implement access lists

➤ Troubleshoot an access list

➤ Evaluate rules for packet control

Review Questions

1. What is an advantage of using named lists?

2. What is the advantage of using extended lists over standard lists?

3. Which Cisco IOS version allows you to use named lists?

10

PPP AND ISDN

Labs included in this chapter

➤ Lab 11.1 Configure PPP with CHAP and PAP

➤ Lab 11.2 ISDN BRI Configuration

CCNA Exam Objectives	
Objective	**Lab**
Implement simple WAN protocols	11.1, 11.2
Perform simple WAN troubleshooting	11.1

LAB 11.1 CONFIGURE PPP WITH CHAP AND PAP

Objectives

The objective of this lab is to configure a serial interface on the router for Point-to-Point Protocol (PPP) with Challenge Handshake Authentication Protocol (CHAP) and Password Authentication Protocol (PAP) authentication. Although the default encapsulation on serial interfaces is High-level Data Link Control (HDLC), PPP is preferred in many cases because of its superior Network layer and authentication functionality.

In this lab you will configure each end of a WAN link for PPP with CHAP and PAP. *This means you must configure a router that has an active serial interface.* You will check the status of the newly configured serial interfaces using the show interface command. Finally, you will confirm Network layer connectivity between the WAN links.

After completing this lab, you will be able to:

➤ Configure PPP with CHAP and PAP on a WAN link

➤ Understand why a WAN link is working or not

➤ Interpret the status line of the show interface command output

Materials Required

This lab requires the following:

➤ The internetworking lab setup used in the labs from Chapters 6, 7, 8, and 9

➤ Completion of the labs in Chapters 6 and 7

Estimated completion time: **30 minutes**

ACTIVITY

ACTIVITY

NOTE

This lab cannot be done on the lab-e router because the router has no active serial interfaces.

1. Start the Windows computer, and begin the HyperTerminal session with the router.

2. Turn on the routers and hubs, if necessary. Press **Enter** to get started, and then type the password **cisco** to reach the user EXEC mode prompt. Type **enable**, and then press **Enter** to access privileged EXEC mode.

3. Type **class**, and then press **Enter** when prompted for the enable secret password.

4. Enter global configuration mode.

5. Enter the command to configure an active serial interface on your router. Which command did you enter?

_____

6. Type **encap ppp**, and then press **Enter**. What does the "encap" abbreviation stand for?

_____

What does the encap ppp command do?

_____

What was the encapsulation before you changed it to ppp?

_____

7. Type **ppp auth chap pap**, and then press **Enter**. What does the "auth" abbreviation stand for?

_____

What does this command do?

_____

_____

8. Type **exit**, and then press **Enter** to return to global configuration mode.

9. Next, configure the username and password for the link. The command syntax is **username [*remote router host name*] password [*password*]**. Use **cannon** as the password. Which command did you enter?

_____

10. Press **Ctrl+Z**.

11. Enter the **show interface** command for the interface that you just configured. What is the status of this interface?

_____

12. If the line protocol is down, what is your explanation for it being down? (*Hint:* Is the other end of the WAN link configured for PPP?)

_____

_____

_____

13. Move to the remote router that you specified in Step 9. This router is on the other end of the WAN link that you just configured. To which router did you move?

_____

14. Enter global configuration mode, and then enter the command to configure the serial interface connected to the serial interface you have already configured. Which command did you enter?

_____

11

15. Type **encap ppp**, and then press **Enter**.

16. Type **ppp auth chap pap**, and then press **Enter**.

17. Press **Ctrl+Z**.

18. Enter the **show interface** command for the interface that you just configured. What is the status of this interface?

19. If the line protocol is down, what is your explanation for it being down? (*Hint*: password)

20. Enter global configuration mode.

21. Configure the username and password for the link, as you did in Step 9. You must use the remote router's host name but the same password, which should be **cannon**. Which command did you enter?

22. Press **Ctrl+Z**.

23. Enter the **show interface** command again for the interface that you just configured. What is the status of this interface?

24. If the line protocol is up, what is your explanation?

25. Ping the other end of the WAN link to confirm connectivity. Which command did you use?

26. Enter the **show ip interface** command for the interface that you configured for PPP. Notice the words "peer address" with the IP address of the remote serial interface in the output. What is the meaning of "peer" in this context?

27. Enter global configuration mode, and then interface configuration mode for the serial interface on which the PPP encapsulation has been configured. Remove the PPP encapsulation from the serial interface. Which command did you use?

28. Exit to global configuration mode, and then use the keyboard and editing short-cuts to retrieve the username command and negate it.

29. Repeat Steps 27 and 28 for the first router that you configured for PPP. Exit to enable mode.

30. Use the **show interface** command to examine the default encapsulation on Cisco WAN interfaces. What is it?

_____

_____

31. Type **logout**, and then press **Enter** to exit the router.

Certification Objectives

Objectives for the CCNA exam:

➤ Implement simple WAN protocols

➤ Perform simple WAN troubleshooting

Review Questions

1. Why is PAP considered a two-way handshake?

2. Why is CHAP considered a three-way handshake?

3. When is Cisco's HDLC used on WAN interfaces?

4. What are the advantages of PPP compared with its predecessor SLIP?

11

LAB 11.2 ISDN BRI CONFIGURATION

Objectives

The objective of this lab is to configure global Integrated Services Digital Network (ISDN) parameters, identify and configure interesting traffic, configure Basic Rate Interface (BRI), and configure call information.

ISDN is a WAN service that is popular because of its relatively low cost, as compared with the cost of a dedicated T1 line; therefore, it is an ideal backup or secondary link. The low cost is further reduced when ISDN BRI is configured using dial-on-demand routing (DDR).

In this lab you will configure the routers shown in Figure 11-1 for ISDN BRI with DDR. This includes CHAP authentication and static Internet Protocol (IP) route configuration.

After completing this lab, you will be able to:

➤ Configure ISDN BRI

➤ Understand why configuring DDR reduces the cost of ISDN

➤ Understand that ISDN can use the PPP encapsulation method, which includes CHAP authentication

Materials Required

This lab requires the following:

➤ Pencil

Estimated completion time: **30 minutes**

ACTIVITY

1. Review Figure 11-1 before beginning this lab.

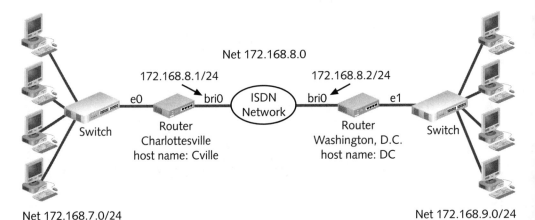

Figure 11-1 ISDN BRI example

2. The routers in Figure 11-1 have a bri0 interface. Are these routers TE1 devices or TE2 devices?

_____

Is a terminal adapter necessary between the routers and the telco BRI lines?

_____

Is an NT1 necessary between the routers and the telco BRI lines?

_____

What is the function of an NT1?

_____

3. In Figure 11-1, the computers off Charlottesville's e0 port require sporadic access to the server off Washington D.C.'s e1 port. This sporadic access does not justify the cost of a leased line. The alternative is to configure these routers to connect only when interesting traffic occurs. What is this configuration called?

_____

_____

4. The switch type in Figure 11-1 is an ni-1. Give the prompt and command to identify the switch type on the Charlottesville router, which has the host name Cville.

_____

_____

5. What is the command to begin configuring the bri0 interface? To what does the prompt change?

_____

_____

11

6. What is the command to configure IP on the bri0 interface of the Cville router?

_____

7. What is the command to configure the SPID number for SPID number 1, which is 3535353535?

_____

8. What are the commands to configure PPP encapsulation with CHAP authentication on the Cville router?

_____

_____

9. What is the command to configure the dialer to map the Washington, D.C., bri0 interface to phone number (202) 555-1212 at a speed of 64 Kbps? The router's host name is DC.

_____

10. What is the command to apply dialer-group 2 to Cville's bri0 interface?

_____

11. What is the command to force the line to disconnect if no interesting traffic occurs for 200 seconds?

_____

12. What is the dialer-list command that is paired with the dialer-group command? The dialer-list command should allow all IP traffic. Which prompt is used with the dialer-list command?

_____

_____

_____

13. What is the command to configure the username and password on the Cville router? The password is cvilledc.

_____

_____

14. What is the command to configure a static route on the Cville router to the DC LAN?

_____

Certification Objectives

Objectives for the CCNA exam:

➤ Implement simple WAN protocols

Review Questions

1. How are the dialer-list/dialer-group commands similar to the access-list/access-group commands?

2. How does DDR save money?

3. Why is ISDN used most often with PPP encapsulation when HDLC encapsulation is the default serial encapsulation?

4. What is the advantage of using static routing rather than dynamic routing on the Cville router in this lab?

FRAME RELAY

Labs included in this chapter

➤ Lab 12.1 Set Up a Test Frame Relay Network

➤ Lab 12.2 Configure the Lab-c Router to Simulate a Frame Relay Switch

➤ Lab 12.3 Configure the Lab-b and Lab-d Routers for Frame Relay

---

CCNA Exam Objectives	
Objective	**Lab**
Implement simple WAN protocols	12.1, 12.2, 12.3
Perform simple WAN troubleshooting	12.1, 12.2, 12.3

LAB 12.1 SET UP A TEST FRAME RELAY NETWORK

Objectives

The objective of this lab is to configure a test Frame Relay network using a router to simulate the Frame Relay switch. As you may know, a Cisco router can be configured to act as a Frame Relay switch. Because a Frame Relay switch acts as a channel service unit/data service unit (CSU/DSU), the router simulating the switch must be configured as the data communications equipment (DCE) on both serial interfaces.

In this lab you will make the physical connections necessary to set up a test Frame Relay network. The lab-c router will act as the switch, and the lab-b and lab-d routers connected to the lab-c router will be configured for Frame Relay, as shown in Figure 12-1. You will also test the DCE.

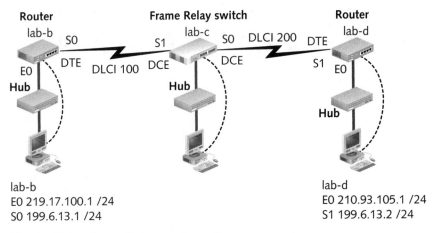

lab-b
EO 219.17.100.1 /24
SO 199.6.13.1 /24

lab-d
EO 210.93.105.1 /24
S1 199.6.13.2 /24

Figure 12-1   Frame Relay configuration

After completing this lab, you will be able to:

➤ Set up a test Frame Relay network

➤ Understand the relationship between the DCE and the data terminal equipment (DTE), and the equipment that comprises each

➤ Test the DCE connection using the show controller serial command

➤ Erase the startup configuration on the routers

Materials Required

This lab requires the following:

➤ The internetworking lab setup used in the labs from Chapters 6, 7, 8, and 9

➤ Completion of the labs in Chapters 6 and 7

Estimated completion time: **30 minutes**

ACTIVITY

1. Make sure that all routers are off. Refer to Figure 12-1 as you work through this lab.

2. Remove the serial cable between the lab-b and lab-c routers.

3. Plug the DCE end into the S1 interface of the lab-c router.

4. Plug the DTE end into the S0 interface of the lab-b router. Why is reversing the serial cable ends necessary in this lab?

   _____

   _____

5. Turn on the lab-b, lab-c, and lab-d routers and the hubs that are connected to them.

6. Turn on the computers connected via the console port to the three routers, if necessary.

7. Open a session in HyperTerminal to connect to the three routers.

8. Move to the lab-c router terminal, which will be the one simulating the Frame Relay switch.

9. Press **Enter** to get started, if necessary, and type the password **cisco** to reach the user EXEC mode prompt. Type **enable**, and then press **Enter** to access privileged EXEC mode.

10. Type **class**, and then press **Enter** when prompted for the enable secret password.

11. Type **show controller serial 0**, and then press **Enter**. Does the command output indicate that it is a DCE port?

    _____

    If the answer is no, something is wrong with the way the cable is connected to the S0 interface, and you must begin troubleshooting. Make sure the correct end of the cable is securely attached to the router interface. If the answer is yes, proceed to Step 12.

12. Type **show controller serial 1**, and then press **Enter**. Does the command output indicate that it is a DCE port?

    _____

    If the answer is no, something is wrong with the way that the cable is connected to the S1 interface, and you must begin troubleshooting. Make sure the correct end of the cable is securely attached to the router interface. If the answer is yes, proceed to Step 13.

12

13. Type **erase start**, and then press **Enter** to erase the startup configuration. Confirm the erase, if necessary. Where is the startup configuration stored?

   _____

14. Type **reload**, and then press **Enter** to restart the router with the empty configuration. If you are prompted to save, press **N** for no. Confirm the reload.

15. Because the startup configuration has been erased, you will be prompted to enter an initial configuration using the system configuration dialog. Press **N** for no and press **Enter**. You may also be prompted to terminate autoinstall. Press **Y** for yes and press **Enter**.

16. Move to the lab-b router terminal.

17. Press **Enter** to get started, if necessary, and then type the password **cisco** to reach the user EXEC mode prompt. Type **enable**, and then press **Enter** to access privileged EXEC mode.

18. Type **class**, and then press **Enter** when prompted for the enable secret password.

19. Type **show controller serial 0**, and then press **Enter**. Does the command output indicate that it is a DTE port?

   _____

   If the answer is no, something is wrong with the way the cable is connected to the S0 interface, and you must begin troubleshooting. If the answer is yes, proceed to Step 20.

20. Type **erase start**, and then press **Enter** to erase the startup configuration. Confirm the erase, if necessary.

21. Type **reload**, and then press **Enter** to restart the router with the empty configuration. If you are prompted to save, press **N** for no. Confirm the reload.

22. Because the startup configuration has been erased, you will be prompted to enter an initial configuration using the system configuration dialog. Press **N** for no and press **Enter**. You may also be prompted to terminate autoinstall. Press **Y** for yes and press **Enter**.

23. Move to the lab-d router terminal.

24. Press **Enter** to get started, if necessary, and type the password **cisco** to reach the user EXEC mode prompt. Type **enable**, and then press **Enter** to access privileged EXEC mode.

25. Type **class**, and then press **Enter** when prompted for the enable secret password.

26. Type **show controller serial 1**, and then press **Enter**. Does the command output indicate that it is a DTE port?

   _____

   If the answer is no, something is wrong with the way that the cable is connected to the S1 interface, and you must begin troubleshooting. If the answer is yes, proceed to Step 27.

27. Type **erase start**, and then press **Enter** to erase the startup configuration. Confirm the erase, if necessary.

28. Type **reload**, and then press **Enter** to restart the router with the empty configuration. If you are prompted to save, press **N** for no. Confirm the reload.

29. Because the startup configuration has been erased, you will be prompted to enter an initial configuration using the system configuration dialog. Press **N** for no and press **Enter**. You may also be prompted to terminate autoinstall. Press **Y** for yes and press **Enter**.

30. In Frame Relay networks, what is the DCE?

_____

_____

In Frame Relay networks, what is the DTE?

_____

_____

You have made and tested the physical connections necessary to make the lab-c router simulate a Frame Relay switch. In the next lab, you will configure the lab-c router with the correct Frame Relay commands.

Certification Objectives

Objectives for the CCNA exam:

➤ Implement simple WAN protocols

➤ Perform simple WAN troubleshooting

12

Review Questions

1. What is the function of a DTE?

2. What is the function of a DCE?

3. In the case of Frame Relay, are the DTE and DCE both customer premises equipment (CPE)?

Lab 12.2 Configure the Lab-c Router to Simulate a Frame Relay Switch

Objectives

If you made the physical connections outlined in Lab 12.1, you are ready to configure the lab-c router to simulate a Frame Relay switch, which is the objective of this lab. This lab involves some commands that, although not normally seen on a router, give you insight into the structure of a Frame Relay network.

In this lab you will configure the lab-c router to simulate a Frame Relay switch that connects the lab-b and lab-d routers.

After completing this lab, you will be able to:

➤ Configure a router to simulate a Frame Relay switch

➤ Understand how a Frame Relay switch operates

Materials Required

This lab requires the following:

➤ The internetworking lab setup used in the labs from Chapters 6, 7, 8, and 9

➤ Completion of the labs in Chapters 6 and 7, and Lab 12.1

Estimated completion time: **30 minutes**

ACTIVITY

ACTIVITY

1. Move to the lab-c router terminal, if necessary. Press **Enter** to get started, and then enter global configuration mode.

2. Type **frame-relay switching**, and then press **Enter**. This command must be entered before the router can perform as a Frame Relay switch.

3. Type **int s1**, and then press **Enter** to begin configuration of the serial port leading to the lab-b router, as shown in Figure 12-1.

4. Type **encap frame-relay**, and then press **Enter**. What does this command do?

_____

_____

5. Type **no ip address**, and then press **Enter**. Why is there no IP address on this router interface?

_____

_____

6. Type **clock rate 1000000**, and then press **Enter**. What is the speed of this link? (Include units in your speed statement.)

   _____

   Why is the clock rate command necessary on this interface?

   _____

   _____

7. Type **frame-relay intf-type dce**, and then press **Enter**. This command sets up the interface as a DCE device on a Frame Relay network. The default is DTE, so you won't normally use this command on a router.

8. Type **frame-relay route 100 int S0 200**, and then press **Enter**. This command configures a static route from the lab-b router to the lab-d router through the switch using the DLCIs.

9. Type **no shutdown** and then press **Enter**.

10. Enter interface configuration mode for the S0 interface, and configure it as you configured the S1 interface using the commands in Steps 4 through 9. The static route command in Step 8 will be slightly different, reflecting a route from the lab-d router to the lab-b router. Which static route command will you use?

    _____

11. Press **Ctrl+Z** to exit to enable mode. In the next lab, you will configure the lab-b and lab-d routers to operate on the simulated Frame Relay network.

Certification Objectives

Objectives for the CCNA exam:

➤ Implement simple WAN protocols

➤ Perform simple WAN troubleshooting

Review Questions

1. Which WAN encapsulation was on the serial interface on the lab-c router before you configured it for Frame Relay?

2. Why don't you typically use the "frame-relay switching" command on a router?

3. What does the Data Link Connection Identifier (DLCI) do?

4. What is the most important parameter to negotiate in a Frame Relay contract with a service provider?

LAB 12.3 CONFIGURE THE LAB-B AND LAB-D ROUTERS FOR FRAME RELAY

Objectives

If you made the physical connections outlined in Lab 12.1, and configured the lab-c router to simulate a Frame Relay switch, as outlined in Lab 12.2, you are ready to configure the lab-b and lab-d routers for Frame Relay, which is the objective of this lab.

In this lab you will configure the lab-b and lab-d routers for Frame Relay with the default Cisco encapsulation for Local Management Interface (LMI) and Inverse ARP enabled. You will then test your configuration using the Frame Relay show commands.

After completing this lab, you will be able to:

➤ Configure a router for Frame Relay

➤ Understand the output of the various Frame Relay show commands

Materials Required

This lab requires the following:

➤ The internetworking lab setup used in the labs from Chapters 6, 7, 8, and 9

➤ Completion of the labs in Chapters 6 and 7, and Labs 12.1 and 12.2

Estimated completion time: **30 minutes**

ACTIVITY

ACTIVITY

1. Move to the lab-b router terminal, if necessary, and then press **Enter** to get started and enter global configuration mode.

2. Configure the IP address on the E0 interface of the lab-b router, per Figure 12-1. Which command did you enter?

_____

3. Type **no shutdown** and press **Enter**.

4. Configure the IP address on the S0 interface of the lab-b router, per Figure 12-1. Include the no shutdown command. Which commands did you enter?

_____

5. Type **encap frame-relay** and then press **Enter**. What does this command do?

   _____

   _____

6. Exit to global configuration mode.

7. Enter the command to configure the router for Interior Gateway Routing Protocol (IGRP) using the autonomous system number 20. Which command did you enter?

   _____

8. Enter the **network** commands to complete the IGRP configuration. Use Figure 12-1 as a reference. Which two network commands did you enter?

   _____

   Notice that when the lab-c router operates as a Frame Relay switch, the serial interfaces on the lab-b and lab-d routers reside on the same network.

9. Press **Ctrl+Z** to return to enable mode.

10. Move to the lab-d router terminal.

11. Using Steps 2 through 9 and Figure 12-1 as a reference, configure the lab-d router for Frame Relay.

12. From the lab-d router, ping the Ethernet port of the lab-b router. Was the ping operation successful?

    _____

    If the answer is no, check your configurations on all three routers and get help from your teammates or instructor if necessary. Make sure that the interfaces are not shut down. In addition, check your routing table. There should be three entries in the routing table of the lab-d and lab-b routers: the two networks to which the router is directly connected and a network that the router learned about via IGRP. Repeat Step 12 from the lab-b router and ping the lab-d router. When the ping operations are successful, proceed to Step 13.

13. Type **show frame-relay pvc** on the lab-b or lab-d router, and then press **Enter**. Are these routers acting as DCEs or DTEs? How do you know?

    _____

    _____

    What is the local DLCI?

    _____

14. Type **show frame-relay map** on the lab-b or lab-d router, and then press **Enter**. To which IP address is the local DLCI mapped?

    _____

15. Type **show interface** on the lab-b or lab-d router. Can you verify that the Frame Relay encapsulation is on the appropriate serial interface?

    _____

12

16. Move to the lab-c router console terminal.

17. Type **show frame–relay route**, and then press **Enter** to look at the Frame Relay switching table. What information is contained in a Frame Relay switch table?

    _____

    _____

    _____

18. Type **show frame–relay pvc**, and then press **Enter** on the lab-c router terminal. Is this router acting as a DCE or DTE? How do you know?

    _____

    _____

19. Log out of all three routers. Turn off the three routers.

20. Switch the ends of the serial cable between the lab-b and lab-c router.

Certification Objectives

Objectives for the CCNA exam:

➤ Implement simple WAN protocols

➤ Perform simple WAN troubleshooting

Review Questions

1. Which show command displays statistics regarding the PVC circuit?

2. How exactly did the Frame Relay map table get built in this lab?

3. Why didn't you have to use the "frame-relay lmi-type" command in this lab?

SWITCHING AND VLANs

13

Labs included in this chapter

➤ Lab 13.1 Configure a Cisco 1900 Switch Using the Menus

➤ Lab 13.2 Configure a Cisco 1900 Switch Using the Command-Line Interface

➤ Lab 13.3 Evaluate Hub Performance

➤ Lab 13.4 Evaluate Switch Performance

➤ Lab 13.5 Understand Switching and LAN Design Concepts and Terminology

➤ Lab 13.6 Configure "Router-on-a-Stick"

CCNA Exam Objectives	
Objective	**Lab**
Customize a switch configuration to meet specified network requirements	13.1, 13.2, 13.6
Perform LAN and VLAN troubleshooting	13.2, 13.6
Troubleshoot IP addressing and host configuration	13.6
Troubleshoot a device as part of a working network	13.2, 13.3, 13.4, 13.6
Describe the Spanning Tree process	13.2
Compare and contrast key characteristics of LAN environments	13.5
Describe the components of network devices	13.5

Lab 13.1 Configure a Cisco 1900 Switch Using the Menus

Objectives

The Cisco 1900 switch can be configured in various ways. You can use the menu or the command-line interface (CLI) when connected via a console cable, or you can use the visual switch manager via a Web browser.

The objective of this lab is for you to become familiar with the 1900 switch series by connecting a terminal to the switch and configuring basic settings using the menus. The Catalyst 1900 series switches have twelve or twenty-four 10-Mbps ports for 10BaseT devices and one 10-Mbps AUI port. In addition to these interfaces, the 1900 provides two 100BaseT ports. The switch has a console port like a router so that it can be configured via a PC by using programs such as HyperTerminal.

In this lab you will connect a workstation to a 1900 series switch via the console port. Next, you will configure HyperTerminal to access the switch. Finally, you will configure the switch using the Management Console, which is a menu-driven configuration utility.

After completing this lab, you will be able to:

➤ Physically connect a Cisco 1900 series switch to a workstation for configuration purposes

➤ Configure the HyperTerminal program to access the switch configuration

➤ Configure the VLANs and set the switching mode using the switch's Management Console utility

➤ Configure a console password on the switch

➤ Reset the switch configuration to factory defaults

Materials Required

This lab requires the following:

➤ One Cisco 1900 series switch with Enterprise Edition software

➤ Power cord for switch

➤ One Windows PC with the HyperTerminal program installed

➤ Console cable for the switch

➤ RJ-45-to-DB-9 or -DB-25 adapter

Estimated completion time: **45 minutes**

ACTIVITY

1. Make sure that the workstation is off.

2. Make sure that the Cisco switch is off. There is no power button on the switch; you have to unplug it to turn it off.

3. Connect one end of the console cable to the console port on the switch.

4. Connect the other end of the cable to the COM1 or COM2 port on the Windows PC. You will need an RJ-45-to-DB-9 or –DB-25 adapter on the PC end of the cable.

5. Plug in the switch and turn on the computer. Wait for the port lights on the front of the switch to go out before continuing.

6. Click **Start**, click **Programs**, click **Accessories**, click **Communications**, and then click the **HyperTerminal** program. If this window does not come up by itself, click **File** on the menu bar, and then click **New Connection**.

The procedure for opening a new connection in HyperTerminal may be slightly different on your Windows computer.

7. Type **SWITCH** in the Name text box, and then press **Enter**.

8. If you are prompted to install a modem, click **No**.

9. In the Connect using: box, choose **COM1** or **COM2**, depending on whether your cable is connected to the COM1 or COM2 port. Click **OK**.

10. Enter the settings as you would when connecting to a Cisco router. In other words, enter the following settings in the appropriate text boxes:

    Bits per Second = **9600**; Data Bits = **8**; Parity = **None**;

    Stop Bits = **1**; Flow Control = **Hardware**

11. Click **OK** to accept the configuration.

12. If there is no response from the switch in the HyperTerminal window, press **Enter**. If it still does not work, ask your instructor or a classmate for help with the configuration. You may have made incorrect cable connections. If you receive a response from the switch, proceed to Step 13.

13. The User Interface menu should be displayed. Type **M** to access the switch via the menu interface.

13

14. The main menu of the switch's Management Console should be displayed. Type **C** to set a console password.

15. At this time, there is probably no password set. It is important to be very careful when setting a switch password. There is no password recovery routine as there is on a Cisco router. Type **M** to modify the password.

16. Type **cisco** for the password, and then press **Enter**. Type **cisco** again to verify the password, and then press **Enter**.

17. Press any key to continue, and then type **X** to exit to the main menu.

18. Type **S** to access the system configuration menu.

19. Type **N** to name the switch, and then type **Cisco1900** and press **Enter**.

20. Type **C**, and then enter *your name* as the contact name.

21. Type **L**, and then enter **Lab Room** as the location.

22. Type **S**, and then set the switching mode to **store-and-forward** by typing a **1** and pressing **Enter**. What is the default switching mode on the Cisco 1900 series switch?

_____

23. Type **X** to exit to the main menu.

24. Type **N** to access the network management menu.

25. Type **B** to investigate the Spanning Tree Protocol settings. Is STP enabled by default?

_____

26. Type **X** to exit to the previous menu level, and then type **X** again to exit to the main menu.

27. Type **V** to access the VLAN menu.

28. Press **A** to add a VLAN.

29. Type **1**, and then press **Enter** to choose the Ethernet VLAN type.

30. Type **V** for VLAN name, type **Engineering** when prompted for the VLAN name, and then press **Enter** to name the second VLAN "Engineering".

31. Type **S** to save and exit.

    How many local VLANs are supported by the switch?

_____

32. Type **A** to add another VLAN.

33. Type **1**, and then press **Enter** to configure the VLAN for Ethernet.

34. Type **N**, type **3**, and press **Enter** to create VLAN 3.

35. Type **V** to name the VLAN, and then type **Finance** and press **Enter**.

36. Type **S** to save and exit.

37. Type **L** to list your VLANs. Type **1, 2, 3** and press **Enter** to list VLANs 1, 2, and 3. What is the name of VLAN 1?

_____

What is the name of VLAN 2?

_____

What is the name of VLAN 3?

_____

If the VLANs do not display correctly, attempt to reconfigure them using Steps 27 through 36.

38. Press any key to continue if instructed to do so.

39. Type **E** for VLAN membership. Have any ports been assigned to the Engineering or Finance VLANs?

_____

40. Type **V** for VLAN assignment.

41. Type **4-8**, press **Enter**, and then type **2** to move ports 4–8 to the Engineering VLAN. Press **Enter** again.

42. Repeat Steps 40 and 41, but this time move ports **9-12** to VLAN 3.

43. Type **X** to exit to the previous menu.

44. Type **X** to exit to the main menu, and then type **X** again to log out of the Management Console.

45. Type **Y** and press **Enter** to confirm.

46. Type **M** to attempt to return to the switch menu interface. Were you prompted for a password?

_____

If you were prompted for a password, type **cisco** and press **Enter**.

47. Type **S** for system, and then type **F** to reset the factory defaults of the switch. Type **Y**, and then press **Enter** to confirm.

48. Close HyperTerminal. Save the switch settings when prompted.

49. Unplug the switch.

50. Remove the console cable from the switch and the PC.

13

Certification Objectives

Objectives for the CCNA exam:

➤ Customize a switch configuration to meet specified network requirements

Review Questions

1. What is the difference between cut-through and store-and-forward switching?

2. Why is fragment-free somewhere between cut-through and store-and-forward in terms of speed and error detection?

3. What do you need to facilitate traffic between different VLANs?

4. What is the benefit of grouping switch ports into different VLANs?

LAB 13.2 CONFIGURE A CISCO 1900 SWITCH USING THE COMMAND-LINE INTERFACE

Objectives

The objective of this lab is to configure a Cisco 1900 series switch using the command-line interface. Using commands rather than the menus provides exposure to an additional way to configure a Cisco switch. Switch commands are part of the CCNA exam.

After completing this lab, you will be able to:

➤ Identify the status of switch ports

➤ Configure the host name, IP address, gateway, and domain name on the switch

➤ Examine the Spanning Tree Protocol settings

➤ Configure port security

➤ Change the switching type

➤ Configure a new VLAN

➤ Configure VTP

➤ Modify the CDP parameters

➤ Copy the switch configuration to a TFTP server

➤ Reset the switch configuration to factory defaults

Materials Required

This lab requires the following:

➤ One Cisco 1900 series switch with Enterprise Edition IOS

➤ A console cable for the switch

➤ RJ-45-to-DB-9 or -DB-25 adapter

➤ Three Windows workstations with NICs installed and with HyperTerminal installed (it is easiest to use the lab-d, lab-e, and TFTP server computers)

➤ One computer must be running TFTP software and be configured with IP address 210.93.105.3

➤ The computer known as lab-d should be configured for IP address 210.93.105.4

➤ The computer known as lab-e should be configured for IP address 210.93.105.5

➤ Two patch cables

➤ One power cord for the switch

13

Estimated completion time: **60 minutes**

ACTIVITY

1. Review Figure 13-1. Plug the console cable into the Cisco 1900 switch console port.

2. Plug the other end of the console cable into an RJ-45-to-DB-9 or RJ-45-to-DB-25 adapter and connect the adapter to a COM port on the lab-e computer.

3. Connect the TFTP server with IP address 210.93.105.3 to **port 1** of the switch with a UTP patch cable.

4. Connect the lab-d computer with IP address 210.93.105.4 to **port 2** of the switch with a UTP patch cable.

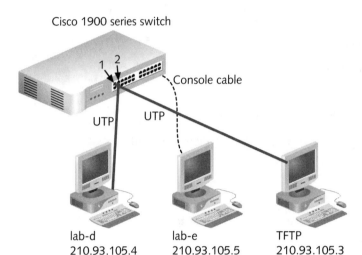

Cisco 1900 series switch

Console cable

UTP   UTP

lab-d   lab-e   TFTP
210.93.105.4   210.93.105.5   210.93.105.3

Figure 13-1   Lab 13.2 configuration

5. Turn on the TFTP server, if necessary.

6. Turn on the lab-d computer, if necessary.

7. Plug in the switch.

8. The port lights on the switch should turn green and all lights should initially be on and not blinking. After a minute or so, port lights without connections should go off. Ports 1 and 2 should turn first to orange and then to green, which indicates readiness. If the port lights with the computer connections are orange and do not turn green, there is a problem, possibly with the cable. Start troubleshooting and ask your instructor for help.

9. On the lab-d computer, open a Windows command prompt window.

10. Type **ping 210.93.105.3** and press **Enter**.

11. Were you able to ping the TFTP server successfully?

_____

If you were not able to ping successfully, start troubleshooting with the help of your instructor.

12. On the TFTP server, open a Windows command prompt window.

13. Type **ping 210.93.105.4** and press **Enter**.

14. Were you able to ping the lab-d computer successfully?

_____

If you were not able to ping successfully, start troubleshooting with the help of your instructor.

15. Turn on the lab-e computer, if necessary.

16. Click **Start**, point to **Programs**, point to **Accessories**, point to **Communications**, and then click **HyperTerminal**. Double-click a saved HyperTerminal connection if there is one. If there is no saved HyperTerminal connection on your computer, create one using the instructions in Lab 13.1, Steps 6 through 11.

TIP

The procedure for opening a new connection in HyperTerminal may be slightly different on your Windows computer.

17. Press **Enter** to generate output from the switch, if necessary.

18. Enter **K** to access the command-line interface. What is the prompt?

_____

What is the mode?

_____

19. Enter the **enable** command. What is the prompt?

_____

20. Enter global configuration mode using the **configure terminal** command. What is the prompt?

_____

13

21. Type **hostname malabar** and press **Enter**. What is the prompt?

_____

22. Type **ip address 210.93.105.10 255.255.255.0** and press **Enter**.

23. Type **ip default-gateway 210.93.105.1** and press **Enter**.

24. Type **ip domain-name cannonball.com** and press **Enter**.

25. Press **Ctrl+Z** to return to enable mode.

26. Enter the **show ip** command. Does your IP configuration reflect the commands you entered in this section?

_____

If the answer is no, try entering your configuration again.

27. Enter the **show mac-address-table** command. How did the switching table get these MAC addresses?

_____

_____

28. Enter global configuration mode using the **configure terminal** command.

29. Enter the **interface e0/1** command to access the Ethernet port. Notice the slot type of "0" is included to reference the interface on this device. All commands entered at this point will affect which port number on the switch?

_____

30. Type **port secure max-mac-count 1** and press **Enter**. What is the purpose of this command?

_____

31. Enter **exit** to move back to global configuration mode.

32. Enter the **interface e0/2** command.

33. Use the **up arrow** to retrieve the **port secure max-mac-count 1** command and press **Enter**.

34. Press **Ctrl+Z** to return to enable mode.

35. Examine the Spanning Tree Protocol settings using the **show spantree 1** command. What does the "1" in the command designate?

_____

_____

36. According to the show spantree 1 command, what are ports 1 through 12 doing?

_____

_____

_____

37. What are ports 25, 26, and 27 doing?

_____

_____

_____

38. What kind of port is port 25 on the Cisco 1900?

_____

39. What kind of port is port 26 on the Cisco 1900?

_____

40. What kind of port is port 27 on the Cisco 1900?

_____

41. Enter the **show interface** command. What is the status of ports 1 and 2?

_____

What is the status of ports 3 through 12?

_____

What is the status of port 25?

_____

What is the status of ports 26 and 27?

_____

42. Enter the **show port system** command. What is the default switching mode of the Cisco 1900 switch?

_____

43. Enter global configuration mode.

44. Type **switching-mode store-and-forward** and press **Enter**.

45. Press **Ctrl+Z**.

46. Type **show port system** and press **Enter**. Did the switching mode change as directed?

_____

47. Enter the **configure terminal** command to enter global configuration mode.

48. Type **vtp server** and press **Enter**.

49. Type **vtp domain cannonball** and press **Enter**. Why do you need to create a VTP domain?

_____

_____

13

50. Press **Ctrl+Z** to return to enable mode.

51. Enter the **show vtp** command. Is the switch operating as a VTP server?

_____

52. Enter the **configure terminal** command again to enter global configuration mode.

53. Enter the **interface f 0/26** command. What does the "f" represent?

_____

What does the "0" represent?

_____

What does the "26" represent?

_____

54. Type **trunk on** and press **Enter**. What does this command do?

_____

_____

55. Press **Ctrl+Z** to return to enable mode.

56. Type the **show vlan 1** command and press **Enter**. Are all ports on VLAN 1?

_____

57. Enter the **configure terminal** command again to enter global configuration mode.

58. Type the **vlan 2 name cannon** command, and press **Enter**. What does this do?

_____

59. Enter the **interface e 0/2** command.

60. Enter the **vlan-membership static 2** command.

61. Press **Ctrl+Z** to return to enable mode.

62. Type **show vlan** and press **Enter**. VLAN 2 should be named "cannon" and port 2 should now be assigned to VLAN 2. Does the output look correct?

_____

If not, attempt to reconfigure the VLAN by returning to Step 57 and redoing the VLAN configuration.

63. Type **show vlan-membership** and press **Enter**. What is the difference between this command and the show vlan command?

_____

_____

64. Type **ping 210.93.105.3** and press **Enter**. Were you able to successfully ping the TFTP server from the switch?

_____

65. Move to the lab-d computer, and then open a Windows command prompt window. Type **ping 210.93.105.3** and press **Enter**. Were you able to successfully ping the TFTP server from the lab-d computer?

_____

Why or why not?

_____

_____

_____

66. Move the patch cable for the lab-d computer from port 2 on the switch to port 3. Now, attempt to ping the TFTP server from the lab-d computer again. The IP address is 210.93.105.3. Was the ping successful? Why or why not?

_____

_____

_____

67. Return to the lab-e computer and the switch. Enter the **show cdp** command. What is the broadcast interval?

_____

What is the holdtime?

_____

68. Enter global configuration mode.

69. Enter the **cdp timer 90** command.

70. Enter the **cdp holdtime 240** command.

13

71. Press **Ctrl+Z**.

72. Enter the **show cdp** command. Did the timer information change per your commands?

_____

If not, redo the commands in this section, beginning with Step 68.

73. Make sure you can ping the TFTP server at 210.93.105.3 from the switch.

74. Open the TFTP server software on the TFTP server, if necessary.

75. Back up the switch configuration to the TFTP server using the following command at the enable mode prompt:

copy nvram tftp://210.93.105.3/1900switch

76. If the copy was successful, you will receive a message indicating success. Was it successful?

_____

What does the "1900switch" in the command designate?

_____

Could you have used a different name?

_____

77. Reset the configuration to the factory defaults using the **delete nvram** command in enable mode. Press **Y** for yes and press **Enter** to confirm the deletion.

78. Unplug the switch and remove the patch cables from the switch ports.

Certification Objectives

Objectives for the CCNA exam:

➤ Customize a switch configuration to meet specified network requirements

➤ Perform LAN and VLAN troubleshooting

➤ Troubleshoot a device as part of a working network

➤ Describe the Spanning Tree process

Review Questions

1. What is the function of a VTP server?

2. What is the VLAN limit on the Cisco 1900 series switch?

3. How many VLANs can STP support on one 1900 series switch?

4. What is a port doing if it is in the forwarding state?

5. What is a port doing if it is in the blocking state?

6. Can you delete a VLAN 1? Why or why not?

13

7. Is CDP enabled by default on the Cisco 1900 series switch?

LAB 13.3 EVALUATE HUB PERFORMANCE

Objectives

The objective of this lab is to illustrate how hubs operate given two different scenarios. The first scenario involves generating data traffic on two ports. The second scenario involves generating data traffic on all active ports.

In this lab you will connect the six computers used in the internetworking lab to a common hub. Next, you will time the transfer of a large folder of files between two of the computers. Finally, you will measure the time it takes to move the folder back to its original location while generating traffic on the rest of the network.

The workstations used in this lab are the same ones used to connect to routers lab-a through lab-e. As such, the workstations are referred to as the lab-a workstation, the lab-b workstation, and so on. The TFTP server workstation is also used.

After completing this lab, you will be able to:

> ➤ Describe how hubs perform when transferring data between two computers

> ➤ Describe how hubs perform when transferring data between many computers

Materials Required

This lab requires the following:

> ➤ The internetworking lab computers: lab-a, lab-b, lab-c, lab-d, lab-e, and the TFTP server

> ➤ Lab workstations with IP addresses configured for the 210.93.105.0 network and with all workstations in the same workgroup

> ➤ One hub

> ➤ Six UTP patch cables

> ➤ A shared desktop on all computers with full access

> ➤ A folder named SWITCHTEST containing enough files to equal at least 100 MB on the desktops of the lab-b, lab-d, and lab-e computers

> ➤ A stopwatch

Estimated completion time: **30 minutes**

ACTIVITY

1. Turn on the lab workstations, if necessary.

2. Review Figure 13-2. Connect all six workstations via UTP from their NICs to a single hub. Make sure that you do not use the uplink port on the hub. Make sure that the hub lights are on.

3. Double-click **My Network Places** on all computers to make sure that every workstation can see every other workstation in the lab setup, including the TFTP server. Sometimes it takes a while for the computers to see each other. If every workstation is not visible in My Network Places, contact your instructor.

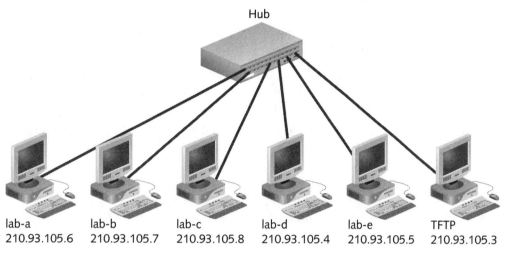

Hub

lab-a   lab-b   lab-c   lab-d   lab-e   TFTP
210.93.105.6   210.93.105.7   210.93.105.8   210.93.105.4   210.93.105.5   210.93.105.3

Figure 13-2   Lab 13.3 configuration

4. Move to the TFTP server, double-click **My Network Places**, double-click the **lab-e** icon, and then double-click the **Desktop** folder.

5. Right-click and drag the **SWITCHTEST** folder from the desktop of the lab-e computer to the desktop of the TFTP server. *When the shortcut menu appears, stop. This is the operation that you will time using the stopwatch.*

6. Using the stopwatch, calculate the time that it takes to move the SWITCH-TEST folder from the lab-e computer to the TFTP server.

7. You and your team should watch the move operation and be prepared to type **A** for All if you are prompted for a confirmation regarding the move.

8. Observe the hub during the move. If there is a collision light, how active is it?

_____

_____

9. Observe the NICs on the six computers. Is there any appreciable activity on the NICs of workstations that are not participating in the move?

_____

10. How long (in minutes and seconds) did it take to move the SWITCHTEST folder from the lab-e computer to the TFTP server?

_____

11. Prepare to move the SWITCHTEST folder simultaneously from the TFTP server to the lab-e computer, from the lab-d computer to the lab-c computer, and from the lab-b computer to the lab-a computer.

13

12. Move to the lab-c computer, double-click **My Network Places**, double-click the **lab-d** icon, and then double-click the **Desktop** folder. You should see the SWITCHTEST folder.

13. Right-click and drag the **SWITCHTEST** folder from the desktop of the lab-d computer to the desktop of your computer, which is lab-c. When the shortcut menu appears, *stop*.

14. Move to the lab-a computer and repeat Steps 12 and 13 in preparation for moving the SWITCHTEST folder from the lab-b desktop to the desktop of the lab-a computer.

15. Move to the lab-e computer and repeat Steps 12 and 13 in preparation for moving the SWITCHTEST folder from the TFTP server to the desktop of the lab-e computer. *This is the only operation that you will time using the stopwatch.*

16. As close to simultaneously as possible, have your team begin moving the SWITCHTEST folder from the lab-d computer to the lab-c computer, from the lab-b computer to the lab-a computer, and from the TFTP server to the lab-e computer. *Remember that one of the team members must time the move from the TFTP server to the lab-e computer.*

17. You and your team should watch the move operations and be prepared to type **A** for All if you are prompted for a confirmation regarding the move. You want to keep traffic moving.

18. Observe the hub during the move. If there is a collision light, how active is it compared with the generated activity on only two ports?

_____

_____

19. Approximately how long did it take (in minutes and seconds) to move the SWITCHTEST folder from the TFTP server to the lab-e computer?

_____

20. Compare your answer in Step 19 with your answer in Step 10. If there is a difference, how do you account for it?

_____

_____

_____

Certification Objectives

Objectives for the CCNA exam:

> ➤ Troubleshoot a device as part of a working network

Review Questions

1. How does regular half-duplex communications through a hub work?

2. Would a hub be used to solve network congestion problems in an Ethernet network? Why or why not?

3. Why did it take so much longer to transfer the files when there was traffic on all connected hub ports?

LAB 13.4 EVALUATE SWITCH PERFORMANCE

13

Objectives

The objective of this lab is to illustrate how switches operate in the two scenarios in which you worked in Lab 13.3. In this lab you will connect the six computers in the internetworking lab to a Cisco 1900 series switch and time the transfer of a large folder between two of the computers. You will then measure the time it takes to move the folder back while generating other traffic on the rest of the network. Finally, a comparison will be made between the times recorded in this lab and the times recorded for the hub in Lab 13.3.

After completing this lab, you will be able to:

> ➤ Understand how switches perform when transferring data between two computers

> ➤ Understand how switches perform when transferring data between many computers

Materials Required

This lab requires the following:

➤ The internetworking lab computers: lab-a, lab-b, lab-c, lab-d, lab-e, and the TFTP server

➤ Lab workstations with IP addresses configured for the 210.93.105.0 network

➤ One Cisco 1900 series switch

➤ Six UTP patch cables

➤ A shared desktop on all computers with full access

➤ A folder named SWITCHTEST containing enough files to equal at least 100 MB on the desktops of the lab-b, lab-d, and lab-e computers

➤ A stopwatch

➤ The completion of Lab 13.3

Estimated completion time: **30 minutes**

ACTIVITY

1. Turn on the lab workstations, if necessary.

2. Review Figure 13-3. Connect all six workstations via UTP from their NICs to a single switch. Use **ports 5** and **6** for the lab-e computer and the TFTP server. Make sure that the switch is turned on and that the port lights on the switch have turned green.

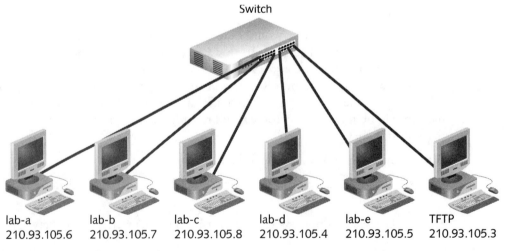

| lab-a | lab-b | lab-c | lab-d | lab-e | TFTP |
| 210.93.105.6 | 210.93.105.7 | 210.93.105.8 | 210.93.105.4 | 210.93.105.5 | 210.93.105.3 |

Figure 13-3   Lab 13.4 configuration

3. Double-click **My Network Places** on all computers to make sure that every workstation can see every other workstation in the lab setup, including the TFTP server. Sometimes it takes a while for all computers to see each other. If every workstation is not visible in My Network Places, contact your instructor.

4. Move to the TFTP server, double-click **My Network Places**, double-click the **lab-e** icon, and then double-click the **Desktop** folder.

5. Right-click and drag the **SWITCHTEST** folder from the desktop of the lab-e computer to the desktop of the TFTP server. When the shortcut menu appears, *stop. This is the operation that you will time using the stopwatch.*

6. Using the stopwatch, calculate the time it takes to move the SWITCHTEST folder from the lab-e computer to the TFTP server.

7. You and your team should watch the move operation and be prepared to type **A** for All if you are prompted for a confirmation regarding the move.

8. Observe the switch during the move. Is there equal activity on each port, or are ports 5 and 6 busier than the other occupied ports?

_____

9. Observe the NICs on the six computers. Is there any appreciable activity on the NICs of workstations not participating in the move?

_____

10. How long (in minutes and seconds) did it take to move the SWITCHTEST folder from the lab-e computer to the TFTP server?

_____

11. Prepare to move the SWITCHTEST folder simultaneously from the TFTP server to the lab-e computer, from the lab-c computer to the lab-d computer, and from the lab-a computer to the lab-b computer.

12. Move to the lab-d computer, double-click **My Network Places**, double-click the **lab-c** icon, and then double-click the **Desktop** folder. You should see the SWITCHTEST folder.

13. Right-click and drag the **SWITCHTEST** folder from the desktop of the lab-c computer to the desktop of your computer (lab-d). When the shortcut menu appears, *stop.*

14. Move to the lab-b computer and repeat Steps 12 and 13 in preparation for moving the SWITCHTEST folder from the lab-a desktop to the desktop of the lab-b computer.

15. Move to the lab-e computer and repeat Steps 12 and 13 in preparation for moving the SWITCHTEST folder from the TFTP server to the desktop of the lab-e computer. *This is the only operation that you will time using the stopwatch.*

13

16. As close to simultaneously as possible, have your team begin moving the SWITCHTEST folder from the lab-c computer to the lab-d computer, from the lab-a computer to the lab-b computer, and from the TFTP server to the lab-e computer. *Remember that one of the team members must time the move from the TFTP server to the lab-e computer.*

17. You and your team should watch the move operations and be prepared to type **A** for All if you are prompted for a confirmation regarding the move. You want to keep traffic moving.

18. Observe the switch during the move. Is there equal activity on each connected port?

_____

19. Approximately how long did it take (in minutes and seconds) to move the SWITCHTEST folder from the TFTP server to the lab-e computer?

_____

20. Record your timings from Lab 13.3 and Lab 13.4 in Table 13-1:

Table 13-1 Hub and switch comparison

Scenario	Transfer Time in Minutes and Seconds
Hub—activity on two ports	
Hub—activity on six ports	
Switch—activity on two ports	
Switch—activity on six ports	

21. There should be a time difference between the two hub experiments. How do you explain this?

_____

_____

_____

22. There should be no appreciable time difference between the switch experiments. How do you explain this?

_____

_____

_____

23. If there was very little time difference between the hub and switch for the two-port activity experiments, how do you explain this?

Certification Objectives

Objectives for the CCNA exam:

➤ Troubleshoot a device as part of a working network

Review Questions

1. In terms of collisions and speed, what are the differences between hubs and switches?

2. How do switches solve network congestion problems on Ethernet networks?

3. What does the term "switched bandwidth" mean?

13

LAB 13.5 UNDERSTAND SWITCHING AND LAN DESIGN CONCEPTS AND TERMINOLOGY

Objectives

The objective of this lab is to make sure you have a good understanding of modern Ethernet LAN design and the associated terminology. In this lab you will match switching and LAN design terms, which are in a bulleted list, with definitions in Table 13-2.

After completing this lab, you will be able to:

➤ Understand the terms and concepts related to switching and LAN design

Materials Required

This lab requires the following:

➤ Pencil or pen

Estimated completion time: **20 minutes**

ACTIVITY

1. Relate the following bulleted terms to the descriptions in Table 13-2 by placing the terms in the correct cell in the Matching Term column. Each term is used only once.

- 10BaseT
- ISL
- Fast Ethernet
- Full-duplex
- Half-duplex
- Shared bandwidth
- Switched bandwidth
- CSMA/CD
- Slot time
- Collision domain
- Broadcast domain
- VLAN
- Latency
- Broadcast storm
- 100BaseT4
- 100BaseTX
- Auto
- Half
- Microsegmentation
- STP
- Cut-through
- Fragment-free
- Store-and-forward
- Management VLAN

Table 13-2   Switching and LAN design concepts and terminology

Description	Matching Term
Should be slightly longer than the time it takes to transmit a 64-byte frame on an Ethernet wire	
Data Link layer protocol defined by IEEE specification 802.1d	
The total network bandwidth is dedicated to each unicast transmission, even if there are multiple unicast transmissions at the same time	
A logical broadcast domain on the LAN created by one or more switches	
Entire transmitted frame is read into the switch's buffer before being forwarded by the switch	
Default setting for 10BaseT switch ports	
All devices are in contention for the total bandwidth of the network	
Increasing the number of collision domains without increasing the number of subnets	
The lag or delay that a device or part of the network media causes	
Alternate one-way communications	
Frame is forwarded immediately after the destination address is read	
Fast Ethernet implementation that uses four pairs of either Category 3, 4, or 5 UTP cable	
Ethernet station must first listen before transmitting on the network. Any station can transmit as long as there are no transmissions active on the network. If two stations transmit simultaneously, a collision will occur, and those stations must detect the collision and reset themselves.	
An error condition in which broadcast traffic is above 126 packets per second and network communications are impeded	

Table 13-2   Switching and LAN design concepts and terminology (continued)

Description	Matching Term
Communication in two directions at once	
Frame is forwarded after the first 64 bytes of the incoming frame are read	
VLAN 1, which cannot be deleted; also known as the default VLAN	
Frames can be transmitted in 90% less time than with standard Ethernet	
A group of devices that will receive broadcast traffic from each other on the LAN	
Fast Ethernet implementation that uses two pairs of either Category 5 unshielded twisted-pair (UTP) or shielded twisted-pair (STP)	
Switch port is set to determine whether the connected device is full- or half-duplex, and it configures itself to match	
Standard Ethernet using UTP cable configured in a physical star	
Cisco proprietary frame-tagging method for VLANs	
A group of devices that are subject to the collisions of each other's traffic	

Certification Objectives

Objectives for the CCNA exam:

> ➤ Compare and contrast key characteristics of LAN environments

> ➤ Describe the components of network devices

Review Questions

1. If you have a 10BaseT network with Category 5 UTP cable and are using Cisco 1900 series switches, what will you have to purchase to upgrade your network to full-duplex? To Fast Ethernet?

2. What are some ways you can limit broadcast traffic on your network?

3. What is the open standard frame-tagging specification defined by IEEE?

13

LAB 13.6 CONFIGURE "ROUTER-ON-A-STICK"

Objectives

You have learned that VLANs cannot communicate with each other without a router to move traffic between the VLANs. This is because each VLAN is considered a different logical network. The router routes the packets between the VLANs in the same way it routes packets between two physically separate networks. Very often, a single physical link is used to connect a router to a switch configured for multiple VLANs. In this case, trunking must be configured on the router and the switch for inter-VLAN routing. This configuration is known as "router-on-a-stick." The objective of this lab is to configure a router and a switch for the "router-on-a-stick" scenario. Unlike previous labs, you will not be given step-by-step instructions. Rather, you will use Figure 13-4 as well as some general instructions and show command output to guide you in your configuration.

After completing this lab, you will be able to:

➤ Configure a router for inter-VLAN routing using ISL

➤ Configure a switch for multiple VLANs and trunking

Materials Required

This lab requires the following:

➤ One Cisco 1900 series switch with Enterprise Edition software or any other Cisco switch that supports ISL trunking

➤ One Cisco 2600 series router or any other Cisco router that supports ISL trunking

➤ Power cords for the switch and router

➤ Three Windows PCs with the HyperTerminal program installed

➤ Two console (rollover) cables

➤ Two RJ-45-to-DB-9 or -DB-25 adapters

➤ Four UTP patch cables

Estimated completion time: **60 minutes**

ACTIVITY

1. Make sure all equipment is turned off.

2. Refer to Figure 13-4 and connect the equipment accordingly. Turn on the equipment once it is cabled correctly.

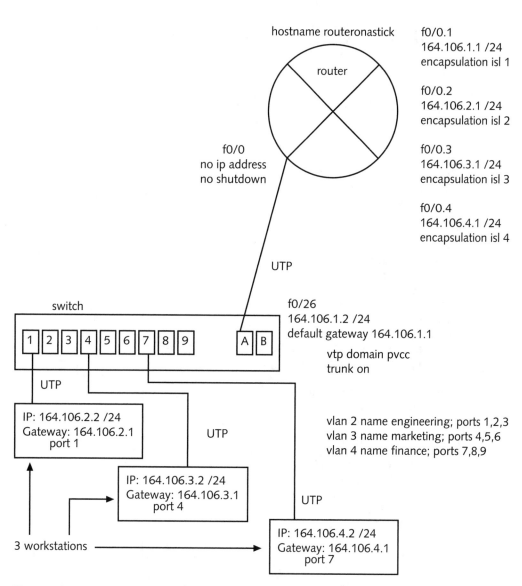

Figure 13-4   Router-on-a-stick

3. Configure the interfaces on the router as shown in Figure 13-4. The show run output for the router is displayed in Figure 13-5. If you have configured the router correctly, your show run output should be similar to that in the figure.

```
hostname routeronastick
!
logging rate-limit console 10 except errors
!
ip subnet-zero
!
!
no ip finger
!
ip audit notify log
ip audit po max-events 100
call rsvp-sync
!
!
interface FastEthernet0/0
 no ip address
 duplex auto
 speed auto
!
interface FastEthernet0/0.1
 encapsulation isl 1
 ip address 164.106.1.1 255.255.255.0
 no ip redirects
!
interface FastEthernet0/0.2
 encapsulation isl 2
 ip address 164.106.2.1 255.255.255.0
 no ip redirects
!
interface FastEthernet0/0.3
 encapsulation isl 3
 ip address 164.106.3.1 255.255.255.0
 no ip redirects
!
interface FastEthernet0/0.4
 encapsulation isl 4
 ip address 164.106.4.1 255.255.255.0
 no ip redirects
!
interface Serial0/0
 no ip address
 shutdown
 no fair-queue
!
interface FastEthernet0/1

 no ip address
```

Figure 13-5   Show run output on the router

```
shutdown
duplex auto
speed auto
!
interface Serial0/1
 no ip address
 shutdown
!
ip classless
no ip http server
!
!
dial-peer cor custom
!
line con 0
 transport input none
line aux 0
line vty 0 4
 login
!
no scheduler allocate
end
```

Figure 13-5   Show run output on the router (continued)

4. Configure the switch for VLANs and trunking as shown in Figure 13-4. The show run, show interface f0/26, and show vlan command output for the switch are displayed in Figures 13-6, 13-7, and 13-8, respectively. If you have configured the switch correctly, your command output should be similar to that in the figures.

5. Configure the IP addresses, subnet masks, and default gateways for the three workstations as shown in Figure 13-4.

6. The connected port lights on the router, switch, and workstations should be on. Make sure the active interfaces on the router and switch are up. If they are administratively down, attempt to bring them up with the no shutdown command. If that doesn't work, there is something wrong with your cabling or configuration and you need to start troubleshooting with the help of your instructor.

13

```
#show run
Building configuration...
Current configuration:
!
!
vtp domain "pvcc"
!
vlan 2 name "engineering" sde 100002 state Operational mtu 1500
vlan 3 name "marketing" sde 100003 state Operational mtu 1500
vlan 4 name "finance" sde 100004 state Operational mtu 1500
!
!
ip address 164.106.1.2 255.255.255.0
ip default-gateway 164.106.1.1
!

interface Ethernet 0/1

  vlan-membership static 2
!
interface Ethernet 0/2

  vlan-membership static 2
!
interface Ethernet 0/3

  vlan-membership static 2
!
interface Ethernet 0/4

  vlan-membership static 3
!
interface Ethernet 0/5

  vlan-membership static 3
!
interface Ethernet 0/6

  vlan-membership static 3
!
interface Ethernet 0/7

  vlan-membership static 4
!
```

Figure 13-6   Show run output on the switch

```
interface Ethernet 0/8

  vlan-membership static 4
!
interface Ethernet 0/9

  vlan-membership static 4
!
interface Ethernet 0/10

!
interface Ethernet 0/11

!
interface Ethernet 0/12

!
interface Ethernet 0/13

!
interface Ethernet 0/14

!
interface Ethernet 0/15

!
interface Ethernet 0/16

!
interface Ethernet 0/17

!
interface Ethernet 0/18

!

interface Ethernet 0/19

!
interface Ethernet 0/20

!
interface Ethernet 0/21

!
interface Ethernet 0/22
```

Figure 13-6   Show run output on the switch (continued)

```
!
interface Ethernet 0/23

!
interface Ethernet 0/24

!
interface Ethernet 0/25

!

interface FastEthernet 0/26

!
   trunk On
!
interface FastEthernet 0/27

!
line console
end
```

Figure 13-6   Show run output on the switch (continued)

```
#show int f0/26

FastEthernet 0/26 is Enabled
Hardware is Built-in 100Base-TX
Address is 0005.9BE0.30DA
MTU 1500 bytes, BW 100000 Kbits
Port monitoring: Disabled
Unknown unicast flooding: Enabled
Unregistered multicast flooding: Enabled
Description:
Duplex/Flow Control setting: Auto-negotiate
Auto-negotiation status:  Full duplex
Enhanced Congestion Control: Disabled
```

Figure 13-7   Show interface f0/26 output

```
# show vlan

VLAN Name              Status     Ports
-------------------------------------------
1    default           Enabled    10-24, AUI, A, B
2    engineering       Enabled    1-3
3    marketing         Enabled    4-6
4    finance           Enabled    7-9
1002 fddi-default      Suspended
1003 token-ring-defau  Suspended
1004 fddinet-default   Suspended
1005 trnet-default     Suspended
-------------------------------------------


VLAN Type         SAID    MTU    Parent RingNo BridgeNo Stp  Trans1 Trans2
--------------------------------------------------------------------------
1    Ethernet     100001 1500    0      0      0        Unkn 1002   1003
2    Ethernet     100002 1500    0      1      1        Unkn 0      0
3    Ethernet     100003 1500    0      1      1        Unkn 0      0
4    Ethernet     100004 1500    0      1      1        Unkn 0      0
1002 FDDI         101002 1500    0      0      0        Unkn 1      1003
1003 Token-Ring   101003 1500    1005   1      0        Unkn 1      1002
1004 FDDI-Net     101004 1500    0      0      1        IEEE 0      0
1005 Token-Ring-Net 101005 1500  0      0      1        IEEE 0      0
```

Figure 13-8   Show vlan output

7. If your active interfaces are up, it is time to test your "router-on-a-stick" configuration. Begin by pinging from the router to the switch address 164.106.1.2. Also ping from the switch to the router address 164.106.1.1. If the pings are successful, proceed to the next step.

8. Every workstation should be able to ping every other workstation, even though they are on different VLANs. If this pinging works, you have successfully configured a "router-on-a-stick." If it doesn't work, start troubleshooting. You can use the following troubleshooting list to help you.

   ■ All connected link lights should be on.

   ■ All active interfaces should be up.

   ■ Double-check the IP addresses, subnet masks, and default gateways on the workstations and the switch.

   ■ Double-check the configuration on the router, paying special attention to the addressing and the ISL configuration.

   ■ Use the **show trunk a** command on the switch to make sure trunking is on and the encapsulation type is ISL.

13

- If you are having a duplexing problem, use the **duplex auto** command on the router.

- Make sure the workstations are connected to the correct ports on the switch.

9. Once you are sure your configuration works, demonstrate this to your instructor.

10. When you finish this lab, use the **erase start** command on the router if you saved your configuration at any time during this lab. Use the **delete nvram** command on the switch to reset it for the next lab group. You should also remove the IP configurations from the workstations.

11. Turn off all equipment and disconnect all cabling.

Certification Objectives

Objectives for the CCNA exam:

➤ Customize a switch configuration to meet specified network requirements

➤ Perform LAN and VLAN troubleshooting

➤ Troubleshoot IP addressing and host configuration

➤ Troubleshoot a device as part of a working network

Review Questions

1. A switch is LAN equipment. Why then is a router necessary for computers on VLANs to communicate?

2. What are the two trunking protocols supported by Cisco?

3. What is the basis for the term "router-on-a-stick"?

4. How are subinterfaces used in the "router-on-a-stick" configuration?

NOTES

NOTES

NOTES

NOTES

Glossary

5-4-3 rule — The rule that stipulates that between stations on a LAN, there can be no more than five network segments connected, the maximum number of repeaters between the segments is four, and the maximum number of segments with stations on them is three.

10 Gigabit Ethernet — IEEE 802.3ae standard that uses Ethernet frames in full duplex mode over fiber only. Used extensively in MANs for distances up to 40 km over single-mode fiber.

10Base2 — An Ethernet standard that specifies a 10-Mbps baseband transmission over thin Ethernet (RG-58); the maximum transmission distance of any single segment is 185 meters.

10Base5 — An Ethernet standard that indicates a 10-Mbps baseband transmission over a maximum segment length of 500 meters; the type of cable used in this standard is called thick Ethernet, or thicknet, and uses RG-8 coaxial cable.

10BaseT — An Ethernet standard that specifies a 10-Mbps baseband transmission over twisted-pair cabling; the maximum segment length is 100 meters.

100Base–FX — A Fast Ethernet implementation over multimode fiber-optic (MMF) cabling. The maximum segment length is 412 meters.

100BaseT — An Ethernet standard that provides a 100-Mbps baseband transfer rate over twisted-pair cabling. Also called Fast Ethernet. Known as IEEE standard 802.3u.

100Base-T4 — A 100-Mbps Fast Ethernet implementation that uses four pairs of either Category 3, 4, or 5 UTP cable. The maximum segment length is 100 meters.

100Base-TX — A Fast Ethernet implementation that uses two pairs of either Category 5 unshielded twisted-pair (UTP) or shielded twisted-pair (STP). 100Base-TX operates at 100 Mbps with a maximum segment distance of 100 meters.

802.11 — The IEEE standard that defines wireless LANs.

802.2 — A standard of the IEEE that specifies the subdivision of the Logical Link Control sublayer from the Media Access Control (MAC) sublayer. These sublayers are part of the OSI Data Link layer.

802.3 — The IEEE standard that defines CSMA/CD or Ethernet networking.

802.5 — The IEEE standard that defines Token Ring networking.

access layer — The layer in the three-layer network model that provides users access to the network. This is the layer in which end systems are connected to the network.

access lists — Permit or deny statements that filter traffic based on criteria such as source address, destination address, and protocol type.

access method — The rules that determine which station can send data and how collisions are managed. The two most popular access methods are CSMA/CD and token-passing. Access method is also known as logical topology.

active hub — A device that connects multiple nodes and/or networks, is connected to external power, and repeats and regenerates signals on a network.

active monitor — The computer in a Token Ring network that is powered on first and manages the beaconing process.

adaptive cut-through — A method of switching whereby the switch uses the cut-through technique unless network errors reach a certain threshold; then, it automatically switches to store-and-forward switching until the error rate returns to an acceptable level. Also known as **error sensing**.

address — The element of the PPP frame represented by the binary sequence 11111111; because PPP is used to create a point-to-point connection, there is no need for PPP to assign an individual address for each host.

Address Resolution Protocol (ARP) — A protocol that works at the Internetwork layer of the TCP/IP networking model; resolves a known IP address to an unknown MAC address, which is the final leg of communication between the source and destination.

adjacencies database — The neighbor database in OSPF.

adjacency — Bidirectional communication formed by EIGRP neighbors.

administration system — The centralized management component that collects and analyzes the information from the managers in a network-management system, such as SNMP or CMIP.

administrative distance — A value used to determine the reliability and desirability of a particular routing table update.

Advanced Data Communication Control Procedures (ADCCP) — The ANSI standard for HDLC.

Advanced Research Projects Agency (ARPA) — The government organization operating in the Department of Defense (DOD) that was responsible for the creation and proliferation of the Internet and the TCP/IP protocol suite.

Advanced Research Projects Agency Network (ARPANET) — The original name of the Internet.

agent — The client software part of the management tool in a network-management system, such as SNMP or CMIP; responsible for collecting the information that is used by the management system; resides on each network device.

alignment error — A frame that has both an FCS error and an entire octet missing from the frame.

alternating current (AC) — Type of current that is delivered to homes and office buildings. It changes polarity cyclically as it is manufactured by power plants.

American National Standards Institute (ANSI) — The organization that guides the process of standardization by ensuring that consensus, openness, and due process are maintained during the development process. ANSI is responsible for the FDDI standard.

American Registry of Internet Numbers (ARIN) — Manages IP address allocation in the United States.

American Standard Code for Information Interchange (ASCII) — A standardized method for formatting binary information and text for communications and printer control. The acronym ASCII is pronounced "ask-ee."

amplifier — A device used to boost analog signals on a broadband network.

analog — A method of signal transmission on broadband networks.

any — A keyword used to represent all hosts or networks; replaces 0.0.0.0 255.255.255.255 in an access list.

AppleTalk Control Protocol (ATCP) — PPP interface protocol for AppleTalk; *see* **Network Control Protocol**.

Application layer — The seventh layer of the OSI model, which is responsible for requesting network services and for providing services to applications. Also, the TCP/IP layer that corresponds to the Application, Presentation, and Session layers of the OSI model.

area — An OSPF concept used to define the confines within which LSAs will propagate.

ARP reply — A reply sent by the device that discovers its own IP address in the IP header of the ARP request frame and includes the requested MAC address.

ARP request — A process used to obtain the correct mapping when a source computer cannot locate a destination MAC address for a known IP address in its ARP table.

ARP table — A table used by a network device that contains MAC to IP address mappings.

Asymmetric Digital Subscriber Line (ADSL) — DSL service that provides from 1.536-Mbps to 6.144-Mbps connections in the United States. Outside the U.S. connections are either 2.048 or 4.096 Mbps.

asymmetric switching — A type of LAN switching that allows for multiple speeds of network communication; a switch that supports both 10-Mbps and 100-Mbps communications is an example of asymmetric switching.

asynchronous — Asynchronous communications rely on start and stop bits to define the endpoints of a transmission; timing mechanisms are not needed to maintain clock synchronization between the source and destination.

asynchronous character map — The piece of information in the LCP field of the PPP packet that allows PPP to encode its transmission properly for the recipient host.

asynchronous serial — Serial connections that are employed in most modems connected to residential phone lines.

Asynchronous Transfer Mode (ATM) — A networking implementation for both high-speed LAN and WAN connectivity.

attachment unit interface (AUI) port — A 15-pin physical connector interface between a computer's network interface card (NIC) and an Ethernet network that uses 10Base5 (thicknet) coaxial cable. On 10Base5 Ethernet, the NIC uses the AUI to connect to a transceiver cable that in turn taps into the main cable.

attenuation — The natural degradation of a transmitted signal over distance.

authentication — The process of verifying the right to complete a connection.

autonomous system (AS) — A group of routers under the control of a single administration.

AutoSPID — A feature of modern ISDN systems whereby SPID numbers do not have to be configured on the router.

AUX line password — A password used to access the router through the AUX port.

AUX port — *See* **auxiliary port (AUX)**.

auxiliary port (AUX) — A secondary port that allows connection to a modem that will be used for direct access to the router for configuration.

B-channel (bearer channel) — An ISDN channel used to carry data; two or more B-channels, each supporting 64 Kbps, are provided with ISDN service.

backbone — Cabling used to connect wiring hubs in an extended star topology; typically, 62.5/125-micron multimode cable is used for this connection. However, 100-ohm UTP, 150-ohm STP, and single-mode fiber can also be used to connect wiring closets to wiring closets, wiring closets to the POP, and wiring closets between buildings; sometimes called vertical cable.

backoff algorithm — A mathematical calculation performed by computers after a collision occurs on a CSMA/CD network, which forces machines to wait a random amount of time before resending the destroyed packet. A backoff algorithm is run by computers to set the length of time for the backoff period.

backoff period — A random interval used by devices that have caused a collision on an Ethernet network, during which the devices cannot send, to prevent them from immediately causing another collision.

backup designated router (BDR) — An OSPF router on broadcast, multiaccess networks that takes over if the DR fails.

Backward Explicit Congestion Notification (BECN) — When congestion is recognized, the Frame Relay switch sends a BECN message to the source router; should reduce the amount of traffic that is sent by the router.

bandwidth — The available capacity of the network. The greater the network bandwidth, the greater the speed in data transfer.

barrel connector — Used in coaxial networks; connects one coaxial cable segment to another, effectively forming a single cable.

baseband — A digital signal used in network transmissions where a single carrier frequency is used to transmit the signal.

Basic Rate Interface (BRI) — An ISDN service that provides two B-channels for data transfers up to 128 Kbps and one D-channel to control the communications.

beaconing — A fault-detection method implemented in Token Ring networks where stations broadcast packets to other stations on the ring in an attempt to find a break in the wire or a faulty interface.

bit stream — The stream of bits, or data, that flows between a source (transmitter) and a destination (receiver); can be communicated by synchronous or asynchronous methods.

bit time — The duration of time to transmit one data bit on a network, which is 100 nanoseconds on a 10-Mbps Ethernet network or 10 nanoseconds on a 100-Mbps Ethernet network.

blocking — A port state on a switch that indicates the port is receiving and sending BPDUs, but is not receiving and forwarding data frames in order to prevent logical loops in the network.

BMP — A Windows Bitmap (BMP) file, a graphical image type used with Microsoft Windows applications.

BNC — A hardware connector for coaxial cable that has a cylindrical shell with two small knobs that allow it to be locked into place when twisted. Depending on the source, the letters BNC are said to stand for Bayonet Navy Connector, British Naval Connector, Bayonet Neill Concelman, or Bayonet Nut Connection. *See also* **barrel connector**.

bonding — Load balancing across the two BRI B-channels to form a 128-Kbps single channel.

bootstrap — A small program used to load a much larger program. In the case of a router or switch, the bootstrap program loads the IOS.

Border Gateway Protocol (BGP) — An Exterior Gateway Protocol used to route between multiple autonomous systems.

bridge — A device that operates at the Data Link layer, used to filter traffic between network segments by evaluating the MAC address of packets that are sent to it.

bridge protocol data unit (BPDU) — An STP management message used to transfer status information about the Spanning Tree configuration of a switched or bridged network. Also known as **configuration bridge protocol data unit (CBPDU)**.

bridging table — A table maintained on a bridge that maps MAC addresses to the bridge port through which they can be accessed.

broadcast — A frame that is addressed to all stations on the broadcast domain. The destination MAC address is set to FFFFFFFFFFFF so that all local stations will process the packet.

broadcast domain — A group of network devices that will receive LAN broadcast traffic from each other.

broadcast storm — An error condition in which broadcast traffic is above 126 packets per second and network communications are impeded. This is typically the result of a software configuration error or programming error.

brouter — A device that functions as a bridge for nonroutable protocols and a router for routable protocols. The brouter operates at both the Data Link and Network layers.

buffer — A portion of memory used to store information that is being sent or created too fast for a system to process.

buffering — A way in which devices on a network are able to handle packet flows that exceed their processing capabilities. Packets are stored in a buffer until the system can process them.

bus — In the physical sense, a network topology where computers are daisy-chained together on the same coaxial cable segment; in the logical sense, refers to the CSMA/CD access method that sends data frames to all other stations simultaneously.

bus/star — A physical bus and physical star can be combined to form a star/bus or bus/star physical topology; hubs that have connectors for coaxial cable as well as twisted-pair wiring are used to form these types of networks. When different topologies are applied to a network, it is often called a mixed-media network.

cable modem — Broadband technology that provides cable TV and high-speed Internet access over existing coaxial TV cable.

cancellation — The desirable situation in which magnetic fields generated by two different wires carrying electronic signals cancel out each other; cancellation provides limited protection from crosstalk and external interference.

capacitive reactance — A naturally occurring opposition to voltage changes in a wire used for electronic signal transmission.

Carrier Sense Multiple Access with Collision Detection (CSMA/CD) — An access method specified by the IEEE Ethernet 802.3 standard. In this method, a node will listen to see if the line is clear and then, if the line is clear, send data. Two nodes may still send at the same time and cause a collision, in which case the two nodes will then perform the backoff algorithm.

Carrier Sense Multiple Access/Collision Avoidance (CSMA/CA) — The network access method used by wireless LANs as outlined in IEEE 802.11. Nodes must first listen to a channel before transmitting. If the channel is busy, nodes configure a random backoff time to wait before transmitting.

carrier signal — A transmitted electromagnetic pulse or wave on the network wire that indicates a transmission is in progress.

CAT 1 — Category 1 unshielded twisted-pair (CAT 1 UTP) is a voice-grade only communication medium that should not be used as network media.

CAT 2 — Category 2 unshielded twisted-pair (CAT 2 UTP) is a voice- or data-grade medium that is rarely used in modern networks but does have the rating to transmit up to 4 Mbps.

CAT 3 — Category 3 unshielded twisted-pair (CAT 3 UTP) is a voice- or data-grade medium that can transmit at 10 Mbps and supports 10BaseT networking.

CAT 4 — Category 4 unshielded twisted-pair (CAT 4 UTP) supports voice or data and is capable of a 16-Mbps transmission rate.

CAT 5 — Category 5 unshielded twisted-pair (CAT 5 UTP) is the most popular installation medium today; this media type supports 100-Mbps transmission rates, but new standards attempt to achieve 1000 Mbps over CAT 5 cabling.

catchment area — The area serviced; for example, the area serviced by a wiring closet is the catchment area of that wiring closet.

Central Office (CO) switch — The telecommunications company location that is part of the PSTN or toll network; point of entry to the toll network from the demarc.

challenge — The query packet, or the action of sending the query packet over a CHAP connection, that is used to verify the participants of the PPP connection.

Challenge Handshake Authentication Protocol (CHAP) — PPP authentication protocol that provides better security than PAP in authenticating devices on PPP connections.

channel service unit/data service unit (CSU/DSU) — A telecommunications company device that provides connectivity between the

WAN service provider network and the customer's LAN.

cheapernet — A reference to RG-58 thin Ethernet cable.

circuit — Path in which electrical current can flow.

Cisco Discovery Protocol (CDP) — A Cisco proprietary Data Link layer protocol that shares configuration information between Cisco devices that are locally connected.

Cisco Internetwork Operating System (IOS) — A router operating system that provides a command-line interface, which allows network operators to check the status of the router and allows network administrators to manage and configure the router.

classful — A routing process that involves using subnet masks with traditional octet boundaries.

classful routing protocol — A dynamic routing protocol that does not carry subnet mask information in its routing table updates and consequently must summarize to major classful network boundaries.

classless — A routing process that allows subnet masks to partition the network and the node portions on any bit boundary.

Classless Inter-Domain Routing (CIDR) — A system of allocating IP network numbers based on arbitrary subnet mask boundaries. CIDR notation uses a prefix to designate the network portion of the subnet mask.

classless routing protocol — A dynamic routing protocol that carries subnet mask information in its routing table updates; allows support for discontiguous subnets and VLSM.

client — A computer that operates on a network and requests and uses the services of other computers on the network, but does not necessarily provide any services to other computers.

client/server — A type of networking in which a few dedicated computers, called servers, share files, printers, disk drives, and other resources with a group of client computers.

collision domain — The area on a network in which collision can occur; a section of network that is not separated by routers, switches, or bridges.

command executive — The user interface that interprets commands and is provided by the Cisco IOS (also known as the EXEC).

Committed Burst Size (CBS) — The maximum amount of data bits that the service provider agrees to transfer in a set period under normal conditions.

Committed Information Rate (CIR) — The minimum average transfer rate of the Frame Relay circuit; usually lower than the access rate because the transfer rate may exceed the CIR during short bursts.

Common Management Information Protocol (CMIP) — A standard developed by the International Organization for Standardization (ISO) to provide a method for monitoring and managing network resources.

compression — Data compression that can be performed on the PPP packet at the source and then uncompressed at the destination.

concentrator — A term used to describe a hub.

conductor — Material with low resistance to electron flow.

configuration bridge protocol data unit (CBPDU) — *See* **bridge protocol data unit (BPDU)**.

configuration register — A feature in Cisco routers that is stored in NVRAM and allows the administrator to control several boot functions.

congestion avoidance — A method by which a system on the network can reduce the flow of packets on a network by sending a message request to the sender to reduce the rate at which packets are being transmitted.

connection-oriented — Network communications that require acknowledgment. On the OSI reference model, the decision to use connection-oriented communications is made at the Transport layer.

connectionless — Network communications that do not require acknowledgment. On the OSI reference model, the decision to use connectionless communications is made at the Transport layer.

console — A physical connection on the back of the router to which you can connect a rollover cable to attach to a PC for router configuration (also known as a console port).

console password — The password that is used to access the router through the console port.

console port — *See* console.

Consultative Committee on International Telephony and Telegraphy (CCITT) — The former name of International Telecommunication Union-Telecommunication Standardization Sector (ITU-T).

content-addressable memory (CAM) — A memory location on a switch that contains the MAC address-to-switch port mapping information, which the switch uses to forward frames to the appropriate destination.

contention — The condition that occurs when computers on a network must share the available capacity of the network wire with other computers.

contention method — The method by which computers on a network must share the available capacity of the network wire with other computers.

context-sensitive Help — Help with the syntax of commands for the router that is based on the current router mode and prompt, as well as any part of a command that is typed.

control — The element of the PPP frame represented by the binary sequence 00000011, which indicates that the transmission of user data will not be sequenced and is to be delivered over a connectionless link.

convergence — The point at which all routers on a network share a similar view of the network.

core layer — The layer that provides fast WAN connectivity for large network designs using the three-layer network model.

cost — The default metric in OSPF, calculated with the following equation: Cost = (10^8 / bandwidth of the link).

count-to-infinity — A routing loop whereby packets bounce infinitely around an internetwork.

counters — Detailed statistics kept by a router about data passing across its interface.

crosstalk — Signal bleed from one cable to another; this type of error usually occurs in poorly wired media.

customer premises equipment (CPE) — Equipment under the customer's control; also known as customer-provided equipment, depending on the publication.

cut-through — A switching technique in which an Ethernet frame is forwarded immediately after the destination address is deciphered. This method offers the lowest latency, but does not reduce packet errors.

cyclical redundancy check (CRC) — The process that ensures that data was not corrupted during transmission. This is accomplished by comparing CRC calculations before and after transmission.

D-channel (data channel) — The control channel used in ISDN communications; can be 16 to 64 Kbps.

data — The LCP field is also known as the Data field. This location contains the LCP information and the data that has been encapsulated from the higher layers. The default size of this field is 1500 bytes, but PPP implementations can negotiate a larger size for this field.

data circuit-terminating equipment (DCE) — Typically, the telecommunications-provided device on the customer side that allows the customer to connect to the WAN; often, a CSU/DSU, but can also be a modem or TA.

Data Link Connection Identifier (DLCI) — Pronounced *dell-see*, information in a Frame Relay connection that is configured on the router and used to identify which path leads to a specific Network layer address (i.e., IP address). The DLCI is only locally significant, meaning that it can, and usually does, change on each physical link.

Data Link layer — The second layer of the OSI protocol stack, which defines the rules for sending and receiving information across the network media. It encodes and frames data for transmission and provides error detection and control. This layer has two parts: LLC and MAC.

data terminal equipment (DTE) — A customer device that is used to connect to the telecommunications company equipment. This device is typically a router, but it can also be a computer or other type of terminal.

datagram — A message or packet that is sent across a network and does not require acknowledgment by the destination station.

DCE (data communication equipment) — Equipment that performs some type of signal conversion between the terminal device and the transmission facility. Usually the DCE is part of the telco provider's equipment.

default gateway — The address to which a host or IP device sends a packet when the destination host is not on its subnet. The default gateway is usually an interface on a router.

default route — A static route that directs all traffic not specified anywhere else in the routing table to a particular route. Same as quad zero route.

default VLAN — The default configuration of every port on a switch. Same as VLAN 1.

defining a maximum — A technique used with distance-vector routing protocols to prevent packets from bouncing infinitely throughout an internetwork by setting a maximum hop count.

demarc — Location that is the responsibility of the telecommunications provider and that connects to the nearest telephone company office.

demarcation — *See* **demarc**.

designated router (DR) — Used on broadcast, multiaccess OSPF networks as a central point for adjacencies and LSAs.

destination unreachable — An ICMP message sent back to the source host when a gateway cannot deliver an IP datagram.

dial-on-demand routing (DDR) — A feature available on Cisco routers that allows you to use bandwidth as needed.

dialer profile — Allows multiple logical BRI or PRI configurations to be bound to a physical BRI or PRI interface on a per-call basis.

Diffusing Update Algorithm (DUAL) — The algorithm used by EIGRP for path selection.

Digital Subscriber Line (DSL) — Telecommunications services that offer high bandwidth over existing copper lines. DSL connections are generically referred to as xDSL because there are several different DSL technologies.

Dijkstra's Shortest Path First Algorithm — A complex algorithm used by OSPF routers to determine a loop-free, lowest-cost path to a destination network.

directed broadcasts — Broadcasts sent to specific segments. For example, a broadcast on segment 192.168.1.0 would be 192.168.1.255.

disabled — A port state on a switch that indicates the port is neither receiving BPDUs nor forwarding frames.

discard-eligible (DE) — During times of congestion, DE frames are discarded to provide a more reliable service to frames that are not discard-eligible.

diskless workstation — Workstations configured to download their operating systems from a central server. These workstations typically do not have a hard drive.

distance-vector — A routing protocol that functions by broadcasting the entire routing table periodically to all connected neighbors; examples include RIP and IGRP.

distribution layer — Provides the backbone for a network; this layer is used in the three-layer network model to allow for access and protocol control and to increase security on the network.

Domain Name System (DNS) — A hierarchical naming service that is used on the Internet and IP networks to provide host name to IP address resolution.

down-when-looped — A Cisco router command that shuts down an interface when looping is detected; used to prevent testing scenarios from causing troubleshooting problems in a production environment.

dynamic NAT — A type of network address translation in which the valid external IP addresses to be mapped to internal addresses are floating or not fixed. The NAT router can then dynamically assign any of the available external addresses to any of the hosts on the internal network.

dynamic random access memory (DRAM) — *See* **random access memory (RAM)**.

dynamic routing protocol — A protocol that builds the routing table automatically. Examples include RIP, IGRP, EIGRP, and OSPF.

E1 — European 30-channel digital line capable of supporting up to 2.048-Mbps data transmissions.

echo request/reply — The most commonly used ICMP message. ICMP echo request/reply messages are used to check the availability of a remote host, the devices along a network path (intermediate gateways), and to verify the installation of the TCP/IP protocol on the local source host.

EIA/TIA — *See* **Electronic Industries Alliance** and **Telecommunications Industry Association**.

EIA/TIA-568 — Defines and describes operational parameters for various grades of unshielded twisted-pair cabling.

EIA/TIA-568A — A wiring method used to indicate which colors are assigned to which pin for UTP cable.

EIA/TIA-568B — A wiring method used to indicate which colors are assigned to which pin for UTP cable.

EIA/TIA-569 — Describes various network media configurations, such as those for horizontal pathways, entrance facilities, wiring closets, equipment rooms, and workstations.

electromagnetic interference (EMI) — Electronic noise that disrupts signals on cables. This noise is frequently caused by motors and generators, but can also be caused by sunspots and other natural EMI-producing phenomena.

Electronic Industries Alliance (EIA) — The organization that provides standards that define how cabling should be configured on a network; often, these standards are done as a joint operation with the TIA.

enable mode — Another name for the privileged EXEC mode. The enable or enable secret password must be entered in order to access this mode.

enable mode prompt — The prompt that indicates operation in privileged EXEC or enable mode. It has two elements: the host name of the router and the pound (#) symbol.

enable password — The password that protects enable mode in the event that the enable secret password has been removed.

enable secret password — An MD5-encrypted password that is not visible when viewing the system configuration; supersedes the enable password.

encapsulation — A process that occurs during transmission through the protocol stack, in which data from the higher layers is wrapped in a protocol header and/or trailer.

end system — The location and/or set of controls that the user can manipulate to interact with a computer or a network.

Enhanced Interior Gateway Routing Protocol (EIGRP) — A proprietary Cisco routing protocol developed to overcome some of the limitations associated with distance-vector protocols. EIGRP is considered a hybrid routing protocol.

error sensing — *See* **adaptive cut-through**.

established — A keyword that requires traffic to have originated inside the trusted network.

Ethernet — A standard networking architecture that defines the physical layout, lengths, and types of media that can be used. There are many variations of Ethernet but most use the CSMA/CD network access method. *See* **Carrier Sense Multiple Access with Collision Detection (CSMA/CD)**.

Excess Burst Size (EBS) — The amount of excess traffic (over the CBS) that the network will attempt to transfer during a set period; can be discarded by the network, if necessary.

EXEC — *See* **command executive**.

expectational acknowledgment — A TCP acknowledgment process in which the acknowledgment number refers to the sequence number expected next. If the expected sequence is not received within an expected time interval, a retransmission is requested.

Extended Binary Coded Decimal Interchange Code (EBCDIC) — A standardized formatting method for both binary and text files for communications and printer control. IBM developed EBCDIC. The acronym EBCDIC is pronounced "eb-see-dick."

extended IP access lists — IP access lists that filter traffic by source IP address, destination IP address, protocol type, and port number.

extended mode ping — When you type the word "ping" at the privileged EXEC prompt, and then press the Return or Enter key, you will be presented with ping options. Extended mode ping options include the destination address of the ping, the protocol, repeat count, and datagram size.

Exterior Gateway Protocol (EGP) — A gateway protocol used to route between multiple autonomous systems.

extranet — An area of a company's network allowed access by non-employees such as business partners, vendors, and suppliers.

Fast Ethernet — Defined in IEEE 802.3u, and includes any of the following 100-Mbps Ethernet LAN technologies: 100Base-T4, 100Base-TX, 100Base-FX. *See* **100BaseT**.

fast forward — Indicates that a switch is in cut-through mode.

feasibility condition — A condition (RD < FD) that allows a route to become a feasible successor.

feasible distance (FD) — The lowest-cost metric to a destination.

feasible successor — A backup route in the EIGRP topology table.

Fiber Distributed Data Interface (FDDI) — Describes the general specifications for the use, installation, configuration, and limitations of fiber-optic networking; pronounced "fiddy;" this standard is the responsibility of ANSI.

fiber-optic cable — A type of cable that conducts light signals through glass or plastic to generate network signals. Fiber-optic cable allows for transmission rates of 100 megabits per second or greater. It is impervious to electromagnetic interference because it sends light signals rather than electric signals along the cable.

File Transfer Protocol (FTP) — A part of the TCP/IP protocol suite that provides reliable file transfers across the Internet or other TCP/IP networks. FTP uses TCP to transfer files.

flag — A field placed at the beginning and end of an HDLC and PPP frame to mark the beginning and end of the frame.

flash memory — Erasable, programmable, read-only memory (EPROM). The content of flash memory is maintained when the router is rebooted. Flash memory contains the working copy of the Cisco IOS and it is the component that initializes the IOS for normal router operations.

flood — The process of multicasting packets onto a network.

flooded broadcasts — A broadcast for any subnet that uses the IP address 255.255.255.255. Routers do not pass flooded broadcasts.

flush interval — The time at which a route is totally removed from the routing table.

Forward Explicit Congestion Notification (FECN) — Message sent to the destination router on a Frame Relay circuit that tells the router that congestion was experienced on the virtual circuit.

forwarding — The state of a port on a switch or bridge that indicates it will learn MAC addresses and forward frames out that port.

fractional E1 — A service that offers some number of channels less than the 30 (64-Kbps) digital channels provided by a full E1 connection.

fractional T1 — Instead of leasing a full T1 connection, customers may decide to lease the less-expensive fractional T1 connections. Connections range from one 64-Kbps channel up to the full T1 connection of 24 channels.

fragment-free — A method of switching whereby the switch reads the first 64 bytes of the incoming frame before forwarding it to the destination port(s).

frame — A segment of data. The words "frame" and "data packet" are often used interchangeably, although technically a frame is found at layer 2 of the OSI model and a packet is found at layer 3.

Frame Check Sequence (FCS) — A mathematical computation placed at the end of the frame, used to ensure that the frame was not corrupted during transmission.

frame check sequence (FCS) error — An error that occurs when the calculation in the FCS field indicates that a frame was not received intact.

frame filtering — A technique used on early VLAN implementations that employed the use of multiple switching tables.

frame identification — *See* **frame tagging**.

Frame Relay — A Data Link layer protocol that relies on high-speed, reliable connections; can operate between 56 Kbps and 45 Mbps over a WAN connection.

Frame Relay access device (FRAD) — The device that the Frame Relay customer uses to connect to a Frame Relay network; also known as the Frame Relay assembler/disassembler.

Frame Relay assembler/disassembler — *See* **Frame Relay access device (FRAD)**.

Frame Relay map — A table that defines the interface to which a specific DLCI number is mapped.

Frame Relay network device (FRND) — The device that the Frame Relay provider supplies as the connection to the Frame Relay network; the acronym FRND is pronounced *friend*.

Frame Relay switch — A telecommunications company device that is used to support Frame Relay connections from customer locations; used to route Frame Relay traffic inside the public data network.

Frame Relay switching table — A table that is maintained on a Frame Relay switch; used to route Frame Relay traffic via virtual circuit DLCI numbers.

frame tagging — A method of VLAN identification endorsed by the IEEE 802.1q specification that calls for an additional four-byte field in the VLAN frame after the source and destination addresses in the data packet. Also known as **frame identification**.

full-duplex — A connection that allows communication in two directions at once; common telephone connections are typically full-duplex because people can talk and listen at the same time.

function groups — Used in ISDN communication to describe a set of functions that are implemented by a device and its software; a terminal adapter (TA) is a function group.

gateway — A combination of hardware and software that translates between different protocols on a network.

giant — *See* **long frame**.

Gigabit Ethernet — New 802.3 standard that allows 1-Gbps transmission, usually across fiber-optic cable. Known as IEEE 802.3z.

global configuration mode — A router mode that allows manipulation of most of the router's generic settings. The prompt for global configuration mode is router(config)#.

half-duplex — A connection that allows communication in two directions, but not simultaneously; the circuit can be used for sending or receiving bits in only one direction at a time.

hexadecimal — A base 16 numbering system that uses numerals 0 through 9 and the letters A through F to represent numbers. MAC addresses and IPv6 addresses are displayed in hexadecimal.

hierarchical design — In network design methodology, a network that is structured in a layered hierarchical fashion, such as the one-layer, two-layer, and three-layer network models; the opposite would be a mesh design.

High-bit-rate Digital Subscriber Line (HDSL) — Symmetric digital communication service capable of 1.536 Mbps in the United States and 2.048 Mbps in Europe.

High-level Data Link Control (HDLC) — A Data Link layer encapsulation protocol that is a superset of the SDLC protocol. HDLC is a WAN protocol that can be used for both point-to-point and multipoint connections.

High-Speed Serial Interface (HSSI) — A type of serial device developed by Cisco and T3Plus Networking that operates at speeds of up to 52 Mbps over distances of 15 meters.

hold-down timers — A technique used to stop routing loops in which updates from an inferior source are not allowed for a certain interval. Used by routers to stabilize routing tables and to prevent erroneous routing table updates.

hop count — A count of the number of routers a packet must pass through to reach a destination network.

horizontal cabling — Media that connect workstations and wiring closets.

host — A keyword for an extended IP list that specifies that an address should have a wildcard mask of 0.0.0.0.

hub — An active or passive device that connects network segments. Passive hubs are connection points; active hubs repeat and regenerate signals.

Hypertext Transfer Protocol (HTTP) — A protocol used for communications on the World Wide Web. Web servers are HTTP servers.

ICMP flood — A large quantity of ICMP echo requests sent to a target device by a malicious person or program in an attempt to crash or greatly reduce the performance of the target device.

IEEE 802 — Standard that focuses on the Physical and Data Link layers of the OSI model; developed in 1980.

IEEE 802.10 (FDDI) — A frame-tagging method used to identify VLANs trunked across Fiber Distributed Data Interfaces (FDDI).

IEEE 802.1q — The IEEE standard that defines VLAN implementations and recommends frame tagging as the way in which switches should identify VLANs. Used by Cisco switches for compatibility with non-Cisco switches.

IEEE 802.3u — The IEEE standard that defines Fast Ethernet implementations, including 100Base-T4, 100Base-TX, and 100Base-FX.

impedance — Measure of the total opposition to electron flow, changes in current, and changes in voltage in cable; causes attenuation.

implicit deny any — Blocks all packets that do not meet the requirements of the access list. Exists at the end of all lists.

inbound — A direction parameter used when applying an access list. Direction is into the router.

inductive reactance — Opposition to the changes of electrical current in a wire.

information request/reply — ICMP messages that are typically used to determine the subnet mask used by the destination. This message allows a host to determine the number of the network it is on.

infrared (IR) — One of the wireless technologies defined in IEEE 802.11. This technology requires line-of-sight between the transmitter and receiver. It is low power but cannot be intercepted. Invisible light at the upper end of the electromagnetic spectrum. It is used in most hand-held remote control devices for televisions, stereos, and videocassette players. It is also used in some types of computer networking, especially for data transfers between laptop and desktop systems.

initial sequence number (ISN) — Sequence numbers that allow communicating hosts to synchronize their communications in a TCP three-way handshake. When the communication is initiated, two hosts communicating over TCP will synchronize their initial sequence numbers.

Institute of Electrical and Electronics Engineers (IEEE) — A technical professional society that fosters national and international standards. Its Web site is *www.ieee.org*.

Integrated Services Digital Network (ISDN) — A service provided by most major telecommunication carriers, such as AT&T, Sprint, and the RBOCs; operates over existing phone lines and transfers both voice and data.

Inter-Switch Link (ISL) protocol — A frame-tagging method for VLANs proprietary to Cisco devices. Uses a 26-byte header.

interesting traffic — Network traffic for which you feel it is worth activating or maintaining an ISDN link that is configured with DDR.

interface configuration mode — A router mode that allows you to configure the Ethernet and serial interfaces. The prompt for this mode is router(config-if)#.

interframe gap — The time required between the transmission of data frames on the network: 9.6 microseconds.

Interior Gateway Protocol (IGP) — A gateway protocol used to route within one autonomous system.

Interior Gateway Routing Protocol (IGRP) — A proprietary Cisco distance-vector routing protocol that uses delay and bandwidth as its default metrics.

intermediate distribution facility (IDF) — Dependent upon the MDF in a star topology;

another wiring closet used to support devices on a network.

International Organization for Standardization (ISO) — A multi-industry association that attempts to standardize and define items that increase communication and compatibility in many different industries.

International Telecommunication Union-Telecommunication Standardization Sector (ITU-T) — A standards organization based in Europe, but with membership worldwide; involved in telecommunications standardization.

Internet Assigned Numbers Authority (IANA) — The regulatory agency originally responsible for subdividing and administering the address hierarchy used on the Internet. IANA has been replaced by ICANN.

Internet Control Message Protocol (ICMP) — A protocol in the TCP/IP protocol suite at the Internetwork layer. ICMP messages control and manage IP protocol communications.

Internet Corporation for Assigned Names and Numbers (ICANN) — The global government-independent entity responsible for the Internet.

Internet Engineering Task Force (IETF) — Organization that defines Internet operating protocols; defines the serial line protocols PPP and SLIP.

Internet Protocol (IP) — The Network layer (Internetwork layer) protocol that is responsible for addressing which allows IP to be routed.

internetwork — A large network comprised of smaller interconnected networks.

Internetwork layer — The layer of TCP/IP that is equivalent to the Network layer of the OSI model.

Internetwork Packet Exchange/Sequence Packet Exchange (IPX/SPX) — A routed protocol stack developed by Novell for use with the Netware network operating system.

interpacket gap (IPG) — *See* **interframe gap**.

intranet — The part of a company's network that is restricted to employee use only.

inverse mask — *See* **wildcard mask**.

IP address — A 32-bit binary address used on TCP/IP networks; consists of a host portion and a network portion.

IP addressing — The act of assigning (unique) IP addresses to devices on the network.

IP Control Protocol (IPCP) — PPP interface protocol for IP; *see* **Network Control Protocol**.

IPv4 — The currently deployed system of IP addressing involving 32-bit numbers expressed as decimal numbers in four octets.

IPv6 — The newest version of IP addressing that involves 128-bit addresses expressed as hexadecimal numbers.

IPX Control Protocol (IPXCP) — PPP interface protocol for IPX; *see* **Network Control Protocol**.

ISDN Digital Subscriber Line (IDSL) — A telecommunications service that makes an ISDN connection into a 128-Kbps DSL connection. Unlike ISDN, IDSL only supports data communications (not analog voice or video).

ISDN modem — A modem used in ISDN communications that must be installed at ISDN subscriber locations.

ISDN phone number — *See* **Service Profile Identifier (SPID)**.

jabber — A frame that is longer than the 1518 bytes acceptable for transmission between stations and that also has an FCS error.

jam signal — A 32-bit signal that is sent by the first station to detect a collision on an Ethernet network; ensures that all other stations are aware of the collision.

keepalive frames — Data frames sent between two hosts to ensure that the connection between those hosts remains open.

keepalive packets — Data packets sent between devices to confirm that a connection should be maintained between them.

LAN emulation (LANE) — A frame-tagging method used for VLANs on Asynchronous Transfer Mode (ATM) devices.

late collision — A situation that occurs when two stations transmit more than 64 bytes of their frames before detecting a collision.

latency — A delay on a network caused by a variety of factors, including the addition of devices.

LCP link configuration — A process that modifies and enhances the default characteristics of a PPP connection; includes the following actions: link establishment, authentication, link-quality determination, Network layer protocol configuration negotiation, and link termination.

learning — A transitory state on a bridge or switch port that indicates it is trying to learn new MAC addresses and correct its bridge table before forwarding frames on the network; used to prevent loops during the election of a new root bridge.

legacy DDR — Each ISDN BRI or PRI channel inherits the physical BRI or PRI interface's configuration.

line configuration mode — A router mode that allows you to configure the virtual terminals, console, and AUX lines that let you access the router. The prompt for this mode is router(config-line)#.

link — An OSPF router interface.

Link Access Procedure Balanced (LAPB) — A derivative of the HDLC WAN protocol; adapted to provide WAN services over X.25 networks.

Link Access Procedure-D (LAPD) — A Data Link layer WAN protocol adapted from HDLC; used on D-channel over ISDN lines.

Link Control Protocol (LCP) — Used to establish, configure, maintain, and terminate PPP connections.

link establishment — The process of opening and configuring a PPP connection before any data can be transferred over the link.

Link Quality Monitoring (LQM) — PPP feature that checks the reliability of the link by monitoring the number of errors, latency between requests, connection retries, and connection failures on the PPP link.

link termination — The process of disconnecting a PPP connection when the call is complete, which is determined by the PPP hosts that made the connection.

link-quality determination — The process of checking the quality of a PPP link and monitoring its reliability.

link-state — A routing protocol that uses cost when calculating the best path between two points. It considers items such as network traffic, router congestion, bandwidth, reliability, and other factors that could affect network performance.

link-state advertisement (LSA) — A routing information packet used by link-state routing protocols to advertise their local network link information to neighbor routers in an internetwork.

link-state packets (LSP) — Packets used to send out link-state advertisements.

listening — A transitory state on a bridge or switch port that is used during the election of a new root bridge; the port does not learn MAC addresses, nor does it forward data frames when in this state.

local access rate — The speed of the line that indicates transfer rate; common U.S. access rates are 64 Kbps and 128 Kbps, provided by ISDN connections, and 1.544 Mbps, provided by T1 connections.

local area network (LAN) — A group of computers and other devices typically connected by a cable. A LAN is normally located in a single geographic region such as a building or floor in a building.

local loop — The connection between the demarcation and the telephone company (WAN service provider) office.

Local Management Interface (LMI) — A standard signaling mechanism between the CPE and the Frame Relay connection; can provide the network server with a local or global DLCI; can provide keep-alive and status information to the Frame Relay connection.

logical addresses — Layer 3 addresses (also referred to as Network layer addresses) that allow routing protocols to determine the best path to a particular host.

Logical Link Control (LLC) sublayer — A networking sublayer defined by the IEEE to further modularize the software functions versus the hardware functions (defined by the MAC sublayer) of the OSI Data Link layer.

logical loop — A situation that occurs when a packet can be routed in an endless loop around a network, because bridging tables and routing tables reference each other as the destination for a given address.

logical topology — Describes the way a signal travels in a network, which is a function of the access method; the logical topology is usually a bus or a ring.

long frame — An Ethernet frame that is over the 1518 bytes acceptable for transmission between stations.

loopback — The TCP/IP Class A address 127.x.x.x that is reserved for diagnostic purposes. Any address on this network allows you to check if TCP/IP has been properly installed on the system. (Specifically, the IP address 127.0.0.1 is the address usually given as the loopback.)

loopback command — A Cisco router command that places an interface in a looped-back state, which means that all outgoing data will be redirected as incoming data without going out on the network; used for testing purposes.

magic number — Unique numbers added by the router to a packet, which allows it to detect a looped-back link.

main distribution facility (MDF) — The central wiring closet in an extended star topology; typically, an MDF houses the POP, patch panel, and network-interconnection devices (bridges, routers, switches, repeaters, and concentrators).

Management Information Base (MIB) — A central repository of network statistics used by SNMP and CMIP; allows management protocols to maintain network statistics; can be modified to control workstations and other network devices.

management VLAN — The default configuration of every port on a switch. Same as VLAN 1.

manager — A centralized software component that is used to manage the network in a network-management system, such as SNMP or CMIP.

maximum receive unit size — The piece of information in the LCP field of the PPP packet that sets the receive buffer size for the LCP connection, typically 1500 bytes.

MD5 — Message digest 5, an algorithm used to produce a secure hash of shared secret passwords.

media — The cable, glass, or telephone lines that host the signal from one computer to another on a network.

Media Access Control (MAC) layer — A sublayer of the Data Link layer that defines the hardware address of the physical network interface. In addition, it discards corrupted packets and identifies which packets were directed to the local system.

media access method — *See* **access method** and **network access method**.

mesh design — In network design methodology, a network that has no organized structure; the opposite would be a hierarchical design.

metric — A value used to define the suitability or desirability of a particular route.

metropolitan area network (MAN) — An intermediate specification that defines networks confined to a fairly restricted geographic area, such as a campus, town, or city. These private networks span multiple geographically separate locations that are near one another.

microsegmentation — The type of segmentation that occurs through the use of virtual circuits between switches and nodes. Each connection enjoys the total bandwidth. Bandwidth is not shared as it is through hubs.

mixed media — When different physical topologies are applied to a network, it is often called a mixed media network; for example, the bus and star topologies can be combined to form a star/bus or bus/star physical topology.

modified cut-through — *See* **fragment-free**.

multicast — A frame that is addressed to a group of systems; typically used in radio- or television-style broadcasting on the network.

multicast address — A special subdivision of IP categories reserved for data streaming. Multicast addresses are used to send information to groups of computers. The range for multicasting addresses is 224.0.0.0 to 239.255.255.255.

multicasting — The sending of a stream of data to multiple computers simultaneously.

multilink — Allows multiple transmission devices (such as two modems) to send data over separate physical connections; defined in RFC 1717.

multimode fiber-optic (MMF) cable — Fiber-optic cabling that allows for multiple simultaneous light transmissions.

multiplexed — Combining different traffic streams onto a single physical medium. The traffic is separated (demultiplexed) at the receiving end.

multipoint — The configuration of a single interface or subinterface to use multiple virtual circuits.

multiport bridge — Another name for a switch.

Multistation Access Unit (MAU) — The central device in a Token Ring architecture; forces the signal to be transmitted in a logical ring topology.

named access list — An access list that uses names instead of number ranges.

near end crosstalk (NEXT) — A measure of crosstalk performed at the location nearest the cable tester; the cable tester injects a signal of varying frequencies on a wire and measures signal bleed between other pairs of wires.

nearest active downstream neighbor (NADN) — The station on a Token Ring network that, during normal operations, receives the token from its nearest active upstream neighbor (NAUN).

nearest active upstream neighbor (NAUN) — The station on a Token Ring network that, during normal operations, passes the token to its NADN.

network — Two or more computers connected by some type of media.

network access method — The process by which network interface cards and devices communicate data on a network; an example is CSMA/CD. Also known as **media access method**.

network address translation (NAT) — A method for using a router to separate an internal network from an external network (usually the Internet), which is defined in RFC 3022. Internal hosts with private or unregistered IP addresses can effectively use one or more public registered IP addresses to communicate with external systems.

network analyzer — A device that can collect and analyze information obtained by monitoring network traffic; may be able to query and manage network devices; also called protocol analyzer.

network architecture — A network's physical and logical topology, including its physical structure or layout, the media used, the network access method, and the standards and protocols employed.

Network Control Protocol (NCP) — A functional field that contains codes, which indicate the type of protocol that is encapsulated; allows PPP to encapsulate multiple protocols including IP, IPX, and AppleTalk.

Network File System (NFS) — A file system associated with the UNIX operating system that allows for network communications between hosts.

network interface card (NIC) — A hardware device that transmits and receives electronic signals on a network.

Network Interface layer — In TCP/IP, the layer that is equivalent to the Physical and Data Link layers of the OSI model.

Network layer — The third layer of the OSI conceptual networking model, which allows communications to be routed on a network. It provides a logical address for computers on a network.

Network layer protocol configuration negotiation — The process of determining a Network layer protocol to use over a PPP connection that is common to both PPP hosts.

network monitor — A program that collects information by monitoring network traffic; typically, does not have the advanced features of analysis and device management common to network analyzers.

network operating system (NOS) — Operating software that has networking components built into its structure.

Network Termination 1 (NT1) — A small connection box that is attached to ISDN BRI lines. This device terminates the connection from the Central Office (CO).

Network Termination 2 (NT2) — A device that provides switching services for the internal network.

nibble — Equal to four bits. There is one hexadecimal digit in a nibble.

NIC error — An error that indicates a NIC is unable to transmit or receive a packet.

node — A connection point or junction on the network. A node can be a terminal or computer connected to the network.

nonbroadcast multiaccess (NBMA) — A rule used in Frame Relay that does not allow broadcasts to be sent to multiple locations from a single interface.

nonroutable protocols — Protocols that do not contain Network layer addressing and therefore cannot pass between multiple networks.

nonvolatile random access memory (NVRAM) — A special type of RAM that is not cleared when the router is rebooted. NVRAM is where the startup configuration file for the router is stored.

one-layer network model — Includes WAN connectivity equipment and organizes a network so that it can be easily adapted to the two- and three-layer design models in the future.

Open Shortest Path First (OSPF) — A classless link-state routing protocol that uses areas to provide for hierarchical network design.

Open Systems Interconnection (OSI) — A seven-layer reference model created by the International Organization for Standardization (ISO) to define and separate networking hardware and software into distinct layers and functions. This model makes it easy for developers and manufacturers to ensure that their networking implementations are compatible with other implementations in the industry.

optical repeater — A network device that uses LEDs or diode lasers to amplify optical signals.

oscillations — Undesirable, irregular signals (noise) riding on top of the desired signal.

out of band signaling — The practice of controlling an ISDN connection on a channel other than the channel(s) on which data is transferred.

outbound — A direction parameter used when applying an access list. Direction is out of the router.

overlapping — When an organization wants to connect to the Internet, but its internal addressing scheme is registered to another entity. Instead of renumbering the internal network, the organization uses NAT to translate its internal addressing scheme to the addresses that it was assigned by the ISP.

overloading — A type of NAT that allows multiple internal hosts to use one or more external IP addresses. The NAT router uses a table to keep track of the IP addresses and ports of each host, dynamically mapping each internal socket to a valid external socket.

oversubscription — When the sum of the data arriving over all virtual circuits exceeds the access rate.

packet — A group of data that is transmitted across a network.

Packet Internet Groper (ping) — A troubleshooting utility that uses ICMP to verify that a remote host is currently running and accessible.

packet-switched — A WAN connection in which data is broken into smaller packets and then routed to the destination over multiple paths.

parameter problem — An ICMP message sent whenever incorrect datagram header information is received. The message identifies the octet in the datagram that caused the problem.

partial masking — When an octet in a wildcard mask contains a mix of binary 1s and 0s.

passive hub — A device that connects network segments, but does not perform signal regeneration.

Password Authentication Protocol (PAP) — PPP authentication protocol that provides some security in verifying the identity of devices using PPP connections.

patch cable — See **patch cord**.

patch cord — Cables used to terminate communication circuits in a wiring closet or between a workstation and a telecommunications outlet. See also **cross-connect jumpers**.

patch panel — A device that includes ports and pin locations used to connect devices in a wiring closet to devices on the network; acts as a switchboard for the network.

peer communication — The method of communication among the levels of the OSI model, in which each protocol in the OSI protocol stack encodes its own protocol data unit into the network hierarchy, so that it can communicate with the equivalent layer on the destination computer.

peer-to-peer networks — Small networks, normally consisting of fewer than 10 computers, in which each computer can give and receive network services.

permanent virtual circuit (PVC) — A connection to the WAN that is established by the network administrator at the customer location; not expected to be terminated and therefore remains active.

physical address — Also called the MAC address. It is burned into the network interface card (NIC) during the manufacturing process.

Physical layer — The first layer of the OSI conceptual networking model, which defines the physical media and electronic transmission methods used in networking.

physical path loops — A loop that occurs when network devices are connected to one another by two or more physical media links.

physical ring — *See* **ring**.

plenum — A space or enclosure in which air or gas is at a higher pressure than that of the outside atmosphere; a rating for network cable that specifies that the cable does not give off a toxic gas when burned.

point of presence (POP) — The point of interconnection between the telephone company and the building, floor, or company.

point-to-point — The configuration of one or more interfaces or subinterfaces to connect to multiple virtual circuits. Each circuit will be on its own subnet. Acts like a leased line.

Point-to-Point Protocol (PPP) — An Internet standard WAN protocol defined in RFCs 2153 and 1661; used to provide router-to-router, host-to-router, and host-to-host WAN connections.

policy-based connectivity — A method that the network administrator uses to control access. The network administrator creates policies, such as "no video streaming is allowed at site 1," then implements them on the network, using equipment such as routers and switches.

port — A connection point, usually for network cable, on a device such as a hub, bridge, switch, or router.

port address translation (PAT) — A process used in overloading that allows multiple internal, unregistered IP addresses to use a single external registered address.

port forwarding — A method for sending packets from an external host system through a firewall or NAT router to an internal device. In this way, the internal device IP address is hidden from the external network, yet the internal device can still service requests from the external network.

port-based memory buffering — A memory buffer on a switch assigned by port, equally; doesn't allow for dynamic allocation of buffer space according to the activity level of a port.

Post Office Protocol version 3 (POP3) — A protocol used by client machines, which allows users to download their e-mail from an e-mail server.

power-on self-test (POST) — A diagnostic program in ROM that runs when the router is powered on. POST checks hardware availability.

preamble — Binary timing information that precedes an Ethernet frame; used by the receiving station to synchronize its clock circuits so the frame can be received correctly.

prefix — A way of designating the subnet mask that involves a forward slash followed by the number of binary ones in the mask; in other words, the network portion.

Presentation layer — The sixth layer of the OSI network model, responsible for data formatting and encryption.

Primary Rate Interface (PRI) — An ISDN service that provides 23 B-channels for data transfers up to 1.544 Mbps and one D-channel for controlling communications.

privileged EXEC mode — A router mode used to configure the router.

propagation delay — *See* **latency**.

protocol — A definition of rules for communication between two or more computers. Computers must have a common protocol (or a translator) in order to communicate. Also, the element of the PPP frame represented by two bytes used to identify the protocol that is encapsulated.

protocol analyzer — A hardware or software device that can capture and analyze network packets, help you analyze traffic flow and packet errors, and track network problems. *See* **network analyzer**.

protocol data unit (PDU) — Information added to a data packet by the layers of the protocol stack. It can be header or trailer information that is attached to the data packet prior to transmission.

Protocol Dependent Modules (PDMs) — A component of EIGRP that allows it to support multiple routed protocols such as IP, IPX, and AppleTalk.

public data network (PDN) — A telecommunications network that connects telephones around the country. These services can be provided by AT&T, Sprint, MCI, and RBOCs.

Public Switched Telephone Network (PSTN) — A telecommunications network that connects telephones around the country.

punch tool — Used to punch down cable at the patch panel or RJ-45 wall jack; completes the connection while simultaneously removing excess wire.

quad zero route — *See* **default route**.

R — The point between non-ISDN equipment (TE2) and the TA.

R-interface — The wire or circuit that connects TE2 to the TA.

radio frequency interference (RFI) — Electronic signal interference caused by radio transmissions.

RADIUS server — RADIUS is an authentication and accounting server.

random access memory (RAM) — Memory that stores the working copy of the router configuration. This configuration is erased if the router is rebooted, unless it is saved to the startup configuration.

read-only memory (ROM) — Memory that contains the necessary routines to boot the system and check its hardware. It also contains a limited version of the Cisco IOS for use only when the primary copies of the IOS in flash memory or on a TFTP server are accidentally lost.

redirect — An ICMP message sent to source hosts requesting that they change routes because the one they chose was not optimal. This packet is used to update a source host's internal routing table.

reference points — Used in ISDN communications to identify specific connection points along the ISDN connection, including the cables that form those connections; *see* **U** and **U-interface**.

Registered Jack (RJ) — A type of telecommunications connector that is used for twisted-pair cabling.

Reliable Transport Protocol (RTP) — A Transport layer protocol used by EIGRP.

remote login application (rlogin) — A utility that allows remote computers to connect to other computers or devices.

Remote Procedure Call (RPC) — A method used to establish communications between computer systems at the Session layer.

repeater — A device that repeats and cleans signals on the network, and extends the usable distance of the network.

reported distance (RD) — The distance an EIGRP router advertises to its neighbors for a network.

Requests for Comments (RFC) — A group of Internet-related documents that specify Internet protocols and standards.

reset packet (RST) — A packet indicating that the receiver should delete the TCP connection without further interaction.

resistance — Opposition to the flow of electrons in a wire.

Reverse Address Resolution Protocol (RARP) — A protocol used to resolve the client's unknown IP address to the client's MAC address for the final leg of communication between an IP source and destination. RARP clients broadcast a request for their IP address. A RARP server has a table of IP to MAC mappings and responds to the client with a RARP reply.

RG-58 — A type of thin coaxial cable that meets the 10Base2 Ethernet specification.

RG-8 — A type of thick coaxial cable that meets the 10Base5 Ethernet specification.

ring — A physical topology in which computers or other devices are connected in a circle or ring.

RJ-45 to DB-25 — A connector that ships with the router to enable connection to a PC with a DB-25 COM port to the router console port.

RJ-45 to DB-9 — A connector that ships with the router to enable connection to a PC with a DB-9 COM port to the router console port.

RJ-45 to RJ-45 rollover cable — A cable that connects the console port on the back of the router to an RJ-45 to DB-9 or RJ-45 to DB-25 connector on the back of a PC. This cable ships with the router.

ROM Monitor — A bootstrap program that runs during the power-on self-test and checks basic operations of hardware, including CPU, memory, and interfaces.

ROM monitor mode — A router mode that allows you to configure your router in the event that there is no valid IOS file in your flash memory.

root bridge — The bridge or switch that is designated the point of reference (point of origin) in STP operations. Also known as a root device.

root device — *See* **root bridge**.

root port — The communications port on a non-root bridge device that is used for BPDU communication between itself and the root bridge.

Route Switch Module (RSM) — A router placed on a switch blade; common with high-end Cisco switches such as the Catalyst 6500.

routed protocol — A protocol that contains enough OSI Network layer information that its

packets can be routed from a source to a remote destination on an internetwork.

router — A device that connects multiple segments, subdivides a network, filters broadcast traffic, and maintains a routing table. A router uses the logical address to move data packets from point to point.

router configuration mode — A router mode that allows you to enable routing protocols such as RIP and IGRP. The prompt for router configuration mode is router(config-router)#.

router ID — A router identifier used in OSPF Hellos and updates; normally the highest configured loopback or interface address.

router# — *See* **enable mode prompt**.

router> — *See* **user EXEC mode**.

routing by rumor — The learning of routes through secondhand information, and not directly from the router experiencing the change. Routing by rumor is characteristic of distance-vector routing protocols.

Routing Information Protocol (RIP) — A distance-vector routing protocol that uses hop count as its only metric.

routing loops — A network state in which packets are continually forwarded from one router to another in an attempt to find the destination network.

routing protocols — Protocols used by routers to define and exchange routing table information in an internetwork.

routing table — A table used by a router to determine which of its interfaces is connected to the destination network.

runt — *See* **short frame**.

RxBoot mode — A configuration mode that can be entered when changes to a system make it impossible to boot from the flash memory and a valid IOS image cannot be located.

S — The point between the ISDN customer's TE1 or TA and the network termination, NT1 or NT2.

S-interface — A four-wire cable from TE1 or TA to the NT1 or NT2, which is a two-wire termination point.

S/T — When NT2 is not used on a connection that uses NT1, the connection from the router or TA to the NT1 connection is typically called S/T. This is essentially the combination of the S and T reference points.

segment (noun) — A section of a network that has been subdivided by routers, switches, or bridges.

segment (verb) — To subdivide a network with a networking device, such as a bridge, switch, or router.

segmentation — The process of breaking a network into smaller broadcast or collision domains.

Serial Line Internet Protocol (SLIP) — A protocol that was originally used for IP connections over serial lines. It was replaced by the more efficient and versatile PPP.

server — A computer that shares resources with other devices on a network.

Service Access Point (SAP) — A protocol located in the Logical Link Control layer; defines how data can be passed up to higher layers.

Service Profile Identifier (SPID) — A reference number assigned to ISDN channels; functions like a phone number.

Session layer — The fifth layer of the OSI model, which controls the connection between two computers sharing data. It maintains, defines, and recovers connections that are established between two computers.

shared memory buffering — Dynamic memory buffer that is shared by all switch ports and allocated according to the needs of the ports; ports that have more activity and larger frames to process are allowed to use more memory buffer space.

shielded twisted-pair (STP) — Describes a type of cabling in which pairs of wires are twisted around one another inside a wire bundle; the wire bundle is then shielded by a foil coating, which protects it from external interference.

short frame — A frame that is smaller than the 64-byte minimum frame transmission size required by Ethernet.

Shortest Path First (SPF) algorithm — A complex algorithm used by link-state routing protocols to determine the best path in an internetwork.

signal injector — Puts traffic on a wire so that a cable tester can measure attenuation and crosstalk.

signal reference ground — Zero-volt reference point on a computer cabinet or chassis; incoming signals are measured against this ground to determine if they are a "one" or a "zero."

Simple Mail Transfer Protocol (SMTP) — The main protocol that transfers electronic mail on the Internet between e-mail servers.

Simple Network Management Protocol (SNMP) — A protocol that provides network administrators the ability to centrally control and monitor the network.

simplex — A circuit that is unidirectional is called simplex because data can only be transmitted in one direction.

sliding windows — A feature of TCP used to control the flow of communications between two hosts. The size of the TCP sliding window regulates how often acknowledgments will be sent to the transmitting host from the receiving host.

slot time — 512 bit times, which should be slightly longer than the time it takes to transmit a 64-byte frame on an Ethernet wire.

source quench — An ICMP message request to reduce the rate at which the sender is transmitting packets to the destination. This message is used for flow control, when packets arrive too fast (the receiving host runs out of buffer space for the message), or if the system is near capacity (network is congested).

Spanning Tree Algorithm (STA) — The algorithm used by STP to ensure that logical loops are not created in the presence of physical loops on a network.

Spanning Tree Protocol (STP) — The Data Link layer protocol used by switches and bridges to prevent logical loops in a network, even though physical loops may exist.

split horizon — A technique used by routers to prevent routing loops. In short, a router will not send an update for a route via an interface from which it originally received knowledge of that route.

split horizon with poison reverse — A split horizon in which the router responds to attempts to update a route with an update that marks the route in contention as unreachable.

spread spectrum — One of the wireless technologies defined in IEEE 802.11. This technology involves radio frequency transmission with the deliberate spreading of the signal over different frequencies.

stable state — The normal states of ports when the root bridge is available and all paths are functioning as expected.

standard IP access lists — Access lists that filter traffic based on source IP address.

star — Most popular physical topology in which computers are connected to a central device, usually a hub or a MAU.

star-bus — A network architecture that uses a physical star topology with a logical bus topology.

star-ring — A network architecture that uses a physical star topology with a logical ring topology.

start frame delimiter (SFD) — The one-octet binary pattern (10101011) that indicates the preamble is over and that the following information should be considered the actual data frame.

static address to DLCI Frame Relay map — A Frame Relay map that has been manually created by a network administrator.

static NAT — A type of network address translation (NAT) that allows for a one-to-one mapping of internal to external addresses. One internal address is mapped to one specific external address.

static route — A route manually added by a network administrator to the routing table of a router.

statistical multiplexing — A method for transmitting several types of data simultaneously across a single line; bandwidth is dynamically allocated to the virtual circuits on a packet-by-packet basis.

sticky-learn — A term used when a switch automatically learns MAC addresses during communications and configures them as permanent, due to a limit set by an administrator on the number of MAC addresses that can use a particular port.

storage area network (SAN) — A subsystem of networked storage devices that are physically separate from the servers.

store-and-forward — A switching method in which the entire transmitted frame is read into a switch's buffer before being forwarded by the switch. This method offers the greatest error reduction, but the highest latency. *See* **cut-through** and **adaptive cut-through**.

Structured Query Language (SQL) — A computer language used to query, manipulate, and communicate with databases.

stub network — A network with only one route to the Internet.

stub router — A router that is last in a chain of routers. There is only one path for all hosts connected to this router to get to the outside world.

subinterface — A logical division of an interface; for example, a single serial interface can be divided into multiple logical subinterfaces.

subnet — A portion of a network that has been separated from the main network by using a different subnet mask.

subnet mask — A required component for all IP hosts used in combination with an IP address to determine to which subnet the local host belongs. The local host uses this information to determine if the destination is local or remote to the source. Based on this information, the source will either broadcast information on the local network or send its packet to the default gateway for delivery to a remote network.

subnetting — The act of subdividing a network logically with subnet masks.

subnetwork — A portion of the network created by manipulating a network address and breaking it down into smaller parts.

successor — The best route to a destination in an EIGRP network.

summarization — The advertisement of many routes as a single route to reduce the total number of route table entries on a router.

supernetting — Also known as summarization or route aggregation. Done by moving the network/node boundary in the subnet mask to the left to include more than one network in an advertisement.

switch — A device used between nodes on a network or between networks to create virtual circuits between two points. A switch increases bandwidth by isolating traffic between two points.

switched bandwidth — A switching technique whereby the total network bandwidth is dedicated to each unicast transmission, even if there are multiple unicast transmissions through the switch at the same time. Unicast traffic between devices on a switch do not share the total bandwidth of the network.

switched virtual circuit (SVC) — A temporary virtual circuit created when a network device calls the WAN to establish a connection; is terminated when the connection is terminated.

symmetric switching — A type of LAN switching that requires all devices to be operating at the same speed; it does not allow for a mix of 10-Mbps and 100-Mbps communications.

Symmetrical Digital Subscriber Line (SDSL) — A symmetric digital communication service that uses a combination of HDSL and the regular telephone system.

synchronous — Communications that rely on a clock. The clocks of the source and destination must be synchronized so that the destination can pick up and interpret the transmitted frames correctly.

Synchronous Data Link Control (SDLC) — A protocol that was developed by IBM in the 1970s to allow IBM host systems to communicate over WAN connections; can be used for point-to-point or point-to-multipoint connections between remote devices and a central mainframe.

synchronous serial — The type of serial connection used with ISDN lines.

system configuration dialog — An automated setup routine that runs if you type "setup" from privileged EXEC mode or if the router is started/restarted without a configuration file.

T — The point between NT1 and NT2, which is also the T-interface; a four-wire cable that is used to divide the normal telephone company two-wire cable into four wires, which then allows you to connect up to eight ISDN devices.

T-connector — Used with coaxial cabling to connect a workstation NIC to a coaxial network.

T-interface — *See* **T**.

T1 — A leased line from a telecommunications carrier capable of carrying both voice and data with a 1.544-Mbps bandwidth.

T1C — North American 48-channel digital line capable of supporting up to 3.152-Mbps data transmissions.

T2 — North American 96-channel digital line capable of supporting up to 6.312-Mbps data transmissions.

T3 — A leased line from a telecommunications carrier that provides the bandwidth of 28 T1 connections, which equals 44.736 Mbps.

T4 — North American 4032-channel digital line capable of supporting up to 274.176-Mbps data transmissions.

TCP/IP — *See* **Transmission Control Protocol (TCP)** and **Internet Protocol (IP)**.

Telecommunications Industry Association (TIA) — Provides standards that define how cabling should be configured on a network; often, these standards are done as a joint operation with the EIA.

Terminal Access Controller Access Control System (TACACS) — An authentication protocol that allows Cisco routers to offload user administration to a central server. TACACS and Extended TACACS (XTACACS) are defined in RFC 1492.

terminal adapter (TA) — An adapter that allows non-ISDN terminals to operate on ISDN lines.

terminal emulation protocol (telnet) — A connection-oriented, Application layer utility that allows TCP/IP clients to log in to a remote system and operate on that system as if the connection between the two were local.

Terminal Equipment 1 (TE1) — A device that supports ISDN standards and can be connected directly to an ISDN network connection.

Terminal Equipment 2 (TE2) — A non-ISDN device, such as an analog phone or modem, which requires a TA to connect to an ISDN network.

terminator — A device used at the end of a coaxial segment to absorb a signal and prevent it from reflecting back along the wire.

thick Ethernet — *See* **thicknet**.

thicknet — An Ethernet networking standard that employs RG-8 coaxial cabling; a thicknet network can have segments of up to 500 meters and provides a 10-Mbps baseband transmission rate.

thin Ethernet — *See* **thinnet**.

thinnet — An Ethernet networking standard that employs RG-58 coaxial cabling; the specification includes a 10-Mbps baseband transmission rate and up to 185-meter segments.

three-layer network model — Divides a network into three connectivity layers: core, distribution, and access.

three-way handshake — The method used by TCP to negotiate a reliable connection between two hosts on a network. This process involves the exchange of three data packets before the communication process begins.

throughput — The observed transfer rate of a network; transfer rate is affected by device latency, network traffic, and capacity of source and destination to send and receive traffic.

Time Division Multiplexing (TDM) — A method for transmitting several types of data simultaneously across a single line; each path (circuit) has dedicated bandwidth allocated to it for the duration of the call; less efficient than statistical division multiplexing.

time exceeded — An ICMP message sent whenever a packet's time-to-live (hop count) reaches zero and the datagram is dropped.

time-domain reflectometer (TDR) — Cable tester that can detect the overall length of a cable or the distance to a cable break or opening by measuring the distance to where the signal is reflected anytime the wiring is open.

time-to-live (TTL) — The number of hops (routers) that a packet can make before it is discarded. The router discards a packet when its TTL is zero, which prevents a packet from looping endlessly around the network. Routers normally decrement the packet TTL by one before passing the packet to the next router.

timestamp request/reply — ICMP messages that are used to synchronize clocks by requesting the destination machine's current time of day value, which is given in milliseconds since midnight Universal Time.

Token Ring — A networking method developed by IBM that organizes the network into a physical or logical ring. The token is a logical device, and because stations may only broadcast on the network when they have the token, traffic does not collide.

token-passing — A network access method that employs a data token to enable a computer to transmit information.

toll network — A section of a WAN that is owned by a telecommunications provider; a monthly billed connection or a per-minute billed connection for the customer.

topological database — A database that holds the common view of the network formed from the link-state advertisements that are received. It allows the router to run the Shortest Path First algorithm and find the best path to a network.

topology — The physical layout of network components. The topology can take the form of a ring, star, or bus.

trace — A utility that uses ICMP messages to determine the path between a source and destination host. Trace can discover all of the hops (routers) along the path between two points.

transceiver — A device that converts a data signal into an electronic signal for transmission; designed to attach to a specific type of wiring or network media; transceivers for thinnet and UTP are on the NIC; transceivers for thicknet are usually attached to a vampire tap on the cable itself.

transformer — Device that steps voltage up or down where the hot lead originates and the neutral wire is grounded.

transitory state — The operating states of ports that prevent logical loops during a period of transition from one root bridge to another.

Transmission Control Protocol (TCP) — The protocol that guarantees the delivery of a packet by sending an acknowledgment for each window of data received. This protocol operates at the Transport layer and sends its data encapsulated in the IP protocol. TCP communications are also known as connection-oriented because TCP negotiates a communication path between hosts on the network.

Transmission Control Protocol/Internet Protocol (TCP/IP) — Routed protocol stack developed in the late 1960s for use on the precursor to the Internet; protocol stack of the modern-day Internet.

transmission time — The time it takes for a transmission to go from the source host to the destination host.

Transport layer — The fourth layer of the OSI reference model, which segments and reassembles data frames. It also provides for connection-oriented and connectionless communications. Also, the TCP/IP layer that maps directly to the OSI model Transport layer.

triggered updates — Updates that occur due to network topology changes, not periodic routing table advertisements.

Trivial File Transfer Protocol (TFTP) — A file transfer utility used on the Internet. TFTP uses UDP to transfer files and is therefore less reliable than FTP, which uses TCP in transferring files.

Trivial File Transfer Protocol (TFTP) server — A computer that provides TFTP services and can be used to maintain the IOS and configuration file of a Cisco router.

two-layer network model — Divides a network into two connectivity layers: core and access.

U — The point that defines the demarcation between the user network and the telecommunications provider ISDN facility.

U-interface — The actual two-wire cable, also called the local loop, which connects the customer's equipment to the telecommunications provider.

unicast — A frame that is sent or addressed to a single destination host; compare with multicast and broadcast.

Universal Time Code (UTC) — Based on the time in the city of Greenwich in the United Kingdom. All other time zones are either plus or minus hours of the clocks in Greenwich.

unshielded twisted-pair (UTP) — A type of cabling in which pairs of wires are twisted around one another inside a wire bundle.

User Datagram Protocol (UDP) — The protocol that operates at the Transport layer and transports data unreliably over IP. This is sometimes known as connectionless communication because the messages are sent without expectation of acknowledgment.

There is no connection negotiation process as in TCP. The packets that are sent by UDP are also known as datagrams. Because UDP does not negotiate a connection, it is faster than TCP.

user EXEC mode — A router mode that allows a network operator to check router status, see if the interfaces are operational, and review several of the router settings.

user mode — *See* **user EXEC mode**.

variable length subnet masking (VLSM) — The use of different masks on different subnets, which allows for more efficient IP address allocation. Supported by advanced routing protocols such as RIP version 2, OSPF, and EIGRP.

vertical cabling — *See* **backbone**.

Very-high-data-rate Digital Subscriber Line (VDSL) — A digital subscriber technology that supports 51.84-Mbps connections over unshielded twisted-pair cable.

virtual circuit — A private connection between two points created by a switch that allows the two points to use the entire available bandwidth between them without contention.

virtual LAN (VLAN) — A logical broadcast domain on a LAN, created by one or more switches, that is not constrained by the physical configuration.

virtual private network (VPN) — A private communications link over public communications infrastructure, such as the Internet.

virtual terminal password — A password that is used to access the router over a telnet connection.

virtual terminals (VTY) — Terminals provided with each Cisco router that can be used by telnet sessions to configure the router.

VLAN trunking protocol (VTP) — A Data Link layer protocol used to track VLAN membership changes across trunk links between VTP-enabled devices.

volatile — Contents of memory that are lost when the power is turned off. RAM is an example of volatile memory.

VTP client — A VTP device that receives and shares VTP information, but does not add, modify, or delete information and does not store the VTP database in NVRAM.

VTP domain — A group of VTP-enabled devices configured under one name to share VLAN information.

VTP pruning — An option configured for an entire VTP domain that prohibits the forwarding of VTP updates about VLANs disabled on specific trunk links.

VTP server — A VTP device that is capable of adding, modifying, sending, and deleting VTP configuration information.

VTP transparent — A device that does not participate in receiving or managing VTP domains, but will forward VTP information through its trunk ports.

VTY — A Cisco IOS abbreviation for virtual terminal used in commands to reference virtual terminals.

WAV — A Windows Audio file, an audio file format used with Microsoft Windows applications.

Well Known Port numbers — TCP and UDP ports from 0 through 1023 on which client applications expect to find common Internet services.

wide area network (WAN) — A network that spans two or more geographically diverse locations and typically uses public telecommunications carriers to connect its individual segments.

wildcard mask — Applied to IP addresses to determine if an access list line will act upon a packet. Zeros are placed in positions deemed significant, and ones are placed in nonsignificant positions.

wire map — A function that displays the connections of UTP wiring from point to point; used to see if the connectors were properly wired.

wireless — Communications that are not conducted over physical wires or cables. These communications can include infrared, radio, and other types of transmissions that are sent through the air between two or more locations.

wireless access point — A network device that contains a radio transceiver, which allows wireless clients to connect to a WLAN.

wireless local area network (WLAN) — A local area network consisting either entirely of wireless clients or a traditional LAN that contains wireless access points.

wiring closet — A central junction point, usually located in a separate room, used for interconnecting various network devices.

X-Windows — A standard graphical user interface (GUI) used on UNIX systems.

xDSL — *See* **Digital Subscriber Line**.

Index